Sunderland College
Hylton Library

This book is due for return on or before the last date shown below
Please be aware that fines are charged for overdue items
Renew online: http://library.citysun.ac.uk
Renew by phone: call 5116231

TOURISM

dent

Author HALL, C.   Loc. Code TO

Class. No. 338.4791   Acc. No. 0024924

HAL.

21-DAY LOAN

We work with leading authors to develop the strongest educational materials in social policy, bringing cutting-edge thinking and best learning practice to a global market.

Under a range of well-known imprints, including Prentice Hall, we craft high quality print and electronic publications which help readers to understand and apply their content, whether studying or at work.

To find out more about the complete range of our publishing please visit us on the World Wide Web at: **www.pearsoned.co.uk**

TOURISM: RETHINKING THE SOCIAL SCIENCE OF MOBILITY

C. Michael Hall

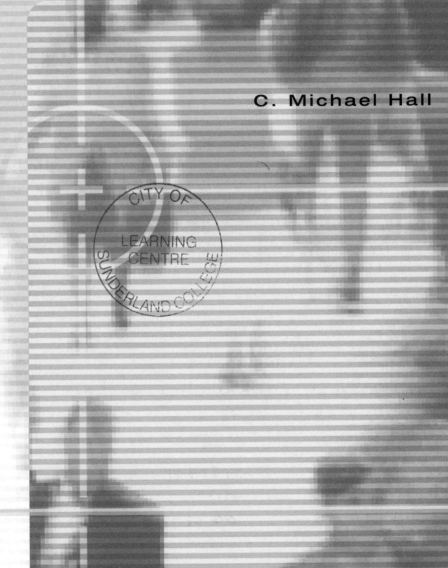

PEARSON

Prentice
Hall

Harlow, England • London • New York • Boston • San Francisco • Toronto • Sydney • Singapore • Hong Kong
Tokyo • Seoul • Taipei • New Delhi • Cape Town • Madrid • Mexico City • Amsterdam • Munich • Paris • Milan

Pearson Education Limited
Edinburgh Gate
Harlow
Essex CM20 2JE
England

and Associated Companies throughout the world

Visit us on the World Wide Web at:
www.pearsoned.co.uk

First published 2005

© Pearson Education Limited 2005

ISBN-10: 0-582-32789-X
ISBN-13: 978-0-582-32789-4

British Library Cataloguing-in-Publication Data
A catalogue record for this book is available from the British Library

10 9 8 7 6 5
11

Typeset in 10pt Book Antiqua by 3
Printed by Ashford Colour Press Ltd., Gosport

The publisher's policy is to use paper manufactured from sustainable forests.

For friends lost and found in the mobile life that we lead

Contents

Supporting resources
Visit **www.pearsoned.co.uk/hall** to find valuable online resources

Companion Website for students
- Exercises for each chapter
- Extra case, concepts and thematic material
- Extra colour images from around the world
- Further reading suggestions
- Suggestions for general research
- Links to relevant sites on the web

For instructors
- Extra zonal case studies with images
- PowerPoint slides that can be downloaded and used as OHTs

For more information please contact your local Pearson Education sales representative or visit **www.pearsoned.co.uk/hall**

List of Figures

List of Tables

List of Plates

Preface and Acknowledgements

Tourism is now a major area of academic study and publishing. There has been a proliferation of tourism courses at tertiary institutions around the world since the late 1980s. Publishers have responded to the growth in student demand for relevant material with a corresponding increase in the publication of texts and reference material. Nevertheless, despite the growth in tourism texts, there are still relative few 'global' introductory texts for university students to the field of tourism studies from a social scientific perspective. This book is designed to fill some of that gap by providing a broad international introduction at a macro-level perspective to tourism development issues and the wider field of tourism studies. However, I would be the first to acknowledge that while global in scope, the international dimension is constrained by a dependence on academic literature in the English language. Where possible, however, reference is made to work in other languages.

The text is designed to meet the demands of undergraduate tertiary tourism students as a core social science text in their degree, although it should also be of some utility for graduate students in tourism as well. Ideally, it will also be useful for students in cognate areas, such as geography, recreation and leisure. The use of key ideas of accessibility, mobility, globalisation and localisation are utilised in order to try to provide a coherent framework for understanding and discussing the development, myths, nature and issues surrounding a phenomenon such as tourism, which is simultaneously both local and global in scope. Moreover, as the reader will see, the book also uses these concepts to help ground the disciplinary context of tourism in the social sciences beyond that of being a specific set of institutional arrangements for the academy.

This book has been several years in coming. It continues on various themes contained in *Tourism Planning* (Hall 2000), with a number of elements of that book (e.g. systems, networks, collaboration and place competition) being carried over into the present book. But by no means is this book a new edition of the planning text. Rather this book has aimed to reconsider the wider context within which tourism has developed as well as the development of tourism as an area of academic study itself and its theoretical capacity to explain tourism mobility. This book, as with tourism itself, has also been impacted by global events such as the terrorist attacks of September 11, 2001, the outbreak of foot and mouth disease in the UK in 2001, the terrorist attacks in Bali in 2002, and the SARs scare in 2003. Accompanying these events have been substantial economic, political and social convulsions, which quickly made large sections of some chapters virtually obselete before they arrived at the publishers. To further complicate matters serious illness in my family also delayed completion. In essence, then, this book has already been through two editions before the publishers even saw it, and here the support of Andrew Taylor and his predecessor, Matthew Smith, and all at Pearson Europe is acknowledged.

Although the author is usually the one held responsible for the contents of any book, research and scholarship rarely occur in splendid isolation. In undertaking this book I have been extremely fortunate to have been able to discuss or undertake collaborative work with a number of colleagues whose influence and comments I would like to gratefully acknowledge: Sue Beeton, Peter Burns, Richard Butler, David Christensen, Tim Coles, Chris Cooper, David Duval, Dave Fennell, Thor Flognfeldt, Lotte Frändberg, Stefan Gössling, Tuija Härkönen, Derek Hall, Atsuko Hashimoto, James Higham, Tom Hinch, John Jenkins, Donna Keen, Neil Leiper, Alan Lew, Simon McArthur, Alison Macintosh, Richard Mitchell, Dieter Müller, Stephen Page, Felicity Picken, Robert Preston-Whyte, Chris Ryan, Jarkko Saarinen, Annadorra Saetorsdottir, Dani Schilcher, Liz Sharples, Kevin Smith, Dave Telfer, Rhodri Thomas, Dallen Timothy, John Tonbridge, Peter Treloar, Hazel Tucker, Gustav Visser, Geoff Wall, Brian Wheeler, and Allan Williams. As always, however, the attribution of any brickbats or bouquets with this book lie squarely with the author and not with these colleagues. Other significant influences include Jackson Browne, Jeff Buckley, Nick Cave, Billy Connolly, Elvis Costello, Joe Jackson, Keith Jarrett, Paul Kelly, Ed Kuepper, Morphine, The Sundays, Matthew Sweet, David Sylvian, Neil Young, Lucinda Williams and Chris Wilson. As well I must particularly thank Di, Melly and Monica (aka Madam Lash) for keeping the office going, my appointments organised and the printer working.

As one who firmly believes that one's writing and theorising are influenced by where you are in time and space (see Chapter 13) I would also like to acknowledge the opportunity to visit colleagues and speak to classes and at conferences in the process of developing this book. The book was helped to completion by visits to universities in the Nordic countries in the late northern summer of 2003 and early 2004 so I would particularly like to acknowledge the assistance of colleagues and graduate students at the universities of Joensuu (Savonlinna campus), Lund (Helsingborg), Oulu, Umeå as well as the Finnish University Network of Tourism Studies. Indeed, all the figures and tables in this book were used in lectures and presentations while in Scandinavia in 2003 and 2004. I am not sure if my lectures on current issues in tourism research were of interest to the audience, but they certainly helped me to solidify and represent ideas! I would also like to acknowledge that several of the chapters first saw light of day as conference presentations at Launceston (1995) (Chapters 3 and 8), Jyvaskyla (2000, 2002) (Chapter 6), Rotorua (NZHTC 2002) (Chapter 11), Savôlinna (2003) (Chapters 1, 3 and 4), Umeå (2003) (Chapters 6 and 8), Brisbane (CAUTHE 2004) (Chapters 12 and 13), and Naples (ATLAS 2004) (Chapter 5). These opportunities were vital not only for feedback but also to actually think about mobility while being away from home and the concept of home itself and the multiple place attachments I have in the Nordic countries, the UK, Canada, Australia and New Zealand. Finally, therefore, I must give my heartfelt thanks to Jody for putting up with my mobile academic life. Hopefully we shall both be mobile in the near future.

C. Michael Hall
City Rise, New Zealand and Umeå, Sweden

Publisher's Acknowledgements

We are grateful to the following for permission to reproduce copyright material:

Table 1.2 adapted from ATLAS 97, reproduced by permission of the European Association for Tourism and Leisure Education; Tables 3.1, 3.2, 3.3 and 3.4 are from Hall, C.M. 2003c, 'Tourism and temporary mobility: circulation, diaspora, migration, nomadism, sojourning, travel, transport and home', paper presented at the International Academy for the Study of Tourism (IAST) Conference, 30 June-5 July 2003, Savonlinna, Finland.

In some instances we have been unable to trace the owners of copyright material, and we would appreciate any information that would enable us to do so.

Part I

The context of tourism and tourism studies: understanding mobility

Introduction: Tourism Studies and Tourism

1

Key Concepts

- Disciplinary approaches to tourism
- Growth of tourism studies as a field of research and knowledge
- Defining tourism
- Temporary mobility
- Leisure mobility
- Time-geography

In the early part of the twenty-first century tourism has had a higher international profile than ever before. The impacts of the terrorist attacks of 11 September 2001 in the United States, the foot and mouth disease outbreak in the United Kingdom, terrorist bombings on tourist targets on the resort island of Bali in 2002 and, in 2003 and 2004, the SARS outbreak in East Asia and Canada, the American-led invasion of Iraq, and the bombings in Madrid, Spain, and the Indian city of Mumbai have all affected where, how and why people travel. Perhaps more significantly, the negative impacts of these events on the tourism industry have reverberated around the world, not only directly impacting levels of tourist expenditure and employment but having substantial flow-on effects to those businesses that supply the tourism industry. Tourism, for so long a seemingly invisible industry, except when people went on holiday, came to be recognised as a significant economic and social force throughout contemporary society.

However, the above events also raise fundamental questions about how we understand the phenomenon of tourism. Why do events in one part of the world affect individual travel decisions in another? Is tourism more crisis prone than other industries? How do we understand wider patterns and processes in tourism? This book seeks to answer these questions. In doing so it aims to provide not just an overview of the field of tourism but also examine emerging challenges and issues as well as the concepts by which they may be best understood. Moreover the book emphasises that the study of tourism is not just about the tourism and hospitality industry, as important as this is. Instead, this perception needs to be substantially rethought given the extent to which tourism can be grounded in a rich theoretical framework regarding the consumption and production of leisure mobility. This opening chapter aims to provide the context for what follows. It seeks to address two key areas: first, to outline the field of tourism studies; and second, to define tourism. Clearly, these issues are related. However, in analysing these concerns it also seeks to posit new ways forward in understanding the development and management of the tourism phenomenon and its broader contribution to the social science of mobility.

Tourism Studies: Discipline or Indiscipline?

One of the points of debate in the study of tourism is the disciplinary context of the field. As Bull (1991, p. xiii) observed: 'There are few human activities which can simultaneously attract academic attention from economists, geographers, environmental scientists, psychologists, sociologists, and political and management researchers. Tourism is one.' Similarly, Jafari and Ritchie (1981, p. 22) noted that tourism studies, 'like its customers who do not recognize geographical boundaries, does not recognize disciplinary demarcations'. The study of tourism is therefore a multifaceted area of research and scholarship (Meethan 2001) to which numerous disciplines may contribute. Figure 1.1 outlines the relationships of some of these disciplines to the field of tourism studies while Table 1.1 outlines the focus for disciplinary contributions as well as exemplars of these particular approaches.

In contrast to a multidisciplinary approach to tourism, which combines elements of different disciplines, writers such as Leiper (1979, 1981) and Stear (1981) argued for the creation of a new discipline of tourism studies. Indeed, Leiper (1981) went so far as to claim that a multidisciplinary base is an impediment to tourism education, and argued that 'while different disciplines will always have specialized contributions to make to the study of tourism, a need exists for a different approach to form the central ground' (1989, p. 32). Instead, Leiper (1981) believed that an interdisciplinary approach which integrates con-

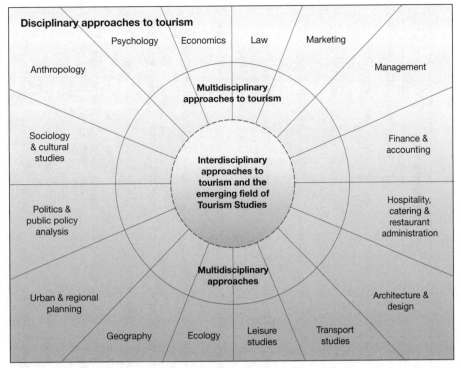

Figure 1.1   The disciplinary spaces of tourism

cepts and ideas from different disciplines or fields within the one approach was required for the study of tourism. Similarly, Jafari believed the interdisciplinary approach to be 'more expedient, productive and meaningful' (1977, p. 8). The selection of a 'best' approach to tourism has not been resolved, depending as it does on the context within which research is taking place. Tribe (1997), in examining the 'indiscipline' of the field of tourism studies, even suggested that the search for tourism as a discipline should be abandoned, and that the diversity of the field should be celebrated. Instead, he described tourism analysis as interdisciplinary, multidisciplinary and 'conscious of its youthfulness' (1997, p. 638). Indeed, the predominant attitude among many tourism researchers is perhaps best summed up by Bodewes, who argued that 'tourism is usually viewed as an application of established disciplines, because it does not possess sufficient doctrine to be classified as a full-fledged academic discipline' (1981, p. 37). A more critical perspective is adopted by Rojek and Urry (1997, p. 1):

> We will begin by interrogating the very category of 'tourism'. Is there such an entity? Does the term serve to demarcate a usefully distinct sphere of social practice? Where does tourism end and leisure or hobbying and strolling begin? This book [*Touring Cultures*] is based on the view that tourism is a term that is waiting to be deconstructed. Or as Marx might have said it is a chaotic conception, including within it too wide a range of disparate phenomena. . . . It embraces so many different notions that it is hardly useful as a term of social science, although this is

Table 1.1   Disciplinary traditions contributing to the study of tourism

Discipline	Areas of contribution	Exemplar texts
Anthropology	Relationship between host and guest, social impact analysis, cultural change	V. Smith 1989; Harrison 1992a; Nash 1996
Sociology & cultural studies	Tourism as a phenomenon in contemporary society; tourism and postmodernity; tourism and transnationalism; tourism performance	Urry 1990; Dann 1996; Selwyn 1996; Rojek & Urry 1997
Politics & public policy analysis	Understanding the tourism policy process and decision-making; the role of interest groups; international relations; political-economy and the exercise of power	Hall 1994a; Hall & Jenkins 1995; Elliott 1997
Urban & regional planning	Tourism development studies, regional development, planning of tourism; public participation, urban tourism development	Gunn 1979; Inskeep 1991; Hall 2000a
Geography	Spatial analysis of tourism, understanding tourism places, movements of people, historical geography, national park and outdoor recreation management, social and environmental impact assessment	Pearce 1987; Shaw & Williams 1994; Towner 1996; Hall & Lew 1998; Hall & Page 2002; Hall & Williams 2002a
Ecology	The impact of tourism on the physical environment; maintenance of biodiversity; national parks, wildlife tourism, ecotourism	Edington & Edington 1986; Newsome et al. 2001
Leisure studies	Understanding the nature of leisure, policies, activities and motivations	Bramham et al. 1989a, 1993; Collins & Cooper 1997
Transport studies	The provision and use of tourist transport services and associated infrastructure	Page 1994, 1999; Lumsdon & Page 2004
Architecture & design	The development and design of tourism infrastructure, landscape architecture, resort design, heritage conservation	Lawson & Baud-Bovy 1977; Lawson 1995
Hospitality, catering & restaurant administration	The provision of accommodation, convention and hospitality services to tourists; casinos and club management; food and beverage management; gastronomy	Jones & Lockwood 1989; Jones & Merricks 1996; Knowles 1998
Finance & accounting	Tourism business management, feasibility analysis, tourism real estate development	Harris 1995; Owen 1998
Management	The management of tourism businesses in relation to operations, service and human resources; business strategy	Leiper 1995; Medlik 1995; Tribe 1997
Marketing	The marketing of tourism attractions, products, businesses and destinations; tourist consumer behaviour; tourism advertising and promotion	Morrison 1989; Heath & Wall 1992; Horner & Swarbrooke 1996; Kotler et al. 1997
Law	The legal and regulatory framework for tourism; tourism businesses and government, including environmental, planning and resource management law	Corke 1993; Downes & Paton 1993; Pannett & Boella 1996
Economics	The economic contribution of tourism to national, regional and local economies; economic evaluation of tourism costs and benefits	Bull 1991; Sinclair & Stabler 1997
Psychology	Why people travel, tourist behaviour	Pearce, 1982, 2005 (in press); Ross 1994

paradoxical since Tourism Studies is currently being rapidly institutionalised within much of the academy.

Despite Rojek and Urry's concerns as to its usefulness as a term, the field is, as they rightly noted, increasingly becoming institutionalised in academic terms (Rojek and Urry 1997) and recognised as a legitimate area of study in its own right (Ryan 1997). Indeed, Walton (2002, p. 111) observes that 'a whole new discipline of tourism studies is gathering momentum'.

Tourism has many of the characteristics of a discipline. Johnston (1991), in his landmark review of Anglo-American geography, identified three key characteristics of a discipline:

● a well-established presence in universities and colleges, including the appointment of professorial positions;

● formal institutional structures of academic associations and university departments; and

● avenues for academic publication, in terms of books and journals. Indeed, 'It is the advancement of knowledge – through the conduct of fundamental research and the publication of its original findings – which identifies an academic discipline; the nature of its teaching follows from the nature of its research' (Johnston 1991, p. 2).

These characteristics clearly apply to the field of tourism studies.

A well-established presence in universities and colleges, including the appointment of professorial positions

There are departments and/or degree programmes established throughout the world, although in countries such as Australia and the United Kingdom they have less frequently been located in older established universities. University involvement in tourism-related education and research originate in the inter-war period. The first professorial positions in tourism were established in Austria and Switzerland in the 1920s, while the first hospitality programme in the United States was established at Cornell University in New York State in 1920. The first European chairs and research programmes were an outgrowth of departments of economics and, to a lesser extent, the field of economic geography. The Cornell programme was developed as the result of an initiative of the American Hotel Association. The first undergraduate degree programme in tourism in the United Kingdom was established at the University of Surrey in 1973. The first programmes in Australia were established at Gatton College (now a part of the University of Queensland) and Footscray College of Advanced Education (now a part of the Victoria University of Technology) in the late 1970s. The study of tourism as an area of academic endeavour has been strongly influenced by its origins in North America and Europe. Until the mid to late 1970s tourism in North America was often regarded as a hospitality trade or professional area which meant that there was only limited involvement of universities. In contrast, in Europe tourism was well established as an area of academic research and scholarship separate from that of hotel schools.

Much of the growth in university and college education in tourism occurred because of the rapid growth of international tourism and the increased recognition by governments of tourism as a tool for economic development and employment generation. Therefore, from the mid-1980s on, there has been a dramatic increase in the number of tertiary courses in tourism and the extent of university involvement in tourism research. For example, in the United Kingdom the Council of National Academic Awards (CNAA) (1992) reported that there were 23 first degrees in tourism in the United Kingdom in 1992 and 17 postgraduate degrees. By 1997 tourism was being offered as a first degree in over 30 institutions. Although many former polytechnics are teaching tourism, a number of more established institutions, such as Nottingham, Stirling, Strathclyde and Surrey, also have degree programmes. Similar growth also occurred in Australia. In 1987 tourism was being offered as a first degree in three tertiary institutions; by 1997 this had grown to at least 23 universities. A review of memberships of North American tourism and professional organisations (e.g. Council of Hotel, Restaurant, and Institutional Education (CHRIE)) and the Society of Travel and Tourism Educators would suggest that there are now over 200 first degrees available in tourism and related subjects, such as hospitality, in Canada and the United States (see CHRIE 1997). In New Zealand five of the eight universities had undergraduate programmes in tourism by 2000, while throughout Europe, China, Korea, South Africa, South-East Asia and South America university tourism programmes continue to be established.

Formal institutional structures of academic associations and university departments

There are also a number of institutional structures for tourism both within universities and colleges of higher learning, that is departments and schools of tourism, as well as on a national or international basis. For example, at a national level institutions such as the Council for Australian University Tourism and Hospitality Education (CAUTHE), the Tourism Society in the United Kingdom, and the Finnish University Network for Tourism Studies (FUNTS) run annual research conferences and provide a forum for discussion on tourism education.

At the international level social scientific unions in the fields of anthropology and ethnology, economic history, geography, history and sociology have specific commissions or working groups to study tourism issues. For example, the International Geographical Union Commission on Tourism, Leisure and Global Change, which was established in 2000, has existed in various guises as a commission or study group since 1972. The International Union of Anthropological and Ethnological Sciences has had a Commission on Tourism since 1993. A number of other international tourism research and education organisations also exist and these have made substantial contributions to tourism studies. For example, the first refereed academic journal on tourism, *Revue de Tourisme/The Tourist Review* was established as early as 1946, as the official organ of l'Association Internationale d'Experts Scientifiques du Tourisme (AIEST), based in Switzerland. The Council of Hotel, Restaurant and Institutional Education (CHRIE), which has a strong tourism component and which publishes *Journal of Hospitality & Tourism Research* and *Journal of Hospitality & Tourism Education*, was also established in 1946 in the United States although it now has a substantial international orientation. The Tourism and Travel Research Association (TTRA) had its beginnings in the merger of the Western Council of Travel Research and the Eastern Travel Research Association in 1970. Although it retains a strong North American base, TTRA now has a substantial international network with a European chapter and over 800 members, and produces the *Journal of Travel Research*. In Europe, the Association for Tourism and Leisure Education (ATLAS) was established in 1991 to develop transnational educational initiatives in tourism and leisure. Since that time ATLAS has expanded rapidly to include chapters from the Asia-Pacific, Africa and the Americas, and working groups on fields as diverse as entrepreneurship, policy and gastronomy. With an institutional membership of over 300 and an active conference, research and publishing programme, ATLAS is now one of the most significant international tourism education and research organisations. Its significance has also been enhanced with the development of a draft core body of tourism knowledge which enables the transfer of students and credits between European institutions.

Tourism Insight: The ATLAS Tourism Body of Knowledge

With the growth of university research, scholarship and teaching, increased recognition has been given to the development of a body of tourism knowledge which meets both academic and industry criteria. Indeed, one of the most notable developments in tourism education around the world has been the emphasis given to research and scholarship as opposed to the 'technical' education traditionally associated with community colleges, polytechnics and colleges of TAFE (Technical and Further Education) (e.g. Weiler et al. 1991; Wisch 1991; O'Halloran and O'Halloran 1992; Koh 1995; Wells 1996; Hing and Lomo 1997; Walle 1997). The development of a research base for tertiary tourism education is now seen as essential for industry recognition and the professionalisation of the area. As Pavesic (1991, p. 39) stated, industry credibility for tourism and hospitality education 'ultimately starts with academic excellence'. The key theme which emerges from a review of the tourism education literature and the statements of professional associations is that it is important the universities imbue their tourism graduates with the traditional bases of a university education while remaining cognisant of the voices of industry and other stakeholders. Examples of the manner in which tourism education goes beyond 'technical training' and reflects wider concerns incorporated in university education are evidenced by the extent to which concerns over ethics (e.g. Whitney 1989; O'Halloran 1991), social responsibility (e.g. De Franco and Abbott 1996) and multiculturalism (e.g. Bartlett and Farrar 1997) are expressed in the tourism education literature.

The development of a core body of knowledge recognised by universities and industry has been the subject of much discussion within educational and professional bodies, including the Council of Hotel, Restaurant, and Institutional Education (CHRIE) in North America, the Tourism Society in the United Kingdom and the European Association for Tourism and Leisure Education (ATLAS). It has also been the subject of government reports (e.g. Council of National Academic Awards 1992).

One of the most developed accounts of an appropriate core body of tourism knowledge is that of the SOCRATES Thematic Network in tourism and leisure managed by ATLAS. In September 1996 ATLAS started a three-year project to create a European Thematic Network (ETN) for tourism and leisure education (SOCRATES) with the support of DGXXII of the European Commission. The Thematic Network projects are designed to bring groups of academics in a single subject area together on a European-wide basis to discuss issues of common interest. The stated aim of the ETN is to 'define and develop a European dimension within a given academic discipline ... through cooperation between university faculties or departments and academic associations. Such cooperation should lead to curriculum development which will have a lasting and widespread impact across a range of institutions.' One of the basic goals of the European Thematic Network is 'to define the scope and content of the study area at European level, by developing a "body of knowledge" for tourism education' (European Association for Tourism and Leisure (ATLAS) 1997; hereafter ATLAS 1997).

The ATLAS draft tourism body of knowledge is designed to provide a common basis for tourism courses in higher education in Europe, which can be used to inform lecturers, students and employers about the essential agreed elements which they can expect to find in tourism courses. The body of knowledge is also designed to facilitate the international recognition of tourism courses and the qualifications they provide, and facilitate the process of student exchange, particularly within the European Union. The body of knowledge outlined by ATLAS is intended to represent a *minimum* area of knowledge required to understand tourism by those in higher education (ATLAS 1997). However, it should be seen as a facilitating statement rather than one which seeks to exclude other approaches to tertiary tourism education. Moreover, it should be seen as a body of knowledge appropriate for an undergraduate tourism degree. Those students who take a minor in tourism or individual courses will only be exposed to a segment of the wider body of knowledge, while some students at both the graduate and undergraduate levels may undertake tourism specialisations such as sustainable tourism, ecotourism, conventions and events, or sports tourism or degree courses in leisure, recreation and hospitality.

The details provided in the body of knowledge were based on work on a common core curriculum for tourism carried out in the UK by the National Liaison Group for Higher Education in Tourism (NLG) (CNAA 1992), which was itself based on work by the Tourism Society in the early 1980s (Airey and Nightingale 1981; Airey and Middleton 1984). It was subsequently refined by the Core Group of the ATLAS Thematic Network in Tourism and Leisure Education. The draft content of the tourism body of knowledge (ATLAS 1997) is outlined in Table 1.2.

In addition to the core body of knowledge, universities have developed various specialisations, either sector-specific or thematic in focus. Examples of these specialisations include courses in event management, ecotourism, conventions and meetings management, special interest tourism, heritage management and tourism economics (Wells 1996). Many tourism degrees are grounded in business principles and, if not stand-alone departments, centres or faculty, are often associated with faculties of business and commerce (CNAA 1992; Wells 1996; CHRIE 1997; Walle 1997). However, just as significantly, many tourism degrees and courses have a significant broader social sciences or cultural studies dimension. Even with the development of a draft body of tourism knowledge significant debate still exists over the content of, and approaches to, tourism education. This is also reflected in the nomenclature of tourism degrees.

Nomenclature for degrees appears to have developed according to the origins of tourism research and scholarship in each country or region. In the United States approximately 75% of degrees are designated as a Bachelor of Science (BSc), often with a specific reference to either tourism or hospitality as the specialism (CHRIE 1997). In the United Kingdom there is primarily a mix between Bachelor of Commerce (B.Comm.)/Bachelor of Business (B.Bus.) and Bachelor of Tourism (B.Tour)/Bachelor of Tourism Management (B.Tour.Man.) with a small number of Bachelor of Arts (BA) offerings. Specifically named tourism degrees appear to be becoming more common as new developments occur. In Australia and New Zealand tourism degrees are primarily named degrees in business and commerce, with the most recent developments being specifically named tourism degrees. Arguably, the development of specifically named tourism degrees is a reflection not only of institutional recognition of tourism studies but the development of tourism as a field of academic study and research in its own right.

As with many other areas of academic endeavour the field of tourism also has an academy which was established to recognise outstanding scholarship and contribution to the field. The International Academy for the Study of Tourism, which was founded in 1990, is limited to 75 active members as well as emeritus members. However, the academy includes members who have been included by virtue of their administrative contributions (e.g. journal editorship or promotion of tourism education), rather than just on the quality or impact of publications. In addition, membership is heavily biased towards Anglo-American scholarship in tourism and is primarily white and male.

Table 1.2   Draft contents of the ATLAS tourism body of knowledge

1. The meaning of tourism
   * definitions of tourism
   * approaches to the study of tourism
   * history of tourism
   * types of tourism
   * tourism determinants and motivations
   * tourism systems and actors
   * tourism and change

2. The tourism industry
   * tourism production system
   * generating area sectors, destination area sectors and transit sectors
   * operating characteristics, organisational characteristics, interrelationships and structures

3. The dimensions and measurement of tourism
   * scope and patterns of demand
   * geographical perspectives and knowledge (including spatial distribution of resources)
   * measurement of demand and supply
   * sources of tourism data and interpretation and uses of information

4. The significance and impact of tourism
   * economic, psycho-sociological, cultural, environmental, political and other interactions
   * host–guest encounters

5. Marketing of tourism services
   * marketing theory and its application in tourism
   * consumer behaviour

6. Tourism planning and development
   * political context
   * public sector policy and organisations
   * destination and site development
   * sustainable tourism
   * public and private sector interface
   * regulation of tourism

7. Management of the tourist experience
   * interpretation
   * service management and quality (including monitoring and control)
   * visitor and management issues
   * tourism eduction and training

Source: ATLAS 1997

Although some may question the membership, exclusivity or value of such an organisation, from an institutional perspective its existence remains important because of the parallels it makes with other established disciplines.

Avenues for academic publication, in terms of books and journals

Communication of research and scholarship has traditionally been a central element of academic disciplines. In terms of the advancement of knowledge, there is now a substantial body of tourism literature, as evidenced in journals, books, conference proceedings and electronic publications. Table 1.1, for example, identified just a small number of the texts that are available in English. There are also numerous thematic, regional and international academic conferences which focus on tourism. These include not only conferences held by academic associations but also conferences that focus on specific areas such as ecotourism, nature-based tourism, tourism economics, climate change, tourism in peripheral areas, as well as regional conferences for Asia, Africa and the Nordic countries. Nearly all of these conferences produce proceedings which also add to the sum of tourism knowledge.

Tourism has also witnessed enormous growth in the number of published refereed journals (Table 1.3) (Hall, Williams and Lew 2004). *Tourism: An International Interdisciplinary Journal* (formerly *Turizam*) was first published in 1952, while the *Revue de Tourisme/The Tourist Review* was established by AIEST in 1946. The noted North American journals, the *Cornell Hotel & Restaurant Administration Quarterly* and the *Journal of Travel Research* (the journal of the Tourism and Travel Research Association), commenced in 1959 and 1972 respectively. Other notable general tourism journals include *Annals of Tourism Research* (commenced publication in 1973), *Tourism Recreation Research* (1975, and also significant because it is published in India), *Tourism Management* (1979) and *Current Issues in Tourism* (1998). Journals also exist within specific disciplinary areas (e.g. *Tourism Economics* (1995), *Tourism Geographies* (1999) and *Journal of Travel and Tourism Marketing* (1992)) and in thematic areas (e.g. *Journal of Sustainable Tourism* (1993), *Journal of Sports Tourism* (1995) and *Journal of Convention & Exhibition Management* (1998)). There are also regionally focused journals (e.g. *Scandinavian Journal of Hospitality and Tourism* (2001) and *ASEAN Journal on Hospitality and Tourism* (2002)). In a review of the field of tourism studies, Hall, Williams and Lew. (2004) identified 75 journals, published in English either in full or in part, as having had a substantial academic component devoted to tourism research, including journals in cognate fields such as hospitality and leisure. In analysing the list of journals, Hall et al. (2004) also observed that the journal field has been marked by increased specialisation in subject matter, which may again be interpreted as part of the maturing of the field of tourism studies. To academic tourism journals can be added the many trade journals in which some research may be reported, while many researchers also publish in disciplinary-oriented journals.

Tribe (1997, p. 638) observed that tourism studies was 'conscious of its youthfulness'. Although such statements about tourism studies are widespread, they

Table 1.3   Rate of establishment of academic journals in tourism and cognate fields

Time period	Number of journals established
pre-1960	3
1960–69	2
1970–79	8
1980–89	10
1990–99	31
2000–	21
Total	75

Source: Derived from Hall, Williams and Lew 2004

fail to understand that the study of tourism within the social sciences has a far longer history than is often imagined, and is far less 'youthful' than Tribe implies (Hall, Williams and Lew 2004). For example, with respect to the geography of tourism, Hall and Page (2002) charted an Anglo-American and European tradition of social scientific scholarship on tourism that dates to the 1920s and 1930s (see Carhart 1920; Graves 1920; Leopold 1921; McMurray 1930; Jones 1933; Brown 1935; Selke 1936; Carlson 1938; Gilbert 1939) and, as noted above, the first chairs in tourism were established in the 1920s. Instead, comments regarding the supposed novelty of tourism research reflect a lack of appreciation of the substantial amount of research which has been conducted in the past. Undoubtedly there has been a growth in the amount of tourism research as well as a growth of research outputs. However, in this tourism is no different from many other endeavours in the arts and sciences. One possible reason for a relative lack of appreciation of the history of tourism as a field of academic study is that no history of the sociology of tourism knowledge has yet been written (Hall 2004a). Another could be that students of tourism increasingly rely on electronic versions of journals in which such historic material is not listed and the art of browsing the library shelves has been lost! Nevertheless, regardless of the reasons, the key point to make is that the field of tourism studies bears the hallmarks of a discipline as identified by Johnston (1991). However, Johnston (1991, p. 9) also went on to reflect that

> there is no fixed set of disciplines, nor any one correct division of academics according to subject matter. Those disciplines currently in existence are contained within boundaries established by earlier communities of scholars. The boundaries are porous so that disciplines interact. Occasionally the boundaries are changed, usually through the establishment of a new discipline that occupies an enclave within the pre-existing division of academic space.

Undoubtedly, the growth of tourism studies and tourism institutions has helped to reshape such boundaries, as well as being influenced by them (Hall, Williams and Lew 2004). That stated, despite the clear institutionalisation of tourism studies in the academy, a further reason why tourism has been criticised is because of its theoretical base which is often perceived as being 'borrowed' from other disciplines as well as being conceptually 'weak' (Mowforth and Munt 1998). For example, as Meethan (2001, p. 2) commented, '... for all the evident expansion of journals, books and conferences specifically devoted to tourism, at a general analytical level it remains under-theorised, eclectic and disparate'. Franklin and Crang (2001, p. 5) also note that tourism studies is relatively new and has grown dramatically, but then they also claim

> that tourist studies has been dominated by policy led and industry sponsored work so the analysis tends to internalize industry led priorities and perspectives ... this effort has been made by people whose disciplinary origins do not include the tools necessary to analyse and theorize the complex cultural and social processes that have unfolded.

Despite being rather condescending, Franklin and Crang's (2001) assessment does point at one of the persistent tensions in tourism research, between the often contradictory requirements of critical social science and the extent to which industry and policy-makers influence the research agenda, particularly through funding and commercialisation strategies (Hall, Williams and Lew 2004). However, it should be noted that this tension exists throughout the physical and social sciences, given the increased intervention of government and the private sector in university teaching and research priorities. Just as significantly, the above discussion highlights the difficulties inherent in defining tourism and the complexities that competing conceptualisations of tourism provide for the student of tourism. It is to these definitional issues therefore that we will now turn.

Defining Tourism

An understanding of the definition of tourism is important at both a practical and a theoretical level. At a practical level it enables us to gain a better understanding of the myriad sources of tourism data and information, while at a theoretical level it illustrates the broad dimensions and character of tourism. At its most basic the definition of tourism helps distinguish not only what we study but also how we analyse and govern it. For example, how can government set policy for tourism unless they have a clear understanding of what it is? Burkart and Medlik (1981, p. 41) observed that the concept of tourism refers to the 'broad notional framework, which identifies the essential characteristics, and which distinguishes tourism from the similar, often related, but different phenomena'. Although such an approach may be useful for general research purposes it does not help much in determining tourist patterns and flows.

Therefore, more technical definitions have evolved over time as researchers modify and develop appropriate measures for statistical, legislative and operational reasons, implying that there may be various technical definitions to meet particular purposes (Hall and Page 2002).

Leiper (1979) classified definitions of tourism as 'economic', 'technical' or 'holistic', depending on their intention. However, as S.L.J. Smith (1988) observed, Leiper's (1979) goal of a single, comprehensive and widely accepted definition of tourism is beyond hope of realisation. Nevertheless, students of tourism should heed Smith's comment that 'practitioners must learn to accept the myriad of definitions and to understand and respect the reasons for those differences' (1988, p. 180). In the United States as well as some other countries there is also a tendency to use the term 'travel' as a synonym for tourism. However, it is widely acknowledged that the two terms are used in isolation or in unison to describe three core concepts:

- the movement of people;

- a sector of the economy or an industry; and

- a broad system of interacting relationships of people (including their need to travel outside their communities and services that attempt to respond to these needs by supplying products) (Chadwick 1994; Hall and Page 2002).

Technical definitions of tourism are used by organisations seeking to measure a specific population and there are three principal features which normally have to be defined:

- Purpose of travel (e.g. the type of traveller, be it business travel, holidaymakers, visits to friends and relatives or for other reasons such as education or health).

- The time dimension involved in the tourism visit, which requires a minimum and a maximum period of time spent away from the home area and the time spent at the destination. Most jurisdictions utilise a minimum period of a stay of more than 24 hours away from home and a maximum of less than one year.

- Those situations where tourists may or may not be included as tourists (e.g. travel for military service, migration or travel by refugees).

Definitions of tourism tend to share a range of common elements (Hall and Page 2002; Hall 2003a):

- Tourism is the temporary, short-term travel of non-residents along transit routes to and from a generating area and a destination.

- Tourism may have a wide variety of impacts on the destination, the transit route and the source point of tourists.

- Tourism may influence the character of the tourist.

- Tourism is primarily for leisure or recreation, although business is also important.

- An additional, and usually unstated, aspect of defining tourism is that such movement is also voluntary.

Of significance to all definitions of tourism are concepts of space (i.e. travel away from a home area) and time (i.e. the time spent away from a home area). Yet the boundaries which are selected as determinants of what constitutes short-term travel are increasingly fluid. For example, in order to improve the collection of statistics and improve understanding of tourism, the United Nations (UN) (1994) and the World Tourism Organisation (WTO) (1991) recommended differentiating between visitors, tourists and excursionists (daytrippers). The WTO (1991) recommended that an international tourist be defined as: 'a visitor who travels to a country other than that in which he/she has his/her usual residence for at least one night but not more than one year, and whose main purpose of visit is other than the exercise of an activity remunerated from within the country visited'; and that an international excursionist (e.g. cruise ship visitors) is defined as 'a visitor residing in a country who travels the same day to a country other than that in which he/she has his/her usual environment for less than 24 hours without spending the night in the country visited and whose main purpose of visit is other than the exercise of an activity remunerated from within the country visited'. Similar definitions were also developed for domestic tourists, with domestic tourists having a time limit of 'not more than six months' (WTO 1991; United Nations 1994). As Hall and Page (2002) noted, the inclusion of a same-day travel, 'excursionist' category in UN/WTO technical definitions of tourism makes the division between such categories as recreation and tourism, or daytrips and tourism, even more arbitrary, and they observed that there is increasing international agreement that 'tourism' refers to all activities of visitors, including both overnight and same-day visitors (United Nations 1994, p. 5). Indeed, the UN (1994: p. 9) stated, 'day visits are important to consumers and to many providers, especially tourist attractions, transport operators and caterers'.

One of the long-time themes in tourism research is the relationship of tourism to recreation and leisure (e.g. Ryan 1991, 2003; Williams 1998; Pigram and Jenkins 1999; Hall and Page 2002). For instance, in the 1980s Bodewes (1981) believed tourism to be a recreational phenomenon, while Pearce (1987, p. 1) noted the 'growing recognition that tourism constitutes one end of a broad leisure spectrum'. Authors such as Pigram also took the view that 'tourism is carried on within an essentially recreational framework' (1985, p. 184), while others, such as Murphy (1985) conceptualised recreation as one component of tourism. Nevertheless, as Pigram (1985, p. 184) argued:

> Little success has been afforded to those attempting to differentiate between recreation and tourism and such distinctions appear founded on the assumption that outdoor recreation appeals to the rugged, self-reliant element in the population, whereas tourism caters more overtly for those seeking diversion without too much discomfort.

Historically, research in outdoor recreation, which also has its own set of academic institutions and structures, has developed independently of tourism research. As Crompton and Richardson (1986, p. 38) noted: 'Traditionally, tourism has been regarded as a commercial economic phenomenon rooted in the private domain. In contrast, recreation and parks has been viewed as a social and resource concern rooted in the public domain.' Yet they went on to note that the demarcation line between recreation and tourism is rapidly becoming 'fuzzy and overlap is now the norm' (Crompton and Richardson 1986, p. 38). Although the division between public and private activities may have held relatively true from the end of the post-war period through to the early 1980s, since then political philosophies regarding the appropriate intervention of the state in leisure, recreation and tourism provision, and the corresponding division between public and private sector activities, has substantially altered in Western countries (Hall and Jenkins 1995). Therefore, as Williams (1998, p. 4) commented, 'in approaching the study of tourism ... we need to understand that the relationships between leisure, recreation and tourism are much closer than the disparate manner in which they are treated in textbooks might suggest'. According to Moore et al. (1995, p. 74), there are common strands in the 'relationships between the various motivating factors applicable to both leisure and tourism'. And as Leiper (1990a) argued, tourism represents a valued category of leisure, where there is a degree of commonality between the factors motivating both tourist and recreational activities and many of the needs, such as relaxation, can equally be fulfilled in a recreational or tourism context. Although there is some merit in Leiper's (1990a) approach, grouping leisure into one amorphous category assumes that there are no undifferentiated attributes that distinguish tourism from leisure (Hall and Page 2002). The distinction between tourism and recreation may therefore be regarded as one of degree (Hall 2003a). In addition, many of the theoretical concepts in leisure and recreation studies are readily utilised by tourism researchers in their own studies (e.g. Ryan 1991; Williams 1998; Hall and Page 2002).

Some of the various dimensions of the relationships between leisure, recreation and tourism and other related concepts are noted in Figure 1.2. The boundaries between tourism, recreation and leisure, as well as work, which is often seen to be opposite to leisure, should be seen as permeable. Nevertheless, for the purposes of expressing relationships between concepts, work is differentiated from leisure, with there being two main realms of overlap: first, business travel, which is seen as a work-oriented form of tourism in order to differentiate it from leisure-based travel; and, second, 'serious leisure', which refers to the breakdown between leisure and work pursuits and the development of leisure career paths with respect to hobbies and interests (Stebbins 1979, 1982). The category of pilgrimage is included because, although a significant travel component, it reflects notions of religious duty rather than being a leisure or recreational activity. Daytripping is included because of its recreational travel dimension, as noted above, while second home tourism is also regarded as a significant form of leisure-oriented travel, although it is different from other forms of tourism because it usually implies the ownership of property in the destination (Hall and Müller 2004a). Hospitality is not included as it refers to a specific type of production or supply of services to those who consume them.

Figure 1.2 is useful because it helps illustrate the relationships between key concepts in tourism and tourism studies. It also describes various forms of consumption through reference to travel activities and motivations. However, its utility in describing the relationships between such travel activities and forms in space and time is somewhat limited.

Figure 1.3 provides a two-dimensional representation of some of the key concepts in tourism in space and time. The figure also illustrates the critical points of time for definitional purposes in that 24 hours or overnight stay away from home is usually used to differentiate between daytripping and tourism. Depending on the jurisdiction, time is also used to classify migration and tourism: in some countries it is six months away from the country of permanent residence, in others it is 12 months. However, tourism has historically been classified as much by space as it is by time. For example, the crossing of a national border separates domestic from international tourism as it does domestic from international migration. Moreover, space is also used as the determinant of regional and local tourism statistics. Although these are usually based on political boundaries, other distances may also be used to differentiate between different classifications of mobility. For example, the Western Australian Tourism Commission (WATC) (1997) estimated that in 1996 over 10 million pleasure-oriented daytrips were undertaken in Western Australia with a total expenditure of just under A$200 million. The definition of 'daytrip' used by the WATC was 'a trip taken mainly for pleasure which lasts for at least 4 hours and involves a round trip distance of at least 50 km. For trips to national parks, state forests, reserves, museums and other man-made attractions the distance limitation does not apply' (WATC 1997, p. 1).

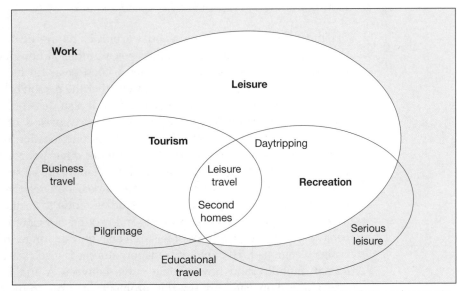

Figure 1.2   Relationships between leisure, recreation and tourism and cognate concepts

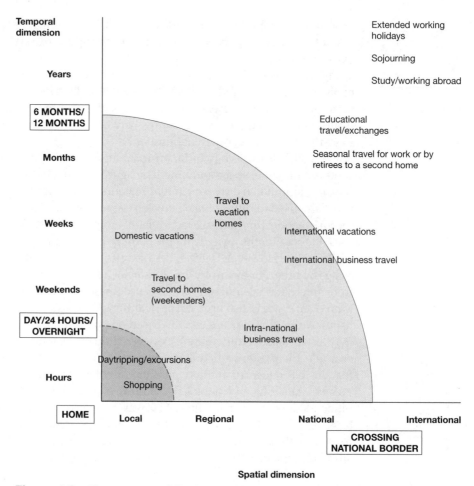

Figure 1.3   Temporary mobility in space and time

Figure 1.3 highlights the essential arbitrary nature of delineating tourism from other forms of human mobility. For example, although at first glance the location of a political border provides a good basis for determining tourism statistics, it does not take into account whether the person being classified lives 20 km or 220 km away from such a border. It also does not take into account how fast people are travelling within a given period of time. Obviously, someone travelling by a very fast train from one location to another may be able to undertake in less than 24 hours what other people may take several days to do. Furthermore, such space–time relationships also have implications for the study of human mobility. Figure 1.4 posits the relative location of disciplinary studies on mobility. Leisure studies tends to focus on leisure in the home or in near-home environments and is often associated with daily leisure behaviours although studies of leisure behaviour on longer trips (i.e. holidays) is also recognised. The field of transport studies is also clearly concerned with human mobility and how people move between A and B. Much transport research is concentrated on the problems arising from daily commuting although long-distance travel is also a significant concern. Tourism studies has historically tended to concentrate on overnight travel behaviour although, as noted above, daytripping is becoming a significant interest, while the touristic dimensions of longer-term travel behaviours are also being recognised. Migration studies are concerned with permanent mobility. Indeed, in their otherwise excellent introductory text on contemporary migration Boyle et al. (1998, p. 33) note that 'the importance of temporary movement ... cannot be underestimated' but then go on to mention it only once more in the remainder of the book. However, given the increasing rates of mobility of a substantial proportion of the population in developed countries, the notion of permanence is itself increasingly contested, while temporary travel to a location may be the precursor to longer-term migration (Hall and Williams 2002a).

Nevertheless, Figure 1.4 indicates that there are a number of disciplines with clear interests in explaining the patterns and processes of human mobility, to this we may of course add other areas, such as geography and sociology, for which mobility has also become a significant issue in recent years. Yet, what is remarkable is the historical lack of interplay and cross-fertilisation between these fields. This is especially evidenced in the case of the study of human mobility, with the difficulties to be encountered in finding overlap between national and international surveys of tourism, migration, and studies of short- and long-term travel undertaken in transport studies. This may have occurred because of the relative lack of seriousness given to the tourism phenomenon in the wider social sciences until very recently. Alternatively, it may have arisen because while transdisciplinary and interdisciplinary research are often seen as good because of the potential new insights they can bring, the reward systems of academic research and the nature of academic institutions and avenues for publication are actually usually more geared towards disciplinary outcomes than that of encouraging research at the intersection of disciplines. This stated, it is apparent that a number of researchers are seeking to find a new common ground for the study of human mobility.

Mobilities

As the above discussion indicates, in addition to being defined in relation to its production and consumption, tourism is therefore increasingly being interpreted as but one, albeit highly significant, dimension of temporary mobility and circulation (Bell and Ward 2000; Urry 2000a, 2000b; Williams and Hall 2000, 2002; Larsen 2001; Hall and Williams 2002a; Sheller and Urry 2003; Coles et al. 2004; Hall and Müller 2004a). Figure 1.5 presents a model for describing different forms of temporary mobility, such as those noted in Figures 1.2 and 1.3, in terms of three dimensions of space, time and number of trips. Figure 1.5 therefore illustrates the decline in the overall number of trips or movements, time and distance away from a central generating point which would often be termed as 'home'. The number of movements declines the further one travels

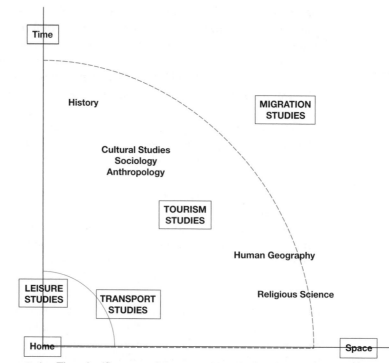

Figure 1.4   The significance of time–space relationships for disciplinary studies

in time and space away from the point of origin. The relationship represented in Figure 1.5 holds whether one is describing the totality of movements of individuals over their life spans from a central point (home) or for an extended period of time or whether one is describing the total characteristics of a population. Such distance decay effects with respect to travel frequency have been well documented (e.g. Holmes and Brown 1981; Smith 1995; Hanink and White 1995; Hanink and Stutts 2002) (see Chapter 2 for a fuller explanation of distance decay). In addition, the figure illustrates the relationship between tourism and other forms of temporary mobility, including various forms of what is often regarded as migration or temporary migration (Bell and Ward 2000; Williams and Hall 2002). Such activities have increasingly come to be discussed in the tourism literature, including travel for work and international experiences (e.g. Mason 2002), education (e.g. Weiler and Kalinowski 1990; Kalinowski 1992; Kalinowski and Weiler 1992; Brewer 1993–94; Kraft et al. 1993–94; Hsu and Sung, 1996, 1997; Field 1999), health (e.g. Goodrich and Goodrich 1987; Becheri 1989; Goodrich 1993, 1994; Hall 2003b), as well as travel to second homes (e.g. Coppock 1977; Müller 1999; Hall and Müller 2004a) and return migration (e.g. Duval 2002, 2003b, 2004d; Opsequio-Go and Duval 2003). It is therefore increasingly evident to those seeking wider perspectives on tourism that such forms of leisure-oriented mobility are highly interrelated and need to be incorporated into our understanding of tourism (Frändberg 1998; Aitcheson 1999; Crouch 1999a, 1999b; Aitcheson et al. 2000; Williams and Hall 2000; Williams et al. 2000; Hall and Williams 2002a; Coles et al. 2004).

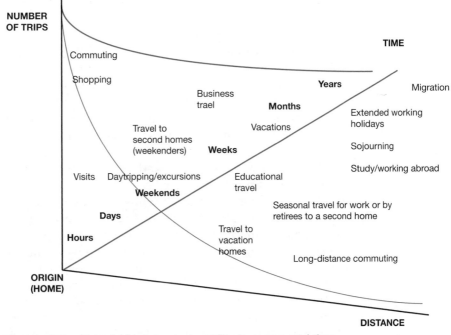

Figure 1.5 Extent of temporary mobility in space and time

From the perspective illustrated in Figure 1.5, tourism may therefore be interpreted as an expression of leisure or recreation lifestyle identified either through voluntary travel or a voluntary temporary short-term change of residence. However, Figure 1.5 also highlights that there are a number of different components of such travel behaviour which, as noted above, are increasingly studied under the rubric of tourism, including travelling for education both in the short and long term, business travel, health tourism, leisure shopping, second home travel, daytrips, the combining of work and travel, and amenity-oriented migration, because of their leisure mobility orientation. Arguably, some of these categories could be described as 'partial tourists' (Cohen 1974), nevertheless the leisure dimension remains important as a motivating factor in their travel behaviour. It should be noted that migration is often not permanent and individuals may return to their original home many years after they left on either a permanent basis (e.g. for retirement) or a temporary basis (e.g. to a second home). Furthermore, for many migrants relationships to the country of origin may be maintained through visits that are invariably described as tourism. Consideration of leisure mobilities also assists us in relating tourism to the broader consideration in the social sciences of the social relationships and identities that often span multiple localities (e.g. Lee 2003). Therefore, *the study of tourism must be willing to formulate a coherent approach to understanding the meaning behind the range of mobilities undertaken by individuals, not just tourists* (Coles et al. 2004).

This therefore allows us to see tourism within a wider social context over the life span of individuals as well as gain a greater appreciation of the constraints that prevent or limit leisure mobility. This also means that tourism is roughly and conceptually analogous in scope and meaning to other voluntary forms of movement (e.g. travel to second homes, return migration, emigration). As Coles et al. (2004) have argued, by extension, the conceptualisation and development of theoretical approaches to tourism should therefore consider relationships to other forms of mobility. Moreover, such a grounded approach necessitates reconfiguring tourism within those social, economic, political and technological forces that have enhanced mobility and the creation of extended networks of kinship and community at regional, national and global scales. Nevertheless, accounts of macro-level patterns and flows of tourist movement should not lose sight of the individual body moving in space and time.

Models of spatial interaction and diffusion or descriptions of transnational communities are collective representations of individual mobilities or time geographies. Time geography examines 'the ways in which the production and reproduction of social life depend upon knowledgeable human subjects tracing out routinised paths over space and through time, fulfilling particular projects whose realisations are bounded by inter-locking capability, coupling and steering constraints' (Gregory, p. 297). Based on the work of authors such as Hägerstrand (1967a, 1967b), Carlstein (Carlstein et al. 1978), Thrift (1977a, 1977b) and Pred (1981a, 1981b), time geography has been influential in seeking to understand individual space–time patterns as well as underlying significant developments in social theory such as Giddens' (1984) notion of structuration (see Chapter 3).

According to Giddens (1984, p. 116), 'Time-geography is concerned with the constraints that shape the routines of day-to-day life and shares with structuration theory an emphasis upon the significance of the practical character of daily activities, in circumstances of co-presence, for the constitution of social conduct', while also stressing the 'routine' character of daily life 'connected with features of the human body, its means of mobility and communication, and its path through the "life cycle" ' (1984, p. 111). Significantly, however, time geographies were not related to tourism, which was seen as being an occurrence outside that of the routine, a perspective which continues to the present day in much tourism writing (Wang 2000). For example, Aronsson (2000, p. 57) argues, '[W]e are prisoners in the present-day time–space structure that we have created for our lives.' Yet such perspectives fail to acknowledge the extent to which space–time compression has led to fundamental changes to individuals' space–time paths and overall global connectivity or extendibility in recent years. The routinised space–time paths of those living in 2004 are not the same as those of people in 1984 when Giddens was writing or in the 1960s when Hägerstrand was examining routine daily space–time trajectories. Instead, because of advances in transport and communication technology, for a substantial proportion of the population in developed countries or for elites in developing countries being able to travel long distances to engage in leisure behaviour (what one would usually describe as tourism) is now a part of their routine activities (Orfeil and Salomon 1993; Schafer 2000; Schafer and Victor 2000).

People's travel time budgets have not changed substantially, but the ability to travel further at a lower per unit cost within a given time budget (Schafer

2000) has led to a new series of social encounters, interactions and patterns of production and reproduction as well as consumption (Suvantola 2002). The locales in which this occurs are sometimes termed destinations, and represent a particular type of lifestyle mobility that, when it occurs away from the home environment, is usually termed 'tourism'. Just as significantly, space–time distantiation through both tourism and changes in communication technology have provided for the development of often dense sets of social, cultural and economic networks stretching between the two ends of the mobility spectrum from daily leisure mobility through to migration and thereby promoting the development of transnational communities in which movement is the norm (Coles et al. 2004).

Arguably, the use of mobility as a key explanatory concept in tourism studies may serve to address some of Rojek and Urry's (1997, p. 1) concerns, noted above, regarding the need to interrogate 'the very category of "tourism"'. Hopefully, by focusing on mobility, we can make sense of some of the 'chaotic conception' of tourism in that its nature can be explicitly addressed in terms of different forms of movement through space and time. Much of this can be done through the use of analogues. Analogue theory is a formal theory of model building which provides for the selective abstraction of elements from an empirical domain and their translation into a simplified and structured representation of a particular system (Chorley 1964). Within the social sciences the use of such analogues is now so widespread that their implications are little considered (Livingstone and Harrison 1981). Indeed, a significant contribution to tourism theory such as the Tourism Area Cycle of Evolution (TACE) of Butler (1980) is itself such an analogue model.

However, for reasons that will be illustrated in the following chapters, envisioning tourism in terms of space–time relationships is not just a simple analogue device, useful as it is. It will also be argued that focusing on movement through time and space also allows not only different forms of mobility to be analysed but also the means by which mobilities are constrained or encouraged at collective and individual levels.

Interrogating Tourism: Outline of the Book

The chapters of this book are divided into four sections. Part I, which includes the present chapter, provides the context for analysing tourism mobilities by focusing on broad issues of consumption and production. A concentration on changing mobilities over time also brings into central focus processes of globalisation and the means by which time and space have become 'flattened' due to technological innovations, particularly in transport and communications, and the socio-cultural and political dynamics of such processes. This is the subject of Chapter 2 and again helps link the subject matter of tourism to one of the key concepts of the social sciences. Chapter 3 examines the concept of mobility over space and time at both a macro-level, including models of spatial interaction, as well as at the level of the individual, through a focus on individuals' life trajectories or life courses. Chapter 3 also investigates some of the constraints and enabling elements of mobility, including not only access to money and time but also such factors as employment, class and race.

As noted above, destination promotion and competition need to be seen in terms of attracting mobility, whether it be capital (for investment) and/or people (as tourists, as labour or as desired residents). Typically, this is a function of tourism production whether at the level of the firm or the destination. Part II deals with these issues. Therefore, the production of tourism by government, industry and labour is the subject of Chapter 4. This chapter discusses the notion of place competition – a concept which itself is a key outcome of processes of globalisation. In order to attract mobility the state, or government, often intervenes (Chapter 5) in a partially industrialised industry that has substantial difficulties in cluster and network formation (Chapter 6). Chapters 5 and 6 also examine some of the issues associated with tourism planning and destination management, including some of the key locational factors in attracting tourism businesses and the implications that this has for tourism development.

Part III examines what happens when tourism consumption and production come together with respect to urban tourism (Chapter 7), rural and peripheral area tourism (Chapter 8) and ocean and marine tourism (Chapter 9). Building on some of the insights gained early in the book, these chapters highlight the importance of accessibility as a defining factor with respect to different tourism environments and their relative capacity to develop tourism.

Part IV examines tourism futures, in relation to major issues that arise out of mobility and which also may serve to constrain mobility. Chapter 10 contextualises Part IV through examining some of the main social, economic, political and technological trends, many of which have also been briefly commented on throughout the book. For example, factors such as demographic change will have an enormous impact on future leisure mobility in terms of both travel opportunities and constraints. As well as discussing issues of terrorism and political instability, Chapter 11 uses an expanded notion of security to introduce not only the extent to which tourism is a political target in terms of ideas of individual and political security, but also ideas of environmental and economic security, that are expanded upon in the following chapter. Chapter 12, on tourism and global environmental change, also examines ways in which tourism both affects and is affected by the environment in which it occurs. Finally, Chapter 13 briefly reflects on the future of tourism studies itself and discusses what factors will influence the directions in which the subject will go, particularly in relation to the question of for what and for whom is tourism knowledge generated. The last chapter also returns us to the potential role that the concept of mobility may have in our understanding of tourism and the relationship of tourism mobilities to other forms of mobility. Yet, by doing so, will this lead to the end of the subject of tourism?

Disciplining Tourism, Rethinking Tourism

This chapter has provided an overview of the disciplinary context of the field of tourism studies. It notes that, at least in terms of its institutional character-istics, tourism studies is now well established in many parts of the world. It also refutes the oft-made charge that tourism is a new area of study. It isn't! Although the mass institutionalisation of tourism is relatively recent, the study of tourism as a phenomenon is now over 70 years old, while tourism as a form of leisure mobility in terms of both production and consumption is much older still. Indeed, the present author actually argues in lectures these days that because of an increased dependency on the internet and downloadable journal articles, the old art of browsing in the library has been lost. We don't look at old books or journals any more (perhaps also because many university libraries have a bad habit of throwing old books out!). The reward system of academic publishing to make your book or journal article look as current as possible also means that many excellent accounts of the tourism phenomenon from the 1970s, 1960s and 1950s, or even earlier, have been lost to contem-porary knowledge. It is therefore with a little irony that the present book focuses on mobility as being a key concept in defining and understanding the tourism phenomenon.

The central role of mobility in understanding tourism and leisure is not new. For example, Perloff and Wingo (1962), writing in the landmark Outdoor Recreation Resources Review Commission (ORRRC) *Trends in American Living and Outdoor Recreation* study, noted that '[o]ne dimension of affluence is mobility, and it is the mobility of the urban population across the Nation which elevates outdoor recreation to the status of an important national problem'. Perhaps more succinctly, in an observation almost as true for the present day as when it was written, Wolfe (1966, p. 7) observed that 'most students of rec-reation concentrate on the reasons for travel, but few have much to say about the significance of mobility. [Mobility is] at the very heart of certain aspects of leisure activity today – outdoor recreation in particular, and, by definition, rec-reational travel.' As you will see, this book, written almost 40 years after Wolfe's insights, clearly agrees. Hopefully, it will help reinforce not only the central significance of mobility for understanding tourism and its study, but also highlight the potential understandings that over a half a century of study of tourism and destination concepts might bring to rethinking the contribution of tourism to the wider social sciences and society.

Plate 1.1 The Acropolis has been a tourism destination for well over 2,000 years and was featured in Ancient Roman guidebooks to Greece. Here a group of American college students are visiting the Acropolis as part of a study tour of Greece. (Details of this World Heritage listed property can be found at http://whc,unesco.org/sites/404.htm)

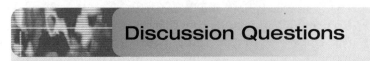

Discussion Questions

1. What are the implications for how one defines tourism?

2. Is there a difference between 'tourism' and the 'tourism industry'?

3. How might changes in temporary mobility in time and/or space affect definitions of activities?

4. Do you think that tourism is now part of everyday life?

Further Reading and Websites

There are a number of very good overviews of the tourism field. Lew et al. (2004) is arguably one of the best in terms of the social sciences outside the immediate business sphere, with a comprehensive coverage of social science subjects. Also see Gartner and Lime (2000) (although this has a strong North American emphasis), Hall and Page (2002), Ryan (2003), Shaw and Williams (2004). For those seeking something of an outdoor feel to examining mobility, see Pigram and Jenkins (1999). Interestingly, the disciplinary anxiety of tourism studies bears strong similarities to other areas, such as international business (see Peng 2004; Shenkar 2004) or even the navel gazing of geography (see Johnston 1991). Such anxiety may also be attached to the rapidly changing world under conditions of contemporary global capitalism.

ALTIS (a UK service designed to 'provide a trusted source of selected, high quality Internet information for students, lecturers, researchers and practitioners in the area of hospitality, leisure, sport and tourism'): http://altis.ac.uk

Tourism Officers Worldwide Directory: www.towd.com

United Nations Environment Programme, Production and Consumption Branch has a website that covers a wide range of tourism issues: www.uneptie.org/pc/tourism/home.htm

The World Tourism Organisation website: www.world-tourism.org

The World Travel and Tourism Council website: www.wttc.org

Globalisation and Tourism: Production, Consumption and Identity

2

Key Concepts

- Globalisation
- Time–space convergence
- Space–time distantiation
- Space–time compression
- Financial deregulation
- Technological change
- Product innovation
- Media and communications systems
- Transport cost
- Production
- Consumption
- Reflexivity
- Placeless social interaction
- Identity
- Sense of place

- Scale of analysis

- Diaspora

- Transnationalism

Globalisation has been a central concept of the Western social sciences over the past two decades. It has 'become a key word for organizing our thoughts as to how the world works' (Harvey 2000, p. 53). Contemporary globalisation 'refers both to the compression of the world and to the intensification of the consciousness of the world as a whole' (Robertson 1992, p. 8). The current dramatic changes in global economy and technology have even been described as the end of organised capitalism (Urry and Lash 1987, p. 97) because of the globalisation 'of economic, social and political relationships which have undermined the coherence, wholeness and unity of individual societies'. Globalisation and related issues of identity and (post)modernity have been the subject of much discussion and contestation as individuals have attempted to come to terms with their, and others', place in a rapidly changing world. Interestingly, tourism has not been a major focus of the globalisation debates in the wider social sciences, even though it has been recognised as a potentially significant factor in the contemporary global culture and economy (e.g. Friedman 1994). Globalisation, in the sense of referring to tourism's role within a global economic system is not a new idea. Indeed, it has been related to concepts of development, international competitiveness and business strategies. For example, Go and Pine (1995, p. 13) note that 'in relation to the hotel industry, globalization is popularly understood as a process designed to establish worldwide a hotel company's presence. Globalization is commonly perceived to have a standardizing impact in that products and institutions originally offered domestically appear on a worldwide scale.' However, from more critical and theoretically informed perspectives, discussed below, globalisation is seen as a far-reaching idea which embraces nearly all aspects of contemporary culture, economy, governance and identity.

Globalisation

Globalisation, like the concept of development, 'can be viewed as a process, a condition, or as a specific kind of political project' (Harvey 2000, p. 54). In tourism all of these perspectives have currency. Globalisation is 'a concept with consequences' (Hirst 1997, p. 424). Globalisation has had the effect of changing the 'rules of the game' in the struggle for competitive advantage among firms, destinations and places within, as well as between, countries and regions (Higgott 1999). However, globalisation is a complex, chaotic, multiscalar, multitemporal and multicentric series of processes operating in particular structural and spatial contexts (Jessop 1999). Globalisation should therefore be seen as an emergent phenomenon which results from economic, political, socio-cultural and technological processes on many scales rather than a distinctive causal mechanism in its own right. It is both a structural and a structuring phenomenon, the nature of which depends critically on processes occurring at the sub-global level.

Global interdependence typically results from processes which operate at various spatial scales, in different functional sub-systems, and involve complex and tangled causal hierachies rather than being a simple, unilinear, bottom-up or top-down movement (Jessop 1999; Dicken et al. 2001). Such an observation clearly suggests that globalisation is developing unevenly across space and time. Indeed, according to Kelly and Olds (1999, p. 2), 'a key element in contemporary processes of globalisation is not the impact of "global" processes upon another clearly defined scale, but instead the relativisation of scale'. Such relativities occur in relation to time–space convergence (Janelle 1968, 1969, 1973, 1974, 1975) through both 'space–time distantiation' and 'space–time compression'. The former refers to the stretching of social and economic relations over time and space, for example through the utilisation of communications technology such as the internet and by advances in transport technology, so that they can be controlled or coordinated over longer periods of time, greater distances, larger areas, and on more scales of activity. The latter involves the intensification of 'discrete' events in real time and/or increased velocity of material and non-material flows over a given distance. Again this is related to technological change, including communication, transport and social technologies (Jessop 1999). An example of this is provided in Figure 2.1, which illustrates changes in travel time between London and Edinburgh. The growth of tourism mobility at a global level is further illustrated in Figure 2.2 and Table 2.1.

Reductions in the cost and time of movement over space has long been a focus of innovations in transport technology and a feature of the increasing connection between different parts of the globe and growth in mobility. For example, in mapping time–space Forer (1978) referred to 'plastic space', noting the manner in which time–space compression had shrunk the United States in relative travel time with each advance in transport technology. In the case of Germany, Lanzendorf (2000) reports that the average kilometres travelled per person per year for leisure and vacation increased from 600 km in 1976 to just under 1,000 km in 1996. For work-related travel it increased 300 km to 500 km in the same period. However, the consequences of contemporary globalisation for tourism are much more than just changes to travel times and the extent of travel. For example, Damette (1980) introduced the concept of 'hypermobility' to describe the accelerated switching of investment between locations as the turnover time of fixed capital is reduced, in part because the state may take over parts of the costs for individual investments. Harvey (2000) identified four recent shifts in the dynamics of globalisation which signify why it has become so important over the last three decades: financial deregulation, technological change and innovation, media and communications, and the cost and time of moving commodities, all of which impact tourism.

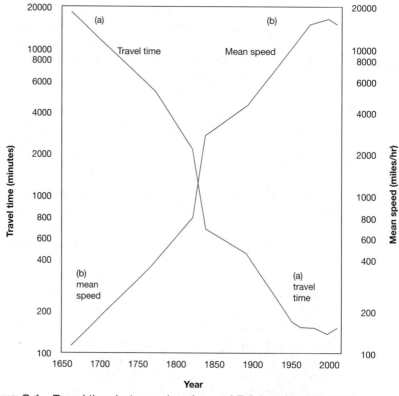

Figure 2.1   Travel time between London and Edinburgh, 1650–2000

Note: Air travel time includes estimate for journey to/from central London to Heathrow airport. Levelling off of travel time and mean speed has occurred because of increased traffic congestion in London and arguably has even increased since 2001 because security requirements have meant being at Heathrow earlier. Indeed, potential delays at Heathrow because of air traffic requirements have not been included in this figure nor the ongoing capacity of baggage handlers to put the author's backpack onto the wrong flight.

Sources: Based on Janelle 1968; Marchand 1973; and the author's personal experience.

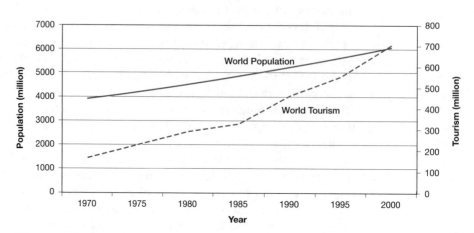

Figure 2.2   Growth in world population versus world tourism

Table 2.1 World population compared to world tourism

Date	World population (m)	International tourism arrivals (m)	International tourism arrivals as a percentage of world population	No. of cars in the world (m)	No. of cars as a percentage of world population
1950	2520.0	25.3	1.00		
1960	3020.0	69.3	2.30		
1970	3912.1	165.8	4.24	200	0.05
1975	4205.1	222.3	5.29		
1980	4520.1	287.5	6.36		
1985	4858.8	327.9	6.75	375	0.08
1990	5222.7	457.3	8.76	500	0.96
1995	5614.0	552.3	9.84	671	1.20
2000	6034.5	696.7	11.55		
2001	6122.4	692.7	11.31		

Sources: United Nations 1999; World Population 2003; World Tourism Organisation 1997a, 1997b, 2002a; http://hypertextbook.com/facts/2001/MarinaStasenko.shtml

Financial deregulation

Since the early 1970s the global financial system has become increasingly deregulated. This has meant that the international financial system has become more decentralised and operated through the functions of the market. However, this has also provided for increased volatility, witnessed for example in the Asian financial crisis of 1997, the repercussions of which are still being felt. Within the current global financial system capital has the ability to move rapidly around the world in order to take advantages of local economic conditions. The drive for financial deregulation has also been felt in movements towards free trade and the lessening of foreign investment restrictions under the negotiations of the World Trade Organisation. These have affected foreign tourism investments, the formation and development of transnational tourism firms, and have had a broader impact on regulation of labour mobility.

Technological change and product innovation

Although technological change and product innovation have long been a feature of capitalism, the recent rate of change and types of change and the rapid diffusion of innovation have been at a pace never before seen. For example, transport and aviation technology has rapidly advanced in a manner which has revolutionised the nature of mass tourism. Historically, the relationship between technology and tourism trends has usually been seen as a result of advances in transport technology (e.g. Burkart and Medlik, 1981). Undoubtedly, changes in transport technology have been profound in terms of their physical and perceptual impacts. For example, when the Jules Verne novel *Round the World in Eighty Days* was first published in 1873 it described an almost impossible feat of rapid travel, but by 1959 it was possible to circumnavigate the globe in 611 hours. By the early 1980s the same journey could be made on scheduled air routes in 32 hours. In 1981 the American manned space shuttle circled the globe once every 90 minutes (Mills 1983).

Media and communications system

The so-called 'information revolution' has changed the way in which we receive information and how we see the world for those in the developed countries and for some in the less developed world. The personal computer and internet have led to the increasing development of 'knowledge-based' economies and the increasing separation of the information-haves and have-nots. Access to travel information, for example, is increasingly becoming geared to using the internet rather than traditional face-to-face travel agents. Moreover, knowledge of destinations is also gained through a wider range of media.

Tourism Insight: Lonely Planet and Accessibility

Arguably, the most influential travel guides are the *Lonely Planet* guides which by the end of 2003 were selling approximately 5 million books a year with 650 different titles put together by a staff of 500 and a pool of 150 authors from 20 countries (Lansky 2003). According to Tony Wheeler, founder of Lonely Planet, 'These days ... in some countries, it seems like everyone is travelling. You're almost expected to do it. ... It's not uncommon to start at 18' (quoted in Lansky 2003, p. 32). In terms of cross-cultural exchange and the economic benefits of tourism, Tony believes the books have had a positive effect on the whole. The most noticeable one, according to Tony, is that 'they've made exotic places more accessible' (Lansky 2003, p. 33).

Cost and time of moving commodities, services and people

The cost and time of moving commodities, services and people have dramatically reduced in recent years. The real cost of travelling internationally has fallen sharply, as has the time it takes to travel long distances. For example, in the 1970s jet aircraft between Eastern Australia and the West Coast of North America would travel via Fiji and Hawaii. In the 1980s improved aviation technology and fuel efficiency meant that aircraft could travel via Hawaii alone. In the 1990s further developments, particularly the addition of winglets to the wings of long-haul aircraft, meant that you could fly non-stop between Sydney and Los Angeles in 12.5 hours. Non-stop commercial passenger flights are now available between Singapore and the United States. In the first decade of the twenty-first century marginal increases in the time saved may be achieved but, more significantly, the same flight will be undertaken by double-decker jumbo jets carrying almost twice as many people as the 'traditional' jumbo jet.

The four shifts identified by Harvey (2000) should not be seen as isolated entities. Most importantly, they are highly interrelated and synergistic in character. For example, as noted above, reductions in the costs and time of moving people cannot be separated from technological change and innovation. Similarly, the changes in the international financial system have been dependent in great part on the development of new communication technologies and innovations. Moreover, the four shifts have also been accompanied by a number of other important features which Harvey (2000, p. 63) regards as being 'perhaps best thought of as derivative from the primary forces at work', including the natures of production and organisational forms, consumption and place.

Production and Organisational Forms

One of the most influential frameworks in the analysis of global economic change is that of 'post-Fordism' which represent a distinct break from the past economic structures associated with a dominant era of 'Fordism' (Leborgne and Lipietz 1992). Fordism refers to the dominance of large, vertically integrated companies producing homogeneous or standardised products for a market based primarily on price competition. 'Post-Fordism', also described within the context of 'flexible regimes of accumulation' and 'flexible specialisation', refers to the creation of a more specialised and rapidly changing marketplace that necessitates the use of more flexible/responsive forms of production if consumer demands are to be met (Milne 1994). Associated with the development of more flexible/responsive forms of production is the extent to which production has often moved offshore from the original 'home' country of corporations. The reduced costs of commodity and information movement, the attraction of cheap labour and efforts by governments to attract increasingly mobile capital has meant that the geographical dispersal and fragmentation of production systems, divisions of labour and specialisations of tasks have occurred, 'albeit often in the midst of an increasing centralization of corporate power through mergers, takeovers, or joint production agreements that transcended national boundaries' (Harvey 2000, p. 63).

Within the tourism context, post-Fordist ideas have received considerable attention in the work of Poon (1989, 1990), who described these new industrial structures as part of 'new tourism'. The focus on flexibility has considerable significance for the internal and external operations of tourism organisations.

Plate 2.1 Developments in transport technology have been integral for both globalisation and mobility. Ferry services and car transport have become critical for many remote destinations such as here in the west of Scotland which otherwise may have limited air or train access as they offer access at reasonable cost. (The Caledonian MacBrayne ferry service details are at www.calmac.co.uk)

Internally, the corporate structure of a flexible tourism business revolves around the division of the labour force into core and peripheral groupings (Milne 1994; Shaw and Williams 1994). While such flexible labour forces increasingly appear to be utilised by tourism business, particularly in national economies where economic and employment deregulation has occurred, there is some debate over whether contemporary tourism labour force structure is a result of economic globalisation or the specific temporal and spatial nature of tourism demand itself or some combination of the two (Shaw and Williams 1994).

However, although the idea of flexible economic response, whether it be by firms or destinations, is one of the dominant notions of the enterprise culture being promoted by governments in the developed world (see Corner and Harvey 1991), the empirical and theoretical foundations on which our understanding of contemporary economic processes in tourism is based are relatively weak. As Milne et al. (1994) observed, our understanding of the nature of contemporary capitalism has been weakened by the lack of attention paid to economic activities outside the manufacturing sphere and the narrow range of regional settings in which studies have been conducted (Ioannides and Debbage 1998). Service industries, such as tourism, on which many of the economic goals of place marketing are based (see Chapter 7), may therefore have been inadequately conceptualised with respect to their place within post-Fordist and flexible modes of production. Moreover, the flexibility of services industries such as tourism with respect to the development of 24-hour workplaces and increased part-time, contract and casual labour will also have implications for the consumption and production of leisure and the characteristics of leisure lifestyles over the life course (Redmond 1988; Reid 1989; Elchardus 1991; Rosenberg 1992; Gershuny 1993; Reilly 1994; Presser 1995).

The discourse of globalisation clearly goes further than the simple description of contemporary economic and social change. It also carries with it the power to shape material reality via organisational and institutional restructuring and policy formulation and implementation (Gibson-Graham 1996; Leyshon 1997; Kelly and Olds 1999). It can also construct a view of geographical space that implies the deferral of political options from the national to the supranational and global scales, and from the local to the national. In effect, the idea of globalisation has itself become a political force (Piven 1995). Far from being inevitable, 'so-called "globalization" must be seen as a politically rather than a technologically induced phenomenon' (Weiss 1997, p. 23).

In addition to the 'structural context' of globalisation noted above, authors such as Ohmae (1995), Jessop (1999) and Higgott (1999) point to a more strategic interpretation of globalisation, which refers to individual and institutional actors' attempts to promote the global coordination of activities on a continuing basis within different orders or functional systems, for example interpersonal networking, inter-firm strategic alliances, the creation of international and supranational regimes to govern particular fields of action, and the broader development of modes of international and supranational systems of governance (see Chapters 5 and 6). Therefore, given the multiscale, multitemporal and multicentric nature of globalisation, we can recognise that globalisation 'rarely, if ever, involves the full structural integration and strategic coordination across the globe' (Jessop 1999, p. 22). Instead, processes usually considered under the rubric of 'economic globalisation' include:

- the formation of regional economic and trading blocs – particularly in North America (North American Free Trade Area (NAFTA)), Europe (European Union (EU)) and East Asia-Pacific (Asia-Pacific Economic Cooperation (APEC), Association of South East Asian Nations (ASEAN)) – and the development of formal links between those blocs (e.g. the regular conduct of Asia–Europe meetings);

- the growth of 'local internationalisation', 'virtual regions', through the development of economic ties between contiguous (e.g. 'border regions'), or non-contiguous local and regional state authorities (e.g. growth regions and triangles), in different national economies which often bypass the level of the nation state but which still retain support at the national level;

- the widening and deepening of international and supranational regimes which cover economically relevant issues and which may also provide for regional institutionalised governance (e.g. the further expansion of the EU in May 2004);

- the internationalisation of national economic spaces through growing penetration (inward flows) and extraversion (outward flows) typically related to the development of new social and economic networks;

- the extension and deepening of multinationalisation by multinational and transnational firms. In the tourism sector this particularly applies to the activities of transport (e.g. Connex and Stagecoach) and accommodation firms (e.g. Accor); and

- the 'emergence of globalisation proper through the introduction and acceptance of global norms and standards, the development of globally integrated markets together with globally oriented strategies, and "deracinated" firms with no evident national operational base' (Jessop 1999, p. 23).

Consumption

Consumption and production cannot be separated; they are two sides of the same coin. As Laurier (1993, p. 272) observed:

> To build binary opposites is to make one dependent on the other, and so there cannot be consumption without production ... it is apparent that they merge in many places and that each process certainly does have effects on the other ... even if they are causal or may never be explicable.

It should not be surprising, therefore, that in the same way that the nature of production is regarded as having changed, then so has the nature of consumption (Glennie and Thrift 1992). For example, Stuart Hall (1988, p. 24) noted 'greater fragmentation and pluralism, the weakening of older collective solidarities and block identities and the emergence of new identities associated with greater work flexibility [and] the maximisation of individual choice through personal consumption'. Arguably, this is related not only to the enhanced mobilities of some but also the opportunities for enhanced communicative interaction between distant parts of the world. In a review of late twentieth-century consumption, Thrift and Glennie (1993) identified five important, though relatively new and distinctive processes.

Growth of reflexivity

The growth of a high degree of 'reflexivity' of self-consciousness among the populations of contemporary industrial societies is a development in the ability of human subjects to reflect upon the social conditions of their existence. The growth of reflexivity has tended to be regarded as one of the hallmarks of postmodernity (Lawson 1985; Gergen 1991; Lash and Urry 1994). By this is meant that modern societies have reached a point where not only are they forced to reflect on themselves but that they also have the capability of reflecting *back* on themselves. For Giddens (1990, 1991) this has meant the capacity for greater personal, individual self-reflexivity while for Beck (1992) it is societal self-reflexivity through social monitoring and social movements (Beck et al. 1994). Indeed, Giddens (1984, p. 3) argues that reflexivity 'should be understood not merely as "self-consciousness" but as the monitored character of the ongoing flow of social life. To be a human being is to be a purposive agent, who both has reasons for his or her activities and is able, if asked, to elaborate discursively upon those reasons (including lying about them).'

The growth of reflexivity creates new possibilities for social relations in a wide variety of spheres, 'for intimate relations, for friendship, for work relations, for leisure and for consumption' (Lash and Urry 1994, p. 31). Judgements about the value of different social and physical environments, such as those which may be desirable both to consume and reproduce for tourist benefit, are regarded as being increasingly based on aesthetic considerations. In a manner which has substantial implications for discussions of tourism attractions and experiences, for example, Thrift and Glennie (1993) argue that the growth of aesthetic reflexivity has had significant effects on the practices of consumption because there are so many aesthetic authorities to choose from and to interpret. It therefore potentially becomes much more difficult for any one person, agency or whatever to control the meaning of commodities, for example in terms of the interpretation of history at any particular heritage site. And in a manner which reflects the concern by some commentators over the authenticity of the heritage experience, Thrift and Glennie (1993, p. 43) observe that, 'the growth of aesthetic reflexivity has produced a different attitude to authenticity, one which is more bound up with aesthetic illusions (for example in modern advertising) than with a quest for the real or the deeply spiritual'.

Increase in 'placeless' social interaction

There has been a massive increase in social interaction mediated by electronic means (e.g. the internet). This has resulted in the operation of an extended public sphere with the experience of community no longer requiring individuals to share a common locale (Thompson 1991). Indeed, lifestyle and the type of consumption that is undertaken may be a greater basis of a common identity for some than where one lives. For example, virtual travel communities now exist in which 'word-of-mouth' information and recommendations occur without the participants ever making direct physical contact. Similarly, MacCannell (1999, p. 32) writes of the meeting grounds of tourists where '[s]trangers who have the same cultural grounding can come together in a cultural production, each knowing what to expect next, and feel a closeness or solidarity, even where no empirical closeness exists. Their relationship begins before they meet.'

Attention to individuality

The increase in reflexivity that characterises many in contemporary developed societies can also be regarded as an expression of heightened individualism (Kumar 1995). There has been a greater degree of attention paid to the fostering of individuality, particularly in relation to ideas of self-actualisation, with the concept of individuality both broadening and deepening (see Gergen 1991). According to Thrift and Glennie (1993), this has resulted in:

- the entry of more and more groups in consumption culture;

- the growth of various social groupings which may be committed to a particular pattern of consumption (e.g. conservation groups, ecotourism organisations, alternative trade organisations);

- a massive increase in the scale and the power of the consumer movement;

- the business of marketing individuality (through the design of products, shops and so on), which has consequently become more reflective, with niche marketing both creating and constituting new modes of individuality; and

- the shaping of personality as a more reflexively systematic concern with appearance and body presentation coming to express self.

Attention to individuality is also demonstrated in the way in which tourism businesses increasingly focus on lifestyle as a selling feature for their branding and products. For example, in 2000 Ansett Australia, then Australia's second international airline after Qantas, developed an advertising campaign based on an entirely new branding strategy. According to Shane O'Hare, Ansett's manager of customer communications: 'The reality of the marketplace – with globalisation and so on – meant that it was important to re-engineer the business.' The first phase of new advertising, 'Go your own way', was launched in March 2000 and was pitched at 'corporate soldiers', 25–50-year-old business travellers who, said O'Hare, were travelling a lot more: 'E-commerce has increased the need to travel, not decreased it. Also the process of globalisation requires more travel' (Light 2000, p. 60). The launch commercials for the campaign with music provided by Simply Red (*Coming Home to You*) and The Who (*My Generation*) had little to do with flying. Instead, the advertisements showed customers and staff engaged in 'scenes of playful anarchy; playing soccer and cricket, singing, partying, generally having raging good times. The ads could be selling shows' (Light 2000, p. 60). However, according to O'Hare, 'Lifestyle is an extension of business now. Business is everywhere. ... In terms of cut-through [awareness], it is our most successful campaign in at least 10 years' (in Light 2000, p. 60).

The forging of new spaces and places

New modes of consumption are regarded as having led to the establishment of new spaces for both consumption itself and the sustenance of diverse consumption discourses. Integrated urban developments, such as new city centres, festival marketplaces or shopping malls, are part of the recomposition of the city as a dense network of communicative and social interaction (see Chapter 7). This is being done to meet the need to provide different social groups with different sets of information in the same place.

Sense of place

Despite the new patterns of consumption there is still a need to provide a 'sense of place' and, according to Thrift and Glennie (1993, p. 47), 'this sense of a distinctive locality to which a range of social groups belong (complete with their diverse consumption discourses and practices) is something that the city of interaction can still provide against the placeless "hyperspace" of advertising through the mass media'. Such a notion remains important for both heritage tourism, in which heritage may represent something secure and constant in a changing world, and lifestyle migration and travel, in which tourists seek to locate themselves within idealised landscapes. Indeed, increased mobilities may lead to multiple senses of place affiliation and home with corresponding implications for identity as to where one belongs and how you define yourself (Case 1996; Moore 2000), an observation which has been paramount in recent writings on the relationships between tourism, identity and transnationalism in which the 'betweenness' of migrant belongings represents a significant strand of research (Fortier 2000; Duval 2004a, 2004c).

According to Coles et al. (2004), a transnational framework of analysis within tourism studies would allow for the recognition of interconnected social networks and the resulting movement between and among multiple

Plate 2.2   Many shopping mall developments create new spaces of consumption. This photograph from the West Edmonton Mall highlights the extent to which a high street façade has been brought inside into a controlled environment that seeks to encourage consumption and may also exclude undesirable elements from such private space that may otherwise limit consumption. (see www.westedmall.com)

localities. In other words, such interconnected transnational networks mean that movement, or temporary mobility, by transnational actors is perhaps another means by which tourism can be viewed. Such social networks and linkages may account for a significant amount of global tourism, especially when viewed in the context of migrant mobilities (Duval and Hall 2004). Nevertheless, the reality is that very little tourism literature has explored the tourist in the context of transnational behaviour (Duval 2004b, 2004c).

Issues of dislocation and identity are also to be found in recent interest in the intersections of tourism, diaspora and postcolonialism (Shuval 2000; Coles and Timothy 2004; Coles et al. 2004; Hall and Tucker 2004a, 2004b). Clifford (1997), for example, noted that diasporic *routes* are as crucial in identity formation as the (geographical) *roots*. Notwithstanding inter- and intra-diasporic variations, Coles and Timothy (2004) observe that diasporas precipitate a number of different modes of travel and tourism inspired by the collision between their migrational histories (their 'routes'), their attachment to the 'home' country (their 'roots'), and their experiences of and in the host country (their 'routine'). Perhaps most predictably, diaspora tourists travel back to their original, ancestral homeland in search of their roots and family background (e.g. Bruner 1996; Stephenson 2002). More systematic, highly structured journeys of self-discovery that are focused on the search for tangible artefacts of forebears have also been termed 'genealogical' (Nash 2002), 'family history' or 'ancestral' tourism (Fowler 2003). The second mode represents the first in reverse as residents of the original 'homeland' travel into the diaspora, while the third involves intra-diasporic travel to the far-flung destinations beyond 'home' occupied by diaspora(s). The fourth, spaces of transit in the scattering process along diasporic trajectories, may assume sacred importance and motivate trips. For example, Ellis Island and the Statue of Liberty have become popular sites of pilgrimage for many European-Americans to pay homage to their forebears and to their migrational achievements (Ashworth and Tunbridge 1996), although, as Ioannides and Cohen (2002) highlight, spaces of transit are not necessarily restricted to points of entry or departure. Finally, various diasporic home spaces and vacation spaces may also be significant for the decision to travel. One of the most interesting aspects, therefore, of recent writing on transnationalism, diaspora and mobility is that one set of movements leads to another. Displacement from one place to another and the subsequent implications that this has for identity may therefore mean that tourism becomes a perhaps unexpected beneficiary of postcolonial dislocation.

Globalisation, Consumption and Identity

The goods and services that people consume, including tourism, have consistently been a vital way in which people have effectively constituted their sense of self and other. According to some theorists, the emergence of style as identity (Hebdidge 1979) and consumption as a form of self-definition (Baudrillard 1988a) have gone hand in hand with an increasingly reflexive and aesthetic appreciation hastened by the proliferation of visual images and the electronic media (Goodwin 1993) and the development of performative body presentation-accumulation strategies (Edensor 2000a; Harvey 2000). However, the postmodern notion 'that individual identities are disappearing into a seductive flux of free-floating signs is questionable. It is, of course, arguable whether individual identities have ever been well-formed wholes' (Thrift and Glennie 1993, p. 47). Instead, we are probably witnessing a situation of more differentiated notions of individualism and individuality based upon a greater number of systems of cultural reference which are themselves founded upon relatedness and interdependence (Gergen 1991). 'Each individual exercises surveillance over and against himself' (Foucault 1977, p. 155) as we manage impressions of ourselves in the social encounters of everyday life (Goffmann 1959). Fashion and taste therefore not only influence how we present ourselves but also affect where and how we travel. Tourism is a form of conspicuous consumption, the value of which is partly derived from its symbolic value (Baudrillard 1988b) and the cultural capital it provides, in that the desire to be fashionable is one of the means by which people indicate their distinctiveness. However, such an observation is not new. For example, Veblen (1934) described fashion as a symbol of the bourgeoisie designed to symbolise their membership of the non-productive leisure classes. If this is the case, does this mean that clothing is not only a materialisation of class taste but of tourism as well? As Bourdieu (1984, p. 56) observed with respect to fashion and taste:

> It unites and separates. Being the product of the conditioning associated with a particular class of conditions of existence, it unites all those who are the product of similar conditions while distinguishing them from others. And it distinguishes them in an essential way, since taste is the basis of all one has ... and all that one is.

How we holiday therefore acts to define who we are not only in terms of other people's perceptions but also perhaps our own. But this 'does not mean that individual identity is necessarily disintegrating, only that it is changing its form' (Thrift and Glennie 1993, p. 47). Therefore, the relationship between place and identity still holds and, indeed, may become even more significant within a period of rapid global change and mobility. As Thrift and Glennie (1993, p. 48) observed, 'paying greater attention to the historical geographies of ... life and consumption – as a variety of discourses and practices tied to different social groups, regions, cities, towns and intra-urban sites – is an essential component of rethinking the standard theorisations of modern consumption'. As Goodwin (1993, p. 149) so cogently observed, regions are 'thus more than a simple coherence of production and consumption (and even this is never guaranteed). It is a complex collection of individuals and communities, which in certain instances develop particular regional and local cultures, formed by social relations and practices outside of capital's narrow logic.'

Despite awareness of individualism and reflexity, there is nevertheless a substantial discourse in tourism studies on the relationship between tourism, globalisation and homogenisation. Here the development of tourism is often seen as an essential symbol and vehicle of modernity and Westernisation (Harrison 1992b; Mowforth and Munt 1998; Meethan 2001; Hall and Tucker 2004b). As Roche (1992, p. 566) observed, 'This has particularly been the case in Third World countries. But this role as both a symbol and vehicle of economic and socio-cultural change and "modernisation" is potentially just as significant for the advanced industrial countries.' Roche's comments indicate the manner in which globalisation, modernity and development have become closely identified. Indeed, much tourism analysis and advertising have romanticised 'tradition' without considering what people who live at the destination and who are part of the production of tourism themselves want. As Tomlinson (1991, p. 28) has recognised, 'we will have to problematise not just those cultural practices characterised as "modern", but the underlying cultural "narrative" that sustains them: a narrative rooted in the culture of the (capitalist) West, in which the abstract notions of development or "progress" are instituted as global cultural goals'.

However, as noted above, the realm of contemporary modernity is problematic in terms of identity (Giddens 1981). The 'us' of 'in-group identification' becomes increasingly difficult to fill with a content, other than those specifically invoked in the ideology of nationalism, ethnicity, religion and heritage, or those established through new lifestyles, in the increasing 'sameness' of commodified modern life. Such an observation is extremely significant within the context of heritage management and heritage tourism which often provides an idealised past which ignores a number of competing histories (Hall and McArthur 1996; Tunbridge and Ashworth 1996). Instead, what we take to be 'our culture' at any given time is a kind of 'totalisation' of cultural memory up to that point. As a consequence, 'our culture' in the modern world is never purely locally produced, but always contains the traces of previous cultural borrowings or influence, which have been part of this 'totalising' and have become, as it were, 'naturalised' (Tomlinson 1991).

Although there is evidence that an unprecedented cultural convergence seems to be occurring at certain levels, this cannot be read in the self-evidently negative terms that the critics of 'cultural homogenisation' or consumerism assume. The notion of cultural homogenisation is far from simple. For those in a position to view the world as a cultural totality, it cannot be denied that certain processes of cultural convergence are underway, and that these are new processes. However, for the people involved in each discrete instance, the experience of Western capitalist culture will have quite different significance (Tomlinson 1991). The spread of capitalism should therefore be seen as the spread of a distinctive 'cultural dominance' in its own right.

The failure of a culture to 'survive' in an 'original' form may itself be taken as a process of adaptation to a new 'environment', that of capitalist industrial modernity. However, homogenisation of consumption or production is not a certainty. Indeed, an awareness of cultural differences may become decisive in oligopolistic markets of the kind that transnational consumer goods manufacturers have already created in many countries of the world. As Sinclair (1987, p. 166) points out: 'When global competition is driven by scale economies, at a certain point everyone gets equalized ... the competitive advantage will go to the companies that are sensitive to individual market developments.' Accordingly, we can find very few products which are true world brands, 'manufactured, packaged and positioned in roughly the same manner worldwide, regardless of individual economies, cultures and lifestyles'. The logic of capitalist competition may therefore point to cultural outcomes other than homogenisation in the crudest form. Nevertheless, as Tomlinson recognises, the critique of homogenisation itself 'may turn out to be a peculiarly Western-centred concern if what is argued is that cultures must retain their separate identities simply to make the world a more diverse and interesting place' (1991, p. 135). Indeed, even in terms of current debates over place promotion (see Chapter 4), the 'sameness' of the city may be quite problematic. For the inhabitants of a city, whether the city looks like somewhere else may not be a problem if they are enjoying it.

Any critique of consumerist penetration of 'other cultures' cannot therefore be separated from the critique of consumerism in the West. As Sinclair (1987, p. 158) noted, less developed countries or indigenous cultures 'should defend the natural innocence of their traditional values against corrupting incursions by Western "materialism". To the extent that this view romanticised wretchedness, conflated all non-Western cultures and patronised genuine Third World aspirations for material improvement, we would not regard it as tenable today' (see also Crick 1989; Tucker 2003; Hall and Tucker 2004a). We are therefore simply not in a position to deny the attractions consumer culture may have for other cultures unless and until we have established a coherent critique of our *own* consumer culture, and tourism's place within it. Consumerism is therefore perhaps best grasped as part of a wider *structural context* of capitalist modernity, and in terms of the 'routine' discontents which this brings. Within a global capitalist system, all cultures are, in a sense, 'condemned to modernity' (Octavio Paz, in Berman, 1983, p. 125) in that they are integrated at a structural level in the orders of the state system and the global capitalist market; but this integration, which is a structural *fait accompli* and not a cultural 'option', alters the terms of culture irrevocably since it entails a one-way journey from 'tradition' to 'modernity' for which communal decisions to 'opt out' cannot be taken (Tomlinson 1991). Modernity, in which tourism is embedded, is not just a style, form or structure, but is a mode of common *cultural experience*, although, as Berman (1983, p. 15) noted: 'To be modern is to find ourselves in an environment that promises us adventure, power, joy, growth, transformation of ourselves and our world – and, at the same time, that threatens to destroy everything we have, everything we know, everything we are.'

The 'lived culture' of capitalist modernity is transmitted by the major social-economic institutions of the West – the market, bureaucracy, science and technology, mass transport and communications and so on – the 'carriers of modernity' (Berger 1974, p. 200). However, the sense in which they are a *cultural* imposition is not so clear because of both the reflexive dimension of modernity and the set of choices that then become available for self-understanding (Tomlinson 1991, 1999a, 1999b). Nevertheless, the extent to which they represent a 'point of no return' raises numerous concerns. When the certainties of the past have faded how do we define ourselves in a complex global environment and generate shared narratives of meaning and orientation? Heritage and roots tourism and the search for nostalgia and authentic other can be regarded as one component of the search for identity. In this we perceive the 'consumption of roots as commodities, the creation of a life space reminiscent of a nostalgic vision or some pastiche of eras based thereupon' (Friedman 1994, p. 191).

Capitalism is the contextualising structure for global processes and tourism as a consumptive and productive element within such processes. Capitalism is not just a set of economic practices but is the set of *central (dominant) positioning of economic practices* within the social ordering of collective existence (Tomlinson 1991). As Bell (1979, p. 14) observed, 'capitalism is an economic-cultural system, organized economically around the institution of property and the production of commodities and based culturally in the fact that exchange relations, that of buying and selling, have permeated most of the society'. The unintended consequences for a shared environment of 'late modern' production and consumption practices include both globalisation and the emergence of global market forces which are incomprehensible to the vast majority of people. Similarly, Jameson (1984, p. 84) noted 'the incapacity of our minds, at least at present, to map the great global multinational and decentred communicational network in which we find ourselves caught as individual subjects', yet he recognised the emergence of a new ' "cultural space" of some new "world system" of late capitalism' (Jameson 1984, p. 88). The latest expansion of capitalism therefore produces a truly 'global' system for some, which

Plate 2.3   Roots tourism is a very important element of the Scottish tourism product given the spread of the Scottish diaspora throughout most of the English-speaking new world. The town of Braemar in Scotland has a number of shops that seek to provide authentic Scottish gifts and mementoes often associated with particular clans. (see www.ancestralscotland.com and www.visitbritain.com)

can be seen not only in the complex networks of international finance and multinational capitalist production, but also in the spatial context of cultural experience that it produces for those who are most able to participate, those with the greatest mobility.

Our everyday experience is necessarily 'local', and yet this experience is increasingly shaped by global processes. 'The cultural space of the global is one to which we are constantly *referred*, particularly by the mass media, but one in which it is extremely difficult to locate our own personal experience' (Tomlinson 1991, p. 177) unless one has substantial mobility. To use Jameson's (1984) term, we need somehow to be able to 'map' the new cultural space of the global.

Globalisation, Localisation and Identity: Towards New Tourism Spaces and Places?

One of the great apparent paradoxes of contemporary globalisation is the extent to which the local or localisation has become significant (e.g. Kearns and Philo 1993a, 1993b; Kotler et al. 1993; Porter 2000a, 2000b). As Porter (1990, p. 19) noted, in economic and business terms: 'Competitive advantage is created and sustained through a highly localised process. Differences in national economic structures, values, cultures, and institutions, and histories contribute profoundly to competitive success.' The production of tourism is intimately connected to the place marketing process because of the way in which it is often used as a focus for regional redevelopment, revitalisation and promotion strategies, and the formation of collective identities. However, if the creation of place identity and 'the promotion of a place-image becomes a matter of commodifying it through a rigorous selection from its many charac-teristics' (Madsen 1992, p. 633), then it becomes vital that we understand the manner in which the new globalised commodities associated with tourism are produced and consumed. Indeed, it is vital that we see tourism as part of a multiscalar process (Figure 2.3).

Tourism is a part of individual and collective identity formation in a glob-alised world. Tourism also assists in the promotion and production of places. However, the question as to whose place and identities are being produced and for whom is often not raised. The instrumental reasoning of contemporary capitalism, its 'social imaginary', provides not only the initial impetus for much tourism development, but also sets the trajectory. Although the forma-tion of collective cultural identity is 'an ongoing process, politically contested and historically unfinished' (Clifford 1988, p. 9), tourism is clearly inseparable from such cultural politics, which can be defined as 'the struggles over the official symbolic representations of reality that shall prevail in a given social order at a given time' (Ortner 1989, p. 200). Therefore, tourism should not be

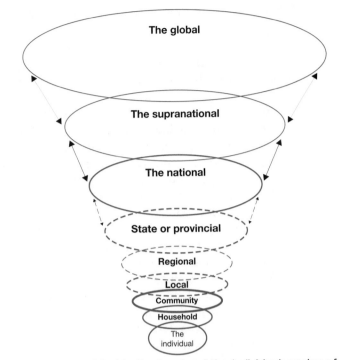

Figure 2.3   From the global to the local and the individual: scales of analysis in tourism

observed in isolation as 'contention over definitions of what is traditional and authentic becomes charged with a variety of additional meanings, as the range of interested parties increases' (Wood 1993, p. 64). Unfortunately, the tourism literature has also not explored the relationship between tourism and transnational behaviour and its relationship to the interplay between place and identity (though see Coles et al. 2004; Duval 2004a, 2004b, 2004c).

Transnationalism 'is the existence of links between a community in its current place of residence and its place of origin, however distant, and between the various communities of a diaspora. ... Transnationalism signals that significant networks exist and are maintained across borders' (Spoonley 2000, p. 4). A transnational framework of analysis in tourism would allow for the recognition of interconnected social networks and the resulting movement between and among multiple localities. In other words, such interconnected transnational networks mean that movement, or temporary mobility, by transnational actors is perhaps another means by which tourism can be viewed. Such social networks and linkages may very well, in reality, account for a significant amount of global tourism, especially when viewed in the context of migrant mobilities (Coles et al. 2004).

There is clearly a need for viable communities of cultural judgement: for communities on a scale to which individuals can relate, and which can provide satisfying accounts of how and why we live as we live (Tomlinson 1991, 1999b). Tourism should be part of providing that need. However, oftentimes in the focus on ecotourism, green tourism, heritage tourism, cultural or whatever other category of tourism we might like to name, the bigger picture of where tourism mobilities fit into contemporary global economic and social processes is often lost and probably not even considered.

Tourism is very much a child of modernity. For Wang (2000), travel distinguishes 'us' from 'others' who are not modern. Travel can be broken down into essential and non-essential travel. 'We' travel for pleasure and fun because 'we' are moderns. 'They' don't travel because 'they' are socially and economically constrained from doing so, and hence are still outside the modern lifestyle. 'The rate of national participation in tourism becomes one of the indicators of a demarcation between the traditional and the modern' (Wang 2000, p. 29). Nevertheless, not only does tourism reflect modern lifestyles and fashions, but it also reflects access to money, time (especially non-essential time), and a relative absence of other social, cultural, political and gender constraints. Indeed, Mowforth and Munt (1998) suggest possible connections between new forms of tourism and the continuous process of social class formation. Yet regardless of the underlying collection of reasons it is apparent that tourism mobilities provide the 'other' and a reference point for identities whether it be in the consumption or production of such mobility. Nevertheless, there is very little utility in reducing the world to a spaceless abstraction (Crang and Thrift 2000, p. 2), as the next chapter will highlight that the consideration of space and time is essential to understanding the local and global processes within which tourism mobilities are implicated. Although the following comment from Marshall McLuhan (1964, p. 16) undoubtedly finds resonance today, neither space nor time have been abolished: 'Today, after more than a century of electronic technology, we have extended our central nervous system itself in a global embrace, abolishing both space and time as far as our planet is concerned.' Indeed, places and regions may be regarded as 'nexuses of untraded inter-dependencies' (Storper 1995) that underpin the relationships of traded dependencies that signify success in the market. The logic of the capitalist production process, validated a posteriori by the sale of commodities in markets, presumes the consumption of what is produced. Such consumption has considerable importance for meanings and identities. Changes in consumption through the emergence of a more product-differentiated flexible production system clearly have implications for individual identities, both for those who can afford to consume the new, often niche, commodities and those who cannot. Equally, the emphasis on places competing with one another for capital, employment, people and visitors within an often global marketplace has involved policies and strategies to (re)create and (re)image the identities of places and the people within them (see Chapter 4). Such strategies have also been enabled by regressive income distribution policies that have greatly increased the disposable incomes of a small minority of middle-class consumers (Curry 1993) who are the focus for the commodity and place marketers and who constitute the most mobile members of society.

Many students of tourism are also the children of modernity, relatively safe within a university world which is increasingly dependent on government and private sector 'partnerships', and are usually filled with the expectation that they will themselves travel. These two factors are implicated within the dominant world view or *episteme* of mainstream tourism studies, which often focuses on the local and on the immediate business concerns of the tourism industry. However, if tourism as an area of study is to make a positive contribution to the lifeworlds and life courses of those we study, there is a clear need for grounding tourism within social scientific theorisations that provide the global context for local and individual actions. And it is perhaps here, with a fuller recognition of the context within which tourism occurs and the rich web of relationships, interactions and linkages in which it is located, that we might, to paraphrase Tomlinson (1991), begin to imagine, theorise and work towards different spaces of mobility.

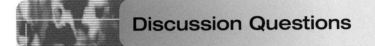

Discussion Questions

1. Why is the concept of globalisation relevant to tourism?

2. How does time–space convergence affect tourism?

3. How does the 'information revolution' affect tourism?

4. Do you think that globalisation is evenly distributed over the world?

5. How might the idea of 'sense of place' be significant for tourism?

6. Do you think that where and how we holiday helps define who we are?

Further Reading and Websites

On globalisation, see Harvey (1989b, 2000), especially the latter work. On tourism and global change, see Skelton and Allen (1999). Cooper and Wahab (2000) and Meethan (2001) deal with issues of the interrelationship between tourism and globalisation. For a critical account of processes of cultural imperialism and the supposed dominance of Western values in contemporary global culture, see Tomlinson (1991, 1999a, 199b). For a critique of cultural and social relations between tourist, tourism and local, see Tucker (2003) and Hall and Tucker (2004b). Hall and Tucker (2004a) provides a number of chapters that examine the relationships between tourism and postcolonialism. One of the best descriptions of the potential relations between travel and identity by the frequent traveller in terms of travel writing is to be found in Iyer (2000).

A.T. Kearney/Foreign Policy Magazine Globalization Index (utilises international arrivals and departures as an indicator of global links): www.atkearney.com/

United Nations Conference on Trade and Development (contains a wide range of useful information on economic globalisation, transnational corporations and foreign direct investment): www.unctad.org

World Bank website on globalisation: www1.worldbank.org/economicpolicy/ globalization/index.html

You will find that entering globalisation into your search engine will soon provide many options!

Tourism Mobility: Systems, Spatial Interaction and the Space–Time Prism of Mobility

3

Key Concepts

- Models
- Systems
- Multipliers
- Tourist system
- Space
- Gravity model
- Distance decay
- Spatial interaction
- Intervening opportunity
- Travel behaviour
- Distance
- Trips
- Space–time prism
- Structuration
- Constraints

- Travel money budget
- Travel time budget
- Extensibility
- Positionality
- Performity
- Routinisation
- Life course
- Locales
- Place
- Leisure time

This chapter seeks to describe tourism mobility through the use of various models of interaction, mobility and constraint. It first explains why such model building is significant. It then goes on to describe one of the most common reference points for explaining tourism with respect to the use of systems approaches. The chapter then discusses charting mobility at both the macro- and the micro-level and the relationships that exist between individual and group or mass travel behaviour. The reader should note that at various times formulae are used. These are supplied to help illustrate certain points. Guides to further reading on the use of some of these concepts are provided, but the reader is urged to consider broad principles rather than worry too much about how to remember formulae!

Why Construct Models to Describe Tourism Mobility and the Nature of Tourism?

Reality is so complex that it is impossible to reproduce all its features, all its functional relationships, and the whole web of interdependences that exist in the world. To represent the world we must simplify. Model building is attractive as it provides a means to represent real-world processes. As noted in Chapter 1, such analogue models can be powerful descriptive tools to illustrate processes of mobility in space and time and may be based on quantitative and/or qualitative research. According to Haggett et al. (1977), model building is attractive because of its:

1. *Inevitability*: models may be regarded as theories, laws, structured ideas, relations, synthesis of data, or equations which state a set of beliefs about the universe we think we see and so, therefore, we cannot avoid them.

2. *Efficiency*: model building is economical because it enables the development of generalised information in a highly compressed form.

3. *Stimulus*: although models may 'over-generalise' they also serve to highlight areas where 'improvement' is necessary and therefore can act to promote further research through the 'testing' of models.

Hagget et al.'s (1977) approach to model building is quite broad and represents the perspectives of many in the social sciences. In contrast, in the physical sciences a narrower perspective of modelling is generally used which regards a model as 'any rule that generalises outputs from inputs' (Haines-Young and Petch 1986, p. 145), or 'any device or mechanism which generates a prediction' (p. 144). Such an approach tends to see modelling as part of a hypothetico-deductive mode of explanation that enables theories to be exampled (Haines-Young 1989). However, from the perspective of the broader social sciences it is important to recognise that 'it is not necessarily positivist and functionalist simply because it is [often] a mathematical approach' (Wilson 1989, p. 64). Indeed, Robinson (1998, p. 190) puts it eloquently when he states: 'Models are simplified representations of reality in which a complex state of affairs is reduced to something more simple but containing key characteristics.' It should be noted that the generalisation of characteristics often involves mathematisation, in which a set of deterministic relations is established in mathematical or statistical form. This is often encountered by students of tourism in economics, geography and finance, and, as we will see, is used in understanding the broader social science of mobility.

Systems Models of Tourism

Systems analysis is a stylised abstraction of complex relationships between linked variables which are treated as the set of elements being examined. Within general systems theory there are links between the elements as well as the 'system' of variables and the system's environment (von Bertalanffy 1950). At its simplest level a system is an integrated whole whose essential properties arise from the relationships between its constituent parts. To put it another way, systems analysis therefore attempts to represent the interactions within a particular system so that simple relationships such as $A = f(B)$ can be seen as being mediated through other relationships.

Systems thinking has been and still is a very powerful conceptual and analytical tool. Systems and systems thinking has greatly influenced fields of study such as biology, ecology and physics, from which some of the first ideas regarding systems were developed early in the twentieth century, through to engineering, building construction, transport, sociology, geography, planning and, of course, tourism (Hall 2000a). A system is an object of study. A system comprises:

- a set of elements (sometimes also called entities);

- the set of relationships between the elements; and

- the set of relationships between those elements and the environment.

Systems analysis is valuable because simple linear relationships and casual chains, while being the realm of high school science and 'learn by numbers' business texts, cannot adequately describe or explain many of the complex situations encountered in either the physical or social sciences. Instead, we are often faced with the problem of trying to explain the multiple and complex interactions which take place in everyday life. A system is therefore a means of abstracting from reality in a manner which makes it more understandable. Some of the values of using systems analysis (Chisholm 1965) therefore include:

- studying more than individual and isolated phenomena;

- potentially identifying basic and general principles which govern the operation of the system; and

- the development of analogues that may describe the interrelationships between the elements of the system as well as the overall nature of the system.

Criticisms of systems analysis include that it can be highly deterministic in application and that its value is dependent on it being able to identify the relevant elements of a system from which an analogue is being drawn.

The structure of a system is composed of elements and the relationships between elements. Elements are the basic unit of a system. However, part of the art of systems analysis and definition will be the construction of a set of entities that form a relatively coherent object of study which has a well-defined relationship with its environment. Systems analysis cannot proceed without such abstraction. As Ashby (1956, p. 16) observed, any real system will be characterised by 'an infinity of variables from which different observers (with different aims) may reasonably make an infinity of different selections' (see also Ashby 1970; Conant 1981; Klir and Rozehnal 1996; Klir and Elias 2003).

One of the most substantial problems in understanding the elements within a system is that of scale. Systems are embedded within systems. What we regard as an element of a system at one level of analysis may itself constitute a system at a lower level of analysis. For example, we often examine the flows of tourists within an international tourism system by analysing the flows of tourists between different countries, which are the elements of such a system. However, if we change our resolution, we may then examine the flows of tourists within a country, by looking at the intra-regional flows of tourists. In the latter example it is the country that is the system and the regions are the elements. How we define an element therefore depends on the scale at which we conceive the system, otherwise referred to as the resolution level. The other component in the structure of a system is the relationship or links between the elements that make up a system. Three basic forms of relationship can be identified. First, a series relation (in which A leads to B), which is the characteristic cause-and-effect type relation of classical science. Second, a parallel relation in which two elements are affected by another element. Third, a feedback relation, which describes a situation in which an element influences itself. Both the elements and the relationships between them are part of the environment, which is most simply thought of as everything there is.

Another important element in systems analysis is defining the boundaries of a system. In mathematical terms this is extremely easy. However, in operational terms it can be extremely difficult. Sometimes the boundary of a system may be set by defining it in terms of something which is self-evident in terms of the questions being asked. For example, if one was examining a political systems problem, then an appropriate boundary may be a government boundary. Similarly, a problem of water resource management may be dealt with in ecological terms through selecting a watershed as a boundary (Brunckhorst 2000; Curtis and Lockwood 2000). However, tourism planning problems typically emerge when the different boundaries of different systems overlap, making management extremely difficult, a point to which we will return later. Many boundaries are not so easy to identify. Therefore, boundaries may be imposed through the application of judgement as to where a system begins and ends and in relation to the problem that is trying to be solved. This does not mean that such boundaries are arbitrary, rather that they should be related to the goals of the study and experience of such systems, as clearly the selection of a boundary can have a major impact on research results, for example with respect to the economic analysis of tourism.

Systems analysis relates to the abstraction rather than the reality (Harvey 1969). However, this does not make systems thinking 'unreal'. We all have our ideas, models or theories about how the world or people operate. These are our abstractions which we use to understand the world, explain what is happening, and act accordingly in various situations. In the physical sciences or in engineering some of the systems models may be isomorphic, that is the abstracted model and the original system will be symmetrically related in terms of the elements within them and the relationships between such elements. The vast majority of abstractions though, particularly in the social sciences, are homomorphic, that is the relationship to the original system is asymmetrical. For example, imagine yourself on a walk in the countryside reading a map. Think of the relationship between the map (which is an abstraction) and the countryside (reality/the original system). Every element in the map can be assigned to an element in the countryside, yet the countryside contains many elements (or entities to use the terms above) which are not recorded on the map. The geometric relationships (physical distances) represented on the map also hold in the countryside, but there are many geometric relationships around you in the countryside which cannot be portrayed on the map. 'We may treat the map as a model of the countryside, but we cannot treat the countryside as a model of the map' (Harvey 1969, p. 471). Nevertheless, we may get easily lost without a map. So it is therefore that other abstractions based on systems modelling may be most useful in helping us find our way through the complexity of tourism and tourism planning.

Tourism Insight: Tourism Multipliers

A multiplier may be regarded as 'a coefficient which expresses the amount of income generated in an area by an additional unit of tourist spending' (Archer 1982, p. 236). It is the ratio of direct and secondary changes within an economic region to the direct initial change itself. The size of the tourist multiplier is a significant measure of the economic benefit of tourism because it will be a reflection of the circulation of the tourist dollar through an economic system. In general, the larger the size of the tourist multiplier the greater the self-sufficiency of that economy in the provision of tourist facilities and services. Therefore, a tourist multiplier will generally be larger at a national level than at a regional level (e.g. state, province, county), because at a regional level leakage will occur in the form of taxes to the national government and importation of goods and services from other regions. Similarly, at the local level, multipliers will reflect the high importation level of small communities and tax payments to regional and national governments. As a measure of economic benefit from tourism, the multiplier technique has been increasingly questioned, particularly as its use has often produced exaggerated results (Bull 1994). One reason is that the selection of the boundary of the economy being studied is so critical. The smaller the area to be analysed, the greater will be the number of 'visitors' and hence the greater will be the estimate of economic impact, while the selection of the boundary will also affect the extent to which there is leakage out of the system, for example through the importation of goods and services for tourism. Boundary selection is therefore a key determinant in influencing the result of any analysis of an economic system (Burns and Mules 1986).

The idea of a system has been extremely influential and has been used in numerous texts as an analogue of the way in which tourism operates (e.g. Mill and Morrison 1985; Pearce 1987; Leiper 1989, 1990a, 1990b; Farrell and Twining-Ward 2004). At a geographical level four basic elements may be identified:

- *The generating region*: this is the source region of the tourist and the place where the journey begins and ends.

- *The transit region or route*: this is the region which the tourist must travel through to reach his destination.

- *The destination region*: this is the region which the tourist chooses to visit and where the most obvious consequences of the system occur.

- *The environment* within which the travel flows are located and with which the tourist interacts.

Figure 3.1 indicates these basic geographical elements of a tourist system. However, it does so in relation to its associated psychological and industrial elements. These are significant as when we travel we are not just physically moving in space and time but our psychology also changes depending on where we are in the journey. Moreover, as we move we consume different elements of the tourism industry and the environment within which we are travelling. These components are illustrated in Figure 3.2. Many elements of the tourism system are obviously directly produced for the consumption of tourists (e.g. accommodation and hospitality). However, much of that which the tourist consumes is not directly produced for the tourist even though they may be commodified or packaged for the tourist (e.g. landscape and culture). Indeed, one of the greatest issues in tourism development is how do you manage those elements of tourism which the tourist may seek, but for which no direct payment is received, and when people at the destination may not even want their environment, culture and community consumed by visitors. Importantly, thinking of tourism as a system means that we need to consider how it operates over all aspects of production and consumption. Arguably, much research in tourism only examines specific elements in the system rather than the interplay between those elements. This issue becomes especially important in considering the impacts of tourism, with most studies only looking at the impact of tourism at the destination rather than over space and time in all stages of tourism mobility. For example, in considering the environmental impacts of tourism, it becomes vital that such impacts are studied over all aspects of a trip rather than just at a destination (Gössling 2002; Gössling et al. 2002). Similarly, we are also seeking ways in which we can describe collective and individual mobilities.

Mobility and Spatial Interaction

Space is always in a state of becoming, known only in and through time (Unwin 2000). Spatial interaction models are one means that has been developed to describe the travel behaviours of aggregates and groups or, alternatively, the collective travel patterns of an individual over time. Spatial interaction is the movement of people, commodities, capital and/or information over geographic space that results from a decision process. The term therefore encompasses such diverse forms of mobility as migration, commuting, shopping, recreation, leisure travel, commodity flows, capital flows, communication flows, transport passenger traffic, and attendance at events (Haynes and Fotheringham 1984). In each case, an individual or a firm trades off the benefit of the interaction with the costs that are necessary in overcoming the spatial separation between the individual and the possible destination. The pervasiveness of this type of trade-off in spatial behaviour, which has made spatial interaction modelling an important subject in human geography and regional science through its utilisation in tourism studies, has been relatively limited. Spatial interaction models are therefore used to predict spatial choices

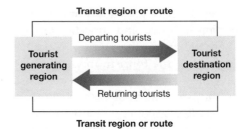

Relationship of geographical elements to other elements

Geographical elements	Psychological elements	Industrial elements
Generating region	Decision to travel/decision to purchase	Travel agencies/ wholesalers destination marketing, promotion and imaging Transport infrastructure such as airports
Transit route	Travel to destination	Transport and transit route infrastructure such as motels, highway cafés and restaurants, service stations, information services
Destination region	Behaviour and activities at destination/social interaction with hosts/ effects on hosts/ demonstration effects	Tourist accommodation, restaurants, tourism information services, attractions, retailing, events, conventions and meetings, tourism business districts, vacation and second homes, souvenir shops
Transit route	Travel from destination	Transport and transit route infrastructure such as motels, highway cafés and restaurants, service stations
Generating region	Recollection stage/ activities and behaviours on return home/reverse demonstration effects	Ongoing efforts by travel agencies, destination and businesses within destination to encourage return visits

Figure 3.1   Geographical elements of a tourist system and associated psychological and industrial elements

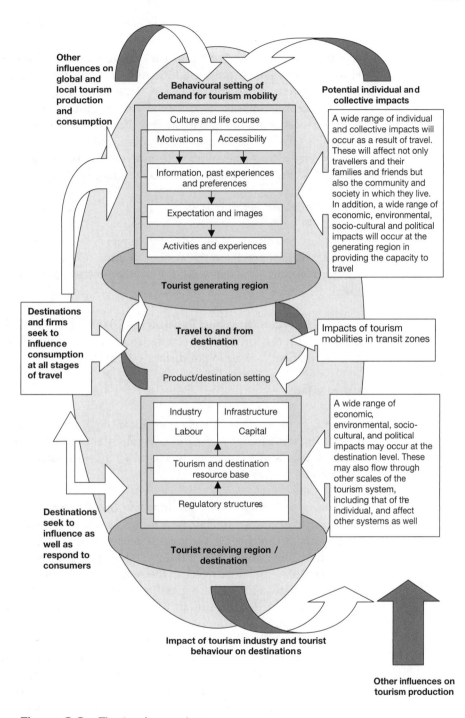

Figure 3.2   The tourism system

reflected in flows of goods or people between origins and destinations. They express trade-offs between the accessibility of alternative destination opportunities and the perceived intrinsic 'attractiveness' of these opportunities. However, they are surprisingly little utilised in tourism studies although they are a major research tool in migration, retail and transport studies (Smith 1995).

The most commonly used model for examining the spatial interactions between locations is the gravity model, which is a direct analogy with Sir Isaac Newton's (1642–1727) Law of Gravitation. This stated that any two bodies in the universe attract each other with a force proportional to the product of their masses and inversely proportional to the square of the distance between them:

$$F = G(m_1 m_2)/R^2 = Gm_1 m_2 R^{-2}$$

where F = magnitude of the attractive force; G = a gravitational constant, the size of which depends on the system of units used, and which is a universal constant; m_1 and m_2 = masses of the two bodies; and R = the distance between them.

The English demographer Ravenstein (1885, 1889) used the gravitational analogy with the formulation of a series of 'laws of migration' (Wrigley 1980) which described the notion of distance decay:

$$I_{ij} = kM_i M_j d_{ij}^{-\beta}$$

where I_{ij} = interaction between two locations i and j; M_i and M_j = 'masses' measuring the 'strength' of i and j, usually the population number of the two settlements, i and j, respectively, P_i and P_j; d_{ij} = the distance between i and j; and k and β = constants.

According to Tobler (1970), the first law of geography is that everything is related to everything else, but near things are more related than distant things (Boden and Molotch 1994; for further debate on this law, see also Barnes 2004; Goodchild 2004; Miller 2004; Phillips 2004; Smith 2004; Sui 2004; Tobler 2004). Distance decay therefore refers to the notion that the degree of spatial interaction (flows between regions, e.g. travellers) is inversely related to distance. The importance of a distance decay function has long been noted in studies of human mobility. For example, in the papers by Ravenstein noted above, he reported that in the case of migrants there was a relationship between the distance and frequency of moves. The empirical regularity of this relationship became developed into demographic laws of spatial interaction which have been applied to a wide range of movements, including not only human movements and the transport of goods, and the relative attraction of retailing, but also the movement of ideas and concepts (e.g. Stewart 1947; Zipf 1949; Stewart and Warntz 1958; Haggett 1965; Taylor 1971; Wrigley 1998; Cole 1989; Axhausen 2001). In the case of the above formula, the value of β can be altered to influence the distance decay of the interaction, with it usually varying between 0.5 and 2.5, the former giving a gradual decline with distance, usually associated with the developed countries, and the latter a sharp decline in difference usually associated with the less developed world because of the relative access to transport technology (Robinson 1998).

Gravity models consider three basic elements (Sheppard 1984):

- the number of trips generated by a place;

- the degree to which attributes of a particular destination attract trip-makers; and

- the inhibiting effects of distance – this refers to the attributes of a location's situation.

Mathematical distance decay functions are convenient formulations designed to reflect real behaviour and perception and response to distance (Morrill and Kelley 1970). The most simple distance decay function expresses the relative attractiveness of equivalent opportunities with increasing distance. Therefore a simple measure of attractiveness (A) is

$$A = 1/D^{b-1}$$

where D = distance; and b is the exponent.

However, it has long been recognised that different functions correspond to different perceptions of distance (e.g. Morrill 1963). Nevertheless, the friction of distance – the decay of interactions such as trips and communication over space – is well recognised in the social sciences but its implications have only been lightly touched on in tourism studies (Smith 1995). Arguably, this may be a result of the issues which arise out of the study of distance decay curves. For example, while such curves may be empirically identified, 'it is not clear to what extent their form depends on the model structures used to replicate them' (Robinson 1998, p. 229). Moreover, the nature of the relationships between interaction, mass (population size) and accessibility are inherently complex.

The basic form of the gravity model (see Haynes and Fotheringham 1984) may be expressed as

$$T_{ij} = f(V_i, U_j, S_{ij})$$

where T_{ij} = interaction between i and j; V_i and U_j = vectors of origin and destination attributes; and S_{ij} = vector of separation attributes.

However, different models have focused on different components of the equation, with some focusing on origin attributes (V_i) (origin-specific, production-constrained gravity models) (see Crouchley 1987b), on destination attributes (U_j) (destination-specific, attraction-constrained models) (see Thomas and Huggett 1980), or on the balance between the two, referred to as doubly constrained models (see Thomas and Huggett 1980; see also Pooler 1994). Figure 3.3 presents an estimation of travel flows between four different

Tourism Insight: Distance Decay

Distance decay forms can be classified into six standard forms, of which the Pareto model is the most common function used in spatial interaction research, although it has been criticised for its over-estimation at shorter distances (Taylor 1971, pp. 223–4). The functions are a family of exponential curves of the form

$$I = k\,e^{-bf(d)}$$

or in linear form

$$\log I = a - bf(d)$$

where I = a measure of interaction intensity over distance d, $f(d)$ = a monotonically decreasing function of distance, and $a = \log k$.
The family includes the following:

1. The Pareto model: $\log I = a - b \log d$
2. The log-normal model: $\log I = a - b(\log d)^2$
3. The exponential model: $\log I = a - b^d$
4. The normal model: $\log I = a - bd^2$
5. The square-root exponential model: $\log I = a - b\sqrt{d}$

cities. Despite their equal size, cities B and C experience different levels of interaction (travel flows) with A because C is nearer to A. Therefore distance decay or gravity effects occur because the amount of interaction between any two places will be directly proportional to the products of the two populations and inversely proportional to some power of the distance between them, itself related to the quality of transport facilities and the ease of transport (transferability) (Chapman 1983).

Among the most commonly used spatial interaction models with potential implications for tourism are intervening opportunity models. The basic premise of intervening opportunity models can be demonstrated with reference to the following example. If there is a city (A) and three similar tourist attractions (X, Y, Z) in the surrounding daytrip zone, people in A may prefer to visit attraction X rather than Y or Z if X is closer and therefore represents an intervening opportunity. If X, Y and Z were all located closer to A, the same preference may still apply if X is still the nearest attraction to A, as it is the relative rather than absolute distance that is significant in the establishment of intervening opportunities.

The concept of intervening opportunities was developed by Stouffer (1940) to help account for the pattern of human migration (although distortions may occur because of cultural and linguistic barriers). There are two basic

I

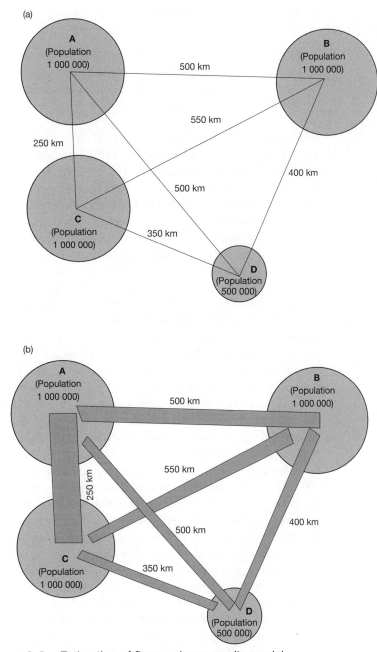

Figure 3.3   Estimation of flows using a gravity model

differences between a gravity model and an intervening opportunity model (Robinson 1998):

1. In the latter the basic characteristics of a destination are measured as the number of opportunities available there.

2. Rather than distance per se influencing the chance of a trip being made, the crucial factor is the number of other opportunities closer to the trip's origin than any particular destination being considered by a traveller, that is the number of intervening opportunities (Stouffer 1940).

Clearly, from the perspective of rational choice behaviour, 'the probability of a trip-maker stopping at the closest destination is proportional to the number of opportunities there' (Robinson 1998, p. 239). In both the intervening opportunities model and the gravity model the number of trips from i to j increases as the number of opportunities at j increases and the number decreases as the distance between i and j increases. However, both models can only be applied practically in situations where data are available on the observed distribution of trips and on attributes of the destinations (Robinson 1998).

Fotheringham (1983a, 1983b) observed that gravity models are essentially based on a decision-making process in which expected net utility derived from interacting with any particular destination is compared with the expected utilities for all other destinations, and interactions are predicted on the basis of this comparison. However, many types of spatial interaction are part of a two-stage process. First, individuals choose a broad region with which to interact. Then they choose a specific destination from a set of alternatives within the selected region. For example, in the selection of a holiday location a potential tourist is likely to select a suitable destination offering desired benefits before then searching for a specific accommodation opportunity (Fesenmaier and Jeng 2000). This two-stage process can apply to a wide range of spatial interaction processes. If the region selected is a macro-destination, then the volume of interaction terminating at the latter varies according to the number of other destinations there are at that same distance. Nevertheless, this distorts one of the assumptions of the gravity model as it can be shown that 'the more accessible a destination is to all other destinations in a spatial system, the less likely it is that that destination is a terminating point for interaction from any given origin' (Fotheringham 1983a, p. 20). For interactions terminating in close proximity to the origin this can mean that a gravity model can under-predict the volume of interaction. In contrast, for origins relatively inaccessible to destinations, interactions terminating at specific destinations will be larger than those predicted by a gravity model. This reflects the fact that gravity models do not include a variable that explicitly measures the relationship between interaction and competition between destinations. If such a variable is added, the model is termed a competing destinations model. For example, for an origin-specific production-constrained competing destinations model, the model can be represented as

$$I_{ij} = A_i O_i W_j X_{ij}^{di} C_{ij}^{-\beta}$$

where I_{ij} = interaction between i and j; A_i = the balancing factor; O_i = outflow from i; W_j = attractiveness of destination j; X_{ij} = the accessibility of destination j to all other destinations available to origin i as perceived by the residents of origin i; d_i = a distance decay exponent; C_{ij} = the cost of travel from i to j; and $ß$ = a distance decay exponent.

The relative attractiveness of a destination is therefore a function of the accessibility of the destination and the personal utility derived from the destination.

The importance of demonstrating the various mathematical expressions of distance decay is not just that it indicates a quantitative basis for understanding macro-level travel behaviour. It is also to demonstrate some key principles with respect to travel behaviour in space and time (Garner 1967).

1. *The distribution of travel behaviour in space and time reflects an ordered adjustment to the factor of distance.* Distance is basic to travel behaviour. This means that an understanding of space and time is central to understanding tourism mobility. However, the search for order in travel behaviour must be accompanied by flexibility in how we think about distance. Most importantly, people behave with respect to relative or non-physical space, which does not possess metric properties of distance, rather than the absolute space of Euclidean geometry (Gatrell 1983). Such relativist notions of space in a non-physical sense (Chapman 1983) include:

   - time-distance, which is the time taken to travel between locations (Figure 3.4 portrays the interrelationships between urban form and accessibility (Janelle 1995));

   - economic distance (cost-distance), which is the monetary cost incurred in overcoming physical distance (Figure 3.5);

   - cognitive distance (perceived distance), 'which are judgements regarding the spatial separation of locations. Cognitive distance is particularly important, for example, to the ways that actual or potential travellers collect, structure and recall information with respect to locations in physical space and establish mental maps (Horowitz 1977; Ankomah and Crompton 1992; Walmesley and Jenkins 1992; Jenkins and Walmesley 1993; Walmesley and Lewis 1993); and

   - social distance, which is a distance component associated with differences between social classes (which possess different socio-economic characteristics) which may be expressed in terms of the locational characteristics of class.

2. *Travel and locational decisions are generally taken in order to minimise the frictional effects of distance.* This concept is otherwise referred to as the 'law of minimum effort' (Losch 1954, p. 184) or the 'principle of least effort' (Zipf 1949). According to Zipf (1949, p. 6), 'an individual's entire behaviour is subject to the minimizing of effort'. Zipf's concept of the 'economy of geography' was essentially based on the interrelationship between the principle

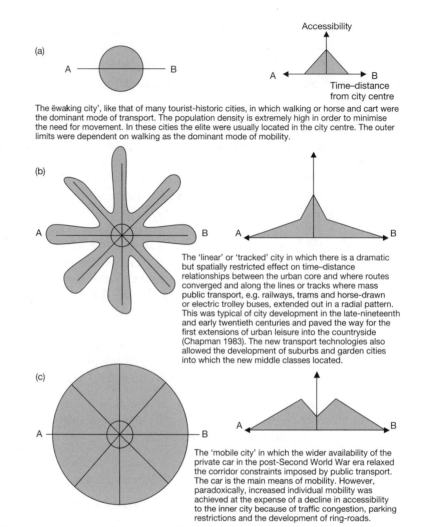

The ëwaking city', like that of many tourist-historic cities, in which walking or horse and cart were the dominant mode of transport. The population density is extremely high in order to minimise the need for movement. In these cities the elite were usually located in the city centre. The outer limits were dependent on walking as the dominant mode of mobility.

The 'linear' or 'tracked' city in which there is a dramatic but spatially restricted effect on time–distance relationships between the urban core and where routes converged and along the lines or tracks where mass public transport, e.g. railways, trams and horse-drawn or electric trolley buses, extended out in a radial pattern. This was typical of city development in the late-nineteenth and early twentieth centuries and paved the way for the first extensions of urban leisure into the countryside (Chapman 1983). The new transport technologies also allowed the development of suburbs and garden cities into which the new middle classes located.

The 'mobile city' in which the wider availability of the private car in the post-Second World War era relaxed the corridor constraints imposed by public transport. The car is the main means of mobility. However, paradoxically, increased individual mobility was achieved at the expense of a decline in accessibility to the inner city because of traffic congestion, parking restrictions and the development of ring-roads.

Figure 3.4   A model of the relationship between accessibility, transport technology and urban form

of least effort and the effect of distance as a barrier to mobility. The empirically observed regularities in movement patterns, which are reflected in the distance decay relationships described above, are ultimately based on the fact that travel decisions generally attempt to overcome this barrier. Therefore, in many situations, minimising the effort expended in movement is achieved by minimising the distance travelled. In tourism, exceptions to this rule apply when the trip itself is part of the attraction or is the destination (e.g. cruising or historic train travel). However, even in these situations time and space limitations still apply.

3. *Destinations and locations are variably accessible with some destinations more accessible than others.* Accessibility is a variable quality of any location but basically refers to the ease of getting to a place and is closely related to the concept of movement minimisation, especially when this is measured by

(d)

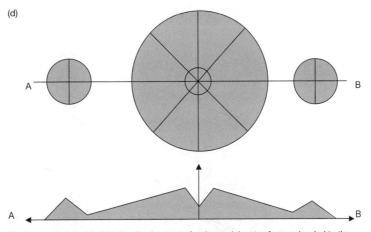

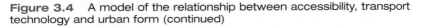

The 'motorway' city in which the development of main arterial routes for cars has led to the development of new suburbs or 'edge cities' as a response to time–distance relationships (in a similar fashion to the linear city but at a different scale). In this case the motorway interchanges represent points of greater accessibility relative to the main city centre (Chapman 1983). In these situations the middle classes have tended to occupy the new edge suburbs and towns (or have even moved into the rural-urban fringe as part of a process of counter-urbanisation) or have moved back to the inner city as part of a process of gentrification. Such shifts may also be related to the notion of social distance. Changes in transport technology and urban form have also influenced locations for employment as well as leisure. In all of the models of the relationship between accessibility, transport technology and urban form an accessibility maximisation strategy is employed by those who can afford it.

Figure 3.4   A model of the relationship between accessibility, transport technology and urban form (continued)

the costs involved in overcoming distance (Forbes 1964). In a technical sense, accessibility is a relative quality accruing to a location by virtue of its relationship to a system of transport. In an operational sense, it is the variable quality of centrality or nearness to other functions and locations (Garner 1967; also see Moseley 1979).

4. *There is a tendency for human activities to agglomerate to take advantage of scale economies.* Scale economies mean the savings in economic and time-distance costs made possible by concentrating activities, such as firm operations, at common locations. However, it can also apply to social relationships. Even in the age of the so-called virtual world there are still advantages to be gained through co-location strategies (Porter 2000a, 2000b; Scott 2001; Amin 2002; see also Chapter 6). Krugman (1991, p. 98), in his influential series of lectures on geography and trade, emphasised that because of economies of scale and 'the costs of transactions across distance', 'producers have an incentive to concentrate production of each good or service in a limited number of locations':

the preferred locations for each individual producer are those where demand is large or supply of inputs is particularly convenient – which in general are the locations chosen by other producers. Thus concentrations of industry, once established, tend to be self-sustaining: this applies both to the localisation of individual industries and to . . . grand agglomerations.

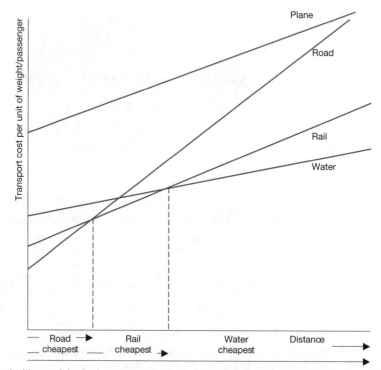

Note: In this case it is also important to recognise that travel is not time-sensitive. Even though travel by one mode of transport may be more expensive than another, many passengers will use the faster mode because time becomes the parameter by which the friction of distance will be measured.

Figure 3.5   Hypothetical relationships between distance and mode of transport

5. *The organisation of spatial and non-spatial aspects of human activity is essentially hierarchical in nature.* In part this occurs as a result of interrelationships between agglomeration tendencies and accessibility. More accessible locations appear to be the sites of larger agglomerations and vice versa. One of the implications of this is that there exists in an area a *hierarchy* of locations in terms of accessibility (Garner 1967). For example, this is something which becomes readily apparent when considering relationships between city population size and airport traffic, as well as other transport nodes (Page 1999).

6. *Human activities and occupance are focal in character.* The nodes about which human activity is organised are agglomerations of varying size. Since these are *hierarchically* arranged, it follows that there is a *hierarchy* of differently sized focal regions (Garner 1967). Again, this becomes evident when considering the order ranking of airports in any given country and the relative size of the regions that they service. Therefore, 'movement-minimization, accessibility, agglomerations and hierarchies are linked together to form a system of human organization in space' (Garner 1967, p. 305).

Such travel behaviours lie at the heart of the definition of the various forms of tourism mobilities outlined in Chapter 1. As noted, Figure 1.5 presented the relationships between tourism mobilities in terms of distance decay in space and time away from a central origin point, which could also be referred to as home. This chapter has indicated that such distance decay effects can be grounded in mathematical analysis of macro-level data. However, one of the major problems in estimating some of the distance decay functions of contemporary mobility is that different surveys are conducted on different aspects of mobility at different scales. For example, domestic travel, international travel, commuting, long-distance travel and migration studies are often conducted by different agencies and organisations for different purposes and with relatively little overlap between such studies or recognition of their relationships in terms of gaining an overall picture of human movement (Madre and Maffre 2001; Hall and Page 2002). Tables 3.1–3.5 (Hall 2003c) represent an attempt to indicate some aspects of the space–time relationships of mobility by amalgamating some of these survey results for different countries; please note that a number of these figures are only estimates derived from a wide number of sources and may not match those of official statistics. Indeed, in developing such tables it should be noted that some countries may even have different statistics for the same category. The tables should therefore be regarded as estimates only.

As can be seen in each of the countries that are presented in Tables 3.1–3.5, there is a clear distance decay function occurring with the number of people engaged in a particular type of mobility. Nevertheless, if one selected a small country in the middle of Europe, such as San Marino or Monaco, it would be quite easy to have its residents engaged in more international travel than domestic recreational travel. In this situation transport travel surveys may well be better suited to illustrate distance decay effects on trip behaviour and here

Table 3.1 Mobilities table for the United States (000s)

Year	Commuting trips	Domestic travel	Outbound travel	Departing permanently^
1980	224 385 000*	–	–	3 362
1990	8 799 000+	–	44 623	3 294
1994	7 949 000+	941 000	46 450	3 845
1995	7 763 000+	966 000	50 835	3 136
1996	7 948 000+	967 000	52 311	3 359
1997	8 374 000+	999 000	52 944	3 167
1998	8 666 000+	1 004 000	56 288	3 372
1999	9 058 000+	987 000	57 598	3 728
2000	9 403 000+	998 000	60 891	3 106
2001	410 969 000*	1 018 000	57 963	2 457
2002	–	1 021 000	56 359	–

Note: ^ US financial year ending
Source: Hall 2003c (derived from + Bureau of Transportation Statistics, * US Department of Transportation, Travel Industry Association of America, Office of Travel and Tourism Industries, US Census Bureau, *various*)

Table 3.2   Mobilities table for Australia (000s)

Year	Commuting trips	Daytrips	Domestic travel	Outbound Short-term	Long-term	Departing permanently
1985	–	–	45 250*	1 512	51	19
1990	–	–	49 962	2 170	66	30
1991	–	–	48 997	2 099	66	30
1992	–	–	48 235	2 276	67	28
1993	–	–	47 878	2 267	64	28
1994	–	–	48 113	2 355	66	27
1995	–	–	57 898	2 519	69	28
1996	1 495 895	–	63 028	2 732	71	29
1997	–	–	62 780	2 933	77	30
1998	–	153 130	73 811	3 161	81	33
1999	–	170 939	72 981	3 210	84	38
2000	–	161 464	73 771	3 498	88	44
2001	1 627 136	146 008	74 585	3 443	93	48
2002	–	–	75 047	3 461	90	49

Notes: Short term = less than 12 months. Measurements for domestic travel changed in 1998, therefore time series data cannot be directly compared. * = estimate
Source: Hall 2003c (derived from Australian Bureau of Statistics, Bureau of Tourism Research, Department of Industry, Tourism and Resources, Australian Bureau of Statistics, Department of Immigration and Multicultural and Indigenous Affairs, *various*)

the results again support the distance decay function (Madre and Maffre 2001). In the case of Europe, for example, the long-distance trip-making (e.g. journeys to destinations beyond 100 km from home or current base) that is usually associated with tourism constitutes a very small share of all journeys (about 0.5%), but represents a much larger share of the total kilometres or miles travelled (about 20%) and therefore of the commercial and environmental impacts of travel (Axhausen 2001; Gössling 2002). For example, according to the *1995 American Travel Survey*, journeys over a 100-mile minimum distance threshold account for about 0.5% of all trips and cover approximately 25% of the person-miles travelled in the United States (Bureau of Transportation Statistics 1997). However, while such macro-level descriptions of trip-making provide important insights into the impacts of tourism and, as we will discuss throughout the book, the relative accessibility and competitiveness of destinations and firms, it needs to be remembered that such movements are based upon the travel behaviour of individuals. Therefore in the next section we will look at individual travel mobility as the basic building block of tourism mobility.

Table 3.3 Mobilities table for Canada (000s)

Year	Commuting trips (000)	Daytrips			Overnight trips			Total domestic tourism	Outbound	Emigration*
		Intra	Inter	Total	Intra	Inter	Total			
1990	1 530 000	–	–	–	–	–	76 599	–	–	213
1995	1 372 200	–	–	–	–	–	–	–	18 206	229
1996	1 363 100	–	–	–	–	–	80 885	–	18 973	229
1997	1 393 600	–	–	–	–	–	65 727	–	18 206	270
1998	1 430 000	71 653	3 605	75 258	67 439	16 521	83 960	159 218	17 644	270
1999	1 460 000	74 373	3 861	78 234	68 637	17 225	85 862	164 096	18 362	270
2000	1 490 000	75 148	3 520	78 668	66 441	16 997	83 438	162 106	19 109	270
2001	1 481 000	67 266	3 078	70 344	58 284	15 575	73 859	144 203	18 350	270

Note: * = estimate including permanent and long-term departures.
Source: Hall 2003c (derived from Transport Canada, Canadian Tourism Commission, Statistics Canada, various)

Table 3.4   Mobilities table for the United Kingdom (000s)

Date	Public transport passengers	Daytrips	Domestic travel	Outbound	Departing permanently
1990	4 850 000	–	–	31 120	–
1991	4 665 000	–	–	30 809	–
1992	4 480 000	–	–	33 850	281.1
1993	4 385 000	–	–	36 720	266.3
1994	4 420 000	–	–	39 640	237.6
1995	4 383 000	–	147 790	41 345	236.5
1996	4 350 000	1 200 000	154 220	42 050	263.7
1997	4 330 000	–	162 230	45 957	279.2
1998	4 248 000	1 300 000	148 820	50 872	251.5
1999	4 281 000	–	173 100	53 881	290.8
2000	4 309 000	–	175 400	56 837	320.7
2001	4 434 700	–	163 100	58 281	307.7
2002	–	–	167 300	59 377	–

Source: Hall 2003c (derived from National Statistics, Statistics on Tourism and Research (STAR), *various*)

Table 3.5   Mobilities table for New Zealand

	Commuting trips	Daytrips	Overnight trips	Outbound (short-term)	Departing permanently/ long-term
1990	–	n/a	n/a	717 278	47 514
1995	–	n/a	n/a	920 107	49 077
1996	–	n/a	n/a	1 092 879	54 212
1997	–	n/a	n/a	1 131 682	60 012
1998	–	n/a	n/a	1 166 418	64 485
1999	–	43 961 077	16 889 492	1 184 920	68 772
2000	–	37 000 135	17 070 122	1 283 439	74 306
2001	327 590 640	38 932 409	16 557 255	1 287 296	71 368
2002	–	–	–	1 293 935	48 726*

Notes: Domestic travel information not collected between 1989 and 1998. Commuting figure estimate only.
* = 2002 figures to October only.
Source: Hall 2003a (derived from Statistics New Zealand, Tourism Research Council New Zealand, *various*)

The Space–Time Prism of Mobility

In the same way that we can chart collective travel behaviour in time and space, we can also chart the movements or paths of individuals. Indeed, it must always be remembered that the collective flows and patterns of domestic and international tourism mobilities represent the sum of individual paths. Social scientists, including many of those who examine tourism, have failed to construct their thinking around the modes in which social systems are constituted across time–space (Giddens 1984). For Giddens, such an observation is extremely important, as 'fixity' in time and space usually also implies social fixity – in terms of the substantially 'taken-for-granted' character of normally highly routinised day-to-day life. Yet by investigating the routinised life paths of the individual Giddens argues that we may be able to detect the extent to which our life courses are themselves set by the institutions which govern society.

Central to the development of Giddens' concept of structuration, which is concerned with the intersection between individual human actors and the wider social structures and systems in which they are implicated (see Chapter 2), is the study of time geography. Time geography examines the ways in which the production and reproduction of social life are connected with features of the human body and agency trace out routinised paths in terms of mobility and communication over space and through time, fulfilling particular projects whose realisations are bounded by various constraints (Gregory 1985, 1986). Time geography has its origins in the work of Swedish geographer Torsten Hägerstrand and his associates at the University of Lund. Hägerstrand's (1965, 1967a, 1967b, 1970, 1973, 1982, 1984) work on time geography was based on three central principles: (i) that human life is temporally and spatially ordered; (ii) that human life has a physical and social dimension; and (iii) that the activities constituting human life are limited by certain temporal and spatial constraints that condition various individual and group-based combinations of possible activities. Such constraints are:

1. The indivisibility of human beings, and of other living and inorganic entitities. Corporeality imposes strict limitations upon the capabilities of movement, and perception of human beings.

2. The finite nature of human life. This essential element of the human condition gives rise to certain inescapable demographic parameters of interaction across time–space. This also means that time is a scarce resource for individual human beings.

3. The limited capability of human beings to engage in more than one activity or task at once, coupled with the fact that every task has a specific duration.

4. Movement in space also consumes movement in time.

5. The limited 'packing capacity' of time–space, that is space has a limited capacity in its ability to accommodate in a particular space. No two human

bodies can occupy the exact same space at the exact same time; physical objects clearly have the same characteristic. Therefore, any zone of time–space can be analysed in terms of constraints over the two types of object which can be accommodated within it (see also Chapin 1974; Thrift 1977a, 1977b; Carlstein et al. 1978; Giddens 1984).

Encounters into which individuals enter in the trajectories of daily life are subject to various constraints which can be classified into three types:

- *Capability constraints*: when individuals' physical capabilities or the facilities they can command affect the ability of travel. They also define an individual's prism, which contains a set of feasible space–time paths flowing through a constellation of stations, for example workplace, school, university, shops, home or, in a touristic setting, airports and railway stations. Locales can also be described as stations within which the paths of different individuals intersect.

- *Coupling constraints*: when individuals and groups are required to be in certain places at certain times and which define space–time bundles.

- *Authority constraints*: when individuals are precluded from being in certain places at set times. Authority constraints therefore restrict people's movements through time and space in the form of 'pockets' or domains.

Authority constraints are similar to Foucault's (1980) emphasis on the 'net-like organisation' through which power is exercised in different domains – for example, with respect to such things as gender, in which gendered space can be seen as being socially constructed. To this Carlstein (1982) adds the notion of 'ecological constraints' which derive from three modes of 'packing':

1. The packing of materials, artefacts, organisms and human populations in settlement space–time.

2. The packing of time-consuming activities in population time-budgets.

3. The packing of bundles of various sizes, numbers and durations in the population system, that is group formation because of the indivisibility and continuity constraints of individuals.

The above constraints are interactive rather than additive and together delineate a series of possible boundaries that individuals may follow in seeking to undertake particular projects as they pass through a web of space–time relations (Figure 3.6). Hägerstrand (1973) noted that the competition between different projects to use particular pathways was mediated by specific institutions. Interestingly, such an observation has strong resonance with the significance of the regulation of time for the development of commercial transport operations in the nineteenth century, which was clearly essential for the viability of mass human mobility, including tourism (Urry 1995).

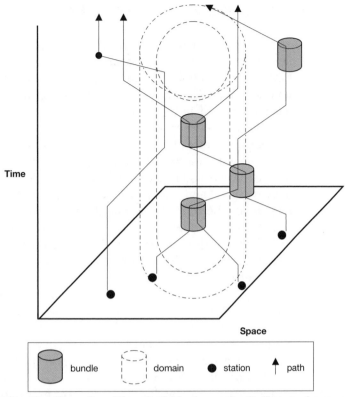

Figure 3.6 The life paths of four individuals moving in time and space

The mobility of people is therefore constrained by a space–time prism (Figure 3.7), with different potential path spaces depending on the modes of transport used and the route of such transport (Figure 3.8) (see Miller 1991, 1998; Miller and Wu 2000, for the application of a space-time prism to transport accessibility questions using GIS). For most people in societies around the world mobility is relatively constricted within such a prism as not only does one need money to access transport to enhance mobility beyond that of walking, but one also needs access to time resources in order to undertake particular tasks (or projects). This is a way one can argue that tourism, and international tourism in particular, is the domain of the wealthiest members of our planet because they are the ones who are time and money rich and can therefore engage in substantial mobility (Hall 2003c, 2004b). In one sense the prism can almost be referred to as a prison as it is impossible to move beyond it, although with increased access to resources it may be possible to extend it. For example, consider the enormous costs involved with space tourism or even travelling at supersonic speed between London and New York when the Concorde still used to undertake the route. However, whether one is rich or poor, migrant or tourist, nearly all time–space paths involve a return in space. Relationships can also be drawn between the space–time prisms of time geography and the spatial interaction models which detail the macro-accessibility of potential destinations, with potentially critical implications not only for our understanding of travel behaviour, but also the competitiveness of certain destinations in terms of their relative distance from tourism generating regions. According to Schafer (2000, p. 22): 'Aggregate travel behavior is determined largely by two budgets: the share of monetary expenditure and the amount of time that individuals allocate to transportation. However, neither budget is unique.' Given that a travel money budget represents the fraction of disposable income devoted to travel, a fixed travel money budget establishes a direct relationship between disposable income and distance travelled, provided average user costs of transport remain constant (see Schafer and Victor 2000). If people are on a fixed time budget, then those who are willing to pay the increased costs will likely shift from one mode of transport to another so as to increase speed and therefore reduce the amount of time engaged in travelling relative to other activities within the constraints of the overall time budget.

Substantial evidence exists for the ways in which various constraints including age (Rosenbloom 1989; Rosenbloom and Waldorf 2001), childcare responsibilities (McEnroe 1991; Lee et al. 1992; Presser 1995; Turner and Niemeier 1997), gender (Hanson and Johnston 1985; Elchardus 1991; Blumen 1994; Pashigan and Bowen 1994; Manrai and Manrai 1995; Pol et al. 1995; Presser 1995; Hanson and Pratt 1999), income, race (Polzin et al. 2001), cultural context (Jamal and Badawi 1995; Manrai and Manrai 1995) and consumer culture (Wilson and Jolman 1984; Pashigan and Bowen 1994; Zmud and Arce 2001), affect travel behaviour. In the case of the United States the various national travel surveys provide a rich vein of data for research on constraints (Transportation Research Board 2001). For example, both the elderly and those

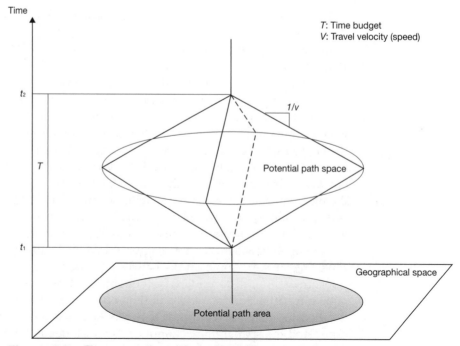

Figure 3.7 The space–time prism of mobility

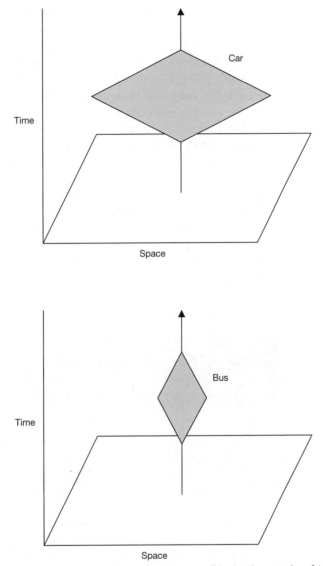

Figure 3.8   Different space–time prisms according to the mode of transport indication, given the potential area that could be travelled within the same time period

on a low income have significantly lower long-distance mobility when compared to other segments of the population (Georggi and Pendyala 2001). Data from the 1995 American Travel Survey and the 1995 Nationwide Personal Transportation Survey show that recreation trips (RTs) undertaken in a private vehicle (PV) make up about 14% of all local trips, 23% of all long-distance trips, and about 15% of total vehicle kilometres travelled in the United States (Mallett and McGuckin 2000). However, recreation trips are not equally distributed among the population. For example, African Americans report about half the amount of recreation automobile trips and one-third the average distances travelled as whites. Research by Mallett and McGuckin (2000) indicates that people in households earning US$75 000 or more made about 1.7 long-distance PV-RTs each, more than four times the number made by people in households earning less than US$25 000 (0.4 trips per capita). However, people in low-income households are more dependent on a PV to make long-distance RTs than people in high-income households, with the gap widening as trip length increases. For people in households with an annual income over US$100 000, flying becomes a significant option for trips of 644–805 km (400–500 miles) away from home. About 30% of all PV and air trips combined for recreation are taken by air at this distance. For households with an income less than US$25 000, this 30% threshold is not approached until trips of 1290–1450 km one-way (800–900 miles) or 2575–2896 km round-trip (1600–1800 miles) (Mallett and McGuckin 2000, pp. 7–8). Similarly, from the same survey data Mallett (2001) also indicated that people in low-income households made less than half the annual number of long-distance trips (defined as a round-trip to a destination at least 100 miles or more from home) per person than the population as a whole. On average, low-income people made 1.6 long-distance person trips in 1995 compared with 3.9 trips for the entire population. In contrast, persons in households with medium-low income made 2.6 trips a year, medium-high income 4.2 trips, and high income 6.3 trips (Mallett 2001, p. 170).

Tourism Insight: **Travel Constraints and the Findings of the 1995 US National Travel Survey with Respect to Age, Income, Race and Long-Distance Travel**

Age

- There is a decline in trip generation with age, with the greatest decrease occurring in the 75 or over age group; this group is also associated with the lowest household income and car ownership levels.
- The elderly are significantly more dependent on bus transport than the rest of the population.
- Recreation/vacation trip generation decreases dramatically at age 75 or over.
- Both the average one-way trip distance and overall trip duration were found to increase with age; the elderly of 75 years or over showed the highest average values for these variables. This is likely to be an outcome of family members having moved away and because of second home ownership.
- Both income and car ownership elasticities of long-distance trip generation are found to increase with age, but only until the onset of old age, indicating that physical and other limitations may play a role in inhibiting long-distance travel even if car ownership and income were to increase.

Income

- There is an increase in long-distance trip generation with income; the trip generation rate almost triples when one transfers from the very low-income group to a very high-income group. Whereas 46% of the lowest income group households made zero long-distance trips, just 17% of the highest-income group did so.

- Lower income groups were much more likely to travel by road (either by car or bus) when compared to other income groups.
- The share of air travel steadily increased with rising income levels.
- Higher income levels were associated with higher percentages of business trips.
- The absolute number of recreation/vacation trips increased with income.
- As income rises, usage of air transportation increases, as does the distance of the average one-way trip. No substantial differences were noticeable with respect to overall trip duration.
- Income elasticities of long-distance trip generation were found to decrease with increasing income.

Race

- 20% of African Americans live in households without vehicles while only 3% of Whites live in zero-vehicle households.
- Hispanic and African-American household incomes were only 74% and 70% respectively of the national average in 1995.
- On average Hispanics and African Americans are younger, have lower levels of educational attainment, are more likely to live in single-adult households with children, spend fewer dollars but spend larger shares of their income on transportation, and have proportionately fewer licensed drivers.

Sources: Georggi and Pendyala 2001; Mallett 2001; Polzin et al. 2001

When low-income individuals travel they do it to visit friends and relatives and on personal business. They travel much more rarely for leisure or on business (Mallett 2001). The US data also revealed that low-income individuals travel shorter distances than people in higher-income groups. The average (mean) round-trip distance among low-income adults under age 65 was 650 miles compared with 990 miles by high-income people. This is primarily related to the fact that the low-income individuals travel much less often by air because the average long-distance trip (excluding air) by all income groups was about the same (approximately 550 miles). Because they travel less often and less by air, low-income individuals travel less miles overall than other groups: low-income people travelled about 1350 miles in 1995 compared with 2300 miles by medium-low earners, 3650 miles by medium-high earners, and 7250 miles by those with high incomes (Mallett 2001, p. 173).

Similarly, Axhausen (2001), in a review of European travel surveys, notes that income is a significant determinant of frequency of travel, distance covered and main modes used. For the Portuguese from the relatively poor north of the country, long-distance travel is a rare event (0.02 journeys per person per week and about 1 journey per person per year), while the Northern European residents have between 0.10 and 0.14 journeys per week (between five and seven journeys per year). Air travel is the dominant mode of transport in Denmark and Sweden, while in northern Portugal the coach is the most prominent (Axhausen 2001). Such data provides rich empirical evidence for the changing socio-economic basis of markets for tourist areas with the relative cost-distance accessibility of destinations in part determining destination choice.

Constraints can also exist with respect to particular activities. For example, Gilbert and Hudson (2000) investigated the constraints facing both skiers and non-skiers and found that economic factors were the major constraints for non-skiers, but they also faced a number of intrapersonal constraints. They perceived skiing to be harder to learn than other sports, and thought the activity would make them cold and wet, and that it would be dangerous, expensive and too stressful. There was the feeling that skiing is an elitist sport, and that they were not 'chic and glamorous enough' to go. Skiers, on the other hand, were constrained by time, family or economic factors.

Time–space convergence can be plotted to describe the potential outer bounds of space–time prisms (see Chapter 2, especially Figure 2.1). The size of these prisms will be very strongly influenced by the degree of time–space convergence in transport as well as in broader terms by communication. Indeed, the media of transportation were the main factor in space–time convergence until the separation of the media of communication from the media of transportation (Giddens 1984; Urry 1995). Until that time the positioning of one life path with another required co-presence.

The space–time prism concept therefore allows us further insights into the impacts of globalisation on identity, as time–space convergence implies greater social interaction with others, whether it be through face-to-face or virtual contact. Social interaction for those with a high degree of mobility not only potentially includes access to individuals from another culture which is distant in space but also virtual access through television and other media. The enlarged space–time prisms of many in the West have therefore contributed to new ways of seeing others, in a manner that was hard to imagine before the industrial revolution of the nineteenth century and, associated with that, the growth in mass tourism (Squire 1994; Crang 1997, 1999; Crawshaw and Urry 1997; Löfgren 1999; Osborne 2000; Crouch and Lübbren 2003). However, such interaction also brings the life paths of others with small space–time prisms in contact with those that are large, creating a new dialectic of social relations and ways of looking at the other that are tied up with the notion of the impact of various world views or gazes on how the world is perceived and understood (Urry 1990). Janelle (1973) uses the notion of extensibility to describe the extent to which the social relations of many individuals in the developed world have increasingly become extended over time and space, often without people even realising it (e.g. by what they watch on television or listen to on the radio). In such a situation personal boundaries in space–time change and we (here referring to most people who will read this book) in effect bring globalisation home (see Adams, 1995, 1999), with corresponding changes to relative accessibility (Janelle and Hodge 2000).

As noted in the previous chapter, such new sets of social relations have significant effects on social relations, senses of belonging, and identity in which tourism is deeply implicated. Therefore, the degree of potential interaction and the implications of one gaze for another depend upon the 'positioning' of individuals in the time–space contexts of activity. For example, Pred (1981a, 1981b) notes the role of structuration in the temporal changes he observed in social and economic development and recognises four antithetical 'dynamics' in the impact of technological and institutional innovations:

1. Individual versus societal: everything that affects an individual affects society and vice versa.

2. Daily path versus life path: anything that affects an individal's daily activities affects his/her life as a whole and vice versa.

3. External versus internal: movement along the daily and life paths leads to the accumulation of mental experiences that shape intentions and influence movements.

4. Path convergence versus path convergence: any new 'coming together' destroys old paths but creates new contacts.

Positionality and performity

Giddens (1984) sees the positioning of the body in serial encounters across time–space as fundamental to social life. All social life occurs in, and is constituted by, intersections of presence and absence of others across space and time (Giddens 1984, p. 132). Positioning occurs through the immediate co-presence of the body in relation to others whether it be corporeal or virtual. However, the individual is simultaneously positioned in mutiple ways: in the flow of day-to-day life; over one's life span; in the duration of 'institutional time'; in the 'supra-individual' structuration of social institutions and locales; and within social relations conferred by specific social identities. Here Giddens (1984) highlights the importance of different scales of structure within which the agency of the individual body is positioned. Such a relational perspective has recently had much influence on tourism theorisation in which the tourist may be conceived as performing over a path in time and space in relation to the various domains and locales in which he/she is travelling (Adler 1989; Veijola and Jokinnen 1994; Edensor 1998, 2000b, 2001; Desmond 1999; Parinello 2001; Coleman and Crang 2002; Crouch 2002; Bærenholdt et al. 2004). Moreover, the study of performity provides an opportunity to integrate the findings of qualitative research with some of the quantitative research that underlies many spatial interaction studies (Nash 2000).

Routinisation of tourism consumption and production

The routinisation of space–time has substantial implications for tourism consumption and production. As an industry, tourism and hospitality are based on

Tourism Insight: Qualitative Research

Qualitative research is not 'easier' than quantitative research. If it is done properly it may require even more time and effort and requires strong theory if generalisations are to be made. Qualitative research should be seen as complementary to quantitative research and a natural concomitant of investigations of meaning, value and context. Moreover, qualitative research requires a need for reflexivity in which the researcher is aware of her/himself in juxtaposition, interaction and relation to the subject of enquiry. This implies a continual interrogation of self and subject. According to Hakim (1987), qualitative research involves:

- being able to see through the eyes of the subject or taking the subject's perspective in understanding his/her lifeworld (Seamon 1979);
- describing the detail of a setting from the perspective of participants;
- understanding actions and meanings in their social context;
- emphasising time and process;
- favouring open and relatively unstructured research designs; and
- is an approach in which the formulation and testing of concepts; and theories proceed in conjunction with data collection.

providing people with services needed when they are away from home, regardless of how close or how far home might be. As Shaw and Williams (1994) noted, the temporal variation in demand is far greater than is experienced in any branch of manufacturing or even in other service sectors. The rhythm of demand varies between seasons, between working days and weekends/public holidays, and at different times of the day (Figures 3.9 and 3.10) (Jakle et al. 1976). Each trip type will have its own distance decay effects (Figure 3.11) (Wheeler and Stutz 1971; Stutz 1973; Jakle et al. 1976), as well as activity linkages (Figure 3.12) (Wheeler 1972; Jakle et al. 1976) that will also impact consumption and demand of hospitality and tourism services. Product cycles for seasonal work not only affect products such as skiing but even the timing of agricultural produce will influence the availability of students on short-term work visas and therefore the pattern and flow of mobility. Regulations which govern holiday-taking and retirement also influence temporal variation in demand (Table 3.6) as, of course does the relative attractiveness of the resource itself in seasonal terms and the time–space characteristics of particular products (Baum and Lundtrop 2001). Nevertheless, the overall result is that tourism services have to be delivered to customers in both temporal and spatial clusters, with one implication of this being the provision of a flexible labour force (Bagguley 1987, 1990; Urry 1990) as well as the relative competitiveness of such clusters in relation to market accessibility. Externally, the concept of flexible production is also tied in with the production of places as commodities to be promoted and sold to consumers (Gershuny 1993; also see Chapter 4). 'Place marketers do not see their task as purely promoting and advertising, but also as adapting the "product" (that is, the place) to be more desirable to the "market" ' (Holcomb 1993, p. 134; also see Fretter 1993). Similarly, for Kotler et al. (1993, p. 345), flexibility is inherent in the notion of place marketing: 'Place marketing is a continual activity that must be adjusted to meet changing economic conditions and new opportunities.'

Life courses

A further implication of time geography for tourism is that positioning in the time–space paths of day-to-day life, for every individual, is also positioning within the 'life course', 'life cycle' or' life path' of individuals (Giddens 1984, p. 85). Although the idea of a life cycle has had considerable influence in tourism marketing, the notion of a life course has not been significantly incorporated into tourism analysis (although, in the context of second homes, see McHugh et al. 1995; McHugh and Mings 1996; Hall and Müller 2004a).

As originally envisaged, the lifestyle model has been subject to substantial

Table 3.6   Statutory leisure time in select countries

	Statutory leave (days per year)	Public holidays (days per year)	Retirement age Male	Female
Australia	20	8	65	61
Austria	30	13	65	60
Brazil	maximum of 30	10	65	60
Canada	2 weeks rising to 3 after 5 years	11	65	65
China	10	7	60	50
France	25	11	60	60
Germany	24	9–13	65	65
Italy	20	12	65	60
Japan	10–20	14	65	65
Korea	22	18	60	60
Malaysia	8 increasing to 16	13	55*	50*
Netherlands	20	8	65	65
Singapore	7 plus 1 day per year of service up to 14	11	62	62
South Africa	14	12	55	55
Switzerland	20	8	65	62
UK	20	8	65	60
USA	nil – in practice commonly 10 days	9	65	65

Note: * refers to Malaysian government employees.
Source: Derived from World Tourism Organisation 1999

(a) Regularly scheduled activities (work, university, dinner, prayer)

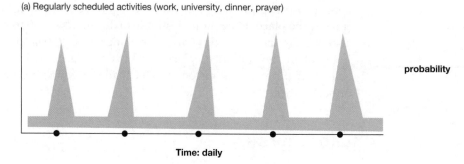

Time: daily

(b) Trips to purchase regularly needed item (shopping for food)

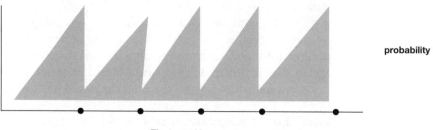

Time: weekly

(c) Trips to time-contiguous activities which occur at various locations at relatively irregular intervals (playing sport)

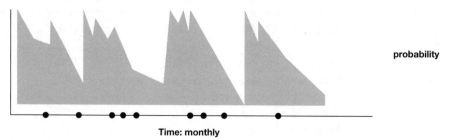

Time: monthly

(d) Visits to family for occasions such as Easter, Thanksgiving and Christmas or other statutory holidays

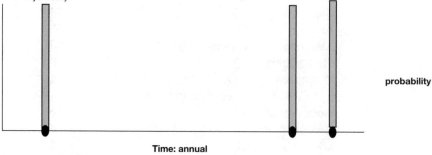

Time: annual

• Occurrence of an activity

Figure 3.9   Relationships between time and the probabilities of trips to different activity locations

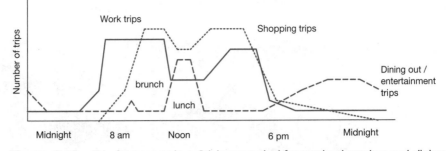

Figure 3.10   Trip frequency in a 24-hour period for work, shopping and dining out/entertainment trips

criticism (Glick 1947; Young 1977). In particular it has been stressed that human life paths are not constituted by the endless repetition of orderly sequences, 'the deterministic implication that life is irreversibly leading something back to where it came from' (Bryman et al. 1987, p. 2). Instead, personal time, like historical time, is linear not cyclical (Harris 1987, p. 22). In addition, the notion of family life cycle, as it was (and still is) usually elaborated (Glick 1947), refers to the family circumstances of white urban middle-class Americans in the 1950s and 1960s – a far more child-oriented period in the developed world than at present (Murphy 1987). Similarly, Warnes (1992) noted that with hindsight the formulation seemed plausible for middle-class white Americans in a dominantly private sector housing market but that it is inappropriate for black Americans or for low-income Europeans. The notion of a family life cycle was therefore time- and space-specific (Anderson 1985).

In contrast, a life-course approach recognises the diversity in life paths or pilgrimage (Frankenberg 1987), which should be based on normative personal event histories and biographies (Hohn 1987). The essence of the life-course approach is that the unit of analysis becomes the individual sited in geographical, social, historical and political space and time, and that the study of the individual, household or family becomes the study of conjoined or

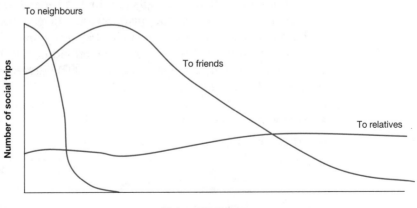

Figure 3.11   Distance decay for different types of social/visiting-friends-and-relations trip

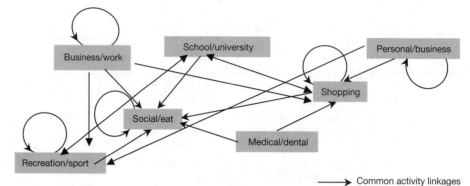

Figure 3.12   Activity linkages related to the probability of going from one activity to another in the context of a multipurpose trip

interdependent life courses or paths (Elder 1987; Harris 1987), thereby recognising that social interactions influence decisions with respect to mobility behaviour. A life-course approach seeks not to impose a normal or ideal life path; instead, what is central to the concept of the life course is not the concept of stage but that of transition (Boyle et al. 1998). Early transitions have implications for later ones with transitions occurring in 'personal time', 'historical time' and 'family time'. The life-course paradigm therefore emphasises that changes in one dimension of the household-ageing process, for example, are necessarily linked to changes in other dimensions. As Harris (1987, p. 25) noted, 'the study of the life course involves an examination of what transitions the members of different social categories within a given cohort typically experience and puts the question as to whether those transitions are of such a nature and so timed as to constitute life transitions'. Such an analysis clearly has strong resonance with time geography and has implications for understanding tourism behaviour.

Motivations are undoubtedly an important variable in explaining travel behaviour (Fodness 1994). However, motivations can change during the course of a trip let alone over the course of a lifetime. Rather than examine tourism motivations and activities in isolation, tourist behaviour and demand should be seen in a wider context than just previous travel experiences (as important as the notion of a travel career might be). They should also be seen in the broader context of the life course of the individual and the events that influence life paths. For example, Warnes (1992) identifies several life-course transitions that will also influence travel careers:

- leaving parental home
- sexual union
- career
- family
- children (income high/low)
- career promotion
- divorce or separation

- cohabitation and second marriage
- retirement
- bereavement or income collapse
- frailty or chronic ill-health.

An important methodology for examining changes in the life course focuses on the events themselves, and measures the intervals between events. Event-history analysis uses event-history data (data on the change from one state to another), from which it is possible to construct or examine life courses (Allison 1984; Courgeau and Lelièvre 1992). A model for understanding the implications of a life-course approach for understanding travel behaviour is illustrated in Figure 3.13 in which the life-course domain is shown to be related to the accessibility domain and the mobility domain (Salomon 1983; Hall 2004b). Past travel and life experiences influence future travel destination choices, with Sönmez and Graefe (1998) noting that past reasons for travel determine future travel decisions and can affect an individual's perception of risk. For example, Page and Meyer (1996) noted that tourists' experiences with accidents and illness while on holiday can greatly impact on future travel decisions (Page and Meyer 1996). Indeed, such a conception assists in integrating various forms of mobility, such as return migration (Duval 2002, 2003b, 2004b), into the wider account of leisure-oriented mobility. For example, return migration is a very strong motivating force in explaining temporary and permanent mobility in the Chinese population. This supports the hypothesis that Confucian belief in *Ye lo hui gen* (falling leaves return to their roots) plays a very important role in return migration in China with migrants making great efforts to return home, especially when they are old (Li and Li 1995).

Tourism Insight: The Youth Market

Bywater (1993) noted that the youth market is a multi-million dollar business but has not yet captured sufficient significance in academia. Recognising this gap, Chadee and Cutler (1996) examined student motives for undertaking international travel with a survey administered to students of the University of Auckland in New Zealand. Further significant studies (Carr 1998, 1999) show that despite the youth travel markets' importance, research has neglected this target group, resulting in a disregard of its potential by both academics and marketers. These studies suggest that the youth market should not be ignored as it could serve as an indicator of future travel trends. The Federation of International Youth Travel Organisations (FIYTO) suggested that 80 million trips annually, which totals 20% of all international travel, are accounted for by the student travel market (FIYTO 2002). Arguing from a similar point of view, Loker-Murphy and Pearce (1995) stated in their studies that every sixth international arrival is a youth tourist. Moreover, it was suggested that more and more younger people from developed countries postpone the entrance into 'real life' through an intensive and longer travel period.

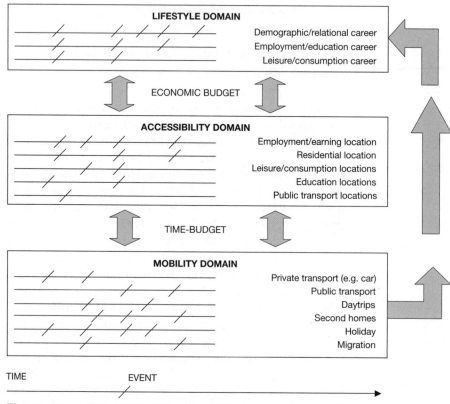

Figure 3.13   The construction of mobility biographies and life courses (Hall 2004b)

Locales

As settings for interaction, locales constitute important contexts to the life paths of individuals. Giddens (1984) sees such locales as being regionalised in terms of the zoning of time–space in relation to routinised social practices. Similarly, a domain also constitutes an important regionalisation of time–space. One can, for example, consider the night-time as a frontier of social activity in which there are certain mores associated with behaviour in a particular time–space which do not exist in the same space during daytime. Indeed, the attractiveness of some locations is based on such domains and reference can be made to the 'entertainment' or 'nightlife' cities in urban tourism research (Janelle and Goodchild 1983; Goodchild and Janelle 1984; Janelle et al. 1998; Page and Hall 2003), in which specific locales may even be deliberately commodified and marketed to others and visiting them may also serve to reinforce certain identities (Giddens 1991).

Locales are therefore points at which the various life paths of individuals intersect. This is important for more than just the individual. Recognition of the economic potential of such intersections, as well as the potential influence available to such locales, has therefore reinforced the ways in which locales (places) may themselves be deliberately commodified and promoted to encourage particular types of intersection and merging of life paths to the perceived benefit of such places. Nevertheless, recognition of the significance of the notion of a locale only serves to reinforce the importance of place as a central construct in tourism because of the role of destinations in tourism analysis.

Structuration theory emphasises that individuals and structures are embedded within each other. However, the relationships between structure and agency do not occur in a vacuum; they occur in places. Places are continually becoming, and may be conceptualised as 'an historically contingent process' emphasising institutional and individual practices as well as the structural features with which those practices interact (Pred 1984, p. 279). Agnew (1987) identifies three main elements of place:

- Locale: the settings in which objective social and economic relations are constituted.

- Location: the objective geographical area encompassing the setting for social interaction as defined by social and economic processes operating at a wide scale.

- Sense of place: the local structure of subjective feeling associated with an area.

To Relph (1976), an authentic sense of place involves a sense of belonging. In contrast, inauthentic places – placelessness – are the prevalent mode of industrialised mass society and Relph often equated them with the realms of many tourist places and the supposed globalising and homogenising capacities of tourism. Placelessness is a 'weakening of the identity of places to the point where they not only look alike, but feel alike and offer the same bland possibilities for experience' (Relph 1976, p. 90).

Places are produced by the complex intersection of processes that operate across spatial scales from the local to the global. Places are therefore made up of complex webs and flows that are never static and instead should be recognised as relatively fluid spaces in which identities are continually being negotiated. Indeed, much of the concern over authenticity in tourism also needs to be reinterpreted in terms of the fluidity of place and representation. Identities are selected at different places and times for a variety of reasons, some of which may relate to intensely personal understandings of heritage, but they are also often invented and promoted for commercial or political reasons. Nevertheless, it must be recognised that locales and places are imbued with significance. Arguably, as some people become even more mobile, many places will become imbued with more meaning as people establish multiple relationships to place, for example by having both a permanent and a second home, or by the capacity to visit some places more often, or even by virtue of having a diasporic or roots connection to a locale. Indeed, Peet (1998) identified a number of experiences of place in terms of the positioning of people in relation to place:

- existential outsiderness, in which all places assume the same meaningless identity;

- objective outsiderness, in which places are viewed scientifically and passively;

- incidental outsiderness, in which places are experienced as little more than backgrounds for activities;

- vicarious insiderness, in which places are experienced in a second-hand way;

- behavioural insiderness, which involves emotional and empathetic involvement in a place;

- existential insiderness, when places are experienced without deliberate reflexion, yet are full of significance.

It may well be that 'increasingly, pure experience, which leaves no material trace, is manufactured and sold like a commodity' (MacCannell 1999, p. 21). However, at some level experience is tied to place. Indeed, as the following chapter indicates, place, and the creation of place, is a central element in the consumption and production of tourism.

Tourism Mobilities, Modernities and the Cage of Routine

Most empirical work in time geography has been limited to small-scale, short-term and essentially individual-level research (Pred 1990). Nevertheless, its broader influence on the social sciences has been substantial (Giddens 1984; Ellegaard 1999; Gren 2001), while clear relationships exist between macro-level studies of spatial interaction and the micro-level studies of time geography. For example, this has been applied in the context of shopping time and frequency of consumption (Baker 1985; Baker and Garner 1989), integrated with environmental psychology (Gärling and Golledge 1993), transport (Tanner 1979; Wigan and Morris 1981; Jones 1990; Vilhelmson 1999) and to a broader understanding of the relationships between accessibility, transport and geographic information systems (Miller 1991, 1998, 1999; Miller and Wu 2000). However, it has been surprisingly little associated with tourism studies despite the potential it holds for the field (Hall 2003c, 2004b; Coles et al. 2004), particularly given the insights that it may provide into understanding how tourism fits into the routinisation of everyday life.

Tourism has often been held as being an occurrence outside that of the routine, a perspective which continues to the present day in much tourism writing. For example, as noted in Chapter 1, Aronsson (2000, p. 57) argued:

[W]e are prisoners in the present-day time–space structure that we have created for our lives, we often use the free time we have in the evenings, at week ends and during our holidays to change this state of affairs through, for instance, a change of environment or, if you will, a change of time-space.

Similarly, Wang (2000, p. vii) observes that tourism is 'a kind of social action which distances the paramount reality' both in time and geography and in terms of culture. Yet such perspectives fail to acknowledge the extent to which space–time compression has led to fundamental changes to individuals' space–time paths in recent years and, hence, their mobile lifestyles and extensibility. The routinised space–time paths of those living in 2004 are not the same as those of people in 1984 when Giddens was writing, or even more so in the 1960s when Hägerstrand was examining daily space–time trajectories. Instead, because of advances in transport and communication technology, for a substantial proportion of the population being able to travel long distances to engage in various forms of leisure behaviour (what one would usually describe as tourism) or even to vicariously experience other cultures via the National Geographic or Discovery Channel is now a part of their space–time prism. The more mobile people are the more travel and tourism become routinised.

The notion of leisure time, for example, can be seen as part of the domain of life paths that engage in tourism practices. Leisure or free time is defined by Wang (2000, p. 116) as a 'socially and culturally approved way of spending a certain period of time that is legitimately exempt from the work ethic, obligations, and working tempos'. Indeed, Wang (2000) argues that under modernity, it is actually expected that people will designate some of their resources in order to acquire new experiences geographically remote from their daily life as part of their leisure time. For some, tourism may be part of a 'distancing action' or escapism (Tuan 1998), but for many it also provides opportunities for social interaction and the chance to travel through other locales. But just as importantly, because of the space–time prisms within which we operate, one can never truly escape. Figure 3.14 details the relative flexibility of some travel activities in time and place.

People's travel time budgets have not changed substantially, but the ability to travel further at a lower per unit cost within a given time budget (Schafer 2000) has led to a new series of social encounters, interactions and patterns of production and reproduction as well as consumption. The locales in which this occurs are sometimes termed destinations, and represent a particular type of lifestyle mobility that, when it occurs away from the 'home environment', is usually termed 'tourism' (Hall 2004b).

Individual space–time trajectories are shifting, leading to greater social and economic interaction in various, often transnational, domains, or what Giddens (1984, p. 116) prefers to call 'the regionalization of time–space: the movement of life paths through settings of interaction that have various forms of spatial demarcation' over increasingly larger distances in space and time. Moreover, the potential for individuals to develop close relationships to multiple localities either through migration, second homes or employment not only spawns temporary movement that is inherently culturally influenced and predicated by previous mobility and the path of the life course, but also interrogates the

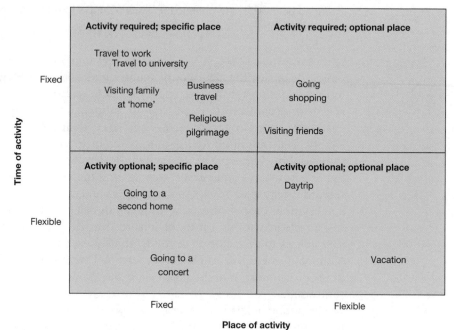

Figure 3.14   Categorisation of travel activities by time and place requirements

notion of a 'singular' home itself. Just as significantly, as noted in the previous chapter, space–time distantiation has provided for the development of often dense sets of social, cultural and economic networks stretching between the two ends of the mobility spectrum, from daily leisure mobility through to migration, from the local to the global, and thereby promoting the development of communities in which movement is the norm and in which place becomes one of the key bases for attracting the leisure mobile over space and time.

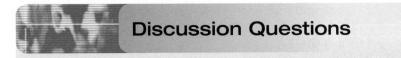

Discussion Questions

1. Why is model building important for undertaking tourism research?

2. In what ways are the geographical and psychological elements of a tourist system (Figure 3.1) related?

3. How might distance influence tourism and what are the different forms that distance can take?

4. How do time budgets affect your leisure mobility?

5. How might the size of an individual's time–space prism influence his or her understanding of the world?

6. How might tourism consumption and production be routinised?

7. Do you think that we are, as Aronsson (2000, p. 57) argued, 'prisoners in the present-day time–space structure that we have created for our lives'?

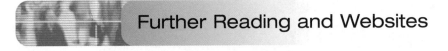

Further Reading and Websites

On concepts of mobility in tourism, see Coles et al. (2004), which provides an overview of the relationship of tourism mobility to a wide body of social science literature. Also look at work in relation to tourism and migration (Williams and Hall 2000; Hall and Williams 2002a), second homes (Hall and Müller 2004a), diaspora (Coles and Timothy 2004) and sociology and cultural studies (Urry 2000a, 2000b; Verstraete 2001; Kaufmann 2002; Verstraete and Cresswell 2002). McHugh's (2000) argument for the use of ethnographic approaches to migration apply equally well to tourism, while Stopher (1992) notes the use of activity diaries. Gustafson (2002) is an excellent collection of papers on issues that arise out of the relationships between place, place attachment and mobility, while Marchetti (1994), Levinson and Kumar (1995) and Vilhelmson (1999) provide excellent accounts of the patterns of daily mobility. Elsud (1998) is an interesting account of time creation in travelling by female backpackers.

Useful accounts of issues of accessibility and mobility in relation to transport can be found in Hansen (1959), Ingram (1971), Burns (1979), Pooler (1995), Handy and Niemeier (1997), Kwan (1998, 1999, 2000), Miller (1999), Pooley and Turnbull (2000), Kenyon et al. (2002) and McQuaid et al. (2004). For some examples of space and/or time budget research undertaken in a tourism context, see Pearce (1988), Debbage (1991), Fennel (1996) and Bærenholdt et al. (2004), while issues of distance decay and other dimensions of spatial interaction and spatial economy are well illustrated in the work of Dean Hanink; see Hanink (1995a, 1995b), Hanink and White (1999), and Hanink and Stutts (2002).

Eco-Tour a European network 'tourism with soft mobility': www.eco-tour.org

European Spatial Planning Research and Information Database: www.esprid. org

Transport Direct (promoted as the world's first natonal, integrated, door-to-door, transport advice website): www.transportdirect.info

West Virginia University, Regional Research Institute, The Web Book of Regional Science (excellent free source of material on a number of topics examined in this book): www.rri.wvu.edu/regscbooks.htm

Part II

Place, governance and management: competing destinations

Place Competition in the Global Economy

4

The study of place and region, for long the domain of human geographers, has recently become a major element for the study of tourism. Indeed, as noted in the previous chapters, throughout the social sciences there has been an increased focus on the significance of place and region, particularly in the light of contemporary globalisation processes. Moreover, government and industry have also focused on the concept of place within the context of regional development and promotion, reflecting the role of places as new actors in the world economic scene (Kotler et al. 1993). Within the tourism and marketing literature, the concepts of 'place marketing' (e.g. Madsen 1992), also sometimes described as 'selling places' (e.g. Burgess 1982; Kearns and Philo 1993a, 1993b), 'geographical marketing' (e.g. Ashworth and Voogd 1988) or 'reimaging strategies' (Roche 1992; Hall 1994a), have come to receive significant attention as key elements of the tourism system (Hall and Page 2003). As Ashworth and Voogd (1988, p. 65) argue, the process of place marketing reflects a paradigm that structures 'the way the complex functioning of cities is viewed [as] many urban activities operate in some kind of a market ... in which a planned action implies an explicit and simultaneous consideration of both the supply-side and the demand-side [and] such an approach has implications for ... the way the cities are managed'.

Arguably, the core of this paradigm is the view that places, cities and regions are now a commodity to be promoted and sold in order to attract mobile capital, investors, people and tourists (Philo and Kearns 1993; Kneafsey 2000; Page and Hall 2003). Therefore, places are now commodities to be produced and consumed. The competitive ethos of the marketplace became translated into a burgeoning 'place market' (Sadler 1993). 'The primary goal of the place marketer is to construct a new image of the place to replace either vague or negative images previously held by current or potential residents, investors and visitors' (Holcomb 1993, p. 133), in order to effectively compete with other places within the constraints of a global economy for a share of mobile international capital (Harvey 1987, 1989a). This marketing operation involves the construction of particular identities, images and representation of place, which are enmeshed with 'the dynamics of the global economy and legitimised particular conceptions of what were "appropriate" state policy responses' (Sadler 1993, p. 175). The new rhetoric of 'the local' therefore has to be seen as deeply embedded in processes of global accumulation, in which competitive places try to secure a lucrative development niche (Swyngedouw 1989).

The notion of competition for rapidly circulating international capital within the global economy is also implicit in the work of Kotler et al. (1993), probably the major place marketing text which is oriented within the mainstream empiricist marketing tradition. According to Kotler et al. (1993, p. 18), a central proposition of *Marketing Places: Attracting Investment, Industry, and Tourism to Cities, States, and Nations* is that the

> marketplace shifts and changes occur far faster than a community's capacity to react and respond. Buyers of the goods and services that a place can offer (i.e. business firms, tourists, investors, among others) have a decided advantage over place sellers (i.e. local communities, regions, and other places that seek economic growth).

Kotler et al. (1993) referred to the need for places to adopt a process of 'strategic place marketing' for urban and regional revitalisation in order to design a community that satisfied the needs of its 'key constituencies'. Such a process embraces four interrelated core activities:

- designing the right mix of community features and services;
- setting attractive incentives for the current and potential buyers and users of its goods and services;
- delivering a place's products and services in an efficient, accessible way; and
- promoting the place's values and image so that the potential users are fully aware of the place's distinctive advantages.

To Kotler et al. (1993) place marketing means designing a place to satisfy the needs of its target markets in the same way as one would sell any other product, with various investments being made to a place to improve its attractiveness for living in, investing in, and visiting, a process made up of the four components of place:

- place as character;
- place as a fixed environment;
- place as a service provider; and
- place as entertainment and recreation (Kotler et al. 1993).

However, in all of this what has become of the notion of place as people, locales and webs which reveal a number of different intersections of life courses? For Kotler et al. (1993) this means that a place succeeds when citizens and businesses are pleased with their community, and it meets the expectations of visitors and investors. Yet, in objectifying place as a commodity, as an object to be bought and sold, as within the empiricist tradition of the majority of tourism marketing, the people constituting place have been placed outside the place marketer's frame of reference. As noted in the previous chapter, a locality is not just a space in which to work for a wage, but a place where people are socialised human beings with deep attachments rather than just being labour commodities. As Hudson (1988, pp. 493–4) recognised: 'These localities are places that have come to have socially endowed and shared meanings for people that touch on all aspects of their lives and that help shape who they are by virtue of where they are.'

   In commodifying place as a product that can be revitalised, advertised and marketed, places are presented not so much as foci of attachment and life courses, but as bundles of social and economic opportunity *competing* against one another in the marketplace for a share of the cake of mobile capital and people (Philo and Kearns 1993). The 'terrain of thinking' about local economic policies and political forms has therefore been shifted (Duncan and Goodwin

Tourism Insight: Cebu

When Cebu first started promoting itself to investors and tourists it referred to itself as 'an island in the Pacific'; any reference to the fact that it is a province of the Philippines 600 km to the south of the capital Manila was omitted. Cebu's strategy was one built not only on its cultural and language differences but also on independent provincial policies that differentiated promotion as well as tax incentives for business investment. Instead of a corporate tax of 30%, select companies receive a flat 5% levy on their gross income. According to Hookway (2003, p. 43), 'as Cebu has found, an increasingly interconnected global economy has given cities or islands the chance to decouple from their countries and carve out their own niches in the world market'. Cebu has some natural advantages in terms of accessibility such as its central location in the Philippine archipelago and a natural deep-water harbour. These advantages have since been reinforced by the development of an international airport and even its own airline, as well as its location outside the usual cyclone paths in the region. However, such development has not been without its problems, particularly with respect to inmigration, slum development, congestion and pressure on infrastructure. In response, rather than seek assistance from Manila, members of the local political and economic elite have sought to have greater political and economic independence. According to Emilio Osmena, former Governor and a leading independence advocate, 'The only connection we have with Manila is that they use us as their milking cow. ... China has a one-country, two-systems policy in regard to Hong Kong. We can do that too. ... We want to shed the inefficient colonial system' (quoted in Hookway 2003, pp. 43–4).

1985a, 1985b, 1988) so that a range of local institutions have now internalised the idea that the interests of a place are best served by lifting the 'dead hand' of regulation and by opening it to the sway of market forces as being 'natural' (Philo and Kearns 1993). However, such normative arguments also lie within the academic terrain and was a central thrust of the work of Kotler et al. (1993, p. 325), who stated: 'The public sector, being largely monopolistic in character, often lags behind the private sector in being responsive to the needs and service requirements of its citizens.' This is a truly remarkable comment given the lack of a polity for the private sector and the ongoing responsiveness in the developed world of the various levels of the state to the demands of elections.

It is important to note that theories are also policies (Hall and Jenkins 1995). Academic, government and industry arguments as to the role of the local state are intimately related. The 1980s onwards witnessed the re-emergence of political structures and ideologies which were based around the notions of privatisation and deregulation, twin processes which supposedly promote the unfettered operation of so-called 'market forces' (Cloke 1992). Throughout the developed world the infrastructure previously provided by government in the public interest has become increasingly privatised. 'Where public agencies were once seen as an essential part of the solution to any urban crisis, they are now viewed as part of the problem itself' (Goodwin 1993, p. 148). Thus, it is ironic given that Kotler et al.'s (1993) discussion of strategic place marketing fails to address the means by which the citizenry can actually participate in the place marketing process to decide how their city or region should be presented to consumers, if at all. Within this context, normative assumptions about equal individual access to power and decision-making pervade much of the marketing literature. Yet, clearly, individuals do not have equal access to power and decision-making. As Hall and Jenkins (1995) argued, business interest groups dominate the tourism policy-making process, while Harvey (1988) highlighted the role of growth coalitions in urban redevelopment. Similarly, Harvey (1989a) and Lowe (1993) commented on the power of regional entrepreneurs (such as a charismatic mayor, a clever city administrator or a wealthy business leader) in moulding the contemporary urban landscape. Therefore, to return to a question which haunted much urban planning in the late 1960s and early 1970s (Johnston 1991), in whose interests are cities and places being constructed, promoted and revitalised? Furthermore, the command and control functions of an increasingly spaced-out global economy will doubtless continue to locate within the global cities, economic winners but marked by deep social divisions (Sassen 1991). Are we witnessing the creation and promotion of places in the gaze of white, marketing academic, middle-class notions of what constitutes civil society?

Packaging Place

Places are therefore often packaged around a series of real or imagined cultural traditions and representations, often focusing on a particular interpretation of the enterprise history of a place – typically without any labour disputes! Under the enterprise economy, 'the ideology of locality, place and community becomes central to the political rhetoric of urban governance which concentrates on the idea of togetherness in defence against a hostile and threatening world of international competition' (Harvey 1989a, p. 14). The packaging of cultural images and traditions is recognised as being significant for place marketing in the work of Kotler et al. (1993). However, whereas Kotler et al. see this as an appropriate means of forging new images in the marketplace, other commentators argue that this may be an inappropriate form of political socialisation whereby images of places are manipulated in order to manufacture an apparent cultural and political consensus designed to convince people, often disadvantaged and potentially disaffected, 'that they are important cogs in a successful community and that all sorts of "good things" are really being done on their behalf' (Philo and Kearns 1993, p. 3). Indeed, the more intangible phenomenon of place marketing is the process by which cultural resources are mobilised in an attempt to engineer a sense among residents 'that beyond the daily difficulties of urban life which many of them might experience the city is basically "doing alright" by its citizens' (Kearns and Philo 1993a, p. ix). Not only are internal marketing campaigns utilised to make citizens of a community feel better about themselves, for example the 'Absolutely, Positively, Wellington' campaign in Wellington, New Zealand, or the 'State on the Move' campaign in Victoria, Australia, but culture, in the form of heritage, history, traditions and lifestyles, are also sold as commodities to be consumed and utilised as mechanisms to create a unified image or history where none existed before.

Central to the activities subsumed under the heading of 'selling places' is often a conscious and deliberate manipulation of culture not only for those who live in a place but also to those from outside in an effort to enhance the appeal of places, especially to the relatively well-off and well-educated workforces of high-technology industry, but also to 'up-market' tourists and meetings and event organisers. In part this manipulation of culture depends upon promoting traditions, lifestyles and arts that are supposed to be locally rooted and which have an 'authentic' quality (Philo and Kearns 1993). Issues of authenticity and inauthenticity, for example the creation of a 'consensus' when one does not exist, have become a major area of interest for students of cultural and heritage tourism. However, the means by which *places* are created, and the authenticity they have for tourists and the people which make up those places, particularly in Western cities and regions, has not drawn much attention within the mainstream tourism literature in recent years, although it has been an issue of concern within cultural studies and social theory. 'If particular places project a dominant, even hegemonic, image of what they are and what they are meant to become, then this has not arisen naturally but is a product of political debate and struggle' (Hudson 2000, p. 26).

A 2003 advertisement in the SAS airlines magazine for the Advantage West Midlands development agency, centred on Birmingham in England, is typical of many place promotions used to attract business investment and relocation. According to the advertisement:

The UK is Europe's leading business location and the West Midlands, situated at the very heart of the UK, can offer your business the ideal base you need to succeed here. We already have over 2,100 overseas owned companies from 40 countries worldwide who have been attracted by our:

- central location at the heart of the UK's road and rail network, with 75% of the UK's population within a five hours' truck drive

- excellent international access with direct flights to all European business centres as well as locations in North America, the Middle East and Asia

- highly competitive operating costs, with a range of buildings in a variety of locations to suit your needs

- young, skilled and dynamic labour force of over 2.6 million

● intellectual base of 10 universities and 10% of all the UK graduates

● business and professional services centre which is the largest outside London

● superb quality of life

● potential grant assistance. (Advantage West Midlands 2003, p. 90)

The advertisement contains most of the main elements to persuade mobile capital to relocate: accessibility, relative costs of location, educated labour force, quality of life/amenity values, and possible state assistance for location.

The culture of a place, however this might be understood, is intimately bound up with the history of that place and with the histories (which may *not* always be locally rooted, for example in the case of migrants) of the peoples who have ended up living in that place (Philo and Kearns 1993). However, the past is often appropriated and manipulated for the presentation of a particular picture or image of the past and designed for consumption by external consumers, as well as internal consumers – the people who live there. The outcome has been described as 'the city as theme park', in which the architecture of the inner city utilises historic façades 'from a spuriously appropriated past' to generate consumption within an atmosphere of nostalgia and display. 'The result is that the preservation of the physical remnants of the historical city has superseded attention to the human ecologies that produced and inhabit them' (Sorkin 1992, p. xiv). For example, Burgess and Wood (1989) argued that as a result of the London dockland redevelopment and associated marketing, the richness and diversity of the specific localities within East London have been reduced to a commodity to be packaged and sold, with many of those who lived in the district prior to the redevelopment not benefiting from the newly 'revitalised' areas because they do not have the educational or social capital that can provide them with the employment and social access to such a newly created place (Page and Hall 2003).

The reality of place is always open, making its determination an inherently social and political process. Therefore, one of the great ironies, given that the enterprise culture of place marketing extols the virtues of competition and choice, is the manner in which debate over representation and redevelopment of place is denied. Throughout much of the Western world, in order to ensure that specific urban development projects are carried out, local authorities have had planning and development powers removed for those locations and handed to an unelected public–private institution (Goodwin 1993). Harvey (1989, p. 7) recognised that 'the new entrepreneurialism has, as its centrepiece, the notion of a "public–private partnership" in which a traditional local boosterism is integrated with the use of local government powers to try [to] attract external sources of funding, new direct investments, or new employment sources'. However, the partnership does not include all members of a community. Those who do not have enough money, are not of the right lifestyle, or simply do not have sufficient power are ignored (see Sadler (1993) with respect to Derwentside in the United Kingdom as an example).

As Harvey (1993, p. 8) asked, '[t]he question immediately arises as to why people accede to the construction of their places by such a process'. In many cases they do not. Communities may resist such change. However, while wins in short-term battles may save the physical fabric of inner-city communities, this will not usually win the war. The social fabric will usually change through gentrification and touristification of many areas, leaving only façades and a new set of place relations. Furthermore, the very 'rules of the game' by which planning and development decisions are made will often favour business over community interest groups (Hall and Jenkins 1995). Indeed, Harvey (1993, 2000) also notes that resistance has not checked the overall process of place competition. A mixture of coercion and co-optation centred around maintenance of real estate values, assumptions regarding employment and investment generation, and an assumption that growth is automatically good has led to the creation of local growth coalitions (see Chapter 6 for an exposition of the reasons behind this). However, place packaging is not just the result of micro-political factors. It should also be placed within the context of cultural fashions and social theory, particularly as identified in Chapter 2. In this sense, contemporary architects, designers and other place-makers, with their penchant for the postmodern, are as responsible for the commodification of place as the real estate developer or place marketer wanting to package their product. Moreover, it should be noted that the territorially bounded conception of place is subject to substantial critique given the extent to which such boundaries may be relatively discontinuous and permeable (Allen et al. 1998). Despite the attempts of some place marketers to provide rather simplistic impressions of place, it must be emphasised that they are instead endowed with multiple, and often contested, identities and meanings. Places are complex condensations of overlapping and different social relations in a particular envelope or location of space and time, 'with the density, variety and types of social relations that intersect there helping to define different types of place' (Hudson 2000, p. 25).

A good example of the extent to which place competition has led to attempts to simplify place identity is to be found in the development of national branding strategies. A number of countries, such as Australia, New Zealand and South Africa, have public–private brand councils which seek to assist in the development and promotion of national brands. Australia has formed a brand council in order to promote 'brand Australia' and obtain support for a more unified approach to promoting Australia internationally. Members of the organisation include the Australian Tourist Commission, the Australian Film Commission, Fosters (a beer brand) and RM Williams (a country clothing and footwear manufacturer and retailer). In addition to advising companies that export or operate abroad on how best to market themselves, the council will also advise organisations, sports teams and high-profile Australians on how to be 'brand ambassadors' for Australia (Lee and Dennis 2004). The formation of the brand council was aimed to coincide with a new A$27 million Australian Tourist Commission marketing campaign which would highlight 'Australian traits such as inclusiveness, openness and optimism – characteristics to be incorporated into guidelines to be used by the brand council' (Lee and Dennis 2004, p. 14). According to the Chief Executive of the Australian Tourist

Commission, Ken Boundy, 'A lot of people reel back from the idea that you can build a nation into a brand. There are obviously a lot more variables in a country than, say, the branding of a car or a clothing label, but it can be done' (quoted in Lee and Dennis 2004, p. 14). Such enthusiasm is matched by that of the Federal Tourism Minister, Joe Hockey, who stated:

> Australia sells thousands of bottles of wine a minute around the world, and if we can turn them into liquid postcards just imagine the benefits for Australia and its image overseas. . . . We want every Australian, and every international visitor, to become ambassadors for Australia. (quoted in Lee and Dennis 2004, p. 14)

However, while political enthusiasm for developing national brands remains strong, it is ironic that on the same day that the development of a national brand council was announced there was also substantial promotion occurring for state and regional brands in the same newspaper in which the council announcement was contained. *The Age Good Weekend* magazine included:

- A one-page advertisement for Shoalhaven on the New South Wales south coast urging people that they were 'Free to go at your own pace. . . . That's the beauty of the Shoalhaven', with the advertisement sponsored by Shoalhaven City and 'Feel Free' New South Wales (The Age 2004, p. 9).

- A one-page advertisement for South Australia featuring a natural attraction called Wilpena Pound, telling the reader that 'if you're after a totally wild time, you've come to the right place'. The advertisement was sponsored by 'Discover the Secrets of South Australia' (The Age 2004, p. 17).

- A two-page advertisement for travel to northern Tasmania, with messages written in the style of a man who had recently visited the area, telling readers that with 'Cruising to Tasmania I felt like a new man. Luckily my wife didn't.' The advertisment was sponsored by Tasmania 'A rejuvenating journey' (The Age 2004, pp. 24–5).

- A one-page advertisement for Queensland which featured a quote from St Ambrose: 'If you are elsewhere, live as they do', and the tag line for the state being 'Where else but Queensland' (The Age 2004, p. 28).

Indeed, the extent to which place competition occurs between the various Australian states was demonstrated in that on the day after the Australian brand council was announced the Victorian state government announced an A$7 million two-year campaign to sell Victoria's culture to tourists in the lead up to the 2006 Commonwealth Games (Simpson 2004).

Plate 4.1   The 'London eye' viewing wheel has become an important part of London tourism since its construction as a millennium project not only because it is an attraction in its own right but because it has assumed an important role in the place promotion of London. (The official visitor site for London is www.visitlondon.com/)

The Learning Economy

In addition to places seeking to reimage or promote themselves, competitiveness and economic success are also increasingly seen to be grounded in types of knowledge and knowing – what has become known as the learning economy. The term 'learning economy' signifies a society in which the capacity to learn, and therefore to innovate, is critical to economic success (Lundvall and Johnson 1994) and in which knowledge is recognised as a strategic resource. Lundvall (1992) highlighted the national context of innovation systems and learning and the significance of shared language and culture, as well as formal regulatory legislative frameworks in shaping trajectories of learning and innovation – regulatory frameworks. However, there are different forms or varieties of knowledge (Bathelt et al. 2004) with knowledge often being 'collective rather than simply individual, locally produced and often place specific' (Hudson 2000, p. 95). Indeed, depending on the sectoral context within which innovation occurs (Metcalfe and Miles 2000), regional and locality-based knowledge can be of great significance (Malmberg and Maskell 1997, 2002; Lawson and Lorenz 1999; Maskell and Malmberg 1990a, 1990b; Lundvall and Maskell 2000; Maskell 2001). This may particularly be the case for some types of tourism which seek to provide added value to visitors through either interpretative skills, for example with respect to heritage and nature, or with specific activity skills, such as in various forms of adventure tourism or sports tourism. Indeed, various language or inter-cultural communication skills, often the product of international mobility as well as formal education (Inkson et al. 1997; Joint Standing Committee on Migration 1997; Inkson et al. 1999; Kinnaird 1999; Lowell 1999; Aitken and Hall 2000; OECD 2002; Rosenkopf and Almeida 2003) may also prove to be valuable for the development of tourism products, particularly given the growth of cultural capital and therefore the importance of understanding consumer tastes (Aitken and Hall 2000).

In most industries intensive competition and shorter product life are creating closer linkages of research and development (R&D) with production in order to provide innovative products and meet market demands. However, there is very little consideration of innovation and R&D processes in tourism, although network development has been seen as one avenue for sharing intellectual capital, while government, sometimes in conjunction with university or private providers, usually are the major providers of market research information to the tourism industry. However, spatial clustering of tourism firms does not necessarily lead to knowledge sharing. Instead, it is organisational proximity as opposed to simple spatial proximity, in which the existence of shared knowledge of the environment is presupposed, that allows for flows of information and collective learning (Hudson 2000).

This is not to deny the significance of spatially embedded knowledge, which is potentially significant for tourism, but rather highlights the importance of dense horizontal and vertical networks for the flow of knowledge and information whether it be intra- or inter-firm (Sadler 1997). Nevertheless, ideas of 'institutional thickness' (Amin and Thrift 1994), social capital (Jacobs 1961; Coleman 1988; Putnam 1993, 1995a, 1995b, 2000, 2002) and Storper's (1995) notion of 'regions as a nexus of untraded interdependencies' all reinforce the fact that 'the region is a key, necessary element in the "supply architecture" for learning, knowledge development and innovation that underlies much place competitiveness' (Storper 1995, p. 210). Such concepts suggest that by virtue of certain cultural and institutional characteristics there is a stronger basis for developing and sharing knowledge and for cooperative behaviour than in other regions (Feldman 2000; Hotz-Hart 2000; Storper 2000; Bathelt 2003; Bathelt and Glückler 2003). This may be because of shared values and meanings, as well as the role of institutions, such as universities or the local state, that reproduce such knowledge. Such factors are extremely important for the overall competitiveness of regions but may not have that much direct influence per se on tourism, although significant indirect benefits may accrue in certain situations. Indeed, one of the greatest problems of innovation in tourism is the extent to which innovations in tourism can be sustained at the levels of the firm or the destination as there is a tendency towards the erosion of temporarily conferred competitive advantage by the diffusion of knowledge as information and of technological innovation (Hudson 2000). As one Finnish tourism entrepreneur told the author in 2003, 'any innovation I introduce will last only one season'. The reason of course is that tourism product or service innovations are extremely hard to protect through any form of intellectual property rights and can be very easily copied. Indeed, in this situation a differentiated competitive strategy for a destination may actually serve to reinforce local attributes and resources, such as culture and nature, as they may be the hardest thing to copy by another destination. Yet regional institutional thickness on its own is no guarantee of successful economic adaptation and innovation as it can constrain rather than facilitate processes of collective learning and change if it does not provide openness and the sharing of debated ideas (Hudson 2000). Therefore, concerns with equity and the distribution of power with places and clusters remain fundamental to understanding the winners and losers that arise from development strategies and processes (Bathelt and Taylor 2002).

Accessibility and Place Competition

Tourism does not occur randomly in space. While notions of the learning or the knowledge economy and place competition are important for the relative success of destinations, it should not be forgotten that 'old-fashioned' variables of economic competitiveness, such as accessibility and cost (which can be interpreted as a particular type of accessibility), remain important for tourism. Therefore, some of the principles of spatial interaction discussed in the previous chapter can provide substantial insights into how destinations compete. The time/distance sensitivity of tourist-related travel leads to specific spatial patterns related to distance from origin. Space–time constraints exist for a range of accessibility relations between a point of origin and a destination (Hägerstrand 1970; Pred 1977; Burns 1979). The space–time framework recognises that participation in activities, such as leisure, has both spatial and temporal dimensions, that is activities occur at specific locations for finite temporal durations. In addition, the transportation system dictates the velocities at which individuals can travel and therefore the time available for activity participation at dispersed locations (Miller 1999).

Figure 4.1 presents an idealised model for leisure travel which extends from an urban core in relation to car-based mobility. The model not only highlights the nature of the distance decay effects of leisure travel, but identifies a zone of overnight stay within the hinterland of the urban centre. The zone of overnight stay refers to an area in which the tendency for travellers to stay overnight increases and the likelihood of same-day return trips decreases as a result of:

- availability of time to travel (time budget) and engage in tourist-related activities;

- limitations related to the need for rest while travelling (i.e. tourists cannot continue to drive continuously without sleep); and

- time/distance trade-offs between returning home to sleep and the travel time involved versus stopping overnight.

The time sensitivity of leisure travel because of individual space–time prisms means that the location of overnight stays from a tourist generating region tends to cluster at a location related to time/distance from a point of origin. Typically, a tourism generating area will be a large city but a gateway may also act as such a point of origin. Figure 4.2 represents this clustering in terms of the density of overnight stays with respect to a highly simplified model of an isolated central tourism generating location surrounded by a uniform plane. Individuals and households, possessing perfect knowledge of the distance costs, select a tourism area location that maximises their utility subject to their time/distance constraints. However, a uniform plane clearly does not occur in the real world and travel distances are highly affected by transport networks as well as the distribution of amenity areas which are sought by leisure tourists and weekend second-home purchasers and provide much of the utility function of tourism mobilities. Such a constraint is accounted for by Miller's (1991) notion of Potential Path Space (PPS), defined in terms of the space–time prism that delimits all locations in space–time that can be reached by an individual based on the locations and duration of mandatory activities (e.g. home, work) and the travel velocities allowed by the transportation system. Assume an individual located at time t_1 at the point of origin $(X0, Y0)$ (see Figure 3.7). Again assume that at time t_2 the individual has to be back at the origin. Then the available time for all activities is given by

$$t = t_2 - t_1$$

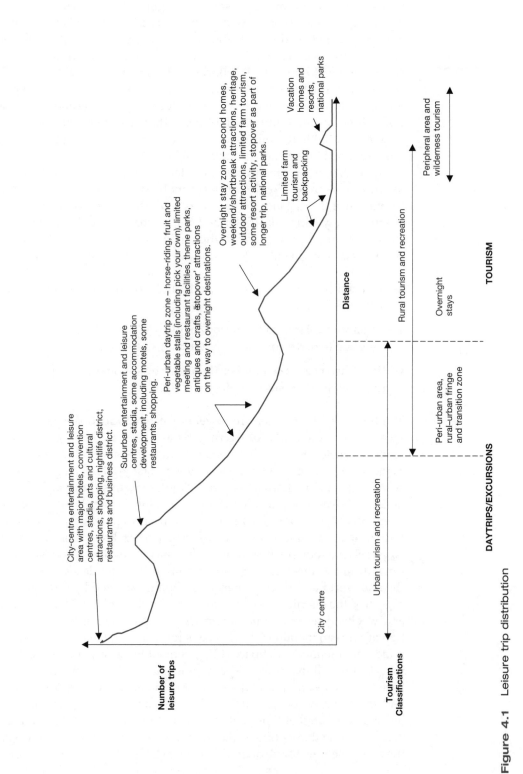

Figure 4.1 Leisure trip distribution

The projection of PPS on to two-dimensional XY-space represents the potential path area that an individual can move within, given the available time budget.

Figure 4.3 presents a hypothetical pattern of density of overnight stays in relation to optimal range for overnight stays and location of tourist areas given the presence of arterial transport networks along the X and Y axes. Significantly, the figure postulates that the density of overnight stays will change over time – presented as t_1 and t_2. Such changes can occur because of improvements in transport technology (e.g. a shift between or within technologies), or transport infrastructure (e.g. improvement in road quality allowing for faster travel). It should also be noted that population growth and urbanisation processes will also encourage such changes because of the relationships between accessibility, transport technology and infrastructure and urban form (refer to Figure 3.4). These changes can also be represented as a wave analogue in which changes in time/distance from a central point of origin will lead to different densities d of overnight stay at a specific location L over times t_1, t_2, in relation to the overall distribution of overnight stays as a function of distance from origin (Figure 4.4).

The use of analogue theory – a formal theory of model building which provides for the selective abstraction of elements from an empirical domain and their translation into a simplified and structured representation of a particular system – was an important component of the quantitative revolution that existed in geography in the 1950s and the 1960s. Within geography and elsewhere in the social sciences the use of analogues is now so widespread that its implications are little considered (Livingstone and Harrison 1981). Indeed, Butler's (1980) Tourism Area Cycle of Evolution (TACE) is itself such

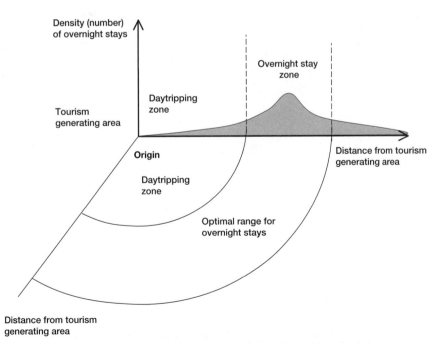

Figure 4.2   Location of overnight stays in relation to points of origin

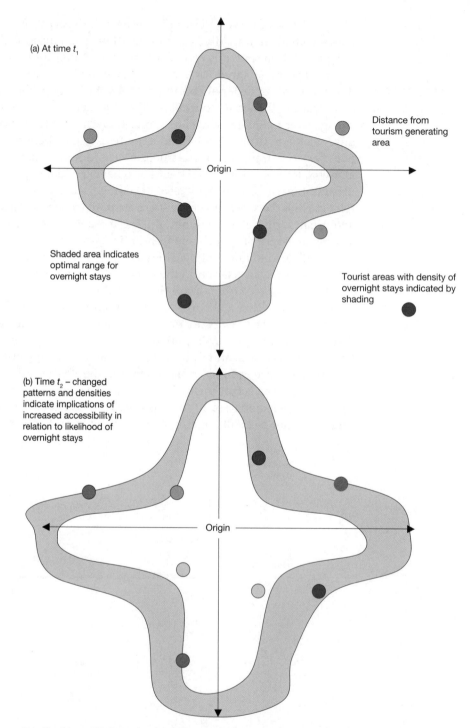

(a) At time t_1

Distance from
tourism generating
area

Origin

Shaded area indicates
optimal range for
overnight stays

Tourist areas with density of
overnight stays indicated by
shading

(b) Time t_2 – changed
patterns and densities
indicate implications of
increased accessibility in
relation to likelihood of
overnight stays

Origin

Note: Tourist areas that were formerly in the overnight stay zone and are now in the daytrip zone are
accessibile to a larger potential market, however their product will need to be modified to meet the
changed market characteristics.

Figure 4.3   Hypothetical pattern of density of overnight stays in relation to the
optimal range for overnight stays and the location of tourist areas

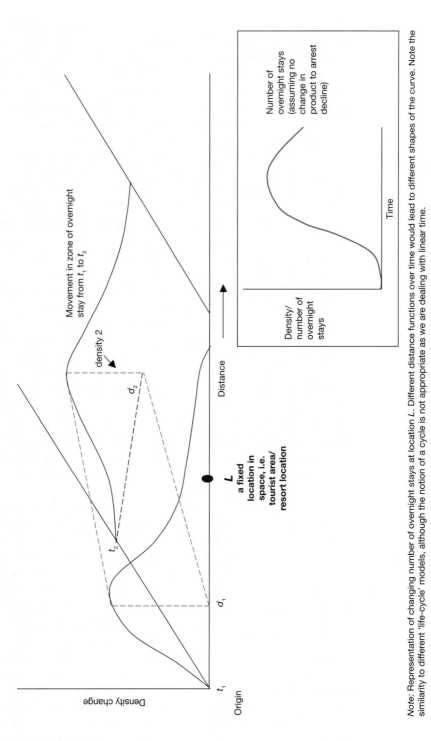

Note: Representation of changing number of overnight stays at location *L*. Different distance functions over time would lead to different shapes of the curve. Note the similarity to different 'life-cycle' models, although the notion of a cycle is not appropriate as we are dealing with linear time.

Figure 4.4 A wave analogue model of the implication of changed accessibility for a fixed location in space

an analogue model, with Hall (2005) noting the importance of accessibility as a basis for the 'life cycle' model, as TACE is often referred to (e.g. Strapp 1988; Cooper and Jackson 1989; Cooper 1992; Oppermann 1996; Graber 1997; Russell and Faulkner 1998; Johnston 2001). For example, Butler (1980) cited Wolfe's (1952) research on summer cottaging in Ontario as an example 'that each improvement in the accessibility to a recreation area results in significantly increased visitation and an expansion of the market area' (Butler 1980, p. 11). In addition to Wolfe's work, Butler also cited the research of Stansfield (1972, 1978) as highlighting the importance of accessibility as a factor in influencing change in tourism destinations. Stanfield's (1978) discussion of Atlantic City and a cycle of resort change is particularly instructive with respect to transport and accessibility issues, with Stansfield noting the influence of transport-related time/distance on the development of Atlantic City as a 'surf and sand' (1978, p. 242) destination: 'Connecting customers with the resort is the basis of all resort development; all recreation and tourism patterns take place within a time and space frame. Atlantic City's time-distance and cost-distance relative to Philadelphia were a successful blend of shortest straight line distance and the efficiency of the railroad', also noting that changes in time–space functions can affect the relative attractiveness of destinations (Stansfield 1978, p. 242). Unfortunately for Atlantic City, its dependence on the railroad meant that with the growth of automobile infrastructure and greater individual mobility through increased car ownership levels, the competitiveness of Atlantic City as a destination decreased. A morphology that had developed in relation to the point-to-point mobility of railroad users could not easily adapt to the demands of the car. As Stansfield (1978, p. 246) noted, 'The new highways that brought vacationers to Atlantic City also facilitated their going to other resorts, or their commuting into Atlantic City from less expensive locations. Highway improvements even increased the "day-trip" hinterland of the city.' Changing patterns of accessibility were therefore integral to Stansfield's understanding of the relative competitiveness of destinations and resorts.

Wave analogues have been used to describe phenomena as distinct as urban density and the development of the urban fringe (e.g. Boyce 1966), and innovation (e.g. Hägerstrand 1952, 1967a). As noted above, in the case of TACE the chapter argues that within the context of the Butler (1980) model a tourist area/destination should not be primarily conceived as an aspatial product in marketing terms. Instead, the destination should be primarily conceptualised as a geographical place, for example as a point in space which is subject to a range of factors which influence locational advantage and disadvantage. Most significant to these is the movement outwards from a tourist generating origin of travellers or trips as a function of distance. Such travel movement cannot be adequately represented in the classic linear form of a distance decay model whereby the location of numbers of trips or people travelling at any given time is highest closer to the generating area and diminishes in relation to distance. Instead, factors which influence travel behaviour, such as decisions relating to overnight stays and time to undertake leisure-oriented activities, as well as overall amenity values, create a series of peaks and troughs in relation to distance from the generating area. Moreover, for any given form of transport there will be a different set of distance/time functions at which overnight stays will need to be made, but all, out of the necessity of travellers to stop, can be represented through a series of peaks and troughs rather than as a straight line (or alternatively as a route/trip behaviour model (see Figure 4.5).

Given the above assumptions, then changes in distance (whether time, cost, behavioural or network) between the tourist generating origin and the surrounding hinterland will lead to corresponding changes in the number of travellers for any given point in the spatial system. However, locations within the spatial system are spatially fixed. Towns and cities do not suddenly get up and move away in order to maximise advantageous distance functions, although they do change and adapt over time in relation to new networks and patterns of accessibility. Similarly, tourist areas/destinations are full of plant and infrastructure that are also spatially fixed. Therefore, as Figure 4.4 indicates, if the numbers of tourist bed-nights (or other measures of tourism-related density) at a spatially fixed point 'destination' (L) are drawn at t_1, t_2, t_3, in relation to the changed accessibility with respect to a tourist generating region or trip origin, then this provides a representation of overnight stay density at a specific location which is analagous to that of the TACE when presented in its standard two-dimensional form (Butler 1980).

The wave analogue approach to tourism is potentially far richer than the basic model presented here. For example, as well as direct-line distance, the notion of distance can, and should, be expressed in terms such as network distance, time–distance, cost–distance, behavioural distance (including perceived distance) and multidimensional measures combining time, money and effort spent in travelling between origin and destination. Space–time functions can be developed for all these ways of considering distance, both at the level of the individual and at the macro-level. Perhaps more significantly there is the issue of multiple origin points as well as different forms of transport. However, in the case of both of these concerns it should be noted that given data availability the relative role of different origin points in determining the accessibility of a given location should be assessable while different space–time prisms clearly exist for different forms of transport.

Significantly, spatial interaction models can also be developed, given the availability of necessary data, of the total cost of travel (which may be variously defined) as well as cost as a proportion of total economic budget. For example, in international terms the relative value of currencies will often be an extremely important factor in the attractiveness of destinations, not only in terms of the direct attraction of visitors but also in relation to domestic and international investment decisions (Crouch 1993). When destinations are competing in terms of the relative cost of their destination product for international visitors, the local tourism industry will often be strongly in favour of a lower value currency so as to help the destination remain competitive in price terms with their competitors. Nevertheless, this may only be a viable strategy in the short term. For example, Reed (2003b) notes that one of the big challenges for South Africa is to become more competitive by means other than rand depreciation. Furthermore, recognition of the spatial interaction of tourism areas with origin areas provides a potentially powerful explanatory tool with respect

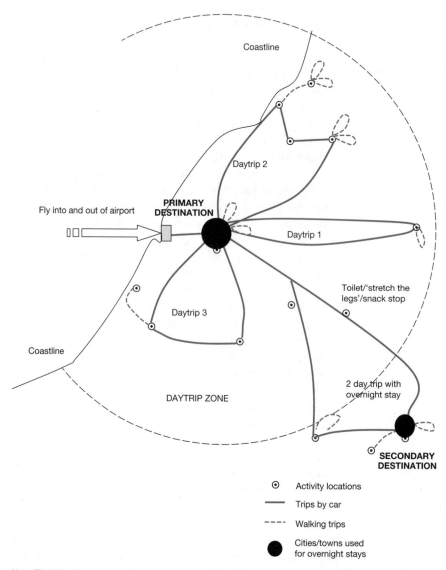

Coastline

Daytrip 2

Fly into and out of airport

PRIMARY DESTINATION

Daytrip 1

Toilet/'stretch the legs'/snack stop

Daytrip 3

Coastline

2 day trip with overnight stay

DAYTRIP ZONE

SECONDARY DESTINATION

⊙   Activity locations

——   Trips by car

- - - -   Walking trips

⬤   Cities/towns used for overnight stays

Note: Trip behaviour portrays a five-night fly/drive FIT (free and independent travel) holiday itinerary with hire car pick up and drop off at airport in which three daytrips are undertaken using the main city as the base and one overnight stay (two-day trip) is undertaken. Each stage of the trip is operating within a space–time prism, as is the trip overall as account also needs to be given to the time to fly in and out of the destination.

Figure 4.5   Trip behaviour model

to the characteristics of tourism markets and their accessibility to any given destination.

Hall (2003d, 2004b, 2005) has argued that an analogue model which incorporates distance as a variable within the spatial interaction between a tourist generating origin and a tourist area provides a far greater degree of explanatory power than that provided in the original Butler (1980) model and subsequent (re)interpretations. As Smith (1985, p. 151) observed, 'it appears

Tourism Insight: The Mallorca Pensioner Market

Economic circumstances are an important macro- and micro-determinant of tourism mobility. For example, at the start of the 2003–04 winter tourist season on the Spanish tourist destination of Mallorca it was reported that the German pensioner market which traditionally holidays there had not arrived in anticipated numbers. The island's hotel federation reported in October that nearly half of all hotels were closing early while only 30% of hotels were likely to stay open over winter. Bookings for October 2003 were 20% down on the previous year. The lack of elderly German tourists was being blamed on the growing economic problems of Germany, which had had almost two years of recession, leading German pensioners to either travel somewhere cheaper or stay within Germany. In contrast, the hotels which were doing well in terms of occupancy were those geared to Spanish pensioners from the mainland. 'Spain's social welfare department offers subsidised holidays in Mallorca for the bargain basement price of €132 (£92) a week' (Harding 2003, p. 15). Nevertheless, retired Germans are still important to the region's economy with approximately 25 000 Germans living permanently or semi-permanently on the Balearics, forming the largest expatriate community.

that the geographic [spatial] variables are more important as predictors of vacation travel patterns than traditional aggregate socioeconomic variables'. Just as importantly, a spatial interaction approach highlights the fact that tourism areas need to be understood in relation to origin areas. Tourism areas do not occur in isolation. The dynamic magnitude and nature of tourism activity reflect the strength of interaction between origins and destinations and their associated environments. Changes in tourism activities which are reflected in changes in spatial interactions may lead to qualitative and/or quantitative economic, environmental and social change at destinations. Changes in the environment, such as changes in amenity values, may induce changes in tourism activities and consequently the interactions between origins and destinations. New networks and patterns of connectivity and accessibility will also affect the interaction between origins and destinations and corresponding changes in the tourism activities and their impact.

Clearly, when utilising a spatial interaction model to examine the relative accessibility and utility of destinations, it is apparent that for any given region with comparable access to another then other factors become key competitive factors in their attractiveness. Assuming costs to be equal and perfect knowledge on behalf of the consumer, it is then that amenity values become extremely significant.

Location-specific amenities are non-traded goods (Graves 1979a, 1979b, 1983; Graves and Linnemann 1979) that can only be obtained when needs or demands arise, through travel to the place in which they are present. Amenities are therefore spatially fixed. Boyle et al. (1998) noted that

Plate 4.2   Inverary in Scotland originally became accessible to holiday makers from Glasgow through paddle steamer connections which meant that it was typically an overnight destination. However, with the demise of the steamers and the growth of motorcar access it has instead become a daytrip destination from Glasgow with overnight holidaymakers instead tending to come from further afield.

equilibrium models assume that amenities can compensate for variations in wages and other economic factors, with overall quality of life – expressed in terms of economic opportunity plus amenity factors – in relative equilibrium over space. Such an observation is extremely significant in relation to the role that the life course plays in the purchase of second homes, often later to become retirement homes, as well as holidaying in general (Mings 1984; Murphy and Zehner 1988; Mullins and Tucker 1988; McHugh and Mings 1991; Haas and Serow 1993; McHugh et al. 1995; Hall and Müller 2004a). Indeed, the importance of climate has long been noted (Graves 1980; Clark and Cosgrove 1991) but other amenity variables, such as access to the sea, ski slopes, mountains, natures and lakes, and attractive scenery are as significant factors in rural areas as restaurants, museums, sport and nightlife are in urban areas. To this can also be added the amenity values available by locating near or holidaying with people of a particular class, as well as the utility values that can be gained through access to family in certain situations. However, it should be noted that the relative amenity value of a location will change over the life course (Graves 1979b; Graves and Regulska 1982; Graves and Waldman 1991). For example, security is particularly significant for the elderly, and it is an amenity value included in the selection of many destinations.

Therefore, security and political stability are also important dimensions in place competition. For example, South Africa, which in the immediate post-apartheid period was characterised by appallingly high crime rates, including the murder and rape of tourists, is gradually being recognised as an increasingly attractive location to visit and in which to invest. According to a 2003 *Financial Times* special report on investing in South Africa, 'Tourists steering clear of northern hemisphere trouble spots have been visiting South Africa in record numbers. Portfolio investors have been pouring money into South African debt securities in pursuit of high returns but also in recognition of the country's solid macroeconomic management' (Reed 2003a, p. 1). Similarly, Carole Mason, head of equities with Investec, said, 'As a result of the rise in terrorism, South Africa has almost come to be seen as a safe haven' (quoted in Reed 2003a, p. 1). Indeed, the idea of maximising amenity values through short- and long-term mobility behaviour is closely related to the notion of quality of life which is a particularly important aspect of second home purchase and holidaying in general (Porell 1982).

The understanding of accessibility and amenity values is regarded as critical to identifying and predicting the actual and potential patterns of tourism development at specific locations in space. Indeed, the product life cycle so influential in consideration of TACE is itself a space–time wave analogue related to innovation diffusion processes (Hägerstrand 1952, 1967a), a point seemingly lost in nearly all of the discussion which has taken place on tourism destination life cycles. Hägerstrand's pioneering work in Sweden on innovation diffusion as a spatial process (1967a) likened the innovation diffusion process to a wave-like pattern which loses its strength as it moves away from the initial point of origin. In his initial work, Hägerstrand noted that a distance decay function was operating in the expansion diffusion process in which probabilities of adoption were higher in the neighbourhood of an earlier adoption and decreased with distance away from an early adoption. Hägerstrand also recognised that there were irregularities in the wave-like form that were produced by the presence of different barriers: a physical barrier (e.g. a border) which completely stopped the flow of information (though stoppage may be only temporary), a reflective barrier that deflects an innovation pulse back on itself (e.g. settlement along a coastline), although cultural and perceptual barriers may be far more significant than physical barriers.

Such an observation also highlights the potential for spatial interaction modelling to provide a better understanding of the development of information regarding potential destinations through the analysis of information fields, a technique long-established in the geographical literature (Morrill and Pitts 1972) because the trip process is not just a spatial process but is also a communicative and social process by which information is exchanged. This is one of the reasons why preventing the flow of travellers between countries was so long a strategy to either keep information in or keep it out (e.g. as in the case of North Korea), although the financial value of tourists and the modern communications revolution through the internet, radio and satellite television have meant that most restrictions on travel to authoritarian countries have finished (although of course, when you get there, you may not be encouraged to speak to those who are 'unauthorised'!).

Tourism Insight: Innovation Diffusion

The wave-like pattern can be represented as a normal curve (Figure 4.6a) or as a logistic curve. Underlying this regularity is a decision-making process that follows the sequence of an individual being made aware of information, showing interest in the innovation, evaluating the innovation, and then adopting it. Those among the first to adopt innovations (initiators) tend to be young, better educated, more widely travelled, willing to take risks and have closer contact with scientific information sources. The late adopters and laggards tend to be older, have more traditional views, are more likely to be socially isolated and tend to be suspicious of agents of change (M.A. Brown 1980). There are implications for tourism not only in the uptake of innovations, such as technology, but also in terms of information flow about a product or destination. The S-shaped curve depicted in Figure 4.6(b) is likely to be adhered to if:

- potential users of a technological innovation become adopters under the influence of previous adopters in the course of direct personal contacts;
- potential users have different degrees of resistance to change;
- resistance to change may be overcome by an adequate number of messages from adopters. This is sometimes referred to as 'conversion through conversation' (Robinson 1998, p. 298).

The logistic curve may be expressed as

$$p_t = (1+e^{a-bt})^{-1}$$

where p_t = the proportion of adopters at time t; a = the intercept; and b = the slope coefficient. Similarly,

$$y_t = k(1+ e^{a-bt})^{-1}$$

where y_t = the number of adopters; and k = the maximum possible number of adopters, that is the saturation level.

Nevertheless, it is important to note that a number of factors will influence uptake of an innovation, including, at the firm level in particular, economic factors. It is also important to note that it is not just the information that determines adoption but the social context within which the information is received (Robinson 1998). L.A. Brown (1981) stressed market and infrastructure perspectives in the study of diffusion and argued that it is often institutional behaviour that holds the key to innovation adoption. Brown argued for the importance of diffusion agencies as well as implementation strategies as being critical for innovation adoption, a conclusion now accepted by many governments in their economic development strategies.

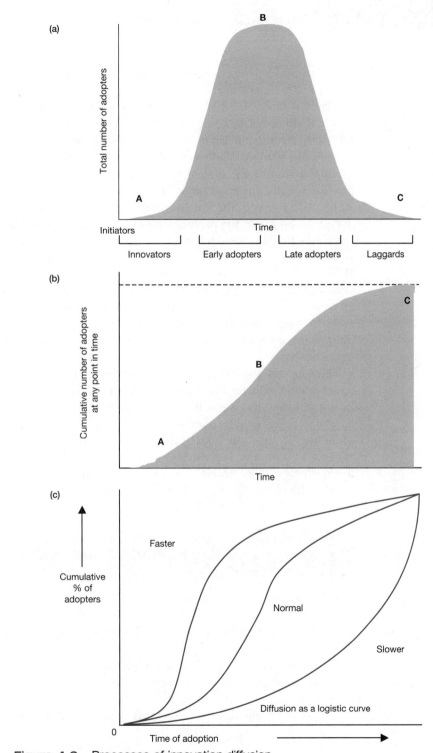

Figure 4.6   Processes of innovation diffusion

Competing Places and Spaces

This chapter has emphasised a number of different dimensions of place competition. The attractiveness of places to tourists is seen to be based, in substantial part, on accessibility and amenity. However, it also emphasised that in a time of place competition there is also a conscious attempt to package places in order to market them to the mobile as well as to develop appropriate images and brands. While some of this happens organically, that is via word of mouth, or indirectly, that is via various media, there are also attempts to provide specific information by the private and public sectors at destinations. At its various levels, the state develops and moulds specific information, often in conjunction with the private sector and often in the public–private partnerships which govern much of tourism policy and development. In this situation we are seeing the emergence of the negotiated economy (Amin and Thomas 1996, p. 99) in which the state fulfils a distinctive role as arbitrator and facilitator of relations between autonomous organisations, 'a mode of regulation' positioned between the market and hierarchy through which the enabling state seeks to 'create the conditions for a dialogic approach to conflict resolution and policy formation in general and innovation, knowledge creation and learning in particular'.

These issues and others regarding the role of the state in tourism and its development will be discussed in the following chapters. However, in finishing this chapter, we will conclude with a cautionary quote regarding the dangers of engaging in place competition and the development of a learning economy: '... for those regions that do successfully embark on the "high road" to regional economic success, this very success raises new problems in terms of a requirement continuously to learn and anticipate, if not create, market trends. Moreover, if some regions "learn" and "win", many more will fail to do so and "lose" ' (Hudson 2000, p. 106).

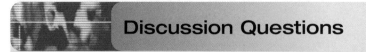

Discussion Questions

1. Do you think that it's possible to actually sell places?

2. How important is asscessibility to competing tourism destinations?

3. Why might some localities be better able to innovate in terms of their tourism products than other areas?

4. How might the relative value of currencies influence the attractiveness of destinations?

5. How might amenity values change over someone's life course?

Further Reading and Websites

An overview of the contribution of the Tourism Area Life Cycle (Butler 1980) to the tourism field is to be found in Butler's (2005) two-volume edited work on TALC. Volume 1 examines conceptual and theoretical issues, while volume 2 looks at applications and modifications. Kearns and Philo (1993b) and Harvey (1989b, 2000) provide excellent accounts of place marketing processes in a broad context. Kotler et al. (1993) represents an extremely instrumental and uncritical approach to place marketing, although it is representative of what many places seek to do.

For overviews of some of the recent thinking regarding regions and locales as focal points of economic generation and social and economic networks, see Hudson (1999, 2000). Gieryn (2000), Clark et al. (2000), and Sheppard and Barnes (2002). Interestingly, the Clark et al. (2000) and Sheppard and Barnes (2002) collections do not address the role of tourism in economic geography, even though its significance has been argued by those studying tourism (e.g. Debbage and Daniels 1998; Ioannides and Debbage 1998; Shaw and Williams 2002, 2004).

West Virginia University, Regional Research Institute, The Web Book of Regional Science (excellent source of material): www.rri.wvu.edu/regsc books.htm

Use your search engine to look for regional economic development agency websites and destination promotion websites, examples include:

East Tennessee Economic Development Agency (USA): www.etada.org/

Greater Columbus Georgia Chamber of Commerce: http://208.62.83.218/ed/ The page on the tourism cluster is particularly interesting: http://208.62.83.218/ed/clusters/tourism.cfm)

Northwest Regional Development Agency (UK): www.nwda.co.uk/

South East England Development Agency (UK): www.seeda.co.uk/

Gauteng Economic Development Agency (South Africa): www.geda.co.za/

Halifax Regional Development Agency (Canada): www.hrda.ns.ca/

European Association of Regional Development Agencies: www.eurada.org

Destination New Zealand: www.newzealand.com/travel/

Australian Tourist Commission: www.australia.com/

Western Australia (for tourists): www.westernaustralia.com/en

Western Australia (for industry): www.westernaustralia.com/en/Industry

Governance and State Intervention

5

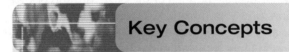

Key Concepts

- Governance
- Regulation
- The nation state
- The local state
- Sub-state actors
- Supranational organisations
- Multilayered governance architecture
- Transnational relations
- Intermestic policy
- Networks
- Planning
- Boosterism
- Community-based planning
- Regulation
- Sustainability

- Public interest
- Stimulation
- Tragedy of the commons
- Place-ownership

The greater interdependence between national and local states during the current period of globalisation has arguably led to a transformation of power and regulatory practices among polities which, in turn, may serve to reinforce such interdependencies. This has meant that state authority, power and legitimacy have ceased to be bounded on a strict territorial framework, which has been the basis for sovereign governance for most of the past 150 years. Instead, in the condition of post-sovereign governance, the governance of key cultural, economic and financial issues will be increasingly handled 'by the transfer of goal-specific authority from states to regional or multilateral organizations and to local or subnational polities'. Under this set of conditions the governance of a number of issue areas will be maintained, not just by territorial state-bounded authorities, as in much of the past, 'but rather by a network of flows of information, power and resources from the local to the regional and multilateral levels and the other way around' (Morales-Moreno 2004, p. 108).

In this context there is therefore the need to examine not only the role of the nation state in tourism, but perhaps more critically, the roles and interactions of international and supranational bodies, private actors such as transnational corporations and non-governmental organisations, and the increasingly international role of the local state. These new policy actors, along with the regulatory mechanisms of the nation state, are contributing to the development of a new post-sovereign multilayered governance architecture (e.g. Maier 1987; Taylor 1991; Kooiman 1993a, 1993b; MacCormick 1993, 1996; Rhodes 1996; Castells 1998; Delanty 1998; Scholte 2000; Hooghe and Marks 2003; Kooiman 2003), to which tourism is contributing and by which, in turn, it is affected.

The term 'governance' has a number of meanings (Rhodes 1997a, 1997b), and, in particular, has come to imply changes in the public sector that minimise the role of formal governmental actors. For example, Rhodes (1997b) adopts a definition of governance that assumes that government has lost its capacity to govern, and that governance is now the product of self-organising, inter-organisational networks. Similarly, Kooiman (1993a, p. 6) also argues that governance has become an inter-organisational phenomenon, and that it is best understood through terms such as 'co-managing, co-steering and co-guidance', all implying more cooperative methods for identifying and achieving policy goals. Kooiman (1993b, p. 258) defines governance as: 'The pattern or structure that emerges in a socio-political system as a "common" result or outcome of the interacting intervention efforts of all involved actors. This pattern cannot be reduced to one actor or group of actors in particular.'

Although not denying the importance of decentralisation, Peters (1996, 1998; Peters and Savoie 1996) nevertheless emphasises that governance implies 'steering', or the employment of some mechanism(s) of providing coherent direction to society by nation state governments. This theme is also picked up by Morales-Moreno (2004, pp. 108–9) who argues that 'we could define governance as the capacity for steering, shaping, and managing, yet leading the impact of transnational flows and relations in a given issue area, through the inter-connectedness of different polities and their institutions in which power, authority, and legitimacy are shared'. The identification of transnational relations here is significant as there are many issues which are not transnational and yet clearly remain in the domain of territorially based state sovereignty. However, tourism is one area which is marked by substantial transnational flows and relations, although their political and policy significance has often not been fully appreciated (Hall 1994a).

Indeed, sovereignty is still largely in the hands of the nation states, which clearly remain the main actors in the international sphere, especially when some states do not fully ascribe to the notion of a multi-levelled polity. In the case of Europe, it may even be argued that the power of the state has been increased as a result of integration rather than eroded, since the tendency does appear to be for the supranational European Union to take over from the state those functions which the state performs less well under contemporary conditions of globalisation, for example regulation of financial markets and international trade (Milward et al. 1993; Majone 1996; Delanty 1998). The notion that the state is finished or is a 'hollow' vessel may therefore be substantially premature (Dunn 1995; Hirst and Thompson 1996).

Of course, as Peters (1998) observes, 'the capacity of states to behave as a unitary actor is sometimes greatly overstated in the "state" literature, but it still appears easier to begin with that more centralized conception and find the exceptions than to begin with a null hypothesis of no order and find any pattern'. However, there is no disputing the tremendous transformation of sovereignty that has occurred and which points to the formation of a multi-levelled polity (Close 1995; Delanty 1997, 1998) which has a number of implications for tourism that will be examined below and in the following chapters. However, these can be dealt with under five headings. First, the significance of new actors and structures (e.g. new supranational regulatory regimes) within the transformation of state power and authority. Second, the development of multilayered governance architecture for explaining the new relationships between states, power, markets and non-government actors. Third, the new role of sub-state actors, including tourism destination organisations, in international relations. Fourth, the significance of networks as a competitive strategy within the so-called networked economy. Fifth, the potential for place-owned firms and organisations as a basis for effective regional development and distribution of desired externalities from tourism.

The Significance of New Actors and Structures within the Transformation of State Power and Authority

A number of new actors and structures have developed to deal with governance under globalisation. These include the development of new regulatory structures, such as that of the World Trade Organisation and the associated rounds of trade negotiations, as well as more specific tourism-related structures such as the World Tourism Organisation (WTO) and those related to aviation and conservation. The WTO provides an example of an international actor that serves to act as a regulatory regime, for example with respect to the collection of statistics, as well as be an actor in its own right, for example in terms of its influence on individual governments and regions' tourism policies and tourism development strategies.

Some of these international organisations and less institutionalised international regimes may constrain the autonomy of nation states and limit their capability for exercising governance in a number of policy areas that may have once been almost purely domestic considerations. However, arguably, these are largely governmental organisations that may actually enhance the capacity of the member governments to steer their own societies and economies. In the case of the European Union for example, probably the most significant example of a powerful supranational organisation, there is considerable evidence of the development of regulatory or inter-governmental aspects of governance arrangements rather than merely the construction of a new polity (Peters 1998).

The development of international law and regimes for human rights, security, investment and the environment also has significant implications for tourism. New security and mobility agreements regarding border entry are obviously important for influencing the flow of people, including tourists, between countries. Environmental issues are also extremely significant. For example, the potential implications of climate change on tourism are substantial, as is the development of regulatory agreements to manage such change. In addition to state-related supranational sectors there are also significant numbers of private transnational actors that include corporations and private and public non-government organisations. Examples of a significant actor here in tourism terms is the World Travel and Tourism Council (WTTC) – a private-sector based organisation that is by invitation only. 'WTTC's mission is to raise awareness of the full economic impact of the world's largest generator of wealth and jobs – Travel & Tourism. Governments are encouraged to unlock the industry's potential by adopting the Council's policy framework for sustainable tourism development' (http://www.wttc.org/framesetaboutus.htm). The WTTC has been extremely influential in achieving its goals, including the adoption of tourism satellite accounts and, perhaps more controversially, its focus on a neo-liberal agenda of liberalisation in the tourism sector (an agenda that also holds considerable sway within the WTO).

The Development of Multilayered Governance Architecture

The growth of supranational organisations and regimes is only one, albeit significant, element in the development of multilayered governance architecture. At the same time that the supranational component has grown so too have changes occurred in the context of the regional and local state, as well as the role of producer and non-producer groups, including single-issue groups which concentrate on concerns such as human rights, fair trade in tourism and child sex tourism (Table 5.1). These developments have meant that, on many issues, such as the environment and international trade, there is substantial interaction between levels of government as they seek to achieve policy goals as well as various producer and non-producer groups.

The area of transnational relations, that is 'direct interactions between agencies (government subunits) of different governments where those agencies act relatively autonomously from central government control' (Keohane and Nye 1976, p. 4), is therefore becoming of increasing importance in tourism policy and planning, particularly as regions seek to attract increasing amounts of international visitors in a complex and competitive market. Two types of trans-government relations may be distinguished. First, where the sub-national government is a primary actor when it engages directly in international relations, for example through direct international promotion. Second, where the sub-national government is a mediating actor and seeks to affect international relations by attempting to influence the central government in its policy deliberations and actions for the purpose of promoting policies that will be beneficial to local conditions, for example trade policy and targeted international tourism promotion (Fry 1998, 1999). Further, it should be noted that increasingly it is not just provincial/state governments which are playing such an international role, but also cities (e.g. see Cohn and Smith 1996). For example, in the case of tourism and place competition (Chapter 4), cities are increasingly lobbying to host international events, such as the Olympics and International Expositions, and are also competing to be able to attract international investment for tourism infrastructure, such as conference and exhibition centres and sports stadia.

The increasing activity of regional and municipal agencies in tourism promotion and planning may create substantial tensions between different levels of government and further increase the difficulties that exist in coordinating government activities. Therefore, the growing importance of sub-governments in international tourism has significant implications not only for international relations but also for intermestic and domestic relations between central and regional governments (Figure 5.1).

Table 5.1 Examples of tourism organizations in multilayered governance architecture

	Government and intra-government organisations	Producer organisations	Non-producer organisations	Single-interest organisations
International	World Tourism Organisation; World Heritage Committee (UNESCO); Committee for the Development of Sport; OECD (Organisation for Economic Cooperation and Development)	World Travel and Tourism Council; International Air Transport Association; Tourism Sport International Council; International Olympic Committee	Tourism Concern; World Wildlife Fund (WWF); World Leisure and Recreation Association; Greenpeace; Friends of the Earth; ATLAS	World Congress Against the Commercial Sexual Exploitation of Children
Supranational	APEC tourism working group; Tourism Council of the South Pacific; ASEAN Promotion Centre on Trade and Investment; European Commission	Pacific Asia Travel Association (PATA); Baltic Sea Tourism Commission; Play Fair Europe; National Olympic Committees	Sierra Club; International Downtown Association; Travel and Tourism Research Association	End Child Prostitution in Asian Tourism (ECPAT)
National	Indonesian Directorate General of Tourism; Countryside Commission; Australian Tourist Commission; Irish Tourist Board (Bord Fáilte)	British Sports and Allied Industries Federation; Tourism Task Force; Institute of Leisure and Amenity Management (ILAM); Irish Tourish Industry Confederation	National Trust; Australian Conservation Foundation; Australian Consumers' Association	The Wilderness Society; Hispanic Association for Corporate Responsibility; Child Wise
Regional (including provincial and state)	Tourism Alberta; West Australian Tourism Commission (WATC); Scottish Tourist Board; Tourism British Columbia	Tourism Council Australia (WA Division); Scottish Confederation of Tourism; Shannon Development; Coalition of Minnesota Business	Western Australian Conservation Council	The Wilderness Society
Local	Local government involvement in leisure and tourism provision, e.g. Tourism Dunedin; Calgary Economic and Development Authority; Tourism Vancouver	Local chambers of commerce and industry associations; local sporting clubs and private sport and leisure centres	Ratepayers and resident associations, e.g. Waikiki Improvement Association	Single-issue organisations such as a 'friends of a park' or a group which has been formed in order to prevent particular developments such as a hotel or airport

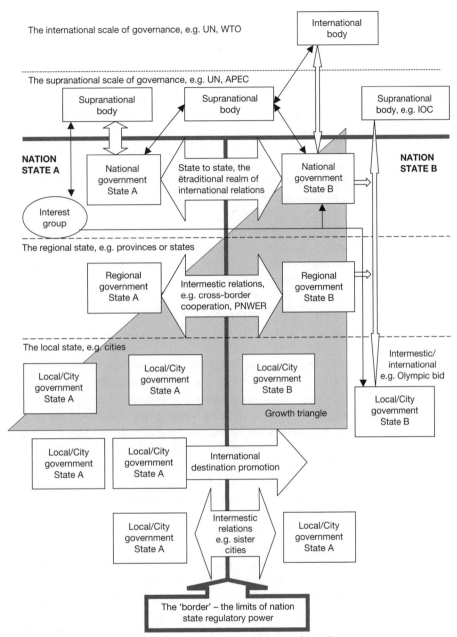

Figure 5.1   International and intermestic relations of tourism

The New Role of Sub-state Actors in International Relations

Although models of international relations are well developed to deal with the activities of nation states, the growth of sub-governmental actors as international actors provides significant challenges to our understanding of economic globalisation and its spatial and policy implications. In the United States, four states maintained offices abroad in 1970, compared with 37 states and Puerto Rico, which had 241 offices or designated representatives in more than 30 different countries as of the end of 2003 (Fry 2003). Moreover, in an era of economic globalisation, the rise of 'new' supranational policy issues such as the environment, fair trade, human rights and labour mobility are profoundly different in scope from the traditional strategic and security issues of international relations. Such issues may be described as 'intermestic' in nature, that is they are simultaneously both domestic and international policy issues which, while being of substantial domestic concern, cross international boundaries thereby creating international interest in the setting of policy (Manning 1977; P. Smith 1992, 1993; Cohn and Smith 1993, 1996).

Within North America, Canadian provincial governments have signed hundreds of agreements with the US states and many governors and legislators already work very closely with their fellow premiers and legislators in Canada. The Quebec and Ontario governments have even been accorded an associate status in the US Council of State Governments, and the Alberta and British Columbia governments work closely with the US Council of State Governments West and the Western Governors' Association.

One good example of local internationalisation is the Pacific NorthWest Economic Region (PNWER) which consists of the American states of Alaska, Idaho, Montana, Oregon and Washington, plus the Canadian provinces of Alberta, British Columbia and Yukon Territory, as well as numerous private sector members. The combined gross domestic product (GDP) of the region is in excess of US$350 billion annually. If it were a single country, the Pacific NorthWest Economic Region would rank tenth among the world's industrial economies. Initially established in 1989 as the Pacific NorthWest Legislative Leadership Forum, PNWER was created in 1991 by statutes in all seven states and provinces. PNWER brings together legislative, government and private sector leaders to work towards the development of public policies that promote the economies of the Pacific Northwest region in the global marketplace. 'The objective of PNWER is to build the necessary critical mass for the region to become a major player in the new global economy' (PNWER 2000a). According to PNWER (2000b), '[i]ncreasing competition requires economic policies that build on the strengths of the region, increase efficiency through cooperation and collaboration, and create ongoing opportunities for policy development beyond the state, provincial, and federal level'.

The six original working groups of PNWER reflected the region's strengths, including environmental technology, tourism, recycling, value-added timber, workforce training and telecommunications, with further working groups being established in transportation (1993), export (1994), government procurement (1994) and agriculture (1995). The Tourism Working Group has undertaken work in a number of areas, including creating regional tourism partnerships; developing a list of barriers to tourism in the region; successfully lobbying for an open skies policy between Canada and the USA; recommending the expansion of the visa waiver, CANPASS and other barrier reducing programmes; and sponsoring a regional tourism marketing summit (PNWER 2000c). The activities of PNWER are similar to other local internationalisation initiatives around the world. However, the full impact of such activities is still to be adequately examined.

Tourism is increasingly being recognised as an intermestic policy issue particularly as sub-national actors such as states, provinces, regions and cities respond to an increasingly globalised business environment and seek to attract investment, employment and tourists. Moreover, the role of tourism in establishing regional images through place marketing processes may see it being given closer attention as a factor in supranational policy development (C.M. Hall 1997a). Nevertheless, the understanding of the policy and territorial dimensions of tourism's functions in economic integration remains a poorly developed though potentially highly significant subject of study.

Plate 5.1 Vancouver Convention and Exhibition Centre. Vancouver is a significant international sub-state actor through its various activities such as hosting the 1986 Expo and the 2010 Winter Olympics in addition to promoting itself as a major Pacific Rim transport and economic hub. (The Centre's website is www.vanconex.com; The Tourism British Columbia website is www.hellobc.com)

The Significance of Networks as a Competitive Strategy

In the new global order networks are also seen as a key competitive strategy. Many economic development regions are therefore now regarded as consisting of clusters of interrelated industrial sectors that are better described as networks rather than as unconnected 'industries' (see Chapter 6), the basic organisational 'unit' being the interaction between firms linked together in chains of production, exchange and distribution. Firms, or even decentralised divisions within firms, maintain a degree of autonomy in the chain, but all significant activity is, in some way, coordinated with other organisations in the network. Such network relations have been facilitated by the willingness of government to encourage overseas investment, often in partnership with local industry, and by the development of policy settings which have sought to reinforce freer trade and investment in the region, thereby encouraging the further internationalisation of economic spaces through growing penetration (inward flows) and extraversion (outward flows).

In the case of Asia three sets of interrelated factors underpinned the extension of production networks which provided much of the region's economic growth in the early 1990s and which contributed to greater economic integration at the supranational level but which, interestingly, also left it vulnerable to the problems of the Asian financial crisis in the late 1990s. The first set of factors was the change in relative factor costs within the region. For companies in North-East Asia (Japan, Korea and Taiwan) seeking to increase their production of relatively mature products, the costs of undertaking the investment necessary to increase domestic capacity were far in excess of those of establishing new facilities elsewhere in the region, where labour, infrastructural and land costs were much lower.

The second group of factors was political. The original tensions over trade imbalances and market access between Japan and the United States, and later Japan and Europe and Australasia, were extended to Korea and Taiwan in the late 1980s. International tensions in turn generated domestic political forces that interacted with and reinforced underlying economic change. For instance, the Japanese government encouraged corporations to increase both their foreign direct investment and their sourcing from their overseas subsidiaries. In tourism terms it is notable that Japan utilised outbound tourism as a means of improving trade relations and providing its trading nations with a source of funds to purchase Japanese manufactured goods (Hall 2000a, 2000b).

The third set of factors is related to changes in the production process which have facilitated flexible production techniques through the advent of the micro-electronics and communications revolution. These, in turn, decreased the significance of economies of scale thereby opening up markets for a whole range of non-standardised products. Smaller companies have therefore been able to gain a footing in increasingly regionalised production chains.

All these factors have been influential in the development of networks elsewhere, particularly where they are competing for the international tourist, but also, for some locations, when they are competing against other regions for domestic travellers. Network thinking clearly also has substantial implications for how we consider competition at the level of both the destination and the firm. Indeed, network considerations also become a key element in the promotion of greater public–private relations.

The Role of the State in Tourism

The state can be conceptualised as a set of officials with their own preferences and capacities to effect public policy, or in more structural terms as a relatively permanent set of *political institutions* operating in relation to civil society (Nordlinger 1981). The term 'state' encompasses the whole apparatus whereby a government exercises its power. It includes elected politicians, the various arms of the bureaucracy, unelected public/civil servants, and the plethora of rules, regulations, laws, conventions and policies which surround government and private action. The main institutions of the state include: the elected legislatures, government departments and authorities, the judiciary, enforcement agencies, other levels of government, government-business enterprises and corporations, regulatory authorities, and a range of para-state organisations, such as labour organisations (Hall and Jenkins 1995). Although the boundaries of the state are becoming more and more blurred in many jurisdictions as emphasis is increasingly placed on the creation of public–private partnerships and reducing government intervention in the economy, it should be noted that the state still sets the regulatory framework within which public and private activity occurs.

Government helps shape the economic framework for the tourism industry (although international economic factors relating to exchange rates, interest rates and investor confidence are increasingly important), helps provide the infrastructure and educational requirements for tourism, establishes the regulatory environment in which business operates, and takes an active role in promotion and marketing. In addition, tourism may be politically and economically appealing to government because it can potentially give the appearance of producing results from policy initiatives in a short period of time in terms of visitor numbers and/or employment generation (Hall and Jenkins 1998; Jenkins et al. 1998). For example, the European Union argued that 'The importance of tourism in a region's development is due in particular to its job-creating capacity, to its contribution to the diversification of economic regional activities and to various indirect effects of expenditure by tourists' (European Union 1998, sec. 74).

A number of roles of government in tourism can be identified, although there will be variation from place to place in terms of the extent to which they apply. The forerunner to the WTO, the International Union of Tourist

Organisations (IUOTO) (1974), in their discussion of the role of the state in tourism, identified five areas of public sector involvement in tourism: coordination, planning, legislation and regulation, government as entrepreneur, and stimulation (including tourism promotion) (also see Jenkins and Henry 1982; Mill and Morrison 1985). To this may be added two other functions: a social tourism role, and a broader role of protector of public interest (Hall 1994a, 2000a). The present section will discuss these seven roles of government in tourism.

Coordination

Coordination is necessary both within and between the different levels of government in order to avoid duplication of resources between the various government tourism bodies and the private sector, and to develop effective tourism strategies. Given the large number of public organisations which have an interest in tourism matters, one of the main challenges for government is being able to bring the various organisations and agencies together to work for common policy objectives. Furthermore, in several jurisdictions government has often served to help coordinate private sector activities as well.

Planning

Public planning for tourism occurs in a number of forms (e.g. development, infrastructure, land and resource use, promotion and marketing), institutions (e.g. different government organisations) and scales (e.g. national, regional, local and sectoral) (Hall 2000a). In several nations, notably the island states of the Pacific (Hall and Page 1996), national tourism development plans have been drawn up in which government identifies which sectors of the industry will be developed, the appropriate rate of growth and the provision of capital required for expansion. Throughout many parts of the world regional tourism development plans are also a common government initiative (Hall and Page 1999a), particularly where such regions are attempting to utilise tourism as a response to problems of economic restructuring (Jenkins et al. 1998). Nevertheless, while planning is recognised as an important element in tourism development, the conduct of a plan or strategy does not by itself guarantee appropriate outcomes for stakeholders, particularly as issues of implementation and the policy–action relationship need to be addressed. Indeed, one of the major problems for public tourism planning is the extent to which tourism-specific agencies, which usually have a very limited legislative base of responsibility, have the authority to direct other government organisations to meet tourism-specific policy goals.

Tourism Insight: Approaches to Tourism Planning

Typologies provide a useful frame of understanding for those trying to understand a subject area. In the wider planning literature three forms of debate have occurred with respect to planning (Yiftachel 1989):

- The analytical debate: 'What is urban planning?'
- The urban form debate: 'What is a good urban plan?'
- The procedural debate: 'What is a good planning process?'

To a limited extent these debates have also occurred within tourism planning (Getz 1987; Hall 2000a), particularly with respect to issues of sustainable tourism. One of the most useful typologies of the field of tourism planning was provided by Getz (1987), who identified four broad traditions of tourism planning:

- 'boosterism';
- an economic, industry-oriented approach;
- a physical/spatial approach; and
- a community-oriented approach which emphasises the role that the host plays in the tourism experience.

To this Hall (2000a) added a fifth approach, that of sustainable tourism. As Getz (1987, p. 5) noted, the 'traditions are not mutually exclusive, nor are they necessarily sequential. Nevertheless, this categorisation is a convenient way to examine the different and sometimes overlapping ways in which tourism is planned, and the research and planning methods, problems and models associated with each.' The various approaches to tourism planning are outlined in Table 5.2.

Boosterism

Boosterism has long been the dominant tradition towards tourism development and planning since mass tourism began. Boosterism is a simplistic attitude that tourism development is inherently good and of automatic benefit to the hosts. Under this approach little consideration is given to the potential negative economic, social and environmental impacts of tourism and instead cultural and natural resources are regarded as objects to be exploited for the sake of tourism development. However, boosterism has had a marked impression on the economic and physical landscape.

Elements of the idea of boosterism have their origins not only in nineteenth-century European *laissez-faire* economic utilitarianism and North American frontier capitalism, but also in the relatively small size of organised tourism for much of the past 150 years. When tourist numbers were so small and natural resources so overwhelming in some areas, such as in the United States where the first national parks were created, then the effects of tourism were relatively small, with the perception of tourism as a benign, 'smokeless' industry not changing until extremely recently.

The economic tradition: tourism as an industry

Under the economic tradition, tourism is seen as an industry which can be used as a tool by governments to achieve certain goals of economic growth and restructuring, employment generation, and regional development through the provision of financial incentives, research, marketing and promotional assistance. Although the economic model does not claim tourism to be the panacea for all economic ills, the approach does emphasise the potential value of tourism as an export industry, sometimes nebulously defined, which can positively contribute to national and regional imbalances in such things as terms of trade, balance of payments or levels of foreign exchange. Within the economic tradition, government utilises tourism as a means to promote growth and development in specific areas. Therefore, the planning emphasis is on the economic impacts of tourism and its most efficient use to create income and employment benefits for regions or communities. Attention is given to the means by which tourism can be defined as an industry in order that its economic contribution and production can be measured, and so the role of government regulation and support can be adequately appraised. Arguably, as Chapter 4 discussed, the notion of entrepreneurial places may well be shifting as a subset of the economic tradition to one which may be described as an approach to tourism planning in its own right.

The land use/physical/spatial approach

The physical/spatial approach has its origins in the work of geographers, urban and regional land use planners and conservationists who advocate a rational approach to the planning and development of natural resources. Land use planning is one of the oldest forms of environmental protection. Physical or spatial planning refers to 'planning with a spatial, or geographical, component, in which the general objective is to provide for a spatial structure of activities (or of land uses) which in some way is better than the pattern existing without planning' (P. Hall, 1992, p. 4). Typically, spatial planning is multidimensional and has many objectives. Within this approach, tourism is often regarded as having an ecological base with a resultant need for development to be based upon certain spatial patterns that would minimise the negative impacts of tourism on the physical environment. One of the main focuses within this framework are the related issues of physical and social carrying capacity (e.g. Mathieson and Wall 1982), environmental thresholds, and limits to or acceptable/desirable rates of change (e.g. McCool 1994; Wight 1998) as well as the overall management of visitor impacts.

Community-oriented tourism planning

Since the late 1970s increasing attention has been given to the negative environmental and social impacts of tourism. Indeed, Craik (1988, p. 26) argued that despite difficulties in quantifying the social impacts of tourism 'in the same way as carrying capacities, bed requirements and even environmental impacts … it is perhaps the most important aspect of tourism development'. Therefore, an examination of the social impacts of tourism came to be regarded as essential not only from an ethical perspective of the need for community involvement in decision-making processes but also because without it, tourism growth and development may become increasingly difficult. As Ross (1994, p. 157) observed: 'If pleasant and satisfying experiences involving local residents are important in the destination images of tourists, and in their decision-making processes, then a consideration of the well-being of local residents in the context of tourist development would seem critical.'

One of the clearest and most influential statements of the community approach to tourism development is to be found in Murphy's (1985) seminal book *Tourism: A Community Approach*. Murphy (1985) advocated the use of an ecological approach to tourism planning which emphasised the need for local control over the development process. One of the key components of the approach is the notion that in satisfying local needs it may also be possible to satisfy the needs of the tourist, a 'win-win' philosophy that is immensely attractive. Nevertheless, despite the undoubted conceptual attraction to many destinations of the establishment of a community approach to tourism planning, substantial problems remain in the way such a process may operate and how it may be implemented (Haywood 1988; Murphy 1988), although the approach has proven to be attractive in the tourism planning literature (e.g. Getz 1994; Ryan and Montgomery 1994; Simmons 1994; Singh et al. 2003).

A significant problem in utilising a community approach to tourism planning is the structure of government. The nature of systems of governance leads to difficulties in ensuring that tourism policies at different levels of government are adequately coordinated and that decisions and policies at one level are not at odds with decisions at another. For example, a locally based community decision not to allow tourism development at a particular site may well be at odds with a regional or national tourism plan which has been drawn up by a superior level of government. Alternatively, a local government decision to proceed with a tourism-related development may be opposed at another level if it impinges on legislative requirements or policy settings. However, if tourism resource conflicts are to be resolved at the community level, then the institutional arrangements for decision-making processes related to management also need to be based at the local level (Millar and Aitken 1995). One major concern with such measures is the role that local elites may have in skewing decisions towards their own interests rather than wider community needs. However, the holding of reserve powers at higher levels of government can often act as a restraint on the roles of local elites (Ostrom 1990).

A sustainable approach to tourism planning: towards integration of planning and development?

Sustainable development has a primary objective of providing lasting and secure livelihoods which minimise resource depletion, environmental degradation, cultural disruption and social instability. The World Commission on Environment and Development (the Bruntland Commission) (1987) report extended this basic objective to include concerns of equity; the needs of economically marginal populations; and the idea of technological and social limitations on the ability of the environment to meet present and future needs. While tourism ostensibly seeks to meet the primary objective of sustainable development (i.e. 'not to foul its own nest' and in so doing to continue over time to return benefits to society), there are many contradictions within both the concept of sustainable development and the nature of tourism which will mean that implementation of the concept will be extremely difficult (e.g. see Dutton and Hall 1989; Bramwell and Lane 1993; Hall and Butler 1995; Hall and Lew 1998). For example, Pearce et al. (1988) and Mowforth and Munt (2003) noted that sustainability implies an infinite time horizon, whereas practical decision-making requires the adoption of finite horizons. Although these factors complicate the attainment of sustainable development planning objectives, they are not 'hard barriers'. Rather, they serve to emphasise the preconditions for tourism to become a sustainable land use (Tisdell 1995; Farrell and Hart 1988; Kadak 2000; Hamblin 2001). Paramount among these is an effective coordination and control mechanism – a system which is able to give practical and ongoing effect to the policy and planning intent of sustainable development (Butler 1990, 1991).

Lew and Hall (1998), in a review of research on sustainable tourism development, identified a number of 'lessons' regarding sustainable tourism that do provide something of the context which planners need to understand in order to be able to make principles of sustainability work:

- Sustainable tourism represents a value orientation in which the management of tourism impacts takes precedence over market economics, although tension between the two are ever present.
- Implementing sustainable tourism development requires measures that are both scale and context specific.
- Sustainable tourism issues are shaped by global economic restructuring and are fundamentally different in developing and developed economies.
- At the community scale, sustainable tourism requires local control of resources.
- Sustainable tourism development requires patience, diligence and a long-term commitment.

Nevertheless, sustainable tourism development has turned out to be as much of an ideal as having practical impact on tourism planning and development.

Perhaps most significantly of all, for example, is the issue of the scale at which we are seeking to be sustainable (Rollings and Brunckhorst 1999). For instance, it may be possible for a firm or site to be sustainable but not the surrounding region. Sustainability therefore implies that the impacts of tourism need to be evaluated at all stages of the travel process and not just on-site. This observation is particularly important given that, in terms of energy use, for instance, the vast majority of impact occurs in getting to and from a destination, not just at the site, which is where most of the attention of trying to 'green' the tourism industry is actually located.

Legislation and regulation

Government has a number of legislative and regulative powers which directly and indirectly impinge on tourism. Government involvement in this area ranges from authority on passports and visas matters, through to environmental and labour relations policy. However, substantial issues for tourism often emerge because of the extent to which tourism policy needs to be integrated with other policy areas. With the possible exception of island micro-states which are highly economically dependent on tourism, tourism policy tends to be only a relatively minor area of government policy initiatives. Nevertheless, policy decisions undertaken in other policy jurisdictions, for example economic policy and environmental and conservation policy, may have substantial implications for the effectiveness of policy decisions undertaken in tourism. For example, general regulatory measures such as industry regulation, environmental protection and taxation policy will significantly influence the growth of tourism (C.M. Hall 1998).

The level of government regulation of tourism tends to be a major issue for the various components of the tourism industry. Undoubtedly, while industry recognises that government has a significant role to play, particularly when it comes to the provision of infrastructure, marketing or research, the predominant argument by industry throughout most of the world is that the industry must be increasingly deregulated. However, governments simultaneously call for increased regulation of tourism, especially with respect to the desire for environmental protection (Bramwell and Lane 1993), and, increasingly, human rights and social justice, especially with respect to the rights of indigenous peoples (e.g. Smith and Eadington 1992).

Capitalist regulation chronically involves the interaction of a set of regulatory practices, many of which are incompatible and in conflict with one another (Painter and Goodwin 1995; Goodwin and Painter 1996). The issue of regulation in the context of tourism and the environment has been well described by McKercher (1993). As a predominantly private sector-driven industry, development decisions by tourism enterprises must be geared to function at a profit, resulting 'in preference for investment in profit centres (such as swimming pools) rather than in cost centres (such as sewage systems). ... Mitigation protection programmes will receive lower priorities, unless there is an opportunity for profit generation or a legislative imperative forcing such

Table 5.2 Tourism planning approaches: assumptions, problem definition, methods and models

Planning tradition	Underlying assumptions and related attitudes	Definition of the tourism planning problem	Some examples of related methods	Some examples of related models
Boosterism	• tourism is inherently good • tourism should be developed • cultural and natural resources should be exploited • industry as expert • development defined in business/corporate terms	• how many tourists can be attracted and accommodated? • how can obstacles be overcome? • convincing hosts to be good to tourists	• promotion • public relations • advertising • growth targets	• demand forecasting models
Economic	• tourism equal to other industries • use tourism to create employment, earn foreign revenue and improve terms of trade, encourage regional development, overcome regional economic disparities • planner as expert • development defined in economic terms	• can tourism be used as a growth pole? • maximisation of income and employment multipliers • influencing consumer choice • providing economic values for externalities • providing economic values for conservation purposes	• supply–demand analysis • benefit–cost analysis • product-market matching • market segmentation • development incentives	• management processes • tourism master plans • motivation • economic impact • economic multipliers • hedonistic pricing
Physical/spatial	• tourism as a resource user • ecological basis to development • tourism as a spatial and regional phenomenon • environmental conservation • development defined in environmental terms • preservation of genetic diversity	• physical carrying capacity • manipulating travel patterns and visitor flows • visitor management • concentration or dispersal of visitors • perceptions of natural environment • wilderness and national park management • designation of environmentally sensitive areas	• ecological studies • environmental impact assessment • regional planning • perceptual studies	• spatial patterns and processes • physical impacts • resort morphology • LAC (limits of acceptable change) • ROS (recreational opportunity spectrum) • TOS (tourism opportunity spectrum) • destination life cycles

Community	• need for local control • search for balanced development • search for alternatives to 'mass' tourism development • planner as facilitator rather than expert • development defined in socio-cultural terms	• how to foster community control? • understanding community attitudes towards tourism • understanding the impacts of tourism on a community • social impact	• community development • awareness and education • attitudinal surveys • social impact assessment	• ecological view of community • social/perceptual carrying capacity • attitudinal change • social multiplier
Sustainable	• integration of economic, environmental and socio-cultural values • tourism planning integrated with other planning processes • holistic planning • preservation of essential ecological processes • protection of human heritage and biodiversity • inter- and intra-generational equity • achievement of a better balance of fairness and opportunity between nations • planning and policy as argument • planning as process • planning and implementation as two sides of the same coin • recognition of political dimension of tourism	• understanding the tourism system • setting goals, objectives and priorities • achieving policy and administrative coordination in and between the public and private sectors • cooperative and integrated control systems • understanding the political dimensions of tourism • planning for tourism that meets local needs and trades successfully in a competitive marketplace	• strategic planning to supersede conventional approaches • stakeholder audit • raising producer awareness • raising consumer awareness • raising community awareness • stakeholder input • policy analysis • evaluative research • cooperative approaches • political economy • aspirations analysis • environmental analysis and audit	• systems models • integrated models focused on places and links and relationships between such places • resources as culturally constituted • environmental perception • business ecology • learning organisations and regions

Source: After Hall 2000a

investment' (McKercher 1993, p. 10). According to McKercher (1993), the very nature of the tourism industry makes voluntary compliance with environmental programmes virtually impossible, therefore creating a regulatory vacuum in which government must operate in order to establish clear environmental guidelines. Given this situation, conservation groups will often seek the extension of government regulation to ensure that tourism remains 'controlled', particularly in environmentally and politically sensitive areas such as national parks or the coastal zone. In many cases, especially when companies are using the environment as part of their branding and competitive strategy, the regulatory conflict is perhaps not so much should controls be in place but rather what the nature of the controls should be, with industry often seeking to place the locus of control on themselves (e.g. self-regulating), while conservationists will usually seek to have control placed in a government body, such as an environmental protection authority, which is distinct from the tourism industry (Hall 2000a).

Government as entrepreneur

Government has long had an entrepreneurial function in tourism. Governments not only provide basic infrastructure, such as roads and sewage, but may also own and operate tourist ventures, including hotels and travel companies. Governments at all levels have had a long history of involvement in promoting tourism through bureaux, marketing ventures, development of transport networks through national airline and rail systems, and the provision of loans to private industry for specific tourism-related developments. According to Pearce (1992, p. 11), 'because of the scale of development and the element of the common good, provision of infrastructure is a widely accepted task of public authorities and one which can greatly facilitate tourist development and selectively direct it to particular areas'. However, the entrepreneurial role of government in tourism is changing in a climate in which less government intervention is being sought (see Chapter 4). This has meant the development of increasing public–private arrangements in tourism-related redevelopment projects and the conduct of such developments on a commercial basis where substantial direct economic return is being sought for government authorities rather than development occurring for the notion of a wider public good.

The role of the state as entrepreneur in tourism development is closely related to the concept of the 'devalorisation of capital'. This is the process by which the state subsidises part of the cost of production, for instance by assisting in the provision of infrastructure, by investing in a tourism project where private venture capital is otherwise unavailable or even in the provision of incentives for the location of events. In this process what would have been private costs are transformed into public or social costs. The provision of infrastructure, particularly transport networks, is regarded as crucial to the development of tourist destinations. There are numerous formal and informal means for government at all levels to assist in minimising the costs of production for tourism developers. Indeed, the offer of government assistance for development is often used to encourage private investment in a particular region or tourist project, for instance through the provision of cheap land, tax breaks or government-backed low-interest loans. Table 5.3 indicates some of the incentives provided by Malaysian state and local authorities to the MICE sector (Meetings Incentives Conventions and Exhibitions).

Table 5.3   Malaysian state and local authorities' incentives for MICE

Kuala Lumpur City Hall	• Complimentary cultural performance for conference of at least 25% of foreign delegates with minimum of 200 pax participants • Supply of Kuala Lumpur City Hall's promotional materials
Penang State Tourism Industry Committee	• Hosting of cultural performances • Cultural welcome reception at the point of entry into Penang for incentive groups of more than 100 pax and meeting groups of more than 50 pax upon arrival • Penang tourism collaterals
Langkawi Development Authority	• Cultural performance for a convention's welcome reception • Assistance in customs and immigration clearance • Discount for entrance fee to tourism products in Langkawi Island • Supply of Langkawi promotional materials
Sabah Tourism Promotion Corporation	• Complimentary cultural performance for minimum of 300 persons at one time • Cultural welcome at Kota Kinabalu International Airport or sea port for incentive groups of more than 100 persons and meeting groups of more than 50 conference delegates per arrival (also applies to cruise ships that dock at Sabah port for the first time) • Express lane airport clearance • Supply of Sabah promotional materials • Welcome beads for minimum of 100 persons
Sarawak Tourism Board	• Welcome at the airport with Sarawak Traditional Dance performance • Welcome beads necklace for foreign groups of 75 persons and above • Supply of promotional materials

Source: Derived from Tourism Malaysia 2003

Stimulation

Similar to the entrepreneurial role is the action that government can take to stimulate tourism development. According to Mill and Morrison (1985), governments can stimulate tourism in three ways. First, financial incentives such as low-interest loans or a depreciation allowance on capital. For example, the creation of incentives to encourage foreign investment in the tourism sector has been closely tied to the creation of new tourism development bodies at the state level in India. Concessions at the state level have also been matched by central government fiscal incentives for tourism projects, including income tax exemptions on 50% of the profits from foreign exchange earnings, exemption on the remaining 50% if the amount is reinvested in new tourism projects, and exemption on import duty for hotel projects. In an effort to use tourism as a tool for regional development, the Indian federal government has explicitly sought to encourage regional tourism development by providing interest subsidies on term loans from eligible financial institutions for hotels in cities other than main centres such as Mumbai (Bombay), Delhi, Calcutta and Chennai (Madras), with higher rates of subsidy available for hotel development in designated tourist areas and heritage hotels. The provision of financial incentives for tourism by the Indian central government in the 1990s is indicative of not only increased attention by government to tourism's potential for generating employment and foreign exchange, but also the wider deregulation of the Indian economy to provide for competition and foreign investment. For example, in the accommodation sector the federal government now allows foreign management and up to 51% foreign ownership of hotels (Hall and Page 1999a).

A second aspect of government stimulation of tourism is through sponsoring research for the general benefit of the tourism industry rather than for specific individual organisations and associations. The third dimension of the stimulation role is that of marketing and promotion, generally aimed at generating tourism demand, although it can also take the form of investment promotion aimed at encouraging capital investment in tourism attractions and facilities. However, such is the size of the role that government plays in promotion that it is usually recognised as a separate function.

Tourism promotion

One of the main activities of government is the promotion of tourism through tourism marketing campaigns (Ascher 1984). Tourist commissions and agencies have the task of identifying potential target markets, the best methods of attracting them, and once they want to buy the tourist product, where to direct them. Furthermore, as well as encouraging visits by foreign travellers, tourism promotion agencies will sometimes attempt to retain as many domestic tourists as possible through the conduct of domestic marketing campaigns in order to ensure the minimum of 'leakage' from outside the national, state or regional tourism system.

Given calls for smaller government in Western society in recent years, there have been increasing demands from government and economic rationalists for greater self-sufficiency by industry in tourism marketing and promotion (Jeffries 1989). The political implications of such an approach for the tourism industry are substantial. As Hughes (1984, p. 14) noted: 'The advocates of a free enterprise economy would look to consumer freedom of choice and not to governments to promote firms; the consumer ought to be sovereign in decisions relating to the allocation of the nation's resources.' Such an approach means that lobbyists in the tourism industry may be better shifting their focus on the necessity of government intervention to issues of externalities, public goods and merit wants rather than employment and the balance of payments (Hall 1994a). 'Such criteria for government intervention have a sounder economic base and are more consistent with a free-enterprise philosophy than employment and balance of payments effects' (Hughes 1984, p. 18). However, the conduct of government involvement in tourism promotion is as much a legacy of effective political lobbying as it is the conduct of economic rationalism, if not more so (Craik 1990, 1991a, 1991b).

Nevertheless, as Pearce (1992, p. 8) has recognised, 'general destination promotion tends to benefit all sectors of the tourist industry in the place concerned; it becomes a "public good". ... The question of "freeloaders" thus arises, for they too will benefit along with those who may have contributed directly to the promotional campaign.' However, the freeloader or freerider problem can be regarded as rational business behaviour in the absence of some form of government intervention in tourism promotion. As Access Economics (1997, p. 29) observed: 'There will be a strong incentive for individual producers of tourism/travel services to minimalise their contribution to cooperative marketing, or even not to contribute at all, and other private sector producers have no power to coerce such producers and the beneficiaries of tourism activity, anyway.'

Given the supply-side fragmentation of tourism and the substantial degree of market failure that exists with respect to generic destination promotion, government may need to determine the most appropriate form of government intervention in order to fulfil their tourism planning and policy goals. In the Australian context, Access Economics (1997) reviewed a number of different forms of intervention including:

- forcing businesses to pay a funding levy;

- 'user pays'/cooperative funding systems;

- levies on foreign exchange earnings;

- making government funding conditional on industry funding;

- levies on tourism investment;

- funding from a passenger movement charge;

- a bed tax;

- funding out of consolidated revenue; and

- funding out of a possible Goods and Services Tax (GST) [similar to VAT] that emerges from tax reform measures.

After examining the different potential forms of government intervention, Access Economics concluded that the most appropriate form of government intervention is the appropriation of funds from consolidated revenue funds through budget processes. Several reasons for this conclusion were put forward:

- the inability to capture the benefits of generic marketing activity is severe in the light of the fragmented nature of the tourism industry;

- levies, 'user pays' charges and business tax arrangements, including bed taxes, will institutionalise the 'freerider' or 'freeloader' problem; and

- the benefits of successful generic promotion as a travel destination are dispersed across the community.

One of the more unusual features of tourism promotion by government tourism organisations is that they have only limited control over the product they are marketing, with very few governments actually owning the goods, facilities and services that make up the tourism product (Pearce 1992). This lack of control is perhaps testimony to the power of the public good argument used by industry to justify continued maintenance of government funding for destination promotion. However, it may also indicate the political power of the tourism lobby, such as industry organisations (Craik 1990, 1991a, 1991b; Hall and Jenkins 1995), to influence government tourism policies.

Social tourism

Social tourism can be defined as 'the relationships and phenomena in the field of tourism resulting from participation in travel by economically weak or otherwise disadvantaged elements of society' (Hunzinger, quoted in Murphy 1985, p. 23). Social tourism involves the extension of the benefits of holidays to economically marginal groups, such as the unemployed, single-parent families, pensioners and the handicapped. The International Bureau of Social Tourism defines social tourism as meaning 'the totality of relations and phenomena deriving from the participation in tourism of those social groups with modest incomes – participation which is made possible or facilitated by measures of a well defined social character' (Haulot 1981, p. 208).

According to Murphy (1985, p. 24), 'Social tourism has become a recognized component and legitimate objective for modern tourism. By extending the physical and psychological benefits of rest and travel to less fortunate people it can be looked upon as a form of preventative medicine.' Haulot (1981, p. 212) further extended this perspective by noting that: 'Social tourism

... finds justification in that its individual and collective objectives are consistent with the view that all measures taken by modern society should ensure more justice, more dignity and improved enjoyment of life for all citizens'. However, the desire of conservative elements in society to reduce the extent of government intervention in economic and private life and focus on individual as opposed to public interest has meant a substantial decline in support for social tourism around the world in recent years. Indeed, in July 2004 the Conservative Party Opposition in Britain stated that they would end 'state tourism' by privatising the Forestry Commission's log cabins which made a loss of £3.7 million in the previous financial year. According to Tony Caplin, a member of a Conservative Party committee seeking ways to make savings if they return to government: 'We see no justification for the state to continue to subsidise, at taxpayers' expense, a loss-making forest holidays business currently operated by Forest Enterprise. ... This must be one of the few examples left of a state-run tourist industry. There are plenty of opportunities for people to stay in log cabins: we do not need [the Department of Environment, Food and Rural Affairs] trying to compete with the private sector' (Watt 2004).

Government as public interest protector

The final role that government plays in tourism is that of interest protector. Although not necessarily tourism-specific, such a role will have major implications for the development of tourism policy. Indeed, public tourism planning, particularly from the community and sustainable approaches in which equity is a major consideration, serves as an arbiter between competing interests. The defence of local and minority interests has traditionally occupied much government activity, particularly as government has had the role of balancing various interests and values in order to meet national or regional public interests, rather than narrow, sectional, private interests, such as that of a specific industry such as tourism. This does not, of course, ignore the fact that various tourism interests are represented within the structure of government. 'Statutory authorities and a myriad of state agencies were established to protect sectional groups, to represent key interests in the policy process, and to protect the social order via welfare provisions to many sections of business and society in general' (Davis et al., 1993, p. 26). Nevertheless, tourism policy needs to be considered as being potentially subsumed beneath a broader range of government economic, social, welfare and environmental policies. Ideally, policy decisions will reflect a desire to meet the interests of the relevant level of government (e.g. national, provincial/state or local), rather than the sectionally defined interests of components of the tourism industry (Hall 1994a).

The issue of government as protector of the common or public interest lies at the heart of questions surrounding the role of government in tourism planning. It also causes us to question the democratic nature of planning and policy-making – the extent to which planning and policy decisions are open to public scrutiny and debate and therefore provide for such decisions to be seen as legitimate in the public sphere. As Saul (1995, pp. 115–16) states: 'Democracy is simply about the nature of legitimacy and whether the repository of that legitimacy – the citizens – are able to exercise the power its possession imposes upon them. We are having great difficulty today exercising the power of legitimacy. It has ... shifted away into other hands.'

Tourism Insight: Public Interest and the 'Tragedy of the Commons'

Purely economic and self-interested individual preferences can easily lead to the continuing degradation and depletion of resources. One of the best examples of this idea, and one of the theoretical underpinnings of contemporary understandings of the problems of sustainability, is Garret Hardin's (1968) well-known 'Tragedy of the Commons'. According to Hardin, the state of the environment resembles an open pasture that is open to all. Each herder tries to keep as many cattle on the common land as possible. Each herder sees the utility of adding one more animal to his herd, with an advantage of +1. In contrast, the personal disadvantage to the herder of such a move is only a fraction of −1 as any effects of overgrazing will be shared by all the herders. The tragedy is that all herders who are seeking to maximise their position economically will arrive at the same conclusion and the herders as a collective then proceed to exceed the carrying capacity of the land.

Hardin's (1968) tragedy of the commons was based on an understanding derived from the work of eighteenth-century philosopher David Hume, that if citizens respond only to private incentives, then public goods will be inadequately provided and public resources will be overused. As noted above, the problem was originally stated with respect to the grazing of cattle but visitor use of a public resource such as a high amenity landscape can be substituted for reasons of explanation (Figure 5.2).

If businesses seek to maximise returns from their visitors they will each seek to increase the number of visitors they bring to a site. However, the amount of return associated with each increase in numbers of visitors brought to the site will fall as the amount of the site available to each visitor falls. If some businesses increase their visitor size and other businesses do not, those who do not will have the returns from their business reduced as a consequence of the depletion of the scenic resource. In contrast, those increasing their visitor size will have a net gain on their returns despite

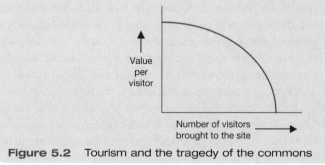

Figure 5.2   Tourism and the tragedy of the commons

sharing in the negative costs of scenic damage. Therefore, it is in the interests of every business to increase the size of their visitor numbers. The consequences of such actions are a fall in the value of each visitor and a progressive depletion of the common scenic resource. This is the tragedy. Although the long-term scenario is one of destruction of the scenic resource, the short-term one is of increasing numbers of visitors.

Many issues regarding the sustainability of tourism resources, for example impacts of tourists in wilderness areas, accommodation or second home development without consideration of sewage disposal, air pollution in national parks or destruction of the ozone layer by jet aircraft, all illustrate that issues of sustainability are related to such concepts as 'collective action', the 'public good' and the 'public interest'. Therefore, as Ophuls (1977, p. 186) recognised, 'environmental imperatives are basically matters of principle that cannot be bargained away in an economic fashion'. Clearly, 'not all of us think of ourselves primarily as consumers; many of us regard ourselves as citizens as well' (Sagoff 1988, p. 27). Notions of public good or public interest are therefore central to ideas of sustainability and tourism planning. Issues surrounding sustainability call for a politics of the common good and consequently for interventionism (Hall 2000a). Cooperation may be regarded as one antidote to such a tragedy in that businesses may cooperate in order to maximise long-term benefits to each other through both allowing a certain amount of visitation while ensuring maintenance of the resource (e.g. Ostrom 1990) (see Chapter 6).

The Potential for Place-owned Firms and Organisations

As with production and consumption, globalisation and localisation cannot be separated. Globalisation is about the achievement of new global–local relations. 'Globalization is like putting together a jigsaw puzzle: it is a matter of inserting a multiplicity of localities into the overall picture of a new global system' (Robins 1991, p. 35). Nevertheless, as Robins argues, we should not idealise the local:

> We should not invest our hopes for the future in the redemptive qualities of local economies, local cultures, local identities. It is important to see the local as a relational, and relative, concept. If once it was significant in relation to the national sphere, now its meaning is being recast in the context of globalization. (Robins 1991, p. 35)

But 'local' in this sense does not correspond to any specific territorial configuration. 'Local' should not be mistaken for 'locality'. The 'local' should be seen as a fluid and relational space, constituted only in and through its relation to the global. For the global corporation, the local might, in fact, correspond to different regional spheres of activity depending on the product and the constituency of the market. However, place marketers have equated place with the local state. Cities and regions are positioning themselves in an attempt to gain access to scarce international mobile capital in order to redevelop themselves, with the help of architects, as postmodern cities of pastiche and image, so that they can, again, go in search of economic and cultural capital with which then to compete against other places. 'Whether it is to attract a new car factory or the Olympic Games, they go as supplicants. And, even as supplicants, they go in competition with each other: cities and localities are now fiercely struggling against each other to attract footloose and predatory investors to their particular patch' (Robins 1991, pp. 35–6).

In the era of globalisation, greater interconnections exist within and between each level of the state. Local states are now international actors in tourism, not only in terms of their advertising and promotional campaigns to attract tourists but also in terms of their attempts to attract investment and events. Yet in a global economy capital not only has to be attracted, it also has to be retained. In this situation the local state needs to be considering place-based ownership models in which enterprises are owned and controlled in a more collective or community-oriented fashion because of the potential this provides for enterprises being rooted in place and therefore not so subject to the hypermobility of capital. Six models of place ownership can be mooted: community-owned corporations, non-profit corporations, municipal enterprises, consumer cooperatives, employee ownership and community development corporations (Imbroscio et al. 2003). To many North Americans and Europeans there is, of course, nothing new in such strategies. However, significantly, they are at odds with the desire for liberalisation espoused by the WTO and the WTTC, for example. Missions which seem more akin to a desire to achieve a political agenda than one which necessarily meets the needs of the people who live and work in tourism destinations. In our quest to bring governance and globalisation together, we therefore arrive at a place in which the state very clearly has a major role to play in terms of its intervention in tourism and steering towards certain policy goals.

Conclusion: The State is Dead, Long Live the State

The state is still very much a key player in contemporary governance, albeit within a multilayered architecture. Its regulatory roles remain substantial. Moreover, governance is a differentiated activity in which the nation state can still exert considerable influence at the domestic level. The regulatory literature also provides evidence of government organisations that adapt their modes of behaviour to cope with the changing nature of the industries being regulated, as well as changing political and social values. Firms typically will attempt to evade the controls placed upon them, but once again that evasion usually is not the end of the game and regulatory organisations have been shown to be very adept at developing new instruments for pursuing their goals. Some of those instruments may involve the self-enforcement of regulations, albeit always with the capacity of the regulator to withdraw that privilege if abused (Peters 1998). Finally, and perhaps most importantly, in the Western political tradition governance requires some mechanism for public accountability if the decisions made through the process are to be legitimate. This fundamental requirement for any political process appears to give pause for thought to the advocates of 'governance without government', as well it should (see Rhodes 1997b, pp. 55–9). And in critiques of public–private relationships in tourism, as well as the growth of some supranational organisations, it is this potential for policy and democratic closure that is arguably of most concern in contemporary governance of the so-called network economy.

Discussion Questions

1. To what extent might coordination be an issue with respect to the development of multilayered governance architecture for certain issues, such as the environment?

2. How significant is the role of sub-state actors in international relations with respect to tourism?

3. What is the appropriate role of the state with respect to tourism?

4. To what extent does an economic agenda dominate tourism development and planning?

5. Are sustainable tourism and sustainable developement the same thing?

Further Reading and Websites

Surprisingly, there is very little written about governance issues in tourism in terms of the relationships between different levels of governance although there is some writing on the role of the state in tourism, particularly with respect to destination planning and marketing. On the political dimensions of tourism, see Hall (1994a) and Elliott (1997), while Hall and Jenkins (1995) provide an account of public policy analysis with respect to tourism. A number of political and policy themes are brought together with tourism planning issues in Hall (2000a), on which several sections of this chapter are based. Other useful material to refer to includes a 2001 special issue of *Current Issues in Tourism* on tourism policy-making (vol. 4 (2–4)), Jenkins (2001), Kerr (2003) and Hall (2003f). On general issues of governance, see Peters (1996, 1998),

Peters and Savoie (1996), and Rhodes (1997a, 1997b). Although not originally intended for a tourism audience, the work of Cohn and Smith (1993, 1996) on the role of Vancouver and the British Columbian provincial government as a sub-national government actor provides useful comparisons with many other competing places around the world. Gössling (2003) provides a range of interesting chapters relating to tourism and development on tropical islands from a political ecology perspective, while Wilkinson (1997) and Dieke (2000) provide overviews of tourism politics and policy with respect to the Caribbean and Africa respectively.

Governments on the WWW (an extremely useful metasite that includes surpranational organisations as well as government websites and tourism agency websites, however it is not as well maintained as it used to be! Remember that much tourism governance is actually not undertaken within national tourism organisations): www.gksoft.com/govt/en/

United Nations Environment Programme, Production and Consumption Branch, Section on government and policy support: www.uneptie.org/pc/tourism/policy/home.htm

Europa (the European Union online): http://europa.eu.int/

US State and Local Governments on the Net (a directory of official state, city and city government websites, primarily US but does have some international links): www.statelocalgov.net/index.cfm

US Government's official web portal: www.firstgov.gov

Government of Canada portal: http://canada.gc.ca/main_e.html

UK Government web portal: www.direct.gov.uk/Homepage/fs/en

Australian Federal Government portal: www.australia.go.au

New Zealand Government portal: www.govt.nz/

Singapore Government portal: www.gov.sg/

Developing Destinations

6

Key Concepts

- Destination
- Regionalism
- Development
- Production
- 'Growth machine'
- Use value
- Exchange value
- Regional development
- Networks
- Cooperation
- Partial industrialisation
- Value chain
- Consumption
- Supply chains
- Tourism product

- Common pool resources
- Clusters
- Trust
- Cornerstone firms
- Entrepreneurship
- Lifestyle entrepreneurship
- Copreneurship
- Massification
- Experience economy

Despite destinations being a focal point for much tourism research, there is still confusion as to what the concept actually means (Davidson and Maitland 1997; Ringer 1998; Hall 2000a; Leiper 2000b; Framke 2002). Metelka (1990, p. 46) defines a destination as the 'geographic location to which a person is traveling', and Vukonic (1997) equates the term to that of a 'resort', with Gunn (1994, p. 107) describing the idea of a destination as that of a 'travel market area'. Gunn makes the distinction between three different scales – the site scale, the destination zone scale and the regional scale. He defines destination zone as 'a geographic area containing a critical mass of development that satisfies traveller objectives' (Gunn 1994, p. 27). Similarly, Medlik (1993, p. 148) defines a tourism destination as '[c]ountries, regions, towns or other areas visited by tourists'. What is significant with the use of the concept is that it does reinforce the spatial dimension of tourism and particularly indicates the idea of specific regions within which tourism occurs. Smith (1995) provides a number of ways in which regionalisation may be identified in tourism research through such measures as cartographic regionalisation, perceptual regionalisation, cognitive mapping, functional regionalisation and destination zone identification. Drawing on the work of Gunn (1979), Smith (1995, p. 199) identified a number of criteria that might be applied in the identification of destination zones, and these are rooted in deeper attempts in geography to identify the attributes of regions (e.g. Grigg 1967; see also Johnston 1991; Hall and Page 2002):

- The region should have a set of cultural, physical and social characteristics that create a sense of regional identity.

- The region should contain an adequate tourism infrastructure to support tourism development. Infrastructure includes utilities, roads, business services and other social services necessary to support tourism businesses and to cater to tourists' needs.

- The region should be larger than just one community or one attraction.

● The region should contain existing attractions or have the potential to support the development of sufficient attractions to draw tourists.

● The region should be capable of supporting a tourism planning agency and marketing initiatives to guide and encourage future development.

● The region should be accessible to a large population base. Accessibility may be by road, scheduled air passenger service or cruise ships.

Nevertheless, despite the value of such an approach, precise boundaries will still be difficult to identify (Smith 1995). As Grigg (1967, p. 478) observed: 'If a region is thought to be a real entity then it must be presumed to have clear and determinable limits.' Moreover, from a public planning perspective it should also be noted that perceptual regions or destination zones may run over different government boundaries, making land use planning and often tourism promotion extremely difficult as it raises the potential for conflicts between different jurisdictions that may even have competing development objectives. In attempting to overcome such difficulties, Davidson and Maitland (1997, p. 4) defined destinations in terms of 'a single district, town or city, or a clearly defined and contained rural, coastal or mountain area' which share a number of characteristics:

● a complex and multidimensional tourism product based on a variety of resources, products, services and forms of ownership;

● other economic and social activities, which may be complementary to or in conflict with the various aspects of tourism;

● a host community;

● public authorities and/or an elected council with responsibility for planning and management; and

● an active private sector.

Davidson and Maitland's approach towards tourism destinations is useful as it highlights the complexity of destinations. Although some tourism marketers, promoters and planners may sometimes seem to propose otherwise (see Chapter 3), a destination is not just another 'product' or 'commodity'. Destinations are places in which people live, work and play, and to which they may have a strong sense of attachment and ownership. The difficulty in identifying a destination as a spatial unit is that it has different meanings depending on whether one is approaching the concept from the perspective of consumption or from that of production. From the perspective of the consumer, a destination is an abstract location of reality in which consumption of the tourism product occurs. Until it is visited it remains nothing more than an idea. Destinations are usually 'other' until they have been visited, possibly more than once. Then they start becoming imbued with directly experienced meaning and then they become transformed into locales. At this point destinations do not merely mark the end of a trip but often become something more, a place, or may even be described as another home.

However, while such abstract ideas of place may be interesting in terms of how places are perceived, they do not assist us greatly in understanding how destinations are brought into the complex web of place competition. Indeed, the fact that the 'objectifying' term 'destination' is used to describe the places travellers are going to is significant because, as originally used, the term implies an end point or destiny. Instead, within the context of tourism mobility we know that a destination is actually only a temporary stopping point, albeit perhaps a significant one, within the life course. Yet in terms of the production of tourism we can understand that a destination can be regarded as a particular point in space to which a consumer has moved and stopped, albeit temporarily. Within the various stages of a trip there are often multiple destinations, although we can refer to main destinations and secondary destinations. Clearly, the longer a person is travelling away from home the greater will be the number of destinations that he/she will encounter. Places are wanting to be seen as destinations by travellers, that is as locations in which they will stop, spend money, and hopefully stay overnight and spend even more money.

Destinations are locations of tourist consumption. More than that, destinations are commodified through the place competition process and the activities of the state, which actively encourages tourist consumption within its border, invariably in cooperation with the private sector. Destinations can only exist if the state allows it, as without the permission of the state you cannot enter specific spaces. Destinations are therefore regulated and often highly commodified spaces that are an outcome of shifts in the nature of the production process that have been accompanied by broader changes in regulation, governance, state intervention as well as the focus on the region as an economic unit. As Logan and Molotch (1987, pp. 43-4) note: 'A place is defined as much by its position in a particular organizational web – political, economic, and culture – as by its physical makeup and topographical configuration. Places are not "discovered", as high school history texts suggest; people construct them as a practical activity.' Such a statement may be rather gloomy for some readers as not only are we trapped within a space-time prism but destinations are also regulated and commodified in character. Indeed, here is one of the ironies of tourism – that while the industry often seems to promote the idea of freedom and escape, the reality is that the nature of late capitalist society has seemingly commodified almost everything. But people still travel! The individual does have agency! As MacCannell recognised in his notion of the second gaze, in identifying the construction of our existence the second gaze 'refuses to leave this construction to the corporation, the state, and the apparatus of touristic representation. ... It looks for the unexpected, not the extraordinary, objects and events that may open a window in structure, a chance to glimpse the real' (2001, p. 36). Nevertheless, in seeking to understand the way in which destinations seek development we need to understand the objectives of such development and the means by which development occurs.

Development

Tourism development is one of the most commonly used, but least understood, expressions in the tourism lexicon. Development means different things to different people. As Friedmann (1980, p. 4) observed: 'Development is one of the more slippery terms in our tongue. It suggests an evolutionary process, it has positive connotations, in at least some of its meanings it suggests an unfolding from within.' Much of the ambiguity over the use of the term 'development' arises because it refers to an objective, a process, and a state, with the state of development deriving from the economic, social, political and cultural processes which have caused it (Pearce 1989). Furthermore, development is always of something (Friedmann 1980).

Pearce (1989), drawing on the work of Mabogunje (1980), has five different ways in which the concept of development is used:

- economic growth;

- modernisation;

- distributive justice;

- socio-economic transformation; and

- spatial reorganisation.

To these Hall (1994a) has added three further categories: the analysis of the impacts of tourism; the idea that tourism development may be made sustainable (Bramwell and Lane 1993; Hall and Lew 1998); and, in a narrow sense, the production of facilities, infrastructure, labour and services to meet the needs of tourists. As Pearce (1989) noted, development is therefore a dynamic concept, interpretations of which have changed over time. From a primarily economic orientation, 'development' has also come to reflect broader social, political and cultural values, and attributes such as self-reliance and regional development (D.R. Hall, 1991a, 1991b).

Tourism development is an essentially political concept in that it is imbued with a set of values about how tourism should occur. The pursuit of tourists by governments around the world, and the perceived benefits of such development raise questions about the economic, social and political dimensions of the development process and the directly political manner in which overt and covert development objectives are pursued at the expense of other objectives. Political philosophy and ideology will have a substantial impact on tourism development processes. The selection of particular tourism development objectives represents the selection of a set of overt and covert values. Both the selection and implementation of these values will depend on the relative power of 'winners' and 'losers' in the political processes surrounding tourism development.

However, in the early twenty-first century it would be true to say that there are very few places that are not actively pursuing tourists. Furthermore, not only is the development process political, but so is its analysis. The selection of a particular theory or approach to development by the researcher or policy analyst will set the boundaries within which research is conducted, conclusions are reached and recommendations are made (Hall and Jenkins 1995). For many years students of tourism tended to concentrate on the economic dimensions of tourism development. More recently, greater attention has been given to environmental, socio-cultural and political considerations, but the economic imperative of tourism development studies still predominates. This is perhaps because tourism studies cannot easily transcend the capitalistic nature of most travel and tourism consumption and production on which many researchers are dependent (Britton 1991). Moreover, in a time of place competition, don't we need to attract tourists to survive and assist 'our place'?

While the social and environmental impacts of tourism are undoubtedly important, the reality is that it is the perceived economic benefits of tourism, such as employment and regional development, that drive the desire to attract tourists to destination regions. The policies of the national and local state are geared around the search for economic growth. As Roche (1992, p. 567) noted, 'probably the main political and social stimuli and motivations for developing a tourism industry at all derive from its assumed potential to generate employment'. It is extremely rare that a destination will put up a 'No Tourists' sign, even if some of the people who live there would like to at times. The reality is that nearly everywhere on the planet believes that mobility (although in some places it is more regulated than in others) is good for them, and if tourists come to your locale, you are told that it is good for you.

Tourism production is part of what Molotch (1976) termed 'the growth machine'. According to Logan and Molotch (1987), growth machine activists are largely free of concern for what happens within production processes (e.g. the flexibility of the labour supply), for the actual use of the products that are available locally (e.g. heritage buildings, streetscapes), or for spillover consequences in the lives of residents (e.g. negative environmental or social consequences of tourism) (see Chapter 4). There may be some disagreement between growth activists as to how the value of aggregate growth may be shared, but they all agree on the issue of growth itself. Fundamental to the nature of growth is the social context in which commodities are used and exchanged. Any given piece of real estate in a market economy has both a use value and an exchange value (Harvey 1973, 1982; Logan and Molotch 1987). For example, a rental apartment building provides a 'home' for residents (use value), while simultaneously generating rent for the owner (exchange value). People differ as to whether use or exchange is most crucial at different stages in their lives. For some, place is 'home', a residence, or a production site. For others, places represent a commodity for realising exchange value, via buying, selling or renting. The sharpest contrast, and what Logan and Molotch (1987) believe to be the most important, is between residents, who essentially use place to satisfy needs, and place entrepreneurs, who strive for financial return, usually through intensifying the use to which property is put and maximising economic rent. The pursuit of exchange values in places does not necessarily lead to the maximisation of use value for others, thereby providing a basis for locational conflict (Cox 1978,

1979, 1981; Ley and Mercer 1980; Mercer 1995), which is a feature of much tourism development. Indeed, use value may even be reduced, However, because 'the market' has come to be seen as the primary legitimising mechanism for determining what is to be produced, and the determinant of where and how production should occur, so therefore, with few exceptions, do governments or communities evaluate a product by its social or environmental worth or value to human life. As a result, locational and production decisions are portrayed as a public good if they contribute to economic activity and aggregate growth. Moreover, because the amount of mobile capital is always finite, no matter how hypermobile it is, so must the growth coalition in each area compete with that of others in an arena of place competition to attract scarce investment and, in the case of tourism, to attract those who satisfy the demands of tourism production. Moreover, to facilitate aggregate growth, places at one level will seek resources from the tiers above in order to attract capital and become more competitive, for example by seeking assistance in developing transport infrastructure or in bidding for and hosting an event. Therefore, the local state will typically seek to attract resources from the regional state and the nation state and even beyond. It is this interrelationship of exchange value and the market which drives place competition and tourism as a part of that phenomenon in an increasingly globalised, mobile world.

The mixture of public and private interests puts environmental, land use, social and even some economic conflicts at the intersection of two different sets of rules. In the public realm, arguments about the public interest, justice and equity make sense. Democratic procedures such as elections and public participation procedures are viewed as appropriate means of determining the best course of action and public opinion is significant. However, in the market realm the guiding ideas are efficiency and/or profit. Therefore, from a market-oriented perspective, the collective good is neither the focus of debate and public opinion nor a legitimate resource unless it is expressed through consumption (Dietz 2001) (see also comments regarding Kotler et al. (1993) in Chapter 4).

Although opposition does exist, for example through some aspects of the environmental movement, social justice campaigns or even community activism, the reality is that most responses from the growth machine only occur at the margin, so business now becomes 'green' or 'sustainable' or is 'socially responsible' and engages in 'fair trade'. But to what extent is this merely new branding rather than a fundamental change in behaviour? Indeed, because political and economic philosophies have shifted to embrace the values of the market in so much of the Western world, and supranational and global institutions have been created to sustain such dominance, many attitudes to the market have become myopic. Any intervention in the functioning of 'the market' can run the risk of generating substantial hostility. As Logan and Molotch (1987, pp. 47–8) recognised, 'This lack of understanding of markets leads to an ongoing ideological asymmetry between those struggling over use and exchange, with those pursuing exchange having the advantage. Through their institutional power and a potent ideological context, [place] entrepreneurs have the hegemonic edge.'

Regional Development and Tourism

The competitiveness of mass production changed its form from the late 1970s to different ways of preserving firm and regional competitiveness. New forms of production organisation began to emerge along with the reorganisation of capital–labour relations in the labour market and at the point of production. However, the nature of these changes has been open to multiple interpretations. For some, it heralded the transition from 'Fordism' to 'post-Fordism' as a set of organising and regulatory principles. For others, it was marked by new forms of high-volume production such as 'lean production' (Womack et al. 1990), while the role of small firms linked into competitive industrial districts also became significant (Amin 1989). However, according to Hudson (2000, p. 23):

> what was involved was a much more uneven and nuanced set of changes, generating novel and more complex forms of uneven development [that] involved re-shaping relations (competitive *and* cooperative) between capital and labour in various ways ... new ways of selecting workers, new forms of work, new ways of organizing the labour process, new forms of industrial and labour relations and often new geographies of employment and production.

Regions which had been affected by economic change and restructuring, such as rural and former industrial areas, from the early 1970s on, have commonly perceived tourism as a mechanism to bring employment and income back to the region. In the case of the European Union, tourism is regarded as having a core role in regional development (Williams and Shaw 1999; Roberts and Hall 2001; D. Hall 2004). The European Union has long attempted to encourage development in economically peripheral regions, but tourism is a more recent mechanism to achieve economic and social objectives.

The European Regional Development Fund was established in 1975 as a means of implementing the then European Community's regional policy. Tourism has become an essential part of the shift in EU development strategies because it is perceived as being highly labour-intensive and a counter-balance, along with other service industries, to job loss in 'traditional' agricultural and manufacturing sectors. Nevertheless, such statements tend to obscure the somewhat problematic success of tourism as a tool for regional development. For example, while globally there has been a general growth in employment in service sector industries such as tourism, many of these positions are part time. In the case of Britain's hotel and catering sector, Robinson and Wallace (1984) noted that, while there had been extensive growth in part-time female employment, such workers were badly paid and earned about 4% less than the average for part-time female workers in all industries. Similar issues with respect to the part-time, casual and highly gendered nature of much tourism employment was reported in Australia in the 1990s (Industry Commission 1995). The highly seasonal nature of many tourist destinations may also serve to mitigate some of the potential economic goals of regional tourist development strategies. Indeed, Urry (1987, p. 23) has observed that 'the more exclusively an area specialises in tourism the more depressed its general wage levels will be', a situation that, if it holds true, has substantial implications for the use of tourism as a development mechanism.

Regional development through tourism is established not only by the stock of its man-made capital (e.g. transport and energy infrastructure, housing, production of goods), or of its natural capital (wilderness, natural resources, national parks, green space, high-value species), but also by its human capital (professional skill, training, individual knowledge, education) and social capital (subjects' ability to coordinate their own actions and choices in view of common goals) (Ostrom 1990; Fukuyama 1995). Human and social capital therefore become critical requirements for sustainable nature-based tourism development as they are not the consequence of development, but rather its prerequisite. A region is rich if it has human capital and social capital because these are the means by which other forms of capital are produced and specific aspects of the natural environment are turned into tourism resources. Nevertheless, the relative absence of human and social capital also becomes one of the development challenges of many regions (Hall and Boyd 2005, in press).

The potential for tourism to contribute to regional development will depend on a broad range of economic, social and political factors, including the degree of linkage among the various sectors within the regional economy, the pattern of visitor expenditure and the extent of leakage from the regional economic system. Where substantial imports of goods and services are necessary to maintain the tourism industry, the relative worth of the industry may be somewhat doubtful from the perspective of national economic and social policy. The question of 'who benefits?' should be fundamental to the assessment of development policies.

Perhaps in many economically peripheral areas the creation of some jobs is better than no jobs at all, but given the substantial amounts of money that governments place in regional development schemes, a closer examination of the redistributive effects of tourism development within a region is warranted. For example, while tourism may be relatively labour-intensive compared to some other industries, it is that labour input which is most vulnerable to minimisation by owners in order to restrict costs, therefore creating the situation in which employment is often casual, part-time, under labour award rates and, at least in many Western countries, heavily centred on women because of the possibility of paying lower wages. In the situation in which tourism is promoted as an alternative to other economic activities, such as marginal agricultural or forestry operations or the mining industry, the ability of employees to transfer from those sectors to the tourism industry is somewhat limited unless there is both massive investment in retraining schemes and dramatic shifts in traditional gender roles. Therefore, in many situations, the ability for tourism to provide an employment alternative is extremely limited. At a gross level the same or even a greater number of jobs may exist in a region, but employment patterns may dramatically shift by gender, with a corresponding potential for the development of social problems because of breakdowns in traditional roles.

At a micro-level, regional development schemes may also reinforce existing disparities. For example, farm or rural tourism is often promoted as a mechanism to support regional agricultural communities. However, there is a substantial body of evidence which suggests that while farm tourism may bring visitation and income into a region, it is the farmers with surplus capital or at least enough capital to reallocate from agricultural activities into touristic activities which have the most to gain from rural tourism strategies. The most economically marginal farms, and the ones for whom such policies are often supposedly developed, are those with the least flexibility to participate in tourism enterprises because of their lack of capital. Rural tourism strategies may therefore reinforce existing income disparities for households within a region, although on a per capita or household level incomes may be maintained or rise (Bouquet and Winter 1987). Nevertheless, tourism is clearly of significance to many governments as a mechanism to promote national and regional development. However, the analysis of the economic impacts of tourism indicates that our understanding of its effects is incomplete, not only in terms of macro- and micro-economic impacts but also in terms of its social consequences. Policies do not always lead to desired outcomes.

Regional Development, Networks and Cooperation

The increased emphasis by tourism organisations on partnership arrangements is closely related to developments in management and policy theory as well as changes in the nature of the state. For example, government tourism organisations are now encouraged to engage in a greater range of partnerships, network and collaborative relationships with stakeholders. Such a situation has been described by Milward (1996) as the hollowing out of the state in which the role of the state has been transformed from one of hierarchical control to one in which governing is dispersed among a number of separate, non-government entities. As noted in the previous chapter, this has therefore led to increased emphasis on governance through network structures as a '*new* process of governing; or a changed condition of ordered rule; or the *new* method by which society is governed' (Rhodes 1997a, p. 43). However, it should be emphasised that the recognition of a growing variety of forms of production organisation has led to renewed interest in the diverse forms of cooperation as well as competition that shape inter-firm relationships as well as state–firm relationships, although the regulatory functions of the state virtually ensure its involvement in network development at one level or another.

As emphasised in Chapter 4, the focus on territory rather than company as one of the key bases for competitive success has meant a renewed attention to the internal characteristics of regions, including their cognitive and institutional assets (Amin and Thrift 1994), their capacity to be intelligent, learning regions (Morgan 1995; Hudson 1999), and the relational forms between firms that may be maximised for firm and regional advantage. The metaphor of relational webs and social and economic networks provides a useful, descriptive way of capturing a conception of relational social dynamics that exist in tourism development and, of course, in everyday life. Governance, which is the management of the common affairs of political communities, may serve to sustain or transform relational webs. Spatial planning systems provide a framework to manage the various connections between networks which co-exist in a locality (Healey 1997). Increasingly, the role of the private tourism manager or the public tourism planner is to assist in the development and maintenance of networks, whether it be for reasons of tourism development (Jamal and Getz 1995), the management of heritage sites (Hall and McArthur 1998), or the maintenance of agency support.

Networking refers to a wide range of cooperative behaviour between otherwise competing organisations and between organisations linked through economic and social relationships and transactions. Current government interest in networking stems from the view that the networked firm appears to be an important component of both successful national economies and of highly performing regional economies (e.g. Cooke and Morgan 1993) and may offer considerable potential to assist in cushioning the effects of economic restructuring, particularly in rural and peripheral areas.

Networks are a distinct, hybrid mode of coordinating economic activity that are alternatives to organisation by markets or within firms (hierarchical transactions) (Harper 1993). Networks involve firms of all sizes in various combinations, they can be locally or internationally based, they can occur at all stages of the value chain, and they range from highly informal relationships through to contractual obligations. Network development has received enormous attention in both academic and government circles in recent years. However, networking is not a new phenomenon and has long been a hallmark of innovative organisations. The innovation literature attests to 'the central importance of external collaboration with users and external sources of technical expertise [and] these empirical studies of innovation demonstrated the importance of formal and informal networks, even if the expression "network" was less frequently used' (Freeman 1991). Nevertheless, as Freeman goes on to observe, 'there has been a major upsurge of formal and semi-formal flexible networks in the 1980s, including some new types of network'. Networks are defined as arrangements of inter-organisation cooperation and collaboration. Such collaboration occurs, for example,

> where firms cooperate in production and marketing, to exchange know-how and market intelligence, to jointly train their employees, to develop research capacities and new markets, to purchase raw materials in bulk, to share equipment and infrastructure, and so on. If the collaborators also compete in input and product markets – as is often the case – networks are said to encompass the cooperative elements of otherwise competitive relationships. (Bureau of Industry Economics 1991, p. 5)

Similarly, in a much cited work, Powell notes that in networks, '[t]ransactions occur neither through discrete exchanges nor by administrative fiat, but through networks of individuals or institutions engaged in reciprocal, preferential, mutually supportive actions. ... Complementarity and accommodation are the cornerstones of successful production networks' (Powell 1990, p. 78). Yet despite increasing recognition of the significance of networks, there is an absence of a common set of factors for describing and explaining the development of networks as the conditions which give rise to network formation are quite diverse. Network arrangements have multiple causes and varied 'historical trajectories' (Powell 1990, p. 323), in some cases, the creation of networks 'anticipates the need for [network] form of exchange; in other situations, there is a slow pattern of development which ultimately justifies the form; and in still other circumstances, networks are a response to the demand for a mode of exchange that resolves exigencies that other forms are ill-equipped to handle'.

Business and regional strategic thinking now places substantial emphasis on relations with stakeholders as part of the development process while the emergence of concepts of collaboration (e.g. Gray 1985, 1989; Wood and Gray 1991) and network development (e.g. Powell 1990; Freeman 1991; Cooke and Morgan 1993) highlights the importance of the links to be made between stakeholders in processes of mediation, promotion and regional development. For example, in Australia the Federal Government has invested substantial funds into promoting network development between businesses in a number of sectors including tourism (e.g. AusIndustry 1996), while network development is an important common element in many European Union regional development programmes such as LEADER (e.g. Zarza 1996).

Awareness of the need of tourist organisations to create links with stakeholders is, of course, not new. The community tourism approach of Murphy (1985, 1988) emphasised the importance of involving the community in destination management because of their role as key stakeholders, although in actuality this often meant working with industry and community-based groups in a destination context rather than through wider public participation mechanisms. The difficulty in implementing community-based tourism strategies is reflective of wider difficulties with respect to effective destination management and tourism planning (Davidson and Maitland 1997), namely the diffuse nature of the tourism phenomenon within the economy and society and the problem this creates with respect to coordination and management. Hall (2000a) argued that the partially industrialised nature of tourism means that tourism, like the environment, should be regarded as a meta-problem which represents highly interconnected promotional, planning and policy 'messes' (Ackoff 1974), which cuts across fields of expertise and administrative boundaries and, seemingly, becomes connected with almost everything else. Tourism, therefore, 'is merely an acute instance of the central problem of society' (P. Hall 1992, p. 249) of creating a sense of the whole which can then be effectively planned and managed.

In retrospect I think the above is only partly true. Partial industrialisation, the condition by which only certain firms and agencies that provide goods and services directly to tourists are regarded as part of the tourism industry, is important. According to Leiper (1989, p. 25): 'The proportion of (a) goods and services stemming from that industry to (b) total goods and services used by tourists can be termed the index of industrialisation, theoretically ranging from 100% (wholly industrialised) to zero (tourists present and spending money, but no tourism industry).' As Hall (2000a) noted, some of the major consequences of the partial industrialisation of tourism are its significance for tourism development, marketing, coordination and network development.

Although we can recognise that many segments of the economy benefit from tourism, it is only those organisations which perceive a direct relationship to tourists and tourism producers that become actively involved in fostering tourism development or in cooperative marketing. However, there are many other organisations, such as food suppliers, petrol stations and retailers, sometimes described as 'allied industries', which also benefit from tourists but which are not readily identified as part of the tourism industry. Therefore, in most circumstances, businesses which regard themselves as non-tourism businesses will often not create linkages with tourism businesses for regional promotion unless there is a clear financial reward. It will often require an external inducement, such as promotion schemes established by government at no or minimal cost to individual businesses, or regulatory action such as compulsory business rating tax for promotion purposes, before linkages can be established.

Yet to the issue of partial industrialisation we must also add that the sheer fact that tourism consumption occurs over space and time must also create substantial difficulties in firm relations, even with the advent of improved communication systems, particularly as product demand shows substantial, though often quite regular, shifts in consumption. Arguably, however, both the partial industrialisation and the space–time dimension are also wound up in the very structure of tourism consumption and production and the nature of the tourism value chain. Tourism value chains are the collection of firms and organisations involved in producing, distributing and selling a related set of products from raw material to the consumer. Porter (1990) argued that competitive advantage is increasingly a function of how well a company or place can manage the value chain or 'value system', as Porter refers to it. In tourism the value chain comprises a complex web of firm and place interrelationships.

If one accepts that tourism is consumption, in that consumption (albeit variable) occurs throughout all stages of the trip process from decision to travel, travel to a destination, at the destination, from the destination, and even consumption in recollection, then you are dealing with a form of consumption that is stretched over space and time and in which there are multiple experiences of the tourism product at different scales (Figure 6.1). Indeed, the tourism product is actually made up of four separate products that range from individual service encounters/experiences, to firm-level products, to destination products, and then to the total tourism trip product (Figure 6.2). This is a service experience that is unlike what is usually described in the service management texts as there is a succession of service/product experiences on an ongoing basis through the various stages of the trip which will typically be produced by different providers, and in which the level of satisfaction occurs not just at each individual point of consumption with specific firms but over the totality of the tourism experience. Some readers may find it offensive that non-firm experiences are included as part of the service product, because this involves interaction with others who are 'nothing to do with the tourism industry' (e.g. individuals or communities or even just pleasant sights). Yet this is still part of what a destination is selling. Tourism commodifies a bundle of space–time for your consumption. This is what you purchase when you travel – people, places and their landscapes. This is the promissory note we receive from the place promoters in destination brochures and virtual tours via the web if we purchase this locale. And this is what you don't see if you just think about tourism at the level of individual service experiences in specific firms (as important as they are) rather than through all stages of the trip and the larger frame of production and consumption.

This therefore means that at the level of the trip not only are there are multiple supply chains within the context of the overall trip, but that different trips produce different configurations of the supply chain, with different value adding and through different distribution channels. This makes it extremely difficult to provide a standardised product but attempts are made, for example through the development of package tours, often in conjunction with particular horizontal, vertical and diagonal integration strategies. These may be achieved both within the firm or externally to the firm through networks. However, even here it is impossible to manage every experience. Therefore pleasant surprises or serendipity continues to be an important part of the overall level of satisfaction with the tourism or destination product. Indeed, it may be quite possible to contrive such surprises. Nevertheless, within the web of inter-firm relationships that are available in tourism, a number may be deliberately linked together in order to maximise the likelihood of a flow of tourists to particular destinations and particular firms. This is a reflection of the situation that every coordinating activity that improves organisational efficiency, reduces transaction costs, speeds up flow through the economic system, or makes possible a more intensive use of the factors of production is likely to improve the performance of the destination/regional economic system (Chandler and Daems 1979; Williamson 1981). This may be done through bundling firm offerings together in a commercial product or it may even be done through individual advice and recommendation. Either way the intention is to encourage the consumer to stay within a particular bundle of space–time for a period that maximises consumption.

Notions of collaboration, coordination and partnership are closely related within the emerging network paradigm. Networks refer to the development of linkages between actors (organisations and individuals) where linkages become more formalised towards maintaining mutual interests. The nature of such linkages exists on a continuum ranging from 'loose' linkages to coalitions and more lasting structural arrangements and relationships. Mandell (1999) identifies a continuum of such collaborative efforts as follows:

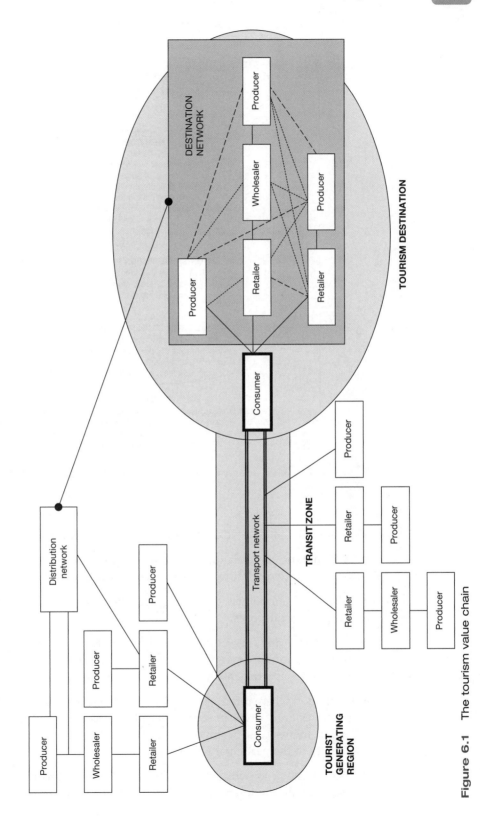

Figure 6.1 The tourism value chain

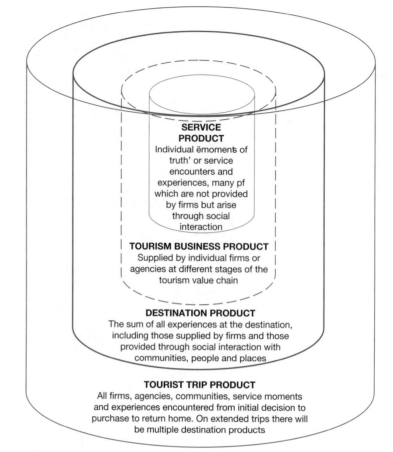

SERVICE PRODUCT
Individual ëmoments of truth' or service encounters and experiences, many pf which are not provided by firms but arise through social interaction

TOURISM BUSINESS PRODUCT
Supplied by individual firms or agencies at different stages of the tourism value chain

DESTINATION PRODUCT
The sum of all experiences at the destination, including those supplied by firms and those provided through social interaction with communities, people and places

TOURIST TRIP PRODUCT
All firms, agencies, communities, service moments and experiences encountered from initial decision to purchase to return home. On extended trips there will be multiple destination products

Figure 6.2   What does the tourist consume? The multiple nature of the tourism product

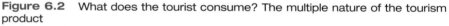

- linkages or interactive contacts between two or more actors;

- intermittent coordination or mutual adjustment of the policies and procedures of two or more actors to accomplish an objective;

- *ad hoc* or temporary task force activity among actors to accomplish a purpose or purposes;

- permanent and/or regular coordination between two or more actors through a formal arrangement (e.g. a council or partnership) to engage in limited activity to achieve a purpose or purposes;

- a coalition where interdependent and strategic actions are taken, but where purposes are narrow in scope and all actions occur within the participant actors themselves or involve the mutually sequential or simultaneous activity of the participant actors; and

- a collective or network structure where there is a broad mission and joint and strategically interdependent action. Such structural arrangements take on broad tasks that reach beyond the simultaneous actions of independently operating actors.

Tourism Insight: Collaboration and the Management of 'Common Pool Resources'

Ostrom (1990) uses the term 'common pool resources' to denote natural resources used by many individuals in common, such as fisheries and groundwater basins. In the tourism context, 'common pool resources' include landscapes and public attractions. Such resources have long been subject to over-exploitation by individuals acting in their own interests because of the characteristics of commons (Hardin 1968). Conventional solutions usually involve either centralised governmental regulation or resource privatisation. But, according to Ostrom (1986, 1987, 1990, 1998a, 1998b, 1998c; Blavin 2000), there is a third approach to resolving the problem of the commons: the design of durable cooperative institutions that are organised and governed by the resource users themselves. Characteristics of resources conducive to self-organised commons management include:

- *Feasible improvement:* resource units are not deteriorated to a point that there would be no advantage in organising.
- *Indicators:* reliable and valid indicators of the condition of the resource system are available at a relatively low cost.
- *Predictability:* the flow of resource units is relatively predictable.
- *Spatial extent:* the resource system is of an appropriate size, given the transportation and communication technology in use, that users can develop accurate knowledge of the internal characteristics and external relationships of the system.

Characteristics of users conducive to self-organised commons management include:

- *Salience:* users place a high value on the resource system.
- *Common understanding:* users have a shared image of how the resource system operates and how their actions affect each other and the resource system.
- *Discount rate:* users use a low discount rate in relation to future benefits to be achieved from the resource.
- *Distribution of interests:* users with substantial economic and political assets within the system are adversely affected by a lack of coordinated patterns of appropriation and use. Therefore it is in their self-interest to cooperate.
- *Trust:* users trust one another to keep promises and relate to one another with reciprocity.
- *Autonomy:* users are able to determine access and use rules without external authorities countermanding them.
- *Previous organisational experience:* users have previously gained organisational skills through participation in other associations.

Plate 6.1 Rhinoceros are a very significant tourism resource in South Africa. Their survival is linked to cooperation between the industry, conservationists and local communities. Unless communities have 'ownership' over the conservation process it is extremely difficult to minimise the impacts of poaching on such animal populations. Tourism therefore acts as a very important financial incentive to ensure the survival of the species as tourism means it is worth more as a living resource than being sold on the black market. (see the KwaZulu-Natal Tourism Authority www.kzn.org.za/kzn/; Tourism South Africa www.tourism.org.za; and the South African Department of Environmental Affairs and Tourism www.environment.gov.za)

Undoubtedly, as Buhalis and Cooper (1998, p. 338) observed, networking does allow small and medium-sized tourism enterprises (SMTEs) to:

● pool their resources in order to increase their competitiveness;

● draw up strategic management and marketing plans;

● reduce operating costs; and

● increase their know-how.

Similarly, arguments have been made with respect to the wine and food tourism sector. Yet, despite the focus on trust as the basis for collaboration and network formation, the fierce competition between small firms at the lower levels of the supply chain and its implications for inter-firm relations arguably makes tourism no different from that of other sectors (Hudson 2000). Nevertheless, it is apparent that substantial change in the form of the contractual relationships linking companies, has led to an increased recognition of the emergence of longer-term strategic alliances and joint ventures, which then have a number of direct and indirect consequences for geographies of production (Dicken and Oberg 1996), particularly when combined with the drive for place promotion. For example, with respect to Baltic Sea tourism destinations, the World Tourism Organisation's Chief of Quality of Tourism Development, Henryk Handszuh, commented that the region's 'tourism image must be strengthened, enhanced and, to the extent possible, coordinated. Coordination here does not mean any formal intervention, but identifying and working towards common objectives by tourism enterprises in the region and by their support bodies in the public and private sectors' (World Tourism Organisation 1998f). Indeed, allied to the spatial dimension of the network paradigm is the emphasis given to clusters.

Industry clusters exist where there is loose geographic concentration or association of firms and organisations involved in a value chain producing goods and services and innovating. A cluster is defined as a concentration of companies and industries in a geographic region that are interconnected by the markets they serve and the products they produce, as well as by the suppliers, trade associations and educational institutions with which they interact (Porter 1990). Such exporting chains of firms are the primary 'drivers' of a region's economy, on whose success other businesses, such as construction firms, for example, depend in terms of their own financial viability. An industry cluster includes companies that sell inside as well as outside the region, and also supports firms that supply raw materials, components and business services to them. These clusters form 'value chains' that are the fundamental units of competition in the modern, globalised world economy. Clusters in a region form over time and stem from the region's economic foundations, its existing companies and local demand for products and services (Waits 2000). Firms and organisations involved in clusters are able to achieve synergies and leverage economic advantage from shared access to information and knowledge networks, supplier and distribution chains, markets and marketing intelligence, competencies, and resources in a specific locality. The cluster concept focuses on the linkages and interdependencies among actors in value chains (Enright and Roberts 2001).

Although one of the lessons of cluster development programmes around the world 'is that there is no precise, "right" (one size fits all) formula for developing industry clusters' (Blandy 2000, p. 80), a number of factors have been recognised as significant in the development of clusters and the associated external economy which serves to reinforce the clustering process. These include:

- the life-cycle stage of innovative clusters;
- government financing and policies;
- the skills of the region's human resources;
- the technological capabilities of the region's R&D activities;
- the quality of the region's physical, transport, information and communication infrastructure;
- the availability and expertise of capital financing in the region;

- the cost and quality of the region's tax and regulatory environment; and

- the appeal of the region's lifestyle to people who can provide world class resources and processes.

Hall (2001a) identified several other factors which may be significant in cluster and network success:

- spatial separation: the existence of substantial spatial separation between elements of a cluster that inhibit communication;

- administrative separation: the existence of multiple public administrative agencies and units within a region;

- the existence of a 'champion' to promote the development of a network; and

- the hosting of meetings to develop relationships.

Tourism Insight: Wine Clusters

Suggesting that business clusters add value to a region implies an entirely new set of public policies, one that shifts the focus of attention from an individual place or individual firm to a region and clusters of businesses and the interaction between them (Rosenfeld 1997). Rosenfeld (1997, p. 9) argues that to all intents and purposes, networks are a result of mature and animated clusters. Wine has been recognised as one industry in which clustering is a significant competitive factor. Porter (1990) used the California wine industry as an example of successful cluster development in his seminal work on competitive strategies. Blandy (2000, p. 21) uses the South Australian wine industry as 'the classic example of a successful industry cluster . . . a group of competing, complementary and interdependent firms that have given strong economic drive to the State through the cluster's success in exporting its products and know how nationally and internationally'. Similarly, Marsh and Shaw (2000) commented that clustering and collaboration have been the primary reason for the success of the Australian wine industry in terms of its export growth.

Cluster formation is regarded as a significant component in the formation of positive external economies for wine firms, with tourism being recognised as an important contributor of the cluster (Porter 1990). Telfer (2000) argued that clustering was a useful concept to describe the development of a wine and food network in the Niagara region of Ontario, Canada, Tastes of Niagara, which is a Quality Food Alliance of Niagara food producers, winemakers, chefs, restaurateurs and retailers (http://www.tourismniagara. com/tastesofniagara/index.html). However, Hall (2004d) has argued that in the case of Porter's (1990) citing of the wine industry of California as an example of a cluster and Blandy's (2000) reference to the South Australian wine industry cluster, both authors failed to recognise that in each case the wine industry had been in place for well over 100 years (often with the establishment of substantial family networks over that period) and that tourism was a late, and often incidental, arrival in both cases as a component of the cluster. Furthermore, given that the areas had been wine regions for such a long period and that wine is an environmentally dependent resource, it is not surprising that certain elements of a cluster formation had developed in this time. Perhaps a more significant question is therefore how can we use existing work on clusters to help us identify the factors in developing new clusters, particularly in rural areas which have undergone fundamental economic restructuring? In this case Hall stated that trust and factors such as being champions for innovations were extremely important (also see Henton and Walesh 1997), but he also noted the significance of the institutional characteristics of each region.

However, geographical co-location does not necessarily lead to cluster development and activation. Instead, communicative relationships need to be established between partners. Without an appropriate cluster champion and associated relationship-creating strategy (formal or otherwise) co-location may as much lead to rivalry that works against cluster development as behaviours that do. The creation of trust becomes a critical component in this exercise and outside independent knowledge brokers appear extremely important in providing an understanding of the economic and social context of cluster development. Such an observation is significant, as Audretsch and Feldman (1997) have argued that the generation of new economic knowledge tends to result in a greater propensity for innovative activity to cluster during the early stages of the industry development, and to be more highly dispersed during the mature and declining stages.

What is remarkable in many of the accounts of cluster development, with Blandy's (2000) review being typical, is that few of the models or accounts of clusters adequately capture and describe the underlying dynamics of clusters. They do not explain how they actually 'work' or answer questions of whether and how firms interact and produce synergy. Scale is only part of the reason that clusters and their regions prosper. In the case of the wine industry it could be argued that wine clusters form because of the environmental determination of where one can produce wine. Equally important to the circuitry of the system is the 'current', or the flow of information, knowledge, technological advances, innovations, skills, people, and capital into, out of, and within the cluster, from point to point (Rosenfeld 1997). Conventional data cannot distinguish between a simple industry concentration and a working cluster. As Doeringer and Terkla (1995, p. 228) observed: 'Although interindustry transactions incorporated within production channels can sometimes be detected in input–output tables, neither the character of relationships among firms nor the benefits of clustering can be discerned in this way.' However, in a cluster, the social ecology is as important as the agglomeration economies. As Rosenfeld

Plate 6.2   Featherstone Vineyard in Niagara region of Canada emphasises its relationship to the Grapegrowers of Ontario association in its promotion to wine tourists (www.featherstonewinery.ca)

(1997, p. 10) comments: 'The "current" of a working production system is even less easily detected, often embedded in professional, trade and civic associations, and in informal socialization patterns. ... The "current" depends on norms of reciprocity and sufficient levels of trust to encourage professional interaction and collaborative behaviour.'

In light of the role of trust as a strategic factor in regional tourism development (Hall 2000a), Rosenfeld (1997, p. 10) redefined clusters as '[a] geographically bounded concentration of interdependent businesses with active channels for business transactions, dialogue, and communications, and that collectively shares common opportunities and threats'. Importantly, this definition asserts that 'active channels' are as important as 'concentration', and without active channels even a critical mass of related firms is not a local production or social system and therefore does not operate as a cluster. Without such active channels it is extremely unlikely that the various firms in a region, large or small, can actively cooperate in order to achieve regional aims (e.g. see Saxenian 1994). Therefore, in seeking to understand the processes of cluster development, recognition of social capital and the relative efficiency of channels of social exchange become vital components of the networking process. As Théret (1994) noted, successful modes of regulation generally involve a range of formal and informal institutions, extending from habits and routines to societal wide routines. Indeed, without sufficient social capital, the co-location of firms may at times lead to a lack of social exchange as often as it does to a posi-

Plate 6.3   Wine tasting at Olssens of Bannockburn in Central Otago, New Zealand. The Winery cooperates with a number of other wineries in the region to promote their wines and attract visitors to sample their wines. (For information on wineries in the region see www.otagowine.com and for New Zealand wine in general see www.nzwine.com)

tive sharing of knowledge and ideas unless the firms are seen to have some shared interests on which they communicate.

However, one of the most significant aspects of networks is that not only do they represent flows of corporate information, for example research and promotion, but, from a tourism perspective, they may also represent flows of tourists on the ground as well as economic transactions between firms. In other words, the economic and social characteristics of networks influence the flow of goods and services, including tourists (Figure 6.3). In many situations the informal network of the individual flows into the formal linkages of the organisation network, although obviously the borders between these relationships remain extremely blurred at the level of many small tourism businesses that may be one- or two-person operations (Table 6.1).

Communicative relationships therefore affect a range of business, community, economic, social and political relationships both at the destination level – horizontal networks – but also within firms that associate on the basis of specific common features, for example special interest tourism, ecotourism, art galleries and museums – vertical networks. Important to the operation of networks are cornerstone firms or organisations that act to keep the network together. The cornerstone organisation is a firm or agency which lies at the centre of many networks and which works actively to promote and maintain the network. However, the largest companies are not necessarily the cornerstone of networks (Blumberg 2004; Lindroth and Soisalon-Soininen 2004). Instead, it may be a local champion who sees the destination's interests in relation to her/his own interests. Often such individuals have substantial social capital in terms of the relationships they have in the destination community and this serves as a basis on which networks can be established. In many situations the role of a network cornerstone may be one of the interventionist activities of the local state through their support of a tourist information office or, more actively, destination management officials. Interestingly, the very notion of destination management in a business sense is quite different from many other management functions undertaken at the level of the firm. This is because the product offered by destinations is not owned by them even though they are commodifying and selling it, a situation in common with the activities of travel agents (Holloway 1994; Lawton and Page 1997), as well as other destination marketing organisations. Therefore, classic command and control functions cannot operate in all but the most authoritarian of states. Instead, the development of collaborative relationships and trust in working together towards common goals is central in destination network development. From a place competition perspective, the formation of such networks may not only bring benefits to individual firms but also to the destination because of the potential to retain as much consumption as possible within the destination.

The strategies of some tourism SMEs (small and medium-sized enterprises) may well be aimed as much towards maintaining the desired lifestyles of the owners as they are towards profit maximisation or growth-oriented strategies (Lynch 1998; Ateljevic and Doorne 2000; Getz and Carlsen 2000; Miciak et al.

Table 6.1   Organisational and personal dimensions of the network construct in tourism

Network dimension	Inter-organisational	Personal
Actors	Organisations: private (e.g. firm), public (e.g. tourism ministry), public–private (e.g. tourism promotion board), non-government organisation (e.g. environmental group)	Individuals, copreneurs, entrepreneurs
Type of link	Formal	Informal
Common categorisations	Economic transactions, economic network, marketing network, vertical network, horizontal network	Social network, social relationships, communication

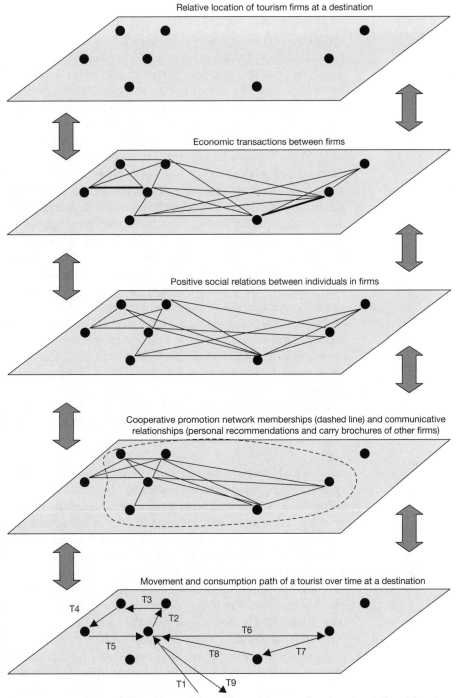

Figure 6.3 Interrelationships of the different forms of network relationship at a destination and the relationship to tourist consumption

2001). Nevertheless, a survey of bed and breakfast operators in New Zealand (Hall and Rusher 2004) indicated that the attitudes of owners to the issues of applying strict business principles to a business that is known for its lifestyle benefits demonstrated evidence of a strong business philosophy being balanced against the personal goals of the business owners to enjoy a good lifestyle. Indeed, for vast majority of the operators *lifestyle is a strategic business objective*, therefore illustrating the need to incorporate lifestyle goals within the development of models of the entrepreneurship process within tourism and, arguably, within much small business knowledge (e.g. Gibb and Davies 1990, 1992; Perren 1999; Glancey 1998; Greenbank 2001). Interestingly, at least two other consequences emerge from understanding the importance of lifestyle as a strategic business objective of small tourism businesses. First, our understanding of small business performance and entrepreneurial success would need to incorporate lifestyle 'quality-of-life' measures as an important component (Hornaday and Aboud 1971; Keats and Bracker 1988). Second, lifestyle and amenity factors also become a significant factor in decision-making regarding the location of new small tourism business ventures (Williams and Hall 2002). Third, copreneurship (Marshack 1994), that is when life partners share the entrepreneurial process, appears to be a very significant dimension of the business process, although this requires substantial study because, while related, there are clearly some different properties to the notion of family business operations (Getz et al. 2004), to which they may be a precursor, thereby reinforcing the importance of undertaking a life-course approach to mobilities advocated in Chapter 3.

Hall and Rusher's (2004) study of the New Zealand bed and breakfast sector also indicated that the sector was characterised by poor formal linkages with tourism industry associations, regional tourism organisations and other sectors of the tourism industry. Quite possibly one of the most significant reasons for poor linkages is the different goals of small businesses within emergent tourism networks. For example, the lifestyle goals of many tourism entrepreneurs may well be at odds with some of the profit maximisation goals of other entrepreneurs within a tourist destination. These conflicts were observed first-hand by the authors within their study area. Comments from members of economic development agencies or tourism organisations that such lifestyle entrepreneurs are 'hippies' or 'a danger to the industry' were not uncommon. Many New Zealand tourism organisations often perceive such lifestyle businesses as being 'unprofessional'. However, the evidence from Hall and Rusher (2004) suggested that this was not the case, although there are potentially significant areas for goal conflict in terms of business objectives, particularly in terms of 'opening hours' and service quality. In addition, substantial conflict can also occur over the different regulatory structures and costs incurred by the 'formal' hospitality and tourism sector, for example hotel chains, motels and pubs versus those incurred by 'informal' providers, many of which were not even registered as businesses. From a network development perspective such issues clearly need to be addressed if regions are to effectively maximise the economic and social benefits of tourism development (Hall 2000a).

Another interesting dimension of the development of tourist firms is the extent to which massification has affected service provision and the nature of the tourism firm, particularly with respect to the hospitality and restaurant sector. For example, Baum (1999) argued that the development of chains may be the prototypical form of contemporary organisational development, and Ritzer (1996), in his extremely influential work on service sector industries, has described the McDonald's chain as a new and dominant model for organisational growth. Partly as the result of Ritzer's work, restaurants have been singled out as the quintessential example of chain store organisation (also see Leidener 1993). However, the restaurant sector is in fact highly diverse, with substantial distinctions between full-service and fast-food restaurants, not only in terms of the nature of the meal and the experience, but also of the labour force. The traditional restaurant industry is maintained with elaborate menus and individualised production of customer orders. In contrast, as Parcel and Sickmeier (1988, p. 43) noted: 'The fast-food industry has grown up with different labor needs. Clearly the skill requirements differ across these two related industries, with the low-skill-crewperson job growing at the expense of the more diversified semiskilled food preparation jobs in traditional restaurants.' However, Nelson's (2001) research on restaurants in the United States indicated that in spite of the increasingly huge size of the restaurant market, substantial segments of the industry remain composed of single, independent establishments. He concluded that despite claims as to massification of the restaurant sector, proximate markets grow oppositionally and that the full-service sector – with its extensive menus, service, on-site preparation, and higher labour costs – provided few opportunities for the high-profit margins of interest to large-scale capital development.

Overall, restaurants were not as commonly chained as Ritzer (1996) suggested. Instead, 'different profit environments generate different market structures and different strategies for survival' (Nelson 2001, p. 134). Interestingly, in relation to the discussion regarding the role of fashion and taste in tourism in Chapter 2, Nelson (2001) goes on to reflect on the potential implications of the environments in which commodities are produced, distributed and consumed, so that 'consumption should always be based on the recognition of distinct systems of provision across commodities' (Fine and Leopold 1993, p. 5), noting that fashion intensifies in industries without the opportunity to generate mass production or distribution essential to lower prices. Nevertheless, the growth of the forms of organising production and the accompanying new forms of individualised pay and remuneration has implications for relationships between workers but also has impacted divisions of class, ethnicity and gender (Beck 1992; Yates 1998). For example, in many service sector occupations, such as in the hospitality industry, personal appearance and social skills have become key recruitment and retention criteria, rather than technical skills (McDowell 1997), while female migrants tend to play a very important role in back-of-house duties in the accommodation sector.

Developing Destinations

The terrain of thinking regarding the nature of regional development and tourism's role within that has shifted rapidly since the early 1970s. These shifts have paralleled globalising and localising processes and the growth in place competition. These changes have been well described by Hudson (2000, p. 130): a shift 'in the characteristic form of social organisation from standardized production and mass consumption patterns (orchestrated via extensive state involvement in economic and social life) to a new, more diverse pattern', associated with 'the new regime ... a fluidity of production arrangements, labour markets, financial organization and consumption' (Harvey and Scott 1987, pp. 2–3). Tourism is invariably tied up with such fluidity of production because of the associated fluidity of consumption, while some elements of mass customisation (Pine 1993) are clearly to be found in tourism at different levels of the tourism product, particularly in terms of packaging.

The notion of the experience society has recently entered writing on tourism (Autero 2003; Stamboulis and Skayannis 2003). According to Pine and Gilmore (1999), the experience society is a new stage of industrialised development, with experiences being distinguished from services (also see Jensen 1999). Yet the provision and commodification of experiences have clearly long been a part of the tourism product and it is unfortunate that Pine and Gilmore did not pay more attention to the substantial literature on the importance of experiences in selling tourism products as we have been part of the experience society for many years. The destination provides the framework for the provision of much of the tourism product and its significance has grown as places have increasingly come to compete against each other. Central to this competition is the development of networking and collaborative strategies by which firms cooperate towards common goals, often in conjunction with agencies of the local or even nation state. Networking can provide a basis by which particular experiences and firms can be linked together to bundle or package products for visitors. Networks, like most tourism production, are highly fluid in nature. Although much attention has been given to the massification of tourism, there is still substantial variation in the forms of production of tourism services. However, these issues of destination development do not occur in the abstract; they reflect real issues in the development and promotion of specific places and environments, and it is to these issues that the next three chapters will now turn.

Discussion Questions

1. Is it true to say that tourism development is an essentially political concept?

2. What are the differences between use value and exchange value and what might be the implications of these differences for tourism development issues?

3. What might be the barriers to forming collaborative relationships between tourism firms?

4. What are the factors which might encourage and discourage cluster formation?

5. What are the similarities and differences between the management of destinations and the management of firms?

Further Reading and Websites

On the concepts that surround the idea of tourism development, see Sharpley and Telfer (2002). On the characteristics of tourism firms, see Page et al. (1999), Thomas (2000, 2004) and Getz et al. (2004). O'Donnell et al. (2001) provide a useful general overview of the network construct in entrepreneurship research, while Bramwell and Lane's (2000) collection on collaboration and partnerships in tourism probably remains the best general overview of the field in tourism. Nordin (2003) provides a useful though uncritical overview of several examples of clustering and innovation. The recent work by Kozak (2004) on benchmarking destinations demonstrates more managerialist approaches to ideas of destination development. Hall (2000a) provides an approach to tourism planning that concentrates on the implications of system, scale and processes. Murphy and Murphy (2004) updates Murphy's seminal (1985) contribution with respect to notions of community tourism. Ritchie and Crouch (2003) provide an approach to destination competitiveness that is in keeping with the approach of Kotler et al. (1993), however it is interesting that distance and accessibility issues are only briefly examined. Campbell-Hunt (2000) provides an excellent meta-review of competitive strategy, and provides substantial criticism of over-concentrating on Porter's (2000a, 20000b) competitive strategies.

The Competitiveness Institute: The Cluster Practitioners Nework (a not-for-profit alliance of cluster practitioners): www.competitiveness.org/

Governments on the WWW (tourism institutions): www.gksoft.com/govt/en/tourism.html

West Virginia University, Regional Research Institute. The Web Book of Regional Science (excellent source of material): www.rri.wvu.edu/regsc books.htm

A search through the web will reveal a number of tourism cluster strategies. Some examples include: Scotexchange (the official website of the Scottish tourism industry) has useful links to enterprise agencies, the route development fund, as well as tourism cluster strategies: www.scot exchange.net/index.htm

The Experience Enterprise and Tourism Cluster, Missoula, Montana, USA: www.missoula cultural.org/mbca/clusters/

Niagara Economic and Tourism Corporation (see the information regarding strategic clusters): www.niagaracanada.com

Part III

When production meets consumption: understanding development issues

Urban Tourism: Development and Issues

7

Key Concepts

- Urban tourism
- Redevelopment
- Revitalisation
- Regeneration
- Economic restructuring
- Imaging
- Hallmark events
- Mega-event
- Sports tourism
- Olympic Games
- Migrant populations
- Serial monotony
- Authenticity
- Mixed use
- Heritage
- Capital cities
- World city

..., and urban tourism in particular, has become a key component of the ...titutional forms of economic regeneration (Hudson 2000), particularly ... areas. Despite the potential for the movement of capital through place ...ion, the major cause of job loss in manufacturing and heavy industry ... developed countries may be capacity closure and restructuring to ...abour productivity rather than capital flight and relocation abroad. ...less, these impacts, when associated with rationalisation and privat-... ...may be massive. For example, in the north-east of England ...yment in the traditional coal mining, iron and steel production, and shipbuilding industries had fallen from almost 300 000 in the mid-1950s to fewer than 10 000 jobs in the early 1990s (Hudson 2000).

The redevelopment and revitalisation of urban areas through the creation of new tourism and leisure precincts have been regarded by some commentators (e.g. Bramham et al. 1989) as being indicative of a crisis of the local state in which the importance of traditional welfare functions has been lessened and entrepreneurial functions increased. However, in a broader context, the current use of tourism to re-image and redevelop areas of the city may also be seen as a response by urban elites to the globalisation of capital and the changing nature of the role of the state in society. Regardless, it is apparent that a major shift has occurred in the political and economic context of city development, from the late twentieth century on, which has led to tourism contributing to new social and spatial segregation and new private and public cultures (Mommaas and van der Poel 1989). Hudson (2000) identified five new institutional forms of response to economic restructuring:

Plate 7.1 City as spectacle I: Singapore waterfront (The official website for tourist information for Singapore is www.visitsingapore.com; For policy and statistical information visit the Singapore Tourism Board http://app.stb.com.sg/asp/index.asp)

1. *Productionist solutions*, which have a focus on small and medium-sized manufacturing firms and the enterprise culture. Here tourism becomes implicated in the development of small firms and self-employment opportunities.

2. *Productionist solutions*, with the focus on the attraction of large firms and the branch plant economy. This generally applies to other industries apart from tourism, although some elements of this institutional strategy are related to the development of airport and transport infrastructure as well as the attraction of some tourism company administrative headquarters or branches.

3. *Consumptionist solutions*, which reveal a shift from working-class production spaces to tourism based on the heritage of working-class production, for example industrial and waterfront museums and leisure spaces. Nevertheless, it is interesting to note that, according to Hudson (2000, p. 233), such a strategy in 'many old industrial areas represents a sort of politics of despair, born of a lack of alternatives in terms of manufacturing industry or other types of service sector activity'.

4. *Consumptionist solutions*, which indicate a shift from working-class production space to middle-class residential and consumption spaces. Here tourism becomes an integral component of the development of integrated tourism/leisure/retail/entertainment spaces often located in inner-city areas that are targeted for regeneration. These locations indicate a profound and selective demographic and social composition in terms of their being sites of middle-class residence and consumption. Such locations also often reveal the role of development corporations.

5. Finally, a *welfare state solution*, in which people move from being industrial workers to clients of the welfare state. However, even here tourism is seen to have a particular role as sport and leisure activities are seen as serving a key role not only in regeneration but also in controlling anti-social or deviant behaviour.

Given the implication of tourism in all of the above institutional urban regeneration strategies, to various degrees it is readily apparent that the creation of urban leisure spaces and the hosting of hallmark events in order to establish new images for cities and attract mobile capital and people has substantial implications for the interests of groups within urban areas, especially in the inner-city areas which are most susceptible to re-imaging strategies, as well as the role of the local state.

Although urban centres have long served to attract tourists, it is only in recent years that cities have consciously sought to develop, image and promote themselves in order to increase the influx of tourists. Following the deindustrialisation of many industrial and waterfront areas in the 1970s and 1980s, particularly related to the impact on container shipping technology, tourism has been perceived as a mechanism to regenerate urban areas through the creation of leisure and tourism space. This process appears almost universal in the developed world (e.g. see Law 1985; Cameron 1989; P. Hall 1992; Judd and Parkinson 1990; Watson 1991; Bianchini and Parkinson 1993; Page 1993). Such a situation led Harvey (1988, cited in Urry 1990, p. 128) to ask: 'How many museums, cultural centres, convention and exhibition halls, hotels, marinas, shopping malls, waterfront developments can we stand?' Similarly, Urry (1990, p. 119) observed that 'in recent years almost every town and city in Britain has been producing mixed development waterfront schemes in which tourist appeal is one element'. Almost 15 years later nothing has fundamentally changed. Waterfront redevelopment remains a major mechanism of tourism-led urban regeneration. However, according to Mommaas and van der Poel (1989, p. 263), the development of a more economically oriented city develop-ment policy style, aimed at the revitalisation of the city, led to projects, developed in public–private partnerships, which were meant not for the inte-gration of disadvantaged groups within society, even though the rhetoric of development often talked about regeneration, 'but for servicing the pleasures of the well-to-do'. Indeed, it can be argued that much regeneration is physical and economic in nature rather than aiming to meet the social and economic development needs of disadvantaged groups.

The concept of regeneration includes both physical (i.e. concerned with architecture and image) and social dimensions (i.e. concerned with improving the quality of life of those who already live in target areas) (Page and Hall 2003). This split was noted in the comments regarding the delivery of urban regeneration in *Towards an Urban Renaissance: The Report of the Urban Task Force*, chaired by Lord Rogers of Riverside for the British Government (Department of the Environment, Transport and the Regions 2000a): 'There are neighbour-hoods where regeneration can only be achieved through comprehensive packages of measures to tackle not just the physical environment, but also the economic and social needs of local people.'

However, if the social aspects of regeneration programmes are to be achieved, then it is apparent that physical and social regeneration goals need to be brought together in an integrated package. A review conducted by the Department of the Environment, Transport and the Regions (DETR) of urban regeneration policies in the United Kingdom provides interesting insights into the success of such initiatives. The DETR-sponsored evaluation defined 're-generation' as broadly consisting of area-based initiatives (ABIs) mainly introduced by the Department of the Environment and/or DETR, in England, since 1990. Such ABIs were introduced to address cumulative, social, economic and physical problems in disadvantaged areas. In the 1980s and early 1990s, many regeneration measures were oriented towards land and property-led economic regeneration. Initiatives included projects such as City Challenge and the Single Regeneration Budget (SRB) Challenge Fund, which placed a stronger emphasis on comprehensive regeneration through partnership working, and the more recent New Deal for Communities (NDC) projects which target substantial resources at deprived neighbourhoods of 1000–4000 households. Although the evaluation reported that the schemes have made improvements to areas on some indicators, substantial issues remain, particu-larly with assisting those who live in such areas. Indeed, it concluded that

Plate 7.2   City as spectacle II: Toronto (The Tourism Toronto (Toronto Convention and Visitors Association) website is www.torontotourism.com. The Ontario Ministry for Tourism and recreation website is www.tourism.gov.on.ca/english/)

'Physical regeneration has, in many cases, played an important role in improving neighbourhood identity and external image, and in attracting employment opportunities into the area – although most jobs have not been secured by residents of deprived neighbourhoods' (DETR 2000b).

The primary justification for the redevelopment of inner-city areas for tourism is the perceived economic benefits of tourism. Since the mid to late 1970s the nature of the urban core has changed substantially in the developed world. Although the commercial function of central business districts is still important, leisure and tourist functions are increasing in their significance. Jansen-Verbeke's (1989, p. 233) claim that '[t]he entire urban core is presently looked upon as a recreational environment and as a tourism resource' is something of an exaggeration as most urban cores, with the exception of some very specific tourism destinations such as Las Vegas, remain multifunctional in nature. Indeed, even here, because of the sheer size of the resident community, there is still some blend of functions. Nevertheless, there has clearly been a transformation in the way that urban cores and some areas in the suburbs and the rural–urban fringe have been developed and commodified as tourism–leisure spaces. In fact, it should be emphasised that when we talk about urban tourism there are many areas in the cities which are not focal points of tourism activity, especially in the suburbs. Instead we are talking about specifically commodified spaces. Indeed, the distribution of leisure trips within and outside cities (see Figure 4.1), as well as the distribution of overnight stays (Figure 7.1), indicates that cities are simultaneously both destinations and generators of tourism mobility. Moreover, the zone of influence of cities means that there is a substantial daytrip zone that is utilised by urban dwellers and those visiting cities. Such urban tourism hinterlands, though often promoted as rural destinations, are actually extremely dependent on the flow of urban capital and populations.

The urban imaging processes intrinsic to urban tourism production are clearly significant for urban governance, planning and tourism development. Contemporary urban imaging strategies are important elements in policy responses to the social and economic problems associated with deindustrialisation and economic restructuring, urban renewal, multiculturalism, social integration and control (Roche 1992, 2000). Indeed, the imaging of the city in order to attract the middle-class employment market, mobile capital and visitors, and the associated focus on the economic benefits of tourism have only reinforced the idea of the city as a kind of commodity to be marketed.

The principal aims of urban imaging strategies are to attract tourism expenditure, to generate employment in the tourist industry, to foster positive images for potential investors in the region, often by 're-imaging' previous negative perceptions (e.g. the attempted transformation of the image of Sheffield from an 'industrial' to a 'modern' city through the hosting of sports events), and to provide an urban environment which will attract and retain the interest of professionals and white-collar workers, particularly in 'clean' service industries such as tourism and communications. Urban imaging processes are characterised by some or all of the following:

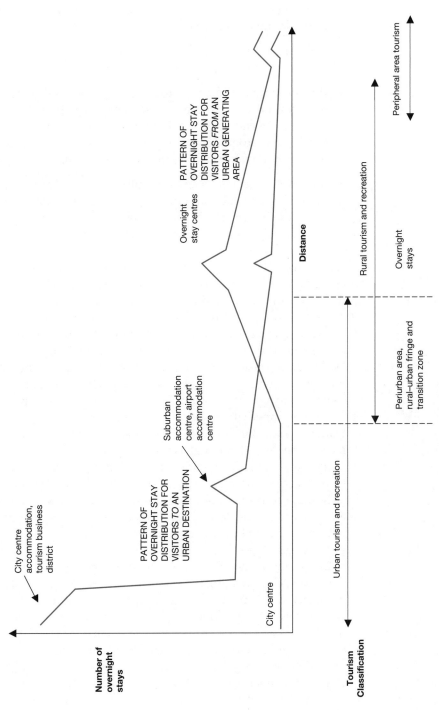

Figure 7.1   Distribution of overnight stays in an urban region and its hinterland

- the development of a critical mass of visitor attractions and facilities, including new buildings/prestige centres (e.g. the Inner Harbor development in Baltimore, Darling Harbour in Sydney and the dockland redevelopment in London);

- hallmark events (e.g. Olympic Games, World Fairs and the hosting of Grand Prix and major street car races);

- the development of urban tourism strategies and policies often associated with new or renewed organisation and development of city marketing (e.g. in New Zealand the Wellington City Council's 'Absolutely Positively Wellington' promotional campaigns as well as a restructuring of city organisations to develop an integrated tourism, event and retailing agency); and

- the development of leisure and cultural services and projects to support the marketing and tourism effort (e.g. the creation and renewal of museums and art galleries and the hosting of art festivals, often as part of a comprehensive cultural tourism strategy for a region or city).

According to Harvey (1989a, 1989b), imaging a city through the organisation of spectacular urban space is a mechanism for attracting capital and people (of the right sort) in a period of intense inter-urban competition and urban entrepreneurialism in which 'even whole built environments became centrepieces of urban spectacle and display (Harvey 1987, p. 276). For example, Harvey (1990) argued that the redevelopment of the inner harbour in Baltimore in the United States was a response to the social unrest of the late 1960s in which what was initially a space of civil unity gradually became a space of commercialism, conspicuous consumption and property development.

The new inner-city space of leisure consumption is reflective not only of particular values but also of particular interests. Values and interests are inextricably linked: the 'new' civic values reflect those of the local elites which influence urban redevelopment and planning processes. However, in focusing on one set of economic and social interests, other community interests, particularly those of traditional inner-city residents of lower socio-economic status, are increasingly neglected, given that their lifestyles do not, arguably, mesh with those desired by the mobile leisure classes.

The creation of a 'bourgeois playground' (Mommaas and van der Poel 1989, p. 263) in the name of economic progress may create considerable tension in the urban policy-making environment. For example, the integration of tourism functions in the inner city may contest with traditionally different functions such as lower socio-economic group residential areas. The redevelopment of the inner city in terms of visitor attractiveness can lead to the transformation of the community-based organisation of local spaces and populations into an individual or family-based organisation, or what Castells (1983) characterised as the 'disconnection of people from spatial forms'. The implications of the transformation of the core of many cities for lower socio-economic groups is amplified by the reallocation of local state resources from social welfare to imaging functions, because at the same time as the inner city is being promoted and developed as a leisure resource public spending on social programmes has also decreased.

According to some commentators, the above situation has been related to a crisis of the local state in developed countries (Bramham et al. 1989). The crisis of the local state is bound up in a crisis of legitimacy in which certain groups in society, particularly the powerless and disadvantaged in the inner cities, have become disenchanted with the existing political arrangements which have failed to deliver needed social, economic and infrastructural improvements in inner-city areas. In addition, it may be asked whether city centres, the focal point of the new urban tourism, are gaining resources at the expense of the interests of those in the suburbs. A second crisis is what may be termed a 'fiscal crisis', in which the local state has been faced with increased demands for both welfare services and local economic development while at the same time having a declining tax base and/or receiving less funds in real terms from central government.

The two crises are intimately related and may be regarded as two sides of the same coin, with the reallocation of scarce financial resources only serving to exacerbate the frustration of certain groups in society to achieve desired social and welfare ends. However, while many civic governments claim that by encouraging the development of visitor attractions they will also be creating new employment, it should be recognised that many of the jobs do not go to those who were most affected by such developments in the first place because they often do not have the requisite skills or, if they do gain employment, it will often be at the most unskilled and menial levels. Nevertheless, it may be argued that the so-called crisis of the local state has not eventuated in ways envisaged in the 1980s simply because those who most seek the desired welfare ends are also those least able to influence local state policy-making. Therefore, while the real issues of inequalities in society and the plight of the homeless, the poor and the unemployed remain in many urban areas, the problem has been defined away in terms of the advocacy of certain growth and place competition strategies, as well as the philosophical translocation of responsibility for such a situation from the collective to the individuals themselves.

Large-scale redevelopment projects and tourist events are almost universally upheld as a component of urban imaging programmes because of their supposed economic and social benefits. Nevertheless, it has long been recognised that large-scale tourist developments also 'create a political and economic context within which the hallmark event is used as an excuse to overrule planning legislation and participatory planning processes, and to sacrifice local places along the way' (Dovey 1989, pp. 79–80). Despite the potential for negative economic and social impacts on certain sections of the community, hallmark events are almost invariably seen by urban elites, politicians and governments as beneficial at both collective and individual levels because of their ability to promote appropriate images of places and attract investment and tourism (C.M. Hall 1992a). Events may therefore act to strengthen dominant ideologies or further individual interests, legitimise hegemonic relationships and change the meaning and structure of place. Furthermore, events can even be used to legitimise what would otherwise be unpopular decisions, particularly in the area of urban development because of the climate of urgency they can create within the planning and development process. Indeed, Law (1993, p. 107) observed that the mega-event 'acts as a catalyst for change by persuading people to work together around a common objective and as a fast track for obtaining extra finance and getting building projects off the drawing board'. Although, as he went on to note, '[t]his is not without its problems, since some would argue that it gives priority to development issues over those of welfare' (Law 1993, p. 107).

Perception by some groups, such as conservation, ratepayers or resident action organisations, of the prospect of unwanted impacts, such as resident displacement and architectural pollution, may give rise to interest group politics and a call for greater public participation in the planning process. However, the importance and prestige attached to hallmark events by government often mean a commitment to 'fast track' planning practices which ignore community resistance to either the hosting of the event or the construction of associated infrastructure (C.M. Hall 1989a, 1989b, 1992a; Roche 1992). Given the importance of events to contemporary urban tourism, it is to this form of temporary attraction that we will now turn.

Events

Tourist events, otherwise referred to as hallmark, special events or mega-events, are major, large-scale fairs, festivals, expositions, cultural and sporting events (Table 7.1) which are held on either a regular or a one-off basis, which often require a substantial financial input of public funding and/or support and which serve as major mechanisms for physical redevelopment and/or re-imaging strategies (C.M. Hall 1992a; Roche 1992) (see Chapter 4). While the term 'mega-event' is often used interchangeably with the terms 'hallmark' and 'special' event (e.g. see Getz 1991; C.M. Hall 1992a), mega-events may be defined separately (Table 7.2). Ritchie and Hu's (1987) categorisation of a mega-event corresponds to Ritchie's earlier definition of hallmark events, while the 1987 Congress of the Association Internationale d'Experts Scientifiques du Tourisme resolved that mega-events could be defined in three different ways: by volume (1 million visits), by a money measure (Can.$500 million, DM 750 million, FFr 2500 million), and in psychological terms (by reputation: 'Must see', '*Muss miterlebt werden*', '*Il faut absolument voir*') (Marris 1987, p. 3). Nevertheless, while substantial disagreement remains over the definition and interpretation of what constitutes a mega-event, it is apparent that several key and related factors occur in the study of large-scale events: redevelopment, imaging and place promotion, and their impacts (Hall 1996a) (Table 7.3).

Mega-events have assumed a key role in urban and regional tourism marketing and promotion strategies (Roche 1994; Page and Hall 2003). Their

Table 7.1   A classification of hallmark tourist events

Classification	Examples and locations
Religious and sacred events	The Haj (Mecca) Christmas in the Holy Land (Bethlehem and Jerusalem) Papal tours RamLila
Cultural events Carnivals and festivals	Mardi Gras (Rio de Janiero) Spoleto Festival (Spoleto and Melbourne) Gay and Lesbian Mardi Gras (Sydney) Festival of the Pacific Oktoberfest (Munich, Waterloo) British royal weddings (London) New year celebrations
Historical milestones	United States Bicentenary (1977) Australian Bicentenary (1988) 500th Anniversary of the Sailing of Columbus (1992) Celebration of new millennium (2000)
Commercial events and expositions	World and International Expositions Agricultural shows World Travel Fair
Sports events	Olympic Games (Summer and Winter) Commonwealth Games Pan-American Games World Cup Soccer World Cup Athletics World Cup Rugby Union World Cup Cricket Australian Football League Grand Final (Melbourne) National Football League (NFL) Superbowl Baseball World Series Football Association (FA) Cup Final (Wembley) The America's Cup Formula 1 Grand Prix racing Melbourne Cup (Melbourne) The Grand National (Aintree)
Political events	Party conventions International Monetary Fund/World Bank conferences Visits by the British monarchy Expansion of the European Union
Conferences	Rotary International conference International Geographical Union Congress

Table 7.2   Characteristics of events

Market	Major level of public financial involvement	Organisation and leadership	Examples	Associated descriptions of event
International	National	Establishment of special event authorities by central government	Olympic Games, World Fairs, World Cup soccer, World Cup rugby	Mega-event, special event, hallmark event
International/National	National/Regional	Coordination between various government levels, often using inter-governmental committees. Leadership role shared between central and regional government	Grand Prix, America's Cup, Commonwealth Games, World Cup cricket, Superbowl, Australian Rules, grand final	Special event, hallmark event
National/Limited International	National/Regional	Limited local involvement, leadership role shared by regional and central government	Touring international art exhibitions, cricket test match, soccer international, baseball world series	Hallmark event
National/Regional	National/Regional	Consultative government role only	Arts and cultural festivals, such as Festival of Adelaide, Grey Cup Canada	Hallmark event
Regional/Limited National	Regional/Local	Major role for regional tourism bodies, local business and government	Arts and cultural festivals such as the Festival of Sydney	Hallmark event
Regional/Local	Local	Leadership and organisation provided from within host community	Local festival, e.g. Shaw Festival, Festival of Perth	Sometimes referred to as community events
Local (event designed for local consumption)	Minimal local government expenditure, social rather than economic considerations	Local control	Community fêtes and celebrations, local festival, e.g. Dunedin Festival	Community events

Sources: Hall 1989a, 1989b, 1992a; Page and Hall 2003

Table 7.3 Potential positive and negative impacts of events on host communities

Type of impact	Positive	Negative
Economic	• Increased expenditures • Creation of employment • Increase in labour supply • Increase in standard of living • Increase in property values and rents	• Inflated prices during event • Real estate speculation • Failure to attract tourists • Better alternative investments • Inadequate capital • Inadequate estimation of long-term costs of event, including facility use • Locals unable to access event because of cost or restricted ticket availability
Tourism/Commercial	• Increased awareness of the region as a travel/tourism destination • Increased knowledge concerning the potential for investment and commercial activity in the region • Creation of new attractions and accommodation • Increase in accessibility	• Acquisition of a poor reputation as a result of inadequate facilities, improper practices or inflated prices • Negative reactions from existing enterprises due to the possibility of new competition for local human resources and state assistance
Physical/Environmental	• Construction of new facilities • Improvement of local infrastructure and facilities • Heritage preservation • Environmental clean up	• Environmental damage • Changes in natural processes • Architectural pollution • Destruction of heritage • Overcrowding
Social/Cultural	• Increase in level of local interest and participation in types of activity associated with event • Strengthening of regional values and traditions • Greater awareness of human rights	• Commercialisation of activities which may be of a personal or private nature • Modification of the nature of the event to accommodate tourism • Changes in community structure • Potential increase in crime • Social dislocation • Acceleration of gentrification process • Potential human rights abuse
Psychological	• Increased local pride and community spirit • Increased awareness of non-local perceptions	• Tendency towards defensive attitudes concerning host regions • Possibility of hostility of host community towards visitors
Political/Administrative	• Enhanced international recognition of region and values • Development of skills among planners.	• Economic exploitation of local population to satisfy ambitions of growth coalition • Distortion of nature of event to reflect values of elite • Inability to cope or achieve aims • Increase in administrative costs • Use of event to legitimate unpopular decisions • Legitimation of particular ideology

Sources: Hall 1989a, 1989b, 1992a, 1997a, 1997b; Olds 1998; Page and Hall 2003

primary function is to provide the host nation, region and/or city with an opportunity to secure high prominence in the tourist and business marketplace (Ritchie and Smith 1991). Mega-events are therefore a significant ingredient in the desire of many cities to promote themselves not just to attract tourists and generate employment, but also to attract investment. Events and their physical infrastructure become part of the cultural capital of places as they seek to compete with other destinations. Mega-events are also extremely significant not just because of their visitor component but also because they may leave behind legacies which will have an impact on the host community far greater than the period in which the event took place. When asked as to the 'most likely legacy' of the Victoria Commonwealth Games, a readers' poll in *Monday Magazine* ranked debt, new pool, higher taxes, increased tourism, and higher real estate prices as being the Games' legacies (McCaw,1994). Such an assessment may well be quite astute (Hall 1996a). Mega-events such as the Olympic Games or World Fairs have been associated with large-scale public expenditure, the construction of facilities and infrastructure, and the regeneration of urban areas which may have substantial impacts on local communities (Hughes 1993; Law 1993; Mount and Leroux 1994). For example, the Olympic planners for the 2004 Athens Summer Olympics stated that overall costs had exceeded the US$5.6 billion budget. According to the *Financial Times* (2004, p. 4) 'some analysts forecast the debt could weigh heavily on the Greek economy for years'. Nevertheless, the Olympics is a major opportunity for place promotion. For example, in April 2004 the Market Promotion Conference on Olympic Economy, organised by Invest Beijing International and also the Beijing Engineering Consulting Company and sponsored by 14 Beijing municipal and regional authorities, was advertised as 'New Beijing, New Olympic Games: Business opportunities to China and the rest of the world', with readers being asked 'Do you want to make the most of the business opportunities created by the Olympic Games? Do you want to know how to do business in Beijing?' (Invest Beijing 2004, p. 15).

The 'Olympic Games are concerned not only with athletics. They are also about politics, ego, and the compulsion of cities to prove themselves' (Thomas 1984, p. 67). Moreover, it has been argued that the spectacles, such as the Olympic Games and World Fairs, have come to symbolise the power of commodity relations and global capital within modern society (e.g. Debord 1973). For example, the 1984 Los Angeles Olympics were as much a celebration of American capitalism and the processes of capitalist accumulation as the 1980 Moscow Olympics attempted to show the supposed success of state Marxism to the Western world. Cities compete to 'win' the rights to host the Olympics regardless of who incurs the costs. Therefore, given the attention paid to sports tourism and events, we will now turn specifically to the relationship of sports events to urban regeneration.

Sports Tourism and Urban Regeneration

The issue of regeneration has become a major theme for urban policy and planning over the last three decades in much of the industrialised world. The impacts of seemingly ongoing economic restructuring, globalisation, and technological and policy change have meant that the basis for many urban economies has undergone fundamental shifts within which certain areas have high levels of social exclusion and deprivation. The change in the urban economy has therefore led policy-makers to rethink the means by which employment may be created and some of the impacts of restructuring overcome. Much of this is undertaken under the rubric of regeneration.

Both sport and tourism have long been perceived as urban regeneration mechanisms (C.M. Hall 1992a; Law 1992, 1993; Page 1995; Page and Hall 2003). For example, sport is often seen as a mechanism to overcome anti-social problems and youth delinquency (e.g. Sugden and Yiannakis 1982; Purdy and Richard 1983; Hastad et al. 1984; Coalter 1988; Glyptis 1989; Tsuchiya 1996; Witt and Crompton 1996; Institute of Leisure and Amenity Management 1999), a mechanism which has proven enormously influential on government policy-making at all levels. Typical of this perspective is that of the UK Policy Action Team 10 report, which suggested that sport (and the arts) can contribute to 'neighbourhood renewal by improving communities' "performance" on four key indicators – health, crime, employment and education' (Department of Culture, Media and Sport 1999, p. 22).

Sport is often unquestionably regarded as playing a positive role with respect to community development (McDonald and Tungatt 1992; Coalter and Allison 1996; Keller et al. 1998; Long and Sanderson 1998). This received wisdom has meant that sport has often been integrated into regeneration strategies in the form of both facilities and infrastructure and programmes to encourage participation. For example, the statement by the Wirral Partnership (2001) in the UK that '[s]port brings with it benefits for the economy, for the area's health and provides a positive focus for individual and community motivation' is commonly held among state agencies. Nevertheless, the issue of the real benefits that sports bring to disadvantaged areas is increasingly under question (Coalter and Allison 1996; Long and Sanderson 1998), particularly as unemployment and low income are at the root of social exclusion and urban deprivation rather than whether or not people are good at sport (Roche and Annesley 1998; Coalter et al. 2000).

With respect to the employment possibilities of sports-related development, a number of reports have suggested that such employment can contribute to 'neighbourhood renewal' (e.g. Department of Culture, Media and Sport 1999) and community development (e.g. McDonald and Tungatt 1992). However, there is little research on the *regenerative* potential of investment in sport, or the long-term benefits to local communities of sports-led investment strategies (Gratton 1999; Coalter et al. 2000). For example, existing economic impact studies of local areas (Henley Centre for Forecasting 1989) have simply estimated the value of the sports industry, rather than addressed issues of regeneration *per se* (Leisure Industries Research Centre 1997). Similarly, Coalter et al. (2000, p. 6.4) report on a study of the economic importance of sport in the northern region of Lincoln and Stone which concluded that 'although many claims are made for the contribution that this sector makes in terms of economic welfare, these are frequently based on assertion rather than concrete evidence'. Formal evaluation of sport development and its contribution to regeneration is generally not forthcoming and, where they are conducted, the findings are often not encouraging in terms of the original expectations for sports-generated economic development (e.g. see C.M. Hall 1992a, 2001a; Crompton 1995; Gratton 1999; Page and Hall 2003). Despite such misgivings, a number of cities have embarked on large-scale sporting developments associated with regeneration strategies, usually in relation to the hosting of major sports events such as the Olympics (e.g. Sydney, Barcelona), the Commonwealth Games (e.g. Kuala Lumpur, Manchester, Melbourne), and the World Student Games (e.g. Sheffield), as well as large cultural and industrial events such as World Fairs. For example, Manchester has positioned itself as a sports city in terms of its own regeneration strategy, in competition with nearby Sheffield, with the development of the Eastlands Sports City to host the Commonwealth Games, followed by the redevelopment of the main stadium to host Manchester City Football Club (Manchester City Council 2001).

Sports-related tourism is typically perceived as a key component for the effectiveness of sports-related regeneration strategies, associated as they are to the re-imaging of locations in order to attract and retain capital and people. Undoubtedly, the 'intangibles' of sport have a powerful influence on decision-makers with respect to the role of sport in economic development (Baade 1996; Whitson and Macintosh 1996; Page and Hall 2003). Baim (1994) examined financial data from 15 subsidised stadia in the United States and found that, with very few exceptions, the sole rational justification for stadia built to receive or keep a sports franchise revolve around the external benefits (e.g. civic pride, tourism and leisure time options) brought to a city. However, the costs to the taxpayer varied widely depending upon the lease negotiations for each facility, noting that the smaller the market size, the more likely that the market accrued external benefits. Nevertheless, such a position could be negated because the per-capita subsidy tends to be higher, and the lease terms far more generous to teams from smaller cities because of the substantial competition between medium-sized markets to attract sporting teams (Whitford 1993). For example, the Los Angeles Rams moved from Anaheim Stadium in Orange County, California – where they were losing $6 million a year – to St Louis' new municipally funded $276 million domed downtown stadium for the 1995 season. In exchange, the Rams organisation received a stadium lease with rent of only $250,000 for the whole season, $13 million in moving expenses, half of game day expenses paid by the city, a separate practice facility, all the revenues from boxes, club seats and regular tickets, guaranteed sales of deluxe seats, most of the advertising and concession profit, and $27 million to pay off the lease in Anaheim (Sickman 1995). Indeed, a common characteristic of studies of the economic impacts of sports stadia and facilities and the events that fill them is that their positive effects are usually grossly overestimated (Burns et al. 1986; C.M. Hall 1992a; Cromption 1995; Economists at Large 1997).

The potential attraction of sports tourism for urban areas is illustrated by the case of sports development in Indianapolis, USA. According to Rawn (1990), sports events helped create service jobs in Indianapolis which make up for employment loss in the manufacturing sector. However, in a later analysis of the investments, policies and strategy behind Indianapolis' US$172.6 million sports-related economic development strategy, Rosentraub et al. (1994) determined that the sports strategy actually had little impact on development and economic growth in Indianapolis versus other middle-sized cities in the region (Rosentraub 1996). Similar to Manchester and Sheffield in the UK, the Indianapolis strategy entailed substantial municipal capital investment in five major facilities, a National Institute for Fitness and Sports and the hosting of seven governing bodies of sport. However, although the strategy generated a substantial employment in the service sector and associated spin-offs from attendance at sporting events, Rosenbtraub et al. (1994) calculated that sports-related employment accounted for only 0.32% of all employment in the Indianapolis economy (an increase of 0.03%) and the sports-related payrolls accounted for less than 0.5% of the total payrolls of all Indianapolis businesses. Rosenbtraub et al. (1994, p. 238) concluded that while not minimising the publicity that sports achieved for the city, investments in other sectors may have generated better returns: 'Given how small sports is as an industry and the low pay associated with the numerous service sector jobs created by sports activities, sports is not a prudent vehicle around which a development or redevelopment effort should be organised.'

It is therefore perhaps not surprising that in their review of event-specific evaluations, Coalter et al. (2000, p. 6.7) concluded that 'there is little evidence about the medium to long-term economic effects of such sports event-led economic regeneration strategies.... In particular, there is a lack of available data on the *regenerative impact* of sports investments on local communities.' Nevertheless, despite such caution, sport and event tourism continues to be integral to regeneration strategies. For example, as part of its regional strategy the Northwest Development Agency (NWDA) in the UK states that a long-term programme of arts, sport and cultural events will help 'with engendering pride and raising aspirations. It brings in and helps to retain the more skilled and talented members of the community – people whose leadership skills are needed to sustain the capacity of every community' (NWDA 2000, p. 34). More significantly for tourism, they later go on to claim: 'Quality infrastructure for sport, arts and museums can help to build the region's image and is part of the package needed to attract and retain those with the highest levels of talent and skill. These facilities are major tourist and visitor attractions too' (NWDA 2000, p. 50). Undoubtedly, facilities can generate employment, particularly through the construction phase, and may generate some employment in the longer term, though in the case of event employment much of it will be part time or casual and low-skilled, and integral to the successful contribution of job recreation will be the extent to which facilities have a policy to train and employ people from within the target area.

An example of the use of sport and sports tourism for urban regeneration was that of the bid by Cape Town to host the 2004 Olympics. The bid was unsuccessful but nevertheless significant as it explicitly linked the hosting of a mega-event to development needs (Page and Hall 2003). The Cape Town bid sought to add a fourth 'pillar' of 'human development' to the Olympic Movement's pillars of sport, culture and the environment. The Bid Book argued that every aspect of hosting the Olympics 'should contribute to the upliftment and quality of life of the people of the city ... we place special emphasis on our disadvantaged communities' (in Hiller 2000, p. 441). Rather than merely focus on urban regeneration through the provision of new infrastructure and an increase in city profile, the Cape Town bid sought to be transformative in a social as well as economic sense. Therefore, the Cape Town bid introduced two innovative ideas into the role of hosting the Olympics. First, the Olympics would serve as a catalyst for improving the social and economic conditions of the historically disadvantaged. Second, they would act to redesign the apartheid city and create new linkages between people and cultures. The bid aimed to achieve these objectives through a number of measures (Hiller 2000; Page and Hall 2003):

- *A transformational catalyst accelerating change*: using the Olympics as a mechanism to effect immediate short-term change in the physical and social well-being of the city as well as longer-term impacts.

- *The construction of facilities in disadvantaged areas*: of the 42 activity sites for competitions in the Cape Town region, seven were planned for disadvantaged areas. However, 66 of the 77 proposed training sites were planned for disadvantaged areas, thereby creating a substantial permanent resource in those urban areas most substantially impacted by the legacy of apartheid.

- *Facilities as 'kick-start' initiatives*: the development of new facilities and the upgrading of some existing ones were seen as a mechanism for community revitalisation as part of a wider redevelopment strategy to attract new housing, retailing and investment to disadvantaged areas.

- *Quality sports facilities supporting community sports programmes*: sport and recreation provision was seen as a means of improving the quality of life as well as reducing crime and improving community pride.

- *A human resource opportunity*: it was projected that 90 000 permanent jobs would be created in South Africa as a result of hosting the Olympics.

- *Contribution to the stock of affordable housing*: it was expected that the Olympic developments, including the athletes' and media accommodation, would make a small though significant contribution to the housing stock in Cape Town.

- *Support for small business*: the bid explicitly sought to assist small businesses through an economic empowerment policy which offered 50% of its business transactions to enterprises from previously marginalised communities.

- *Urban integration of the transport system*: 70% of the transport system development funds were earmarked for projects that would directly benefit disadvantaged areas by linking those areas more effectively into the wider urban structure.

- *Community consultation*: the Olympic bid group explicitly sought to involve the community in the bid process through a variety of mechanisms, including local Olympic Steering Committees, a Community Olympic Forum and a Strategic Environmental Assessment process.

As Hiller (2000, p. 455) noted, 'the idea of harnessing a mega-event to a broader urban agenda that moves beyond the interests of finance capital, developers, inner-city reclamation and the tourist city is a relatively new idea. This is especially so given the preoccupation with winning IOC votes internationally and the minimization of local costs and dissent'. However, it is notable that Cape Town did not win its bid (coming third in the final vote). Therefore, the Cape Town Bid Company's argument that in awarding the bid to Cape Town, the International Olympic Committee would have demonstrated that the Olympic Movement was not 'beholden to gigantism and commercial exploitation' and was instead 'devoted to the progress of all people and must therefore also offer opportunity to those still struggling for their place in the economic sun' (quoted in Hiller 2000, p. 442) holds considerable weight in judging why events are located where they are. Nevertheless, what is also significant in the Cape Town bid is that it demonstrated that the hosting of sporting events can be utilised as much for the broader public good as for the regeneration of cities as places of consumption, entertainment and leisure (Hannigan 1995; Hiller 2000; Page and Hall 2003). The Cape Town bid, as with bids by Toronto to host the Summer Olympics in 2008 (Hall 2001), also reflects the growing recognition that the hosting of mega-events, as perhaps with all large-scale urban regeneration projects, needs to be perceived as part of a broader social contract (Page and Hall 2003). Indeed, one of the most significant aspects of large-scale urban regeneration strategies, such as mega-sports events, is that they often exclude participation from urban social democracy while at the same time requiring such large public investments that, if they do not work as revitalisation strategies, then their actual and opportunity costs are substantially modified (Page and Hall 2003). Reflecting Law's (1993, p. 23) observation: 'Urban policies are concerned with both winning economic growth for a city and regenerating the core areas, goals which may not always be coincident.'

The potential contribution of sports tourism to urban regeneration therefore needs to be seen in context. Municipal regeneration strategies frequently see sport and tourism and the relationships between them as integral to regional development. Benefits are usually perceived in terms of infrastructure development and the hosting of sporting events which utilise such infrastructure which then contribute to both employment and the generation of a positive image which, in turn, may then assist in attracting and retaining capital, employment and people. Sports facilities can make an important contribution to the physical infrastructure of communities, providing a social focus for a community and affecting people's perception of their neighbourhood and can also contribute to the quality of life of communities (Coalter et al. 2000). Nevertheless, the contribution of sports infrastructure and sports and events tourism in the wider context is open to substantial debate, plagued as it is by the often gross overestimation of the economic benefits of sport tourism both in the short and longer term. In particular, the opportunity costs of investing in sport as opposed to other redevelopment options in terms of employment generation are rarely undertaken. However, as Hall (2005, in press) observed, sport is extremely hard to argue against. The inherent belief of many that sport is good for you, makes for better citizens, creates pride in the community and generates a positive image is hard to overcome. This belief and a relative lack of criticism mean that in terms of urban regeneration many large-scale projects and events are going to continue to be funded as it provides opportunities for politicians and civic boosters to cut ribbons, reveal plaques and be seen with sporting winners. Yet, the reality is that urban regeneration requires much more than just sport and tourism to generate social and economic capital and create jobs (Page and Hall 2003).

Tourism Insight: 'The Biggest and Most Costly Mega-Project in the History of Toronto'

In the late 1990s Toronto made an unsuccessful bid to host the 2008 Summer Olympic Games. Toronto's bid, as with its previously unsuccessful bid for the 1996 Games, was built on a waterfront redevelopment strategy which sought to revitalise the harbour area through the development of an integrated sports, leisure, retail and housing complex. However, as in the case of many other mega-events with substantial infrastructure requirements, questions can be asked about the process by which the event is developed and as to who actually benefits from hosting the event.

One of the most striking features of the 2008 Toronto bid was the extent to which information on the bid was either unavailable or provided only limited detail on the costs associated with hosting the event. Toronto was fortunate to have a non-profit public interest coalition, Bread Not Circuses (BNC), actively campaign for more information on the bid proposal and for government to address social concerns. BNC argued that given the cost of both bidding for and hosting the Olympics, the bidding process must be subject to public scrutiny. 'Any Olympic bid worth its salt will not only withstand public scrutiny, but will be improved by a rigorous and open public process' (Bread Not Circuses 1998a). BNC also argued that Toronto City Council should make its support for an Olympic bid conditional on:

- the development and execution of a suitable process that addresses financial, social and environmental concerns, ensures an effective public participation process (including intervenor funding), and includes a commitment to the development of a detailed series of Olympic standards. A time-frame of one year from the date of the vote to support the bid should be set to ensure that the plans for the participation process are taken seriously;

- a full and open independent accounting of the financial costs of bidding and staging the Games; and
- a full and open independent social impact assessment of the Games.

From a public participation perspective, other elements promoted by BNC included:

- a full, fair and democratic process to involve all of the people of Toronto in the development and review of the Olympic bid;
- an Olympic Intervenor Fund to allow interested groups to participate effectively in the public scrutiny of the bid;
- an independent environmental assessment of the 2008 Games, and strategies should be developed to resolve specific concerns; and
- the development of a series of financial, social and environmental standards governing the 2008 Games, similar to the Toronto Olympic Commitment adopted by the City Council in September of 1989 (Bread Not Circuses 1998a).

In addition to the factors identified by BNC, it should also be noted that the city's previous experiences with stadia and events raised significant questions about the public liability for any development. For example, in 1982, the then Metropolitan Toronto Chairman Paul Godfrey promised that Toronto's SkyDome, a multipurpose sports complex used for baseball and Canadian football, could be built for Can.$75 million, with no public debt. However, the final price of the development was over Can.$600 million, with taxpayers having to pay more than half. BNC also noted that even the previous Toronto bid costs were 60% over budget, 'with a great deal of spending coming in the final, overheated days of the bidding war. . . . There was no public control, and little public accountability, over the '96 bid', while 'There was virtually no assessment of the social, environmental and financial impact of the Games' (Bread Not Circuses 1998c).

For the 2008 bid BNC lobbied various city councillors on whether or not they would support a bid. Only one councillor out of 55 voted against the Olympic bid proposal even though they only had a 20-page background information document about the proposal. Thus, when city councillors voted on the project, they did not have:

- an estimate of the cost of bidding for the Games;
- a list of the names of the backers of 'BidCo', the private corporation that was heading up the Olympic bid;
- a reliable estimate of the cost of staging the Games;
- a plan for the public participation process, the environmental review process or the social impact assessment process; and
- a detailed financial strategy for the Games.

Such a situation clearly had public interest organisations, such as BNC, worried as to the economic, environmental and social costs of a successful bid. The history of mega-events such as the Olympic Games indicates that such a situation was not new (Olds 1998). The International Olympic Committee (IOC) have already sought to ensure that the Games are environmentally friendly, perhaps it is now time to see that they are socially and economically friendly and build wider assessment of the social impacts of the Games into the planning process as a mandatory component of the bidding process. In this vein, Bread Not Circuses (1998b), in a letter to the IOC President, requested 'that the IOC, which sets the rules for the bidding process, take an active responsibility in ensuring that the local processes in the bidding stage are effective and democratic' and specifically address concerns regarding the 'financial and social costs of the Olympic Games'. They proposed:

1. An international network of human rights and housing rights groups, academics and experts, NGOs (including local groups in cities that have bid for and/or hosted the Games).
2. A set of standards regarding forced evictions, etc., would be developed and adopted by the network.
3. A plan to build international support for the standards, including identification of sympathetic IOC, National Olympic Committee and other sports officials, would be developed and implemented.
4. The IOC would be approached with the request that the standards be incorporated into the Olympic Charter, Host City Contracts and other documents of the IOC (Bread Not Circuses 1998b).

Such a social charter for the Olympics would undoubtedly greatly assist in making the Games more place-friendly and perhaps even improve the image of the IOC. However, the books of the Olympic bids have never been fully opened for public scrutiny, while there has been no set of social standards established for the Olympics. Toronto was unsuccessful in its bid and the IOC continues to try to repair its tarnished image in the aftermath of questions about the means by which it selects host cities and runs its own activities. Nevertheless, in the meantime, another Canadian city, Vancouver, has won the right to host the 2010 Winter Olympics over Pyeongchang in South Korea and Salzburg in Austria. Yet even here questions are being asked about the benefits of hosting the event. As *The Economist* reports the bid: 'Nor do many Vancouverites, except hotel and restaurant owners, imagine the games will do them good. In opponents' minds, the Olympics mean mostly debt and higher taxes; Montreal, after all, has only just paid off its debt from the games it hosted in 1976' (*The Economist* 2003, p. 37). Nevertheless, the British Columbia government has engaged in an extensive promotional campaign on the back of the successful Olympic bid. For example, in March 2004 Canada's national newspapers, *The Globe and Mail* and the *National Post*, featured full-page advertisements with the copy: 'Spirit of 2010. British Columbia be here. In 2010, British Columbia will host the world for the Olympic and Paralympic Winter Games. Today, you can see what we live and breathe. It's the spirit of discovery, enterprise and opportunity.' The advertisements highlighted the province's business environment and noted that the budget was balanced 'with future surpluses on the horizon'. The advertisements also included claims that British Columbia leads the nation in terms of:

- lowest personal income tax rates;
- highest job growth rate;
- best housing growth;
- first in small business confidence;
- top destination for investor migrants; and
- longest life expectancy in nation.

See the British Columbia website: www.gov.bc.ca, also Bread not Circuses: www.breadnotcircuses.org

Cities: Just Commodities for Consumption?

Everything now seems to be a commodity available for consumption. Of course, it is not. Instead, it has to be a commodity of a certain type with a given symbolic value which reinforces preferred lifestyles and representations of identity and which can be 'bundled' by place promoters. These commodities are not evenly distributed in urban space. They are presently disproportionately located in the inner-city areas, with many of the outer suburbs forgotten by those who seek to re-image the city, even though that is where the majority of residents live. These commodities not only include the typical developments of re-imaging strategies, for example stadia, convention centres and retail outlets, but increasingly also include concentrations of ethnic populations which provide 'colour', particularly with respect to ethnic foods, culture and restaurants.

Given the interrelationship of identity, image and urban place promotion, it is not surprising that the association of particular and different ('the other') ethnic, cultural and migrant groups with particular places and locations has been commodified for the purposes of tourism promotion. This can assume several forms, whether it be with respect to promoting the availability of national and regional cuisines or the commodification of entire locales, such as Chinatown, Little Italies, or ethnic and national identities. For example, Julesrosette (1994) argued, with respect to Afro-Antillian Paris, that the transformation of the locales of everyday life into tourist sights connected with the identity of a particular foreign ethnic population is part of the process of postmodern simulation in tourism. Cultural identities may be explicitly utilised in the branding of places at particular scales, for example Scotland, as well as becoming integrated with tourism policy in order to achieve domestic political aims, as in the case of Singapore (Chang 1997; Hall and Oehlers 1999). However, the role of migrant communities in these situations is actually problematic as the utilisation of the commodified ethnicity of migrant communities is dependent on contemporary political realities and sensitivities. In some locations ethnicity is only commodified as a heritage product (with contemporary ethnic realities ignored), in other circumstances commodification focuses on more recent migrant settlement, while in many jurisdictions the migrant other is ignored as tourist product.

Tourism Insight: Migrant Populations: Spatial Confinement, Acquiesence and Commodification

While access to international business networks, international business skills, and new markets is one dimension of the desire of growth coalitions to incorporate some migrant communities from a place promotion perspective, such measures may not be sufficient to attract large numbers of tourists from outside the social networks of the migrant groups. Instead, migrant culture needs to be commodified. This can be done through several means, such as the hosting of events and festivals, or support for artistic groups. However, the most attractive option for tourism promotion purposes is to be able to identify certain accessible locations or places that have identifiable 'otherness' associated with migrant groups. For this to occur there needs to have been substantial migrant co-location in inner-city areas or in large suburban hubs at least. Moreover, they need to be shop-front visible. Large numbers of migrants from given populations in suburban areas is not a visitor attraction; a high street or several blocks with characteristics that may be associated with migrant populations is.

Such spatially identifiable areas may have historical associations with migrant populations, such as that often associated with Chinese ghettos, only to be later rebranded as Chinatowns. More often than not their continued existence may actually be encouraged through planning regulations and promotional funding which maintain such locations of otherness over time. Such locations may also become established as a result of principles of business advantage at the level of the firm which takes advantage of the presence of migrant communities. Over time, as such communities become increasingly dispersed over urban space, locational advantage may be maintained only for some specific types of business, particularly restaurants, whose products are now consumed by a much larger population. Indeed, many restaurant districts around the world (excepting those of the malls and the central business district) tend to have their origin in the migrant ghettos. Such identifiable locations serve not only as attractors to other urban residents but also as locations for the tourist lifestyle consumer, while their continued existence over time may reflect something of Gans' (1979) notion of symbolic ethnicity.

Migrant group acquiescence to the process of tourist commodification is

Plate 7.3   Chinatown in Victoria, Canada. Although the precinct has a long association with the Chinese ethnic population the commodification of space through the use of a gateway as a marker is primarily oriented towards tourism and leisure oriented consumption. (see the Tourism Victoria website at www.tourismvictoria.com)

also an important part of the place promotion process as conflict is anathema to tourism development. Often the 'local colour' provided by migrant restaurants and shops, as well as people, will be utilised in tourism promotion activities without the local community being immediately aware that it is happening. However, for longer-term commodification and promotion success migrant communities will need to be supportive. This usually occurs through migrant group associations and migrant business people (one should also note that this often tends to be a highly gendered process of commodification). Nevertheless, while some resistance can occur, the business members of such migrant groups usually see such location promotion as a business opportunity rather than a loss of culture.

The promotion of new urban images, of new lifestyles and of new 'city myths' is often a necessary prelude to the establishment of new urban economies. Migrant communities are an important element of the new urban economy in many ways. Not only may they provide new international business skills and networks or, in many cases, cheap service labour, but they may also become an important part of the place product. In some cases, if a migrant community is accepted by local growth coalitions, the intangible capital of culture and ethnicity available through migrant communities may serve to reinforce the potential power of cultural commodities as a means of delivering place advantage in the global (cultural) economy. In short, migrant otherness becomes an essential element of place differentiation. Moreover, such otherness may not only be able to promote something attractive as a visitor experience, but it may also be able to promote broader brand values of security, harmony, cosmopolitanism and multiculturalism that may also prove attractive to capital and certain sought-after migrant groups.

New brands, new developments, the hosting of events and the creation of new leisure and retail spaces are all signs that 'something has been done' by the local state in response to problems arising from globalisation and restructuring, including greater flexibility in production. The greatest beneficiaries of this, though, are the growth coalitions, not those who suffer most from the casualisation of employment or the potential for unemployment or who wonder how to cope with what seems like constant change. However, for those who are able to visit many cities around the developed world on a regular basis we can note that even though they are trying to re-image themselves as places which are different, they also look the same. Harvey's (1989a, 1989b) concern over the 'serial monotony' of the redeveloped and re-imaged city is reinforced. Concerns over the supposed monotony of such places also belong to those who have the capacity to be highly mobile. For those who do not, and even many who do, the spaces of consumption of the urban waterfront or the mega-mall may still be locales of social relations and enjoyment.

The homogenisation of 'public' life and space, sometimes referred to as disneyfication, is a major criticism of tourism and contemporary cultural process. Indeed, to paraphrase Holcomb (1993), at first glance it might be assumed that place marketing, with its enthusiastic embrace of place, its appeal to the supposedly unique attractions of particular locations, and its passionate text, is anything but homogenising. 'Yet ultimately, the deconstructed discourses of the packed newly post-industrial cities replicate the same images, amenities, and potentials and contain the same silences with respect to poverty, race and blight' (Holcomb 1993, p. 141). Nevertheless, it does not have to be like that. Hall (2000a) argued that with appropriate design and planning authentic lived social, economic and environmental urban spaces could be created, with this still being attractive to many visitors to cities. 'Authenticity can perhaps be viewed as the attainment of an integrated, unstrained totality derived from ... meaningful dialectical relationships between ... different contexts' (Beng 1995, p. 218). Rapid, large-scale adaptations typical of most tourism-oriented urban redevelopments may work in the short term but in the long term they are the least easy to alter as environmental conditions again change. 'Instant-gratification, universal-standard buildings *are* corrupting. What is called for is the slow moral plastic of the "many ways" diverging, exploring, insidiously improving. Instead of discounting time, we can embrace and exploit time's depth. Evolutionary design is healthier than visionary design' (Brand 1997, p. 221).

The pattern of ownership of land and property is extremely important for the way in which places change. Small lots allow for ongoing fine-grain change as opposed to the sudden wholesale change that can occur with large parcels of land. The more owners the more gradual and adaptive will be the change (Hall 2000a). Appropriate urban tourism development may well mean relatively gradual small-scale change with the inclusion of large numbers of stakeholders as opposed to large-scale developments with limited numbers of 'owners' of the project, while the large-scale project may well be a grand gesture which members of the urban growth coalition support by virtue that they are seen to be 'doing something'. The more unspectacular gradual change is likely to be more sustainable (Hall 2000a). For example, in the case of Vancouver in British Columbia, Canada, the gradual redevelopment of Granville Island as a mixed use area which maintained associations with traditional waterfront businesses (e.g. chandlers, boat repairs and moorings), as well as providing for new uses such as a hotel, markets, bookshops and theatres, has proven to be a far more sustainable development than the large-scale development of other parts of the former dock area through the hosting of the 1986 Expo (Hall 2000a). It was not until 2004 that the last parts of the former Expo site were developed and in the meantime real estate prices in the city continued to increase and ease of access to housing for the poor continued to be a problem. 'The "real" in "real estate" derives from *re-al* – "royal" – rather than *res* – "thing" – which is the root of reality. Realty is in many ways the opposite of reality.... All that is sold melts into cash' (Brand 1997, p. 87). Rapid changes in real estate value are extremely dangerous to the lives of buildings and places. Substantial increases or decreases in value can dramatically affect land use development strategies as well as municipal charges placed on residents and owners. Tourism development is often used by cities in conjunction with private sector partners to try to improve real estate values. However, such developments may have ripple effects across the social and economic fabric of the city (Hall and Hodges 1996; Hall 2000a; Page and Hall 2003).

In thinking about sustainable design, one can consider Brand's (1997, p. 49) statement that 'the product of careful continuity is love'. Unfortunately, many tourist developments are not loved. In part this has been a failure of architects and planners to place such developments in a relevant local context. However, it also reflects the failure to appreciate the role of process and adaptive change

Plate 7.4   Granville Island in Vancouver, Canada has been a successful urban development with substantial tourism emphasis because of the focus on mixed use development utilising small properties available to micro-entrepreneurs as well as larger firms. In addition to a development plan (downloadable from the Island's website) there are also a Cultural Society and a Business and Community Association that play a significant role in the sustainable development of the island (The Granville Island website is www.granvilleisland.com; Tourism Vancouver – Greater Vancouver Convention & Visitors Bureau website www.tourismvancouver.com/docs/visit/index.html)

(Hall 2000a). According to Beng (1995, p. 6): 'The production of tourist architecture distorts both time and place. There is a tendency to homogeneity behind the false fronts.' The loss of historically rooted places, including the attempt to depoliticise them 'decontextualising them and sucking out of them all political controversy – so as to sell ... places ... to outsiders who might otherwise feel alienated or encounter encouragements to political defiance' (Philo and Kearns 1993, p. 24) appears commonplace in urban redevelopment tourism. The approach almost seems to be, 'sorry there's tourists coming, no contention here'. Heritage centres and historical anniversaries often serve to flatten and suppress contested views of history (Hall and McArthur 1996). However, the presentation of one-dimensional views of the past to the tourist and the community is also encountered at the destination and resort level. In her excellent study of tourism, history and ethnicity in Monterey, Norkunas (1993) argued that the rich and complex ethnic history of Monterey was almost completely absent in the 'official' historic tours and the residences available for public viewing.

In Monterey, as in many other parts of the world, heritage is presented in the form of the houses of the aristocracy or elite, not the poor and the oppressed.

It is the 'official' heritage, the heritage of the winners. 'This synopsis of the past into a digestible touristic presentation eliminates any discussion of conflict; it concentrates instead on a sense of resolution. Opposed events and ideologies are collapsed into statements about the forward movement and rightness of history' (Norkunas 1993, p. 36). Narratives of labour, class and ethnicity are typically replaced by romance and nostalgia. Overt conflict, whether between ethnic groups, classes or, more particularly, in terms of industrial and labour disputes are either ignored or glossed over in 'official' tourist histories. The overt conflict of the past has been reinterpreted by local elites to create a new history in which heritage takes a linear, conflict-free form. In the case of Monterey, the past is reinterpreted through the physical transformation of the canneries. 'Reinterpreting the past has allowed the city to effectively erase from the record the industrial era and the working class culture it engendered. Commentary on the industrial era remains only in the form of touristic interpretations of the literature of John Steinbeck' (Norkunas 1993, pp. 50–1).

Tourism Insight: Capital Cities and Tourism: Ottawa and Symbolic Representation

Capital cities represent a special case of urban tourism. Yet, in much of the literature on capital cities the planning and policy significance of tourism is seemingly ignored, while similarly little is made of the significance of capital status in the tourism literature. However, as capitals provide an administrative and political base of government operations there are important spin-off effects for business and convention travel. In addition to business-related travel, capital cities are also significant for tourism because of their cultural, heritage and symbolic functions. They are frequently home to major institutions while also tending to have a significant, wider role in the portrayal, preservation and promotion of national heritage and culture. A concentration of cultural institutions will therefore have implications for the attraction of culturally interested tourists as well as contributing to the image of a city as a whole, particularly when, at times, the negative perceptions many people have of politicians may impact the overall image of a city.

The use of the notion of a capital in terms of branding and culture is especially significant for tourism in terms of place promotion. Indeed, given the growth of place marketing in an increasingly competitive global economic environment such a development is logical in terms of branding places and place competition. However, for the purpose of this discussion the notion of a capital is related primarily to political, administrative and symbolic functions that operate at a national or provincial level. Arguably, such a situation must also provide a significant attraction for tourists as well. For example, if capital status is lost, it can have a marked effect on visitor numbers, as in the case of the transfer of the German national capital from Bonn to Berlin where Berlin has witnessed a dramatic increase in visitor arrivals and Bonn a decline. In fact in the period 1997–99 Bonn was the only German city to experience a decline in overnight stays.

Plate 7.5   Federal Parliament, Ottawa. (The National Capital Commission website is at www.canadascapital.gc.ca/index_e.asp; also see Destination Ottawa www.ottawakiosk.com)

The planning of capital cities, including the planning of tourism, is often somewhat problematic given potentially competing agendas and demands between the national, regional and local level. In great part this relates to the institutional arrangements which have been established as well as the cultural and political framework within which capital cities exist. For example, Washington, DC and Canberra, along with Ottawa, have national government mandated authorities specifically established to reinforce the capital city symbolic function while many capitals do not. Nevertheless, capital cities, as with other major urban centres around the world, are increasingly utilising tourism, leisure and entertainment industries as a direct means of economic diversification and redevelopment, particularly in light of government restructuring and downsizing since the mid-1980s as well as for the creation of urban leisurescapes which may serve to provide amenity values for business and individual location decisions.

However, the establishment of a specific planning development body for a capital does not necessarily mean that it will embrace tourism, although the creation of a specific organisation to promote national or regional identity and symbolism must influence place promotion and tourism strategies. Ironically, in a number of capital city jurisdictions, such as Canberra in Australia, tourism was actively discouraged until the late 1980s as some planners perceived it to be at odds with the 'cultural' aspects of the capital. In contrast, more recently established bodies have actively embraced tourism because of its contribution to the symbolic status of the capital and the economic development values of the tourist dollar, particularly in the Canadian provinces.

Although tourism has become recognised as an important, if not vital, component of the economic base of Canada's capitals (see Plan Canada 2000), its development is not unproblematic. As Dubé and Gordon (2000, p. 6) observed: 'Planning for cities that include a seat of government often involves political and symbolic concerns that are different from those of other urban areas.' Perhaps most significant among these concerns is how nationhood should be represented.

Ottawa, the capital of Canada, presents an excellent case of the difficulties associated with representation. According to the National Capital Commission (NCC) (2000, p. 10), the cultural function of the capital is to represent the achievements, cultural identities, customs and beliefs of the Canadian people. It has the institutions, events, attractions, symbols, landscapes, pathways and associated facilities that are required to present the nation's human and natural resources, and to display Canadian history, creativity and knowledge. It also exhibits the various cultural values, aspirations and traditions of Canadians.

Yet what is being represented? Ottawa is an excellent example of Gottmann's (1983) observation that 'capital cities often act as hinges between different regions of a country'. As the NCC (1999) recognises, Ottawa lies at the border between French- and English-speaking Canada, and is a location of interaction between labour and capital, as well as being a place where different ecological regions also coincide. Such borders tend to be locations of contestation, yet the official representation of nationhood as presented to the visitor in Ottawa seems to deny that such contestation has occurred or still occurs to the present day. For example, Confederation Boulevard is regarded as symbolising a link between English, French and Aboriginal peoples, yet the interpretation that is available to the visitor does not reflect the conflicts that have occurred historically between these groups or the extent to which it is still occurring with respect to the possibilities for land title claims, the re-interpretation of heritage or multiple interpretations of heritage. Providing multiple interpretation means more than just English and French signage. Official interpretation does not deal with the conflicts which surround either Canadian nationhood or even the space of the national core area. Previous representations of heritage are removed and reinterpreted in light of the present-day need. For example, the kneeling Indian at the base of the Champlain Statue overlooking the Ottawa River at Nepean Point was relocated about 150 metres away to Major's Hill Park in 2000. Yet a visit to the statues tells you nothing about the original relationship between them, or why the Indian statue was moved from its position of symbolic subservience. Instead of using the dissonant representations of heritage that the statues created as a means of engaging visitors in the complex story of Canada's history, the potential for revealing difference and conflict is avoided. Similarly, many visitors to Canada, and many Canadians, know that the relationship between English- and French-speaking Canada and Quebec and the other provinces is full of stresses and strains which have at several times almost reached breaking point. Yet, in visiting the central core and in seeing and hearing the story of nationhood, such issues are not dealt with and are seemingly ignored.

Rather than being ignored, such dissonance provides an opportunity for national storytelling far more engaging than much of the interpretation that is currently available to the visitor. If Ottawa is to more accurately exhibit the various cultural values, aspirations and traditions of Canadians, it needs to be able to convey that these have not always happily co-existed. Undoubtedly, many of the nation's politicians may be unhappy about laying bare some of the fractures which exist in Canadian nationhood, yet this would provide opportunity for debate and discussion which, after all, should be part of the political function of the capital's core area.

An excellent example of the possibilities created by allowing dissonance to be observed and expressed in a capital city is provided by Canberra. An Aboriginal Tent Embassy was set up outside Parliament House in 1972 as part of an assertion of Aboriginal rights. Described as an eyesore and torn down by police action it was then rebuilt in 1976. Such is its heritage significance that the Embassy is now listed on the register of Australia's National Estate. Even though Parliament has moved, the Embassy has continued to be a focal point for Aboriginal rights and is seen and visited by many tourists as they travel around Canberra's parliamentary triangle. However, its visual appeal as well as its core message is certainly not in keeping with the more traditional interpretative and symbolic accounts of Australia's history embodied in Canberra's national core.

If the built and natural environments of Ottawa, 'as well as events and programs, educate, instill pride, please the senses, and enrich the quality of life for residents and visitors' and more effectively 'contribute to the memory of Canadians and international visitors alike, as integral parts of the Capital's symbolic image' (NCC 1998, p. 114), then reconsideration needs to be given to the national capital's interpretative and visitor strategies. If Ottawa really is to become a meeting place for Canadians and those interested in Canada, then the multiple stories and voices of Canadians need to be heard, including the attendant discord. The development of a national meeting place does not mean the construction of yet another conference centre. Instead, the opportunity exists for the development of an interpretative centre which seeks to challenge the visitor as to what it means to be Canadian in light of the reality of the Canadian experience rather than the sanitised or 'safe' versions of history revealed in current interpretation and symbols.

One location which presents itself as a place in which such an interpretative centre could be established is Victoria Island, which lies in the middle of the Ottawa River in easy walking distance from the national parliament and the highest court in the land. The island is both a physical and symbolic meeting place between industry and capital (complete with ruins); the English-speaking, French-speaking and indigenous peoples of Canada; and even different ecologies. It is therefore a contested space in which the different voices of the Canadian experience find physical expression. However, to utilise this space in a manner which provides for the presentation of dissonant heritage will not be easy, not because it is not technically or interpretatively feasible, but because of the political implications of such a proposal (see also Jones and Birdsall-Jones 2003).

Many people come to Ottawa to learn about Canada's national experience through visits to institutions or by looking at the symbolic landscapes of the capital core. The nature of this experience could be made richer by developing new forms of heritage interpretation that seek to challenge and stimulate the visitor. Perhaps what is therefore being argued is that as a capital city the symbolism of the Ottawa core needs also to reflect that Canada is mature enough to accept that there are multiple voices in the national story which need to be heard by visitors and that some of the dissonance that exists needs to be located in a place which encourages discussion, debate and openness. Such political and cultural symbolism would not only be an asset from a tourism standpoint, but would also provide a powerful message about the function of Canada's political centre in the twenty-first century.

See National Capital Planning Commission: www.ncpc.gov

Cities that compete are increasingly a site of spectacle, a 'dreamscape of visual consumption' (Zukin 1991, p. 221). Is it therefore not surprising that at a time when little competitive edge can be found for cities in terms of the reconstruction of their physical space then emphasis is placed on the lifestyle opportunities they offer to those who are able to afford them? If there are no lasting benefits and no identifiable economic opportunity costs from selling the city for those who live in such places, then we are left with the proposition of Bourdieu (1984) that 'the most successful ideological effects are those which have no words' (quoted in Harvey 1989a, p. 78). The function of a flagship development such as hosting an Olympics, a World Fair, a Commonwealth Games, a Grand Prix or a major waterfront redevelopment scheme is then 'reduced to inducing social stability, assuming the generated experience is sustainable for enough people over a long period and is targeted towards those who are potentially the harbingers of disruption' (Smyth 1994, p. 7). What, then, is the purpose of marketing the city? This is a question that is particularly appropriate for former heavy industrial areas in Australia, Europe and North America which now focus on tourism that is often integrated with industrial heritage development. As Hudson (2000, p. 233) recognised:

There may be circumstances in which promotion of such activities might appropriately form one element in local economic development strategies, but to rely upon them as their main, or sole, basis is a very risky course of action. For it places such areas in competition with the vast array of locations, scattered around the globe, that seek to sell themselves to tourists in various ways. There is no guarantee that a tourism based on nostalgia for a departed industrial past will prove more attractive to consumers than one based on sun, sea and sand in southern Europe or the mystic delights of distant continents as the tourist industry becomes increasingly globalised.

Despite the conscious development of space in a manner which aims to attract the visitor and the investor, places can still resist commodification. Indeed, it is the very complexity of place, with its dense social networks, which ultimately makes them interesting, though not always easily accessible for the visitor. As Hewison (1991, p. 175) observed, 'the time has come to argue that commerce is not culture, whether we define culture as the pursuit of music, literature or the fine arts, or whether we adopt Raymond Williams' [1983] definition of culture as "a whole way of life". You cannot get a whole way of life into a Tesco's trolley.' Such arguments are important because they run counter to the notions of commodification of place and culture as product, which are intrinsic to place marketing.

Murphy and Watson (1997) described Sydney as a 'city of surfaces'. Such a comment may also apply to many other cities around the world that are competing to be a 'world city', as well as attempts to image entire countries and regions. However, while the spaces are the same, the places are different. Place has a distinct location which it defines, place is fixed. Space, in contrast, is composed of intersections of mobile elements with shifting often indeterminate borders (de Certeau 1984; Larbalestier 1994). As Daniels and Lee (1996, p. 5) suggest, 'reading human geography ... is a complex and critical act of interpretation and, as readers, we are engaged in interpreting writers' interpretations ... of worlds which are already construed, or misconstrued, by meaning or imagery'. Fortunately, city places and spaces are continually read 'in various ways, by a variety of people pursuing a variety of endeavours, in walking, in working, in reading, in speaking, in all or any of our everyday practices' (Larbalestier 1994, p. 187). In design as in planning, 'at each level of scale, it is those actually using the space who understand best how it can be made/altered to have the character of being conducive to the work, and this group should be given sole control over that space' (Alexander, quoted in Brand 1997, p. 173). While space is being constructed by urban growth coalitions in the desire to re-image the city, places remain open to negotiation and interpretation.

Discussion Questions

1. To what extent does a focus on physical regeneration through the development of tourism-related facilities and infrastructure improve the capacity for economic and social regeneration?

2. What are the principal aims of urban imaging strategies?

3. How are hallmark events used as imaging strategies? How successful are they?

4. Why is the pattern of ownership of land and property significant for how places change?

Further Reading and Websites

The best general overview of urban tourism is to be found in Page and Hall (2003). Other useful accounts of urban tourism include Selby (2004), Judd and Fainstein (1999) and Law (1996). For critical studies on the concept of urban regeneration, see Bassett (1993) and Furbey (1999). A useful analysis of the role of events in commodifying place and how this process is related to the political economy of place is Gotham (2002). Graham (2002) also provides a useful critical analysis of heritage in the urban context. On sports tourism, see Hinch and Higham (2003) and Ritchie and Adair (2004). Olds (1998b) provides an excellent examination of the social impacts of urban hallmark events. Timothy (2005) provides a good review of retail and shopping-related tourism, much of which occurs in urban fields. DRI.WEFA (2002) provides an overview of the economic significance of tourism in 100 US cities as well as the effects of September 11 on urban tourism in that country. Bahaire and Elliott-White (1999) provide a detailed case study of community participation in urban tourism planning, paying particular attention to the intersection between ideals of participation and the political climate of entrepreneurial cities.

ALTIS provides some links to urban tourism sites: http://altis.ac.uk/

Ontario Ministry of Municipal Affairs and Housing, Managing Downtown Revitalization:
www.reddi.gov.on.ca/redtool/default.jsp?lang=e&page=strategies&sub=downtown

Use your search engine to examine city tourism and convention agencies and their websites, examples include:

Las Vegas Tourism Bureau: www.lasvegastourism.com/

New York official website: http://www.nycvisit.com/home/index.cfm

Greater Glasgow and Clyde Valley Tourist Board: www.seeglasgow.com/

Visit London (the official visitor organisation for London; UK): www.visit london.com/

London, Ontario, Canada: www.londontourism.ca/

Melbourne, Australia, official site: www.visitmelbourne.com/

Tourism Victoria (official tourism site of Victoria, Canada): www.tourismvic toria.com/

Dunedin Tourism, New Zealand: http://www.DunedinNZ.com/tourism/ Like many locations, see how many unofficial sites there are as compared to official sites. An unofficial site for Dunedin is: www.dunedintourism .info/

(However, if visiting or intending to visit an urban destination in the South Island of New Zealand, Christchurch may prove to be more attractive given the information available: www.christchurchnz.net/.)

Tourism in Rural and Peripheral Areas: Development and Issues

8

Key Concepts

- Rural tourism
- Peripheral areas
- Restructuring
- Rurality
- Regional development
- Second homes
- Lifestyle migration
- Retirement migration
- Amenity
- Attraction fields
- Visitor fields
- Core–periphery
- Imperialism
- Location
- Policy measures
- Intangible capital

Rural areas have long been seen and used as appropriate locations for recreation and tourism activities (Towner 1996). However, with increased personal mobility for the urban population since the 1950s as a result of increased car ownership, the relationships between the rural setting and tourism and leisure activities have changed significantly (Cloke 1993). Just as significantly, the restructuring of rural areas and population loss from many areas have meant that tourism has also assumed greater economic and employment importance in many rural and peripheral regions. Along with other economic change, the growth of agro-business and social processes (e.g. urbanisation), this has contributed to substantial changes to the rural landscape and notions of what constitutes rurality.

Rural economies are much more open to global forces, they are more economically, culturally and environmentally diverse and their populations are becoming more concentrated in larger regional centres. Prior to the Second World War, although the widespread shift into commercial agriculture had produced regions of greater or lesser viability, the rural system overall retained a degree of homogeneity and distinctiveness. Subsequent to the Second World War in many regions in the developed world this structure has been either destroyed or weakened. 'Across the rural regions of the developed world the issues of population decline, economic change and community regeneration are almost universal' (Lane 1994, p. 7). Weakness is a result of at least three types of restructuring, namely: the collapse of peripheral areas unable to shift to a more capital-intensive economy; the selective and reductionist process of agro-industrialisation with the loss of many family-held farms; and the pressures of urban and peri-urban development. The result is an agricultural rural system suffering absolute decline along its extensive margins and the rural–urban interface, with the intervening core area weakened by decoupling of farm and non-farm sectors and the shift of decision-making to urban-based corporations and governments. Restructuring has created a fragmented and reduced rural system which seems to lack most of the criteria for sustainability in either economic or community terms (Burch et al. 1996; Troughton 1997; Burch et al. 1999). Indeed, while the rhetoric of free trade is otherwise heard in international trade negotiations, substantial agricultural subsidies maintain agricultural production in Canada, Europe, Japan and the United States, with the unfortunate irony that this has only exacerbated development problems in much of Africa, Asia and South America. Yet even given massive state intervention to support rural areas, whether it be for reasons of maintaining lifestyle and identities or because of the power of the rural vote, the nature of rural areas continues to alter.

Changes to rural areas have been inextricably linked to developments in both global and local economies, and tourism has emerged as one of the central means by which rural areas can 'adjust' to the new global environment. The regional restructuring associated with globalisation has usually involved attempts by regions to widen their economic base to include tourism as part of a 'natural' progression towards a tertiary economy, as employment in traditional Western agriculture declines and farm sizes diminish (Hudson and Townsend 1992, p. 64). This implies the selective expansion of tourist flows designed to achieve one or more of the following goals (Hall and Jenkins 1998):

- to sustain and create local incomes, employment and growth;

- to contribute to the costs of providing economic and social infrastructure (e.g. roads, water, sewage and communication);

- to encourage the development of other industrial sectors (e.g. through local purchasing links);

- to contribute to local resident amenities (e.g. sports and recreation facilities, outdoor recreation opportunities, and arts and culture) and services (e.g. shops, post offices, schools and public transport); and

- to contribute to the conservation of environmental and cultural resources, especially as scenic (aesthetic) urban and rural surroundings are primary tourist attractions.

Nevertheless, as Butler et al. (1998a) observed, while much has been written on the subject of the changing character of rural areas, of agriculture, and of the countryside (e.g. Bowler et al. 1992; Ilbery 1998), relatively little has been written on the linkages between leisure, tourism and the social, cultural and economic elements of rural and peripheral areas. This is surprising given the substantial emphasis placed on the potential economic impacts of tourism alone and the hyperbole that often surrounds tourism development in rural regions, such as the claim 'Rural tourism to the rescue of Europe's countryside' (World Tourism Organisation 1996a).

Constructing the Rural

The notion of rural is difficult to define. In international terms there are no universally accepted technical terms for what constitutes rural and urban. Different countries use different size or distance parameters. In the developed world many people's notion of rural tourism actually occurs within the daytrip zone of the urban recreational hinterland. This zone is the border area between the rural and the urban, with the market being driven by urban recreationists. Moreover, this area is also substantially utilised by other settlers who live in this peri-urban area (peripheral urban) but who commute into the urban area for their employment as well as by those who seek an easily accessible second home for weekend or overnight stay. Indeed, in tourism terms, the 'true' rural area is that beyond the daytrip zone as it is here that overnight stays become essential for travellers and there are therefore qualitative and quantitative differences to the nature of tourism, including the sheer numbers of people travelling to such areas.

As well as difficulties in defining the notion of rural in demographic or spatial terms, it must also be noted that the idea of rurality has been socially constructed, particularly under the influence of the media. As Butler et al.

(1998a) noted, in the nineteenth century, for example, images of the British countryside for many of the new urban middle class came not only from their own personal experience, but also from their exposure to novels (e.g. those by Thomas Hardy), poetry (e.g. that of Wordsworth), and paintings (e.g. those of Constable). Ironically, the newly idealised British rural landscape was itself a product of the agricultural restructuring that was begun with the enclosure movement and reinforced by the industrial revolution. It was within this social environment that the countryside was set in opposition to the 'evils' of industrial cities, and the image of a rural arcadia or idyll was established (Lansbury 1970), which masked the poverty, displacement and poor working conditions of many rural inhabitants.

In the twentieth century, the media continued to portray images of a 'simpler' rural life to its primarily urban audience, through television (e.g. *All Creatures Great and Small*, the television serialisation of the books by James Herriot on veterinary life in the Yorkshire Dales), radio (*The Archers*, 'An everyday story of simple country folk'), and lifestyle magazines (e.g. *Country Life*, *Country Style*). However, in the late twentieth and early twenty-first centuries, with time–space compression, rural images from outside Britain are exerting a greater influence of the romanticised rural image at a wider scale. For example, the idealised Provence of Peter Mayle's books and subsequent television programme, *A Year in Provence*; cooking books and television shows from rural Italy presented by celebrity chefs, for example Antonio Carluccio; and the promotion of a 'clean, green, image for New Zealand' via media such as the film trilogy of *Lord of the Rings*.

Nevertheless, contemporary rurality is not just consumed via the media. Elements of the countryside, real or imagined, are also transported to urban areas through the growth of shops which specialise in 'cottage' and 'heritage' furniture and household goods (e.g. kitchenware and basketware), by which urbanites are able to bring the country into the city in symbolic and, sometimes, functional forms. Moreover, the relation to rural places is also reinforced through consumption of geographically designated products such as Tuscan olive oil and Marlborough wine. However, images of British rurality are not dead and are used in the promotion of both domestic and international tourism: images of thatched cottages, the village pub and, to a lesser extent, cricketers playing on the village green are still used in both public and private sector tourism advertising. As Britton (1991, p. 475) observed: 'As a major, yet typically unappreciated and unacknowledged, avenue of accumulation in the late twentieth century, tourism is one of the most important elements in the shaping of popular consciousness of places and in determining the creation of social images of those places.'

The countryside is a cultural landscape in which ideas of rurality are socially constructed. Despite attempts by some (e.g. Hoggart 1989, 1990) to do away with the rural, and the increasing recognition that both urban and rural areas are subject to the same global transitions in economic, political and social structures (e.g. Cloke 1989), notions of 'rural' and 'rurality' remain important not only for the everyday lives of people in the city and the country but also for planners and policy-makers. The categories of 'rurality' and 'rural' consump-

Tourism Insight: Art, Landscape and Identity

Elite group and intellectual perceptions of nature and rurality are important for the transformation of broader landscape and leisure taste. In the case of the Krkonoše (Giant) Mountains in the Czech Republic, an area which is now a national park and a biosphere reserve of over 55 000 hectares, including 29 towns and over 27 000 people, its original attractiveness for leisure visitors arose through the activities of artists from the end of the eighteenth century onwards. According to Petrikova (2001, p. 38): 'Czech and German painters were coming to Krkonoše to picture the mountain landscape according to the ideals of classicism and romanticism. At the same time a number of guide-books were published [giving] details about the beauties of the mountains.'

Similarly, the attractiveness of the Finnish national landscape of Koli National Park in eastern Finland was derived in great part from the activities of artists who saw Koli as the 'culmination of the Kalevala landscape. During the time called the "Golden Era of Finnish Art" Koli became one of the most important sites for pilgrimages of the so-called Karelianists. These were national romantic artists in different fields, who were fascinated by the Finnish national epic, the Kalevala, and wanted to travel to the source of its stories, Karelia' (Oinen-Edén 2001, pp. 66–7). In this period culture and art were used as an expression of cultural independence from Russia: 'When the Finns needed means to enforce their national identity in a way that would surpass Russian censorship, they hung on the wall Järnefelt's impressive Koli painting "Autumn view from Lake Pielinen" from 1899 or played music of Sibelius' (Oinen-Edén 2001, p. 67).

tion and production are therefore essential in providing the context within which tourism occurs. As Harvey (1989c, p. 72) recognised, the rural 'lingers in the realms of ideology with some important results'. Similarly, although Cloke and Goodwin (1993, p. 168) denied that 'rurality is in itself a deterministically casual mechanism', they went on to note that people 'behave as though rural is real to them and is influential in their locational decisions'. New ways of seeing the countryside are developed with each round of capital that is invested in the countryside (Cloke and Goodwin, 1993; Ilbery and Bowler 1998). Tourism and recreation, along with other forms of consumption, rely on the marketing of a rural idyll in order to attract both visitors and investment. Constructions of rurality therefore play a vital role in determining not only the rate of change in the countryside but also how tourists see the country and how the rural community see themselves (Aronsson 1994; Crouch 1994; Lane 1994), even with respect to the supposed spiritual relationships available in connections with nature (Heintzmann 2000). It is perhaps ironic that rural tourism appears based on images of an unchanging, simpler and problem-free countryside when the reality has been one of change, although, admittedly, change has been uneven and has 'taken different forms and has proceeded at different scales at different

Plate 8.1   Lake Saimaa, Finland. The Finnish lake landscape is an essential element of Finnish national identity which is reinforced through tourism promotion and advertising. (see Finnish Tourist Board www.visitfinland.com)

Plate 8.2   Olavinlinna Castle, which was built in 1475, is not only a significant tourist attraction in its own right, including the hosting of opera and other cultural events, but it has long been utilised by artists in the presentation of a Finnish national landscape that serves to reinforce Finnish identity. (see www.travel.fi/int/savonlinna/ as well as visiting the municipal website which has some information in English, www.savonlinna.fi)

times in different rural areas' (Cloke and Goodwin 1993, p. 327). In addition, as Butler and Hall (1998a) noted, given its importance in determining tourism flows and the patterns of tourism development, it is also perhaps ironic that the vast majority of academic research on rural tourism has missed understanding the means by which the rural is created and sold to the visitor and local alike.

Blake (1996, p. 211) also recognised that rurality is no longer dominated by concepts of food production and notes that new uses of the countryside are redefining the idea of what constitutes the rural landscape. In Britain, as in many other industrialised countries, these non-agricultural or traditional uses are placing extreme pressures and creating new conflicts not only in terms of rural policy-making and its relationship to agriculture but also between themselves. For example, Blake (1996) reported that, according to a Countryside Commission survey, 76% of the English population visited the countryside in 1990. Such a high level of visitation inevitably requires the transformation of villages, and the creation of tourist facilities and infrastructure such as car parks and toilets. However, at the same time, 89% of people now believe that the English countryside should be protected at all costs, but, as Butler and Hall (1998a) observed, presumably as long as this cost would not result in the exclusion of those who wanted it saved.

Countryside change and the promotion of place image therefore reflects the same national and international shifts in economic, political and social structures as do urban areas (Cloke 1989, 1993; Marsden et al. 1996). Rural imaging processes are characterised by some or all of the following:

- the development of a critical mass of visitor attractions and facilities (e.g. the development of heritage sites);

- the hosting of events and festivals (e.g. Highland Games or produce-based events, such as wine and food festivals);

- the development of rural tourism strategies and policies often associated with new or renewed regional tourism organisations and the related development of regional marketing and promotional campaigns (e.g. 'Hardy Country' or 'Herriot Country' in England);

- the development of leisure and cultural services and projects to support the regional marketing and tourism effort (e.g. the creation and renewal of regional museums, heritage listed buildings and support for local arts and crafts);

- the maintenance of the rurality of the landscape, often through support for systems of economic production that are otherwise no longer economically viable; and

- encouragement of second home development and retirement homes in areas with an excess of housing stock.

Indeed, a rural counterpart to Harvey's question of redevelopment of the inner city may well be 'How many heritage trails, folk museums and villages, historic houses, roadside stalls, authentic country cooking, country fairs, country 'shoppes', and Devonshire teas can we stand?'

Tourism as a Policy Response

Tourism as a policy response to the economic problems of rural areas has gone through a number of phases in recent years. Until the mid-1980s rural tourism was primarily concerned with commercial opportunities, multiplier effects and employment creation (e.g. Cornwall and Holcomb 1966; Clout 1972; Canadian Council on Rural Development 1975). In the late 1980s policy guidance shifted to the message that the environment is a key component for the tourism industry. Under this notion, 'tourism is an additive rather than extractive force for rural communities' (Curry 1994, p. 146). Tourism was regarded as 'sustainable', stressing the intrinsic value of the environment and, in some countries, the rural community as a tourist resource (although in Australia sustainability was defined primarily in ecological terms) (Ecologically Sustainable Development Working Groups 1991). In the early to mid-1990s an additional layer was added to the policy responses of government to tourism and regional development, which returns to the earlier economic concerns. This is the perceived role of rural tourism as a major mechanism for arresting the decline of agricultural employment and therefore as a mechanism for agricultural diversification (Rural Development Commission 1991a, 1991b). In the case of Europe, for example, the identification of specific rural development areas, in which tourism development is funded by the European Union, has occurred through a number of development programmes, often in conjunction with member states, the local state and the private sector. Australia provides a good example of governments' belief in the development potential of tourism. As the Commonwealth Department of Tourism (Department of Tourism (Commonwealth) 1993, p. 24) noted, 'diversification of traditional rural enterprises into tourism would provide considerable benefits to local rural economies', including:

- wider employment opportunities;

- diversifying the income base of farmers and rural towns;

- additional justification for the development of infrastructure;

- a broader base for the establishment, maintenance and/or expansion of local services;

- scope for the integration of regional development strategies; and

- an enhanced quality of life through extended leisure and cultural opportunities.

According to the Commonwealth Department of Tourism (1993, p. 2): 'Tourism creates jobs, stimulates regional development and diversifies the regional economic base. With the decline in many traditional industries in rural and regional areas, tourism offers an opportunity to revitalise regional Australia and spread the social benefits of tourism.' However, tourism 'can be a tool in regional development or an agent of disruption or destruction' (Getz 1987, pp. 3–4). As Getz (1987) suggested, there is a growing recognition that neither an economic approach nor an environmental approach to rural tourism development is, by itself, sufficient to meet both the policy agendas of government and the real needs of the people who live in the rural areas that are the focus of most of the discussion on regional tourism development. There is therefore a need to *integrate* economic and environmental interests with the social dimensions of regional development as well as recognise the factors that make places competitive or provide for the development of a diverse economy.

The concept of integration provides us with a number of significant points about the nature of regional development. First, all the dimensions of development need to be considered. Second, it implies the need for us to be aware of the various linkages that exist between the elements of development. Third, it also implies that 'successful' regional development will require coordination and, at times, intervention in order to achieve desired outcomes. Nevertheless, rural policy is often poorly developed and fails to integrate the different development impacts of various sectors in rural areas as well as the various forms of state intervention (Murdoch 1993; Whatmore 1993).

As Butler and Hall (1998b) noted, much of the discussion on applications of sustainability has been in individual components of rurality, for example attempts at developing sustainable agriculture, rather than a comprehensive approach to integrate the socio-cultural, economic and environmental components of both sustainability and rurality. For example, the Rural White Paper entitled *Rural England: A Nation Committed to a Living Countryside* (Department of the Environment and Ministry of Agriculture, Fisheries and Food (DoE/MAFF) 1995) was the first specifically rural policy from a British government for 50 years (Blake 1996). Indeed, in many rural areas of the developed world tourism policy is inextricably bound up with broader agricultural policies. Nevertheless, the rural tourism industry does not have the same political power as the agricultural industry, in terms of being able to attract subsidies or other forms of financial support.

| Tourism Insight: | Monastery of the Transfiguration of Christ at New Valamo |

In various Christian cultures there has long been a tradition of monasteries being located in peripheral, relatively isolated areas in order for the occupants to contemplate and meditate. However, at the same time, such centres may become important destinations for pilgrimage, either religious or secular. This brief case study outlines the history of a monastery that has moved over time and has also drawn visitors, more recently through state assistance for its upkeep as well as for earnings from visitors.

The original monastery was started by the monk Sergei on the island of Valamo in present-day Russia in the year 1329. In 1611 the monastery was destroyed by the Swede Jacob de la Gardie and was left unoccupied until

1716 when Czar Peter the Great ordered its rebuilding. However, the monastery did not have any great religious prominence until the appointment of the priestmonk Nazari as the new igumen (abbot) in 1786. In 1786 Valamo was a third-class monastery but by 1822 it was regarded as a first-class monastery. By the time of Igumen Damaskin in 1840 the monastery was receiving 8000 visitors a year, a figure which was generally maintained (except through times of war) until the early 1930s. In 1934 the monastery received 10 000 visitors and 20 000 in 1939. However, the growth in visitor numbers is in stark contrast to the numbers of people who undertake the religious life. In 1913 the brotherhood had 359 monks and 562 novices. However, following Finland's independence from Russia in 1917, the border was closed and no new novices could enter from Russia. Accordingly, the number of members of the brotherhood had dropped to 200 by 1939. In February 1940 the monastery was evacuated because of the Finno-Russian War (also known as the Winter War), with control of the island reverting to Russia. In the summer of 1940 the brotherhood bought the Papinniemi Estate in the county of Heinävesi from Yrjö Herman Saastamoinen, a Minister in the Finnish Cabinet, and established a monastery at what was called New Valamo.

In the early 1970s the number of monks had diminished to the point that the divine services were performed by just one monk. However, dramatic changes occurred in 1977 which improved the fortunes of the monastery. In that year Church Slavonic was replaced by Finnish and the Gregorian Calendar was adopted. A new main church was built with the aid of funds from the Finnish government. Completed in 1977 the new church houses one of the main spiritual treasures of the Orthodox Church of Finland, the supposedly miracle-working icon of the Mother of God of Konevitsa. By the late 1990s the average number of monks was seven.

In 2002 the monastery received an estimated 200 000 visitors. In September 2003 the monastery housed 12 monks and had a staff of 30, with many volunteers. Although no figures were kept on individual nationalities of monks, interpretation was available in English, French, German, Swedish and Russian, as well as Finnish. The cultural centre houses the monastery library, the icon conservation laboratory, a museum and conference facilities for up to 200 people. The monastery's hotels and guest houses can host around 70 people. The old church is only open for services in summer while the new church is open all year round. In summertime a boat cruise sails regularly between the monastery and the nearby convent of Lintula.

For further information see the website: www.valami.fi

Despite the imaging of rural areas as somehow simpler and more pleasant locations, there are many conflicts implicit in the diverse nature of rural areas (Curry 1992; Cloke and Little 1997; Chaplin 1999). Many of these owe their origins to changing tastes and preferences among the ever-changing user populations of rural areas and the shifting spatial influences of exogenous economic and political forces. They also have origins in the same conflicts between exchange value and use value noted in Chapter 7 in the case of urban areas. For example, the conversion of former farmland into plantation forests and the decline of the family farms to be replaced by agribusiness and, often, a mono-cultural landscape of agribusiness have aroused opposition from a variety of sources because of employment losses as well as reduction in amenity.

In Norway, conflict exists between the commercial interests of farmers and timber producers on the one side and the experience interests of hikers, campers and recreational visitors on the other (Larsen 2001). They compete to use the same areas for mutually exclusive activities. The establishment of national parks is controversial for the same reason, as is the construction of dams and river piping for electricity generation. Larsen (2001) noted that, over time, there will be a growing number of such conflicts as society demands areas and resources for both commercial and experience production.

Similarly, in Britain, opposition to the spread of agribusiness has been voiced by wildlife and landscape conservationists, who note the loss of variety and habitat, and by hiking and other recreational users over the disappearance of long-established footpaths and other means of access in rural areas. Indeed, accessibility within and to the countryside has long been another source of conflict. The decline of public transportation in rural areas, reflecting in part a declining rural population and changed political philosophies over the appropriate role of government in transportation, has meant that 'in rural areas cars are more of a necessity than in cities' (DoE/MAFF 1995, p. 132). The probable growth in automobile use in rural areas, and the subsequent increase in air pollution and demands for better roads may therefore run against desires for a tranquil and unpolluted rural environment (Blake 1996). This problem is further exacerbated by the increasing commuting use of rural areas by urban workers, which is clearly related to issues of the purchase of goods and services outside the immediate resident community, thereby threatening the viability of existing retail and service outlets in such communities.

One of the more difficult issues to resolve in rural areas is the different desires, expectations, perceptions and requirements of long-time residents and new arrivals and changing community power structures that may result, particularly in those areas in which counter-urbanisation is occurring (Halfacree 1994, 1995, 1996), such as in the daytrip zone; where second homes and retirement homes are established (e.g. Coppock 1977; Gartner 1987; Chaplin 1999; Hall and Müller 2004a); and where the development of resort communities attract not only visitors and second home development but also people seeking employment in such locations (Gill 1998; Hall and Müller 2004a).

Second homes are an integral though often neglected component of domestic and international tourism mobility (Coppock 1977; Jaakson 1986; Hall and Page 2002; Hall and Müller 2004a). In many areas of the world second homes, also referred to as vacation homes, cottages, summer houses, recreation homes, cribs and weekend homes, are the destination of a substantial proportion of domestic and international travellers, while the number of available bed nights in second homes often rivals or even exceeds that available in the formal accommodation sector (Hall and Müller 2004b). Second homes are defined by Shucksmith (1983, p. 174) as 'a permanent building which is the occasional residence of a household that usually lives elsewhere and which is primarily used for recreation purposes'. Although the second home may be permanent, the period of residence is not. Indeed, terms used to describe second homing include 'residential tourism' (Casado-Diaz 1999), 'semi-migration' (Flognfeldt 2002), 'summer migration' (Finnveden 1960), and 'seasonal suburbanization' (Pacione 1984). Second homes have a long tradition in Scandinavia, Canada and New Zealand, where they were originally a cheap, accessible means of holidaying and leisure taking, although since the 1950s increases in second home development are primarily explained through the increased personal mobility made possible by car ownership. However, second homes are significant for any analysis of tourism mobility for several reasons, including the motivations for second homing and the insights it may provide into concepts such as 'home' and 'mobility', relations between 'permanent' and second home populations, and the potential contribution to regional development.

Second homeowners are motivated by a number of reasons, many of which have to do with the specific amenity characteristics of a location, including distance from primary residence, physical and social characteristics of the area and availability of recreational opportunities (Coppock 1977; Hall and Müller 2004a), lifestyle (Wolfe 1952; Jaakson 1986; Kaltenborn 1997a; Chaplin 1999; Williams and Kaltenborn 1999; Jansson and Müller 2003), family ties to an area (Jaakson 1986; Kaltenborn 1997a, 1997b, 1998; Löfgren 1999; Jansson and Müller 2003) and retirement planning (Buller and Hoggart 1994; McHugh et al. 1995; Williams et al. 1997; King et al. 2000; Williams et al. 2000; Truly 2002). In many cases second home purchase is related to stages in the life course and travel careers. The identification of a desirable second home environment tend to be related to an environmental search process, of which travel is a key component. Holiday-making provides the opportunities to identify potential second home locations, while second homes may also be a part of a wider lifestyle strategy that utilises second home purchase as a precursor to more permanent retirement or lifestyle migration (Hall and Page 2002). However, in many cases the travel component which leads to the decision to purchase a second home may be related to family ties to a district rather than just leisure and environmental amenity values. In such cases the notion of home may take on very significant personal meaning in terms of a desire to remain connected to a place where, for various reasons, particularly a lack of available employment or the quality of life opportunities in rural areas, it may not be possible to live on a permanent basis.

Accessibility plays a major influence on the use of second homes. The majority of second home owners live close to their property. Even in an international context, long-distance second home ownership is still the exception (Hoggart and Buller 1995). The classification of second homes into weekend or vacation homes is a function of the distance of the second home from the permanent home and the time budget of the user. Weekend homes need to be within daytripping distance in order to be used effectively. Müller (2002b) established empirically that the second home demand decreases in a logistic curve with increasing distance from the primary residence, implying that second home ownership loses attractiveness as soon as the weekend leisure zone is passed. The weekend leisure zone of Müller (2002a, 2002b) is analogous to the identification of a zone of overnight stay within the recreational hinterland of an urban centre (Chapter 3). In the Swedish case, Jansson and Müller (2003) have demonstrated that 25% of all second home owners have their property within 14 kilometres of their primary residence, 50% have less than 37 kilometres to their property, and 75% have less than 98 kilometres. Nevertheless, international second home owners remain significant, including German second home owners in the south of the country (Müller 1999; Müller 2002c, 2002d). Amenity-rich areas disturb the otherwise very regularly declining second home patterns while the development of point-to-point low-cost airline routes has also opened up international second home development in Europe.

Land availability is also a significant factor in the selection of second home sites as land use planning regulations may limit the minimum size of land sections that can be sold, thereby contributing to the scarcity value of desired second home locations. Such government land use controls therefore play a significant role in influencing land and housing stock values and, depending on the local rating or tax system, may even be manipulated so as to maximise rates returns from housing developments. Although such regulatory measures will often be justified by local government on the basis of landscape or environmental protection, they nevertheless will have enormous impacts on the availability of land for second home development (Hall and Müller 2004b). Therefore, weekend homes tend to be in locations that may already be experiencing substantial growth through counter-urbanisation. It is in these locations that much of the conflict between second home development and the existing community occurs as, to a great extent, the likelihood of conflict is dependent on availability in the housing stock.

Nevertheless, second homes do have potential value as a means of economic development in rural and peripheral areas, especially when such areas have excess housing stock and an otherwise limited economic base. Second homes provide a means for regional development through:

- increasing direct visitor expenditure to the region;

- the provision of infrastructure used for both home owners and other tourists;

- the support of service and construction industries, including the utilisation of housing stock that would otherwise be unoccupied; and

- the opportunity for further regional development through owners retiring to their second home.

Though the benefits of second home development to a region are potentially high, they may not always exceed the costs created for government in relation to increases in waste, health care, and other services, as well as the social and

Plate 8.3 Swedish second home. Second homes, often referred to as summer cottages, have long had an important place in Swedish holiday-making and identity and are an important component of the rural economy in many peripheral areas.

Tourism Insight: Second Homes and Low-cost Airlines in Europe

A French court ruling in September 2003, which halted flights by Ryanair, the Irish low-cost carrier, to Strasbourg, was regarded as having a potentially wider impact on Britons owning second homes in France. Following legal action brought by Brit Air, a subsidiary of Air France, over the subsidies paid to Ryanair by the Strasbourg Chamber of Commerce, Ryanair ceased its service. Although Ryanair had mounted an appeal against the decision, the result of the appeal was unknown at the time of writing. The Strasbourg court case, along with a similar court case regarding its Brussels service, was thought to have wide implications for UK holiday home owners and visitors to France. According to Liz Oliver, managing director of French property agency Francophiles, 'The Ryanair service has been marvellous for anyone wanting the option of long weekends in their home, even in the far south' (cited in Glasgow 2003, p. W16).

The economic impacts of low-cost flights to regional airports in France is substantial. Manager of the Pau Pyrenées Airport, Jean-Luc Cohen, reported that in the three months after the Ryanair service started in April 2003, 25 000 passengers arrived; of these, almost 80% were visitors from outside the region, spending a total of €1.4 million on goods and services. According to Cohen: 'That's why we say we're not helping Ryanair with subsidies, so much as running a marketing campaign for our region' (cited in Glasgow 2003, p. W16). Services by Ryanair and other low-cost airlines have also led to an increase in property prices in areas accessed through regional airports. According to Maurice Lazarus at British-based French property agent Domus Abroad, 'Prices across France have gone up perhaps by perhaps 30–40 per cent over the last three years, but in areas that were not previously served by a UK air link, such as Biarritz, they have at least doubled' (cited in Glasgow 2003, p. W16). According to Lazarus, accessibility is vital for the purchase of holiday homes by the British, and he noted that areas within three or four hours of the Channel ports are drive to properties: 'It's more remote hubs such as Carcassonne in the Aude and Rodez in Aveyron – which were effectively opened up to the UK market by Ryanair and have become popular with British buyers – that will feel it. Even Bergerac in the Dordogne, where there are many British owners, is too far to drive comfortably' (cited in Glasgow 2003, p. W16).

As Glasgow (2003, p. W16) noted, if services were withdrawn, the alternatives for the British holiday home owners would be that 'they could drive, which may be tolerable for longer holidays but would rule out long weekends to more distant regions, or they could fly to an international airport, which currently means paying more and travelling further at the other end'. Lazarus puts the situation much more dramatically, 'It would be extremely nasty and bad for tourism in France – they would really be shooting themselves in the foot' (cited in Glasgow 2003, p. W16).

environmental impacts that may also occur (Hall and Müller 2004a). The seasonal nature of some second home locations may also limit the potential benefits of second home development, while also creating extra pressures at periods of peak demand. Examples of social conflict have included disagreement between locals and second home residents regarding the levels of development (Green et al. 1996), conflicts over perceived social inequality (Gallent 1997), and competition for the use of land (Gallent 1997; Gallent and Tewdwr-Jones 2000). Second homes, and the related issues of 'homes for locals' and the maintenance of services, are probably, more than most forms of tourism migration/settlement, the focus of contested space issues (Girard and Gartner 1993). Indeed, a series of letters to the editor in the same edition of *The Times* illustrates well the different perspectives that exist on second homes. For example, Turner (2004, p. 19) highlighted the extent to which the village of Burnham Market in Norfolk has been able to retain facilities: 'We may mourn the passing of another, gentler era, but villages must embrace change, doing what they can to provide affordable housing, jobs and facilities for visitors who add vibrancy and cash. The shopkeepers, too, must encourage the holiday-homers to buy locally.' Bishop (2004, p. 19) noted issues of facilities and infrastructure, and that the fixed costs of services designed to serve the needs of the permanent resident population may then be under-resourced during holiday months: 'A second home is a privilege that should be fully funded by the owner, without financial penalty to the host community, who already suffer the social disadvantage of living amongst empty houses during the winter months.' Finally, Meredith (2004) expressed the concern that although second homes may produce work for local people, particularly through maintenance and construction, however, the increase in housing costs because of the influx of holiday home buyers made it more difficult for some local people to purchase a permanent home.

Tourism Insight: Attraction and Visitor Fields

As emphasised in Chapter 3, consideration of tourism mobility means that all stages of a trip need to be examined in understanding the tourism phenomenon. As Fridgen (1984, p. 33) noted: 'Travel to and from the destination site and experiences associated with these phases have been ignored. A better understanding of travel behavior could assist in the marketing of secondary trips, staging areas, and minor attractions located in the vicinity of larger, more popular destinations.' Flognfeldt (2002) refers to the concept of a primary attraction shadow to indicate the situation in which *en route* tourists, by visiting such an attraction along a route, may not then visit other attractions in the region of the primary attraction. Flognfeldt (2002) classifies attractions as:

- single-visit attractions, 'once in a lifetime' market newcomers; and
- multi-visit attractions or 'ongoing' attraction, the latter visitors mostly having family or a second home in the destination area.

Because of time and location constraints, the mode of transport a tourist uses has substantial impacts on the flexibility of what the tourist can visit. For example, members of coach tours will have little flexibility on where they can go compared to those with their own car. Flognfeldt (2002) reported a 1995 survey of Ottadalen in Norway, an area with several natural attractions (glaciers and summits) and one cultural attraction (the Lom Stave church) which showed that for 26% of tourists Ottadalen was the main destination, 55% were on a round trip, 13% were passing through and 6% were day visitors. In assessing the potential market for an attraction it therefore becomes vital to consider both the visitor field and the attraction field:

- *Visitor field*: how far away from the accommodation unit is a traveller willing to travel within the frame of a daytrip, including the time for visiting attractions and other stops.
- *Attraction field*: how far from an attraction might daytrippers be recruited for a potential single-day visit.

In Norway, many types of travel experience occur at a substantial distance from the accommodation base. For middle-of-the-day visitors to Røros (a World Heritage mining and industrial site), Flognfeldt (2002) traced holiday bases of up to 250 kilometres away, reflecting daytrips of up to 500 kilometres plus a 4–6 hour stay at the destination. Similar distances were measured for alpine ski resorts of Hafjell, Trysil, Hovden, Oppland and Hemsedal, as well as theme parks such as the Hunderfossen Family Park near Lillehammer.

Plate 8.4 Part of the World Heritage mining town of Røros, Norway. Copper was mined from 1644 to 1977 and both the copper works and part of the town are included in the World Heritage listing. Flognfeldt (2002) traced holiday bases of up to 250km away, reflecting day trips of up to 500km plus a 4-6 hour stay at the destination. ((Details of this World Heritage listed property can be found at http://whc.unesco.org/sites)

Tourism in Peripheral Areas

The periphery has long been an important concept in tourism studies. For example, Christaller (1963), in his highly influential account of tourism development, distinguished between pleasure travel, which he saw as primarily oriented towards peripheral areas, and business and education travel, which were regarded as primarily an urban tourism function. Christaller (1963, p. 96) observed that tourism not only made use of peripheral lands that could not otherwise be used for agriculture or forestry, but that '[i]t is typical for places of tourism to be on the periphery.... [D]uring certain seasons peripheral places become destinations for traffic and commodity flows and become seasonal central points.' Indeed, this notion was later picked up by Turner and Ash (1975) in one of the more influential textbooks on tourism of the 1970s, when they referred to the idea of a pleasure periphery for international tourism (in light of the increased mobility of people in the developed world). However, the initial consideration of tourism peripherality by Christaller was primarily grounded in economic location theory and the spatial relationships that exist between metropolitan and peripheral areas. By the time of Turner and Ash (1975), the notion had expanded to include a core–periphery model which not only reflected the spatial organisation of human and economic activity but, more importantly, identified the reasons for such organisation to be grounded in the unequal distribution of power in the economy and society in which the core dominates while the periphery is dependent (Friedmann 1966; Ilbery 1984).

In terms of international tourism studies the notion of peripherality and dependence has historically been most often associated with less developed countries that are characterised by 'dependent development' (e.g. Hills and Lundgren 1977; Hivik and Heiberg 1980; Britton 1982; Francisco 1983; Harrison 1992a, 1992b; Weaver 1998). Yet, increasingly, such concerns are being associated with areas in the developed world (e.g. Botterill et al. 1997; Buhalis 1997; Scott 2000; Hall and Boyd 2005, in press).

Tourism Insight: Tourism, Dependency and Imperialism

Dependency can be conceptualised as an historical process which alters the internal functioning of economic and social sub-systems within a developing country. This conditioning causes the simultaneous disintegration of an indigenous economy and its reorientation to serve the needs of exogenous markets. This internal transformation determines the specific roles and articulation of various modes of production within a country, and thereby creates specialised commodity export enclaves, such as tourism or primary agricultural production and structural inequality between social groups (Britton 1982). The clear concern in most studies of dependency is that the locus of control over the development process shifts from the people that are most affected by development, the host community, to the tourism generating regions. However, fears of the effects of dependency are not just isolated to economic considerations. As Erisman (1983, p. 339) observed, 'beyond economics lies the deeper and generally unarticulated fear that the industry's impact is even more pervasive and insidious, that it will somehow shape and affect in adverse ways the entire fabric of ... society'. Concerns over dependency are also expressed in terms of former colonial relationships. Indeed, to some dependency is the former imperialism of Western nations by another name (Erisman 1983).

Nash (1989, p. 38), in one of the better-known statements concerning tourism as a form of imperialism, argues: 'At the most general level, theories of imperialism refer to the expansion of a society's interests abroad. These interests – whether economic, political, military, religious, or some other – are imposed on or adopted by an alien society, and evolving intersocietal transactions, marked by the ebb and flow of power, are established.' Similarly, Crick (1989, p. 322) argued that tourism was a form of 'leisure imperialism' and represented 'the hedonistic face of neocolonialism'. Arguably, such an approach to ideas of imperialism is far too wide, otherwise every expansion of state interest overseas would be seen as a form of imperialism. Instead, imperialism should be conceived as a particular kind of reality: 'What it denotes is a relationship: specifically, the relationship of a ruling or controlling power to those under its dominion.... What we mean when we speak of empire or imperialism is the relationship of a hegemonial state to peoples or nations under its control' (Lichtheim 1974, p. 10). Nash (1989, p. 39) correctly identified the importance of the relationship between the metropolitan centre and the periphery in that he recognised that: 'Metropolitan centers have varying degrees of control over the nature of tourism and its development.... It is this power over touristic and related developments abroad that makes a metropolitan center imperialistic and tourism a form of imperialism.'

Although elements of the core–periphery relationship between tourist-generating developed Western nations and the developing nations which host tourism are reflective of former colonial relationships, the range of foreign economic and tourist interests in developing countries is usually greater than that which existed during the colonial period (Hall and Tucker 2004a, 2004b). However, the notion of imperialism is often related to that of globalisation (see Chapter 3). The idea of imperialism contains the notion of the intended spread of a social system from one centre of power across the globe. In comparison, the idea of globalisation suggests interconnection and interdependency of global areas in a much less purposeful way. Globalisation tends to develop as the result of economic and cultural practices which do not, of themselves, aim at global integration, but which nevertheless produce it (Tomlinson 1991). Indeed, one of the paradoxes of globalisation is that it implies the decay of previous imperial powers in that national governments are 'less and less able to act autonomously in the political-economic sphere' (Tomlinson 1991, p. 176), given conditions of contemporary governance (see

Chapter 5). Nevertheless, ideas of 'neocolonialism' or 'imperialism' act as powerful metaphors with which to describe the relationship between core and periphery areas, and serve to illustrate the potential loss of control which the host community may have in the face of foreign tourism interests and the actions of local elites. Yet, the extent to which power is able to be exercised, and hence development controlled, in any nation or destination is somewhat problematic. In many destination areas both the range of foreign investors and the sources of tourists are too wide for one country to exercise a degree of control that could be accurately described as 'imperialistic' or 'neocolonial' (Hall and Tucker 2004b). Nevertheless, there are major exceptions, particularly with respect to island micro-states that are often dependent on foreign-controlled aviation routes tied to a specific tourist generating area such as Australia, Japan or the United States (Connell 1988; Duval 2004c).

The dependence of island micro-states on tourism in the Caribbean and the Pacific is often regarded as having numerous negative economic and social impacts. For example, several authors have questioned the employment benefits of tourism in micro-states and other small developing countries (e.g. Finney and Watson 1977; Britton 1983, 1987; Cater 1987; Connell 1988; Lea 1988; Hall 1994a). In a study of tourism development in the Pacific, Hall (1994a) noted that employment in the tourism industry in the region is often marked by low payment levels, a low skills base and seasonal unemployment, although greater indigenous involvement in tourism management does appear to occur over time. However, in the case of many Pacific nations there are few or no other employment or development alternatives in a situation where populations and expectations are rapidly increasing. Therefore, the labour-intensive nature of many hotel and resort developments is seen by island governments as an important employment generator and, hopefully, a mechanism for improving the business skills of the indigenous population. Furthermore, indirect employment is also provided in the construction of hotel and tourism facilities and through improvements in linkages with other sectors in the economy, such as agriculture and fisheries.

According to Hall and Boyd (2005) peripheral areas are characterised by a number of interrelated features that impact the development of tourism, as well as other industry sectors (Botterill et al. 1997; Buhalis 1997; Hall and Jenkins 1998; Jenkins et al. 1998):

1. Peripheral areas tend to lack effective political and economic control over major decisions affecting their well-being. They are particularly susceptible to the impacts of economic globalisation and restructuring through the removal of tariffs and the development of free trade regimes (Jenkins et al. 1998). In addition, the political and economic decisions made by corporations whose headquarters lie elsewhere and political institutions in the capital or at the supranational level may lead to a situation where 'organisations and individuals within the periphery often feel a sense of alienation,

a feeling of governance from afar and a lack of control over their own destiny' (Botterill et al. 1997, p. 3).

2. Peripheral areas, by definition, are geographically remote from mass markets. This not only implies increased transportation costs to and from the core areas but may also increase communication costs with suppliers and the market as well.

3. Internal economic linkages tend to be weaker at the periphery than at the core, thereby potentially limiting the ability to achieve high multiplier effects because of the substantial degree of importation of goods and services (Archer 1989).

4. In contemporary society migration flows tend to be from the periphery to the core. This is a major issue for many peripheral and rural regions because of the impact that this can have not only on the absolute population of a given area but its profile as well. For example, migration outflows tend to be younger people looking for improved employment and education opportunities for both themselves and/or their children. The loss of younger members of communities can then have flow-on effects in terms of school closures, thereby further reinforcing such a vicious cycle of out-migration. In addition, out-migration can also lead to a loss of intellectual and social capital. However, for some peripheral areas, new forms of in-migration may occur with respect to retirement and second home development, although this will tend to be with respect to older age groups. In some situations although such developments may inject economic and human capital into peripheral areas, it may also place further strain on health and social services (Hall and Müller 2004a).

5. Botterill et al. (1997) have argued that peripheries tend to be characterised by a comparative lack of innovation as new products tend to be imported rather than developed locally.

6. Because of the economic difficulties experienced by peripheral regions, the national and local state may have greater interventionist roles than in core regions (Hall and Jenkins 1998). This is illustrated through the establishment of local economic development agencies, the development of special grant schemes for peripheral areas as in the case of the European Union, and/or agricultural subsidy programmes (Jenkins et al. 1998).

7. Information flows within the periphery and from the periphery to the core are weaker than those from the core to the periphery (Botterill et al. 1997). Such information flows may have implications for political and economic decision-making undertaken in core regions, as well as broader perceptions of place, given the difficulties that may exist in changing existing images of the periphery (D. Hall 1997).

8. Peripheral regions often retain high aesthetic amenity values as a result of being relatively underdeveloped in relation to core areas. Such high natural values may not only serve as a basis for the development of nature-based

tourism, but may also be significant for other types of tourism and leisure development, such as that associated with vacation homes (Hall and Müller 2004a).

Unfortunately, many of the expectations for long-term economic development generated by government support for tourism in peripheral areas have often failed to come to fruition (Hall and Jenkins 1998; Jenkins et al. 1998). Indeed, optimism over the potential employment and economic benefits of tourism 'owes much to a policy climate that has been uncritical over a range of issues' (Hudson and Townsend 1992, p. 50). Several reasons can be posited for this. Perhaps most important is the tendency by both government development agencies and tourism researchers to fail to see tourism within the larger development context. Most significantly, while recent government programmes have sought to address peripheral problems and imbalances by way of local and/or regional tourism development programmes, simultaneously, many governments have adopted restrictionist economic policies which have compounded the difficulties of peripheral areas adjusting to economic and social restructuring (e.g. by way of centralisation of health and transport services). In such instances policy-makers appear to be struggling with national versus local priorities (e.g. the restructuring and deregulation of agriculture and other industries versus subsidy provision), a point which also raises the issue of conflict in the values and objectives of the nation state as opposed to the local state (Jenkins et al. 1998).

A second reason for the relative lack of success of tourism development in peripheral areas is that policy-makers are also confronted with inadequate (and sometimes misleading) information on peripheral area issues, and therefore a restricted capacity to identify appropriate policy instruments to select, promote and support industries and other productive capacities as viable and sustainable alternatives. Indeed, a number of industries, and not just tourism, appear to present opportunities to diversify the economic base of peripheral areas, and also to stem the leakage and transfer of labour and capital (and thus community services and infrastructure) from peripheral economies. Nevertheless, some forms of tourism development and a focus on specific markets may actually preclude other development alternatives that may be more extractive in nature. Indeed, in some cases of maximising economic development in the periphery, the best form of tourism may well be no tourism at all. Table 8.1 details some of the macro- and micro-economic measures that the state may use to intervene in regional development policy (Hall 2003g, 2003h).

A third reason for perceived policy failure is that the initial expectations for tourism as a means of regional development were too high. Arguably, this is particularly the case with nature-based tourism which, almost by definition, tends to be very small-scale, often highly seasonal, and fails to attract the large numbers of tourists characterised by mass pleasure tourism. Indeed, policy realism often appears to be lacking with respect to nature-based tourism. Nevertheless, at a local scale such developments can still be extremely significant, allowing population and lifestyle maintenance and possibly even a small

Table 8.1   Macro- and micro-economic policy measures with regional implications

Category	Regional effect
Macro-economic regional policy measures	
Fiscal:	
Automatic stabilisers	Progressive taxes and income support measures, especially unemployment benefit
Discretionary	Regional variation in taxes and central government expenditure (including infrastructure and procurement)
Monetary	Geographical variation in interest rates and credit control
Import controls & tariffs	Protect specific industries which may be localised
Export controls & tariffs	Assist specific industries which may be localised
Currency exchange rate	Affects the competitiveness of domestic production and exports relative to imports
Public investment	Differential regional impact
Micro-economic regional policy measures	
Policies to reallocate labour:	
In situ reallocation	Occupational training and retraining, educational policies, including student support and the location of education and research facilities, journey-to-work subsidies
Spatial reallocation	Migration policies, housing assistance, employment information, improvements in efficiency of labour market
Policies to reallocate capital:	
Taxes & subsidies: inputs	Assistance with capital investment, wage subsidies, operational subsidies, research and development assistance, including new product and product differentiation, and the provision of market information
Taxes & subsidies: outputs	Export rebates, price subsidies, marketing and promotion assistance
Taxes & subsidies: technology	Research and development assistance, innovation assistance, communication access assistance
Subsidies: capital markets	Loan guarantees, export credit guarantees, venture capital provision
Administrative controls	Controls on location of investment, planning controls, reduced administrative controls

Source: Hall 2003g, 2003h

amount of growth, although not the dramatic improvements that many regions and their politicians seek.

One of the greatest difficulties in developing tourism in peripheral areas is understanding the factors by which tourism firms chose to locate successfully (Table 8.2) as well as the means by which government can intervene in assisting the location of private firms. Clearly, if tourist firms are publicly owned, then some of the commercial pressures that influence firm location in market optimal, as opposed to social or place optimal, conditions can be resisted. However, given contemporary philosophies regarding the appropriate role of the state with respect to firm ownership, then even 100% owned public firms will often need to provide a return to government.

Table 8.2   The relative importance of factors in explaining the distribution of the tourism industry

Important		Moderately important		Not important

Accessibility
– road
– aviation/
– airports
– train
– communi-
  cation
  (general)
– pedestrian
	Exchange rate	Amenity
		values
		Infrastructure
		Local linkages
		Business
		services
		Wage rates
		
		Government
		intervention
		– land and
		  premises
		– land prices
		  and rents
		– loans,
		  grants and
		  tax
		  reductions
		– planning
		– advice and
		  assistance
		– support
		  from
		  various
		  levels of
		  government
			Destination
			promotion
			(highly
			targeted and
			specific, e.g.
			special
			interest
			marketing)
			Skilled labour
				Access to
				research
				Industry
				organisation
				Unionisation
				Headquarters
				function
				Destination
				promotion
				(generic)

Source: Hall, 1995, 2003g, 2003h

Nevertheless, this is not to say that rural and peripheral area tourism policy always fails. Indeed, there are a number of successes, particularly in areas that have increased their accessibility, while several other initiatives concerning connections between agriculture, food and tourism have also proven to be extremely successful. Critical to the success of regional business strategies is the development of intangible capital (Henton and Walsesh 1997; Daley 2001; Hall 2002a). For example, many firms and regions have intangible assets – knowledge, relationships, reputations and people. However, only some firms and regions succeed in converting these assets into intangible capital which creates value when captured as intellectual property, networks, brand and talent. Appellation controls have long served to act as a form of intellectual property in terms of rural space as well as product, which have international repercussions in the ability – or otherwise – to copy such names, for example Champagne and Burgundy. More recently, however, regional specialty food and drink products have also come to be registered as intellectual property as designated quality labels within European Union and national law (Ilbery and Kneafsey 2000a), a process which Ilbery and Kneafsey (2000b) appropriately described within the context of globalisation as 'cultural relocalization'. The intellectual property of process, place and product through appellation controls can therefore act as a competitive edge for many food products. Appellation controls may also serve as the basis for place brands and reinforcement between food production and consumption and tourism destinations, as they also serve as a source of differentiation. Talent, or intellectual capital, is also important for peripheral regions as it is often subject to the loss not only of population in general but more specifically those seeking greater educational or employment benefits. Therefore strategies to attract and retain the population are very important to peripheral areas. In this the amenity values of an area, the development of a tourism industry, the deliberate location of infrastructure, such as educational institutions, airports and broad band capabilities, can all be used to attract and retain people. This strategy has been used with success in parts of Iceland, Norway and Sweden. Finally, networks, particularly between sectors such as agriculture and tourism, are arguably even more important in rural areas than in urban ones because of the need to attract and retain as much expenditure as possible in economically marginal locations.

Sustaining Rural and Peripheral Places

This chapter examined tourism in rural and peripheral areas. It noted various issues related to ideas of rurality, the impacts of tourism mobility, conflicts between different users of the countryside, and tourism as a tool in rural regional restructuring and employment generation. Rurality, as well as other conceptions of nature, is part of the cultural economy of the countryside in

Plates 8.5–8.7 Kyle of Tongue, Scotland. This spectacular peripheral landscape is highly attractive to many tourists seeking more 'natural' destinations. However, because of its harsh winter climate and relative inaccessibility the tourist season is extremely short and is limited to the summer period with the hotel closing during winter. Ironically, the attractiveness of its relative inaccessibility therefore also acts as a deterrent as well. New developments in the region such as fish farming may provide some benefits in terms of extending employment opportunities over a longer of period of time as well as providing produce for visitors during the tourist season. However, to some people the fish farm infrastructure does not meet their images of what the countryside should look like and are therefore opposed to some development applications. (see Undiscovered Scotland http://www.undiscoveredscotland. co.uk/tongue/tongue/ as well as the Scottish National Tourism Board website www.visitscotland.com)

which historical social relations are transformed into new relationships which seek to commodify culture for external and local consumption (Kneafsey 2000). For example, Blake (1996, p. 211) recognised that notions of rurality are no longer dominated by concepts of food production and that new uses of the countryside are redefining the idea of what constitutes the rural landscape. However, the more romantic notions of rurality will not disappear overnight. Indeed, they are often reinforced as part of tourism and food promotion. The romantic idea of the winemaker personally crafting wine in a cellar is extremely remote for what is, in many parts of the world, a chemical process more akin to refining. Many rural tourism opportunities do take people out of the urban environment and become an important part of a lifestyle choice to engage in what is regarded by many as a more attractive environment. The issue of whether this represents a break in routine is a moot point. It is a break from urban routine but for many people it is a regular occurrence, especially for those with second homes. This is not to deny that for many people, the immobile in urban society, the rural environment is unknown, perhaps even alien, and only known through the media.

Tourism Insight: Access and Peripherality

Although accessibility is critical to tourism in peripheral areas, it should also be noted that as accessibility to a peripheral location improves not all the benefits will be positive. Obviously, accessibility may not only increase the market area of any destination, but it can also mean that it becomes easier for the residents of an area to travel as well, thereby affecting the overall travel budget (inbound versus outbound). Just as critically, some firms in the destination will have the cost structures of their supply chain affected by new transport costs, while the changed accessibility patterns will likely lead to new market entrants developing in competition with existing tourism firms. New entrants may have better linkages to tourism generating regions and therefore have distinct competitive advantages over existing firms.

Nevertheless, rural and peripheral areas in the developed world have been affected by the same issues of economic restructuring and globalisation as have many urban environments. However, in rural regions, which already have a less complex economy, such factors can have a more marked effect in terms of the loss of infrastructure, as government withdraws services, and often the loss of economic viability for agricultural or forestry production without significant subsidies. These factors, along with changes in technology and mobility, have also contributed to population loss. Indeed, it needs to be emphasised that accessibility and mobility are not a one-way process – people can leave a place as much as they can be attracted to it as mobility options become available. In response to the perceived crisis in rural areas, tourism has become an extremely important development strategy which does hold promise for the economic competitiveness of some locations (see Table 8.3). Nevertheless, in a sometimes desperate search for economic development, a wider tax base and employment generation, inappropriate policies and development programmes may be followed. Policy measures in one sector, such as the attraction of agribusinesses or large foreign investments to a region may lead to a decline of the value to a region of other industries, such as tourism, which are based on adding value to local primary production yet are dependent on particular dimensions of the rural environment. 'Ironically, the very consequences of lack of development, the unspoilt character of the landscape and distinctive local cultures, become positive resources as far as tourism is concerned' (Duffield and Long 1981, p. 409). An integrated approach to rural and peripheral areas is therefore essential if rural development is to assume more sustainable characteristics. However, sustainability does not mean freezing the rural landscape. As Jenkins (1997) observed with respect to rural Australia, government can best assist rural areas to meet the challenges of economic restructuring and change by supporting the development of intangible capital such as leadership and generic skills (education and entrepreneurial skills), and by attaching greater importance to the provision of relevant information that affects decision-making, rather than specifically supporting programmes which encourage brochure production, walking trails and other small-scale local tourism initiatives, such as visitor centres. However, projects to support the relative transport and communication accessibility of locations are also extremely important, as is the overall amenity of a location and the nature of government regulation and intervention. Not all areas can attract large numbers of visitors and a realistic appraisal of the tourism potential of a region is essential. In order to achieve the desired goals for places, tourism in rural and peripheral areas must therefore be seen not only within the wider context of mobility but also within the broader mix of government policies and agendas.

Further Reading and Websites

For a further discussion of rural tourism issues, see Butler et al. (1998b), Hall and Page (2002), while the various chapters in Hall and Müller (2004a) provide an international overview of second home mobility (also see Müller 1999, 2004; Gallent and Tewdwr-Jones 2000). For a North American perspective on rural development, see Galston and Baehler (1995). On managing tourism in natural

Table 8.3 Key factors in the success of regional tourism development

---

- The nature of demand/the market
  - age, population, income, education, education
  - length of stay and pattern of expenditure
- Destination alternatives/competition
- Management/composition/adaptability of local labour force
- Attitudes of local communities towards tourism and second home development
- Appropriate state intervention, including infrastructure provision and land use strategies
- Attractiveness/amenity values
- Cost
- Accessibility
  - distance from population centres
  - distance from main highways
  - travel ease
  - travel time
  - travel distance

Source: Hall 1995

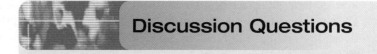

Discussion Questions

1. How are our understandings of what constitutes the image of rural areas constructed?

2. What are the differences and similarities between urban and rural re-imaging processes?

3. How might changes in accessibility, for example through the development of new plane or road routes, affect second home development in rural areas?

4. What are the advantages and disadvantages of second homes as a form of rural or peripheral area regional development?

5. To what extent might it be true to say that core–periphery relationships exist between areas in developed countries? What might be the implications of this for tourism?

6. What might be the critical issues for the successful development of tourism in peripheral areas?

areas, see Newsome et al. (2001). Butler and Boyd (2000) provide an overview of tourism in national parks. On tourism in peripheral areas in the developed world, see Brown and Hall (2000), Hall and Boyd (2005) and Jansson and Müller (2005). For a discussion on mountains, lakes and coastal areas as specific rural and peripheral environments for tourism, see Godde et al. (2000); Härkönen and Hall (2005, in press); and Garrod and Wilson (2003, 2004) respectively. An excellent discussion of notions of social and spatial marginality can be found in Mehretu et al. (2000).

US Department of Agriculture, Rural Development web page: www.rurdev .usda.gov/

Ontario Ministry of Municipal Affairs and Housing, rural tourism strategy: www.reddi.gov.on.ca/redtool/default.jsp?lang=e&page=strategies&sub= ruraltour

Ministry of Agriculture and Forestry, New Zealand, rural tourism resource book: www.maf.govt.nz/mafnet/rural-nz/profitability-and-economics/ emerging-industries/rural-tourism/httoc.htm

UK National Association of Farmers Markets: www.farmersmarkets.net/

UK Countryside Agency: www.countryside.gov.uk/

'Eat the View' project promoting sustainable local produce: www.country side.gov.uk/LivingLandscapes/eat_the_view/index.asp

Coastal and Marine Tourism: Development and Issues

9

Although tourism development has been spatially focused on the coast and the beach, for much of the past century (as witnessed, for example, in the slogan of the four 's's of tourism – sun, sand, surf and sex), coastal, marine and ocean tourism is widely regarded as one of the fastest-growing areas of contemporary tourism in terms of both volume and diversity (Miller and Auyong 1991; Kim and Kim 1996; National Oceanic and Atmospheric Administration 1997; Orams 1999; Bramwell 2003; Garrod and Wilson 2003). Nevertheless, it should be noted that the attractiveness of the coast for tourism is also socially created. Until the end of the eighteenth century the sea was not a focus of leisure activity. It was not until then that the aristocracy and some of the new middle classes went to the newly fashionable coastal spas to take the waters as they had previously in the inland mineral spas. In the Victorian era the attractiveness of the coastal resorts was reinforced by the arrival of the railways and, in some cases, by coastal steamer services from the cities. However, sea bathing in this period was completely different from the present day. Apart from wearing far more body covering, the sexes were usually also segregated. It was only in the 1960s that bikinis became popular. Moreover, it was not until the 1930s that getting a suntan became one of the fashions associated with the beach tourism of the middle classes, as until that time a tan was something which was associated with the working class (by virtue of their working outdoors) (Soane 1993; Walton 1983; Feifer 1985; Taylor 1993; Towner 1996; Shaw and Williams 1997; Simpson 1997).

The exact numbers of people who may be classified as marine tourists remains unknown. Nevertheless, the selling of 'sun, sand and surf experiences', the development of beach resorts and the increasing popularity of marine tourism (e.g. fishing, scuba diving, windsurfing and yachting) has all placed increasing pressure on the coast, an area which is already highly concentrated in terms of agriculture, human settlements, fishing and industrial location (Miller 1993; United Nations Environment Programme et al. 1996; Warner 1999; Tratalos and Austin 2001; Orams 2002). However, because of the highly dynamic nature of the coastal environment, any development which interferes with the natural coastal system may have severe consequences for the long-term stability of the environment (Cicin-Sain and Knecht 1998). Indeed, the United States National Oceanic and Atmospheric Administration (1997) recognises that 'virtually all coastal and ocean issue areas affect coastal tourism and recreation either directly or indirectly'.

This chapter provides an overview of some of the key issues facing ocean and coastal tourism, the environmental impacts of coastal and marine tourism and associated management difficulties.

Defining Marine and Coastal Tourism

The concept of coastal tourism embraces the full range of tourism, leisure and recreationally oriented activities that take place in the coastal zone and the offshore coastal waters. These include coastal tourism development (e.g. accommodation, restaurants, the food industry and second homes) and the infrastructure supporting coastal development (e.g. retail businesses, marinas and activity suppliers) (Bramwell 2003). Also included are tourism activities such as recreational boating, coast and marine-based ecotourism, cruises, swimming, recreational fishing, snorkelling and diving (Miller and Auyong 1991; Miller 1993). Marine tourism is closely related to the concept of coastal tourism but also includes ocean-based tourism such as deep-sea fishing and

Plate 9.1   Estoril, Portugal, is a major coastal beach resort just north of Lisbon. However, the large numbers of tourists in summer creates substantial environmental pressures on the beach system. (see www.estorilcoast-tourism.com as well as the national tourist site at www.portugalinsite.com)

cruising by yacht and ship. Oram (1999, p. 9) defines marine tourism as including 'those recreational activities that involve travel away from one's place of residence and which have as their host or focus the marine environment (where the marine environment is defined as those waters which are saline and tide-affected)'. Such a definition is significant because as well as having a biological and recreational base it also emphasises shore-based activities, such as land-based whale watching, reef walking, cruise ship supply and yachting events, within the overall ambit of marine tourism.

Sustainable Marine Tourism

As with many other aspects of tourism, concerns over the impacts of tourism on the physical environment and related dimensions of sustainable development have become substantial interests influencing research on ocean and marine tourism (Orams 1999). Improvements in technology, including transport (e.g. tourist submarines) and recreational technology (e.g. scuba diving), have also made the oceans more accessible to tourists than ever before. For example, marine parks, coral reefs and areas which are in relatively easy reach of scuba divers have come to be widely regarded by governments and the private sector as significant natural resources which can be developed through tourism (Tratalos and Austin 2001; Rouphael and Inglis 2002).

With respect to using tourism as a tool for economic development, international agencies such as the World Bank have increasingly argued that although marine parks are usually established to help protect endangered ecosystems and maintain biological diversity, trade-offs exist between protection and use, and ways must be found to produce economic benefits from marine areas while still yielding protection benefits. This is a question of particular importance to coastal regions, particularly those of less developed countries and island states, for which marine tourism is an important, if not the major, component of their economy (e.g. see Wong 1986, 1990; Davis and Tisdell 1994; Nijkamp and Verdonkschot 1995; D.R. Hall, 1998; Wrangham 1999; Gössling 2003). For example, Dixon et al. (1993) argued that in the case of the Bonaire Marine Park in the Netherlands Antilles results indicated that proper management can yield both protection and development benefits, although it was noted that questions of ecosystem carrying capacity and retention of the economic benefits of tourism within the country did raise important issues for longer-term sustainability of the marine-based tourism product. Indeed, issues surrounding the impacts of tourism on island micro-states, whose territories are dominated by their maritime areas, comprise a major focus of research on the impacts of tourism in coastal and marine areas (Hall and Page 1996). Nevertheless, the extent to which tourism has been a contributing factor to environmental, economic and social change in coastal areas, and is, in turn, affected by such factors, remains one of the central issues of research on coastal and ocean tourism (Hall and Page 2002). However, while the concept of sustainability has been one of the major factors influencing tourism research (Hall and Lew 1998), concentration on the environmental dimensions of tourism in coastal and marine areas has been the main focus of tourism research.

The Impacts of Tourism

That tourism can have harmful impacts on the physical marine environment is now well recognised (e.g. Beekhuis 1981; Archer 1985; Baines 1987; Hanna and Wells 1992). However, that tourism *automatically* has a negative effect on coastal areas has also become something of a truism. Undoubtedly, unplanned and poorly managed tourism development can damage the natural environment, but the overall understanding of the interaction between tourism and the environment, particularly within coastal areas, is quite poor, with debates over the impacts of tourism development often dealing in generalities rather than the outcomes of scientific research in a specific environment or on a specific species or even on local social and economic systems (Hall 1996b; Bauer 2001; Bellan and Bellan-Santini 2001).

In the majority of coastal regions of the world basic data on tourism and its associated impacts is poor (Wong 1993; Orams 1999; Hall and Page 2002). For example, within the context of the South Pacific, an area that is highly dependent on marine and coastal tourism for its economic well-being (Hall and Page 1996), there has been no systematic study of the environmental impacts of tourism over the region as a whole. Base-line data, that is information regarding the condition of the natural environment prior to tourism development, is invariably lacking or, at best, highly fragmented (German Federal Agency for Nature Conservation 1997; Warnken and Buckley 1998). Even in Australia, one of the most economically developed nations of the region, information about the environmental impacts of tourism on coastal areas is relatively poor, even given attempts to provide a comprehensive overview of coastal zone management in the early 1990s (C.M. Hall 1998; Warnken and Buckley 2000). Indeed, the multiplicity of different agencies involved in managing or developing coastal resources was regarded as a barrier, not only in developing integrated management strategies but also in information sharing and capacity building (Resources Assessment Commission 1992a, 1992b, 1992c; Altman et al. 1993). In addition, development-specific reports, such as environmental impact statements on resort or tourism developments, required by law in many Western countries, are often not required in the less developed countries because environmental legislation is still being developed or, if it exists, is often not adequately implemented (German Federal Agency for Nature Conservation 1997; Briassoulis and van der Straaten 1999; Weaver 2001).

The lack of information on the environmental impacts of tourism in many areas, and in island micro-states in particular, has arisen for several reasons. First, substantial business and political concern over environmental conditions has only emerged in recent years. Second, many of the governments of the less developed world have had far greater priorities (e.g. economic development, health, welfare and education), for their limited financial resources than environmental monitoring or conservation. Third, and as a partial consequence of the above two factors, the resources and scientific expertise were not generally available to undertake the vast amount of research required (Hall 1996b). In recent years, however, greater concern has been expressed over the condition of the coastal and the marine environment. This has not been due to tourism alone. The demise of many fisheries, such as in Atlantic Canada and in the North Sea, has also hastened government and industry concerns about the condition of the oceans and the marine environment. Nevertheless, the increasing economic significance of tourism, the growth of nature-based tourism activities, and the perceived desire of many consumers to experience high-quality natural environments have contributed to an increase in research on the physical impacts of tourism (e.g. Hanna and Wells 1992).

Regional surveys have often proved valuable in identifying the impacts of tourism on marine ecosystems. For example, in the Caribbean, adverse effects that have been reported include damage from small boat anchors, boat groundings, and snorkellers and scuba divers. In addition, island resort development has brought about erosion, pesticide runoff, sewage as well as oil spills and over-fishing. Anchor damage is regarded as one of the most serious threats to marine resources in the Caribbean, particularly given the growing number of medium-sized and large cruise ships operating in the region (Allen 1992). Indeed, the rapid growth of the cruise ship industry in the Pacific Islands (Dwyer and Forsyth 1996, 1998), the Caribbean (J. Hall and Braithwaite 1990) and the world's polar regions (Hall and Johnston 1995) has meant that the impacts of cruising have become a significant area of marine tourism research. Although exact figures are impossible to obtain given the number of smaller cruise tourism operations that operate outside industry assocation, it was estimated that in 2000 cruise lines carried almost 10 million passengers (Kester 2003). According to Kester, the number of berths available increased from 45 000 in 1980 to 212 000 in early 2002. Cruising provides an interesting form of tourism mobility as the transport 'container' is itself part of the attraction (it could possibly be described as a mobile destination or enclave resort), while the spatial limits of tourists at the various stopping points tend to be quite restricted because the majority of time is spent on the mobile cruise ship. Nevertheless, while guests are encouraged to spend money (and therefore time) on board cruise-ships, there is substantial competition between destination to attract cruise-ships.

Cruise tourism is significant for a number of ports because cruise tourists are higher yield tourists, spending, on average, much higher amounts per day than other categories of international tourists (Dwyer and Forsyth 1996, 1998; Ritter and Schafer 1998). In a study of cruise tourism in Australia, Dwyer and Forsyth (1996) reported that home-porting cruise ships in Australia, with a marketing emphasis on flycruise packages for inbound tourists, had the greatest potential for generating large expenditure inflows to Australia. In addition, they reported that because of leakages due to foreign ownership and foreign sourcing of inputs, the average expenditure per passenger per cruise injected into the Australian economy is twice as great for the coastal as opposed to the international cruise. Nevertheless, there is significant debate over the impacts of cruise ships. Ritter and Schafer (1998), for example, argue that the ecological impact of cruises is low, spending by individual tourists is high and accultural processes are minimal. They claim that although the number of jobs directly created as a result of cruises is low, it compares very favourably against most other forms of travel as a development option. In contrast, Marsh and Staple (1995), in a study of cruise tourism in the Canadian Arctic, concluded that given the environmental fragility of much of the region and the vulnerability to impacts of small, remote, largely aboriginal communities, great care should be exercised in using the area for cruise tourism. Similarly, in examining some of the cultural dimensions of the cruise ship experience, Wood (2000) argued that the global nature of the cruise market has meant that cruise ships have become examples of 'globalisation at sea', with corresponding deterritorialisation, cultural theming and simulation. In addition, concern over the environmental impacts of cruise ships led the United States Environmental Protection Agency (EPA) to host a series of meetings in 2000 to solicit input from the public, the cruise ship industry and other stakeholders on the issue of discharges from cruise ships (Rethinking Tourism Project 2000).

Table 9.1 records a number of environmental and ecological impacts associated with tourism development in coastal areas. The range of tourism-related impacts is similar to that for many other environments (Edington and Edington 1986; Hall 1999; Hall and Page 2002). However, tourism impact may arguably be more problematic due to the tendency for tourism development and tourists to concentrate on or near the ecologically and geomorphologically dynamic coastal environment as well as the role of water as a carrier of pollutants. For example, because of the highly dynamic nature of the coastal environment and the significance of mangroves and the limited coral sand supply for island beaches in particular, any development which interferes with the natural system may have severe consequences for the long-term stability of the environment (Hall 1996b). The impact of poorly developed tourism projects on the sand cays of the Pacific has been well documented (Baines 1987; Clarke 1991; Minerbi 1992; Hall 1996b):

● Near-shore vegetation and mangrove clearing exposes the island to sea storm erosion and decreases plant material decomposition on the beach, thereby reducing nutrient availability for flora and fauna.

● Manoeuvring by bulldozer (instead of hand clearing) results in scarring and soil disturbance and makes sand deposit loose and vulnerable to erosion.

● Excessive tapping of the fresh ground-water lens induces salt water intrusion which then impairs vegetation growth and human water use and renders the cay susceptible to storm damage and further erosion.

● Sewage outfall in shallow water and reef flats may led to an excessive build-up of nutrients, thereby leading to algal growth which may eventually kill coral.

● Seawalls built to trap sand in the short term impair the natural seasonal distribution of sand, resulting in the long run in a net beach loss and in a reduction of the island land mass.

● Boat channels blasted in the reef act as a sand trap. In time they fill with sand which is no longer circulating around the island. This sand is replaced by other sand eroded from the vegetated edges, changing the size and shape of the island and in time threatening the island's integrity (Baines 1987).

Another coastal environment which has been substantially affected by tourism in tropical and sub-tropical areas is the clearing and dredging of mangroves and estuaries for marinas, resorts and beaches. Mangroves and estuarine environments are extremely significant nursery areas for a variety of fish species. The loss of natural habitat due to dredging or infilling may therefore have dramatic impacts on fish catches. In addition, there may be substantial impacts on the whole of the estuarine food chain, with a subsequent loss of ecological diversity. A further consequence of mangrove loss is

Table 9.1   Environmental and ecological impacts of tourism on coastal environments

---

Environmental degradation and pollution
- Degradation and pollution of the environment due to tourism urbanisation and developments such as golf courses
- Pollution by littering
- Eutrophication of lagoons and estuaries as a result of increased nutrient inputs

Destruction of habitats and damage to ecosystems
- Poorly managed tourism may result in destruction of high-quality natural environments through either inappropriate development or tourism activities
- Unmanaged human interference and disturbance of specific species of fauna and flora
- Dynamite blasting and overfishing for certain species
- Coral and shellfish species used as souvenirs for tourists
- Trampling by visitors
- Sandy beaches created on coastlines which are not naturally sandy

Loss of coastal and marine resources
- Interference with inland and coastal natural processes
  - excessive ground water extraction by large resorts induces salt water intrusion and deterioration of water quality and recharge of the aquifer
- Coastal ecosystem damage and destruction through tourism development
- Terrestrial runoff and dredging on coastal areas
  - damage to coral reef and marine resources caused by the construction of tourist infrastructure such as runways, marinas, harbours, parking areas and roads, and use of coral limestone in hotels and resort developments
- Damage or destruction by tourist activities
  - damage or destruction of specific elements of the coastal environmental systems such as dune systems, coral reefs, lagoons, mangroves, saltwater marshes, and wetlands due to excessive visitation and/or unmanaged exploitation and development of those resources
  - disturbance to near shore aquatic life due to thrill crafts and boat tours
- Introduced exotic species
  - increased sea and air inter-island traffic creates the danger of accidental importation of exotic species, which can be very destructive to indigenous flora and fauna
- Damage to sand-cay ecosystems
- Damage to mangrove and wetland ecosystems
  - to many tourists mangroves and wetlands are often regarded as unsightly, even though they are highly productive ecological systems; mangroves also provide protection against coastal erosion
- Damage to coastal ecosystems, such as heath land or rainforest
- Loss of sandy beaches, dune systems and shoreline erosion
  - loss of sandy beaches due to onshore development and construction of seawalls

Coastal pollution
- Waste water discharge and sewage pollution
- Coastal water pollution and siltation due to near shore resort construction and runoff from resort areas result in the destruction of natural habitat, coral and feeding grounds for fish
- Marine and harbour pollution
  - coastal oil pollution due to motorised vehicles and ships

Surface water and ground water diversion
- Diversion of streams and water sources from local use to resort use, with resulting decline in water availability for domestic and other productive uses and farming, particularly taro cultivation

---

Sources: After Minerbi 1992; Hall 1996b; German Federal Agency for Nature Conservation 1997; Gormsen 1997; Wong 1998; Gössling 2001a, 2001b; Garrod and Wilson 2003

reduced protection against erosion of the shoreline, thereby increasing vulner-ability to storm surge. Removal of mangroves, of course, has not only impacted the immediate area of clearance, but has also effected other coastal areas through the transport of greater amounts of marine sediment (Clarke 1991). In the case of the Denarau Island resort development in Fiji, 130 hectares of man-grove forest was dredged to construct an 18-hole golf course and create an artificial marina (Minerbi 1992).

One of the most obvious ways in which tourism-related development has impacted the coastal environment is the effect of tourism and tourist activities on coral reefs (Van Treeck and Schumacher 1998; Tratalos and Austin 2001; Rouphael and Inglis 2002; Zakai and Chadwick-Furman 2002). 'Coral reefs are very vulnerable, and adverse human activities may result in a lower capacity to regenerate, or the death of entire coral colonies' (Tourism Council of the South Pacific 1988, p. 12). Tourists can directly impact coral reefs in a number of ways. Skin divers and snorkellers can damage coral by hitting it with their fins as well as through souvenir-gathering. In order to restrict such damage, Vanuatu has been actively educating divers on the importance of maintaining correct buoyancy. In other significant coral reef areas, such as Australia's Great Barrier Reef, reef walking by tourists at low tide has resulted in substantial damage to sections of the reef within easy shore access.

The growth of coastal tourism in the Red Sea has also had substantial impacts on coral reefs in the region in terms of both the effects of construction and infrastructure development as well as the direct effects of snorkelling and diving. According to Hawkins and Roberts (1994), approximately 19% of Egypt's reefs were substantially affected by tourism in the early 1990s, but this figure was expected to rise to over 30% by 2000. Hawkins and Roberts (1994) reported that tourist-related development has already caused substantial damage to inshore reefs near to Hurgharda from infilling, sedimentation and over-fishing for marine curios. Elsewhere in the region, construction of tourist facilities and infrastructure was also beginning to modify reef habitats which, up until the early 1990s, had been generally restricted to the direct effects of diving and snorkelling. While the growth in the numbers of arrivals to the Red Sea area appeared to be sustainable for the planned developments, the authors concluded that the massive expansion planned throughout the northern Red Sea substantially threatened the reef ecosystem and warned that unless the pace of tourist development is reduced the carrying capacity of coral reefs would be exceeded, with widespread reef degradation the likely result (Hawkins and Roberts 1994).

Nevertheless, the major indirect aspect of tourism's impacts on coral reefs is the environmental effects of urban and resort development, land clearing and pollution. Pollutants can come from both land (e.g. resorts), and marine sources (e.g. tourist boats and ships). Land-based pollution is often in the form of excessive nutrients from sewage and fertilisers. While both of these types of pollution may come from non-tourism sources, it should be noted that septic tanks or inadequate sewage systems at resorts, or fertiliser run-off from golf courses may substantially impact reef systems (Kuji 1991). Excessive nutrients promote algal growth at the expense of coral, leading to the smothering of coral and its eventual death. Similarly, sedimentation leads to silting and water cloudiness, which cuts off sunlight to the coral reef also killing it. In the case of the Cape Tribulation Road, constructed near Daintree in northern Queensland by the state government in the mid-1980s in an effort to develop tourism, sedimentation on adjacent coral reefs increased more than six-fold in comparison with undisturbed catchments in the same area (Fisk and Harriott 1989; Partain and Hopley 1990; Hopley et al. 1993).

In his examination of the impacts of tourism development in the Pacific, Minerbi (1992, p. 69) was scathing in his criticism of the environmental impacts of tourism:

> Resorts and golf courses increase environmental degradation and pollution. Littering has taken place on beaches and scenic lookouts and parks. Marine sanctuaries have been run over and exploited by too many tourists.... Tourism has presented itself as a clean and not polluting industry but its claims have not come true.

Yet despite the litany of damage noted by Minerbi, it must be emphasised that the environmental impacts of tourism are certainly less than those of many other industries in the Pacific islands and other coastal regions, such as agriculture, fishing, forestry and mining, as well as wider processes of coastal urbanisation. This is not to deny that tourism has had substantial impacts on the coastal environment, but rather it is to emphasise that specific regional research on environmental impacts is sparse (Milne 1990) and also needs to be seen within the wider context of the effects of different development strategies. Given this situation, it may well be the case that tourism is receiving the blame for various forms of environmental degradation for which it is only partially responsible (Hall 1996b). Other forms of impact, such as overpopulation, inappropriate urban development and land clearance may be far more significant but are perhaps not so easy to blame as an industry as visible as tourism, particularly when businesses will often be owned by foreigners. Correctly managed, therefore, tourism may well be more ecologically sustainable than many other industries in coastal areas.

Management Strategies

The development of management strategies for coastal and ocean tourism needs to be understood in the light of the nature of the management problem, the scale at which the problem is addressed, and the relative extent of intervention by government and quasi-government agencies. Planning for coastal tourism has traditionally focused on land use zoning and site development regulations. However, in recent years, tourism planning has adapted and expanded to include broader environmental and socio-cultural concerns, and the need to develop and promote economic development strategies at local, regional and national scales, particularly within an increasingly globalised tourism environment (Hall 2000a). For example, Gajaraj (1988) argued that UNEP's (United Nations Environmental Programme) Regional Seas Action Plans provide a good basis to find the best practical solutions for the development of environmentally sound coastal tourism because they provide a transnational basis for environmental action. Nevertheless, one of the key problems in coastal and marine tourism management is in the governance of multiple actors at different scales and often in different national jurisdictions.

An understanding of tourism policy processes therefore lies at the heart of broader goals of integrated coastal tourism management (Romeril 1988; Smith 1994). Yet the diverse nature of stakeholders in coastal and marine areas and the wide range of development pressures have meant that the impacts of tourism are often a difficult subject for policy-makers and planners to define and grasp conceptually. This has meant that there have been substantial difficulties for policy-makers in developing appropriate policies, while the coordination of the various elements of the coastal tourism product has also been extremely problematic. As Hall and Jenkins (1995) argued, the formulation and implementation of tourism and recreation public policies present several conundrums. Unrealistic expectations of tourism's potential are unfortunately combined with a lack of understanding by decision-makers of the potentially adverse economic, environmental and social consequences of coastal tourist development that threaten to curtail its benefits (Hudson 1996). Indeed, much of the driving images of coastal and ocean tourism are closely related to perceptions of a relative lack of development (e.g. Roehl and Ditton 1993). In evaluating the effective integration of tourism within coastal areas in a manner which ensures sustainable coastal development, one is forced to conclude that effective government involvement in coastal tourism development has been relatively unsuccessful because of the often *ad hoc* nature of government decision-making and failures in inter-agency cooperation and communication (e.g. Visser and Njuguna 1992; Hudson 1996; White et al. 1997).

The reasons for such failures lie in a lack of understanding of policy processes as well as the governance of complex policy problems which the coastal environment represents. Although the goals of tourism development may be readily apparent at, say, a regional level, they will often not be integrated or related to other policy objectives concerning coastal management and conservation. In the case of coastal and marine tourism, while a range of policy instruments are utilised to achieve management goals, they are often not effectively related to macro-policy goals even if they are at the micro-policy level. The two most widely used types of instrument appear to be regulatory and voluntary measures. For example, regulatory instruments, such as regulations, permits and licences, have a legal basis and require monitoring and enforcement. In the Virgin Islands National Park and in national parks in the Florida Keys restrictions have been placed on anchorings and moorings in an endeavour to reduce environmental impacts (Allen 1992), while a substantial regulatory framework has been established in many countries with respect to controlling whale watching, as well as other forms of marine mammal-based tourism (Orams 2003, 2005).

Voluntary instruments, actions or mechanisms that do not require substantial public expenditure, for example the development of information and interpretative programmes, are often used to educate the public about appropriate behaviours in marine areas (e.g. Hockings 1994; Orams 1995, 1999; Aiello 1998; Lück 2003) or health and safety issues (Wilks and Atherton 1994). The development of voluntary codes of conduct for operators and visitors, as in the case of Antarctic and Arctic cruise ships, may also assist in ensuring that appropriate behaviours occur in coastal and ocean tourism (Hall and Johnston 1995).

With the selection of the most appropriate instrument or, more likely, a range of instruments, being dependent on the particular circumstances of each coastal region or location, there is no universal 'best way' to manage coastal and marine tourism. Instead, each region or locale needs to select the appropriate policy mix for its own development requirements and specific environment (Lagarigue 1988; Briassoulis and van der Straaten 1999). However, as in other environments within which tourism occurs, there is often a strong emphasis on public–private relationships as well as, increasingly, on non-government organisations (NGOs) such as conservation groups. For example, an analysis of the effect of NGOs on socio-economic development in Goa, India, demonstrated that they are essential in managing the adverse impacts on coastal tourism (Singh 1999), whereas in other locations NGOs may only make a minor contribution to coastal management strategies.

Given the potential impacts of tourism on the coastal environment, it is therefore not surprising that organisations such as the Environment and Social Commission for Asia and the Pacific (ESCAP) (1995a, 1995b, 1996a, 1996b) have been trying to encourage sustainable forms of coastal development in Asia and the Pacific. In the United States, the National Oceanic and Atmospheric Administration (1997) regards the sustainable development of coastal tourism as being dependent on:

- good coastal management practices (particularly regarding the proper siting of tourism infrastructure and the provision of public access);

- clean water and air, and healthy coastal ecosystems;

- maintaining a safe and secure recreational environment through the management of coastal hazards, and the provision of adequate levels of safety for the various water users;

- maintenance of the recreational and amenity values of beaches (including beach restoration efforts); and

- appropriate policies for wildlife and habitat protection.

Unfortunately, while the above policy measures are useful, there is usually little or no coordination between programmes that promote and market tourism and those that aim to manage coastal and marine areas (Smith 1994;

Hudson 1996). Environmental or planning agencies often fail to understand tourism, while tourism promotion authorities tend not to be involved with the evaluation of its effects or its planning and management. Implementation strategies often fail to recognise the interconnections that exist between agencies in trying to manage environmental issues, particularly when, as in the case of the relationship between tourism and the coastal environment, responsibilities may cut across more traditional lines of authority. Therefore, one of the greatest challenges facing coastal managers is how to integrate tourism development within the overall tasks of coastal management, and thus increase the likelihood of long-term sustainability of the coastal system as a whole (White et al. 1997; Cicin-Sain and Knecht 1998). Nevertheless, solving such dilemmas will be vital for the many countries which have a substantial interest in marine and coastal tourism, particularly when environmental quality becomes another means to achieve a competitive edge in the tourism marketplace.

Discussion Questions

1. What are some of the key problems associated with evaluating the environmental impacts of tourism in the marine environment?

2. Why is the existence of multiple agencies with administrative responsibilities in coastal zones a potential problem for the achievement of successful coastal zone management strategies?

3. What might be the arguments for and against the adoption of voluntary regulation of activities in coastal zone tourism, e.g. whale watching, reef scuba diving or even walking through sand dunes?

Further Reading and Websites

Issues of marine ecotourism are well covered in Garrod and Wilson (2003), while Bramwell (2003) provides a good collection of papers on the sustainability of mass coastal tourism. Shaw and Williams (1997), Soane (1993) and Walton (1983) provide accounts of British seaside resorts. See Gössling (2003) on tourism and development in tropical islands and Duval (2004c) on tourism in the Caribbean. Orams (1999) is the leading textbook on marine tourism.

Caribbean Environment Programme: www.cep.unep.org/

Coral reefs: http://www.uneptie.org/pc/tourism/sensitive/coral.htm

UNEP Islands website: http://islands.unep.ch/

UNEP Mediterranean Action Plan: www.unepmap.org/

United Nations Environment Programme, Production and Consumption Branch, Coastal zone management: http://www.uneptie.org/pc/tourism/sensitive/coastal.htm

World Wide Fund for Nature has a number of sections on marine and tourism issues: www.panda.org/

Part IV

Tourism futures:
emerging agendas
and issues in
mobility

The Future of Tourism

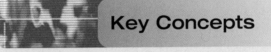

10

Key Concepts

- Futurist
- PEST analysis
- Forecasting
- Longitudinal data analysis
- Time series
- Wildcards
- Demography
- Technology
- Chaos
- Catastrophe
- Space tourism
- X Prize
- Space elevator

Attempts to influence, understand and, perhaps, control the future appear to be inherent to all societies and cultures. Whether it be through divination or prophecy or through more systematic forms of quantitative forecasting, humans seek to determine their futures. Such is the contemporary importance of understanding the future that there is now a well-established set of futurist associations, organisations and individuals that provide advice to governments and businesses. The future is even traded on the stock exchange. At the beginning of the twenty-first century concern over the future in much of the developed and developing world is such that 'our anxiety has naturally enhanced the position of our prophetic politicians, and of our futurologists and forecasters – they have the map of the future, they will tell us how to get there' (Dublin 1991, p. 44).

Such futurists can be extremely influential in not only affecting government and industry decision-making but also shaping popular perceptions of what the future will be (e.g. Beckwith 1967; Kahn and Wiener 1967; Fuller 1969, 1981; Toffler 1972, 1981; Bell 1973; Masuda 1981; Naisbitt 1982; Hawken 1984). Such is the influence of some futurists in policy-making that it could even be argued that they also help shape the future they predict. Nevertheless, the map of the future is often not very accurate. For example, as Hall (2000b) noted in an article on the future of tourism, one of the earliest books on the international tourism industry stated: 'There is, humanly speaking, undoubtedly no more potent force to allay the fears and hatreds which beset nations than the tourist movement' (Norval 1936, p. 149). Written in early 1935, the author could likely not have forecast the chaos about to affect the international tourism industry. In the year the book was published the Spanish Civil War broke out and Japan invaded China. Three years later Europe, which already had substantial cross-border leisure and business travel, became embroiled in the Second World War and international travel for leisure virtually came to a halt. Similarly, forecasts about the international economy and international tourism (e.g. Economist Intelligence Unit 1995; World Tourism Organisation 1995, 1997a; Qu and Zhang 1997; World Travel and Tourism Council 1998) were dramatically shaken in 1997 and 1998 by the Asian financial crisis. Moreover, as Law (2001) noted, not only were forecasting models unable to anticipate the impacts of the financial crisis, but they also performed poorly in predicting the recovery from the crisis in terms of tourism arrival numbers in the Asian region. Indeed, the situation in the region, and for tourism internationally, has become even more confused since the terrorist attacks on September 11, 2001, the SARS outbreak of 2002–03, the American-led invasion of Iraq in 2003, and in 2004 the Asian avian flu outbreak and the terrorist attacks in Madrid. What was at one time seemingly a steady-state situation with respect to international tourism growth has become substantially impacted by the effects of unforeseen, seemingly random events on the international tourism system. All this serves to highlight the difficulties in predicting the future of tourism.

This chapter provides an overview of some of the key issues likely to be associated with the future of tourism as well as briefly noting some of the means by which tourism forecasts are developed. The chapter highlights some of the difficulties associated with forecasting before going on to note key issues that arise in undertaking a PEST (political, economic, social and technological trends) analysis of tourism. This chapter also serves to introduce some of the issues regarding politics and security and global environmental change that will be discussed in more detail in the following chapters.

Predicting the Future

The choice of method to predict the future requires trade-offs between expected accuracy and precision and the various time, human resource and financial resources required for each method. Table 10.1 presents an overview of a number of different approaches towards forecasting tourism. The first three approaches depend upon quantitative approaches whereas the two qualitative approaches rely upon the judgement of experts or consumers. Nevertheless, there is no clear conclusion as to which approaches may prove to be more accurate (Witt and Witt 1992). Indeed, in some cases forecasts may be wildly wrong. For example, in 1973 and 1974 a delphi study was undertaken in the United States of a panel of 904 experts to identify those developments likely to occur in the USA that would influence park and recreation management in the future (Shafer et al. 1974, in Smith 1995). The panel concluded, among other things, that by 2000 (the actual situation is noted in brackets):

● 500 miles (800 km) is considered a reasonable one-way distance for weekend pleasure travel (this is only applicable to the very small minority of the American population who undertake weekend pleasure travel by plane).

● Average retirement age is 50 (average retirement age has remained over 60).

● Middle-class American families vacation on other continents as commonly as they vacation in the USA in the 1970s (middle-class Americans still vacation domestically much more than outside the Americas).

● Electric power or other non-polluting engines replace internal combustion engines in recreational vehicles (very few recreational vehicles use electric power or non-polluting engines though pressure for such use is increasing because of concerns over environmental impacts).

● Travel in large parks is limited to minimal-impact mass transit, for example tramways, air transport and underground rapid transit (travel in large parks is still mainly conducted by cars on roads though some attempts have been made to introduce public transport, for example at the Grand Canyon).

Obviously, the further out from the time of forecast the more likely it is that the prediction will be wrong. Nevertheless, evidence suggests that forecasts

Table 10.1 Summary of requirements and characteristics of tourism forecasting models

	Trend extrapolation	Structural	Simulation	Qualitative (I) (delphi, expert panels, environmental scanning)	Qualitative (II) (consumer/industry surveys)
Technical expertise required	Low to medium	Medium to high	High	Low to medium	Low to medium
Type of conceptual knowledge or data required	Time series data	Cross-sectional data and causal relationships	Time series data, cross-relationships, and change processes	Expert and experiential sectional data, causal	Expert and experiential
Required data precision	Medium to high	High	High	Low to medium	Low
Appropriate forecast horizon	Short	Short to medium	Long	Long	Short
Time required for forecast	Short	Short to medium	Long	Medium to long	Short to medium
Type of problem best suited for	Simple, stable or cyclic	Moderately complex with several variables and known, stable relationships	Complex with known and quantifiable relationships and some feedback effects	Complex with known relationships and elements of uncertainty	Simple to moderately complex, also useful for stable and cyclic problems

Sources: After Smith 1995; Frechtling 1996; Hall 2003

Tourism Insight: Time Series and Longitudinal Analysis

Much tourism forecasting is derived from an analysis of time series and is based on the notion that future values have a probability distribution conditioned by a knowledge of past values. In the analysis of time series three components are usually recognised:

- Long-term or trend components: the broad, smooth undulating motion of the system over a relatively long period of time. These can often be partially isolated by using a moving mean.
- Cyclical or oscillating functions: these move about the trend, often exhibiting a seasonal effect or local variations and as such are extremely important in the analysis of tourist arrival and departure data.
- Random or irregular components: these are revealed when cyclical and trend functions are removed from the time series and are essentially a residual component.

Longitudinal data analysis is extremely valuable in predicting future trends and is usually undertaken in four different ways (Crouchly 1987a; Hand 1996):

1. Repeated cross-sectional surveys 'in which a population is sampled at different points in time but with no attempt to retain the same respondents for each cross-section. This allows for statistical comparison but is not able to isolate change due to population composition versus change due to an individual respondent's behaviour.
2. Classic panel surveys which have the same respondents sampled at different points in time. However, such surveys are often marked by the attrition of respondents in each round of the survey.
3. Rotating panel surveys in which some respondents are retired after each survey and then replaced by new ones, therefore reducing the attrition rates that typically occur in classic panel surveys.
4. Split or mixed panel surveys which combine all of the above in order to maximise the benefits of each.

Three different reasons for variation in the results of a longtitudinal analysis can be identified (Hand 1996; Robinson 1998):

- Heterogeneity: this represents variation between individuals due to both observed and unobserved external forces/influences.
- Non-stationarity: this is the variation of individual choice probabilities over time. These may result from temporal changes or shifts in the values and significance of observed and unobserved exogenous variables (e.g. changes in working hours or business opening hours (observed), changes in tastes, motivations and habits (unobserved).
- Inter-temporal state dependence: this is the dependence of current behaviour on past behaviour and of future behaviour on current behaviour (Hand 1996).

based on expert judgement are seldom accurate. Indeed, there is a very large body of research that suggests that experts in various areas seldom generate better predictions than non-experts who have received some training, and that the predictions of experts are completely outperformed by those made by simple statistical models (e.g. see Camerer and Johnson 1991). However, there are also substantial variations between those who forecast the future proper-ties of physical systems versus those who forecast socio-economic systems. For example, in his review of the work of future-predicting experts, Sherden (1998) concluded that meteorologists were not always correct, but had by far the best accuracy when compared to economists, stock market analysts, population researchers, and business and social trend forecasters (see also Mills and Pepper 1999). Furthermore, most experts overestimate their ability to perform accurately in comparison with non-experts (e.g. Allwood and Granhag 1999), although some exceptions exist with respect to weather forecasters and expert game players (Bolger and Wright 1992). The reason for such over-confidence is usually grounded in greater access to information for experts in comparison to non-experts (Oskamp 1982), with studies demonstrating that, for example, managers and online investors tend to exaggerate the accuracy of their fore-casts (Aukutsionek and Belianin 2001; Barber and Odean 2002). Unfortunately, the accuracy of tourism forecasting has not been subject to the same degree of analysis as other fields of forecasting (although note Law 2001). Indeed, Leiper (2000, p. 808) argues: 'If nobody foresaw the severe downturn in tourism across Asia that began in mid-1997, when all the official forecasting agencies were predicting strong growth, there seems little point in trying to predict, using existing research approaches, what will happen to tourism in the next century.' However, the above discussion does highlight the problems of predicting the future of tourism and tourism research, particularly from someone who may have better access to information than others!

Nevertheless, there are arguably greater degrees of certainty over the future direction of some factors that influence tourism than others. For example, factors related to the physical environment have a greater degree of long-term certainty, with respect to the climate change and ecological regeneration, for instance, while some demographic predictions, such as age structure changes, also have a high degree of predictability at the macro-level (United Nations Population Division 1998) but are less reliable when dealing with specific locations. Even in situations where there is seemingly reasonable pre-dictability, the assumption is that 'wildcards', that is high impact, low probability events which will dramatically affect social and environmental processes, will not occur (e.g. asteroid impact or nuclear conflict). Yet in tourism wildcards, such as September 11, SARS and the Asian financial crisis, clearly have had dramatic impacts at various scales of analysis. This does not necessarily mean that tourism forecasting is without value. Qualitative methods such as environmental scanning and key force identification, as well as the results of quantitative techniques, are an important part of scenario-building for government and industry. They allow 'what if?' questions to be asked so that appropriate preparations can be made in response. What does not occur very often in tourism, however, is backcasting. The selection of desired futures and how they may be reached. Elements of the process are to be found in strategic planning, with the formulation of visions, missions, goals and action plans, but they are generally not sophisticatedly applied to places. Indeed, such a change in direction may be significant as it also gives focus to the question of what sort of future do we actually want, a question which applies as much to the field of tourism as an area of study as it does to forecasting tourism itself. This is an issue which is discussed in more depth in Chapter 13.

A PEST Analysis of the Future of Tourism

The future of tourism is inextricably linked to broader social, political, economic, environmental and technological change. A PEST (political, economic, social and technological trends) framework (Richardson and Richardson 1989; Hall 1997c, 2000b) can be useful in identifying future possible trends in tourism and in the wider environment of which tourism is a part. The PEST analysis is shown in Table 10.2. Note, however, that an environmental category has also been included because although the resource dimension of the physical environment is culturally grounded, such is the significance of environmental issues for the future of tourism and as the ultimate base for sustainable development that they are given their own category. Table 10.2 is divided into short-term (2006–10), mid-term (2011–20) and long-term (2021–50) scenarios. The factors and issues identified in the three scenarios have been derived through trend extrapolation and analysis of existing international situations and agreements. Clearly, the further out from the present, the less likely it is that the trend will have been constant from the present. Nevertheless, trend extrapolation and analysis are useful tools with which to create future scenarios which can inform policy- and decision-making (e.g. Naisbitt 1982).

Political trends

In the immediate future it is likely that continued emphasis will be placed on the importance of free trade in the international economy overall and for travel and tourism in particular (Hall 2000a, 2000b). One of the reasons why free trade will continue to be given emphasis, even though there is growing disquiet about some of its negative impacts on indigenous cultures in terms of job displacement (e.g. Rethinking Tourism Project 1999), is that the institutional arrangements for free trade through both international law and conventions are extremely strong (e.g. http://www.apecsec.org.sg/). However, concerns in the Western countries regarding illegal immigration and the introduction of increased travel security measures following the terrorist attacks of September 11 may also act to limit some aspects of human mobility. Furthermore, one

Table 10.2   A PEST analysis of possible future trends for tourism

Trends	Short-term (2006–10)	Mid-term (2011–20)	Long-term (2021–50)
Political	• Tourists increasingly subject to attack in some developing countries • Increased resistance to free trade agreements as government subsidies are withdrawn, especially in Europe as assistance for rural tourism activities is reduced • Continued financial support for tourism promotion • Normalisation of relations between Cuba and the United States leads to dramatic tourism growth on the island (following election of a Democrat as President and the death of Castro) • Continued security and political measures with respect to human mobility	• Increased conflict between developing and developed countries over global economic development strategies as it becomes apparent to large numbers of the population in developing countries that they will never be able to have Western lifestyles due to population and resource constraints as well as perceived control of international trading and regulatory regimes by the developed countries • Increased tension between the People's Republic of China and the Republic of China (Taiwan) over Taiwanese declaration of independent nation status	• Resource access (to water, land and energy) is now the greatest threat to national security. Resource security problems are multiplied by declining oil reserves and the impacts of global environmental change
Economic	• Asian economic growth returns to early 1990 figures mainly due to the growth of the Chinese economy • Formal horizontal and vertical integration between tourism/leisure/entertainment/sport/communication corporations • Network strategies continue to be utilised by smaller, secondary tourism businesses	• Substantial free trade in APEC area • Japan replaced as major tourism generating market in Asia by China and India • Economic growth targets come under increased pressure because of natural resource constraints, reduced economic growth and higher fuel costs which lead to substantial reductions in the rate of world tourism growth	• Increased use of place-based ownership strategies to prevent firm relocation • Substantially increased costs of long-haul travel because of the price of fuel and the imposition of a carbon tax on fuel. Long-haul destinations are substantially affected, with one response being the encouragement of domestic tourism
Social	• Ageing populations in developed countries increasingly have to rely on their own funds rather than state pensions for their retirement • Cruising continues to grow as a travel market as the population ages • Despite ongoing improvements in communication technology, business and conference travel continues to grow because of the desire for personal contact • Educational travel continues to grow because of the need for lifelong learning and international skills • 'Fast food' and restaurant sector continues to grow as less people prepare their own meals at home	• Development of mass 'health tourism' for the wealthier classes in the developed world as medical technology continues to lengthen lifespan of some • Increasing focus on domestic and short-haul travel as cost of long-haul travel starts to increase due to fuel costs • Religious and spiritual-related travel is increasingly important due to uncertainty and rapid change • Increasing recognition by the tourism industry of the needs of single-parent families • Migration flows continue to reinforce transnational networks	• Continued growth of single-parent families as a result of later parenting options and ageing populations in developed countries • Ageing populations dominate tourism market • Transnational networks are a dominant element in long-haul international tourism

Technology	• Widespread introduction of new generation double-decker jumbo jets further reinforcing development of 'hub and spoke' transport patterns • Dramatic growth in train travel in conjunction with air travel as high speed train systems continue to be integrated with aviation hubs	• Cost of aviation fuel increases as world oil supplies come under increasing pressure, leading to dramatic impacts on visitor arrivals to long-haul destinations • Public transport is given renewed emphasis as the price of fuel increases • Virtual tourism is used to sell visits to destinations • Train travel is possible from Singapore to London	• Space tourism is commercially available though only to a very small number of wealthy individuals or lottery winners • Air balloons are increasingly used for commercial international flights • The train is now a major form of international travel in Europe
Environment	• National parks and reserves continue to be established in order to promote tourism • Biological diversity continues to diminish • Damage to ozone leads to health warnings to international travellers to Australia, New Zealand and southern South America because of the increased danger of skin cancer	• Water shortages start to curtail some resort developments in the south-west United States • Increasing restrictions placed on access to national parks due to impacts of large numbers of visitors – pricing used as a major tool • Ongoing loss of biodiversity. Rainforest areas are particularly hard hit • Several significant species, such as tigers, rhinoceros, elephants, pandas, chimpanzees and gorillas, are all but extinct in their native habitats save for their presence in privately run tourism sanctuaries	• Several island destinations in the Caribbean, the Indian Ocean and the Pacific are evacuated due to sea-level rise • Freshwater shortages severely affect tourism development in many parts of the world • Ski tourism in traditional alpine resorts in Europe, North America and Australasia becomes increasingly expensive due to the unpredictability of snow cover

Source: Adapted from Hall 2000b

possible issue in the future is the focus of free trade proponents on government subsidies for regional development and rural tourism in the same way that agricultural subsidies are presently targeted. Indeed, such an issue has already come under review in the United States' discussions with the European Union over agricultural trade issues (Tagliabue 1998).

Another trend that seems likely to continue in the foreseeable future is the development of partnerships between government and the private sector. Such cooperative relationships exist from the World Tourism Organisation (WTO) through to national, provincial and local governments (World Tourism Organisation 1998a, 1998b, 1998c, 1998d). Indeed, the WTO has been reorganising its structure and processes in a manner which explicitly encourages greater cooperation with the private sector (WTO 1998e). Indeed, in a time when direct government funding for tourism is increasingly under stress in the search for greater return on investment in tourism promotion, the creation of such relationships is hardly surprising.

As Hall (2000b) noted prior to the events of September 11: 'A more insidious trend in the political dimensions of tourism will possibly be the increased targeting of tourists by terrorist groups for political ends and hostage taking of tourists for ransom and/or publicity.' The ability to raise an almost instant international media profile through attacks on Western tourists provides many opportunities for terrorist groups to attempt to achieve their political ends (see Chapter 11). Furthermore, the continuing growth in the numbers of Westerners travelling to peripheral tourism regions can only serve to increase the potential for attacks on tourists, particularly when the division between rich and poor in terms of wealth and access to resources continues to grow in the developing world.

Economic trends

One of the most important driving forces behind travel patterns is that of economic growth. Although economic growth rates in much of the developed world are expected to stay relatively low in the short and mid-term, several countries, and China and India in particular, are expected to maintain relatively high levels of growth (Hall and Page 1999a). The long-term implications of growth in these tourist generating regions for international tourism cannot be overestimated. With their large populations, the emergence in these countries of a new mobile middle class with increased leisure time and greater discretionary income will have repercussions throughout the tourism system. Indeed, it may be likened to the significance of Japanese outbound travel growth in the late twentieth century (Hall, 1997c, 2001b).

Although there is still much debate as to the efficacy of free trade, the institutional arrangements which govern the international economic system are increasingly geared to greater openness in trade and investment. For some this may be interpreted as leading to greater Western hegemony of the global economy, while to others it means the further reinforcement of the role of transnational companies in the circulation of global capital. Either way, the effects will be profound in terms of the influence of foreign investors and foreign capital in many countries' tourism industries (Knox and Agnew 1989).

One of the significant corporate economic trends in tourism is the convergence of the tourism, leisure, gaming, sport, entertainment and advertising industries (e.g. Parkes 2004). Developments in communication technology mean that sports, events and entertainment now have global coverage, so there is greater capacity for these events to increase their television audience. In such a scenario, the desire of growth coalitions to bid for and host events, as well as other forms of mobile capital, may be expected to increase (Harvey 1993). Another dimension of economic globalisation with implications for tourism is the growth of international alliances between various airlines and other parts of the tourism industry, including the accommodation and hospitality sectors. The growth of mega-alliances is likely to continue, with increasing cross-ownership (Cameron and Arnold 2004) and the creation of transnational corporations with a capacity to affect tourism flows to an extent that has not been witnessed before. The actions of these transnational corporations will have dramatic consequences for some destinations as capital shifts according to countries' ability to take advantage of differences in labour costs, exchange rates and tax benefits from government. In addition, the ability of secondary tourism businesses to adapt and survive in the international political economy of tourism in the twenty-first century will likely depend on the creation of appropriate networks between businesses (Buhalis and Cooper 1998).

Social factors

Probably the key demographic factor which will affect the future of tourism is the ageing of the world's population. This substantial demographic change has occurred as a result of dramatic improvements in health care and is predicted to continue so long as the world's resources are able to support the increases in population. As of 1998 11% of the population was aged 60 and above. By 2050, one out of five persons will be aged 60 or older, and by 2150, one out of three will be 60 years or older. However, the older population itself is ageing. The increase in the number of very old people (aged 80+) between 1950 and 2050 is projected to grow by a factor of from eight to ten times on the global scale. On current trends, by 2150, about a third of the older population will be 80 years or older. As well as general ageing of the world's population there are also substantial regional differences in the aged population. For example, currently one out of five Europeans is 60 years or older, but one out of 20 Africans is 60 years or older. In some developed countries today, the proportion of older persons is close to one in five. According to the United Nations, during the first half of the twenty-first century that proportion will reach one in four and, in some countries, one in two (United Nations, Division for Social Policy and Development 1998).

Total fertility rates in the European Union have fallen to fewer than 1.5 births per female lifetime. By 2050 it is predicted that Italy will shrink from 57.5 million people to 45 million, Hungary from 10 million to 7.5 million, Poland from 39 million to 33 million, and Russia from 145 million to 100 million (Colebatch 2004). Given that the vast majority of the world's tourists come from the developed countries, such a demographic shift will clearly have substantial implications for the international tourism industry. Not only may particular types of tourism continue to grow in popularity, such as cruising, but second homes and retirement homes and the provision of health facilities for retirees may become increasingly important in destination development strategies. For examples, locales in areas of Mediterranean Europe, Portugal and the south-west United States and in Florida are already subject to substantial seasonal and permanent retirement migration (e.g. Williams et al. 1997).

However, the demographic shift in many developed countries will also have other impacts on work patterns, pension and taxation policies, retirement age and immigration policies. Eldercare may replace childcare as a work/life issue. A study for the US insurance company Metlife has put the cost to US business of lost productivity due to eldercare at more than US$29 billion a year (Maitland 2004). By 2030 it is predicted that Germany will have seven million fewer people of working age than in 2004, yet 8.5 million more people of retirement age (Colebatch 2004). One in three Germans will be over the age of 60 by 2050. However, the German Institute for Economic Research states that, at present, the over-65s (16% of the population) hold more than a third of the nation's wealth, with an annual buying power of more than €20 billion (Thiessen 2004). In the case of Australia it is predicted that the number of 70 year olds will double in the next 40 years and represent approximately 20% of the population. As of 2004 it was estimated that there were 2000 retirement villages, or lifestyle resorts as they are becoming known, with 50–60 000 village units being run by the commercial sector and the same amount again by the not-for-profit sector. It is expected that there will be a demand for another 30 000 village units by 2020 (B. Brown 2004). Interestingly, the retirement villages are increasingly little different from tourist resorts. According to Bill McClurg, President of the Australian Retirement Village Associations: 'We are starting to see theme-type developments with golf courses, marinas and penthouse-type developments. It's everything the indulgent baby boomer wants' (quoted in B. Brown 2004, p. 8).

With people living longer following retirement the lifestyles of the mature traveller will have a substantial influence on the development and supply of tourism infrastructure. For example, *Modern Maturity*, a North American lifestyles journal for the over 50s, surveyed its subscribers about their travel habits and preferences. Over 37% travelled three to five times a year, 46% preferred car travel over any other type of transportation, 42% indicated that the purpose of their trip was to relax, 39% preferred just their partner as a travelling companion, 46% preferred to go to museums over any other tourist attraction, and 67% stayed in hotels (*Modern Maturity* 1999, p. 12).

Although the ageing of the population will be a dominant demographic factor in tourism trends over the next century, other factors will also be significant. For example, the breakdown of the traditional nuclear family in many Western countries, marked by increased single parenting, people marrying later, more people never marrying, and many people never having children, not only influences demographic characteristics but will also affect the pattern of holiday-taking and leisure travel. In addition, the demographic shift in Western countries is also accompanied by changed employment patterns, particularly the increase in part-time, casual and contract employment in relation to permanent employment. Such changes in social structures have a number of flow-on effects in the tourism and leisure sectors, including the increase of short breaks as opposed to longer holidays, and a growth in the consumption of restaurant and pre-prepared meals compared with meals prepared and eaten in the home (National Restaurant Association 1998). Finally, we should note that continued short- and long-term migration will continue to reinforce transnational flows and networks (Coles et al. 2004).

Tourism Insight: Growth in Urban Slums

Some of the recent interest in pro-poor tourism development pales into insignificance when compared with the growing gap between rich and poor at both national and international scales. One of the most sobering predictions of a 2003 UN study is that within 30 years the urban population in the developing world will double to approximately 4 billion people. During the same period rural populations are expected to only barely increase, with a decline expected after 2020. This means that by 2033 one in every three people in the world will live in urban slums. The report from the UN human settlements programme, UN-Habitat, based in Nairobi, Kenya, found that urban slums were growing faster than expected and that the balance of global poverty was shifting from the rural regions to the cities.

As of 2003 the world's richest countries were home to 2% of slum dwellers. In contrast, 80% of the urban population of the world's 30 least developed nations live in slums. Overall, UN-Habitat estimate that 940 million people, almost one-sixth of the world's population, 'live in squalid, unhealthy areas, mostly without water, sanitation, public services or legal security' (Vidal 2003, p. 13), with Africa having 20% of the world's slum dwellers, including the world's largest slum of 600 000 people in the Kibera district of Nigeria, and Latin America 14%. However, the worst urban conditions are in Asia, where more than 550 million people live in what the UN describe as unacceptable conditions. According to Anna Tibaijuka, the Director of UN-Habitat: 'There is a vacuum developing, because local authorities have no access to the many slums. . . . Extreme inequality and idleness lead people to anti-social behaviour. Slums are the places where all the evils come together, where peace and security is elusive and where young people cannot be protected' (quoted in Vidal 2003, p. 13). The conclusion of the report is also extremely pessimistic in tone, as 'cities have become a dumping ground for people working in unskilled, unprotected and low-wage industries and trades . . . the slums of the developing world swell'.

In this kind of situation what difference does tourism make given that nearly all of the people living in the slums do not possess the same degree of leisure mobility as those of the tourist classes, even though some will undoubtedly travel, particularly for family reasons? Arguably, maybe tourism will make a difference. In some rural and peripheral regions appropriate tourism development may possibly assist through job creation and the development of alternatives to urban migration. Clearly, some projects may create new linkages between the agriculture, hospitality and tourism sectors, providing even greater incentives for local development. However, within all of this, questions may also need to be asked of the extent to which tourism and leisure mobility may even contribute to urban migration through the demonstration effect. Furthermore, what would the environmental impacts of increased travel both to and from these new megalopolises actually be? While these questions are significant, the growth of slum megalopolises and dealing with issues of poverty may likely lie more with the broader process of *laissez-faire* globalisation and new right economic policies than with tourism.

Source: UN-Habitat report on global urbanisation and poverty available at www.unhabitat.org/global_report.asp

Technological factors

In an attempt to maximise profit by minimising per person costs, the next generation of international jet aircraft will seek to travel longer, faster while carrying more people. The impact of such strategies is seen in the Boeing 747, of which nearly 1100 are currently in service, including cargo planes. Accounting for only 8% of the world's fleet, they handle 23% of all airline capacity, although even the biggest 747 has the capacity for only 450 passengers (Page 1999). Despite recent crises facing the aviation industry, Airbus Industrie predicted that 16700 jetliners will be purchased worldwide by 2020 (Hannifin and Le Quesne, 1998) with both Airbus and Boeing forecasting that airline traffic growth will increase on average by just over 5% per annum to 2022 (Done 2004). In 2003 Airbus delivered more aircraft than Boeing for the very first time (Done 2004). However, the aircraft manufacturing companies' strategies for the future are very different.

Airbus Industrie of Europe, which comprises France's Aerospatiale, British Aerospace, Germany's Daimler-Benz and Spain's Casa, has developed the A380 superjumbo, the biggest commercial passenger aircraft ever to be built, in collaboration with some 30 airlines and 70 airport authorities. As of April 2004, 129 firm orders of the 555 passenger, double-decker aircraft had been received, with Singapore Airlines scheduled to be the first to fly the A380 in 2006 (Done 2004). In developing the A380, airlines insisted on 15% to 20% lower operating costs than on 747s, while airports wanted the planes to fit into the same docking space as a 747 and have the same mass-per-wheel (so runways and tarmacs will not have to be reinforced) (Hannifin and Le Quesne 1998). The A380 has cost over US$12 billion (€10 billion) to develop and would break even on a production of 250 aircraft, although Airbus has forecast that the world will need 1138 very large passenger aircraft by 2025 (Done 2004). However, in contrast to Airbus, Boeing is developing the 7E7 Dreamliner as its next generation aircraft to replace the Boeing 757s and 767s. This is a much smaller 200–250 passenger aircraft, which Boeing believes will reflect passengers' preference for more point-to-point, non-stop services between destinations rather than the hub and spoke strategy that the A380 would support, particularly given the stresses that already exist on airport and air traffic control infrastructure (Done 2004). Nevertheless, what is unlikely in the short to mid term is the widespread introduction of supersonic jets given their relative costs in development and the corresponding price for travel on them.

The development of the new range of jet aircraft will also have profound implications for destinations and tourist flows as well as accessibility to destinations. One of the most significant of these may well be further reinforcement of the hub and spoke transport network arrangement with main airports as the hubs of regional transport systems (Wheatcroft 1998). In this situation there is intense competition between countries and airports to encourage the large passenger airlines to use their airport as a hub before passengers are redistributed to other destinations. For example, East Asia has seen a spate of airport development and redevelopment in recent years, for example Bangkok, Hong Kong, Kuala Lumpur and Singapore, in order to compete for hub status (Page 1999). Nevertheless, the continuing development of budget airline routes between secondary airports using smaller jet aircraft will also see ongoing competition for such secondary destination status.

Another major area in which technology has affected tourism is in terms of advances in communication technology (Sheldon 1997). The ability of such technology to convey images almost instantaneously around the world has already been noted. However, one of its most direct impacts has been in terms of the role of the internet in tourism. The internet is significant in terms of its effect on promotional and sales channels and the ability to cut out some tour wholesalers and retailers from the travel product supply chain, enabling direct communication between the producer of the tourism product and the consumer. For example, in April 2004 Continental Airlines announced that as of the end of the year it would eliminate all paper tickets. The company said that it decided to make the change after it discovered that 95% of its domestic customers and 88% systemwide customers used electronic tickets (Reuters 2004).

Environment

The final factor to be examined is the role of the physical environment in influencing tourism. Undoubtedly, relatively natural or wild physical environments are a major drawcard for tourism and tourism research. The continued attractiveness of environmental resources for tourists often requires intensive management strategies in order to ensure that the environment is not unduly degraded. However, growth in tourist numbers and overall pressures stemming from mobility and population growth, particularly in developing countries, will mean that, increasingly, access to some sites will need to be restricted if their environmental values are to be maintained, often by the adoption of a user-pays philosophy in order to maximise return to government or private agencies.

As population and mobility pressures mount in many areas of the developed world, access to nature will become even more contested. Growth of demand for access in rural areas in the developed countries will likely lead to increased conflict with traditional user groups (Butler et al. 1998b). In Britain, as in many other industrialised countries, these new uses are placing extreme pressures and creating new conflicts not only in terms of rural policy-making and their relationship to agriculture but also between themselves (see Chapter 8). For example, Blake (1996) reported that while 76% of the English population visited the countryside in 1990, 89% of people now believe that the English countryside should be protected at all costs. However, as Butler and Hall (1998b, p. 252) observed, presumably this would only be 'as long as this cost would not result in the exclusion of those who wanted it saved'.

Continued interest in the natural environment will undoubtedly lead to further development of the ecotourism or nature-based tourism market. Yet there is a finite amount of such natural areas available for tourist use without the values of such areas being degraded. While tourism can contribute to species and habitat conservation, it comes at a price, which is that not everyone can necessarily have access. Vicarious appreciation of the environment is insufficient to maintain conservation strategies, particularly in the developing world, therefore the delicate balancing act between tourism and conservation will need to be maintained for many years to come. However, perhaps of most concern is the contribution of tourism, and transport in particular, to global climate change. In this situation, whether one is an ecotourist or not at the local level will have very little effect on the energy consumption and carbon contributions of the international air traveller. Yet a number of tourist destinations are already starting to be threatened by the effects of climate change to the stage where some of the attractions, whether they be at the coast or in the mountains, are starting to disappear (see Chapter 12).

Of far greater concern for the future of tourism, indeed for the future of humanity, is the extent to which mobility and population growth and demands for increased material standards of living, including travel, place pressure on the planet's scarce natural resources. Despite the assurances of some futurists that technological solutions will be found (e.g. Naisbitt, 1982) there are still natural limits to growth which the goal and values of sustainable development are seeking to address. In tourism terms, it particularly raises questions about the increased cost of fuel and energy in the future. In relation to longer-term growth of international tourism, it raises issues as to the implications of increased costs of fuel and energy in the future. However, perhaps more fundamentally, it highlights the need for tourism to be seen in the wider context of environment, resources and mobilities if it is ever to become sustainable.

Tourism Insight: Chaos and Catastrophe

In recent years there has been a substantial interest in the natural and social sciences, including tourism, with respect to chaos theory. Chaos theory has been developed from the recognition that apparently simple physical systems which obey deterministic laws may nevertheless behave unpredictably. Chaos is one of three forms that can be taken by non-linear systems, the other two being convergence to an equilibrium or steady state, and periodic behaviour or a stable oscillation (Robinson 1998). Chaos is not unpredictability. Chaotic systems can behave in a predictable and reproducible way. However, the evolution of a chaos system depends very sensitively on its starting conditions, which lead in the longer term to behaviour that is ultimately unpredictable (Dendrinos and Sonis 1990).

Tourism researchers have become interested in chaos theory because of its potential insights into the development of tourism systems, particularly in relation to the evolution of destinations, tourism futures and tourism impacts (Hall 2000a). One particular case of systems theory related to chaos is the concept of catastrophic systems which are discontinuities which occur when there is a qualitative change from one system to another. Catastrophic systems can occur when small, infrequent changes in control variables produce major changes in the state of the system (Poston and Stewart 1978). At the macro-level this may be happening with respect to various elements of global environmental change, while at the micro-level this may occur when a tourism firm that had been one of the cornerstones of a tourism network closes down, leading to repercussions throughout the remaining set of companies and their relations. However, tourism chaos theory has been approached more as an analogue of the behaviour of tourism systems than as a direct mathematical investigation of the actual behaviour of systems.

Dendrinos (1996, p. 240) identified four main difficulties in applying chaos to the social sciences as compared to the natural sciences:

1. Chaotic paths require an enormous amount of data to trace, calibrate and test (Rosser and Rosser 1994).
2. Most social-economic systems do not comprise identical components with highly homogeneous behaviour and most social scientific variables do not produce repetitive measurements under experimentally controlled conditions.
3. Inaccuracies in social science data are problematic when compared with natural science data in which accurate and regular measurement is the norm.
4. There are substantial problems in determining the appropriate levels of disaggregation for spatial datasets and the difficulty of breaking down socio-economic systems into an infinitely self-replicating scale (fractals).

The Future: 2021 and Beyond

Travelling is consuming. This chapter has speculated on a number of possible trends and issues in tourism. The extent to which the factors which affect tourism shift from current trajectories is, of course, unknown. However, even on present terms, the need for sustainable forms of tourism at all scales of analysis is greater than ever. Sustainability shows its relation to the older idea of 'limits to growth' and 'capacity'. 'This does not mean that growth is necessarily limited but it does imply that, in order to be sustainable in the long term, the nature of growth must be such that it respects constraints set by the need to maintain critical environmental capital (and in some interpretations the total value of the environmental capital stock) intact' (Cowell and Owens 1997, p. 17). Nevertheless, as Mowforth and Munt (1998, p. 153) have argued, 'sustainability has proved the perfect ally of the new middle classes, with the social construction and application of ecological concepts such as carrying capacity proving the ultimate justification for normal exclusiveness', thereby excluding those who cannot pay for access in the name of environmental protection and restrictions. As history has demonstrated, maintaining environmental capital is extremely difficult to do within a political-economic system, within which maintaining or increasing levels of economic growth has been a virtually unassailable policy goal.

Appropriately developed tourism has the capacity to maintain the biological, economic and socio-cultural diversity which is essential for survival. Despite the placatory words of government and industry groups and the occasional success story at the local scale, tourism's contribution to sustainability is extremely mixed. For every tourism triumph there are tourism disasters, including those of 'ecotourism', and given the desire of individual destinations, particularly in the developing world, to improve their standard of living, such disasters will continue. Indeed, in terms of creating options for future use, one of the tenets of sustainability, Lynch (1972, p. 115) writes of 'future preservation': 'Our most important responsibility to the future is not to coerce it but to attend to it. Collectively, [such actions] might be called "future preservation", just as an analogous activity carried out in the present is called historical preservation.' In tourism, notions akin to that of future preservation are generally found in the areas of ecotourism, cultural tourism and, to an extent, in sustainable tourism development. Yet, most significantly, part of the future preservation means using a scale of analysis that goes beyond the long-standing focus of impacts at the destination level and instead looks at the system-wide impacts of tourism mobilities that have been ignored until recently, especially with respect to global environmental change (see Chapter 12).

Tourism does have the potential to contribute greatly to economic development, employment creation and the protection of the environment (World Tourism Organisation 1997a; World Travel and Tourism Council 1998). Yet tourism development should not be left to growth coalitions. The direction that tourism takes will be dependent on the interests and values of the people involved, the short- and long-term decisions that they take and, arguably, the development of a conscious appreciation of the impacts that tourism and travel have by travellers, government, industry and the wider community. These concerns are examined in more detail in Chapters 11 and 12 with respect to political and security issues as well as environmental security concerns regarding biosecurity and climate change. Chapter 13 then examines the future of tourism studies and how the field might contribute to the problems of the future and the present.

Tourism Insight:	Space Tourism – The Final Frontier of Tourism Mobility?

Space – the final frontier. These are the voyages of the starship Enterprise. Her five-year mission to seek out new life and new civilizations, to boldly go where no[one] has gone before. Captain James Tiberius Kirk (in Hanley 1997, p. xiii)

Space tourism lies at the very limits of leisure mobility in terms of distance from 'home', although the actual time spent in space is quite small. Nevertheless, space tourism is one of the great dreams of the tourism industry and those who see the commercial exploitation of space (Smith 2003; F. Brown 2004) (Table 10.3 outlines some key dates in the history of space travel). However, the dreams that were generated by the space race of the 1960s between the United States and the Soviet Union have not been fulfilled. Indeed, one of the abiding images of the period was the film *2001 A Space Odyssey* (directed by Stanley Kubrick and based on a book by Arthur C. Clarke), released in 1969 and showing regular scheduled commercial space flights to an orbiting hotel which is part of a space station. Indeed, it was at that time that the Pan Am airline company began taking registrations of interest from individuals interested in travelling to space. More recently, Virgin Atlantic has registered the name 'Virgin Galactic Airways' with the intent of providing space travel in the near future (Duval 2003a). However, the expectations created by the Apollo missions to the moon have not been met, and neither have the hopes for a cheap reusable re-entry vehicle in the form of the space shuttle. There is an international space station in orbit around the Earth but it is only partially built and the unavailability of the space shuttle following another disaster has meant delays in further construction and development.

At the start of 2004, however, interest in space is higher than it has been for many years as a result of the success of Mars Rover missions. At the end of January 2004 two Rover vehicles successfully landed on Mars and began beaming pictures back to the Earth and, over subsequent months, roaming on the surface of the planet. Scientifically, the missions were an incredible success, leading to the identification of geological evidence that confirms that

Table 10.3   Some key dates in space travel

1957	October 4	USSR launches Sputnik 1, the first satellite to orbit the Earth
1957	November 3	Small dog named Laika launched aboard Sputnik 2
1961	April 12	Russian cosmonaut Yuri Gagarin becomes the first man in space aboard Vostok 1
1963	June 16	Russian cosmonaut Valentina Tereshkova-Nikolayeva becomes the first woman in space
1969	July 20	US Apollo 11 astronauts Neil Armstrong and Edwin 'Buzz' Aldrin become the first men on the moon, while Michael Collins orbits in space
1971	January	Apollo 14 astronaut Alan Shepard becomes the first man to hit a golf ball on the moon (possibly the first example of extra-terrestrial recreation)
2001	April	Dennis Tito is the first commercial space tourist
2003	October 15	China becomes the third nation to put a human, Lieutenant Colonel Wang Liwei, into space
2004	January	Two Mars Rovers, successfully landed, reveal that substantial amounts of surface water previously existed on Mars
2004	February	President Bush announces the goals of sending a manned mission to Mars
2004	March	NASA successfully test a scramjet – a high-altitude jet engine capable of very high speeds – for the first time

large amounts of surface water were once present on Mars, further supporting the possibility that life once existed on Mars. Indeed, there is a substantial likelihood that Mars still does support life, given that some water is still present in the polar regions, while it is conjectured that more water may exist below the surface or even in the bottom of some of Mars's canyons. Some evidence for life is being provided by the Mars Explorer orbital surveyor in March 2004, with the identification of significant amounts of methane in the atmosphere, the source of which is likely to be either volcanoes and/or microbial life forms. As well as being a scientific success the American Mars missions were also a political success, with President Bush announcing in February 2004 that he would be charging NASA (National

Aeronautical and Space Administration) to develop a programme to send a manned mission to Mars. Regardless of whether this was part of re-election campaign hype or not, such an announcement did focus attention on the exploration of space and the potential commercial applications of space travel, including tourism.

For all the enthusiasm for space travel, it is important to note that, as of the beginning of 2004, only two space tourists have gone into space. Both paid millions of dollars for the experience and both flew with the Russians. In April 2001, millionaire businessman Dennis Tito became the first private citizen to pay for the privilege to travel to space. Tito's trip to the International Space Station on a Russian Soyuz TM–32 space vehicle was for years only hypothetical. As Duval (2003a) pointed out, while the United States had certainly put private citizens in space on previous occasions through its Space Shuttle Programme, no one was required to pay for the opportunity. Similarly, previous travel by private citizens on Russian space-craft could not be described as commercial space tourism. Therefore, the Russians not only put the first individual in space in April 1961, they also sent up the first tourist almost 40 years later to the day.

Since the so-called 'space race' started in the mid-1950s only Russia and the United States have had the capacity to launch humans into space, although China joined these nations in October 2003 when the first *yuhangyuan* (space traveller) went into orbit. Indeed, China is aiming to launch a manned mission to the moon in 2010, something which has not happened since the early 1970s with the US Apollo programme (Watts 2003). Nevertheless, despite the undoubted national patriotic benefits of the Chinese space programme, '[c]ritics say even if China succeeds in putting a *yuhangyuan* in space, it would merely bring the country up to the level achieved by Russia and America 40 years ago' (Watts 2003, p. 13). Moreover, the sheer cost of the Chinese programme indicates the difficulties in developing space tourism. As Watts (2003, p. 13) noted: 'Since 1992 China is estimated to have spent 19bn yuan (£1.5bn) on the mission, named Project 921. While this is less than a fifth of the amount spent by the US on its space programme, it has made a bigger dent in China's resources, where many among the 1.2 billion strong population still subsist on less than a dollar a day.'

While supporters of the development of space tourism products point to substantial rates of visitation to tourist attractions offering space or astronomical educational themes, such as the Cape Canaveral launching facilities in Florida or the Houston flight control centre in Texas, this cannot realistically be used to accurately forecast demand for a space tourism product. Demand for a product is linked to price and space travel is very expensive. Extensive market research is needed, as Crouch (2001) has pointed out, in order to determine the amount that potential tourists would be willing to pay for a trip to space. As Duval (2003a) observed, interest in space travel will not necessarily translate into purchase. Unless new economies of scale for space travel are generated, the enormous cost of propelling a vehicle into space would likely translate into substantial prices for tourists, and potentially very low levels of realistic demand.

In light of the failure of the space shuttle programme to provide relatively cheap access into space, numerous private companies are now also attempting to enter the world of spaceflight. Central to this goal is the X Prize, a competition 'whose founders hope will jumpstart a private space race and create a space tourism industry' (Schwartz 2003, p. 1). The contest is modelled on the Orteig Prize, the competition that was held for the first transatlantic flight, which was won by Charles Lindbergh with his *Spirit of St. Louis* plane in 1927. The X Prize calls for launching people just over 60 miles, or almost 100 kilometres into sub-orbital space, which is still high enough for any passenger to feel weightless. However, unlike the Orteig's US$25 000 prize, the X Prize carries a winner's purse of US$10 million. According to the creator of the X Prize, Peter Diamandis, 'I was convinced that the marketplace was real, that the technology was readily available.... The only thing missing was the vehicles to jumpstart the market' (quoted in Schwartz 2003, p. 8). Nevertheless, in addition to the technological issues involved, one of those competing for the X prize, John Carmack, also noted that '[t]he environmental impact study is a big, big hassle', with the United States Federal Aviation Administration still trying to determine how to regulate the flights (Schwartz 2003, p. 1).

Rather than develop a new sub-orbiting spacecraft, an alternative approach may be to develop a giant elevator. In 1978 the science-fiction writer Arthur C. Clarke published a book entitled the *Fountains of Paradise*, in which an elevator carried people into space. Some 25 years later the Los Alamos National Laboratory was the sponsor of a three-day conference on such an elevator. The idea of an elevator into space is actually quite old. The Russian scientist Konstantin Tsiolkovsky proposed such a space tower in 1895. Steel, the strongest material available at that time, was too heavy and not strong enough to support such weight. However, the discovery in 1991 of nanotubes, cylindrical molecules of carbon with many times the strength of steel, means that the concept is regarded as viable some time in the first half of the twenty-first century. According to Chang (2003, p. 7): 'Proponents say the economic and technological advances of a space elevator over rockets make it inevitable. They predict it will lower the cost of putting a satellite into space from [US]$10,000 a pound to [US]$100.' Nevertheless, such developments will still be extremely expensive. According to Bradley Edwards (2002), one of the scientists who has worked on the idea at Los Alamos, the cost to build the first elevator is likely to be US$6.2 billion, although it could even double that figure given the uncertainty of research and development costs. Subsequent elevators could then be built at US$2 billion each, because the first elevator would be able to lift materials. By the standards of some space budgets, this could be a relatively cheap figure. For example, the estimated cost of building and operating the International Space Station is likely to be over US$100 billion alone.

The space elevator would be built in three main stages. First, a spacecraft is launched into geosynchronous orbit, where a satellite circles the Earth in exactly one day. Maintaining the same position over the Earth's surface, approximately 22 300 miles above the equator, it would lower a thin nanotube ribbon to the ground where it would be tied to a base station. To strengthen and widen the initial ribbon, mechanical climbers would climb up the original ribbon from the base station, adding additional ribbons. After approximately two and a half years the elevator would be complete. The ribbon would be about three feet wide and thinner than paper but it would be capable of supporting 13 tons of cargo that could be lifted up using the power of lasers on the ground shining on to solar panels on the rising platforms.

Interplanetary travel by humans is the long-standing dream of many space enthusiasts, particularly those used to watching episodes of *Star Trek* or *Doctor Who*. However, such goals appear a long-time away, given the limits and costs of present technology. For example, even with President Bush's enthusiasm for space travel, realistically, NASA is not planning a manned Mars mission until after 2020. This is the earliest time at which an unmanned spacecraft is scheduled to make a round trip to the planet, taking into account favourable distances between Mars and Earth so as to minimise not only fuel costs and weight, but also the time that any astronauts will be in space, given the potential health risks of extended weightlessness and radiation exposure. However, much of the future for interplanetary travel will also depend on the success of present-day programmes such as the International Space Station, the space shuttle programmes and the potential media coverage of unmanned scientific interplanetary exploration to planets such as Mars. Successful missions which return pictures and stories that can be used by the media will undoubtedly increase people's, and hence governments', enthusiasm to financially support expensive manned space programmes, as well as generate interest from potential private sector investors in space travel.

Indeed, as the competition for the X Prize indicates, substantial private sector interest does exist for the commercial development of space tourism, although it is worthwhile noting that the role of public interest groups in space is also significant. For example, The Mars Society is a private organisation of approximately 5000 members who are committed to sending humans to Mars. As part of their research programme they are developing four research stations on Earth to see how individual scientists cope with the rigours of working together in harsh environments. At the end of 2003 one had already been established in the Arctic (and featured on a Discovery Channel documentary regarding the exploration of Mars) and another near Hanksville, Utah, in the United States. Such organisations are significant because of the contribution they can make to research and also because they act to lobby politicians about the value of space travel.

Despite interest in space travel and space tourism, this does not mean that the development of space tourism is without controversy. In the same way that tourism has had undesirable impacts on Earth, so it may also have impacts in space. These impacts include not only the enormous use of energy that is presently required to get people into space and subsequent pollutants that result from such activities, particularly at high altitude, but also the potential impacts on any planets, moons or celestial objects that may be visited. There is already considerable 'space junk' in orbit around the world which is potentially dangerous to orbiting spacecraft. Fortunately, only the larger pieces of such old satellites and spacecraft, return to the earth without burning up. However, pollution of near-Earth space is only one component of the environmental impacts of space travel. Travel to planets, such as Mars and Venus, and moons which have an atmosphere and/or water, such as Io, hold the potential for micro-bacteria to be introduced from Earth. Such organisms can have enormous consequences for the evolution of life on those bodies through the introduction of a potentially competitive species or even the development of new life forms. Furthermore, a reverse situation would exist if life was found to exist on a planet such as Mars – how could we be sure that it was not introduced back to Earth when the spacecraft return? It has already been shown that micro-bacteria and viruses can survive for extended periods of time in incredibly harsh environments on Earth as well as in space. While biosecurity and containment measures can be put in place for space travellers relatively easily (although with a considerable extension of time allocated to any trip), it will be much harder to make an entire spaceship biosecure. Indeed, some people may even think that humankind has done a great job messing up our own planet, so why should we mess up someone else's? Of course, the reverse applies for others in that the terraforming (recreating an Earth environment on an alien moon or planet) of Mars, may well provide another living option for members of the human race.

Using current technology time is also one of the greatest problems in travelling through space. Mars is over a year away and interstellar travel during a person's lifespan is an impossibility. Nevertheless, warp speed, which utilises engines to warp space–time, is a theoretical possibility, as are the transporter machines of *Star Trek* (see Kraus 1995 for a discussion of the physics of *Star Trek*). Time travel presents other problems (Hanley 1997), although these also lie at the frontier of quantum physics. However, for the immediate future, fast human interstellar travel is outside the realm of the space–time prism.

What is one person's space junk or environmental pollution, of course, may one day be another's space heritage. It is quite possible that at some time in the future the sites of the Apollo landings on the moon or Russian and American missions to Mars and Venus may become significant heritage sites visited by space tourists. Indeed, if the history of tourism on Earth is anything to go by, it is readily apparent that vicarious appreciation is not enough, some people just have to go there regardless of the expense or of the time it takes to get there.

Discussion Questions

1. Is it possible that futurists help shape the future they predict?

2. What wildcards may have affected international tourism forecasts since 2000?

3. How might demographic change affect the future of tourism?

4. What are the prospects for interplanetary tourism or even tourist trips to the moon in your lifetime?

5. Will virtual tourism encourage people to stay at home or will it encourage people to visit 'for real' those places they have encountered virtually?

Further Reading and Websites

A useful journal article which overviews space tourism is F. Brown (2004). Crawford (2001) provides an interesting scientific argument of the value of space exploration, while some of the scientific issues regarding new break-throughs in transport technology are also discussed in Kraus (1995) and Allen (2003). Issues regarding the possibility of anti-ageing medicine are well covered in De Grey (2003). On perspectives on the future of science, particu-larly with respect to integrating the physical and social sciences, see Costanza (2003) and Wilson (1998).

Airbus Industrie website: http://www.airbus.com/body.htm

Boeing Space Systems: http://www.boeing.com/bdsg/space.html

International Society to Preserve the Beauty of Space: http://beautyofspace. org/ and www.spacefuture.com

The Mars Society: www.marssociety.org

The Physics of Star Trek links: http://erebus.phys.cwru.edu/~krauss/star links.html

Tourism, Politics and Security: The New Tourism Agenda?

11

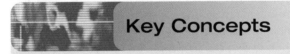

Key Concepts

- Security
- Safety
- Political stability
- Role of the media
- Agenda setting
- Issue–attention cycle
- National security
- Perceived risk
- Common security
- Environmental security
- Economic security

Security is an essential component of the attractiveness of destinations, the routes taken to get to a destination and the mode of transport used. The events of September 2001, the Bali bombing in 2002 and the terrorist attacks in Madrid in 2004 have all highlighted the importance of security for the tourism industry. However, security can be understood in terms of both national security and personal security, although there are likely to be relationships between the two in many cases. Personal security is also often described as personal safety. Safety may be judged by the nature of the physical environment (as in adventure travel, such as whitewater rafting or mountain climbing), by the potential for criminal activity (e.g. pick-pocketing or mugging), the possibility of being caught in a war zone and/or by the potential for politically motivated attacks on tourists. This chapter is primarily concerned with the last two categories of tourist safety, which are intimately related to issues of tourism and political stability. However, it also discusses changing notions of national security as an introduction to the development of a broader notion of the relationships between tourism and security than presently exists in the literature.

The political nature of international tourism has received relatively scant attention in the tourism research literature as compared to other international industries or policy issues (e.g. Matthews 1978; Richter 1989; Hall 1994a). Nevertheless, issues of political stability and political relations within and between states are extremely important in determining the image of destinations in tourist generating regions and, of course, the real and perceived safety of tourists. As Smyth (1986, p. 120) noted in the case of the ongoing conflicts between Loyalists and Republicans in Northern Ireland, 'as an industry, tourism is particularly susceptible to certain exogenous factors and when civil unrest culminated in violence with subsequent media coverage, visitor numbers and expenditure fell'.

This chapter is divided into three main sections. The first section provides a framework for understanding the relationship between tourism and political stability, in which the role of the media is highlighted as influencing tourists' perceptions of the relative safety of destinations. This first section also highlights the two different forms which the tourism–political stability relationship takes: political instability which leads to a decline in tourist numbers; and direct attacks on tourists for political purposes. The remaining sections examine these two dimensions of political instability in detail and provide several case studies of the impact of instability on tourist visitation. The chapter concludes by highlighting the role of the media in determining tourists' perceptions of safety and political stability in tourist destinations.

Tourism and Political Instability

Political instability refers to a situation in which conditions and mechanisms of governance and rule are challenged as to their political legitimacy by elements operating from outside the normal operations of the political system. When challenge occurs from within a political system and the system is able to adapt and change to meet demands placed on it, it can be said to be stable. When forces for change are unable to be satisfied from within a political system and so resort to non-legitimate means of protest, violence, or even civil war to seek change, then a political system can be described as being unstable. Clearly, there are degrees of political instability. For example, Italian governments have tended to have very short life spans due to the nature of the Italian political and electoral system. Nevertheless, the system has generally managed to adapt and change to the demands placed upon it. Similarly, the People's Republic of China has also been reasonably stable even as other state communist regimes collapsed in Eastern Europe. Political stability is therefore not a value judgement as to the democratic nature, or otherwise, of a state. Indeed, it may well be the case that certain authoritarian states which limit formal opposition to government may provide extremely stable political environments in which tourism may flourish. For example, the perceived nature of a political regime as repressive may not necessarily deter international tourism: both Spain and Portugal developed their very considerable international tourism industries under what many would regard as fascist dictatorships (Williams and Shaw 1988).

By their very nature, authoritarian regimes do not have to go through the public consultation measures which are in place in most Western democracies (Hall 1994a). Therefore, tourism development can be fast-tracked through any local, provincial or national planning system that is in place. In the case of Portugal, the development of the tourism industry was accompanied by major shifts in the priority attached to it in government policy in the late 1960s and 1970s (Lewis and Williams 1988). Similarly, in the case of Spain, special laws were passed under the Franco regime to facilitate the creation of new tourist settlements in the zones most favoured by spontaneous tourism (Valenzuela 1988). The authoritarian origins of some of the major coastal tourism developments in Europe is therefore often forgotten in the present day.

The role that authoritarian states have played in tourism development highlights the importance of government, media and tourist perceptions of destinations in determining attitudes towards the political characteristics of the destination and the creation of its tourist image. Figure 11.1 provides a model of the factors that help create images of the political stability of a destination in tourist generating regions as well as potential reactions in the tourism destination region. Critical to market reactions to instability are the media, as they play a major part in conveying the relative safety or security of a destination to the market, along with word of mouth and advertising campaigns that are sponsored by the government(s) of the tourist generating region. Governments, through their foreign policy settings, can also have a dramatic impact on perceptions of potential destinations. For example, travel was encouraged between the former state socialist nations of Eastern Europe in order to support notions of international communist solidarity (D.R. Hall 1991a). Conversely, travel flows between nations may be suspended if political relations are poor, for example the prohibition since the early 1960s on Americans wishing to travel direct to Cuba (Hall 1994a). Indeed, international tourism policy is intimately related to foreign policy objectives, particularly with respect to the visa and passport regulations of tourist generating countries (Richter 1984). Government policy is certainly important in regulating tourist flows and also in influencing tourist visitation through the articulation of national government policies towards current or potential tourist destination regions. However, it is the media which have the greatest influence on the creation of destination images in tourist generating regions (Morgan and Pritchard 1998; Morgan et al. 2002; Hall 2003a).

The media, through books, magazines and newspapers, have always had a substantial influence on images of destination areas. More recently, the telecommunications revolutions of the late twentieth century have created a visual immediacy to image creation unmatched in human history. Thanks to satellites and cable links, events in countries and regions far away from the viewer can now be seen as they happen. For example, in June 1989 Americans and other CNN subscribers around the world were able to watch live as tanks rolled into Beijing's Tiananmen Square to quell the student protests. It can be argued that such images were a major influence in changing travel plans to China for many tourists. Similarly, visual images and the reporting of political events have greatly affected travel to other destinations such as Egypt, Indonesia, Israel, Nepal, Palestine and Sri Lanka when political conflicts have occurred (Goodrich 1991; Sönmez and Graefe 1998; Sönmez et al. 1999).

Therefore a critical point in terms of perceptions of safety and security is the manner in which the media and, to a lesser extent government, mediate as an image filter between the tourist destination and generating regions. Sometimes the filter will emphasise particular issues or events; other times events may be ignored. Either way, the media are a major force in creating images of safety and political stability in the destination region. Indeed, it is the very potential for media coverage that provides some political and terrorist groups with the rationale for attacks on tourists. For example, in the early 1970s elements of the Palestinian Liberation Organisation (PLO) used aircraft hijacking as a means of creating publicity for the plight of the Palestinian people in the Israeli-occupied territories and for promoting the Palestinians' political cause.

Hallmark tourist events also aim to use the media to promote certain images. Hallmark events focus attention on a particular location for a short period of time (Roche 2000). During such events, the host community and nation are able to highlight certain images, themes and values while, at the same time, protest groups may also attempt to use hallmark events in order to obtain publicity, for example, the PLO attack on the Israeli Team at the 1972 Olympic Games in Munich. Security provision for events can also be extremely expensive. For example, security for the 2004 Summer Olympics in Athens cost more than US$800 million, the most expensive in the history of the Games, and three times higher than the security budget for Sydney four years previously (*Financial Times* 2004, p. 4) (Table 11.1 provides details of some of the political dimensions of the Summer Olympic Games). Nevertheless, at the micro-political level hallmark events may be used to improve the international and domestic acceptance of unpopular and/or authoritarian regimes. For example, the 1990 Asian Games in Beijing were used by the Chinese to help improve their image after the Tiananmen Square massacre (Knipp 1990). Indeed, it is a testimony to the power of the media's portrayal of political events that the Square is now a tourist attraction in its own right for many Western visitors to China.

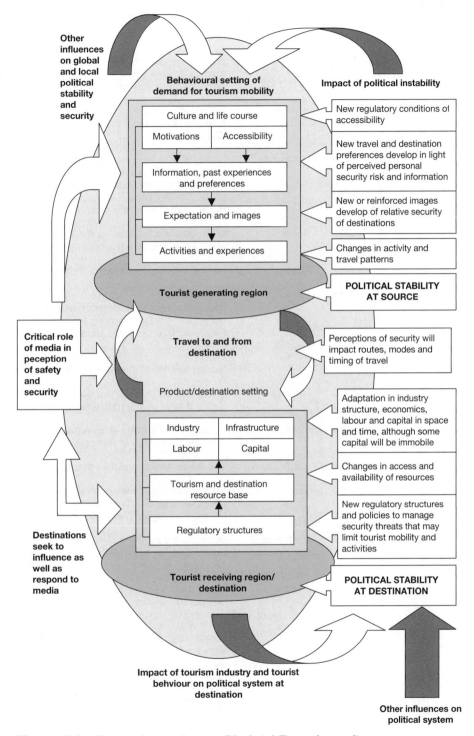

Figure 11.1   The tourism system, political stability and security

Table 11.1   Political events associated with the hosting of the Olympic Games

1936	Berlin	Jesse Owens, a black American sprinter, wins four gold medals, frustrating Hitler's intention of using the Games to prove Aryan supremacy
1952	Helsinki	Soviet Union athletes competing at an Olympics for the first time are housed in a separate athletes' village because of Cold War rivalries
1956	Melbourne	Spain, Switzerland and The Netherlands boycott the Games because of the Soviet invasion of Hungary. Egypt, Lebanon and Iraq withdraw because of the Israeli-led takeover of the Suez canal. The People's Republic of China refuse to participate because of the participation of the Republic of China
1960	Rome	South Africa's last Games for 32 years as the IOC imposes a ban because of apartheid
1964	Tokyo	Restrictions on Japanese outbound travel are lifted
1968	Mexico City	American sprinters Tommie Smith and John Carlos hang their heads and hold gloved hands aloft in a Black Power salute during the medal ceremony for the 200 metres in protest at racial segregation in the United States
1972	Munich	Palestinian terrorists from the Black September movement kidnap and kill 11 members of the Israeli team
1976	Montreal	30 African nations stage a boycott at the inclusion of New Zealand after their national rugby team had toured South Africa
1980	Moscow	65 nations stay away at an American-led boycott because of the Soviet invasion of Afghanistan
1984	Los Angeles	The Soviet Union and 13 other nations boycott the Games
1988	Seoul	South Korea becomes democratic for the Games! All restrictions on South Korean outbound travel are lifted. North Korea, Nicaragua, Cuba and Ethiopia boycott the Games
1992	Barcelona	Boycott-free for the first time since 1972, the Games include a united German team. Although the Soviets are represented by 15 countries, some participate in a unified team
1996	Atlanta	A pipe bomb explodes in the Centennial Olympic Park killing one person and injuring 110
2000	Sydney	North and South Korea march under the same flag. The closing ceremony includes the rock band Midnight Oil wearing T-shirts with 'sorry' on them in reference to the failure of Prime Minister John Howard to apologise for Australia's treatment of its indigenous people
2004	Athens	The most expensive security operation in the history of the Olympic Games
2008	Beijing	Concerns are raised over China's human rights record

The media are not a passive portrayer of events. The media select particular representations and interpretations of places and events from a plethora of potential representations in terms of time, content and images. Therefore, it is the portrayal of political instability rather than political instability itself that becomes uppermost as a factor in tourist destination choice behaviour. Nevertheless, political instability clearly does exist. Political instability can take a number of forms and can be represented as a continuum in terms of the scale and extent of the damage it may have in the tourism marketplace. A number of different dimensions of political instability can be identified within international tourism: international wars, civil wars, coups, terrorism, riots and political and social unrest, and strikes (Lea and Small 1988; also see Pizam and Mansfield 1996). Examples of these different types of political instability are illustrated in Table 11.2.

Warfare, whether it be international or civil, is clearly disastrous for tourism. Apart from the dangers which war presents to the individual, military activity can also damage tourist infrastructure. Although substantially shorter than a civil war, military coups can also have a major effect on tourist arrivals. Nevertheless, military or civilian coups will usually have to be seen as violent or introducing substantial political instability into government before they have a substantial effect on visitor numbers.

Warfare may also have long-term impacts on the image of a destination. For example, South Korea's tourism industry was harmed for a long time by images of the Korean War and conflicts between North and South Korea. A study by Jeong (1988, p. 176) indicated that the 1988 Summer Olympics in Seoul were perceived as a means to overcome the poor image of Korea in the international tourism market as a 'dangerous place to visit', particularly in the United States, because of such factors as *MASH* (the popular television series based on the fictionalised exploits of an American field hospital during the Korean War), the devastation of the country following the Korean War, the shooting down of Korean Airlines flight 007 in the early 1980s, student protests, and the ongoing political instability between North and South Korea. Nevertheless, experience from destinations such as Sri Lanka (Sinclair 1994), Vietnam and Zambia (Teye 1986) indicates that tourism can recover rapidly following cessation of conflict (Richter 1999; Weaver 2000). For example, even in the case of Afghanistan, which had experienced civil war and various invasions since 1979, tourism was slowly returning in 2004 with the most ambitious project in the country being the redevelopment of the five-star, 180-room luxury Kabul Serena hotel by the Aga Khan Development Network. Until the 1979 coup Afghanistan used to receive up to 125 000 tourists a year and was part of an overland route at one time from Europe through to Singapore. According to Aly Mawji, the Development Network's regional representative: 'We would be better off building hotels in other parts of the world. But we felt it was important to demonstrate that a large private company had the confidence to invest here. And tourism is a means of bringing an income into the country' (Bula 2004, p. PT8). Indeed, in the very long term there is some evidence to suggest that war sites and even sites of atrocities can become an attraction in their own right through veterans' tourism, heritage tourism or

Table 11.2   Dimensions of political instability and tourism

Dimension	Examples
International wars	The Iraqi invasion of Kuwait and consequent invasion of Iraq in 1990–91 as well as the American-led invasion of Iraq in 2003 had a massive impact on tourist visitation to the Middle East and broader international tourism in the North American, European and Japanese markets because of the perceived dangers of travel. Since 2000 ongoing conflict between the state of Israel and Palestinian independence groups has also severely damaged the tourism industries of Israel and Palestine.
Civil wars	The break-up of Yugoslavia in 1989 and the conflict between Bosnia, Croatia and Serbia devastated tourist visitation in the former republic for much of the 1990s. Overnight stays of foreign visitors in the communes of the Croatian coast fell from 3.25 million visitors in 1990 to 300 000 in 1991.
Coups	Following the May 1987 coup in Fiji, Japanese visitation was halved during June, and dropped further in July and August. Tourist arrivals from Australia, New Zealand and the United States were cut by almost 75%. From the 85 000 visitors in April, arrivals fell to 5000 in June.
Terrorism	Muslim extremist attacks on tourists in Egypt in late 1992 and early 1993 cut the country's US$4 billion tourist trade by almost half. The terrorist attacks on 11 September in the United States had a major impact on both inbound and outbound travel into the United States that is still being felt in 2004 as new travel security measures are imposed.
Riots/political protests/ social unrest	Following the crushing of the political protests in Tiananmen Square in China, the total number of international arrivals in China fell by 22.7% from 31 694 804 arrivals in 1988 to 24 501 394 in 1989. China's international tourism receipts dropped 17.2% in the same period from US$246 billion to US$186 billion. Political and social unrest may also occur in direct response to tourism development, for example, if the local community are opposed to the development of a tourist resort or infrastructure such as an airport.
Labour strikes and unrest	Following the 1989 Australian domestic air pilots' dispute which lasted several weeks, an estimated 457 000 people cancelled their holiday plans altogether and a further 556 000 had to change their holiday plans due to the dispute.

Sources: Goodrich 1991; National Tourism Administration of the People's Republic of China 1993; Hall 1994a, 1994b; Jordan 1994; Hall and O'Sullivan 1996

what is sometimes referred to as 'dark tourism' (see Foley and Lennon 1996; Evans and Lunn 1997; Graham et al. 2000; Henderson 2000; Lennon and Foley 2000; Dann and Seaton 2001; McKercher and du Cros 2002; Hornstein and Jacobowitz 2003).

Warfare, coups and political strikes or protests may make tourism development or the attraction of visitors problematic, but they do not by themselves pose a direct threat to tourists. However, terrorism constitutes a different nature of threat to tourists because, in this instance, the tourists themselves may be the actual target of terrorist activity. In highlighting the interrelationship between political stability and tourism it is therefore essential to differentiate between tourists and tourism as the direct or indirect victims of political instability, since our ability to comprehend the nature of risk and threat, and hence develop the appropriate managerial response, will be substantially different. The next two sections examine these different types of threat.

Tourism as the Indirect Victim of Political Instability

As noted above, tourism is extremely vulnerable to perceived political instability and lack of safety. Probably one of the best documented examples of the relationship between political instability and tourism was the 4 June 1989 crackdown by Chinese authorities on non-violent student protests in Beijing's Tiananmen Square. As Graham (1990, p. 25) observed: 'The sight of tanks rolling into the Square; the violent battles between students and troops; the steadfastly uncompromising attitude of the Chinese authorities; it was all watched by the world on prime-time television.'

The events in Tiananmen Square and throughout many of China's cities at this time dramatically impacted the country's tourism industry. By late 1989 occupancy levels in Beijing's hotels were 'below 30 per cent at a time when closer to 90 per cent would have been expected ... 300 tour groups totalling 11,500 people were cancelled in May' (Lavery 1989, p. 96). Similarly, Gartner and Shen (1992, p. 47) noted that, 'occupancy rates of 15% was considered high in the months shortly after the conflict'. In addition to the impact on tourist visitation, business visits were also affected by both perceptions of instability and the sanctions that were imposed by many Western governments on their corporations which conducted business in China (Hall 1994a).

The downturn in tourism following Western and Japanese reactions to the quelling of the pro-democracy movement in China had an immediate impact on China's foreign exchange earnings with a drop of 17.2% (US$386.35 million) from 1988 to 1989. Research by Roehl (1990) on American travel agents and by Gartner and Shen (1992) on mature travellers indicated a negative shift in attitudes towards visiting China as a result of the events at Tiananmen Square. However, by 1991 inbound tourism had grown again to exceed pre-Tiananmen levels of visitation. Moreover, some markets, particularly North American and European markets, were far more adversely affected by the events of Tiananmen Square than Asian markets. Several reasons can be put forward for this, including different media coverage of events and different notions of what constitutes the appropriate role of the state in protecting national interests, order and stability against the rights of individuals. Whatever the reason, it is apparent that different markets respond differently to political events and actions.

Indeed, Graham's (1990, p. 25) comment with respect to Tiananmen Square, that 'most people living in free societies felt revulsion and anger; those planning holidays to China cancelled, while those with a vague notion of visiting the country put it on hold for the distant future – if ever', has not come to fruition. Instead, as Cook (1989, p. 64) correctly argued:

> The massacre of Chinese students and civilians in Tiananmen Square put a temporary end to international tourism in China. As history is rewritten in China, however, and as the events of Spring 1989 become back-page news around the world, tourists will return to China. In fact, the number of travellers to China is expected to increase dramatically throughout the 1990s.

For example, in 1991 and 1992 the number of foreign visitors had grown by 55% and 48% respectively. Even events such as the Chinese occupation of Tibet (Klieger 1992) and the lack of popular elections in Hong Kong following transfer to Chinese sovereignty have done little to impact tourism, and, despite concerns surrounding China's human rights record, Beijing will be hosting the 2008 Summer Olympic Games.

This example shows that unless tourists feel directly threatened because of political instability or perceive there to be danger, then they are likely to travel to destinations. The number of people who refuse to travel to a country because of its human rights record, particularly in the post-September 11 environment, therefore appears to be quite small. In the case of China, international economic relations and diplomatic relationships certainly seem to have more weight than any human rights campaign. Since the shift by the Chinese government in 1978 to an 'open door policy' in its relations with non-communist countries and the promotion of the doctrine of a 'socialist market economy', tourism has been regarded as a key element in the modernisation of China and a means to gain important foreign exchange earnings (Richter 1989; Tisdell and Wen 1991; Hall 1994a). The large amount of foreign direct investment in China from Japan, Europe and the United States seems unlikely to be endangered by any tourism and human rights campaign.

In contrast, Europe and the United States have supported a campaign against foreign investment in Myanmar (Burma), a country which had relatively little direct investment by US-based companies. In the case of Myanmar, tourism has been the target of boycott campaigns by several human rights and pro-democracy groups because of the ongoing denial of democracy and human rights by the military *junta*, the focal point of which is the frequent detention of Aung San Suu Kyi, the country's pro-democracy campaigner. As of the end of 2003, she had been detained for a total of 14 years, and had just been put under house arrest again, supposedly for her own protection.

The government of Myanmar seeks to develop tourism partly because of its economic returns but also because of the legitimacy it brings to the government. Myanmar has been accepted into PATA (the Pacific Asia Travel Association) and ASEAN (the Association of South East Asian Nations), and has hosted international trade fairs and Visit Myanmar Years (VMY) to promote the country.

In January 1995, the BBC reported that slave labour was being used to build roads and other infrastructure needed to support the tourism industry. This claim was further documented by John Pilger in *Inside Burma: Land of Fear*, which was screened in June 1996 (Pilger 1996). The documentary showed children and chain gangs being used as slave labour to build roads, bridges, airports, railways, the imperial palace in Mandalay and other tourist attractions. According to Oo and Perez (1996), some two million Burmese, including women and children, have been used as slave labourers in the beautification campaign for VMY. Human rights groups, such as Amnesty International, also charged that forced and prison labour was being used to develop Myanmar's infrastructure and people were being forced to relocate from slum areas so that tourists do not see them (Campbell 1996). The Director-General of Myanmar's Directorate of Hotels and Tourism categorically denied such allegations, stating that those advancing such notions were 'against the government' and 'out of touch with what is really happening in Myanmar' (in Campbell 1996, np).

The actions of the Myanmar government and the boycott campaign of the opposition and international human rights groups raise fundamental questions with respect to the relationship between tourism and politics and the actions that governments should take on tourism issues. According to a *TravelAsia* (1996) editorial: 'It is clear political events have an impact on tourism – from how consumers perceive the country (safe or unsafe) to whether they feel they should support a regime which does not fall in line with their own beliefs.' Yet Oo and Perez (1996) put the issue more bluntly when discussing the 'Visit Myanmar Year' campaign, noting that the Myanmar government, although well-known for its human rights violations, was desperate for the income that foreign tourists and tourism investment generates as well the opportunity to project a good international image. They noted that industry did not seem concerned by human rights issues: 'PATA delegates have generally praised Burmese efforts in opening up the once hermit nation.... And of course, not a single word was spoken on the social costs and impact of "Visit Myanmar Year". For them, money is more important than human rights' (Oo and Perez 1996, np).

The attitude of *TravelAsia* (1996) represented a substantial point of difference from that of human rights groups: 'As travel business professionals, we have to keep a clear head and not take sides. Indeed, the only side we should be on is our customers! The only questions we should ask are, does Myanmar have the products, the infrastructure and the will to become one of Asia's great destinations?' There are no easy answers in trying to determine the most appropriate course of action with respect to tourism in Myanmar. Each government, corporation and individual will have a perspective on this vexed question, depending on their economic and social interests. Within Asia, fellow ASEAN countries such as Thailand and Singapore have invested heavily in Myanmar's tourism industry, whereas the United States and Australia have avoided such actions. Asian countries claim that a constructive engagement through economic and diplomatic relations may be the best means of bringing Myanmar within the sphere of international human rights regimes. In contrast, Western countries and human rights groups believe that sanctions, including encouraging tourists to boycott Myanmar, are the best policy choice in encouraging appropriate behaviours from the Myanmar regime. Either way, it is readily apparent that the growth of intermestic policy issues such as the relationship of human rights and tourism require a detailed analysis with respect to their potential implications for tourist behaviour.

Although the duration of political violence may be shortlived, the longer-term implications for tourism can last for many years, affecting the confidence not only of tourists, but also of potential investors in the tourism industry (Hall 1994a). Given the increasing potential for destination substitution in the highly competitive global tourism marketplace, many destination regions need to pay greater heed to the potential impact of political instability on the image of the destination. Tourism is clearly very susceptible to perceptions of political instability, particularly when such instability is tied to hostilities. In the above cases tourism was an incidental victim of broader political activities. Tourists may sometimes get caught up in a war, a coup or a riot, thereby damaging perceptions of the destination and possibly even the overall pattern of tourism development in the longer term, but they are not the direct target of political violence or social unrest. However, in the case of terrorism, which we examine in the next section, tourism is often a direct and deliberate target of political violence.

The Tourist as Target: Tourism as the Direct Victim of Political Instability

Most of the evidence on tourist motivations points to concerns over safety and insecurity as a major barrier to travel and thus a limitation on the growth of the industry in a number of destinations. In addition to the openly stated fear there may be an expression of lack of interest in travel or changes in travel behaviours, both of which can mask underlying safety concerns. In these circumstances the possibility of terrorists targeting tourists, regardless of how remote the likelihood may be in objective safety concerns, may well have an effect on tourist demand in a number of markets for certain destinations (Buckley and Klemm 1993; Neumayer 2004).

Travellers have long been subject to banditry. Hence, the word 'travail', meaning hard or agonising labour, from which 'travel' derives. However, politically motivated terrorism is a child of the modern era of travel. Images of hijacked aircraft or the taking of tourists as hostages are a relatively common element in television news even though, in objective terms, transport accidents and sickness are far more likely occurrences for any tourist. Indeed, it is the media profile given to tourist loss of life or of hostage situations that likely feeds many terrorist activities. The media profile given to terrorist activities is probably critical in its occurrence, given that 'terrorism is a form of communication, of both the threat or reality of violence and the political message' (Richter and Waugh 1986, p. 230). Therefore, the media which were identified in Figure 11.1 as being significant in establishing tourist perceptions of political stability in destination regions can also serve the communication needs of political terrorists in highlighting their cause in tourist generating regions. Indeed, the internationalisation of the media and increased global political and economic interdependence can only serve to lift the profile of terrorist activities.

According to Hall (1994a), tourism is affected by terrorism through two means. First, terrorist activities can damage a destination's or country's tourist industry by creating an image of lack of safety. Second, tourists or tourist facilities, such as airport terminals or aircraft, may themselves be subject to attack. 'Tourist facilities are logical targets of terrorist violence because they afford opportunity and relative safety for terrorists to act' (Richter and Waugh 1986, p. 233). Although the actual risk of terrorist attack is quite low, it is perceptions that count with the effects of such perceptions on travel decisions usually substantial (Conant et al. 1988).

According to Hall (1994a), attacks on tourists or tourist facilities can be used by terrorists to achieve a range of tactical, strategic and ideological objectives. One of the most common reasons for terrorist attacks is to gain publicity for the terrorist cause. For example, the hijacking of airliners in the early 1970s by the Palestinian Liberation Organisation (PLO) was used to gain publicity for the Palestinian cause. In eastern Turkey in 1993, members of the Kurdistan Workers' Party seeking the establishment of a separate Kurdish state, kidnapped a number of tourists. Australian, French and British tourists were abducted and held hostage in order to raise the profile of the Kurdish separatists in the world media. In August 1994, three tourists travelling on a train between Phnom Penh and Sihanoukville were taken hostage by the Khmer Rouge. They were used as pawns in negotiations with the Cambodian government over foreign military aid and political recognition of the Khmer Rouge. Similarly, in 2003 a group of European tourists was abducted by rebels in Colombia and were then the subject of high-profile negotiations for their release. Terrorist attacks on tourists can also be used to punish nationals of a country which supports the government that the terrorists are trying to overthrow or which is in opposition to their own activities. For example, as long ago as 1986, Richter and Waugh noted that attacks on American tourists could be viewed as a form of punishment of the US government for its foreign policy decisions and military actions.

Events which are used by governments to enhance their legitimacy can also be utilised by opposition groups to undermine support for government and to focus attention on government activities, particularly with respect to authoritarian regimes (Richter and Waugh 1986). For example, it is important to note that the attention given to Islamic extremist groups since the events of September 11 often fails to acknowledge that Islamic terrorist attacks on tourists have been occurring since the early 1990s and, arguably, even longer, along with the many attacks on tourists by non-Islamic terrorist groups.

The situation in Egypt with respect to attacks on tourists is an example of how tourists and tourist facilities can be targeted by terrorist organisations in an attempt to achieve ideological objectives and to strengthen their claims to political legitimacy by making the incumbent government appear weak. The deliberate targeting of tourists in Egypt since late 1992 by fundamentalist Muslim militants marked a change in previous political tactics, and seriously damaged the country's US$4 billion tourist industry for a number of years, cutting the tourism trade by almost half. In August 1994, the El-Gama'a el Islamiya (Islamic Group) attacked a tourist mini-bus near Sohag in southern Egypt, killing a 13-year-old Spanish boy, in order to warn foreigners to stay away from the September United Nations World Population Conference to be held in Cairo. According to one newspaper report, 'The Egyptian Government hoped that by hosting the conference it could promote the image of a peace-loving, democratic country and a safe destination' (*Canberra Times* 1994). Islamic fundamentalists perceived tourism as a soft target and were aware of the role tourism plays in the Egyptian economy and in the regional economy of destinations such as Luxor. Such attacks may also gather a degree of sympathy from the general population because many Islamic fundamentalists are also concerned at the contradiction between the values of some aspects of Western mass tourism and Islam. Indeed, the El-Gama'a el-Islamiya had been warning foreign tourists to stay away from Cairo and Upper Egypt. According to the group: 'The Gama'a has carried out about 20 operations targeting the tourist industry and the casualties among the tourists themselves were negligible, in accordance with our policy of 'tourism not tourists' (Reuters 1993, p. 7). In response, the Egyptian government imprisoned many of the leaders of the fundamentalist movement and have used military forces to help protect convoys of tourist buses, particularly in the south of the country. However, the latter action, while helping to ensure tourist safety, does not enhance perceptions of Egypt as a democratic state which seeks to uphold human rights. In fact concerns over the protection of human rights during campaigns against terrorism is an ongoing theme in many Western nations, let alone countries such as Egypt.

The above examples illustrate the extent to which terrorism can impact tourism. Because of its international visibility tourism is a ready-made target for terrorist groups who are seeking to gain publicity for their objectives. Within this context it becomes imperative for destination areas to understand not only the motivations of terrorist organisations but also the key role that the media play in inadvertently supporting the goals of many terrorist groups. Tourism managers in politically unstable regions and in vulnerable tourist facilities, such as airports, need to develop ways of preventing terrorist attacks against tourists, without giving tourists the impressions that a serious threat is present. If not, there is a likelihood that tourists' behaviour in terms of destination and activity choice may well change.

Safety and Tourism

Perceptions of political stability and safety are a prerequisite for tourist visitation. 'A favourable image is an essential requirement of any tourist destination. The problem with any kind of civil unrest is that unfavourable images are beamed across the world.... It is not so much that the area is dangerous; more that it does not look attractive' (Buckley and Klemm 1993, pp. 193–4). Violent protests, social unrest, civil war, terrorist actions, the perceived violations of human rights, or even the mere threat of these activities, can cause tourists to alter their travel behaviour. Tourism managers and planners therefore need to become far more sophisticated in their approach to crisis management and be more aware of the political dimensions of tourism development. At present, 'when problems arise, the only response the industry knows is to market more vigorously, regardless of the likelihood of success' (Richter and Waugh 1986, p. 232). The sheer scope of the implications of political violence for tourism requires a far more sophisticated understanding of the nature of the international traveller's response to political instability and perceived threats to tourist safety than what has hitherto been the case. Political threats are often not included in assessments of the external environment within which tourist businesses operate, although this has changed to some extent since September 11. This chapter has given a brief introduction to the various means by which political instability and political violence can impact tourism. As noted, the effects of political violence can be both direct or incidental, and may have repercussions far beyond the immediate location in which violence occurs. Political instability can have major effects on the local tourism economy. Since 1990 the tourist economies of Australia, Myanmar (Burma), China, Croatia, Egypt, Fiji, India, Indonesia, Israel, Palestine, Pakistan, Philippines, South Africa, Spain, Sri Lanka and the United States have all been damaged to various degrees by political violence.

Continuing political instability can have a deterrent effect on tourism at a time when regions are most needing the foreign exchange and economic development benefits of tourism, as in the case of the transitional countries of Eastern Europe (D.R. Hall 1991a, 2004) or in less developed nations (Harrison 1992a, 1992b, 2001; Hall 1994b). Currently, there are a number of destinations around the world which may prove potentially dangerous for the traveller and, as a result, are suffering major impacts on their tourist numbers and on tourism development.

Attacks on tourists and actual or perceived political instability may create negative tourist images of a destination which may take years to overcome. In some cases, such as China, changed political conditions and/or favourable media coverage may enable destinations to recover relatively quickly. Indeed, there may even be a 'curiosity' factor whereby tourists are interested in seeing a place they may have seen or read about during a period of political instability and which is now safe to visit. However, where political instability and political violence linger, such as in Kashmir, or some parts of the former

Yugoslavia, it may take many years for visitation figures to reach those of the pre-political instability period. Perceptions of instability can also have long-term effects on tourism development by reducing the likelihood of both foreign and domestic investment in tourist infrastructure, and by increasing the costs of insuring such investments (Hall 1994a).

Politics has major direct and indirect influences on tourism development and on tourist behaviour. The emerging global economy and communications networks, of which the internationalisation of tourism is an integral part, make tourism increasingly subject to the effects of political instability and political violence. In a world of increasing interconnection, the severing of touristic relationships through acts of political violence can have repercussions throughout the entire tourist system, dramatically affecting tourist behaviour, the destination region, nearby destination regions, transit regions and political relationships. Undoubtedly, it is impossible to completely insulate tourism from the effects of political instability. However, to ignore the political dimensions of tourism may lead not only to an incomplete academic appreciation of tourism, but also to an inadequate assessment of the risks associated with tourism development. National security issues are therefore clearly related to tourism development, management and mobility, and these issues will be the subject of the next section.

Tourism, Issue Agendas and National Security

Chapter 10 highlighted some of the relationships between tourism and political instability. However, such a description does not indicate how tourism-related political or security concerns actually become part of the policy agenda for government. This chapter identifies the media as a central player in determining not only how consumers react to issues in the media, but also how politicians and government react. This is not to suggest that governments only react to the media in developing tourism policy, as clearly policies are instigated in relation to other factors such as a perceived problem which does not gain media attention or pressure or advice from the tourism industry. Nevertheless, it is clear that, at least in many developed countries, the media are a major determinant in the policy agenda, not least because of their role in influencing public opinion, although tourism does not often feature as a political news story.

Tourism rarely features as a factor in political elections, particularly at a national level. Instead, tourism is more likely to become a development issue in local government elections. One exception to the involvement of tourism in elections was the 2003 recall election for the state governorship in California, in which casinos on Native American Indian land became a main election issue.

Padgett and Hall (2001) sought to identify the significance of tourism as a political issue in the 1999 New Zealand general election through an analysis of

Tourism Insights: Native American Indian Tribal Casinos and the 2003 Californian Gubernatorial Election

There are approximately 3 million Native Americans in the United States, less than 1% of the population. However, in 2002 Native American casinos took an estimated US$13 billion in revenue (Campbell 2003), a figure which has not only given some tribes a degree of economic independence never seen before but which has also made political enemies, particularly the challenge it provides to the hegemony of existing casinos in Nevada and Atlantic City. In 1988, California, which has the largest number of tribes (109), set up the Indian Gaming Regulatory Act, thereby allowing casinos and other gambling operations to be established as a means of financial independence and economic development.

During the 2003 gubernatorial election in California, the eventually successful candidate, Arnold Schwarzenegger, the one-time body builder and actor, targeted Native American Indian tribal casinos, describing them as 'special interests', and stating that '[t]heir casinos make billions, yet they pay no taxes and virtually nothing to the state. All the other major candidates take their money and pander to them. I don't play that game' (quoted in Campbell 2003, p. 14). In response, Richard Milanovich, the tribal chairman of the Agua Caliente band of the Cahuilla Indians, which operates the Spa resort casino in Palm Springs noted: 'How much influence does General Motors have, or Westinghouse, or Ford, or some construction companies? There's a special interest which Mr Schwarzenegger seems to have his hand out for.' Another tribal chairperson, Mark Macarro, of the Pechanga Band of Luiseno Indians, stated that he was 'astounded by Arnold Schwarzenegger's ignorance' (quoted in Campbell 2003, p. 14). He went on to note that '[i]n 1875, we were forcibly evicted from our land because it had water running through it'. In the eight years that the tribe had been operating a casino they were able to do more in education and health 'than the federal government did in 200 years'. In commenting on Mr Schwarzenegger's campaign advertisements, the chairperson of the National Indian Gaming Association, Ernie Stevens, observed that they 'perpetuated the myth that Indians don't pay taxes and that Indian gaming is not contributing to the state of California.... Indian gaming has created over 40,000 jobs in California while the rest of the state economy is declining' (quoted in Campbell 2003, p. 14). In addition, tribal employees had paid over US$280 million a year in federal income and payroll tax, in addition to the US$100 million paid to California each year through gaming compacts (Campbell 2003).

The extent to which gaming could assist indigenous development is shown by the Spa casino and hotel on the Agua Caliente land. According to Richard Milanovich, 'in 1993 a survey found that half of our members were living below the poverty level, the majority in substandard housing' (quoted in Campbell 2003, p. 14). In contrast, the casino, which opened in 1995, had 2400 employees in 2003 and the revenue has meant that every tribal member receives free health care and can afford to go to college. In 2002 the casino also paid US$9 million to the state of California as part of the compact, which includes money for tribes that do not have casinos as well as for problem gambling.

Some commentators were likening the threat of extermination of the gambling legislation to previous emasculation of Indian rights by the Californian legislature, such as unfulfilled peace treaties and the enaction of the scalping bounty in 1848 – '$50 for a native American man's scalp, $25 for a woman's and $10 for a child's' (quoted in Campbell 2003, p. 14). Yet, despite the failure of tribal support against the recall of Governor Gray Davis in the short term, there was ironically relatively little that Mr Schwarzenegger could do given that many of the state's agreements with the tribes had several years to run, indeed up to 16 years in some cases. However, it is unlikely that the Californian tribes will stop making political donations (US$120 million from 1998 to 2003), given the significance of casinos and gambling for their tribal welfare.

See Northern Californian Indian Development Council ncidc.org; Spa Casino, Palm Springs Sparesortcasino.com; The Schwarzenegger campaign joinarnold.com

four major newspapers. Perhaps an indication of the relative significance of tourism in national elections can be noted in that only four tourism stories were identified during the entire election period! Tourism did not have the same political appeal as economic policies, governance and constitution issues, and taxation regimes. Tourism therefore attracted insignificant media attention compared to its economic significance.

As part of the same study a survey of candidates in the election was also undertaken with respondents stating that tourism contributed significantly to New Zealand's economy and that it would be the basis of the economy in the future. However, candidates were divided over the exact nature of government involvement. The New Zealand tourism industry was considered to be environmentally and ecologically sustainable. Candidates believed that there needed to be a sustainable tourism development strategy and that there was a significant support for government intervention in the protection of the tourism product. Marketing and promotion, another method of government intervention in the tourism industry, was also advocated, yet support for funding was weak. Tourism was generally considered by candidates to be a very important election issue, yet in the context of all issues, it ranked poorly. When asked directly about the importance of tourism as an election issue, candidates rated it as only somewhat important. This was also the attitude taken on the relevance of different political parties' tourism policies for the industry. Many candidates had no knowledge of the other parties' tourism policies. The results suggested that, because candidate knowledge of tourism policies was low, it was unlikely that issues could be successfully debated, therefore tourism was left out of the election campaign. Another policy-related study was undertaken by Richter (1980), who completed a four-month content analysis (CA) of newspaper articles from three daily newspapers in the Philippines. She suggested that tourism might have been used as a propaganda tool in the Philippines to promote the country's beauty and disregarded the fact that martial law had been declared.

One of the main factors in determining government policies in the developed world is the relationship between the media and public opinion (Hester and Gonzenbach 1997). Indeed, some countries may actually try to improve their image internationally or at least in certain key nations through a directed media and public relations campaign in order not only to attract tourists but also to influence broader public opinion surrounding government policies (Zhang and Cameron 2003). A key concept in political science with respect to agenda-setting by government is that of issue attention (Henry and Gordon 2001) and this is examined in the following section with respect to the issue–attention cycle (Downs 1972), the events of September 11, 2001 and the corresponding reaction from government and tourism authorities.

Tourism Policy Concerns and the Media: The Significance of the Issue–Attention Cycle

The terrorist attacks in the United States on 11 September 2001, when three aeroplanes were hijacked and sent crashing into buildings in New York and Washington and a fourth hijacked plane crashed into a field near Pittsburgh, had an enormous immediate impact on international and domestic travel patterns. Not only did the events affect decisions regarding where to travel, but they also influenced choices regarding mode of transport and, in some cases, whether to travel at all. The events clearly raised wider questions about the safety of travellers from terrorist or criminal acts as well as concerns over national security. Just as significantly, the enormity of the events of September 11 and subsequent terrorist attacks in Bali and Spain led many international, national and regional tourism organisations to try to decide not only how to react in the short term but also to pose the question of when the market would regain confidence and return to 'normal'.

Central to these issues is the role of the media in influencing public opinion and perception. The media are clearly seen as very influential when it comes to political and social attitudes. Public perceptions of the relative importance of an issue are largely determined by the news media (Wood and Peake 1998). The media interpret issues, giving them more or less significance through the amount or type of coverage provided. The media, particularly television news, also focus attention on specific events through this same interpretative function (Iyengar and Kinder 1987). However, not only do the media influence general public opinion, they also play a major part in informing consumers' images of destinations and transport modes, their relative safety and security, either directly in terms of being read, heard or watched, or indirectly through the advice given by friends, relatives and other sources of 'word of mouth' information (Fodness and Murray 1997; Swarbrooke and Horner 1999). Moreover, in this age of global communication, events can be played out live on the television screen, therefore potentially having an even greater impact on the viewing public. Therefore, critical to an understanding of the likely longer-term patterns of response to events, such as those of September 11 and other disasters and crises which affect tourism, is an understanding of how the media deal with such issues and how this affects policy and destination management (Faulkner and Vikulov 2001).

One of the most significant concepts in understanding the relationships between the media and consumers is that of the 'issue attention cycle' (Downs 1972). According to Downs (1972), modern publics attend to many issues in a cyclical fashion. A problem 'leaps into prominence, remains there for a short time, and then, though still largely unresolved, gradually fades from the center of public attention' (1972, p. 38). Originally applied to an understanding of social issues in the 1960s, and environmental issues in particular, the notion of an issue–attention cycle has also been found to be extremely important in explaining the relationship between domestic and foreign policy decisions, and the media and the level of public interest in certain issues (Cohen 1963; Walker 1977; Iyengar and Kinder 1987). One of the main reasons for this is the 'ecology of news' in that there is competition between news stories for the finite amount of media space and new stories will usually have greater impact than old ones. In addition, it should be noted that the objective danger of something to tourists will not usually correlate to the amount of news coverage an issue will get. For example, there is a far greater likelihood of being killed in a car crash or catching a tropical disease as a tourist than being killed by terrorists or hijacked. Nevertheless, it is the exceptional event that often seems to grab the headlines and therefore influence public opinion.

The issue–attention cycle is divided into five stages which may vary in duration depending upon the particular issue involved (see Figure 11.2), but which almost always occur in the following sequence:

- the pre-problem stage;

- alarmed discovery and euphoric enthusiasm;

- realisation of the cost of significant progress;

- gradual decline of intense public interest; and

- the post-problem stage.

These stages describe not only current efforts with respect to travel safety measures and policies but are also indicative of wider public opinions towards issues associated with safety and security (Figure 11.1). These stages will now be discussed in relation to the events of September 11.

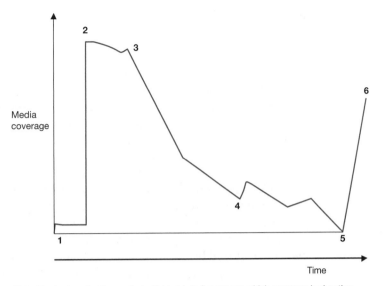

Note: The issue–attention cycle is divided into five stages which may vary in duration depending upon the particular issue involved, but which almost always occur in the following sequence:
1. The pre-problem stage.
2. Alarmed discovery and euphoric enthusiasm.
3. Realising the cost of significant progress.
4. Gradual decline of intense public interest. Sporadic recapture of issue may occur on the anniversary of an event or when a similar event occurs which is related to the overall policy area.
5. The post-problem stage.
6. Issue re-emergence.

Figure 11.2 The issue–attention cycle

Pre-problem stage

At the pre-problem stage an issue only exists for experts and those directly involved. Few members of the public are aware of the issue. It describes well the pre-September 11 situation. Traveller and airline security was an issue, including in relation to terrorist attacks, but primarily for aviation and tourism experts (e.g. World Tourism Organisation 1996b) and it was not high in public consciousness in the Western world. Instead, it was relegated to a problem of the developing world and 'local' tourism security issues. For example, on 24 July 2001 Tamil Tiger separatists attacked Sri Lanka's international airport, leaving 14 dead and 11 military and commercial passenger planes destroyed, and also placing a number of British tourists under fire (BBC 2001). Hall (2002b) recorded 28 terrorist attacks, bomb threats and attempted hijackings on international aircraft for 2001 up to the time of the September 11 attacks (this figure did not include domestic flights or incidents of 'air rage'). All of these events gained some international publicity, albeit relatively briefly, and high-lighted security issues but none of them received as much coverage as the events of September 11. Importantly, they did not receive a high level of sus-tained media coverage in the important international tourism generating regions of North America and Europe.

Alarmed discovery and euphoric enthusiasm

This stage is demonstrated in the immediate response to the events of September 11. The graphic images which were beamed across the world, along with aviation restrictions in US airspace, had an immediate effect on travel plans and pushed an already ailing international aviation industry into deeper trouble. Apart from the immediate shock of the attack, followed by the declaration of the 'war on terrorism', attention was soon given to the adequacy of security measures in American airports, airlines and airports that had connections to the United States, as well as the airlines of countries that were part of the US-led coalition in Afghanistan that might then be subject to attack themselves. Such measures took on an increased urgency in light of anthrax scares and further security breaches shortly after the events of September 11.

The response to recognition that airline and travel security problems existed was characterised by organisational redesign or innovation as a way of demonstrating to the public and business that 'something has been done'. As Poole (2001) commented with respect to American approaches to airport security: 'Federal lawmakers appear to be in quite a rush these days to be seen as "doing something" to combat terrorism'. Although he then cautioned, 'Does it matter to them if that something turns out to be rather foolish?'

What was actually done tended to take the form of the establishment of special committees or working groups, or led to a more fundamental restructuring of government initiatives. For example, in the case of Australia and New Zealand, the tourism ministers established special working groups to provide their perspectives on the impacts of events on tourism and advise the government on initiatives they could undertake (Department of Industry, Tourism and Resources 2001). In the United States the administrative and policy decisions relating to the security issues led to a fundamental reassessment of policies and procedures. For example, the Federal Aviation Administration's (FAA) Civil Aviation Security organisation was integrated into the newly formed Transportation Security Administration (TSA) of the Department of Transportation (DOT) (Federal Aviation Administration 2002, see also http://www.faa.gov/). In addition, a new office of Homeland Security was established. The World Tourism Organisation also undertook a number of measures, including the passing of a resolution against terrorism as well as establishing a crisis committee shortly after the events of 11 September. The committee was later renamed a Tourism Recovery Committee (World Tourism Organisation 2002b).

Realisation of the costs of significant progress

At this stage there is a realisation that solving the security problem comes at a substantial extra cost to consumers and industry stakeholders in terms of both extra fares and/or taxes, but also in changes in services to customers, such as longer check-in times and greater inconvenience. Many regional airports, for example, are now required to install or reinstall expensive security equipment while more personnel are also needed. The extra charges for these services may be perceived by some as a further deterrent to travel by plane and may lead to a switch to other forms of transport where this is possible. In addition, the cost of the quality of security staff and work practices are also debated. Another area in which costs are considered are issues of individual rights and privacy (Peissl 2003; Regan 2003). Some people will baulk at the implications of new security laws which impinge on individual freedoms while concerns may develop in certain communities, particularly the Islamic and certain Middle Eastern communities, that the applications of terrorism and security policies are being targeted at some populations and not others. Many of these issues are still being worked through in the United States and in other countries.

Gradual decline of intense public interest

This phase develops as the original problem loses its novelty to both media and the public. The public also begin to understand how difficult a solution will be, and how costly it has become. Indeed, it may also be acknowledged that some problems, such as those associated with security, are never 100 per cent solvable. As Poole (2001) noted, 'policymakers should admit that nobody yet has "the answer" for implementing more effective and affordable airport security. All sorts of solutions are possible, from better X-ray machines, to sophisticated profiling of high-risk people, to biometric ID cards for employees and frequent fliers – and no one is sure yet how much they will cost or how effective they will be.' Four reactions may result: discouragement, a sense of threat, boredom, or a combination of these feelings (Downs 1972). However, so long as no major breaches of airline security occur or, more particularly, terrorism is seen to be occurring outside the Western world and the primary media space, then public interest, and hence policy concern, will diminish in Western countries. Public attention no longer focuses on the issue but is transferred instead to another problem that is entering stage two, diverting policy attention and government funding with it.

The carrying capacity of the media means that the ecological competition between issues leads to a situation in which new issues arise, replacing the original issue in terms of extent and quality of coverage. Indeed, the amount of attention an issue gets is clearly not always related to its 'seriousness' as an issue. Media coverage is therefore diminished and routinised with only sporadic recapture, review or anniversary stories which mark the effects of the original event on policy and administrative processes. For example, in the week leading up to the first anniversary of the terrorist attacks in Bali on 12 October 2002 which killed 202 people including 88 Australians, the Bali anniversary was the most-mentioned news story in Australia (*The Australian* 2003). Nevertheless, the decline of such attention is also regarded as being related to the decline of political interest in the issue, as well leading to a lack of political impetus to bring about change. From the customer perspective this may be reflected in renewed confidence in travelling and in airline security, even if there are no further substantial changes in policies and procedures. Instead, because the issue has moved towards the media horizon, it has also declined in importance as a consumer concern (Gartner and Shen 1992; Hall and O'Sullivan 1996).

The post-problem stage

In this final stage the problem is managed in an orderly way by agencies through routine programmes and policies. With respect to travel security and airline safety this is the situation that was established after previous breaches of security or acts of terrorism influenced policies, only for them to undergo incremental change or no change at all until another crisis affects the administrative system. In the case of travel security, this stage merges into the pre-problem stage as, despite the most optimistic predictions, it is likely that there will be further attacks on travellers and on the aviation sector in particular. Nevertheless, it is not so much the fact that these attacks occur that is important, but rather it is the extent to which they become the focus of media attention and hence arrive on the radar screens of our politicians so that they recognise that an issue exists and they need to do something about it. Indeed, if terrorist attacks on travellers are seen to become a problem of the developing world again, then it is likely that some procedures put in place in the developed world will be removed over time in order to minimise costs for airlines, airports and destinations.

Throughout the world governments at all levels have sought to take measures to deal with the effects of the events of September 11 and their direct and indirect impacts on travel and tourism. While simultaneously making changes to security measures, many destinations have sought to launch campaigns to persuade people to travel again. In all of this the role of the media and the perception of the public are paramount. Indeed, it should be remembered that there is a difference between the perception of risk and the actual likelihood of risk (Figure 11.3). However, this chapter is arguing that not only is the media significant in terms of the images that surround travel and specific destinations and which influence travel decision-making, but that the media also have a substantial impact on the policy measures which governments take with respect to tourist safety and security. The stringent application of security measures has previously ebbed and flowed in light of responses to terrorist attacks and hijackings, perceptions of risk and security, and subsequent commercial and consumer pressures for convenient and cheaper travel. Even given the undoubted enormity of the events of September 11, it is highly likely that they will ebb and flow again. Moreover, just as importantly, the ebb and flow of the media also influence how other issues may gain the attention of policymakers and politicians, including those discussed in the following chapters with respect to tourism and its relationships to biosecurity and climate change, topics which may mark a new understanding of the relationships between tourism and national security.

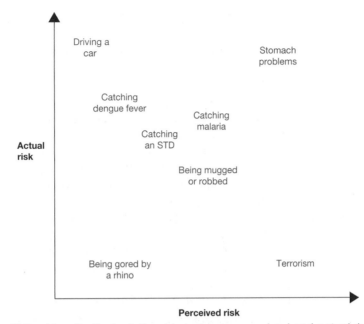

Figure 11.3 Hypothetical relationship between perceived and actual risk of death, sickness or injury while travelling as an international FIT in the tropics (early 2004)

Tourism and the Reconceptualisations of National Security

Security fears are not new to the world. However, the so-called security certainties of the Cold War, at least in relation to notions of friend and foe, have given way to conceptions of security that extend beyond ideas of national security and therefore encompass a wide range of issues at scales ranging from the global to the individual. Under these new concepts of security, threats are generated not just from military actions but also from such global issues as environmental change, resource scarcity, international crime, health, biosecurity, and challenges to sustainable development, to name just a few (Butfoy 1997).

Tourism is irrevocably bound up with the concept of security. Tourist behaviour and, consequently, destinations are deeply affected by perceptions of security and the management of safety, security and risk. Moreover, as events in 2003 related to the war in Iraq, concerns over a new strain of pneumonia, and general travel safety demonstrated, the tourism industry is highly vulnerable to changes in the global security environment. Border security, for example, not only concentrates on terrorist attacks or drug smuggling, but also ensures that unwanted pests and diseases do not cross national or regional borders. However, at least historically, at a macro-analytical level tourism has tended to focus on the threats posed by political insecurity and uncertainty (e.g. Richter and Waugh 1986; Gartner and Shen 1992; Hall and O'Sullivan 1996; Hall and Oehlers 1999).

Although 'Tourism as a Force for Peace' has been a popular positive message relayed by the industry, consultants and some academics in recent years, the reality is that tourism has very little influence on peace and security issues, at least at the macro-level, and that tourism is far more dependent on peace than peace is on tourism. Indeed, as one of the industries which has been hurt the most by the war in Iraq, some may see it as perhaps surprising how quiet industry voices, such as the World Travel and Tourism Council or the World Tourism Organisation (WTO) were regarding the ethics of the invasion (Hall, Timothy and Duval 2004), raising questions as to how possible is it to have ethical tourism unless you see ethics in the wider realm of what happens in the world. Nevertheless, as Hall, Timothy and Duval (2004) noted, recognition by the WTO that various areas of multilateral relations are significant may suggest that environmental, social and economic issues, as well as the system of international governance by which such concerns are governed, now clearly lie within contemporary understandings of security (Boulding 1991).

Hall, Timothy and Duval (2004) noted that contemporary ideas of security have developed from the notion of common security that was articulated in the 1982 Report of the Independent Commission on Disarmament and Security Issues, entitled *Common Security: A Blueprint for Survival* (referred to as the Palme Commission Report, after its chairman, Swedish Prime Minister Olof Palme) (Independent Commission on Disarmament and Security Issues 1982; hereafter referred to as the Palme Commission). While the notion of common security was initially applied to traditional security areas such as armaments, it was soon expanded to include the economy, human rights, welfare, the environment, and food and water as part of a new discourse on security (Brown 1977; Ullman 1983; Mathews 1989; Romm 1993). One area which has become significant for both tourism and national security is that of global environmental change (Hall and Higham 2005). Indeed, David King, the chief scientific advisor to the UK government, has described climate change as a more serious problem than even that of the threat of terrorism (King 2004).

The notion of environmental security arguably developed as an off-shoot of concerns over defence security in the 1970s and 1980s (Myers 1989). Various issues, including the potential impact of a nuclear winter following a nuclear war, the nuclear disaster in Chernobyl, burning oil wells in Kuwait following the liberation of that country in 1991, and global climate change, have all contributed to an appreciation of the security dimensions of ecological interdependence (Levy 1995). At least four sets of relationships between more traditional notions of security and the concept of environmental security may be identified. First, the relationship between environmental security and the potential for 'resource wars' fought over increasingly scarce resources such as oil and water (Gurr 1985; Dolatyar and Gray 2000; Haftendorn 2000; Maxwell and Reuveny 2000). Second, direct threats to environmental health because of environmental change and biosecurity threats, some of which may be deliberately induced by human action (Alexander 2000). Third, the mass migration of ecological refugees who are abandoning resource-poor or damaged areas.

Refugee flows often generate new resource, political, economic and cultural tensions in those nations which receive them (Jamieson 1999). Finally, there is the environmentally destructive capability of the military itself.

Although linked to the concept of sustainable development, the notion of environmental security is not universally accepted. However, it does have a number of significant supporters such as former US Vice President Al Gore (1992) and Norman Myers (1989, 1993). Myers (1993) provided an analysis of a range of case studies (focusing on regional resource wars and global ecological threats) that collectively sought to demonstrate that environmental and resource degradation is inseparable from economic and political insecurities, and that perhaps foresaw some of the oil resource access and ownership issues arising out of the 2003 invasion of Iraq, and some of the potential implications of global climate change. For example, a leaked US security assessment of climate change that was reported in *The Observer* (Townsend and Harris 2004) 'and suppressed by US defence chiefs' 'warns that major European cities will be sunk beneath rising seas as Britain is plunged into a "Siberian" climate by 2020. Nuclear conflict, mega-droughts, famine and widespread rioting will erupt across the world.' According to Townsend and Harris (2004), the report states that climate change 'should be elevated beyond a scientific debate to a US national security concern', and concludes that an imminent scenario of catastrophic climate change is 'plausible and would challenge United States national security in ways that should be considered immediately'.

For Hall, Timothy and Duval (2004) this broader debate on common security provides a link to the development of a relationship between security and sustainable development, the latter being an issue which has already been broadly debated in tourism (e.g. Hall and Lew 1998). As Hall, Timothy and Duval (2004) note, this may pose a new agenda for research on tourism and security, and the development of a broad range of answers to the questions of 'security from what and secure to do what?' Unfortunately, many of the broader security concerns are not exposed to regular discussion in the media and therefore tend to be kept low in the order of government policy priorities unless some kind of environmental disaster occurs. Nevertheless, to some extent several of these issues are already being anticipated in the wider tourism literature, although they are subject to substantial contestation (Hall and Lew 1998; Mowforth and Munt 1998; Butcher 2003). With few exceptions, however, traditional ideas of state security, which have been applied to a set of conditions that guarantees the ability of a nation to protect its territorially bounded community of citizens and pursue its national interests free from both real and imagined impediments and threats, have been applied in tourism. State security concerns clearly have the capacity to affect the flow of international travellers because of the desire of some states to deter undesirable visitors – whether on the basis of wealth, health, creed, or crime. Indeed, in concluding their book on tourism and migration relations, Hall and Williams (2002b) cite Bauman's (1998) discussion of the human consequences of globalisation, which juxtaposes the tourist and the vagabond as the two extreme character types of contemporary mobility and a metaphor for the new, emergent, stratification of global society. As Bauman (1998, pp. 92–3) notes: 'The tourists move because they find the world within their (global) reach irresistibly attractive – the vagabonds move because they find the world within their (local) reach unbearably inhospitable.... Vagabonds are travellers refused the right to turn into tourists.'

The following two chapters investigate some of these security matters in more detail, examining biosecurity and climate change issues respectively. Occasionally these issues hit the tourism policy agenda, as well as the media agenda. For example, the foot and mouth outbreak in the United Kingdom in 2002 and the SARS outbreak in Asia and Canada in 2003 both had substantial implications for tourism, while increased concern is being expressed about the potential impacts of climate change. In 1994 Kaplan referred to 'the coming anarchy' with respect to the prospect of greater international conflict in relation to resource and environmental security. Clearly, tourism will likely be implicated not only in how new understandings of security develop, but also in the reality of how such security issues will be managed.

Discussion Questions

1. Is it true to say that political stability is essential for tourism?

2. If human rights are ignored but political stability is maintained in a particular country should tourists then visit that country?

3. How important is the role of the media in influencing people's perception of political stability?

4. Far more tourists are killed each year in car accidents than by terrorists, yet terrorism seems to have a far greater impact in terms of the perceived risks of travellers. Why might this be the case?

Further Reading and Websites

For a broad overview of safety and security issues in tourism, see Hall, Timothy and Duval (2004), Pizam and Mansfield (1996), Pizam (1999), Pizam and Fleischer (2002), Sönmez and Graefe (1998) and Sönmez et al. (1999). Timothy (2001) provides a useful discussion of the role of political borders in tourism, whereas Hall (1994a) examines the broader political dimensions of tourism and Birkland (2004) analyses the agenda-setting dimensions following the September 11 terrorist attacks, in line with those contained in this chapter. For details of issues associated with airline security in 2001 prior to September 11, see Hall (2002b). A fascinating account of the regulation of mobility is to be found in Salter (2004).

Burma Campaign website: www.burmacampaign.org.uk (this is an example of a campaign that explicitly suggests that travellers should boycott Burma as a destination until the junta's record on human rights and democracy is improved)

UK Foreign and Commonwealth Office travel advisories: www.fco.gov.uk

US Department of State travel advisories: http://travel.state.gov/travel/warnings.html

Foreign Affairs Canada travel advisories: www.voyage.gc.ca/

New Zealand Ministry of Foreign Affairs and Trade travel advisories: www.mfat.govt.nz/travel/

Australian Department of Foreign Affairs and Trade travel advisories: www.smartraveller.gov.au/index.html

Lonely Planet Travel Ticker: www.lonelyplanet.com/travel_ticker/ (this site is updated weekly but also includes other information regarding travel and safety and security beyond what is available on the Australian, Canadian, New Zealand, UK and US services)

Tourism and Global Environmental Change: Biosecurity and Climate Change

12

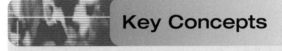

Key Concepts

- Global environmental change
- Biosecurity
- Climate change
- Kyoto Convention
- Governance structures

The world is increasingly mobile. Improvements in transport and communications technology, population growth, deregulation and internationalisation of the world economic system, and moves towards 'free trade' have all encouraged greater mobility of goods, services, ideas, businesses and people. Tourism is an important part of the growth in population mobility. It is therefore perhaps not surprising that tourism is increasingly being implicated in issues associated with global environmental change (GEC) (Gössling 2002). Human impacts on the environment can have a global character in two ways. First, 'global refers to the spatial scale or functioning of a system' (Turner et al. 1990, p. 15). Here, the climate and the oceans have the characteristics of a global system and both influence and are influenced by tourism production and consumption. A second kind of GEC 'occurs on a worldwide scale, or represents a significant fraction of the total environmental phenomenon or global resource' (Turner et al. 1990, pp. 15–16). Issues here can include the destruction of forests, wetlands and biodiversity which are globally cumulative. The transfer of species and diseases through human movement can also constitute GECs. This chapter will examine two areas of GEC: biosecurity and climate change.

Tourism and Biosecurity

Increased movements of people across political and physical borders may have a number of unintended and unwanted consequences. One of the most significant of these is the extent to which travellers and the transport systems they use may act as vectors for diseases or pests, which in themselves may host diseases (e.g. Russell 1987; Carlton and Geller 1993; Berkelman et al. 1994; Bernard and Scott 1995; Wilson 1995; Fidler 1996; Ginzburg 1996; Borgdorff and Motarjemi 1997; Käferstein et al. 1997; Legors and Danis 1998; Cookson et al. 2001; Seys and Bender 2001) (Table 12.1). The impacts of these diseases and pests affect the natural environment and human populations. They may also affect tourism by virtue of the regulatory framework put in place to prevent undesirable movements, by the direct and indirect impact of pests and disease on tourism resources, and by human perception of the desirability to travel to places where perceived personal biosecurity risks may be high (Figure 12.1).

At the start of the twenty-first century several events have already occurred that highlight the global importance of biosecurity. In 2001 there was an outbreak of foot and mouth disease in Britain which had devastating effects not only on farming but also on tourism. In 2003 there was an outbreak of SARS (Severe Acute Respiratory Syndrome) that had a dramatic effect on travel in the Asia-Pacific region, while in 2004 there was an outbreak of bird flu in South-East Asia, which although causing few human deaths did affect tourists' perception on travel in affected regions.

The February 2001 outbreak of foot and mouth disease in the United Kingdom was the first since 1967. Its effect on the countryside was devastating,

Table 12.1 What is carried by humans when they travel

- Pathogens in or on body, clothes and/or luggage
- Microbiologic fauna and flora on body, clothes and/or luggage
- Vectors on body, clothes and/or luggage
- Immunologic sequelae of past infections
- Vulnerability to infections
- Genetic makeup
- Cultural preferences, customs, behavioural patterns, technology
- Luggage may also contain food, soil, fauna, flora and organic material

---

Source: After Wilson; Hall 2004e

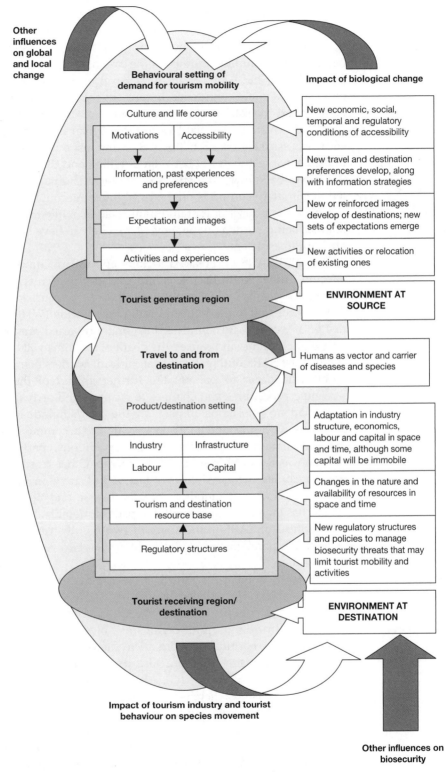

Figure 12.1   The tourism system and biosecurity

and with over 6% of the national livestock herd slaughtered, the effects on those farms that lost their stock were dramatic. Biosecurity measures limited not only the movement of livestock but also the movement of people in the countryside, including tourists. In the case of both agriculture and tourism the outbreak will have long-term impacts: in agriculture because of restocking costs and customer confidence; in tourism because of consumer perceptions of rurality and the safety of the countryside. According to Sharpley and Craven (2001), the overall potential loss to the tourism industry in England alone in 2001 was estimated at £5 billion, while the lost overseas tourism expenditure in Britain was estimated at between £1 billion and £3.5 billion. The final figures will never be known. The effects of the terrorist attacks of 11 September 2001 led to cumulative impacts on the rural tourism economy that make it difficult to isolate the impact of foot and mouth alone, while the impacts of images of animals being burned on huge pyres are likely to have longer-term effects that are hard to ascertain.

The 2003 SARS outbreak, a serious atypical pneumonia which primarily affected China, South-East Asia and Canada (particularly Toronto), caused a number of deaths and severely impacted on the tourism industry (Pottinger 2004). According to the World Health Organisation (WHO), SARS spread in a matter of weeks to 30 countries, infecting a reported number of 8422 humans after eight months, and caused the death of more than 900 people. In the wider context, the SARS outbreak led to significant barriers being placed on people's mobility in order to prevent the further spread of the disease, including screening procedures and changes to customs and arrival forms. Such restrictions had an enormous impact on the tourism industries in the affected countries, with substantial falls in arrivals and accommodation rates as well as the cancellation of conferences and exhibitions, particularly because the disease was featured in much of the media. Other reasons for cancellation of travel included increased costs of health and travel insurance. Just as significant as the fact that mobility spreads disease and pests, is that the rate of spread has increased in line with the pace of mobility. For example, the worldwide spread of SARS in the space of two months can be compared with the Spanish Flu pandemic of 1918–19 which took two years to spread throughout the world.

In order to combat the introduction of pests and diseases many countries and regions have introduced biosecurity strategies. Biosecurity refers to the protection of a country, region or location's economic, environmental and/or human health from harmful organisms. 'Biosecurity involves preventing the introduction of harmful new organisms, and eradicating or controlling those unwanted organisms that are already present' (Biosecurity Strategy Development Team 2001a, sec.1.3). Although tourism is a major focal point for biosecurity measures, there is little discussion of the significance of biosecurity measures in the tourism studies literature. Indeed, the industry itself may be unaware of the role that it plays in biosecurity management. For example, of the 122 submissions received on the *Issues Paper: Developing a Biosecurity Strategy for New Zealand* (Biosecurity Strategy Development Team 2001b), only one came from the tourism industry (Biosecurity Strategy Development Team

2002, p. 4). However, some authors have noted the role of tourism as a factor in health and disease management, and the potential for particular types of tourism, such as ecotourism and food and wine tourism, to introduce diseases, pests and weeds into locations where they did not previously exist (Hall 1992b; Rudkin and Hall 1996), while the outbreak of foot and mouth disease in the United Kingdom in 2001 and the SARS outbreak in 2003 also highlighted the relationship of tourism mobility with respect to biosecurity management. Indeed, the standard response to disease outbreaks is to constrain mobility. For example, in the case of foot and mouth disease, once a case was confirmed, under European Union regulations a protection zone based on a minimum radius of 3 kilometres and a surveillance zone based on a minimum radius of 10 kilometres should be established. In addition, a number of controls were imposed to minimise the risk of the public, including visitors to the country-side, spreading the disease. Not only were the majority of footpaths and other rights of way (i.e. other routes over which the public has a legal right to pass, such as bridleways) closed across the country, but also many rural tourist attractions were closed, and land owned by the Forestry Commission and the National Trust, along with some national parks and forest areas, even some parks in London, were closed to the public (Sharpley and Craven 2001).

Biosecurity measures occur at a number of different scales, all the way from the international level, such as agreements on the movement of agricultural produce across border controls, through to biosecurity practices at individual locations, such as farms. Biosecurity strategies can also be categorised in terms of their utility at the pre-border, border and post-border stages (Biosecurity Strategy Development Team 2001a, 2001b; Green 2001) (Table 12.2).

Tourism is clearly a major area of biosecurity risk and is a focal point of border control activities, particularly in agriculturally based economies and regions. In Australia, the Australian National Audit Office (ANAO) (2001, p. 16) estimates indicated that almost 90% of seizable material arriving by mail, and more than half arriving by international airline passengers, entered Australia undetected. There has been a marked increase in the number of interceptions of pests and diseases at the border, from around 3500 interceptions in 1994 to over 10 000 in 1999 (ANAO 2001). This may be due in part to increased trade and tourism traffic, but is also a likely result of improved biosecurity strategies, particularly as with respect to surveillance – the more you look the more you find. Prohibited items (i.e. those considered as having 'a high risk of carrying pests or diseases and which are seized, treated or re-exported') intercepted at Australian airports increased from 1000 per month in 1998 to 4000 per month in 2000, reflecting the impact of quarantine reform initiatives (ANAO 2001, p. 25). Just as significant is the estimated leakage rate which measures the percentage of all items that have crossed the border but which still contain or possess seizable material. According to ANAO, the leakage rates for airline passengers arriving in Australia have been relatively stable since 1998, at between 3% and 4%. In comparison in 2000 the estimated leakage rate for international mail was 1.2% (ANAO 2001). Using these figures the ANAO, in their audit of quarantine effectiveness in Australia, estimate that 'in excess of half of the seizable material (or 300 000 items per year) carried by international air passengers breaches the quarantine barrier' (2001, p. 27).

Table 12.2   Pre-border, border and post-border biosecurity strategies

Pre-border
- Identifying threats to ecosystems
- Profiling and modelling the characteristics of damaging or potentially damaging organisms and vectors
- Identifying controls (in the country of origin) for selected organisms that pose a threat to destinations
- Analysing and predicting risk pathways for unwanted organisms
- Identifying and collating databases and expertise on unwanted organisms
- Developing systems for rapid access to appropriate data
- Developing import standards and compliance validation methodologies
- Auditing exporting countries' compliance with destination biosecurity standards
- Identifying and locating biosecurity-related risks to animal, plant and human health
- Analysis of public attitudes and perceptions of biosecurity risks and barriers to biosecurity responses in visitor generating areas
- Development of educational programmes in exporting regions so as to reduce the likelihood of introducing unwanted organisms in imported goods
- Development of educational programmes for tourists in both generating and destination regions so as to reduce the likelihood of introducing unwanted organisms

Border
- Developing improved systems, including clearance systems and sampling methodologies, and technologies for intercepting unwanted organisms according to import standards
- Developing border containment and eradication methodologies according to import standards
- Developing profiles of non-compliance behaviour to biosecurity requirements
- Border activities

Post-border (includes pest management)
- Developing rapid identification techniques for unwanted organisms
- Designing and developing methodologies for undertaking delimiting surveys for new incursions
- Developing rapid response options for potential incursions of unwanted organisms
- Analysis of public attitudes and perceptions of biosecurity risks and barriers to biosecurity responses in destination areas
- Developing long-term containment, control and eradication strategies

General
- Analysis of economic and political models for the management of biosecurity threats
- Development of rapid-access information systems, collections and environmental databases on unwanted organisms
- Improve export opportunities for 'clean' products
- Development of industry and public biosecurity education programmes

Source: After Hall 2004e

From a tourism mobility perspective biosecurity strategies occur at different stages of the trip cycle: decision-making and anticipation, travel to a tourism destination or attraction, the on-site experience, return travel, and recollection of the experience. Each of these five stages will have different psychological characteristics with implications for how tourism organisations and businesses establish a relationship with the customer or, in the case of biosecurity, how biosecurity and quarantine organisations establish a relationship with travellers and assist them in undertaking good biosecurity practice. As Fridgen (1984, p. 24) observed: 'People not only act in their present setting, they also plan for subsequent settings. People prepare to arrive in another setting to carry out preplanned behaviors.'

Central to appropriate biosecurity practice by travellers is an improved understanding of biosecurity and quarantine. Improving awareness of biosecurity may lead to a decrease in the number of prohibited items which cross a border. In Australia the ANAO (2001, p. 24) noted that '[a]wareness of quarantine amongst Australians intending to travel, or who have travelled recently, has improved markedly' since implementation of a national campaign by the Department of Agriculture, Fisheries and Forestry to improve public understanding of, and commitment to, quarantine. New Zealand has also recognised the importance of the development of a communications and education programme 'to emphasise the value of biosecurity and the role travellers can play in preserving New Zealand's unique flora and fauna' (Biosecurity Strategy Development Team 2002, p. 11). Such measures apply not only to the international visitor but also to New Zealanders travelling abroad as 'incoming New Zealanders are responsible for 40% of border infringements by passengers' (Biosecurity Strategy Development Team 2002, p. 11). As the 'issues paper' written as part of the development of a biosecurity strategy for New Zealand noted: 'Because the actions of travellers and importers are key to successful biosecurity management, education and awareness programmes may have significant potential to provide low cost gains in biosecurity protection. Education is possibly the major risk management tool available for biosecurity' (Biosecurity Strategy Development Team 2001b, p. 24). Therefore, from a biosecurity perspective, the development team regarded the activities of the tourism industry as essential in assisting implementation of biosecurity measures. 'The tourism industry is well placed to help to improve visitor awareness of the importance of biosecurity to New Zealand, and biosecurity messages could be integrated with tourism promotion campaigns' (Biosecurity Strategy Development Team, 2001b, pp. 24–5), the greatest tangible evidence of this being biosecurity warnings broadcast over plane inflight entertainment systems prior to arrival in New Zealand. However, it is also interesting to note that in the development of the New Zealand strategy only one submission was made to the development team by the tourism industry.

Tourism Insight: Biosecurity and Wine Tourism

Biosecurity issues are of great significance to the international wine industry. For example, since 1998 the state of California has provided US$65.2 million for a statewide management programme and research to combat the glassy-winged sharpshooter and the deadly Pierce's disease (a bacterium, *Xylella fastidiosa*) that it carries. Accidentally introduced in 1989 through imported US nursery stock, 15 counties have been identified as being infested (Wine Institute of California 2002). Another pest which caused havoc in the world's vineyards in the latter half of the nineteenth century is phylloxera. In Western Australia it is estimated that phylloxera could cost affected growers A$20 000 per hectare in the first five years in lost production and replanting costs (Agriculture Western Australia 2000a, 2000b). For many grape diseases, including phylloxera, humans are a significant vector (Pearson and Goheen 1998). Yet despite recognition of the potential role of humans in conveying grape diseases or pests, there is only limited awareness of the biosecurity risks of wine tourism (Agriculture Western Australia 2000b), while Industry stakeholder SWOT analyses of threats to wine tourism in British Columbia (Wilkins and Hall, 2001) and wine and food tourism in New Zealand (Smith and Hall, 2001) both reported disease as a potential threat to future development (Hall, Sharples and Smith 2003).

A survey of New Zealand wineries conducted in 2003 found that only 17% of the 121 respondents had a biosecurity strategy of any form in place. However, the possibilities of the spread of disease or pests through winery visitation are substantial given the growth of wine and food tourism (Hall, Johnson and Mitchell 2000; Hall, Longo et al. 2000). For example, Hall and Johnson (1998) estimated that there were approximately 3 million visits to wineries in New Zealand in 1997, of which 81% were by domestic visitors and 19% by international visitors. Since 1997 the number of wineries has grown from 262 to reach 396 in 2001 (New Zealand Winegrowers 2002, http://www.nzwine.com/statistics/). Moreover, research derived from a national survey of visitors to wineries in New Zealand note that wine tourists tend to travel to a number of wineries in a single trip and that many have visited wineries in their travels over the previous 12 months (Mitchell and Hall 2001). Clearly, such mobility among winery visitors may create significant issues for biosecurity control.

One aspect of biosecurity is the use of customs and passenger declarations as a means of not only gathering customs duty and traveller information and educating travellers about biosecurity but also to alert customs officials to potential biosecurity risks. In addition to containing questions regarding the bringing of plant material, fruit or foodstuffs into the country, of potential interest to the grape growers are questions as to whether passengers have travelled to other rural areas or locations where they might have encountered grape diseases or pests. For example, the Australian incoming passenger card

(Commonwealth of Australia 1999) asks visitors 'Have you visited a farm outside Australia in the past 30 days?' (It should also be noted that they also ask 'Are you bringing into Australia ... soil, or articles with soil attached, i.e. sporting equipment, shoes, etc?') The US custom declaration asks if the traveller or a member of the family has 'been on a farm or a ranch outside the US' (Department of the Treasury no date). In New Zealand incoming passengers are told that 'you must declare' if 'in the past 30 days' a visitor had been 'to a farm, abattoir or meat packing house', as well as having been 'in a forest or hiking, camping, hunting in rural areas or parkland' (New Zealand Customs Service 2001). However, these declarations raise a fundamental question of biosecurity for the wine industry and for those businesses which encourage wine tourism – to what extent do visitors perceive a vineyard or winery as a farm?

In order to undertake an exploratory assessment of biosecurity risks associated with wine tourism, a short convenience survey was undertaken of winery visitors in the Canterbury, Marlborough and Central Otago wine regions of the South Island of New Zealand in January–March 2002. The survey had 324 respondents, of which 69 were international visitors to New Zealand. The responses indicated that over 60% of respondents did not recognise a vineyard as a farm. This response is regarded as significant given the questions posed by customs agencies as to activities undertaken prior to entry into New Zealand. Furthermore, over 90% of respondents had visited a vineyard in the previous 12 months, with almost half of the domestic visitors also having visited a vineyard overseas in the previous 12 months. Perhaps of even greater concern with respect to biosecurity was that 45% of respondents believed that they had worn the same footwear on their last visit to a vineyard as they had on the current visit. In addition, 10% believed they were wearing another piece of clothing they had worn or carried with them on their previous wineyard visit.

These results clearly have significant implications for biosecurity communication and education campaigns. Wine tourists present substantial biosecurity risks not only because of their relative mobility but also because of the use of items of clothing, and shoes in particular, at different vineyard locations on different trips. Despite the potential biosecurity risks and the significance of cellar door sales and wine tourism for their business, few of the wineries in the South Island have any visible biosecurity strategies (e.g. signage or interpretation) to prevent visitors walking in vineyards or taking plant material, within the broader context of a biosecurity framework (Table 12.2). At the agriculture and customs level it also raises concerns as to the applicability of present descriptions of 'at risk areas' in agriculture and customs forms. Arguably, the inclusion of a vineyard or winery category would be a major benefit to the wine industry as a means of risk reduction at customs borders, although given the potential of mobile humans to act as disease or pest vectors it is also important that information regarding biosecurity issues and their management be extended to other relevant ecotourism and rural tourism operations as well as to tourists so as to reduce biosecurity risks in vulnerable rural economies.

Plate 12.1   Phylloxera warning at the Gibbston Valley vineyard and winery, Central Otago, New Zealand (visit www.gvwines.co.nz)

Plate 12.2   Walking path through the Crittenden vineyard, winery and restaurant on the Mornington Peninsula, Victoria, Australia. Note how close the path is to the vines. (www.dromanaestate.com.au)

Tourism and Climate Change

Another major challenge to future development is climate change. Under International Panel on Climate Change (IPCC) (2001a) usage, climate change refers to any change in climate over time, whether it be due to natural or human processes. According to the Framework Convention on Climate Change (the Kyoto Convention), however, climate change refers to changes that can be directly or indirectly attributed to human activity as a result of changes in composition of the atmosphere and that is in addition to natural climate variability observed over comparable time periods.

The IPCC (2001b) conclude that the average surface temperatures of the Earth increased by between 0.6 °C and 0.2 °C over the twentieth century. They estimate that the globally averaged surface air temperature is projected to warm 1.4 °C to 5.8 °C by 2100 relative to 1990, with the globally averaged sea level projected to rise 0.09 mm to 0.88 mm by 2100. However, there will be variation in warming by region, with some areas receiving more rain and others less, and, perhaps even more seriously, there is projected to be changes in climate variability and changes in the frequency and intensity of some extreme climate phenomena (e.g. cyclones, droughts, floods, heatwaves and cold snaps).

Such projections may have enormous impacts on tourism. Higher maximum temperatures may lead to some tourism destinations being regarded as more attractive and others less attractive, yet such effects are variable over time as well as space. In other words, new seasonal variations in the attractiveness of destinations are likely to develop with substantial implications for the consumption and production of tourism in time and space. In addition, increases in sea level combined with likely increases in tropical cyclone peak wind intensities will have enormous impacts not only on tropical and sub-tropical destinations (e.g. the Caribbean, Bali, Thailand, Florida, Hawaii, the Pacific Islands and Queensland), in terms of increased coastal erosion and resort damage, but also in tourists' perceptions of those destinations. Furthermore, there may also be increased damage to the coastal ecosystems that are the basis for the environmental attractiveness of many coastal resorts (e.g. coral reefs and sandy beaches) and activities (e.g. diving). These are areas which in many cases are already under substantial human induced stress (see Chapter 9). As Root et al. (2003, p. 57) argued: 'The synergism of rapid temperature rise and other stresses, in particular habitat destruction, could easily disrupt the connectedness among species and lead to a reformulation of species communities, reflecting differential changes in species, and to numerous extirpations and possibly extinctions.' Species loss and ecosystem change will have enormous impacts on nature-based tourism, especially in peripheral regions. Ironically, these are the very areas that often most need tourism as a tool for regional economic development and as a justification for conservation measures (see Chapter 8; Hall and Boyd 2005), and, by virtue of their peripheral locations, will also be affected by any new regulatory regimes on long-distance travel to combat atmospheric change (Hall and Higham 2005).

Plate 12.3 Ski slope in Scotland. The potential shortening of the ski season due to lack of snow under various climate change scenarios raises substantial questions about the future of many ski resorts. Already a number of ski resorts in Europe, including Scotland, have had to close down because they are now regarded as economically unviable. In early 2004 the Chairlift Company placed the Glencoe and Glenshee resorts on the market, following losses of £1 million over the previous two years, due to lack of snow (Ski Scotland website: http://ski.visitscotland.com/; a Scottish executive report on Climate Change and Changing Snowfall patterns in Scotland is available at www.scotland.gov.uk/cru/kd01/lightgreen/ccsnow_01.htm)

Many ski resorts are at increasing risk from landslides as global warming melts the permafrost that holds mountain surfaces together. As the permafrost melts, resorts are at greater risk of catastrophic landslides and rock falls (National Post 2001). Temperatures in many ski resorts have risen by one degree Celsius over the past 15 years, and with a predicted continuation of global and regional temperatures, skiing destinations will experience less snowfall and shorter skiing seasons. These impacts will be especially pronounced in the lower-lying ski resorts where commercial ventures are already marginal (Viner and Agnew 1999). There are some scientists, however, who suggest that warmer winters could lead to increased precipitation levels in some resorts, but they tend to agree that winter will begin later and spring will begin sooner (Rosa 2001). To thrive without snow many operators have invested heavily in snowmaking equipment. Snowmaking is a critical but expensive investment for many resorts. Buying the machinery and accessing the water, a process than can require protracted negotiations with state authorities and installing dozens of wells and miles of pipes, can cost tens of millions of dollars. In the United States the average snowmaking system covers approximately 67% of terrain (Bender 2000), and most ski resorts there now have snowmaking equipment. Intrawest believes that snowmaking is now an economic necessity. The company has invested US$113 million in snowmaking equipment at its resorts and has an annual operating budget of US$9 million just for making snow (Schreiner 2000). At its 11 resorts, Intrawest turns an average of 1.5 billion gallons of water a season into enough snow to cover 39 000 football fields to a depth of one foot.

Given the potential implications of climate change, it is perhaps not surprising that David King, Chief Scientific Advisor to the UK government (King 2004, p. 176), described climate change as 'the most severe problem we are facing today, more serious even than the threat of terrorism'. Nevertheless, such statements, and their political reception, have illustrated the political and highly contested nature of climate change research. For example, David King's comments were reportedly criticised from within the British government (Connor and Grice 2004), and particularly his targeting of the United States' failure to sign the Kyoto Protocol and general inaction with respect to climate change. However, the results of efforts to reduce greenhouse gas (GHG) emissions are mixed. For example, the European Union reduced its GHG emissions by 2.3% between 1990 and 2001. However, this is only just over one-quarter of the way towards achieving the 8% emissions reduction from base-year levels required by 2008–12 under the Kyoto Protocol. Significantly for tourism, although EU greenhouse gas emissions decreased from most sectors (energy supply, industry, agriculture, waste management) between 1990 and 2001, emissions from transport increased by nearly 21% in the same period, with passenger transport by road being a major contributor. Carbon-dioxide emissions from transport account for 20% of total EU emissions (European Environmental Agency 2003). Nevertheless of greater concern is the fact that, at the time of writing, major industrialised countries such as Australia, Russia and the United States (the latter being the largest polluter of all), add substantial GHGs to the environment.

Figure 12.2 illustrates some of the interrelationships between the tourism system and climate change. All demand and supply facets of tourism are effected by climate change, but just as importantly tourism has direct and indirect effects on climate change itself over all stages of mobility. Conceptualising tourism in terms of wider aspects of human mobility therefore has considerable importance with respect to assessing the complete impacts of tourism on climate change (Høyer 2000; Gössling 2002; Gössling et al. 2002; Frändberg and Vilhelmson, 2003). In addition, tourism and climate change relationships are impacted by other factors that influence global and local change in ways that we are only beginning to identify, such as processes of political, economic and cultural globalisation, technology, especially information technology, megaurbanisation, and environmental change (Johnston et al. 1995).

Within the tourism generating regions climate change affects the tourism decision-making process in a number of different ways. Climate change can directly impact tourist behaviour because of changed perceptions, not only of the climatic appeal and image of certain destinations but also the activities that can be engaged in once there. Moreover, as noted above, climate change may

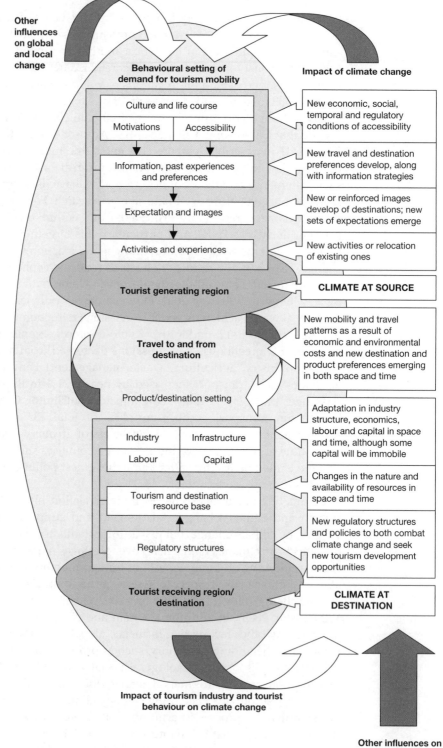

Figure 12.2   The tourism system and climate change

impact patterns of seasonal attraction and associated visitor flows. At a broad scale of analysis climate change will likely mean not that people will stop travelling but that they will change their travel preferences in both space and time (Hall and Higham 2005).

In addition to changes to the nature and use of tourism resources and the development of new regulatory regimes, climate change will also affect tourism capital in its various forms. Some destinations and resorts will have to find new uses for much tourism-related fixed capital and infrastructure (because of its immobility) if they are negatively affected by climate change. Indeed, climate change is already having an impact on insurance and investment strategies for tourism development (see Bürki et al. 2005; Craig-Smith and Ruhanen 2005). The changed accessibility and attractiveness of tourist destinations under conditions of climate change will also have implications not just for tourist mobility but also for labour force mobility. Indeed, the movement of the human capital of tourism will be a flexible response to climate change. However, such movement will obviously have implications for community change and the associated social and economic effects of such change. Nevertheless, such shifts assume that economic, social, regulatory and environmental conditions at the generating region stay relatively constant. Unfortunately, it is likely that this will not be the case in many areas, particularly with respect to impacts on agricultural and manufacturing production as well as the location of human settlements (IPCC 2001b).

Under conditions of rapid human-induced global climate change tourist flows and other human mobility patterns will undoubtedly shift in both space and time. Indeed, the question of whether the Mediterranean is becoming too hot for summer holidays has already been posed (Mather et al. 2004; Perry 2004). Changes in overall mobility patterns will be a result of the development of new destinations and activity locations, while at the same time some existing destinations will cease to be as attractive (in some extreme cases some coastal and island destinations may even disappear), with some transport routes potentially bypassing current destinations as new time and economic budgets develop in the tourist market. The energy demands of tourism transport will undoubtedly be a focal point for new regulatory structures that may act to restrict long-distance travel in particular. For example, with respect to GHG in Europe, the increase in carbon-dioxide emissions from international aviation and navigation was even higher than other forms of transport, with an 82% increase in emissions from 1990 to 2001 as a result of international aviation, 'but these are currently not addressed in the Kyoto Protocol or in EU policies and measures' (European Environmental Agency 2003, p. 13). Yet, arguably, given the potential impacts of climate change, at some stage they will need to be addressed. The environmental effects of travel are substantial. Gössling et al.'s (2002) study of the ecological footprint of travellers to the Seychelles revealed that the major environmental impact of travel was a result of transportation to and from the destination: more than 97% of the energy footprint was a result of air travel. This suggests that efforts to make destinations more sustainable through local energy initiatives can only contribute to marginal savings in view of the large amounts of energy used for air travel. Any strategy towards sustainable tourism must thus seek to reduce transport distances, and, vice versa, any tourism based on air traffic needs per se to be seen as unsustainable. Obviously, these insights also apply to ecotourism based on long-distance travel. (Gössling et al. 2002, p. 208; also see Gössling 2004; Høyer and Aall 2004)

Nevertheless, this is not to suggest that destination-based environmental initiatives are not without some value. But it does emphasise again that the impacts of human mobility need to be considered at the global level, at all stages of the travel experience, and through all modes of consumption, rather than just at site (see Alfredsson 2002, Gössling 2002). Indeed, ultimately, sustainable tourism is about sustainable mobility.

Global Tourism, Global Change

One of the key lessons that we draw from the tourism–climate relationship is that feedback processes within the tourism and climate systems will undoubtedly have unforeseen impacts on numerous locations around the world. Nevertheless, as the various chapters in this book demonstrate for many locations the implications do appear to set numerous policy and management challenges, particularly given the economic role that has been assigned to tourism, as well as demands for tourism consumption. Many people now take mobility as a right – the freedom to travel from one place to another, the freedom to cross borders. However, increasingly, the realisation may be dawning that such mobilities may come at enormous cost at the global scale in terms of energy use, pollution and GHGs. Moreover, global environmental change is entwined with other global social and economic processes that have been a focal point of much of this book. Global environmental change is the corollary in the physical world of globalisation in the human.

The parallels between human and natural system dynamics are, not surprisingly, extremely close. The comment of Root et al. (2003, p. 57) with respect to wild animals and plants, that 'many of the most severe impacts of climate-change are likely to stem from interactions between threats, factors not taken into account in our calculations, rather than from climate acting in isolation', is likely to hold true for the impacts of climate change on tourism as well as other human activities. Indeed, the observations of Root et al. (2003, p. 57) apply to the human species as much as to plant and animal species: 'The ability of species to reach new climatically suitable areas will be hampered by habitat loss and fragmentation, and their ability to persist in appropriate climates is likely to be affected by new invasive species.' Realising the interrelationships between tourism and global environmental change therefore sets a major challenge to the industry in terms of the need to regulate the aviation sector in particular so as to control GHG emissions. Moreover, it highlights that the meta-problem of the impacts of human mobility, as with other global environmental, economic and social issues, requires governance structures that go beyond the self-congratulatory and self-regulatory environmental awards, codes of conduct and branding schemes that operate at the local or site level and ignore the ecological footprint of the total tourist trip from home to destination and back. If one considers the total trip, particularly long-haul international travel, environmental actions at the destination contribute only a fraction to ameliorating the impacts of the entire journey. Arguably, the only truly form of sustainable tourism is local tourism – visit your own country, connect with your locale, perhaps take the train or public transport, but most of all be mindful of one's actions. Unfortunately, in many countries public transport has been devastated by privatisation and user-pays initiatives, yet in other countries, such as Scandinavia, it is apparent that public transport serves important economic, social and environmental goals. Indeed, if a true application of a user-pays approach to travel was to be taken, then we would soon find out just how substantially the private car and the aviation industry are subsidised, and then perhaps we might start to appreciate the true costs and benefits of our mobility.

Discussion Questions

1. Why might biosecurity measures be harder to employ in countries such as Germany or Sweden than in Australia or New Zealand?

2. Aviation fuel is currently not included under the Kyoto Convention. What might be the implications for tourism if it was to be included?

3. Is the only sustainable form of tourism to holiday at home?

Further Reading and Websites

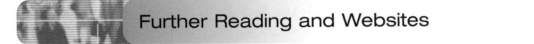

Johnston et al. (1995) provide a useful introduction to issues of global change although not from a tourism perspective. See Wilks and Page (2003) and World Health Organisation (2003) on issues associated with health and security. On biosecurity issues such as foot and mouth disease, see Sharpley and Craven (2001). On tourism and climate change, see the various chapters in Hall and Higham (2005, in press) for a recent overview of the field, while earlier works such as K. Smith (1990, 1993), Ewert (1991), Wall and Badke (1994), Perry (1997), Agnew and Viner (2001) and de Freitas (2003) are also useful. Gössling (2002, 2005) and Gössling et al. (2002) provide a very useful account of tourism and GEC relationships. Høyer and Aall (2005) reinforce the importance of thinking about sustainable mobility in relation to sustainable tourism. The

World Travel and Tourism Council's (2003) *Blueprint for New Tourism* is fascinating for the absence of reference to tourism and GEC.

Global environmental change

Climate Change Research Unit (University of East Anglia) has some useful downloads on tourism: http://www.cru.uea.ac.uk/tourism/

Intergovernmental Panel on Climate Change: http://www.ipcc.ch/

Kyoto Protocol to the United Nations Framework Convention on Climate Change: http://unfccc.int/resource/docs/convkp/kpeng.html

United Nations Environment Programme (site also has links to other aspects of global environmental change): http://grida.no/climate/

United Nations Framework Convention on Climate Change: http://un fccc.int/

United States Climate Change Science Program (as of 2004 the USA has not signed the Kyoto Protocol): http://www.climatescience.gov/

World Health Organisation, Global Change and Health: http://www.euro. who.int/globalchange

Biosecurity

Association of British Travel Agents (worth checking to see what travel information regarding safety is provided to travellers): www.abta.com/

According to Meikle (2004), 'Members of [ABTA] have a code under which customers travelling outside Australasia, North Ameria and Western Europe are advised to contact a health professional, and all customers are supposed to be reminded to check the Foreign Office website for travel advice').

International Society of Travel Medicine: www.istm.org/

US National Center for Infectious Diseases, travellers health information (excellent information source on travel health): www.cdc.gov/travel/

World Health Organisation (contains a range of information on global health issues and is especially useful for tracking AIDS related issues): www.who. int/en/

The Future of Tourism Studies

13

Key Concepts

- Fluidity
- Disciplinarity
- Theory development
- Beliefs
- Values
- Ideas
- Action
- Argument
- Trends

The previous chapters have highlighted major issues which face the future of tourism. This final chapter examines the future of tourism studies as an area of social science research. One of the obvious challenges placed at the beginning of this book is that tourism studies is a discipline. This was argued primarily in terms of its institutional characteristics but, as the book has sought to demonstrate, there are a number of theoretical insights into the nature of temporary mobility, particularly with respect to our understanding of space and time in mobility, place or destination competition, and contemporary social theory with respect to interactions between the global, the local and the individual that provide a rich intellectual basis for the discipline of tourism studies. However, to describe tourism as a discipline is not to suggest that tourism should be closed to other areas. Far from it.

Indeed, in the same way that place and identity are fluid, in the sense that they are open to change because of their relationships with others and with structure, so it is that disciplines, the institutionalised boxes of knowledge that one sees in the academy are also fluid. Astrology becomes cosmology, alchemy becomes chemistry and physics, natural history becomes ecology (and arguably economics!), aspects of philosophy and of the study of religion mutate over time to become a wide range of social scientific subjects, including sociology and politics. Economics and geography fuse together to provide a basis for regional and urban planning and for regional science. Applied social psychology serves as the basis for marketing. Enough! Disciplinary boundaries are not forever set in stone, neither is their content nor the methods and philosophy that underpin the discipline. For example, as Giddens (1984, p. 368) noted with respect to the overall role of space in the social sciences: 'Space is not an empty dimension along which social groupings become structured, but has to be considered in terms of its involvement in the constitution of systems of interaction. The same point made in relation to history applied to (human) geography: there are no logical or methodological differences between geography and sociology' (also see Massey 1999b, 1999c). In one of the author's disciplinary homes, that of geography, there have been enormous shifts in approach and focus over time. There have been theoretical and academic winners and losers, and the field continues to change in response to broader changes in society and institutions as well as in other fields of academic endeavour, let alone what individuals just happen to find interesting and what gets them intellectually aroused (Johnston 1991; Hall and Page 2002). The field of tourism studies is like this. This is not unusual and it is not intrinsically a bad thing. Indeed, if one was to paraphrase Woody Allen's observations regarding relationships in *Annie Hall*, a discipline is like a shark, it either moves forward or it dies.

It is now a truism to claim that tourism comprises an eclectic collection of theories. A theory is a set of ideas about how the world works (Hubbard et al. 2002). In any subject there are usually diverse, evolving and competing ideas or theories that provide a foundation for that area. Much of the humanities and the social sciences, including the field of tourism studies, is characterised by 'epistemological relativism and methodological pluralism' (Gregory et al. 1994, p. 5). Such pluralism is 'no bad thing' (Ward and Almå 1997, p. 626) as 'a continuing, constructive dialogue between different perspectives is clearly preferable to a continued search for a single, new, all-encompassing paradigm' (Hudson 2000, p. 21). Although, as Fincher (1983) argued, there are certainly dangers in the indiscriminate use of theories, a search for all-encompassing paradigms or meta-narratives also seems doomed to failure 'since no theoretical system can provide a complete and satisfactory explanation' (Hudson 2000, p. 21) we perhaps need. Indeed, Massey (1999a, p. 7) observed: 'We continue to define disciplines by exclusion rather than by interrelation: we assume there are areas beyond a discipline's purview. And we define those areas in terms of subject matter rather than in terms of what one might call angle of approach.' Therefore, as Gregory (1994, p. 105) has stated, we need 'to find ways of living – critically and creatively, with theoretical dissonance'. Finding common ground between different disciplinary areas can have many advantages because of the new insights that it can bring. As Massey (1999a, p. 5) observes, 'some of the most stimulating intellectual developments of recent years have come either from new, hybrid places (cultural studies might be an example) or from places where boundaries between disciplines have been constructively breached and new conversations have taken place'. Nevertheless, it should also be noted that some hybrids are infertile.

'Theory making is a process of construction rather than deconstruction and in this respect theory making is doubly contingent: contingent upon the predicament in which we find ourselves and contingent upon the theoretical context in which we work' (Hudson 2000, p. 22). The theoretical context emerges out of the interrelationships between social science philosophy, and various social scientific theories or theoretical domains (Figure 13.1). However, like tourism and tourists, different theories and ideas can also be located in time (linear and non-linear). There is also a spatial dimension that helps explain *why* these ideas were emphasised or de-emphasised at different periods and in different places. For example, political-economy perspectives originated with Adam Smith and Karl Marx in rapidly industrialising England. Such perspectives re-emerged in France in the late 1960s and early 1970s in modified forms in response to social upheaval. These then merged with increasing British and American concerns regarding the participatory and community dimensions of urban renewal (Healey 1997). For example, advocacy planning developed in a United States that was beginning to question the wisdom of government policies, including the Vietnam War and the race issue. Critical theory emerged during the Nazi era in Germany and then blossomed as the intellectual leaders of the approach lived in exile in the United States with its rapidly developing consumer society. The point is that a two-dimensional perspective that emphasises time in a linear sense tells us little about the origin, development or application of theory in differing social, economic and political contexts (Allmendinger 2002). Similarly, in tourism, different ideas have emerged at different times because of the intellectual history of the individuals involved and in terms of the receptivity of such ideas in wider locations. For example, Murphy's (1985) notion of community tourism planning initially found fertile ground in a North America that was already concerned with advocacy issues and was incorporating participation into planning procedures. It did not have such a reception in state communist Eastern Europe, Russia or China, which then had a technical-rational, highly centralised form of planning for tourism as well as everything else.

'Every field of endeavour has its history of ideas and practices and its traditions of debate. These act as a store of experience, of myths, metaphors and arguments, which those within the field can draw upon in developing their own contributions, either through what they do, or through reflecting on the field' (Healey 1997, p. 7). Unfortunately, in the case of tourism, the author

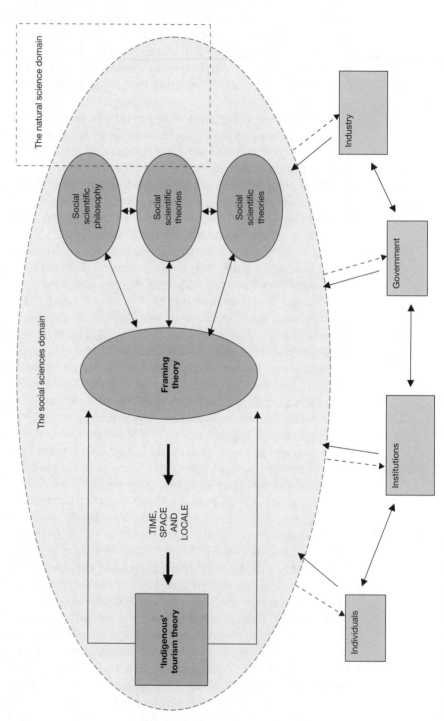

Figure 13.1 Development of tourism theory

would argue that there is not enough reflection and debate. As argued in Chapter 1, tourism is not a brand new area of study. It has antecedents going back to the 1920s and 1930s, and by the 1970s there were already a significant number of books and journals being published and competing approaches were explaining how tourism develops, what is the relationship between tourism and identity, what are the relationships between the tourist and the location in which tourism occurs. Yet much of the enormous amount of literature and the reasons behind its growth, as for the wider institutions of the field, have not been interrogated. There is, unfortunately, as yet no sociology of tourism knowledge in the same way that other social science fields have reflected upon themselves. I am not sure why this is. Perhaps some do not find it interesting. Perhaps, like much of the tourism industry itself, there seems a desire not to debate what may be seen as potentially negative subjects, such as contestation, power, why things do and do not get published, as this may somehow detract from the growth of the field and what is often portrayed as the rational production of tourism knowledge, especially when it comes to dealing with government and industry and not biting the hands that feed. Perhaps also it relates to individual career paths. If I criticise someone else or maybe not reference their work, then maybe they will hold it against me? Indeed, increasingly around the world there seem to be positive incentives not to debate because of the potential fallout in academic reviews through either what or where you publish or how much money you attract. The financial rewards are often a major criterion for gaining professorships in the field of tourism rather than being able to 'profess' or communicate one's disciplinary fields. These are not idle reflections as they strike at the core of understanding how tourism knowledge is produced and what it is that we study. Knowledge management in tourism is therefore also not value free. Questions must be asked about whom we are producing such knowledge for and how it will be used (Ruhanen and Cooper 2004).

Tourism knowledge is not neutral. There is no neutral way of understanding theory. The ability to separate facts and values is rejected, as is the positivist basis to the distinction between substance (analysis) and procedure (process) (Allmendinger 2002). No research, tourism or otherwise, takes place in a philosophical vacuum. Even if it is not explicitly articulated, all research is guided by a set of philosophical beliefs and values (Hill 1981). Neither does tourism knowledge develop in an institutional or environmental vacuum. Instead there is enormous influence at both the personal level, in terms of values, career and relationships, as well as in the environment within which tourism occurs, including institutions such as universities, government, industry, interest groups and significant individuals (Figure 13.2). Institutions have considerable influence on the development of tourism knowledge, particularly through the funding of research but also in the career reward systems that exist. This is not to say that institutions are solely responsible for the generation of tourism knowledge and what academics produce, but that they are extremely influential. In addition, such factors also influence the disciplinary boundaries within which we operate. It is no accident that growth in tourism as an academic study and tourism as an academic unit within universities and colleges has paralleled growth in international tourism and corresponding government interest in using tourism as a means of economic development. Moreover, government and industry are interested in funding tourism education and research (of a certain kind) not just because of the results of research but also because it provides industry with an educated labour force. As Massey (1999a, p. 5) also noted with social science research in general:

> The disciplines into which we are, with varying degrees of success, today corralled are inherited from a particular period and a particular history. And it was a history in which, of course, institutional arrangements and struggles for power played at least as strong a part as any search after the best way of enquiring into the world around us.

In terms of rethinking tourism, we are therefore interested not only in explicitly framing tourism within social science theory, but also in consciously reflecting on how tourism knowledge is used. This means that, as in cognate fields such as planning, there is a complex iterative relationship between ideas and action (Allmendinger 2002). This therefore should make us consider the various values embedded in tourism knowledge and how such values may reveal something about tourism development and policy and, of course, the arguments that the tourism academy use in influencing tourism policy. 'At best, theory making is a process of persuasion and argument both within and outside academia, and choice of theoretical framework is to a degree a political choice' (Hudson 2000, p. 22).

For this author, thinking about tourism therefore has a number of implications in terms of theory development. First, tourism is grounded in

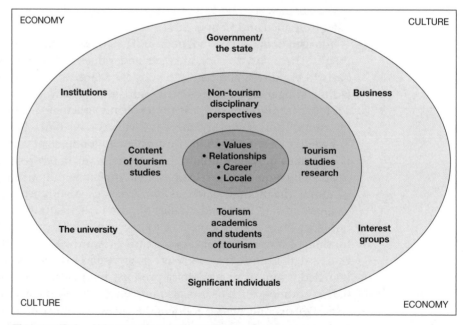

Figure 13.2   Why we do what we do

contemporary capitalism (also see Britton 1991). Thinking about tourism therefore means thinking about the constructions and processes of capitalism and the implications of this for the tourism phenomenon, including aspects of consumption, production, identity and the interaction of structure and agency, at various scales. Second, tourism is global in scope. This implies understanding the processes of mobility as well as globalisation and its corollary of localisation and the significance of place competition. Moreover, a third implication which arises from considerations of mobility has to be asking why people are immobile. What are the constraints that prevent people from travelling? Fourth, ultimately tourism production is grounded in human interaction within the natural environment. Acknowledging the grounding of production in nature has far-reaching implications that imply conceptualising production in terms of relations between the social, spatial and natural. Moreover, introducing environmental concerns raises issues of equity and social justice as well as environmental sustainability (Harvey 1996), and form the basis for a broader understanding of the relationship between tourism and security. Fifth, different forms of mobility are interrelated – movement leads to further movement. This means that the interrelationships between tourism and migration, as well as diaspora, transnationalism and the very notion of home, are of enormous significance for tourism studies. Sixth, concepts of space and time and an understanding of the body moving through space and time are also essential to understanding tourism in different locales. Seventh, I am also part of these implications in that I am both a producer of tourism knowledge, and participate in intellectual debates and struggles as to the competing merits of approaches and theorisations of the subject, and I am also a tourist. This means that positionality is significant. Finally, all of the above implications for rethinking tourism and the social science of mobility do not occur in isolation; they are interrelated and are part of the complex web of human society and mobility.

Inherent in the above is also the notion that the scope of tourism studies is more than just an applied business discipline. Tourism studies is more than just producing a labour force for the industry. It is a means of looking at far wider phenomena that have enormous impacts on contemporary society and the environment. This is not to say that what is in this book is irrelevant to business. Far from it. Understanding the environment within which the industry operates is essential for the development of strategy. In particular, an understanding of mobilities in time and space can contribute not only to marketing but also to firm location and place competitiveness. By rethinking tourism I also do not mean that applied business research and works on the business of tourism are without value. Not at all. However, it does mean that such work needs to be seen within the context of the various theorisations and philosophies of the social sciences and human values.

Tourism as a field of study continues to show remarkable growth. Figure 13.3 illustrates the growth of tourism journals over time (see Chapter 1). The institutions of tourism continue to grow. The growth of tourism studies is, in part, likely to be linked with growth in international tourism. Yet this is not enough to guarantee the future of tourism studies. As noted above, disciplinary boundaries are fluid, subjects rise and fall in their significance. If, as this book has argued, tourism is linked to wider issues of mobility, could this mean that mobility becomes a major subject area in its own right? Possibly. There are already signs that the concept of mobility is beginning to be significant in the first few years of the twenty-first century (e.g. Urry 2000a, 2000b; Williams and Hall 2000, 2002; Gushulak and MacPherson 2001; Pries 2001; Pahl 2001; Kaufmann 2002; Verstraete and Creswell 2002; Coles et al. 2004; Hall and Müller 2004a). But the implications for tourism are as yet unclear. In discussing the significance of trends for the future, Naisbitt (1982, p. xxxii) noted that [t]rends tell you the direction the country is moving in. The decisions are up to you.' Trends are not self-fulfilling prophecies, they are not inevitable. Yet there are signs of disciplinary convergence on the importance of mobility. However, it is an area in which tourism has much to offer other parts of the social sciences, as mobility has always been the subject matter of tourism, even if not explicitly stated. In addition, it is highly unlikely that, given the investment by government, and to a much lesser extent industry, in tourism education and research around the world, the applied nature of tourism business research will suddenly be abandoned.

Nevertheless, tourism studies does face important issues. First, while it has significant institutional strength, tourism studies remains weak in terms of competition for cultural and economic capital with other disciplines and fields of academic endeavour. This is partly a result of perceptions of the field and its subject matter as not being serious and not having academic credibility. This is a result as much of a lack of knowledge by those making such comments and the inherent conservatism of many disciplines as it is based in any reality. More significantly, it is also an outcome of competition for resources through quality assessment exercises and within research institutions. The appropriate response to this is to engage more widely in the social sciences and, arguably, to support the continued development of tourism-specific research bodies that

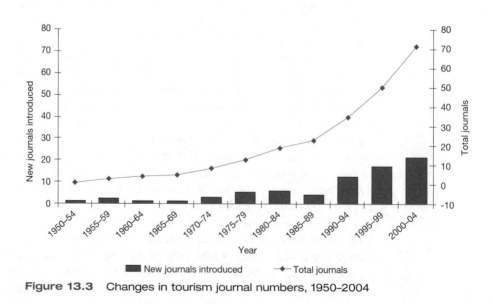

Figure 13.3   Changes in tourism journal numbers, 1950–2004

have a broad mandate, such as ATLAS and the Tourism and Travel Research Association, as well as those with disciplinary associations. Second, it also has to be seen as relevant, not only to industry, but also to policy-makers and the wider community. Here empirical research becomes extremely important. As Johnston (1986, p. 173) argued: 'Empirical research must be used not as an end in itself . . . despite claims that "there is no alternative", empirical research can, and must, show how destinies are created by people interpreting structures and making contexts, how contexts and destinies can be changed, and how structures can be changed. Empirical research is not voyeurism, it is sensitization.'

Tourism and its study are about the generation of new relationships between place and time. Ultimately, therefore, rethinking tourism implies connecting empirical research with theory building, connecting tourism with theory, and ensuring that our work is relevant. Clearly, that begs the response of to what and for whom? And if we are asking those questions then we are already rethinking the social science of mobility.

Discussion Questions

1. Is tourism a discipline? Or is it best described as interdisciplinary, multidisciplinary or even post-disciplinary?

2. Who are the key stakeholders in tourism research and how might the results of such research be made more relevant to them?

3. Is tourism weak in institutional terms at universities and colleges?

4. For what and for whom should tourism research and the dissemination of knowledge be conducted?

Further Reading and Websites

Massey (1999a) provides a stimulating discussion about the issue of disciplinary research in the social sciences. I am also indebted to the work of Johnston (1991) for understanding disciplinarity. On the role of reflexivity in social sciences, see Rose (1997), on its potential role in tourism and on my own reflexivity, see Hall (2004a, 2004c). The more some of us travel the more the concept of home becomes a source of reflexivity (see Miller 2001). According to Morrison (2003, p. 12), 'Classics escape the prism of time. Whichever their era, they belong to every other era. People talk of "contemporary classics" but the phrase is tautologous: classics are contemporary by definition.'

For me there are a small number of classics in tourism. In this group I would include Christaller (1963), Wolfe (1966), Lieper (1979), Butler (1980) and Britton

(1991). In the wider realm, the work of Hägerstrand (1970, 1984) is particularly important for understanding mobility. Harvey's (1989b, 2000) employment of dialectics, as 'both a mode of explanation and a mode of presentation geared to capturing in knowledge the realities of capitalism' (Castree 1996, p. 347), has also been particularly influential (see also Hall 2000a). Two recent books on the ethical and moral dimension of tourism also cast new light on the nature of tourism development and tourism research – see Butcher (2003) and Smith and Duffy (2003).

Biff When all else fails, see: www.biffonline.com

References

Access Economics 1997, *The Economic Significance of Travel & Tourism & Is There a Case for Government Funding for Generic Tourism Marketing*, prepared by *Access Economics*, Tourism Council Australia, Property Council of Australia and Tourism Task Force, Canberra.

Ackoff, R.L. 1974, *Redesigning the Future*, Wiley, New York.

Adams, P. 1995, A reconsideration of personal boundaries in space–time, *Annals of the Association of American Geographers* 85, 267–85.

Adams, P. 1999, Bringing globalization home: a homeworker in the Information Age, *Urban Geography* 20, 356–76.

Adler, J. 1989, Travel as performed art, *American Journal of Sociology* 94, 1366–91.

Advantage West Midlands 2003, Thinking of the United Kingdom? (Advertisement), *Scanorama*, October, p. 90.

Agnew, J. 1987, *Place and Politics*, Allen & Unwin, Boston, MA.

Agnew, M. and Viner, D. 2001, Potential impact of climate change on international tourism, *Tourism and Hospitality Research* 3, 37–60.

Agriculture Western Australia 2000a, *Grape Phylloxera: Exotic Threat to Western Australia, Factsheet No. 0002–2000*, Department of Agriculture, Perth.

Agriculture Western Australia 2000b, *Viticulture Industry Protection Plan*, Department of Agriculture, Perth.

Aiello, R. 1998, Interpretation and the marine tourism industry, who needs it?: a case study of Great Adventures, Australia, *Journal of Tourism Studies* 9, 51–61.

Airey, D. and Middleton, V. 1984, Tourism education course syllabi in the UK – a review, *Tourism Management* 5(1), 52–68.

Airey, D. and Nightingale, M. 1981, Tourism occupations, career profile and knowledge, *Annals of Tourism Research* 8(1), 52–68.

Aitchison, C. 1999, New cultural geographies: the spatiality of leisure, gender and sexuality, *Leisure Studies* 18, 19–39.

Aitchison, C., MacLeod, N.E. and Shaw, S.J. 2000, *Leisure and Tourism Landscapes: Social Constructions of Space and Place*, Routledge, London.

Aitken, C. and Hall, C.M. 2000, Migrant and foreign skills and their relevance to the tourism industry, *Tourism Geographies* 2(1), 66–86.

Alexander, G.A. 2000, Ecoterrorism and nontraditional military threats, *Military Medicine* 165(1), 1–5.

Alfredson, E. 2002, *Green Consumption, Energy Use and Carbon Dioxide Emission*, GERUM Kulturgeografi, Umea.

Allen, J., Massey, D. and Cochrane, A. 1998, *Re-thinking the Region*, Routledge, London.

Allen, J.E. 2003, Quest for a novel force: a possible revolution in aerospace. *Progress in Aerospace Sciences* 39(1), 1–60.

Allen, W.H. 1992 Increased dangers to Caribbean marine ecosystems, *Bioscience*, 42(5), 330–5.

Allison, P.D. 1984, *Event History Analysis: Regression for Longitudinal Event Data*, Sage, Beverly Hills, CA.

Allmendinger, P. 2002, Towards a post-positivist typology of planning theory, *Planning Theory* 1(1), 77–99.

Allwood, C.M. and Granhag, P.A. 1999, Feelings of confidence and the realism of confidence in everyday life, in P. Juslin and H. Montgomery (eds), *Judgment and Decision Making: Neo-Brunswikian and Process-tracing Approaches*, Lawrence Erlbaum Associates, Mahwah, NJ, pp. 123–46.

Altman, J.C., Ginn, A. and Smith, D.E. 1993, *Existing and Potential Mechanisms for Indigenous Involvement in Coastal Zone Resource Management*, Consultancy Report to Coastal Zone Inquiry, Resources Assessment Commission, Canberra.

Amin, A. 1989, Flexible specialisation and small firms in Italy: myths and realities, *Antipode* 21, 13–34.

Amin, A. 2002, Industrial districts, in E. Sheppard and T. Barnes (eds), *A Companion to Economic Geography*, Blackwell, Oxford, pp. 149–68.

Amin, A. and Thomas, A. 1996, The negotiated economy: state and civic institutions in Denmark, *Economy and Society* 25, 255–81.

Amin, A. and Thrift, N. 1994, *Globalization, Institutions and Regional Development in Europe*, Oxford University Press, Oxford.

Anderson, M. 1985, The emergence of the modern life cycle in Britain, *Social History* 10, 69–87.

Ankomah, P.K. and Crompton, J.L. 1992, Tourism cognitive distance: a set of research propositions, *Annals of Tourism Research* 19(2), 323–42.

Archer, B. 1982, The value of multipliers and their policy implications, *Tourism Management* 3, 236–41.

Archer, B. 1989, Tourism and island economies: impact analysis, in C. Cooper (ed.), *Progress in Tourism, Recreation and Hospitality Management*, Vol. 1, Belhaven Press, London, pp. 125–34.

Archer, E. 1985, Emerging environmental problems in a tourist zone: the case of Barbados, *Caribbean Geography* 2, 45–55.

Aronsson, L. 1994, Sustainable tourism systems: the example of sustainable rural tourism in Sweden, *Journal of Sustainable Tourism* 2(1/2), 77–92.

Aronsson, L. 2000, *The Development of Sustainable Tourism*, Continuum, London.

Ascher, B. 1984, Obstacles to international travel and tourism, *Journal of Travel Research* 22, 2–16.

Ashby, W.R. 1956, *Introduction to Cybernetics*, Methuen, London.

Ashby, W.R. 1970, Analysis of the system to be modeled, in R.M. Stogdill (ed.), *The Process of Model-Building*, Ohio University Press, Columbus OH, pp. 94–114.

Ashworth, G.J. and Tunbridge, J.E. 1996, *Dissonant Heritage*, Wiley, Chichester.

Ashworth, G.J. and Voogd, H. 1988, Marketing the city: concepts, processes and Dutch applications, *Town Planning Review* 59(1), 65–80.

Ateljevic, I. and Doorne, S. 2000, Staying within the fence: lifestyle entrepreneurship in tourism, *Journal of Sustainable Tourism* 8(5), 378–92.

Audretsch, D.B. and Feldman, M.P. 1997, *Innovative Clusters and the Industry Life Cycle*, CEPR Discussion Papers 1161, Centre for Economic Policy Research, London.

Aukutsionek, S.A. and Belianin, A.V. 2001, Quality of forecasts and business performance: a survey study of Russian managers, *Journal of Economic Psychology* 22, 661–92.

AusIndustry 1996, *Network News: AusIndustry Business Networks Program* 6 (December), 8.

Australian National Audit Office (ANAO) 2001, *Managing for Quarantine Effectiveness: Department of Agriculture, Fisheries and Forestry – Australia*, The Auditor-General Audit Report No. 47 2000–2001 Performance Audit, Commonwealth of Australia, Canberra.

Autero, J. 2003, The megatrends of the 'Experience Society' guiding future tourism, unpublished paper presented at the 12th Nordic Symposium in Tourism and Hospitality Research, Stavanger, October.

Axhausen, K.W. 2001, Methodological research for a European survey of long-distance travel, in *Personal Travel: The Long and Short of It, Conference Proceedings June 28–July 1, 1999 Washington, D.C.,* TRB Transportation Research Circular E–C026, Transportation Research Board, Washington DC, pp. 321–42.

Baade, R.A. 1996, Professional sports as catalysts for metropolitan economic development, *Journal of Urban Affairs* 18(1), 1–17.

Bærenholdt, J.O., Haldrup, M., Larsen, J. and Urry, J. 2004, *Performing Tourist Places,* Ashgate, Aldershot.

Bagguley, P. 1987, *Flexibility, Restructuring and Gender: Employment in Britain's Hotels,* Working Paper No. 24, Lancaster Regionalism Group, Lancaster.

Bagguley, P. 1990, Gender and labour flexibility in hotel and catering, *Services Industries Journal* 10, 105–18.

Bahaire, T. and Elliott-White, M. 1999, Community participation in tourism planning and development in the historic city of York, England, *Current Issues in Tourism* 2(2–3), 243–76.

Baim, D.V. 1994, *The Sports Stadium as a Municipal Investment,* Greenwood Press, Westport, CT.

Baines, G.B.K. 1987, Manipulation of islands and men: sand-cay tourism in the South Pacific, in S. Britton and W.C. Clarke (eds), *Ambiguous Alternative: Tourism in Small Developing Countries,* University of the South Pacific, Suva, Fiji, pp. 16–24.

Baker, R.G.V. 1985, A dynamic model of spatial behaviour to a planned sub-urban shopping centre, *Geographical Analysis* 17, 331–8.

Baker, R.G.V. and Garner, B.J. 1989, On the space–time associations in the con-sumer patronage of planned shopping centres, *Environment and Planning A* 21, 1179–94.

Barber, B.M. and Odean, T. 2002, Online investors: do the slow die first? *The Review of Financial Studies* 15, 455–87.

Barnes, T.J. 2004, A paper related to everything but more related to local things, *Annals of the Association of American Geographers,* 94(2), 278–83.

Bartlett, A.L. and Farrar, A.L. 1997, Multicultural education in human resource management and organisational behaviour: the case for curriculum trans-formation, *Hospitality & Tourism Educator* 9(1), 49–54.

Bassett, K. 1993, Urban cultural strategies and urban regeneration: a case study and critique, *Environment and Planning A* 25(12), 1773–88.

Bathelt, H. 2003, Geographies of production: growth regimes in spatial per-spective 1 – innovation, institutions and social systems, *Progress in Human Geography* 27, 763–78.

Bathelt, H. and Glückler, J. 2003, Toward a relational economic geography, *Journal of Economic Geography* 3, 117–44.

Bathelt, H., Malmberg, A. and Maskell, P. 2004, Clusters and knowledge: local buzz, global pipelines and the process of knowledge creation, *Progress in Human Geography* 28, 31–56.

Bathelt, H. and Taylor, M. 2002, Clusters, power and place: inequality and local growth in time–space, *Geografiska Annaler* 84B, 93–109.

Baudrillard, J. 1988a, Consumer culture, in *Jean Baudrillard: Selected Writings*, ed. M. Poster, Polity Press, Cambridge.

Baudrillard, J. 1988b, *America*, Verso, London.

Bauer, T.G. 2001, *Tourism in the Antarctic: Opportunities, Constraints, and Future Prospects*, The Haworth Press, New York.

Baum, J.A.C. 1999, The rise of chain nursing homes in Ontario, 1971–1996, *Social Forces* 78, 543–84.

Baum, T. and Lundtrop, S. (eds) 2001, *Seasonality in Tourism*, Pergamon, Amsterdam.

Bauman, Z. 1998, *Globalization: The Human Consequences*, Polity Press, Cambridge.

BBC 2001, Rebels attack Sri Lanka airport, *BBC News*, Tuesday, 24 July. Available at: http://news.bbc.co.uk/hi/english/world/south_asia/newsid_1453000/1453699.stm (accessed 1 February 2002).

Becheri, E. 1989, From thermalism to health tourism, *Revue de Tourisme* 44(4), 15–19.

Beck, U. 1992, *Risk Society: Towards a Modernity*, Sage, London.

Beck, U., Giddens, A. and Lash, S. 1994, *Reflexive Modernization: Politics, Tradition and Aesthetics in the Modern Social Order*, Polity Press, Cambridge.

Beckwith, B. 1967, *The Next Five Hundred Years*, Exposition Press, New York.

Beekhuis, J.V. 1981, Tourism in the Caribbean: impacts on the economic, social and natural environments, *Ambio* 10, 325–31.

Bell, D. 1973, *The Coming of Post-Industrial Society*, Basic Books, New York.

Bell, D. 1979, *The Cultural Contradictions of Capitalism*, Heinemann Educational, London.

Bell, M. and Ward, G. 2000, Comparing temporary mobility with permanent migration, *Tourism Geographies* 2(1), 87–107.

Bellan, G.L. and Bellan-Santini, D.R. 2001, A review of littoral tourism, sport and leisure activities: consequences on marine flora and fauna, *Aquatic Conservation: Marine and Freshwater Ecosystems* 11, 325–33.

Bender, C. 2000, Snowmaking survey, *Ski Area Management* 39(6), 52.

Beng, T.H. 1995, *Tropical Resorts*, Page One Publishing, Singapore.

Berger, P. 1974, *Pyramids of Sacrifice*, Penguin, Harmondsworth.

Berkelman, R.L., Bryan, R.T., Osterholm, M.T., LeDuc, J.W. and Hughes, J.M. 1994, Infectious disease surveillance: a crumbling foundation, *Science* 264, 368–70.

Berman, M. 1983, *All That Is Solid Melts into Air: The Experiences of Modernity*, Verso, London.

Bernard, D.T. and Scott, V.N. 1995, Risk assessment and foodborne micro-organisms: the difficulties of biological diversity, *Food Control* 6, 329–33.

Bianchini, F. and Parkinson, M. 1993, *Cultural Policy and Urban Development: The Experience of West European Cities*, Manchester University Press, Manchester.

Biosecurity Strategy Development Team 2001a, *A Biosecurity Strategy for New Zealand: Strategy Vision Framework Background Paper for Stakeholder Working Groups*, Biosecurity Strategy Development Team, Wellington.

Biosecurity Strategy Development Team 2001b, *Issues Paper: Developing a Biosecurity Strategy for New Zealand: A Public Consultation Paper*, Biosecurity Strategy Development Team, Wellington.

Biosecurity Strategy Development Team 2002, *Developing a Biosecurity Strategy for New Zealand. Submissions on the 'Issues Paper': A Summary Report*, Biosecurity Strategy Development Team, Wellington.

Birkland, T.A. 2004, 'The world changed today': agenda-setting and policy change in the wake of the September 11 terrorist attacks, *Review of Policy Research* 21(3), 179–200.

Bishop, A. 2004, Letters to the Editor: holiday homes and everyday reality, *The Times*, 30 March, p. 19.

Blake, J. 1996, Resolving conflict? The rural white paper, sustainability and countryside policy, *Local Environment* 1(2), 211–18.

Blandy, R. 2000, *Industry Clusters Program: A Review*, South Australian Business Vision 2010, Government of South Australia, Adelaide.

Blavin, J. 2000, Summary report on presentation of Professor Elinor Ostrom, Coping with tragedies of the commons: local lessons, global challenges, Managing Global Issues Seminar Series, Carnegie Endowment for International Peace, 25 February, http://www.ceip.org/programs/global/semostrom.htm

Blumberg, K. 2004, Destination marketing as an exercise in cooperative networking: a case study from Nelson/Tasman region, New Zealand. Paper presented at ATLAS Annual Conference, Networking and Partnerships in Destination Development and Management, Naples, 3–6 April.

Blumen, O. 1994, Gender differences in the journey to work, *Urban Geography* 15(3), 223–45.

Boden, D. and Molotch, H. 1994, The compulsion to proximity, in R. Friedland and D. Boden (eds), *Nowhere: Space, Time and Modernity*, University of California Press, Berkeley, CA, pp. 257–86.

Bodewes, T. 1981, Development of advanced tourism studies in Holland, *Annals of Tourism Research* 8, 35–51.

Bolger, F. and Wright, G. 1992, Reliability and validity in expert judgment, in F. Bolger and G. Wright (eds), *Expertise and Decision Support*, Plenum Press, New York, pp. 47–76.

Borgdorff, M.W. and Motarjemi, Y. 1997, Foodborne disease surveillance: what are the options?, *World Health Statistics Quarterly* 50(1/2), 12–23.

Botterill, D., Owen, R.E., Emanuel, L., Foster, N., Gale, T., Nelson, C. and Selby, M. 1997, Perceptions from the periphery: the experience of Wales, in *Peripheral Area Tourism: International Tourism Research Conference, Bornholm, 8–12 September 1997*, Unit of Tourism Research at the Research Centre of Bornholm, Bornholm.

Boulding, E. 1991, States, boundaries and environmental security in global and regional conflicts, *Interdisciplinary Peace Research* 3(2): 78–93.

Bouquet, M. and Winter, M. 1987, 'Introduction: tourism politics and practice', in M. Bouquet and M. Winter (eds), *Who from Their Labours Rest? Conflict and Practice in Rural Tourism*, Avebury, Aldershot, pp. 1–8.

Bourdieu, P. 1984, *Distinction*, Routledge, London.

Bowler, I., Bryant, C. and Nellis, M. (eds) 1992, *Contemporary Rural Systems in Transition*, 2 vols, CABI, Wallingford.

Boyce, R.R. 1966, The edge of the metropolis: the wave theory analog approach, in J.V. Minghi (ed.), *The Geographer and the Public Environment and Other Papers on Urban Growth and Structure*, BC Geographical Series No. 7, Tantalus Research, Vancouver, pp. 30–40.

Boyle, P., Halfacree, K. and Robinson, V. 1998, *Exploring Contemporary Migration*, Addison Wesley Longman, Harlow.

Bramham, P., Henry, I., Mommaas, H. and van der Poel, H. (eds) 1989, *Leisure and Urban Processes: Critical Studies of Leisure Policy in Western European Cities*, Routledge, London and New York.

Bramham, P., Henry, I., Mommaas, H. and van der Poel, H. (eds) 1993, *Leisure Policies in Europe*, CABI, Wallingford.

Bramwell, B. (ed.) 2003, *Coastal Mass Tourism: Diversification and Sustainable Development in Southern Europe*, Channelview, Clevedon.

Bramwell, B. and Lane, B. 1993, Sustainable tourism: an evolving global approach, *Journal of Sustainable Tourism* 1(1), 6–16.

Bramwell, B. and Lane, B. (eds) 2000, *Tourism Collaboration and Partnerships: Politics, Practice and Sustainability*, Channelview, Clevedon.

Brand, S. 1997, *How Buildings Learn: What Happens After They're Built*, Phoenix Illustrated, London.

Bread Not Circuses 1998a, *Bread Alert!* (Email edition) 2(2), 20 February.

Bread Not Circuses 1998b, *Bread Alert!* (Email edition) 2(3) 26 February.

Bread Not Circuses 1998c, *Bread Alert!* (Email edition) 2(8) 8 April.

Brewer, E. 1993–94, Is 10% realistic? Sending US undergraduates overseas, *Phi Beta Delta International Review*, IV(Fall/Spring), 75–99.

Briassoulis, H. and van der Straaten, J. (eds) 1999, *Tourism and the Environment*, 2nd edn, Kluwer Academic Publishers, Dordrecht.

Britton, S.G. 1982, The political economy of tourism in the Third World, *Annals of Tourism Research* 9(3), 331–58.

Britton, S.G. 1983, *Tourism and Underdevelopment in Fiji*, Monograph No. 13, Australian National University Development Studies Centre, Australian National University, Canberra.

Britton, S.G. 1987, Tourism in Pacific island states: constraints and opportunities, in S.G. Britton and W.C. Clarke (eds), *Ambiguous Alternative: Tourism in Small Developing Countries*, University of the South Pacific, Suva, Fiji, pp. 113–39.

Britton, S.G. 1991, Tourism, capital and place: towards a critical geography of tourism, *Environment and Planning D: Society and Space* 9(4), 451–78.

Brown, B. 2004, Village people play for the boomers, *The Australian*, Wealth section, 14 April, 8–10.

Brown, F. 2004, The final frontier? Tourism in space, *Tourism Recreation Research* 29(1), 37–44.

Brown, F. and Hall, F. (eds) 2000, *Tourism in Peripheral Areas*, Channelview, Clevedon.

Brown, L. 1977, Redefining security. *Worldwatch Paper No. 14*, Worldwatch Institute, Washington, DC.

Brown, L.A. 1981, *Innovation Diffusion: A New Perspective*, Methuen, London.

Brown, M.A. 1980, Attitudes and social categories: complementary explanations of innovation-adoption behavior, *Environment and Planning A* 12, 175–86.

Brown, R.M. 1935, The business of recreation, *Geographical Review* 25, 467–75.

Brunckhorst, D.J. 2000, *Bioregional Planning: Resource Management Beyond the New Millennium*, Harwood Academic Press, Amsterdam.

Bruner, E.M. 1996, Tourism in Ghana: the representation of slavery and the return of the black diaspora, *American Anthropologist* 98, 290–304.

Bryman, A., Bytheway, B., Allatt, P. and Keil, T. 1987, Introduction, in A. Bryman, B. Bytheway, P. Allatt and T. Keil (eds), *Rethinking the Life Cycle*, Macmillan, Basingstoke, pp. 1–16.

Buckley, P.J. and Klemm, M. 1993, The decline of tourism in Northern Ireland. *Tourism Management* June, 185–94.

Buhalis, D. 1997, Tourism in the Greek Islands: the issues of peripherality, competitiveness and development, in Peripheral Area Tourism: International Tourism Research Conference, Bornholm, 8–12 September 1997, Unit of Tourism Research at the Research Centre of Bornholm, Bornholm.

Buhalis, D. and Cooper, C. 1998, Competition or co-operation? Small and medium-sized tourism enterprises at the destination, in E. Laws, B. Faulkner and G. Moscardo (eds), *Embracing and Managing Change in Tourism: International Case Studies*, Routledge, London, pp. 324–46.

Bula, F. 2004, In pursuit of a rare species. *The National Post*, Post Travel section, 27 March, PT1, PT8.

Bull, A. 1991, *The Economics of Travel and Tourism*, Longman Cheshire, South Melbourne.

Bull, A. 1994, *The Economics of Travel and Tourism*, 2nd edn, Longman Australia, South Melbourne.

Buller, H. and Hoggart, K. 1994, *International Counterurbanization: British Migrants in Rural France*, Ashgate, Aldershot.

Burch, D., Goss, J. and Lawrence, G. (eds) 1999, *Restructuring Global and Regional Agricultures*, Avebury, Aldershot.

Burch, D., Rickson, R. and Lawrence, G. (eds) 1996, *Globalization and Agri-food Restructuring*, Avebury, Aldershot.

Bureau of Industry Economics 1991, Networks: a third form of organisation, *Bulletin of Industry Economics* 10, 5–9.

Bureau of Transportation Statistics 1997, *1995 American Travel Survey: Profile*, Bureau of Transportation Statistics, US Department of Transport, Washington, DC.

Burgess, J. 1982, Selling places: environmental images for the executive, *Regional Studies* 16, 1–17.

Burgess, J. and Wood, P. 1989, Decoding docklands: place advertising and decision-making strategies in the small firm, in J. Eyles and D.M. Smith (eds), *Qualitative Methods in Human Geography*, Polity Press, Cambridge.

Burkart, A.J. and Medlik, S. 1981, *Tourism Past, Present and Future*, 2nd edn, Heinemann, London.

Bürki, R., Elsasser, H., Abegg, B. and Koenig, U. 2005, Climate change and tourism in the Swiss Alps, in C.M. Hall and J. Higham (eds), *Tourism, Recreation and Climate Change*, Channelview Publications, Clevedon (in press).

Burns, J.P.A. and Mules, T.L. 1986, A framework for the analysis of major special events, in J.P.A. Burns, J.H. Hatch and T.L. Mules (eds), *The Adelaide Grand Prix: The Impact of a Special Event*, The Centre for South Australian Economic Studies, Adelaide, pp. 5–38.

Burns, J.P.A., Hatch, J.H. and Mules, F.J. (eds) 1986, *The Adelaide Grand Prix: The Impact of a Special Event*, The Centre for South Australian Economic Studies, Adelaide.

Burns, L.D. 1979, *Transportation, Temporal, and Spatial Components of Accessibility*, Lexington Books, Lexington, KY.

Butcher, J. 2003, *The Moralisation of Tourism: Sun, Sand . . . and Saving the World?* Routledge, London.

Butfoy, A. 1997, *Common Security and Strategic Reform: A Critical Analysis*, Macmillan, London.

Butler, R.W. (ed.) 2005, *Tourism Area Life Cycle*, 2 vols, Channelview Publications, Clevedon.

Butler, R. and Boyd, S. (eds) 2000, *Tourism and National Parks*, John Wiley, Chichester.

Butler, R.W. 1980, The concept of a tourist area cycle of evolution: implications for management of resources, *Canadian Geographer* 24, 5–12.

Butler, R.W. 1990, Alternative tourism: pious hope or trojan horse, *Journal of Travel Research* 28(3), 40–5.

Butler, R.W. 1991, Tourism, environment, and sustainable development, *Environmental Conservation* 18(3), 201–9.

Butler, R.W. and Hall, C.M. 1998a, Imaging and reimaging in rural areas, in R.W. Butler, C.M. Hall and J. Jenkins (eds), *Tourism and Recreation in Rural Areas*, John Wiley, Chichester, pp. 115–22.

Butler, R.W. and Hall, C.M. 1998b, Towards sustainable tourism and recreation in rural areas, in R.W. Butler, C.M. Hall and J. Jenkins (eds), *Tourism and Recreation in Rural Areas*, John Wiley, Chichester, pp. 251–8.

Butler, R.W., Hall, C.M. and Jenkins, J. 1998a, Introduction: tourism and recreation in rural areas, in R.W. Butler, C.M. Hall and J. Jenkins (eds), *Tourism and Recreation in Rural Areas*, John Wiley, Chichester, pp. 3–16.

Butler, R.W., Hall, C.M. and Jenkins, J. (eds) 1998b, *Tourism and Recreation in Rural Areas*, John Wiley, Chichester.

Bywater, M. 1993, The youth and student travel market, *Travel and Tourism Analyst* 3, 35–50.

Camerer, C.F. and Johnson, E.J. 1991, The process–performance paradox in expert judgment: how can experts know so much and predict so badly? in K.A. Ericsson and J. Smith (eds), *Toward a General Theory of Expertise: Prospects and Limits*, Cambridge University Press, New York, pp. 195–217.

Cameron, C. 1989, Cultural tourism and urban revitalization, *Tourism Recreation Research* 14(1), 23–32.

Cameron, D. and Arnold, M. 2004, Brussels approves airline alliance. *The Financial Times*, 8 April, p. 18.

Campbell, D. 1996, Myanmar tourism under fire, *Timesnet*, Far East Trade Press and Times Information System (http://web3.asia1.com.sg/timesnet/data/tna/docs/tna2949.html).

Campbell, D. 2003, Tribes' casinos thrown into election mix, *The Guardian*, 6 October, p. 14.

Campbell-Hunt, C. 2000, What have we learned about generic competitive strategy: a meta-analysis, *Strategic Management Journal* 21, 127–54.

Canadian Council on Rural Development 1975, *Economic Significance of Tourism and Outdoor Recreation for Rural Development*, Working paper, Canadian Council on Rural Development, Ottawa.

Canberra Times 1994, Muslims misled by Vatican: Egypt, *Canberra Times*, 29 August, p. 12.

Carhart, A.H. 1920, Recreation in the forests, *American Forests* 26, 268–72.

Carlson, A.S. 1938, Recreation industry of New Hampshire, *Economic Geography* 14, 255–70.

Carlstein, T. 1982, *Time Resources, Society and Ecology*, 2 vols, Allen & Unwin, London.

Carlstein, T., Parkes, D.N. and Thrift, N.J. (eds) 1978, *Timing Space and Spacing Time*, 2 vols, Edward Arnold, London.

Carlton, J.T. and Geller, J.B. 1993, Ecological roulette: the global transport of non-indigenous marine organisms, *Science* 261, 78–82.

Carr, N. 1998, The young tourist: a case of neglected research, *Progress in Tourism and Hospitality Research* 4(4), 307–18.

Carr, N. 1999, A study of gender differences: young tourist behaviour in a UK coastal resort, *Tourism Management* 20(2), 223–8.

Casado-Diaz, M.A. 1999, Socio-demographic impacts of residential tourism: a case study of Torrevieja, Spain, *International Journal of Tourism Research* 1, 223–37.

Case, D. 1996, Contributions of journeys away to the definition of home: an empirical study of a dialectical process, *Journal of Environmental Psychology* 16, 1–15.

Castells, M. 1983, Crisis, planning, and the quality of life: managing the new historical relationships between space and society, *Environment and Planning D, Society and Space* 1: 3–21.

Castells, M. 1998, *End of Millenium*, Blackwell, Oxford.

Castree, N. 1996, Birds, mice and geography: Marxism and dialectics, *Transactions of the Institute of British Geographers* new series, 21, 342–62.

Cater, E.A. 1987, Tourism in the least developed countries, *Annals of Tourism Research* 14, 202–26.

Chadee, D. and Cutler, J. 1996, Insights into international travel by students, *Journal of Travel Research* 35(2), 75–80.

Chadwick, R.A. 1994, Concepts, definitions and measures used in travel and tourism research, in J.R.B. Ritchie and C. Goeldner (eds), *Travel, Tourism and Hospitality Research: A Handbook for Managers and Researchers*, 2nd edn, Wiley, New York, pp. 65–80.

Chandler, A. and Daems, H. 1979, Admistrative, coordination, allocation and monitoring: a comparative analysis of accounting and organisation in the USA and Europe, *Accounting, Organizations and Society* 4, 3–20.

Chang, K. 2003, The edge of reality: an elevator to space, *International Herald Tribune*, 25 September, p. 7.

Chang, T.C. 1997, From 'instant Asia' to 'multi-faceted jewel': urban imaging strategies and tourism development in Singapore, *Urban Geography* 18(6), 542–62.

Chapin Jr., F.S. 1974, *Human Activity Patterns in the City: Things People Do in Time and Space*, Wiley Interscience, New York.

Chaplin, D. 1999, Consuming work/productive leisure: the consumption patterns of second home environments, *Leisure Studies* 18, 41–55.

Chapman, K. 1983, *People, Pattern and Process: An Introduction to Human Geography*, Edward Arnold, London.

Chisholm, M. 1965, General systems theory and geography, *Transactions of the Institute of British Geographers* 42, 45–52.

Chorley, R.J. 1964, Geography and analogue theory, *Annals Association of American Geographers* 54, 127–37.

Christaller, W. 1963, Some considerations of tourism location in Europe: the peripheral regions – underdeveloped countries – recreation areas, *Regional Science Association Papers* 12, 95–105.

Cicin-Sain, B. and Knecht, R.W. 1998, *Integrated Coastal and Ocean Management: Concepts and Experiences*, Island Press, Washington, DC.

Clark, D. and Cosgrove, J. 1991, Amenities versus labor market opportunities: choosing the optimal distance to move, *Journal of Regional Science* 31, 311–28.

Clark, G., Feldman, M. and Gertler, M. (eds) 2000, *The Oxford Handbook of Economic Geography*, Oxford University Press, Oxford.

Clarke, A.C. 1978, *The Fountains of Paradise*, Millennium Books, London.

Clarke, W.C. 1991, Time and tourism: an ecological perspective, in M.L. Miller and J. Auyong (eds), *Proceedings of the 1990 Congress on Coastal and Marine Tourism*, National Coastal Research and Development Institute, Honolulu, pp. 387–93.

Clifford, J. 1988, *The Predicament of Culture: Twentieth-Century Ethnography, Literature and Art*, Harvard University Press, Cambridge, MA.

Clifford, J. 1997, *Routes: Travel and Translation in the Late Twentieth Century*, Harvard University Press, Cambridge, MA.

Cloke, P. 1989, Rural geography and political economy, in R. Peet and N. Thrift (eds), *New Models in Geography*, vol. 1, Unwin Hyman, London, pp. 164–97.

Cloke, P. 1992, *Policy and Planning in Thatcher's Britain*, Pergamon, Oxford.

Cloke, P. 1993, On problems and solutions: the reproduction of problems for rural communities in Britain during the 1980s, *Journal of Rural Studies* 9, 113–21.

Cloke, P. and Goodwin, M. 1993, Rural change: structured coherence or unstructured coherence, *Terra* 105, 166–74.

Cloke, P. and Little, J. (eds) 1997, *Contested Countryside Cultures: Otherness, Marginalisation and Rurality*, Routledge, London and New York.

Close, P. 1995, *Citizenship, Europe and Change*, Macmillan, London.

Clout, H.D. 1972, *Rural Geography: An Introductory Survey*, Pergamon Press, Oxford.

Coalter, F. 1988, *Sport and Anti-Social Behaviour: A Literature Review*, Research Report No. 2, Scottish Sports Council, Edinburgh.

Coalter, F. and Allison, M. 1996, *Sport and Community Development*, Research Digest No. 42, Scottish Sports Council, Edinburgh.

Coalter, F., Allison, M. and Taylor, J. 2000, *The Role of Sport in Regenerating Deprived Urban Areas*, Centre for Leisure Research, University of Edinburgh, The Scottish Executive Central Research Unit, Edinburgh.

Cohen, B. 1963, *The Press and Foreign Policy*, Princeton University Press, Princeton, NJ.

Cohen, E. 1974, Who is a tourist?: a conceptual clarification, *Sociological Review* 22, 527–55.

Cohn, T.H. and Smith, P.J. 1993, International cities and municipal paradiplomacy: a typology for assessing the changing Vancouver metropolis, in F. Frisken (ed.), *The Changing Canadian Metropolis: A Public Policy Perspective*, Institute of Governmental Studies Press, University of California, Berkeley.

Cohn, T.H. and Smith, P.J. 1996, Subnational governments as international actors: constituent diplomacy in British Columbia and the Pacific Northwest, *BC Studies: The British Columbian Quarterly* 110(Summer), 25–59.

Cole, J. 1989, Internal migration in Peru, *Geography Review* 3(1), 25–31.

Colebatch, T. 2004, Europe paying price of ageing population, *The Age*, 9–10 April, p. 6.

Coleman, J. 1988, Social capital in the creation of human capital, *American Journal of Sociology Supplement* 94(S), 95–120.

Coleman, S. and Crang, M. (eds) 2002, *Tourism: Between Place and Performance*, Berghahn Books, Oxford.

Coles, T., Duval, D. and Hall, C.M. 2004, Tourism, mobility and global communities: new approaches to theorising tourism and tourist spaces, in W. Theobold (ed.), *Global Tourism*, Heinemann, Oxford, pp. 463–81.

Coles, T.E. and Timothy, D.J. (eds) 2004, *Tourism, Diasporas and Space*, Routledge, London.

Collins, M.F. and Cooper, I.S. (eds) 1997, *Leisure Management: Issues and Applications*, CABI, Wallingford.

Commonwealth of Australia 1999, *Incoming Passenger Card*, Commonwealth of Australia, Canberra.

Conant, J.S., Clarke, T., Burnett, J.J. and Zank, G. 1988, Terrorism and travel: managing the unmanageable, *Journal of Travel Research* Spring, 16–20.

Conant, R. (ed.) 1981, *Mechanism of Intelligence: Ross Ashby's Writings on Cybernetics*, Intersystems, Seaside, CA.

Connell, J. 1988, *Sovereignty and Survival: Island Microstates in the Third World*, Research Monograph No. 3, Department of Geography, University of Sydney, Sydney.

Connor, S. and Grice, A. 2004, Scientist 'gagged' by No. 10 after warning of global warming threat, *The Independent*, 8 March.

Cook, D. 1989, China's hotels: still playing catch up, *Cornell Hotel Restaurant and Administration Quarterly* 30(3), 64–7.

Cooke, P. and Morgan, K. 1993, The network paradigm: new departures in corporate and regional development, *Environment and Planning D: Society and Space* 11, 543–64.

Cookson, S.T., Carballo, M., Nolan, C.M., Keystone, J.S. and Jong, E.C. 2001, Migrating populations: a closer view of who, why, and so what, *Journal of Emerging Infectious Diseases* 7(3) (Supplement, June), 551.

Cooper, C. and Wahab, S. (eds) 2000, *Tourism and Globalisation*, Routledge, London.

Cooper, C.P. 1992, The life cycle concept and tourism, in P. Johnson and B. Thomas (eds), *Choice and Demand in Tourism*, Mansell, London, pp. 145–60.

Cooper, C.P. and Jackson, S. (1989) Destination life cycle: the Island of Man case study, *Annals of Tourism Research* 16(3), 377–98.

Coppock, J.T. (ed.) 1977, *Second Homes: Curse or Blessing?* Pergamon, Oxford.

Corke, J. 1993, *Tourism Law*, Elm, Huntingdon.

Corner, J. and Harvey, S. 1991, *Enterprise and Heritage: Crosscurrents of National Culture*, Routledge, London and New York.

Cornwall, G.W. and Holcomb, C.J. (eds) 1966, *Guidelines to the Planning, Developing, and Managing of Rural Recreation Enterprises*, Bulletin 301, Cooperative Extension Service, Virginia Polytechnic Institute, Blacksburg, VA.

Costanza, R. 2003, A vision of the future of science: reintegrating the study of humans and the rest of nature, *Futures* 35(6), 651–71.

Council of National Academic Awards (CNAA) (1992) *Review of Tourism Degree Studies*, CNAA, London.

Council on Hotel, Restaurant and Institutional Education (CHRIE) 1997, *A Guide to College Programs in Hospitality and Tourism*, 5th edn, John Wiley & Sons, New York.

Courgeau, D. and Lelièvre, E. 1992, *Event History Analysis in Demography*, Oxford University Press, Oxford.

Cowell, R. and Owens, S. 1997, Sustainability: the new challenge, in A. Blowers and B. Evans (eds), *Town Planning into the 21st Century*, Routledge, London, pp. 15–31.

Cox, K.R. 1978, Local interests and urban political processes in market societies, in K.R. Fox (ed.), *Urbanization and Conflict in Market Societies*, Maaroufa Press, Chicago, IL, pp. 94–108.

Cox, K.R. 1979, *Location and Public Problems: A Political Geography of the Contemporary World*, Basil Blackwell, Oxford.

Cox, K.R. 1981, Capitalism and conflict around the communal living space, in M. Dear and A.J. Scott (eds), *Urbanization and Urban Planning in Capitalist Society*, Methuen, New York, pp. 431–56.

Craig-Smith, S. and Lisa Ruhanen, L. 2005, Implications of climate change on tourism in Oceania, in C.M. Hall and J. Higham (eds) 2005, *Tourism, Recreation and Climate Change*, Channelview Publications, Clevedon (in press).

Craik, J. 1988, The social impacts of tourism, in B. Faulkner and M. Fagence (eds), *Frontiers in Australian Tourism: The Search for New Perspectives in Policy Development and Research*, Bureau of Tourism Research, Canberra.

Craik, J. 1990, A classic case of clientelism: the Industries Assistance Commission Inquiry into Travel and Tourism, *Culture and Policy* 2(1), 29–45.

Craik, J. 1991a, *Resorting to Tourism: Cultural Policies for Tourist Development in Australia*, Allen & Unwin, St Leonards.

Craik, J. 1991b, *Government Promotion of Tourism: The Role of the Queensland Tourist and Travel Corporation*, The Centre for Australian Public Sector Management, Griffith University, Brisbane.

Crang, M. 1997, Picturing practices: research through the tourist gaze, *Progress in Human Geography* 21, 359–73.

Crang, M. 1999, Knowing, tourism and practices of vision, in D. Crouch (ed.), *Leisure/Tourism Geographies: Practices and Geographical Knowledge*, Routledge, London, pp. 238–56.

Crang, M. and Thrift, N. 2000, Introduction, in M. Crang and N. Thrift (eds), *Thinking Space*, Routledge, London.

Crawford, I.A. 2001, The scientific case for human space exploration, *Space Policy* 17(3), 155–9.

Crawshaw, C., and Urry, J. 1997, Tourism and the photographic eye, in C. Rojek and J. Urry (eds), *Touring Cultures*, Routledge, London, pp. 176–95.

Crick, M., 1989, Representations of international tourism in the social sciences: sun, sex, sights, savings, and servility, *Annual Review of Anthropology* 18, 307–44.

Crompton, J.L. 1995, Economic impact analysis of sports facilities and events: eleven sources of misapplication, *Journal of Sport Management* 9(1), 14–35.

Crompton, J.L. and Richardson, S.L. 1986, The tourism connection where public and private leisure services merge, *Parks and Recreation* October, 38–44, 67.

Crouch, D. 1994, Home, escape and identity: rural identities and sustainable tourism, *Journal of Sustainable Tourism* 2(1/2), 93–101.

Crouch, D. 1999a, Introduction: encounters in leisure/tourism, in D. Crouch (ed.), *Leisure/Tourism Geographies: Practices and Geographical Knowledge*, Routledge, London, pp. 1–16.

Crouch, D. (ed.) 1999b, *Leisure/Tourism Geographies: Practices and Geographical Knowledge*, Routledge, London.

Crouch, D. 2002, Surrounded by place, embodied encounters, in S. Coleman and M. Crang (eds), *Tourism, Between Place and Performance*, Berghahn Books, Oxford, pp. 207–18.

Crouch, D. and Lübbgren, N. (eds) 2003, *Visual Culture and Tourism*, Berg, Oxford.

Crouch, G.I. 1993, Currency exchange rates and the demand for international tourism, *Journal of Tourism Studies* 4(2), 45–53.

Crouch, G.I. 2001, Researching the space tourism market. Paper presented at the XXth Annual Conference of the Travel and Tourism Research Association, June 2001, Fort Meyers, FL.

Crouchley, R. 1987a, *Longtitudinal Data Analysis*, Avebury, Aldershot.

Crouchley, R. 1987b, An examination of the equivalence of three alternative mechanisms for establishing the equilibrium solutions of the production-constrained spatial-interaction model, *Environment and Planning A*, 19, 861–74.

Curry, J. 1993, The flexibility fetish: a review essay on flexible specialisation, *Capital and Class* 50, 99–126.

Curry, N. 1992, Recreation, access, amenity and conservation in the United Kingdom: the failure of integration, in I.R. Bowler, C.R. Bryant and M.D. Nellis (eds), *Contemporary Rural Systems in Transition*, Vol. 2, CABI, Wallingford, pp. 141–54.

Curry, N. 1994, *Countryside Recreation: Access and Land Use Planning*, E & FN Spon, London.

Curtis, A. and Lockwood, M. 2000, Landcare and catchment management in Australia: lessons for state-sponsored community participation, *Society & Natural Resources* 13, 61–73.

Daley, G. 2001, The intangible economy and Australia, *Australian Journal of Management* 26, 3–20.

Damette, E. 1980, The regional framework of monopoly exploitation: new problems and trends, in J. Carney, R. Hudson and J. Lewis (eds), *Regions in Crisis: New Perspectives in European Regional Theory*, Croom Helm, London, pp. 76–92.

Daniels, S. and Lee, R. (eds) 1996, *Exploring Human Geography: A Reader*, Arnold, London.

Dann, G.M.S. 1996, *The Language of Tourism: A Sociolinguistic Perspectice*, CABI, Wallingford.

Dann, G. and Seaton, A.V. (eds) 2001, *Slavery, Contested Heritage and Thanatourism*, The Haworth Hospitality Press, New York.

Davidson, R. and Maitland, R. 1997, *Tourism Destinations*, Hodder & Stoughton, London.

Davis, D. and Tisdell, C.A. 1994, Recreational scuba diving and carrying capacity in Marine Protected Areas, Department of Economics, University of Queensland, Brisbane.

Davis, G., Wanna, J., Warhurst, J. and Weller, P. 1993, *Public Policy in Australia*, 2nd edn, Allen & Unwin, St Leonards.

Debbage, K.G. and Daniels, P. 1998, The tourist industry and economic geography: missed opportunities, in D. Ioannides and K.G. Debbage (eds), *The Economic Geography of the Tourist Industry: A Supply-side Analysis*, Routledge, London, pp. 17–30.

de Certeau, M. 1984, *The Practice of Everyday Life*, University of California Press, Berkeley, CA.

De Franco, A. and Abbott, J. 1996, Teaching community service and the importance of citizenry, *Hospitality & Tourism Educator* 8(1), 5–7.

de Freitas, C.R. 2003, Tourism climatology: evaluating environmental information for decision making and business planning in the recreation and tourism sector, *International Journal of Biometeorology* 47(4), 190–208.

De Grey, A.D.N.J. 2003, The foreseeability of real anti-aging medicine: focusing the debate, *Experimental Gerontology* 38(9), 927–34.

Debord, G. 1973, *Society of the Spectacle*, Black and Red, Detroit, MI.

Delanty, G. 1997, Models of citizenship: defining European identity and citizenship, *Citizenship Studies* 1(3), 285–303.

Delanty, G. 1998, Social theory and European transformation: is there a European society?, *Sociological Research Online* 3(1), http://www.socreson line.org.uk/socresonline/3/1/1.html

Dendrinos, D.S. 1996, Cities as chaotic attractors, in L.D. Kiel and E. Elliott (eds), *Chaos Theory in the Social Sciences: Foundations and Applications*, University of Michigan Press, Ann Arbor, MI.

Dendrinos, D.S. and Sonis, M. 1990, *Chaos and Socio-Spatial Dynamics*, Springer, New York.

Department of Culture, Media and Sport 1999, *Policy Action Team 10: Report to the Social Exclusion Unit – Arts and Sport*, HMSO, London.

Department of Industry, Tourism and Resources (DITR) 2001, *Tourism Industry Working Group*, DITR, Canberra, http://www.industry.gov.au/content/ controlfiles/display_details.cfm?objectid=9B158B4B-BFD6-484A-81C27015 800B48DC (accessed 1 February 2002).

Department of the Environment and Ministry of Agriculture, Fisheries and Food (DoE/MAFF) 1995, *Rural England: A Nation Committed to a Living Countryside*, HMSO, London.

Department of the Environment, Transport and the Regions (DETR) 2000a, *Towards an Urban Renaissance: The Report of the Urban Task Force Chaired by Lord Rogers of Riverside*, DETR, http://www.regeneration.detr.gov.uk/utf/ renais/index.htm

Department of the Environment, Transport and the Regions 2000b, *Regeneration Research Summary: A Review of the Evidence Base for Regeneration Policy and Practice*, No. 39 http://www.regeneration.detr.gov.uk/rs/03900/ index.htm

Department of the Treasury (no date) *United States Customs Declaration*, Customs Form 6059B (101695). Department of the Treasury, Washington, DC.

Department of Tourism (Commonwealth) 1993, *Rural Tourism: Tourism Discussion Paper No.1*, Commonwealth Department of Tourism, Canberra.

Desmond, J. 1999, *Staging Tourism: Bodies on Display from Waikiki to Sea World*, University of Chicago Press, Chicago.

Dicken, P., Kelly, P.F., Olds, K. and Yeung, H.W-C. 2001, Chains and networks, territories and scales: towards a relational framework for analyzing the global economy, *Global Networks* 1, 89–112.

Dicken, P. and Oberg, S. 1996, The global context: Europe in a world of dynamic economic and population change, *European Urban and Regional Studies* 3(2), 101–20.

Dieke, P.U.C. (ed.) 2000, *The Political Economy of Tourism Development in Africa*, Cognizant, New York.

Dietz, T. 2001, Thinking about environmental conflicts, in L.M. Kadous (ed.), *Celebrating Scholarship*, College of Arts and Sciences, George Mason University, Fairfax.

Dixon, J.A., Scura, L.F. and Hof, T. 1993, *Ecology and Microeconomics as 'Joint Products': The Bonaire Marine Park in the Caribbean*, World Bank, Washington, DC.

Doeringer, B. and Terkla, D.G. 1995, Business strategy and cross-industry clusters, *Economic Development Quarterly* 9, 225–37.

Dolatyar, M. and Gray, T.S. 2000, The politics of water scarcity in the Middle East, *Environmental Politics* 9(3), 65–88.

Done, K. 2004, Europe hopes gamble on superjumbo will take off, *The Financial Times*, 8 April, p. 16.

Dovey, K. 1989, Old scabs/new scars: the hallmark event and the everyday environment, in G.J. Syme, B.J. Shaw, D.M. Fenton and W.S. Mueller (eds), *The Planning and Evaluation of Hallmark Events*, Avebury, Aldershot, pp. 73–80.

Downes, J. and Paton, T. 1993, *Travel Agency Law*, Longman, Harlow.

Downs, A. 1972, Up and down with ecology – the issue attention cycle, *The Public Interest* 28, 38–50.

DRI.WEFA 2002, *The Role of Travel and Tourism in America's Top 100 Metropolitan Areas*, prepared for the United States Conference of Mayors, The Travel Business Roundtable, The International Association of Convention and Visitors Bureaus, DRI.WEFA, Lexington, MA.

Dubé, P. and Gordon, G. 2000, Capital cities: perspectives and convergence, *Plan Canada* 40(3), 6–7.

Dublin, M. 1991, *Futurehype: The Tyranny of Prophecy*, Viking, New York.

Duffield, B.S. and Long, J. (1981) Tourism in the Highlands and Islands of Scotland: rewards and conflicts, *Annals of Tourism Research* 8(3), 403–31.

Duncan, S.S. and Goodwin, M. 1985a, Local economic policies: local regeneration or political mobilisation, *Local Government Studies* 11(6), 75–96.

Duncan, S.S. and Goodwin, M. 1985b, The local state and local economic policy: why the fuss? *Policy and Politics* 13, 247–53.

Duncan, S.S. and Goodwin, M. 1988, *The Local State and Uneven Development*, Polity Press, Cambridge.

Dunn, J. (ed.) 1995, *Contemporary Crisis of the Nation-State*, Blackwell, Oxford.

Dutton, I. and Hall, C.M. 1989, Making tourism sustainable: the policy/practice conundrum, *Proceedings of the Environment Institute of Australia Second National Conference*, Melbourne, 9–11 October.

Duval, D.T. 2002, The return visit-return migration connection, in C.M. Hall and A. Williams, (eds), *Tourism and Migration: New Relationships between Production and Consumption*, Kluwer, Dordrecht, pp. 257–76.

Duval, D.T. 2003a, Space tourism: another new tourism?, in C.M. Hall (ed.), *Introduction to Tourism: Dimensions and Issues*, 4th edn, Pearson Education, South Melbourne.

Duval, D.T. 2003b, When hosts become guests: return visits and diasporic identities in a Commonwealth Eastern Caribbean community, *Current Issues in Tourism* 6(4), 267–308.

Duval, D.T. 2004a, Conceptualising return visits: a transnational perspective, in T. Coles and D. Timothy (eds), *Tourism, Diasporas and Space: Travels to Promised Lands*, Routledge, London, pp. 50–61.

Duval, D.T. 2004b, Ethnic tourism in post-colonial environments, in C.M. Hall and H. Tucker (eds), *Tourism and Postcolonialism: Contested Discourses, Identities and Representations*, Routledge, London.

Duval, D.T. (ed.) 2004c, *Tourism in the Caribbean: Development, Management, Prospects*, Routledge, London.

Duval, D.T. 2004d, Linking return visits and return migration among Commonwealth Eastern Caribbean migrants in Toronto, Canada, *Global Networks: a Journal of Transnational Affairs* 4(1), 51–68.

Duval, D.T. and Hall, C.M. 2004, Transnational mobilities of Pacific Islanders resident in New Zealand, in T. Coles and D. Timothy (eds), *Tourism and Diaspora*, Routledge, London, pp. 78–94.

Dwyer, L. and Forsyth, P. 1996, Economic impacts of cruise tourism in Australia, *Journal of Tourism Studies* 7(2), 36–43.

Dwyer, L. and Forsyth, P. 1998, Economic significance of cruise tourism, *Annals of Tourism Research* 25(2), 393–415.

Ecologically Sustainable Development Working Groups 1991, *Final Report – Tourism*, Australian Government Publishing Service, Canberra.

Economist, The 2003, Vancouver and the Winter Olympics: somewhat cool. Will the 2010 games do British Columbia any good? *The Economist*, 5 July, p. 37.

Economist Intelligence Unit 1995, *Asia-Pacific Travel Forecasts to 2005*, Economist Intelligence Unit, London.

Economists At Large 1997, *Grand Prixtensions: The Economics of the Magic Pudding*, prepared for the Save Albert Park Group, Economists At Large, Melbourne.

Edensor, T. 1998, *Tourists at the Taj: Performance and Meaning at a Symbolic Site*, Routledge, London.

Edensor, T. 2000a, Moving through the city, in D. Bell and A. Haddour (eds), *City Visions*, Prentice Hall, Harlow.

Edensor, T. 2000b, Staging tourism: tourists as performers, *Annals of Tourism Research* 27, 322–44.

Edensor, T. 2001, Performing tourism, staging tourism – (re)producing tourist space and practice, *Tourist Studies* 1, 59–81.

Edington, J.M. and Edington, M.A. 1986, *Ecology, Recreation and Tourism*, Cambridge University Press, Cambridge.

Edwards, B.C. and Westling, E.A. 2002, *The Space Elevator: A Revolutionary Earth-to-Space Transportation System*, Spageo, San Francisco.

Elchardus, M. 1991, Flexible men and women. The changing temporal organization of work and culture: an empirical analysis, *Social Science Information* 30(4), 701–25.

Elder, G. 1987, Family history and the life-course, in T. Hareven (ed.), *The Family and the Life Course in Historical Perspective*, Academic Press, New York, pp. 19–64.

Ellegaard, K. 1999, A time-geographical approach to the study of everyday life – a challenge of complexity, *Geojournal* 48, 167–75.

Elliott, J. 1997, *Tourism: Politics and Public Sector Management*, Routledge, London.

Elsud, T. 1998, Time creation in traveling: the taking and making of time among women backpackers, *Time & Society* 7(2), 309–34.

Enright, M. and Roberts, B. 2001, Regional clustering in Australia, *Australian Journal of Management* 26, 65–86.

Erisman, H.M. 1983, Tourism and cultural dependency in the West Indies, *Annals of Tourism Research* 10, 337–61.

Environment and Social Commission for Asia and the Pacific (ESCAP, Tourism Unit) 1995a, *Guidelines on Environmentally Sound Development of Coastal Tourism*, ST/ESCAP/1371, ESCAP, Bangkok (http://unescap.org/tctd/rpt_int.htm).

ESCAP 1995b, *Planning Guidelines on Coastal Environmental Management*, ST/ESCAP/1316, ESCAP, Bangkok.

ESCAP 1996a, *Coastal Environmental Management Plan for Pakistan*, ST/ESCAP/1360, ESCAP, Bangkok.

ESCAP 1996b, *Coastal Environmental Management Plan for Macajalar Bay Area, the Philippines*, 2 vols and summary, ST/ESCAP/1359, ESCAP, Bangkok.

European Association for Tourism and Leisure Education (ATLAS) 1997, *SOCRATES Thematic Network in Tourism and Leisure*, Tilburg University, Tilburg.

European Environmental Agency 2003, *Greenhouse Gas Emission Trends and Projections in Europe 2003 Summary: Tracking Progress by the EU and Acceding and Candidate Countries Towards Achieving their Kyoto Protocol Targets*. Office for Official Publications of the European Communities, Luxembourg.

European Union 1998, *Conclusions and Recommendations of the High-level Group on Tourism and Employment*, European Commission DG XXIII, Brussels.

Evans, M. and Lunn, K. 1997, *War and Memory in the Twentieth Century*, Berg, Oxford.

Ewert, A. 1991, Outdoor recreation and global climate change: resource management implications for behaviors, planning and management, *Society and Natural Resources* 77(4), 365–77.

Farrell, A. and Hart, M. 1998, What does sustainability really mean? The search for useful indicators, *Environment* 40(9), 26–31.

Farrell, B.H. and Twining-Ward, L. 2004, Reconceptualizing tourism, *Annals of Tourism Research* 31(2), 274–95.

Faulkner, B. and Vikulov, S. 2001, Katherine, washed out one day, back on track the next: a post-mortem of a tourist disaster, *Tourism Management* 22, 331–4.

Federation of International Youth Travel Organisations 2002, *FIYTO Conference Documents*, http://www.fiyto.org/ (accessed 15 May 2003).

Feifer, M. 1985, *Tourism in History: From Imperial Rome to the Present*, Stein & Day, New York.

Feldman, M.A. 2000, Location and innovation: the new economic geography of innovation, spillovers, and agglomeration, in G. Clark, M. Feldman and M. Gertler (eds), *The Oxford Handbook of Economic Geography*, Oxford University Press, Oxford, pp. 373–94.

Fennel, D.A. 1996, A tourist space–time budget in the Shetland Islands, *Annals of Tourism Research* 23, 811–29.

Fesenmaier, D.R. and Jeng, J.-M. 2000, Assessing structure in the pleasure trip planning process, *Tourism Analysis* 5, 13–27.

Fidler, D.P. 1996, ABA sponsors program on law and emerging infectious diseases, *Journal of Emerging Infectious Diseases*, 2(4), 364.

Field, A.M. 1999, The college student market segment: a comparative study of travel behaviors of international and domestic students at a Southeastern University, *Journal of Travel Research* 37(May), 375–81.

Financial Times 2004, Nato to pay for its role at Olympics. *Financial Times* 2 April: 4.

Fincher, R. 1983, The inconsistency of eclecticism, *Environment and Planning A* 15, 607–22.

Fine, B. and Leopold, E. 1993, *The World of Consumption*, Routledge, New York.

Finney, B.R. and Watson, K.A. (eds) 1977, *A New Kind of Sugar: Tourism in the Pacific*, Center for South Pacific Studies, University of California Santa Cruz, Santa Cruz.

Finnveden, B. 1960, Den dubbla bosättningen och sommarmigrationen: exempel från Hallandskustens fritidsbebyggelse. *Svensk Geografisk Årsbok* 36, 58–84.

Fisk, D.A. and Harriott, V.J. 1989, *The Effects of Increased Sedimentation on the Recruitment and Population Dynamics of Juvenile Corals at Cape Tribulation, North Queensland*, Great Barrier Reef Marine Park Authority Technical Memorandum 20, Great Barrier Reef Marine Park Authority, Townsville.

Flognfeldt, Jr., T. 2002, Developing cultural tourism products in the 'primary attraction shadow', unpublished paper presented at the Reinventing a Tourism Destination International Conference, Dubrovnik, Croatia, October.

Fodness, D. 1994, Measuring tourist motivation, *Annals of Tourism Research* 21, 555–81.

Fodness, D. and Murray, B. 1997, Tourist information search, *Annals of Tourism Research* 24(3): 503–23.

Foley, M. and Lennon, J. 1996, JFK and Dark Tourism: a fascination with assassination, *International Journal of Heritage Studies* 2(4), 198–211.

Forbes, J. 1964, Mapping accessibility, *Scottish Geographical Magazine* 80, 12–21.

Forer, P. 1978, A place for plastic space? *Progress in Human Geography* 3, 230–67.

Fortier, A.-M. 2000, *Migrant Belongings: Memory, Space, Identity*, Berg, Oxford.

Fotheringham, A.S. 1983a, A new set of spatial-interaction models: the theory of competing destinations, *Environment and Planning A* 15, 15–36.

Fotheringham, A.S. 1983b, Some theoretical aspects of destination choice and their relevance to production constrained gravity models, *Environment and Planning A* 15, 1121–32.

Foucault, M. 1977, *Discipline and Punishment*, Penguin, Harmondsworth.

Foucault, M. 1980, *Power/Knowledge: Selected Interviews and Other Writings*, Harvester Press, Brighton.

Fowler, S. 2003, Ancestral tourism, *Insights*, March, D31–D36.

Framke, W. 2002, The destination as a concept: a discussion of the business-related perspective versus the socio-cultural approach in tourism theory, *Scandinavian Journal of Hospitality and Tourism* 2, 93–108.

Francisco, R.A. 1983, The political impact of tourism dependence in Latin America, *Annals of Tourism Research* 10, 363–76.

Frändberg, L. 1998, Distance matters: an inquiry into the relation between transport and environmental sustainability in tourism, Humanekologiska skrifter 15, Human Ecology Section, Göteborg University, Göteborg.

Frändberg, L. and Vilhelmson, B. 2003, Personal mobility – a corporeal dimension of transnationalisation: the case of long-distance travel from Sweden, *Environment and Planning A* 35(10), 1751–68.

Frankenberg, R. 1987, Life: cycle, trajectory or pilgrimage, in A. Bryman, B. Bytheway, P. Allatt and T. Keil (eds), *Rethinking the Life Cycle*, Macmillan, Basingstoke, pp. 122–38.

Franklin, A. and Crang, M. 2001, The trouble with tourism and travel theory? *Tourist Studies* 1(1), 5–22.

Frechtling, D.C. 1996, Practical Tourism Forecasting, Butterworth-Heinemann, Oxford.

Freeman, C. 1991, Networks of innovators: a synthesis of research issues, *Research Policy* 20, 499–514.

Fretter, A.D. 1993, Place marketing: a local authority perspective, in G. Kearns and C. Philo (eds), *Selling Places: The City as Cultural Capital, Past and Present*, Pergamon Press, Oxford, pp. 163–74.

Fridgen, J. 1984, Environmental psychology and tourism, *Annals of Tourism Research* 11, 19–39.

Friedman, J. 1994, *Cultural Identity and Global Process*, Sage, London.

Friedmann, J. 1966, *Regional Development Policy: A Case Study of Venezuela*, MIT Press, Cambridge, MA.

Friedmann, J. 1980, An alternative development?, in J. Friedmann, E. Wheelwright and J. Connell (eds), *Development Strategies in the Eighties. Development Studies Colloquium, Monograph No. 1*, University of Sydney, Sydney, pp. 4–11.

Fry, E.H. 1998, *The Expanding Role of State and Local Governments in US Foreign Affairs*, Council on Foreign Relations Press, New York.

Fry, E.H. 1999, North American cities in an era of economic globalization, in C. Andrew, P. Armstrong and A. Pierre (eds), *World Class Cities*, University of Ottawa Press, Ottawa.

Fry, E.H. 2003, *Substate Strategies in an Era of Globalization and the Information Technology Revolution*, working paper, Department of Political Science, Brigham Young University, Salt Lake City, UH.

Fukuyama, F. 1995, *Trust: The Social Virtues and the Creation of Prosperity*, Free Press, New York.

Fuller, R.B. 1969, *Utopia or Oblivion*, Bantam Books, New York.

Fuller, R.B. 1981, *Critical Path*, St. Martin's Press, New York.

Furbey, R. 1999, Urban 'regeneration': reflections on a metaphor, *Critical Social Policy* 19(4), 419–45.

Gajaraj, A.M. 1988, A regional approach to environmentally sound tourism development, *Tourism Recreation Research* 13, 509.

Gallent, N. 1997, Improvement grants, second homes and planning control in England and Wales: a policy review, *Planning Practice & Research* 12, 401–11.

Gallent, N. and Tewdwr-Jones, M. 2000, *Rural Second Homes in Europe: Examining Housing Supply and Planning Control*, Ashgate, Aldershot.

Galston, W.A. and Baehler, K.J. 1995, *Rural Development in the United States: Connecting Theory, Practice and Possibilities*, Island Press, Washington, DC.

Gans, H.J. 1979, Symbolic ethnicity: the future of ethnic groups and cultures in America, *Ethnic and Racial Studies* 2, 1–20.

Gärling, T. and Golledge, R. (eds) 1993, *Behavior and Environment: Psychological and Geographical Approaches*, North-Holland, Amsterdam.

Garner, B. 1967, Models of urban geography and settlement location, in R.J. Chorley and P. Haggett (eds), *Models in Geography*, Methuen, London, pp. 303–60.

Garrod, B. and Wilson, J.C. (eds) 2003, *Marine Ecotourism: Issues and Experiences*, Channelview, Clevedon.

Garrod, B. and Wilson, J.C. 2004, Nature on the edge? Marine ecotourism in peripheral coastal areas, *Journal of Sustainable Tourism* 12(2), 95–120.

Gartner, W.C. 1987, Environmental impacts of recreational home developments, *Annals of Tourism Research* 14(1), 38–57.

Gartner, W.C. and Lime, D.W. (eds) 2000, *Trends in Outdoor Recreation, Leisure and Tourism*, CABI, Wallingford.

Gartner, W.C. and Shen, J. (1992), The impact of Tiananmen Square on China's tourism image, *Journal of Travel Research* 30(4), 47–52.

Gatrell, A.C. 1983, *Distance and Space: A Geographical Perspective*, Clarendon Press, Oxford.

Georggi, N.L. and Pendyala, R.M. 2001, Analysis of long-distance travel behavior of the elderly and low income', in *Personal Travel: The Long and Short of It, Conference Proceedings* June 28–July 1, 1999 Washington, DC, TRB Transportation Research Circular E-C026, Transportation Research Board, Washington, DC.

Gergen, K.J. 1991, *The Saturated Self: Dilemmas of Identity in Contemporary Life*, Basic Books, New York.

German Federal Agency for Nature Conservation (GFANC) (ed.), 1997, *Biodiversity and Tourism: Conflicts on the World's Seacoasts and Strategies for their Solution*, Springer, Berlin.

Gershuny, J. 1993, Post-industrial convergence in time allocation, *Futures* 25(5), 578–87.

Getz, D. 1987, Tourism planning and research: traditions, models and futures, paper presented at The Australian Travel Research Workshop, Bunbury, Western Australia, 5–6 November.

Getz, D. 1991, *Festivals, Special Events, and Tourism*, Van Nostrand Reinhold, New York.

Getz, D. 1994, Resident's attitudes towards tourism: a longitudinal study in Spey Valley, Scotland, *Tourism Management* 15(4), 247–58.

Getz, D. and Carlsen, J. 2000, Characteristics and goals of family and owner-operated businesses in the rural tourism and hospitality sectors, *Tourism Management* 21, 547–60.

Getz, D., Carlsen, J. and Morrison, A. 2004, *The Family Business in Tourism and Hospitality*, CABI, Wallingford.

Gibb, A. and Davies, L. 1990, In pursuit of frameworks for the development of growth models of the small firm, *International Small Business Journal* 9(1), 15–31.

Gibb, A. and Davies, L. 1992, Methodological problems in the development of a growth model of business enterprise, *The Journal of Entrepreneurship* 1(1), 3–36.

Gibson-Graham, J.K. 1996, *The End of Capitalism (as we knew it): A Feminist Critique of Political Economy*, Blackwell, Oxford.

Giddens, A. 1981, *A Contemporary Critique of Historical Materialism. Vol. One: Power, Property and the State*, Macmillan, London.

Giddens, A. 1984, *The Constitution of Society: Outline of the Theory of Structuration*, University of California Press, Berkeley.

Giddens, A. 1990, *The Consequences of Modernity*, Polity Press, Cambridge.

Giddens, A. 1991, *Modernity and Self-Identity*, Polity Press, Cambridge.

Gieryn, T.F. 2000, A space for place in Sociology, *Annual Review of Sociology* 26, 463–96.

Gilbert, D. and Hudson, S. 2000, Tourism demand constraints: skiing participation, *Annals of Tourism Research* 27(4), 906–25.

Gilbert, E.W. 1939, The growth of inland and seaside health resorts in England, *Scottish Geographical Magazine*, 55, 16–35.

Gill, A. 1998, Local and resort development, in R. Butler, C.M. Hall and J. Jenkins (eds), *Tourism and Recreation in Rural Areas*, John Wiley & Sons, Chichester, pp. 97–111.

Ginzburg, H.M. 1996, Commentary – Needed: comprehensive response to the spread of infectious diseases, *Journal of Emerging Infectious Diseases* 2(2), 151.

Girard, T.C. and Gartner, W.C. 1993, Second home, second view: host community perceptions, *Annals of Tourism Research* 20(4), 685–700.

Glancey, K. 1998, Determinants of growth and profitability in small entrepreneurial firms, *International Journal of Entrepreneurial Behaviour & Research* 4(1), 18–27.

Glasgow, F. 2003, Francophiles clipped at the wings, *The Financial Times*, 27–28 September, Weekend W16.

Glennie, P.D. and Thrift, N. 1992, Modernity, urbanism and modern consumption, *Environment and Planning D: Society and Space* 10, 423–43.

Glick, P. 1947, The family life cycle, *American Sociological Review* 12, 164–74.

Glyptis, S. 1989, *Leisure and Unemployment*, Open University Press, Milton Keynes.

Go, F.M. and Pine, R. 1995, *Globalization Strategy in the Hotel Industry*, Routledge, London.

Godde, P., Price, M.F. and Zimmerman, F.M. (eds) 2000, *Tourism and Development in Mountain Regions*, CABI, Wallingford.

Goffmann, E. 1959, *The Presentation of the Self in Everyday Life*, Penguin, Harmondsworth.

Goodchild, M.F. 2004, The validity and usefulness of laws in Geographic Information Science and Geography, *Annals of the Association of American Geographers*, 94(2), 300–3.

Goodchild, M.F. and Janelle, D.G. 1984, The city around the clock: space–time patterns of urban ecological structure, *Environment and Planning A* 16, 807–20.

Goodrich, J.N. 1991, Industry in a crisis: the impact of the Persian Gulf War on the US travel industry, *Journal of Travel Research* 30(2), 36–7.

Goodrich, J.N. 1993, Socialist Cuba: a study of health tourism, *Journal of Travel Research* 32(1), 36–42.

Goodrich, J.N. 1994, Health tourism: a new positioning strategy for tourist destinations, *Journal of International Consumer Marketing* 6(3/4), 227–37.

Goodrich, J.N. and Goodrich, G.E. 1987, Health-care tourism – an exploratory study, *Tourism Management* 8, 217–22.

Goodwin, M. 1993, The city as commodity: the contested spaces of urban development, in G. Kearns and C. Philo (eds), *Selling Places: The City as Cultural Capital, Past and Present*, Pergamon Press, Oxford, pp. 145–62.

Goodwin, M. and Painter, J. 1996, Local governance, the crisis of Fordism and the changing geographies of regulation, *Transactions, Institute of British Geographers*, new series 21, 635–48.

Gore, A. (1992), *Earth in the Balance: Ecology and the Human Spirit*, Houghton Mifflin, New York.

Gormsen, E. 1997, The impact of tourism on coastal areas, *GeoJournal* 42(1), 39–54.

Gössling, S. 2001a, Tourism, environmental degradation and economic transition: interacting processes in a Tanzanian coastal community, *Tourism Geographies* 3(4), 230–54.

Gössling, S. 2001b, The consequences of tourism for sustainable water use on a tropical island: Zanzibar, Tanzania, *Journal of Environmental Management* 61(2), 179–91.

Gössling, S. 2002, Global environmental consequences of tourism, *Global Environmental Change* 12(4), 283–302.

Gössling, S. (ed.) 2003, *Tourism and Development in Tropical Islands: Political Ecology Perspectives*, Edward Elgar, Cheltenham.

Gössling, S. 2005, Tourism's contribution to global environmental change, in C.M. Hall and J. Higham (eds), *Tourism, Recreation and Climate Change*, Channelview, Clevedon.

Gössling, S., Borgström-Hansson, C., Hörstmeier, O. and Saggel, S. 2002, Ecological footprint analysis as a tool to assess tourism sustainability, *Ecological Economics* 43(2/3), 199–211.

Gotham, K. 2002, Marketing Mardi Gras: commodification, spectacle, and the political economy of tourism in New Orleans, *Urban Studies* 39(10), 1735–57.

Gottmann, J. 1983, Capital cities, *Ekistics* 50, 88–93.

Graber, K. 1997, Cities and the destination life cycle, in J.A. Mazanec (ed.), *International City Tourism: Analysis and Strategy*, Pinter, London, pp. 39–53.

Graham, B., 2002, Heritage as knowledge: capital or culture? *Urban Studies* 39(5/6), 1003–18.

Graham, B., Ashworth, G.J. and Tunbridge, J.E. 2000, *A Geography of Heritage*, Edward Arnold, London.

Graham, M. 1990, Culture shock, *Asia Travel Trade* 22(February), 24–6.

Gratton, C. 1999, *Sports-Related Industry Study: Final Report*, Manchester City Council and Northwest Development Agency, Manchester.

Graves, H.S. 1920, A crisis in national recreation, *American Forestry* 26(July), 391–400.

Graves, P. 1979a, Income and migration revisited, *Journal of Human Resources* 14, 112–21.

Graves, P. 1979b, A life-cycle empirical analysis of migration and climate, by race, *Journal of Urban Economics* 6, 135–47.

Graves, P. 1980, Migration and climate, *Journal of Regional Science* 20, 227–37.

Graves, P. 1983, Migration with a composite amenity: the role of rents, *Journal of Regional Science* 23, 541–6.

Graves, P. and Linnemann, P.D. 1979, Household migration: theoretical and empirical results, *Journal of Urban Economics* 6, 383–404.

Graves, P. and Regulska, J. 1982, Amenities and migration over the life cycle, in D. Diamond and G. Tolley (eds), *The Economics of Urban Amenities*, Academic Press, New York, pp. 211–21.

Graves, P. and Waldman, D. 1991, Multimarket amenity compensation and the behavior of the elderly, *American Economic Review* 81, 1374–81.

Gray, B. 1985, Conditions facilitating interorganizational collaboration, *Human Relations* 38(10), 911–36.

Gray, B. 1989, *Collaborating: Finding Common Ground for Multiparty Problems*, Jossey-Bass, San Francisco.

Green, G.P., Marcouiller, D., Deller, S., Erkkila, D. and Sumathi, N.R. 1996, Local dependency, land use attitudes, and economic development: comparisons between seasonal and permanent residents, *Rural Sociology* 61(3), 427–45.

Green, W. 2001, *Review of Current Biosecurity Research in New Zealand*, Biosecurity Strategy Development Team, Wellington.

Greenbank, P. 2001, Objective setting in the micro-business, *International Journal of Entrepreneurial Behaviour & Research* 7(3), 108–27.

Gregory, D. 1985, Suspended animation: the status of diffusion theory, in D. Gregory and J. Urry (eds), *Social Relations and Spatial Structures*, Macmillan, London, pp. 296–336.

Gregory, D. 1986, Time-geography, in R.J. Johnston, D. Gregory and D.M. Smith (eds), *The Dictionary of Human Geography*, 2nd edn, Blackwell, Oxford, pp. 485–7.

Gregory, D. 1994, Social theory and human geography, in D. Gregory, R. Martin and G. Smith (eds), *Human Geography: Society, Space and Social Science*, Macmillan, Basingstoke, pp. 78–112.

Gregory, D., Martin, R. and Smith, G. (eds) 1994, Introduction, in D. Gregory, R. Martin and G. Smith (eds), *Human Geography: Society, Space and Social Science*, Macmillan, Basingstoke, pp. 1–18.

Gren, M. 2001, Time-geography matters, in J. May and N. Thrift (eds), *Timespace, Geographies of Temporality*, Routledge, London, pp. 208–25.

Grigg, D. 1967, Regions, models and classes, in R.J. Chorley and P. Haggett (eds), *Models in Geography*, Methuen, London, pp. 461–510.

Gunn, C. 1979, *Tourism Planning*, Taylor and Francis, London.

Gunn, C.A. 1994, *Tourism Planning*, 3rd edn, Taylor and Francis, London.

Gurr, T.R. 1985, On the political consequences of scarcity and economic decline, *International Studies Quarterly* 29, 51–75.

Gushulak, B.D. and MacPherson, D.W. 2001, Human mobility and population health: new approaches in a globalizing world, *Perspectives in Biology and Medicine* 44(3), 390–401.

Gustafson, P. 2002, *Place, Place Attachment and Mobility: Three Sociological Studies*, Department of Sociology, Göteborg University, Göteborg.

Haas, W. and Serow, W. 1993, Amenity retirement migration process, *The Gerontologist* 33, 212–20.

Haftendorn, H. 2000, Water and international conflict, *Third World Quarterly* 21(1), 51–68.

Hägerstrand, T. 1952, *The Propagation of Innovation Waves*, Lund Studies in Geography, Series B, Human Geography, No. 4, Department of Geography, The Royal University of Lund, Lund.

Hägerstrand, T. 1965, A Monte Carlo approach to diffusion, *Archives Européennes de Sociologie* 6, 43–7.

Hägerstrand, T. 1967a, *Innovation Diffusion as a Spatial Process* (translated by A. Pred), University of Chicago Press, Chicago, IL.

Hägerstrand, T. 1967b, On the Monte Carlo simulation of diffusion, in W.L. Garrison and D.F. Marble (eds), *Quantitative Geography. Part 1: Economic and Cultural Topics*, Northwestern University Press, Evanston, IL, pp. 1–32.

Hägerstrand, T. 1970, What about people in regional science? *Papers of the Regional Science Association* 24, 7–21.

Hägerstrand, T. 1973, The domain of human geography, in R.J. Chorley (ed.), *Directions in Geography*, Methuen, London, pp. 67–87.

Hägerstrand, T. 1982, Diorama, path and project, *Tijdschrift voor Economische en Sociale Geografie* 73, 323–39.

Hägerstrand, T. 1984, Presence and absence: a look at conceptual choices and bodily necessities, *Regional Studies* 18, 373–80.

Haggett, P. 1965, *Locational Analysis in Human Geography*, Edward Arnold, London.

Haggett, P., Cliff, A.D. and Frey, A. 1977, *Locational Analysis in Human Geography*, Edward Arnold, London.

Haines-Young, R. 1989, Modelling geographic knowledge, in B. Macmillan (ed.), *Remodelling Geography*, Basil Blackwell, Oxford, pp. 22–39.

Haines-Young, R.H. and Petch, J.H. 1986, *Physical Geography: Its Nature and Methods*, Harper & Row, London and New York.

Hakim, C. 1987, *Research Design: Strategies and Choices in the Design of Social Research*, Allen & Unwin, London.

Halfacree, K. 1994, The importance of 'the rural' in the construction of counter-urbanization: evidence from England in the 1980s, *Sociologia Ruralis* 34, 164–89.

Halfacree, K. 1995, Talking about rurality: social representations of the rural as expressed by residents of six English parishes, *Journal of Rural Studies* 11, 1–20.

Halfacree, K. 1996, Out of place in the country: travellers and the 'rural idyll', *Antipode* 28, 42–72.

Hall, C.M. 1989a, The definition and analysis of hallmark tourist events, *Geojournal* 19(3), 263–68.

Hall, C.M. 1989b, The politics of hallmark events, in G.J. Syme, B.J. Shaw, D.M. Fenton and W.S. Mueller (eds), *The Planning and Evaluation of Hallmark Events*, Avebury, Aldershot, pp. 219–41.

Hall, C.M. 1992a, *Hallmark Tourist Events: Impacts, Management, and Planning*, Belhaven Press, London.

Hall, C.M. 1992b, Tourism in Antarctica: activities, impacts, and management, *Journal of Travel Research*, 30(4), 2–9.

Hall, C.M. 1994a, *Tourism and Politics: Policy, Power and Place*, John Wiley, Chichester.

Hall, C.M. 1994b, *Tourism in the Pacific Rim: Development, Impacts and Markets*, Longman Cheshire, South Melbourne.

Hall, C.M. 1995, Tourism and regional development: softening the blows of changing times, in *National Regional Tourism Conference*, Tourism Council Australia, Launceston.

Hall, C.M. 1996a, Hallmark events and urban reimaging strategies: coercion, community, and the Sydney 2000 Olympics, in L.C. Harrison and W. Husbands (eds), *Practicing Responsible Tourism: International Case Studies in Tourism Planning, Policy, and Development*, John Wiley, New York, pp. 366–79.

Hall, C.M. 1996b, Environmental impact of tourism in the Pacific, in C.M. Hall and S. Page (eds), *Tourism in the Pacific: Issues and Cases*, Routledge, London, pp. 65–80.

Hall, C.M. 1996c, Tourism prostitution: the control and health implications of sex tourism in South-East Asia and Australia, in S. Clift and S. Page (eds), *Health and the International Tourist*, Routledge, London, pp. 179–97.

Hall, C.M. 1997a, Geography, marketing and the selling of places, *Journal of Travel and Tourism Marketing* 6, 61–84.

Hall, C.M. 1997b, Mega-events and their legacies, in P. Murphy (ed.), *Quality Management in Urban Tourism*, John Wiley & Sons, Chichester, pp. 75–87.

Hall, C.M. 1997c, *Tourism in the Pacific Rim*, 2nd edn, Pearson, Melbourne.

Hall, C.M. 1998, The institutional setting: tourism and the state, in D. Ioannides and K. Debbage (eds), *The Economic Geography of the Tourist Industry: A Supply-side Analysis*, Routledge, London, pp. 199–219.

Hall, C.M. 1999, Tourism and the environment: problems, institutional arrangements and approaches, in C.M. Hall and S. Page (eds), *Tourism in South and South-East Asia: Critical Perspectives*, Butterworth-Heinemann, Oxford, pp. 94–103.

Hall, C.M. 2000a, *Tourism Planning*, Prentice Hall, Harlow.

Hall, C.M. 2000b, Territorial economic integration and globalisation, in C. Cooper and S. Wahab (eds), *Tourism and Globalisation*, Routledge, London, pp. 22–44.

Hall, C.M. 2001a, Imaging, tourism and sports event fever: the Sydney Olympics and the need for a social charter for mega-events, in C. Gratton and I.P. Henry (eds), *Sport in the City: The Role of Sport in Economic and Social Regeneration*, Routledge, London, pp. 166–83.

Hall, C.M. 2001b, Japan and tourism in the Pacific Rim: locating a sphere of influence in the global economy, in D. Harrison (ed.), *Tourism and the Less Developed Countries*, CABI, Wallingford, pp. 121–36.

Hall, C.M. 2002a, Local initiatives for local regional development: the role of food, wine and tourism, in The Second Tourism Industry and Education Symposium, 'Tourism and Well-Being', 16–18 May 2002, Jyväskylä Polytechnic, Jyväskylä, Finland, pp. 47–63.

Hall, C.M. 2002b, Travel safety, terrorism and the media: the significance of the issue–attention cycle, *Current Issues in Tourism* 5(5), 458–66.

Hall, C.M. (ed.) 2003a, *Introduction to Tourism: Dimensions and Issues*, 4th edn, Pearson Education, South Melbourne.

Hall, C.M. 2003b, Health and spa tourism, in S. Hudson (ed.), *International Sports and Adventure Tourism*, Haworth Press, New York, pp. 273–92.

Hall, C.M. 2003c, Tourism and temporary mobility: circulation, diaspora, migration, nomadism, sojourning, travel, transport and home, paper presented at the International Academy for the Study of Tourism (IAST) Conference, 30 June–5 July 2003, Savonlinna, Finland.

Hall, C.M. 2003d, Institutional arrangements for ecotourism policy, in D. Fennell and R. Dowling (eds), *Ecotourism: Policy and Strategy Issues*, CABI, Wallingford, pp. 21–38.

Hall, C.M. 2003e, Packaging Canada/packaging places: tourism, culture, and identity in the 21st century, in C. Gaffield and K. Gould (eds), *The Canadian Distinctiveness into the XXIst Century*, International Canadian Studies Series, International Council of Canadian Studies and the Institute of Canadian Studies, University of Ottawa Press, Ottawa.

Hall, C.M. 2003f, Politics and place: an analysis of power in tourism communities, in S. Singh, D. Timothy and R. Dowling (eds), *Tourism in Destination Communities*, CABI, Wallingford, pp. 99–114.

Hall, C.M. 2003g, Nature-based tourism development and its local connections, Nature and locality as Tourist Attractions, 7th National Nature-Based Tourism Symposium, Finnish Forest Research Institute (Metla), 27–28 August, University of Lapland and Finnish University Network for Tourism Studies, Punkaharju, Finland.

Hall, C.M. 2003h, North–South perspectives on tourism, regional development and peripheral areas, paper presented at the Perspectives on Tourism in Nordic and Other Peripheral Areas International Conference, 21 August, Umea, Sweden.

Hall, C.M. 2004a, Reflexivity and tourism research: situating myself and/with others, in J. Phillimore and L. Goodson (eds), *Qualitative Research in Tourism*, Routledge, London, pp. 137–55.

Hall, C.M. 2004b, Tourism and mobility, in *Creating Tourism Knowledge, 14th International Research Conference of the Council for Australian University Tourism and Hospitality Education*, 10–13 February, School of Tourism and Leisure Management, University of Queensland, Brisbane.

Hall, C.M. 2004c, The relevance of tourism knowledge: for what and for whom?, *Creating Tourism Knowledge, 14th International Research Conference of the Council for Australian University Tourism and Hospitality Education*, 10–13 February, School of Tourism and Leisure Management, University of Queensland, Brisbane.

Hall, C.M. 2004d, Small firms and wine and food tourism in New Zealand: issues of collaboration, clusters and lifestyles, in R. Thomas (ed.), *Small Firms in Tourism: International Perspectives*, Elsevier, Oxford, pp. 167–81.

Hall, C.M. 2004e, Tourism and biosecurity, in C. Cooper, C. Arcodia, D. Soinet and M. Whitford (eds), *Creating Tourism Knowledge, 14th International Research Conference of the Council for Australian University Tourism and Hospitality Education*, 10–13 February, School of Tourism and Leisure Management, University of Queensland, Brisbane.

Hall, C.M. 2005, Space–time accessibility and the tourist area cycle of evolution: the role of geographies of spatial interaction and mobility in contributing to an improved understanding of tourism, in R. Butler (ed.), *The Tourism Life Cycle: Conceptual and Theoretical Issues*, Channelview Publications, Clevedon.

Hall, C.M. and Boyd, S. (eds) 2005, *Tourism and Nature-based Tourism in Peripheral Areas: Development or Disaster*, Channelview Publications, Clevedon.

Hall, C.M. and Butler, D. 1995, In search of common ground: reflections on sustainability, complexity and process in the tourism system, *Journal of Sustainable Tourism* 3(2), 99–105.

Hall, C.M. and Higham, J. (eds) 2005, *Tourism, Recreation and Climate Change*, Channelview Publications, Clevedon.

Hall, C.M. and Hodges, J. 1996, The party's great, but what about the hangover?: the housing and social impacts of mega-events with special reference to the Sydney 2000 Olympics, *Festival Management & Event Tourism* 4(1/2), 13–20.

Hall, C.M. and Jenkins, J. 1995, *Tourism and Public Policy*, Routledge, London.

Hall, C.M. and Jenkins, J. 1998, Rural tourism and recreation policy dimensions, in R.W. Butler, C.M. Hall and J. Jenkins (eds), *Tourism and Recreation in Rural Areas*, John Wiley, Chichester, pp. 19–42.

Hall, C.M. and Johnson, G. 1998, Wine tourism: an imbalanced partnership', in R. Dowling and J. Carlsen (eds), *Wine Tourism Perfect Partners, Proceedings of the First Australian Wine Tourism Conference,* Margaret River, Western Australia, May 1998. Bureau of Tourism Research, Canberra, pp. 51–72.

Hall, C.M. and Johnston, M. (eds) 1995, *Polar Tourism: Tourism in Arctic and Antarctic Regions*, John Wiley, Chichester.

Hall, C.M. and Lew, A. (eds) 1998, *Sustainable Tourism Development: Geographical Perspectives*. Addison Wesley Longman, Harlow.

Hall, C.M. and McArthur, S. (eds) 1996, *Heritage Management in Australia and New Zealand: The Human Dimension*, Oxford University Press, Sydney.

Hall, C.M. and McArthur, S. 1998, *Integrated Heritage Management*, HMSO, London.

Hall, C.M. and Müller, D. (eds) 2004a, *Tourism, Mobility and Second Homes: Between Elite Landscape and Common Ground*, Channelview, Clevedon.

Hall, C.M. and Müller, D. 2004b, Introduction. Second homes: curse or blessing revisited, in C.M. Hall and D. Müller (eds), *Tourism, Mobility and Second Homes: Between Elite Landscape and Common Ground,* Channelview Publications, Clevedon, pp. 3–14.

Hall, C.M. and Oehlers, A. 1999, Tourism and politics in South and Southeast Asia: political instability and policy, in C.M. Hall and S. Page (eds), *Tourism in South and South-East Asia: Critical Perspectives*, Butterworth-Heinemann, Oxford, pp. 79–94.

Hall, C.M. and O'Sullivan, V. 1996, Tourism, political instability and socal unrest, in A. Pizam and Y. Mansfield (eds), *Tourism, Crime and International Security Issues*, John Wiley, Chichester, pp. 105–21.

Hall, C.M. and Page, S. (eds) 1996, *Tourism in the Pacific: Issues and Cases*, Routledge, London.

Hall, C.M. and Page, S. 1999a, Developing tourism in South Asia: India, Pakistan and Bangladesh – SAARC and beyond, in C.M. Hall and S. Page (eds), *Tourism in South and South-east Asia: Critical Perspectives*, Butterworth-Heinemann, Oxford, pp. 197–224.

Hall, C.M. and Page, S. 1999b, *The Geography of Tourism and Recreation*, Routledge, London.

Hall, C.M. and Page, S.J. 2002, *The Geography of Tourism and Recreation*, 2nd edn, Routledge, London.

Hall, C.M. and Rusher, K. 2004, Risky lifestyles? Entrepreneurial characteristics of the New Zealand bed and breakfast sector, in R. Thomas (ed.), *Small Firms in Tourism: International Perspectives*, Elsevier, Oxford, pp. 83–97.

Hall, C.M. and Tucker, H. (eds) 2004a, *Tourism and Postcolonialism: Contested Discourses, Identities and Representations*, Routledge, London.

Hall, C.M. and Tucker, H. 2004b, Tourism and postcolonialism: an introduction, in C.M. Hall and H. Tucker (eds), *Tourism and Postcolonialism: Contested Discourses, Identities and Representations*, Routledge, London, pp. 184–190.

Hall, C.M. and Williams, A.M. (eds) 2002a, *Tourism and Migration: New Relationships Between Consumption and Production*, Kluwer, Dortrecht.

Hall, C.M. and Williams, A.M. 2002b, Conclusions: Tourism–migration relationships, in C.M. Hall and A.M. Williams (eds), *Tourism and Migration: New Relationships Between Production and Consumption*, Kluwer, Dordrecht, pp. 277–89.

Hall, C.M., Cambourne, B., Macionis, N. and Johnson, G. 1997, Wine tourism and network development in Australia and New Zealand: review, establishment and prospects, *International Journal of Wine Marketing* 9(2/3): 5–31.

Hall, C.M., Johnson, G. and Mitchell, R. 2000, 'Wine tourism and regional development, in C.M. Hall, E. Sharples, B. Cambourne and N. Macionis (eds), *Wine Tourism Around the World: Development, Management and Markets*, Butterworth-Heinemann, Oxford, pp. 196–226.

Hall, C.M., Longo, A.M., Mitchell, R. and Johnson, G. 2000, Wine tourism in New Zealand, in C.M. Hall, E. Sharples, B. Cambourne and N. Macionis (eds), *Wine Tourism Around the World: Development, Management and Markets*, Butterworth-Heinemann, Oxford, pp. 150–74.

Hall, C.M., Mitchell, R. and Sharples, L. 2003, Consuming places: the role of food, wine and tourism in regional development, in C.M. Hall, E. Sharples, R. Mitchell, B. Cambourne and N. Macionis (eds), *Food Tourism Around the World: Development, Management and Markets*, Butterworth-Heinemann, Oxford, pp. 25–59.

Hall, C.M., Sharples, E., Cambourne, B. and Macionis, N. (eds) 2000, *Wine Tourism Around the World: Development, Management and Markets*, Butterworth-Heinemann, Oxford.

Hall, C.M., Sharples, E. and Smith, A. 2003, The experience of consumption or the consumption of experiences?: challenges and issues in food tourism, in C.M. Hall, E. Sharples, R. Mitchell, B. Cambourne and N. Macionis (eds),

Food Tourism Around the World: Development, Management and Markets, Butterworth-Heinemann, Oxford, pp. 314–35.

Hall, C.M., Timothy, D. and Duval, D. (eds) 2004, *Safety and Security in Tourism: Relationships, Management and Marketing*, The Haworth Hospitality Press, Binghampton.

Hall, C.M., Williams, A.M. and Lew, A. 2004, Tourism: conceptualisations, institutions and issues, in A. Lew, C.M. Hall and A.M. Williams (eds), *Companion to Tourism*, Blackwells, Oxford, in press.

Hall, D. 1997, Sustaining tourism development in the fragile Balkan periphery of Europe, in Peripheral Area Tourism: International Tourism Research Conference, Bornholm, 8–12 September 1997, Unit of Tourism Research at the Research Centre of Bornholm, Bornholm.

Hall, D.R. (ed.) 1991a, *Tourism and Economic Development in Eastern Europe and the Soviet Union*, Belhaven Press, London.

Hall, D.R. 1991b, Introduction, in D.R. Hall (ed.), *Tourism and Economic Development in Eastern Europe and the Soviet Union*, Belhaven Press, London, pp. 3–28.

Hall, D.R. 1998, Rural diversification in Albania, *GeoJournal* 46(3), 283–7.

Hall, D.R. (ed.) 2004, *Tourism and Transition: Governance, Transformation and Development*, CABI, Wallingford.

Hall, J., and Braithwaite, R. 1990, Caribbean cruise tourism: a business of transnational partnerships, *Tourism Management* 11(4), 339–47.

Hall, P. 1992, *Urban and Regional Planning*, 3rd edn, Routledge, London and New York.

Hall, S. 1988, Brave new world, *Marxism Today*, October, pp. 24–9.

Hamblin, A.P. 2001, Sustainability indicators: measuring progress towards sustainability, in J. Venning and J, Higgins (eds), *Towards Sustainability: Emerging Systems for Informing Sustainable Development*, University of New South Wales Press, Sydney, pp. 139–64.

Hand, D.J. 1996, *Practical Longitudinal Data Analysis*, Chapman and Hall, London.

Handy, S.L. and Niemeier, D.A. 1997, Measuring accessibility: an exploration of issues and alternatives, *Environment and Planning A* 29(7), 1175–94.

Hanink, D.M. 1995a, The evaluation of wilderness in a spatial context, *Growth and Change* 26, 423–39.

Hanink, D.M. 1995b, The economic geography in economic issues: a spatial-analytical approach, *Progress in Human Geography* 19, 372–87.

Hanink, D.M. and Stutts, M. 2002, Spatial demand for US National Battlefield Parks, *Annals of Tourism Research* 29, 708–20.

Hanink, D.M. and White, K. 1999, Distance effects in the demand for wildland recreation services: the case of national parks in the United States, *Environment and Planning A* 31, 477–92.

Hanley, R. 1997, *The Metaphysics of Star Trek*, Basic Books, New York.

Hanna, N. and Wells, S. 1992, Sea sickness, *In Focus* (Tourism Concern) 5, 4–6.

Hannifin, J. and Le Quesne, N. 1998, Flights of fantasy, *Time Asia* 151(24), 22 June.

Hannigan, J. 1995, The postmodern city: a new urbanisation, *Current Sociology* 43(1), 151–217.

Hansen, W.G. 1959, How accessibility shapes land use, *Journal of the American Institute of Planners* 25, 73–6.

Hanson, S. and Johnston, I. 1985, Gender differences in work-trip length: explanations and implications, *Urban Geography* 6(3), 193–219.

Hanson, S. and Pratt, G. 1999, Geographic perspectives on the occupational segregation of women, *National Geographic Research* 6(4), 376–99.

Hardin, G. 1968, The tragedy of the commons, *Science* 162, 1243–8.

Harding, L. 2003, Mallorca laments missing German tourists, *The Guardian*, 4 October, p. 15.

Härkönen, T. and Hall, C.M. (eds) 2005, *Lake Tourism: An Integrated Approach to Lacustrine Tourism Systems*, Channelview Press, Clevedon (in press).

Harper, D.A. 1993, *An Analysis of Interfirm Networks*, NZ Institute of Economic Research, Wellington.

Harris, C. 1987, The individual and society: a processual approach, in A. Bryman, B. Bytheway, P. Allatt and T. Keil (eds), *Rethinking the Life Cycle*, Macmillan, Basingstoke, pp. 17–29.

Harris, P. 1995, *Accounting and Finance for the International Hospitality Industry*, Butterworth-Heinemann, Oxford.

Harrison, D. (ed.) 1992a, *Tourism and the Less Developed Countries*, Belhaven Press, London.

Harrison, D. 1992b, International tourism and the less developed countries: the background, in D. Harrison (ed.), *Tourism and the Less Developed Countries*, Belhaven Press, London, pp. 1–18.

Harrison, D. (ed.) 2001, *Tourism and the Less Developed Countries*, CABI, Wallingford.

Harvey, D. 1969, *Explanation in Geography*, Edward Arnold, London.

Harvey, D. 1973, *Social Justice and the City*, Johns Hopkins University Press, Baltimore, MD.

Harvey, D. 1982, *The Limits of Capital*, University of Chicago Press, Chicago, IL.

Harvey, D. 1987, Flexible accumulation through urbanisation, *Antipode* 19, 260–86.

Harvey, D. 1988, Voodoo cities, *New Statesman and Society*, 30 September, pp. 33–5.

Harvey, D. 1989a, From managerialism to entrepreneurialism: the transformation in urban governance in late capitalism, *Geografiska Annaler* 71B, 3–17.

Harvey, D. 1989b, *The Condition of Postmodernity: An Enquiry into the Origins of Cultural Change*, Basil Blackwell, Oxford.

Harvey, D. 1989c, *The Urban Experience*, Blackwell, London.

Harvey, D. 1990, Between space and time: reflection on the geographic information, *Annals Association of American Geographers* 80, 418–34.

Harvey, D. 1993, From space to place and back again: reflections on the condition of postmodernity, in J. Bird, B. Curtis, T. Putnam, G. Robertson and L. Tickner (eds), *Mapping the Futures: Local Cultures, Global Change*, Routledge, London and New York, pp. 3–29.

Harvey, D. 1996, *Justice, Nature and the Geography of Difference*, Blackwell, Oxford.

Harvey, D. 2000, *Spaces of Hope*, University of California Press, Berkeley, CA.

Harvey, D. and Scott, A.J. 1987, The nature of human geography: theory and empirical specificity in the transition from Fordism to flexible accummulation, paper presented to the Quantitative Methods Study Group of the Institute of British Geographers, 10 April.

Hastad, D., Segrave, J., Pangrazi, R. and Petersen, G. 1984, Youth sport participation and deviant behavior, *Sociology of Sport Journal* 1, 366–73.

Haulot, A. 1981, Social tourism: current dimensions and future developments, *Tourism Management* 2, 207–12.

Hawken, P. 1984, *The Next Economy*, Henry Holt and Co., New York.

Hawkins, J.P. and Roberts, C.M. 1994, The growth of coastal tourism in the Red Sea: present and future effects on coral reefs, *Ambio* 23(8), 503–8.

Haynes, K.E. and Fotheringham, A.S. 1984, *Gravity and Spatial Interaction Models*, Sage, Newbury Park, CA.

Haywood, K.M. 1988, Responsible and responsive tourism planning in the community, *Tourism Management* 9(2), 105–18.

Healey, P. 1997, *Collaborative Planning: Shaping Places in Fragmented Societies*, Macmillan, London.

Heath, E. and Wall, G. 1992, *Marketing Tourism Destinations: A Strategic Planning Approach*, John Wiley, New York.

Hebdidge, D. 1979, *Subculture: The Meaning of Style*, Methuen, London.

Heintzmann, P. 2000, Leisure and spiritual well-being relationship: a qualitative study, *Leisure and Society* 23(1), 41–69.

Henderson, J.C. 2000, War as a tourist attraction: the case of Vietnam, *International Journal of Tourism Research* 2, 269–80.

Henley Centre for Forecasting (1989) *The Economic Impact and Importance of Sport in Two Local Areas: Bracknell and The Wirral*, Sports Council, London.

Henry, G.T. and Gordon, C.S. 2001, Tracking issue attention, *Public Opinion Quarterly* 65(2), 157–77.

Henton, D. and Walesh, K. 1997, *Grassroots Leaders for a New Economy: How Civic Entrepreneurs are Building Prosperous Communities*, Jossey-Bass, San Francisco.

Hester, G. and Gonzenbach, W. 1997, The environment: TV news, real world cues, and public opinion over time, *Mass Communication Review* 22(1), 5–20.

Hewison, R. 1991, Commerce and culture, in J. Corner and S. Harvey (eds), *Enterprise and Heritage: Crosscurrents of National Culture*, Routledge, London and New York, pp. 162–77.

Higgott, R. 1999, The political economy of globalisation in East Asia: the salience of 'region building', in K. Olds, P. Dicken, P.F. Kelly, L. Kong and H.W. Yeung (eds), *Globalisation and the Asia-Pacific: Contested Territories*, Routledge, London, pp. 91–106.

Hill, M.R. 1981, Positivism: a 'hidden' philosophy in geography, in M.E. Harvey and B.P. Holly (eds), *Themes in Geographic Thought*, Croom Helm, London.

Hiller, H. 2000, Mega-events, urban boosterism and growth strategies: an analysis of the objectives and legitimations of the Cape Town 2004 Olympic bid, *International Journal of Urban and Regional Research* 24(2), 439–58.

Hills, T.L. and Lundgren, J. 1977, The impact of tourism in the Caribbean: a methodological study, *Annals of Tourism Research* 4, 248–67.

Hinch, T. and Higham, J. 2003, *Sport Tourism Development*, Channelview, Clevedon.

Hing, N. and Lomo, E. 1997, Careers for tourism graduates: choice or chance? *Hospitality & Tourism Educator*, 9(1), 77–89.

Hirst, P. 1997, The global economy – myths and realities, *International Affairs* 73(3), 409–25.

Hirst, P. and Thompson, G. 1996, *Globalization in Question*, Polity Press, Cambridge.

Hivik, T. and Heiberg, T. 1980, Centre–periphery tourism and self-reliance, *International Social Science Journal* 32(1), 69–98.

Hockings, M.A. 1994, Survey of the tour operator's role in marine park interpretation, *The Journal of Tourism Studies* 5(1), 16–28.

Hoggart, K. 1989, Not a definition of rural, *Area* 20: 35–40.

Hoggart, K. 1990, Let's do away with rural, *Journal of Rural Studies* 6: 245–57.

Hoggart, K. and Buller, H. 1995, Geographical differences in British property acquisitions in rural France, *Geographical Journal* 161, 69–78.

Hohn, C. 1987, The family life cycle: needs extensions of the concept, in J. Bongaarts, T. Burch, and K. Wachter (eds), *Family Demography: Methods and Their Application*, Clarendon Press, Oxford, pp. 65–80.

Holcomb, B. 1993, Revisioning place: de- and re-constructing the image of the industrial city, in G. Kearns and C. Philo (eds), *Selling Places: The City as Cultural Capital, Past and Present*, Pergamon Press, Oxford, pp. 133–43.

Holloway, C. 1994, *The Business of Tourism*, Pitman, London.

Holmes, J. and Brown, J. 1981, Travel behaviour of isolated rural populations in inland Queensland, in R. Lonsdale and J. Holmes (eds), *Settlement Systems in Sparsely Populated Regions: The United States and Australia*, Pergamon, New York, pp. 215–37.

Hooghe, L. and Marks, G. 2003, Unravelling the central state, but how? Types of multi-level governance, *American Political Science Review* 97(2), 233–43.

Hookway, J. 2003, From Cebu to ceboom, *Far Eastern Economic Review*, 16 October, pp. 42–4.

Hopley, D., van Woesik, R., Hoyal, D.C.J.D., Rasmussen, C.E. and Steven, A.D.L. 1993, *Sedimentation Resulting from Road Development, Cape Tribulation Area*, Great Barrier Reef Marine Park Authority Technical Memorandum 24, Great Barrier Reef Marine Park Authority, Townsville, Queensland.

Hornaday, J.A. and Aboud, J. 1971, Characteristics of successful entrepreneurs, *Personnel Psychology* 24, 141–53.

Horner, S. and Swarbrooke, J. 1996, *Marketing Tourism Hospitality and Leisure in Europe*, ITBP, London.

Hornstein, S. and Jacobowitz, F. (eds) 2003, *Image and Remembrance: Representation and the Holocaust*, Indiana University Press, Bloomington, IN.

Hotz-Hart, B. 2000, Innovation networks, regions, and globalization, in G. Clark, M. Feldman and M. Gertler (eds), *The Oxford Handbook of Economic Geography*, Oxford University Press, Oxford, pp. 432–52.

Høyer, K.G. 2000, Sustainable tourism or sustainable mobility? The Norwegian case, *Journal of Sustainable Tourism* 8(2), 147–61.

Høyer, K.G. and Aall, C. 2005, Sustainable mobility and sustainable tourism, in C.M. Hall and J. Higham (eds), *Tourism, Recreation and Climate Change*, Channelview, Clevedon.

Hsu, C.H.C. and Sung, S. 1996, International students' travel characteristics: an exploratory study, *Journal of Travel and Tourism Marketing* 5(Winter), 277–83.

Hsu, C.H.C. and Sung, S.1997, Travel behaviors of international students at a midwestern university, *Journal of Travel Research* 36(Summer), 59–65.

Hubbard, P., Kitchin, R., Bartley, B. and Fuller, D. 2002, *Thinking Geographically: Space, Theory and Contemporary Human Geography*, Continuum, London.

Hudson, B. 1996, Paradise lost: a planner's view of Jamaican tourist development, *Caribbean Quarterly* 42(4), 22–31.

Hudson, R. 1988, Uneven development in capitalist societies: changing spatial divisions of labour, forms of spatial organisation of production and service provision, and their impacts upon localities, *Transactions of the Institute of British Geographers* new series 13, 484–96.

Hudson, R. 1999, 'The learning economy, the learning firm and the learning region': a sympathetic critique of the limits to learning', *European Urban and Regional Studies* 6(1), 59–72.

Hudson, R. 2000, *Production, Places and the Environment: Changing Perspectives in Economic Geography*, Prentice Hall Pearson Education, Harlow.

Hudson, R. and Townsend, A. 1992, Tourism employment and policy choices for local government, in P. Johnson and B. Thomas (eds), *Perspectives on Tourism Policy*, Mansell, London, pp. 49–68.

Hughes, H.L. 1984, Government support for tourism in the UK: a different perspective, *Tourism Management* 5(1), 13–19.

Hughes, H.L. 1993, Olympic tourism and urban regeneration, *Festival Management and Event Tourism* 1(4), 157–62.

Ilbery, B. 1984, Core–periphery contrasts in European social well-being, *Geography* 69, 289–302.

Ilbery, B. (ed.) 1998, *The Geography of Rural Change*, Longman, London.

Ilbery, B. and Bowler, I. 1998, From agricultural productivism to post-productivism, in B. Ilbery (ed.), *The Geography of Rural Change*, Longman, London, pp. 57–84.

Ilbery, B. and Kneafsey, M. 2000a, Registering regional specialty food and drink products in the United Kingdom: the case of PDOs and PGIs, *Area* 32(3), 317–25.

Ilbery, B. and Kneafsey, M. 2000b, Producer constructions of quality in regional speciality food production: a case study from south west England, *Journal of Rural Studies* 16, 217–30.

Imbroscio, D.L., Williamson, T. and Alperovitz, G. 2003, Local policy responses to globalization: place-based ownership models of economic enterprise, *Policy Studies Journal* 31(1), 31–52.

Independent Commission on Disarmament and Security Issues (the Palme Commission) 1982, *Common Security: A Blueprint for Survival*, Simon & Schuster, New York.

Industry Commission 1995, *Tourism Accommodation and Training*, Industry Commission, Melbourne.

Ingram, D.R. 1971, The concept of accessibility: a search for an operational form, *Regional Studies* 5, 101–7.

Inkson, K., Arthur, M.B., Pringle, J.K. and Barry, S. 1997, Expatriate assignment versus overseas experience: contrasting models of human resource development, *Journal of World Business* 32(4), 351–68.

Inkson, K., Thomas, D. and Barry, S. 1999, Overseas experience – a competitive advantage? *University of Auckland Business Review* 1(1), 1–10.

Inskeep, E. 1991, *Tourism Planning: An Integrated and Sustainable Development Approach*, Van Nostrand Reinhold, New York.

Institute of Leisure and Amenity Management (ILAM) 1999, *The Contribution of the Arts and Sport to Neighbourhood Renewal and Reducing Social Inclusion*, ILAM, Reading.

Intergovernmental Panel on Climate Change 2001b, *Climate Change 2001: Impacts, Adaptation and Vulnerability*, United Nations Intergovernmental Panel on Climate Change, Geneva.

International Panel on Climate Change (IPCC) 2001a, *Summary for Policymakers. Climate Change 2001: Impacts, Adaptation and Vulnerability, A Report of Working Group II of the International Panel on Climate Change*, IPCC, Geneva.

International Union of Official Travel Organisations (IUOTO) 1974, The role of the state in tourism, *Annals of Tourism Research* 1(3), 66–72.

Invest Beijing 2004, Advertisement: Market Promotion Conference on Olympic Economy, *The Far Eastern Economic Review*, 8 April, p. 15.

Ioannides, D. and Cohen, M.W. 2002, Pilgrimages of nostalgia: patterns of Jewish travel in the United States, *Tourism Recreation Research* 27(2), 17–25.

Ioannides, D. and Debbage, K. (eds) 1998, *The Economic Geography of the Tourist Industry: A Supply-side Analysis*, Routledge, London and New York.

Iyengar, S. and Kinder, D.K. 1987, *News That Matters: Television and American Opinion*, University of Chicago Press, Chicago, IL.

Iyer, P. 2000, *The Global Soul: Jetlag, Shopping Malls, and the Search for Home*, Alfred Knopf, New York.

Jaakson, R. 1986, Second-home domestic tourism, *Annals of Tourism Research* 13, 357–91.

Jacobs, J. 1961, *The Death and Life of Great American Cities*, Penguin, Harmondsworth.

Jafari, J. 1977, Editor's page, *Annals of Tourism Research* 5, 11.

Jafari, J. and Ritchie, J.R.B. 1981, Toward a framework for tourism education problems and prospects, *Annals of Tourism Research* 8, 13–34.

Jakle, J., Brunn, S. and Roseman, C.C. 1976, *Human Spatial Behavior*, Duxbury Press, North Scitate.

Jamal, M. and Badawi, J.A. 1995, Nonstandard work schedules and work and nonwork experiences of Muslim immigrants: a study of a minority in the majority, *Journal of Social Behavior and Personality* 10(2), 395–408.

Jamal, T.B. and Getz, D. 1995, Collaboration theory and community tourism planning, *Annals of Tourism Reseach* 22, 186–204.

Jameson, F. 1984, Postmodernism, or the cultural logic of late capitalism, *New Left Review* 146, 53–92.

Jamieson, J.W. 1999, Migration as an economic and political weapon, *Journal of Social, Political & Economic Studies* 24(3), 339–48.

Janelle, D.G. 1968, Central place development in a time-space framework, *Professional Geographer* 20, 5–10.

Janelle, D.G. 1969, Spatial reorganization: a model and concept, *Annals of the Association of American Geographers* 59: 348–64.

Janelle, D.G. 1973, Measuring human extensibility in a shrinking world, *Journal of Geography* 72, 8–15.

Janelle, D.G. 1974, Transportation innovation and the reinforcement of urban hierarchies, *High Speed Ground Transportation Journal* 8, 261–9.

Janelle, D.G. 1975, Time space convergence and urban transportation issues, in C.K. Blong (ed.), *Systems Thinking and the Quality of Life*, The Society for General Systems Research, Washington, DC, pp. 594–600.

Janelle, D.G. 1995, Metropolitan expansion, telecommuting, and transportation, in S. Hanson (ed.), *The Geography of Urban Transportation*, 2nd edn, Guilford Press, New York, pp. 407–34.

Janelle, D.G. and Goodchild, M.F. 1983, Diurnal patterns of social group distributions in a Canadian city, *Economic Geography* 59, 403–25.

Janelle, D.G., Goodchild, M.F. and Klinkenberg, B. 1998, The temporal ordering of urban space and daily activity patterns for population role groups, *Geographical Systems* 5, 117–37.

Janelle, D.G. and Hodge, D. (eds) 2000, *Information, Place, and Cyberspace: Issues in Accessibility*, Springer-Verlag, Berlin.

Jansen-Verbeke, M. 1989, Inner cities and urban tourism in the Netherlands: new challenges for local authorities, in P. Bramham, I. Henry, H. Mommaas and H. van der Poel (eds), *Leisure and Urban Processes: Critical Studies of Leisure Policy in Western European Cities*, Routledge, London and New York, pp. 233–53.

Jansson, B. and Müller, D.K. 2003, *Fritidsboende i Kvarken*, Kvarkenrådet, Umeå.

Jansson, B. and Müller, D. (eds) 2005, *Tourism in High Latitude Peripheries: Space, Place and Environment*, CABI, Wallingford (in press).

Jeffries, D. 1989, Selling Britain – a case for privatisation? *Travel and Tourism Analyst* 1, 69–81.

Jenkins, C. and Henry, B. 1982, Government involvement in tourism in developing countries, *Annals of Tourism Research* 9(4), 499–521.

Jenkins, J. 1997, The role of the Commonwealth Government in rural tourism and regional development in Australia, in C.M. Hall, J. Jenkins and G. Kearsley (eds), *Tourism Planning and Policy in Australia and New Zealand: Cases, Issues and Practice*, Irwin Publishers, Sydney.

Jenkins, J. 2001, Statutory authorities in whose interests? The case of Tourism New South Wales, the bed tax, and 'the Games', *Pacific Tourism Review* 4(4), 201–18.

Jenkins, J. and Walmesley, D.J. 1993, Mental maps of tourists: a study of Coffs Harbour, New South Wales, *GeoJournal* 29(3), 233–41.

Jenkins, J., Hall, C.M. and Troughton, M. 1998, The restructuring of rural economies: rural tourism and recreation as a government response, in R. Butler, C.M. Hall and J. Jenkins (eds), *Tourism and Recreation in Rural Areas*, John Wiley, Chichester, pp. 43–68.

Jensen, R. 1999, *The Dream Society*, McGraw-Hill, London.

Jeong, G.-H. 1988, Tourism expectations on the 1988 Seoul Olympics: a Korean perspective, in *Tourism Research: Expanding Boundaries, Travel and Tourism Research Association, Nineteenth Annual Conference*, Bureau of Economic and Business Research, Graduate School of Business, University of Utah, Salt Lake City, UT, pp. 175–82.

Jessop, B. 1999, Reflections on globalisation and its (il)logic(s), in K. Olds, P. Dicken, P.F. Kelly, L. Kong and H.W. Yeung (eds), *Globalisation and the Asia–Pacific: Contested Territories*, Routledge, London, pp. 19–38.

Johnston, C.S. 2001, Shoring the foundations of the destination life cycle model, part 1: ontological and epistemological, *Tourism Geographies* 3(1), 2–28.

Johnston, R. 1986, *On Human Geography*, Basil Blackwell, Oxford.

Johnston, R.J. 1991, *Geography and Geographers: Anglo-American Human Geography since 1945*, 4th edn, Edward Arnold, London.

Johnston, R.J., Taylor, P.J. and Watts, M.J. (eds) 1995, *Geographies of Global Change: Remapping the World in the Late Twentieth Century*, Blackwell, Oxford.

Joint Standing Committee on Migration 1997, *Working Holiday Makers: More Than Tourists*, Australian Government Publishing Service, Canberra.

Jones, P. (ed.) 1990, *Developments in Dynamic and Activity-Based Approaches to Travel Analysis*, Gower, Aldershot.

Jones, P. and Lockwood, A. 1989, *The Management of Hotel Operations: An Innovative Approach to the Study of Hotel Management*, Cassell, London.

Jones, P. and Merricks, P. 1996, *The Management of Foodservice Operations*, Cassell, London.

Jones, R. and Birdsall-Jones, C. 2003, Native or manufactured? A comparison of indigenous–industrial heritage conflicts in Perth and Ottawa, *Australian-Canadian Studies* 21(2), 73–106.

Jones, S.B. 1933, Mining tourist towns in the Canadian Rockies, *Economic Geography* 9, 368–78.

Jordan, P. 1994, The impact of wars in Croatia and Bosnia-Hercegovina on the tourism of the Croatian coast, paper presented at the International Geographical Union Study Group on Sustainable Tourism Symposium on Tourism Geography, August, Lillehammer, Norway.

Judd, D. and Fainstein, S. (eds) 1999, *The Tourist City*, Yale University Press, New Haven, CT.

Judd, D. and Parkinson, M. 1990, *Leadership and Urban Regeneration: Cities in North America and Europe*, Sage, Thousand Oaks, CA.

Julesrosette, B. 1994, Black Paris: touristic simulations, *Annals of Tourism Research* 21, 679–700.

Kadak, A.C. 2000, Intergenerational risk decision making: a practical example, *Risk Analysis* 20, 883–94.

Käferstein, F.F. Motarjemi, Y. and Bettcher, D.W. 1997, Foodborne disease control: a transnational challenge, *Journal of Emerging Infectious Diseases* 3(4), 503–10.

Kahn, H. and Wiener, A.J. 1967, *The Year 2000*, Macmillan, New York.

Kalinowski, K.M., 1992, Universities and educational travel programs: the University of Alberta, in B. Weiler and C.M. Hall (eds), *Special Interest Tourism*, Belhaven Press, London, pp. 27–35.

Kalinowski, K.M. and Weiler, B. 1992, Educational travel, in B. Weiler and C.M. Hall (eds), *Special Interest Tourism*, Belhaven Press, London, pp. 15–26.

Kaltenborn, B.P. 1997a, Nature of place attachment: a study among recreation homeowners in Southern Norway, *Leisure Sciences* 19, 175–89.

Kaltenborn, B.P. 1997b, Recreation homes in natural settings: factors affecting place attachment, *Norsk Geografisk Tidsskrift* 51, 187–98.

Kaltenborn, B.P. 1998, The alternative home: motives of recreation home use, *Norsk Geografisk Tidsskrift* 52(3), 121–34.

Kaplan, R. 1994, The coming anarchy, *The Atlantic Monthly* (February), 45–76.

Kaufmann, V. 2002, *Rethinking Mobility*, Ashgate, Aldershot.

Kearns, G. and Philo, C. (eds) 1993a, *Selling Places: The City as Cultural Capital, Past and Present*, Pergamon Press, Oxford.

Kearns, G. and Philo, C. 1993b, Preface, in G. Kearns and C. Philo (eds), *Selling Places: The City as Cultural Capital, Past and Present*, Pergamon Press, Oxford, pp. ix–x.

Keats, B.W. and Bracker, J.S. 1988, Toward a theory of small firm performance: a conceptual model, *American Journal of Small Business* Spring, 41–58.

Keller, H., Lamprocht, M. and Stamm, H. 1998, *Social Cohesion Through Sport*, Committee for the Development of Sport, Council of Europe, Strasbourg.

Kelly, P.F. and Olds, K. 1999, Questions in a crisis: the contested meanings of globalisation in the Asia-Pacific, in K. Olds, P. Dicken, P.F. Kelly, L. Kong and H.W. Yeung (eds), *Globalisation and the Asia–Pacific: Contested Territories*, Routledge, London, pp. 1–15.

Kenyon, S., Lyons, G. and Rafferty, J. 2002, Transport and social exclusion: investigating the possibility of promoting inclusion through virtual mobility, *Journal of Transport Geography* 10, 207–19.

Keohane, R.O. and Nye, Jr., J.S. 1976, Introduction: the complex politics of Canadian-American interdependence, in A.B. Fox, A.O. Hero Jr. and J.S. Nye Jr. (eds), *Canada and the United States: Transnational and Transgovernmental Relations*, Columbia University Press, New York.

Kerr, W.R. 2003, *Tourism Public Policy and the Strategic Management of Failure*, Pergamon, Oxford.

Kester, J.G.C. 2003, Cruise tourism, *Tourism Economics* 9(3), 337–50.

Kim, S. and Kim, Y. 1996, Overview of coastal and marine tourism in Korea, *Journal of Tourism Studies* 7(2), 46–53.

King, D.A. 2004, Climate change science: adapt, mitigate, or ignore? *Science* 303(9 January), 176–7.

King, R., Warnes, A.M. and Williams, A.M. 2000, *Sunset Lives: British Retirement to the Mediterranean*, Berg, London.

Kinnaird, B. 1999, Working holiday makers: more than tourists. Implications of the Joint Standing Committee on Migration, *People and Place* 7(1), 39–52.

Klieger, P.C. 1992, Shangri-La and the politicization of tourism in Tibet, *Annals of Tourism Research*, 19, 122–5.

Klir, G.J. and Elias, D. 2003, *Architecture of Systems Problem Solving*, 2nd edn, Kluwer, New York.

Klir, G.J. and Rozehnal, I. 1996, Epistemological categories of systems: an overview, *International Journal of General Systems* 24(1/2), 207–24.

Kneafsey, M. 2000, Tourism, place identities and social relations in the European rural periphery, *Urban and Regional Studies* 7(1), 35–50.

Knipp, S. 1990, A long hard march ahead, *PATA Travel News* (October), 22–3.

Knowles, T. 1998, *Hospitality Management: An Introduction*, 2nd edn, Longman, Harlow.

Knox, P. and Agnew, J. 1989, *The Geography of the World Economy*, Edward Arnold, London.

Koh, K. 1995, Designing the 4–year tourism management curriculum: a marketing approach, *Journal of Travel Research* 34(1), 68–72.

Kooiman, J. (ed.) 1993a, *Modern Governance: New Government–Society Interactions*, Sage, London.

Kooiman, J. 1993b, Findings, speculations and recommendations, in J. Kooiman (ed.), *Modern Governance: New Government–Society Interactions*, Sage, London.

Kooiman, J. 2003, *Governing as Governance*, Sage, London.

Kotler, P., Bowen, J. and Makens, J. 1997, *Marketing for Hospitality and Tourism*, Prentice Hall, London.

Kotler, P., Haider, D.H. and Rein, I. 1993, *Marketing Places: Attracting Investment, Industry, and Tourism to Cities, States, and Nations*, Free Press, New York.

Kozak, M. 2004, *Destination Benchmarking: Concepts, Practices and Operations*, CABI, Wallingford.

Kraft, R.M., Ballatine, J. and Garvey, D.E. 1993–94, Study abroad or international travel? The case of semester at sea, *Phi Beta Delta International Review* IV(Fall/Spring), 23–61.

Kraus, L.M. 1995, *The Physics of Star Trek*, Basic Books, New York.

Krugman, P. 1991, *Geography and Trade*, Leuven University Press, Leuven, and MIT Press, Cambridge, MA.

Kuji, T. 1991, The political economy of golf, *AMPO, Japan-Asia Quarterly Review* 22(4), 47–54.

Kumar, K. 1995, *From Post-Industrial to Post-Modern Society: New Theories of the Contemporary World*, Blackwell, Oxford.

Kwan, M.-P. 1998, Space–time and integral measures of individual accessibility: a comparative analysis using a point-based framework, *Geographical Analysis* 30(3), 191–216.

Kwan, M.-P. 1999, Gender and individual access to urban opportunities: a study using space–time measures, *Professional Geographer* 51(2), 210–27.

Kwan, M.-P. 2000, Gender differences in space–time constraint, *Area* 32(2), 145–56.

Lagarigue, P. 1988, L'exportation des techniques d'aménagement littoral (Exporting coastal development techniques), *Espaces* 90, 30–2.

Lane, B. 1994, What is rural tourism? *Journal of Sustainable Tourism* 2(1/2), 7–12.

Lansbury, C. 1970, *Arcady in Australia: The Evocation of Australia in Nineteenth-century English Literature*, Melbourne University Press, Carlton.

Lansky, D. 2003, Three decades on a lonely planet, *Scanorama* (October), 32–3.

Lanzendorf, M. 2000, Social change and leisure mobility, *World Transport Policy & Practice* 6(3), 21–5.

Larbalestier, J. 1994, Imagining the city: contradictory tales of space and place, in K. Gibson and S. Watson (eds), *Metropolis Now: Planning and the Urban in Contemporary Australia*, Pluto Press, Annandale, NSW, pp. 186–95.

Larsen, E.R. 2001, *Revealing Demand for Nature Experience Using Purchase Data of Equipment and Lodging*, Discussion Papers No. 305, Statistics Norway, Research Department, Oslo.

Larsen, J. 2001, Tourism mobilities and the travel glance: experiences of being on the move, *Scandinavian Journal of Hospitality and Tourism* 1, 80–98.

Lash, S. and Urry, J. 1994, *Economies of Signs and Space*, Sage, London.

Laurier, E. 1993, 'Tackintosh': Glasgow's supplementary gloss, in G. Kearns and C. Philo (eds), *Selling Places: The City as Cultural Capital, Past and Present*, Pergamon Press, Oxford, pp. 267–90.

Lavery, P. 1989, Tourism in China: the costs of collapse, *EIU Travel & Tourism Analyst* 4, 77–97.

Law, C. 1985, *Urban Tourism: Selected British Case Studies*, Working Paper, Department of Geography, University of Salford, Salford.

Law, C. 1992, Urban tourism and its contribution to economic regeneration, *Urban Studies* 29(3/4): 599–618.

Law, C. 1993, *Urban Tourism: Attracting Visitors to Large Cities*, Mansell, London.

Law, C. (ed.) 1996, *Tourism in Major Cities*, International Thomson Business Press, London.

Law, R. 2001, A study of the impact of the Asian financial crisis on the accuracy of tourist arrival forecasts, *Journal of Hospitality and Leisure Marketing* 8(1/2), 5–18.

Lawson, C. and Lorenz, E. 1999, Collective learning, tacit knowledge and regional innovative capacity, *Regional Studies* 33, 305–17.

Lawson, F. 1995, *Hotels and Resorts: Planning, Design and Refurbishment*, Architectural Press, London.

Lawson, F. and Baud-Bovy, M. 1977, *Tourism and Recreation Development: A Handbook of Physical Planning*, The Architectural Press, London.

Lawson, H. 1985, *Reflexivity: Problems of Modern European Thought*, Anchor, London.

Lawton, G. and Page, S. 1997, Evaluating travel agents' provision of health advice to travelers, *Tourism Management* 18(2), 89–104.

Lea, J. 1988, *Tourism and Development in the Third World*, Routledge, London.

Lea, J. and Small, J. 1988, Cyclones, riots and coups: tourist industry responses in the South Pacific, paper presented at Frontiers in Australian Tourism Conference, August, Australian National University, Canberra, Australia.

Leborgne, D. and Lipietz, A. 1992, Conceptual fallacies and open questions on post-Fordism, in M. Storper and A.J. Scott (eds), *Pathways to Industrialization and Regional Development*, Routledge, London, pp. 332–48.

Lee, C., Duxbury, L., Higgins, C. and Mills, S. 1992, Strategies used by employed parents to balance the demands of work and family, *Optimum* 23(2), 60–9.

Lee, H.M. 2003, *Tongans Overseas: Between Two Shores*, University of Hawai'i Press, Honolulu.

Lee, J. and Dennis, A. 2004, Australia's image gets a makeover, *The Age*, 17 April, p. 14.

Legors, F., and Danis, M. 1998, Surveillance of malaria in European Union countries, *Eurosurveillance* 3, 45–7.

Leidner, R. 1993, *Fast Food, Fast Talk: Service Work and the Routinization of Everyday Life*, University of California Press, Berkeley.

Leiper, N. 1979, The framework of tourism: towards a definition of tourism, tourist, and the tourist industry, *Annals of Tourism Research* 6, 390–407.

Leiper, N. 1981, Towards a cohesive curriculum in tourism: the case for a distinct discipline, *Annals of Tourism Research*, 8, 69–74.

Leiper, N. 1989, *Tourism and Tourism Systems*, Occasional Paper No. 1, Department of Management Systems, Massey University, Palmerston North, New Zealand.

Leiper, N. 1990a, *Tourism Systems: An Interdisciplinary Perspective*, Occasional Paper No. 2, Department of Management Systems, Business Studies Faculty, Massey University, Palmerston North, New Zealand.

Leiper, N. 1990b, Partial industrialization of tourism systems, *Annals of Tourism Research* 17, 600–5.

Leiper, N. 1995, *Tourism Management*, RMIT Press, Melbourne.

Leiper, N. 2000a, An emerging discipline, *Annals of Tourism Research*, 27(3), 805–9.

Leiper, N. 2000b, Are destinations 'the heart of tourism'? The advantages of an alternative description, *Current Issues in Tourism* 3, 364–8.

Leisure Industries Research Centre 1997, *A Review of the Economic Impact of Sport: Final Report,* Leisure Industries Research Centre, Sheffield Hallam University, Sheffield.

Lennon, J. and Foley, M. 2000, *Dark Tourism: The Interaction of Death and Disaster*, Continuum, London.

Leopold, A. 1921, The wilderness and its place in forest recreational policy, *Journal of Forestry* 19(7), 718–21.

Levinson, D. and Kumar, A. 1995, Activity, travel and the allocation of time, *Journal of the American Planning Association* 61, 458–70.

Levy, M.A. 1995, Is the environment a national security issue? *International Security* 20(2), 35–62.

Lew, A. and Hall, C.M. 1998, The geography of sustainable tourism: lessons and prospects, in C.M. Hall and A. Lew (eds), *Sustainable Tourism: A Geographical Perspective*, Addison Wesley Longman, Harlow, pp. 199–203.

Lew, A., Hall, C.M. and Williams, A.M. (eds) 2004, *Companion to Tourism*, Blackwell, Oxford.

Lewis, J. and Williams, A.M. 1988, Portugal: market segmentation and regional specialisation, in A.M. Williams and G. Shaw (eds), *Tourism and Economic Development: Western European Experiences*, Belhaven Press, London, pp. 101–22.

Ley, D. and Mercer, J. 1980, Locational conflict and the politics of consumption, *Economic Geography* 56, 89–109.

Leyshon, A. 1997, True stories? Global dreams, global nightmares, and writing globalisation, in R. Lee and J. Wills (eds), *Geographies of Economies*, Arnold, London, pp. 133–46.

Li, W.L. and Li, Y. 1995, Special characteristics of China's interprovincial migration, *Geographical Analysis* 27(2), 137–51.

Lichtheim, G. 1974, *Imperialism*, Penguin, Harmondsworth.

Light, D. 2000, Fly guise, *The Bulletin*, 11 July, p. 60.

Lindroth, K. and Soisalon-Soininen, T. 2004, Regional tourism co-operation in progress, paper presented at ATLAS Annual Conference, Networking and Partnerships in Destination Development and Management, 3–6 April, Naples.

Livingstone, D.N. and Harrison, R.T. 1981, Meaning through metaphors: analogy as epistemology, *Annals of the Association of American Geographers* 71, 95–107.

Löfgren, O. 1999, On Holiday: *A History of Vacationing*, University of California Press, Berkeley.

Logan, J.R. and Molotch, H.L. 1987, *Urban Fortunes: The Political Economy of Place*, University of California Press, Berkeley.

Loker-Murphy, L. and Pearce, P.L. 1995, Young budget travellers: backpackers in Australia, *Annals of Tourism Research* 22(4), 819–43.

Long, J. and Sanderson, I. 1998, Social benefits of sport: where's the proof?, in *Sport in the City: Conference Proceedings*, Vol. 2, 2–4 July, Loughborough University/Sheffield Hallam University/The University of Sheffield, Sheffield, pp. 295–324.

Lösch, A. 1954, *The Economics of Location*, Yale University Press, New Haven, CT.

Lowe, M. 1993, Local hero! An examination of the role of the regional entrepreneur in the regeneration of Britain's regions, in G. Kearns and C. Philo (eds), *Selling Places: The City as Cultural Capital, Past and Present*, Pergamon Press, Oxford, pp. 211–30.

Lowell, L. 1999, Skilled temporary specialty workers in the United States, *People and Place* 7(1), 24–32.

Lück, M. 2003, Education on marine mammal tours as agent for conservation – but do tourists want to be educated? *Ocean & Coastal Management* 46, 943–56.

Lumsdon, L. and Page, S.J. (eds) 2004, *Tourism and Transport: Issues and Agenda for the New Millennium*, Elsevier Science, Amsterdam.

Lundvall, B.-A. 1992, *National Systems of Innovation: Towards a Theory of Innovation and Interactive Learning*, Pinter, London.

Lundvall, B.-A. and Johnson, B. 1994, The learning economy, *Journal of Industry Studies* 1(2), 23–42.

Lundvall, B.-A. and Maskell, P. 2000, National states and economic development: from national systems of production to national systems of knowledge creation and learning, in G. Clark, M. Feldman and M. Gertler (eds), *The Oxford Handbook of Economic Geography*, Oxford University Press, Oxford, pp. 353–72.

Lynch, K. 1972, *What Time is This Place?* MIT Press, Cambridge, MA.

Lynch, P. 1998, Female micro-entrepreneurs in the host family sector: key motivations and socio-economic variables, *Hospitality Management* 17, 319–42.

Mabogunje, A.L. 1980, *The Development Process: A Spatial Perspective*, Hutchinson, London.

MacCannell, D. 1999, *The Tourist: A New Theory of the Leisure Class*, 2nd edn, University of California Press, Berkeley.

MacCannell, D. 2001, Tourist agency, *Tourist Studies* 1(1), 23–37.

MacCormick, N. 1993, Beyond the sovereign state, *The Modern Law Review* 56(1), 1–18.

MacCormick, N. 1996, Liberalism, nationalism and the postsovereign state, *Political Studies* 44(3), 553–67.

Madre, J. and Maffre, J. (2001) Is it necessary to collect data on daily mobility and long-distance travel in the same survey? in *Personal Travel: The Long and Short of It, Conference Proceedings June 28–July 1, 1999, Washington, D.C.*, TRB Transportation Research Circular E–C026, Transportation Research Board, Washington, DC, pp. 343–64.

Madsen, H. 1992, Place-marketing in Liverpool: a review, *International Journal of Urban and Regional Research* 16(4), 633–40.

Maier, S. (ed.) 1987, *Changing Boundaries of the Political*, Cambridge University Press, Cambridge.

Maitland, A. 2004, The growing burden of a labour of love. *The Financial Times*, 8 April, p. 10.

Majone, G. 1996, *Regulating Europe*, Routledge, London.

Mallett, W.J. 2001, Long-distance travel by low-income households, in *Personal Travel: The Long and Short of It, Conference Proceedings June 28–July 1, 1999, Washington, DC*, TRB Transportation Research Circular E–C026, Transportation Research Board, Washington, DC, pp. 169–77.

Mallett, W.J. and McGuckin, N. 2000, *Driving to Distractions: Recreational Trips in Private Vehicles*, Bureau of Transportation Statistics Paper No: 00–1372, Bureau of Transportation Statistics, Washington, DC (accessed at Bureau of Transportation Statistics *Nationwide Personal Transportation Survey 2001*, http://199.79.179.77/nhts/, 3 January 2003).

Malmberg, A. and Maskell, P. 1997, Towards an explanation of regional specialization and industry agglomeration, *European Planning Studies* 5, 25–41.

Malmberg, A. and Maskell, P. 2002, The elusive concept of localization economies: towards a knowledge-based theory of spatial clustering, *Environment and Planning A* 34, 429–49.

Manchester City Council 2001, *Regeneration in Manchester Statement*, http://www.manchester.gov.uk/regen/statemen/.

Mandell, M.P. 1999, The impact of collaborative efforts: changing the face of public policy through networks and network structures, *Policy Studies Review* 16(1), 4–17.

Manning, B. 1977, The Congress, the executive and intermestic affairs, *Foreign Affairs* 55(January), 306–24.

Manrai, L.A. and Manrai, A.K. 1995, Effects of cultural-context, gender, and acculturation on perceptions of work versus social/leisure time usage, *Journal of Business Research* 32, 115–28.

Marchand, B. 1973, Deformation of a transportation surface, *Annals of the Association of American Geographers* 63, 507–21.

Marchetti, C. 1994, Anthropological invariants in travel behavior, *Technological Forecasting and Social Change* 47, 75–88.

Marris, T. 1987, The role and impact of mega-events and attractions on regional and national tourism development: resolutions, *Revue de Tourisme* 4, 3–10.

Marsden, T., Munton, R., Ward, N. and Whatmore, S. 1996, Agricultural geography and the political economy approach: a review, *Economic Geography* 72, 361–75.

Marsh, I. and Shaw, I. 2000, *Australia's Wine Industry: Collaboration and Learning as Causes of Competitive Success*, Australian Business Foundation, Sydney.

Marsh, J., and Staple, S. 1995, Cruise tourism in the Canadian Arctic and its implications, in C.M. Hall and M.E. Johnston (eds), *Polar Tourism: Tourism in the Arctic and Antarctic Regions*, John Wiley & Sons, Chichester, pp. 63–72.

Marshack, K.J. 1994, Copreneurs and dual-career couples: are they different? *Entrepreneurship: Theory and Practice* 19(1): 49–70.

Maskell, P. 2001, Towards a knowledge-based theory of the geographical cluster, *Industrial and Corporate Change* 10, 921–43.

Maskell, P. and Malmberg, A. 1999a, The competitiveness of firms and regions: 'ubiquitification' and the importance of localized learning, *European Urban and Regional Studies* 6, 9–25.

Maskell, P. and Malmberg, A. 1999b, Localised learning and industrial competitiveness, *Cambridge Journal of Economics* 23, 167–85.

Mason, P. 2002, The 'Big OE': New Zealanders overseas experiences in Britain, in C.M. Hall and A.M. Williams (eds), *Tourism and Migration: New Relationships between Production and Consumption*, Kluwer, Dordrecht, pp. 87–102.

Massey, D. 1999a, Negotiating disciplinary boundaries, *Current Sociology* 47(4), 5–12.

Massey, D. 1999b, Imagining globalisation: power geometries of time–space, in A. Brah, M. Hickman and M. Mac an Ghaill (eds), *Global Futures: Migration, Environment and Globalization*, Macmillan, Basingstoke, pp. 27–44.

Massey, D. 1999c, Spaces of politics, in D. Massey, J. Allen and P. Sarre (eds), *Human Geography Today*, Polity Press, Oxford, pp. 279–94.

Masuda, Y. 1981, *Computopia: Information Society as Post-Industrial Society*, World Future Society, Bethesda.

Mather, S., Viner, D. and Todd, G. 2004, Climate and policy changes: their implications for international tourism flows, in C.M. Hall and J. Higham (eds), *Tourism, Recreation and Climate Change*, Channelview, Clevedon.

Mathews, J.T. 1989, Redefining security, *Foreign Affairs* 68(Spring), 162–77.

Mathieson, A. and Wall, G. 1982, *Tourism: Economic, Physical and Social Impacts*, Longman, London.

Matthews, H.G. 1978, *International Tourism: A Social and Political Analysis*, Schenkman, Cambridge.

Maxwell, J.W. and Reuveny, R. 2000, Resource scarcity and conflict in developing countries, *Journal of Peace Research* 37(3): 301–22.

McCaw, F. 1994, Best of Victoria 1994: Monday readers' poll, *Monday Magazine*: 30 June–6 July, p. 20.

McCool, S.F. 1994, Planning for sustainable nature dependent tourism development: the limits of acceptable change system, *Tourism Recreation Research* 19(2), 51–5.

McDonald, D. and Tungatt, M. 1992, *Community Development and Sport*, Community Development Foundation, London.

McDowell, L. 1997, A tale of two cities? Embedded organization and embodied workers in the City of London, in R. Lee and J. Wills (eds), *Geographies of Economies*, Arnold, London, pp. 18–29.

McEnroe, J. 1991, Split-shift parenting, *American Demographics* 13(2), 50–3.

McHugh, K.E. 2000, Inside, outside, upside down, backward, forward, round and round: a case for ethnographic approaches in migration, *Progress in Human Geography* 24, 71–89.

McHugh, K.E. and Mings, R.G. 1991, On the road again: seasonal migration to a sunbelt metropolis, *Urban Geography* 12, 1–18.

McHugh, K.E. and Mings, R.C. 1996, The circle of migration: attachment to place in aging, *Annals of the Association of American Geographers* 86, 530–50.

McHugh, K.E., Hogan, T.D. and Happel, S.K. 1995, Multiple residence and cyclical migration: a life course perspective, *Professional Geographer* 47, 251–67.

McKercher, B. 1993, Some fundamental truths about tourism: understanding tourism's social and environmental impacts, *Journal of Sustainable Tourism* 1(1), 6–16.

McKercher, B. and du Cros, H. 2002, *Cultural Tourism: The Partnership Between Tourism and Cultural Heritage Management*, The Haworth Press, New York.

McLuhan, M. 1964, *Understanding Media*, Routledge and Kegan Paul, London.

McMurray, K.C. 1930, The use of land for recreation, *Annals of the Association of American Geographers* 20, 7–20.

McQuaid, R.W., Greig, M., Smyth, A. and Cooper, J. 2004, *The Importance of Transport in Business' Location Decisions*, Department for Transport, London.

Medlik, S. 1993, *Dictionary of Travel, Tourism and Hospitality*, Butterworth-Heinemann, Oxford.

Medlik, S. 1995, *Managing Tourism*, Butterworth-Heinemann, Oxford.

Meethan, K. 2001, *Tourism in Global Society: Place, Culture and Consumption*, Palgrave, London.

Mehretu, A., Pigozzi, B.W. and Sommers, L.M. 2000, Concepts in social and spatial marginality, *Geografiska Annaler* 82B, 89–101.

Meikle, J. 2004, Tourists 'get poor health advice', *The Guardian*, 28 July.

Mercer, D. 1995, *A Question of Balance: Natural Resource Conflict Issues in Australia*, The Federation Press, Sydney.

Meredith, D. 2004, Letters to the Editor: holiday homes and everyday reality, *The Times*, 30 March, p. 19.

Metcalfe, J.S. and Miles, I. (eds) 2000, *Innovation Systems in the Service Economy: Measurement and Case Study Analysis*, Kluwer, Boston, MA.

Metelka, C.J. 1990, *The Dictionary of Hospitality, Travel and Tourism*, 3rd edn, Delmar Publishers, Albany, NY.

Miciak, A.R., Kirkland, K. and Ritchie, J.R.B. 2001, Benchmarking an emerging lodging alternative in Canada: a profile of the B&B sector, *Tourism Economics* 7(1), 39–58.

Mill, R.C. and Morrison, A.M. 1985, *The Tourism System: An Introductory Text*, Prentice-Hall, Englewood Cliffs, NJ.

Millar, C. and Aiken, D. 1995, Conflict resolution in aquaculture: a matter of trust, in A. Boghen (ed.), *Coldwater Aquaculture in Atlantic Canada*, 2nd edn, Canadian Institute for Research on Regional Development, Moncton, pp. 617–45.

Miller, D. (ed.) 2001, *Home Possessions*, Berg, Oxford.

Miller, H.J. 1991, Modeling accessibility using space–time prism concepts within geographical information systems, *International Journal of Geographical Information Systems* 5, 287–301.

Miller, H.J. 1998, Emerging themes and research frontiers in GIS and activity-based travel demand forecasting, *Geographical Systems* 5, 189–98.

Miller, H.J. 1999, Measuring space–time accessibility benefits within transportation networks: basic theory and computational methods, *Geographical Analysis* 31, 187–212.

Miller, H.J. 2004, Tobler's first law and spatial analysis, *Annals of the Association of American Geographers*, 94(2), 284–9.

Miller, H.J. and Wu, Y.-H. 2000, GIS software for measuring space–time accessibility in transportation planning and analysis, *GeoInformatica* 4, 141–59.

Miller, M. 1993, The rise of coastal and marine tourism, *Ocean and Coastal Management* 21(1/3), 183–99.

Miller, M.L. and Auyong, J. 1991, Coastal zone tourism: a potent force affecting environment and society, *Marine Policy* 15(2): 75–99.

Mills, E.D. 1983, *Design for Holidays and Tourism*, Butterworths, London.

Mills, T.C. and Pepper, G.T. 1999, Assessing the forecasts: an analysis of forecasting records of the Treasury, the London Business School and the National Institute, *International Journal of Forecasting* 15, 247–57.

Milne, S. 1990, The impact of tourism development in small Pacific Island states, *New Zealand Journal of Geography* 89, 16–21.

Milne, S. 1994, The changing structure of the tourism industry: current trends and their economic implications (mimeograph), Department of Geography, McGill University, Montreal.

Milne, S., Waddington, R. and Perey, A. 1994, Toward more flexible organisation?: Canadian rail freight in the 1990s, *Tijdschrift voor Economische en Sociale Geografie*, 85(2), 153–64.

Milward, A., Sorensen, V. and Ranieri, R. 1993, *The Frontier of National Sovereignty*, Routledge, London.

Milward, H.B. 1996, Symposium on the hollow state: capacity, control and performance in interorganizational settings, *Journal of Public Administration Research and Theory* 6(2), 193–5.

Minerbi, L. 1992, *Impacts of Tourism Development in Pacific Islands*, Greenpeace Pacific Campaign, San Francisco.

Mings, R. 1984, Recreational nomads in the southwestern sunbelt, *Journal of Cultural Geography* 4, 86–99.

Mitchell, R. and Hall, C.M. 2001, The winery consumer: a New Zealand perspective, *Tourism Recreation Research* 26(2), 63–75.

Modern Maturity 1999, Results of travel survey, *Modern Maturity*, 12 January.

Molotch, H.L. 1976, The city as a growth machine, *American Journal of Sociology* 82(2), 309–30.

Mommaas, H. and van der Poel, H. 1989, Changes in economy, politics and lifestyles: an essay on the restructuring of urban leisure, in P. Bramham, I. Henry, H. Mommaas and H. van der Poel (eds), *Leisure and Urban Processes: Critical Studies of Leisure Policy in Western European Cities*, Routledge, London and New York, pp. 254–76.

Moore, J. 2000, Continuities and discontinuities of place, *Journal of Environmental Psychology* 20, 193–205.

Moore, K., Cushman, G. and Simmons, D. 1995, Behavioural conceptualisation of tourism and leisure, *Annals of Tourism Research* 22, 67–85.

Morales-Moreno, I. 2004, Postsovereign governance in a globalizing and fragmenting world: the case of Mexico, *Review of Policy Research* 21(1), 107–17.

Morgan, K. 1995, The learning region: institutions, innovation and regional renewal, Papers in Planning Research No. 157, Department of City and Regional Planning, University of Wales, Cardiff.

Morgan, N. and Pritchard, A. 1998, *Tourism Promotion and Power: Creating Images, Creating Identities*, John Wiley & Sons, Chichester.

Morgan, N., Pritchard, A. and Pride, N. (eds) 2002, *Destination Branding: Creating the Unique Destination Proposition*, Butterworth-Heinemann, Oxford.

Morrill, R.L. 1963, The distribution of migration distances, *Papers and Proceedings of the Regional Science Association* 2, 75–84.

Morrill, R.L. and Kelley, M.B. 1970, The simulation of hospital use and the estimation of location efficiency, *Geographical Analysis* 2, 283–300.

Morrill, R.L. and Pitts, F.R. 1972, Marriage, migration and the mean information field: a study in uniqueness and generality, in P.E. English and R.C. Mayfield (eds), *Man, Space and Environment: Concepts in Contemporary Human Geography*, Oxford University Press, New York, pp. 359–84.

Morrison, A. 1989, *Hospitality and Travel Marketing*, Delmar Publishers, Albany, NY.

Morrison, B. 2003, Femme fatale, *The Guardian Review*, 4 October, pp. 12–13.

Moseley, M.J. 1979, *Accessibility: The Rural Challenge*, Methuen, London.

Mount, J. and Leroux, C. 1994, Assessing the effects of a mega-event: a retrospective study of the impact of the Olympic Games on the Calgary business sector, *Festival Management and Event Tourism* 2(1), 15–23.

Mowforth, M. and Munt, I. 1998, *Tourism and Sustainability: New Tourism in the Third World*, Routledge, London.

Mowforth, M. and Munt, I. 2003, *Tourism and Sustainability: New Tourism in the Third World*, 2nd edn, Routledge, London.

Müller, D.K. 1999, *German Second Home Owners in the Swedish Countryside: On the Internationalization of the Leisure Space*, Kulturgeografiska institutionen, Umeå.

Müller, D.K. 2002a, German second home development in Sweden, in C.M. Hall and A.M. Williams (eds), *Tourism and Migration: New Relationships Between Production and Consumption*, Kluwer, Dordrecht, pp. 169–86.

Müller, D.K. 2002b, Second home ownership and sustainable development in Northern Sweden, *Tourism and Hospitality Research* 3, 343–55.

Müller, D.K. 2002c, German second homeowners in Sweden: some remarks on the tourism–migration nexus, *Revue Européenne des Migrations Internationales* 18, 67–86.

Müller, D.K. 2002d, Reinventing the countryside: German second home owners in southern Sweden, *Current Issues in Tourism* 5, 426–46.

Müller, D.K. 2004, Tourism, mobility and second homes, in A.A. Lew, C.M. Hall and A.M. Williams (eds), *A Companion to Tourism*, Blackwell, Oxford.

Mullins, L. and Tucker, R. (eds) 1988, *Snowbirds in the Sunbelt: Older Canadians in Florida*, International Exchange Centre on Gerontology, University of South Florida, Tampa, FL.

Murdoch, J. 1993, Sustainable rural development: towards a research agenda, *Geoforum* 24(3), 225–41.

Murphy, M. 1987, Measuring the family life cycle: concept, data and methods, in A. Bryman, B. Bytheway, P. Allatt and T. Keil (eds), *Rethinking the Life Cycle*, Macmillan, Basingstoke, pp. 30–50.

Murphy, P. and Watson, S. 1997, *Surface City: Sydney at the Millennium*, Pluto Press, Annandale, NSW.

Murphy, P. and Zehner, R. 1988, Satisfaction and sunbelt migration, *Australian Geographical Studies* 26, 320–34.

Murphy, P.E. 1985, *Tourism: A Community Approach*, Methuen, New York.

Murphy, P.E. 1988, Community-driven tourism planning, *Tourism Management* 9(2), 96–104.

Murphy, P.E. and Murphy, A. 2004, *Strategic Management for Tourism Communities: Bridging the Gaps*, Channelview, Clevedon.

Myers, N. 1989, Environment and security, *Foreign Policy* 74(Spring), 23–41.

Myers, N. 1993, *Ultimate Security: The Environmental Basis of Political Stability*, W.W. Norton & Co., New York.

Naisbitt, J. 1982, *Megatrends*, Warner Books, New York.

Nash, C. 2000, Performativity in practice: some recent work in cultural geography, *Progress in Human Geography* 24(4), 653–64.

Nash, C. 2002, Genealogical identities, *Environment and Planning D: Society and Space* 20, 27–52.

Nash, D. 1989, Tourism as a form of imperialism, in V. Smith (ed.), *Hosts and Guests: The Anthropology of Tourism*, 2nd edn, University of Pennsylvania, Philadelphia, pp. 37–52.

Nash, D. 1996, *The Anthropology of Tourism*, Pergamon Press, Oxford.

National Capital Commission (NCC) 1998, *A Capital in the Making*, NCC, Ottawa.

National Capital Commission 1999, *Plan for Canada's Capital: A Second Century of Vision, Planning and Development*, NCC, Ottawa.

National Capital Commission 2000, *Planning Canada's Capital Region*, NCC, Ottawa.

National Oceanic and Atmospheric Administration (NCAA) (1997) *1998 Year of the Ocean – Coastal Tourism and Recreation* (Discussion paper), http://www.yoto98.noaa.gov/yoto/meeting/tour_rec_316.html

National Post 2001, Warming permafrost puts resorts in Alps at risk, *National Post*, 5 January, A10.

National Restaurant Association 1998, *Eating-place Trends: 1998 Restaurant Industry Forecast*, National Restaurant Association, Washington, DC.

National Tourism Administration of the People's Republic of China (NTAPRC) 1993, *The Yearbook of China Tourism Statistics 1993*, NTAPRC, Beijing.

Nelson, J.I. 2001, On mass distribution: a case study of chain stores in the restaurant industry, *Journal of Consumer Culture* 1(1), 119–38.

Neumayer, E. 2004, The impact of political violence on tourism, *Journal of Conflict Resolution* 48(2) 259–81.

New Zealand Customs Service 2001, *New Zealand Passenger Arrival Card – and Notes*, New Zealand Customs Service, Wellington.

Newsome, D., Moore, S.A. and Dowling, R. 2001, *Natural Area Tourism: Ecology, Impacts and Management*, Channelview, Clevedon.

Nijkamp, P. and Verdonkschot, S. 1995, Sustainable tourism development: a case study of Lesbos, in H. Coccossis and P. Nijkamp (eds), *Sustainable Tourism Development*, Avebury, Aldershot, pp. 127–58.

Nordin, S. 2003, *Tourism Clustering and Innovation: Paths to Economic Growth and Development*, Etour, Ostersünd.

Nordlinger, E. 1981, *On the Autonomy of the Democratic State*, Harvard University Press, Cambridge, MA.

Norkunas, M.K. 1993, *The Politics of Memory: Tourism, History, and Ethnicity in Monterey, California*, State University of New York Press, Albany, NY.

Northwest Development Agency (NWDA) 2000, *Regional Strategy*, Northwest Development Agency, Manchester.

Norval, A.J. 1936, *The Tourist Industry: A National and International Survey*, Pitman, London.

Obsequio-Go, M.E. and Duval, D.T. 2003, Return visits among Filipino migrants in Dunedin, New Zealand, *Tourism Review International* 7, 51–5.

O'Donnell, A., Gilmore, A., Cummins, D. and Carson, D. 2001, The network construct in entrepreneurship research: a review and critique, *Management Decision* 39(9), 749–60.

OECD 2002, *International Mobility of the Highly Skilled*, OECD, Paris.

O'Halloran, R.H. 1991, Ethics in hospitality and tourism education: the new managers, *Hospitality and Tourism Educator* 3(3), 33–7.

O'Halloran, R.H. and O'Halloran, C.S. 1992, Hospitality and tourism education: relationships to the core curriculum, *Hospitality and Tourism Educator* 4(4), 56–64.

Ohmae, K. 1995, *The End of the Nation State: The Rise of Regional Economies*, HarperCollins and Free Press, New York.

Oinen-Edén, E. 2001, The cultural project of Koli, in L. Lovén (ed.), *Local and Global Heritage*, Finnish Forest Research Institute, Research Paper 836, Joensuu Research Centre, Joensuu, pp. 65–72.

Olds, K. 1998, Urban mega-events, evictions and housing rights: the Canadian case, *Current Issues in Tourism* 1(1), 2–46.

Oo, A.N. and Perez, M. 1996, Behind the smiling faces, *Newsletter – The International Communication Project*, No. 28, http:/www.comlink.apc.org/fic/newslett/eng/28/page_36.htm

Ophuls, W. 1977, *Ecology and the Politics of Scarcity*, W.H. Freeman, San Francisco.

Oppermann, M. 1996, Travel life cycles, *Annals of Tourism Research* 22, 535–52.

Orams, M.B. 1995, Using interpretation to manage nature-based tourism, *Journal of Sustainable Tourism* 4(2), 81–94.

Orams, M.B. 1999, *Marine Tourism: Development, Impacts and Management*, Routledge, London.

Orams, M.B. 2002, Marine ecotourism as a potential agent for sustainable development in Kaikoura, New Zealand, *International Journal of Sustainable Development* 5(3/4), 338–52.

Orams, M.B. 2003, Marine ecotourism in New Zealand: an overview of the industry and its management, in B. Garrod and J.C. Wilson (eds), *Marine Ecotourism: Issues and Experiences*, Channelview, Clevedon, pp. 233–48.

Orams, M.B. 2005, Dolphins, whales and ecotourism in New Zealand: what are the impacts and how should the industry be managed?, in C.M. Hall and S. Boyd (eds), *Tourism and Nature-based Tourism in Peripheral Areas: Development or Disaster*, Channelview Publications, Clevedon (in press).

Orfeuil, J.P. and Salomon, I. 1993, Travel patterns of the Europeans in everyday life, in I. Salomon (ed.), *A Billion Trips a Day*, Kluwer Academic Publishers, Dordrecht, pp. 33–55.

Ortner, S.B. 1989, Cultural politics: religious activism and ideological transformation among 20th century Sherpas, *Dialetical Anthropology* 14, 197–211.

Osborne, P. 2000, *Travelling Light: Photography, Travel and Visual Culture*, Manchester University Press, Manchester.

Oskamp, S. 1982, Overconfidence in case-study judgments, in D. Kahneman, P. Slovic and A. Tversky (eds), *Judgment under Uncertainty: Heuristics and Biases*, Cambridge University Press, New York, pp. 287–93.

Ostrom, E. 1986, Multiorganizational arrangements and coordination: an application of institutional analysis, in F.X. Kaufmann, G. Majone and V. Ostrom (eds), *Guidance, Control, and Evaluation in the Public Sector*, De Gruyter, Berlin, pp. 495–510.

Ostrom, E. 1987, Institutional arrangements for resolving the commons dilemma: some contending approaches, in B.J. McCay and J.M. Acheson (eds), *The Question of the Commons: The Culture and Ecology of Communal Resources*, University of Arizona Press, Tucson, AZ, pp. 250–65.

Ostrom, E. 1990, *Governing the Commons: The Evolution of Institutions for Collective Action, the Political Economy of Institutions and Decisions*, Cambridge University Press, Cambridge.

Ostrom, E. 1998a, Reflections on the commons, in J.A. Baden and D.S. Noonan (eds), *Managing the Commons*, 2nd edn, Indiana University Press, Bloomington, IN, pp. 95–116.

Ostrom, E. 1998b, Scales, polycentricity, and incentives: designing complexity to govern complexity, in L.D. Guruswamy and J.A. McNeely (eds), *Protection of Global Biodiversity: Converging Strategies*, Duke University Press, Durham, NC, pp. 149–67.

Ostrom, E. 1998c, The institutional analysis and development approach, in E.T. Loehman and D.M. Kilgour (eds), *Designing Institutions for Environmental and Resource Management*, Edward Elgar, Cheltenham, pp. 68–90.

Owen, G. 1998, *Accounting for Hospitality, Tourism and Leisure*, Longman, Harlow.

Pacific NorthWest Economic Region (PNWER) 2000a, *PNWER Profile*, PNWER, Seattle, WA, http://www.pnwer.org/ PNWER Profile (accessed 18 February 2000).

Pacific NorthWest Economic Region 2000b, *Background*, PNWER, Seattle, WA, http://www.pnwer.org/background/backgrou.htm (accessed 18 February 2000).

Pacific NorthWest Economic Region 2000c, *Accomplishments*, PNWER, Seattle, http://www.pnwer.org/background/accompli.htm (accessed 18 February 2000).

Pacione, M. 1984, *Rural Geography*, Harper & Row, London.

Padgett, M. and Hall, C.M. 2001, Case study 4.3: tourism at the polls, in C.M. Hall and G.W. Kearsley (eds), *Tourism in New Zealand: An Introduction*, Oxford University Press, Sydney.

Page, S. 1993, The Wellington waterfront, in C.M. Hall and S. McArthur (eds),

Heritage Management in New Zealand and Australia: Visitor Management, Interpretation and Marketing, Oxford University Press, Auckland, pp. 218–30.

Page, S. 1994, *Transport for Tourism*, ITBP, London.

Page, S.J. 1995, *Urban Tourism*, Routledge, London.

Page, S.J. 1999, *Transport and Tourism*, 2nd edn, Addison Wesley Longman, London.

Page, S.J. and Hall, C.M. 2003, *Managing Urban Tourism*, Prentice-Hall, Harlow.

Page, S.J. and Meyer, D. 1996, Tourist accidents: an exploratory analysis, *Annals of Tourism Research* 23, 666–90.

Page, S.J., Forer, P. and Lawton, G. 1999, Small business development and tourism: *Terra incognita? Tourism Management* 20(4), 435–60.

Painter, J. and Goodwin, M. 1995, Local governance and concrete research: investigating the uneven development of regulation, *Economy and Society* 24, 334–56.

Pannett, A. and Boella, M. 1996, *Principles of Hospitality Law*, Cassell, London.

Parcel, T. and Sickmeier, M. 1988, One firm, two labor markets: the case of McDonald's in the fast-food industry, *Sociological Quarterly* 29, 29–46.

Parinello, G.L. 2001, The technological body in tourism, research and praxis, *International Sociology* 16, 205–19.

Parkes, C. 2004, Nielsen to interact with gaming group, *The Financial Times*, 8 April, p. 22.

Pashigian, P.B. and Bowen, B. 1994, The rising cost of time of females, the growth of national brands and the supply of retail services, *Economic Inquiry* 32, 33–65.

Partain, B.R. and Hopley, D. 1990, *Sedimentation Resulting from Road Development, Cape Tribulation Area*, Great Barrier Reef Marine Park Authority Technical Memorandum No. 21, Great Barrier Reef Marine Park Authority, Townsville, Queensland.

Pavesic, D.V. 1991, Programmatic issues in undergraduate hospitality education, *Hospitality and Tourism Educator* 3(2), 38–9.

Pearce, D.G. 1987, *Tourism Today: A Geographical Analysis*, 1st edn, Longman Scientific and Technical, Harlow.

Pearce, D.G. 1988, Tourists time-budgets, *Annals of Tourism Research* 15, 106–21.

Pearce, D.G. 1989, *Tourism Development*, 2nd edn, Longman Scientific and Technical, Harlow.

Pearce, D.G. 1992, *Tourism Organisations*, Longman, Harlow.

Pearce, D.W., Barbier, E.B. and Markandya, A. 1988, *Sustainable Development and Cost-Benefit Analysis*, IIED/UCL London Environment Economics Centre, LEEC Paper 88–03.

Pearce, P.L. 1982, *The Social Psychology of Tourist Behaviour*, Pergamon, Oxford.

Pearce, P.L. 2005, *Tourist Behaviour: Themes and Conceptual Issues*, Channelview Press, Clevedon (in press).

Pearson, R.C. and Goheen, A.C. (eds) 1998, *Compendium of Grape Diseases*, The American Phytopathological Society, St Paul, MN.

Peet, R. 1998, *Modern Geographic Thought*, Blackwell, Oxford.

Peissl, W. 2003, Surveillance and security: a dodgy relationship, *Journal of Contingencies and Crisis Management* 11(1), 19–24.

Peng, M.W. 2004, Identifying the gig question in international business research, *Journal of International Business Studies* 35(2), 99–108.

Perloff, H. and Wingo, L. 1962, Urban growth and the planning of outdoor recreation, in Outdoor Recreation Resources Review Commission (ORRRC) *Trends in American Living and Outdoor Recreation*, Study Report No. 22, ORRC, Washington, DC, pp. 81–100.

Perren, L. 1999, Factors in the growth of micro-enterprises (Part 1): developing a framework, *Journal of Small Business and Enterprise Development* 6(4), 366–85.

Perry, A. 1997, Recreation and tourism, in R. Thompson and A. Perry (eds), *Applied Climatology*, Routledge, London, pp. 240–8.

Perry, A. 2004, The Mediterranean: how can the world's most popular and successful tourist destination adjust to a changing climate? in C.M. Hall and J. Higham (eds), *Tourism, Recreation and Climate Change*, Channelview, Clevedon.

Peters, B.G. 1996, *The Future of Governing*, University Press of Kansas, Lawrence, KS.

Peters, B.G. 1998, *Globalization, Institutions and Governance*, Jean Monnet Chair Paper RSC No. 98/51, European University Institute, Florence.

Peters, B.G. and Savoie D.J. 1996, *Governance in a Changing Environment*, McGill/Queens University Press, Montreal.

Petrikova, H. 2001, Cultural heritage of the Giant Mountains – a sustainable performance of traditions or a museum show?, in L. Lovén (ed.), *Local and Global Heritage*, Finnish Forest Research Institute, Research Paper No. 836, Joensuu Research Centre, Joensuu, pp. 33–44.

Phillips, J.D. 2004, Doing justice to the law, *Annals of the Association of American Geographers*, 94(2), 290–3.

Philo, C. and Kearns, G. 1993, Culture, history, capital: a critical introduction to the selling of places, in G. Kearns and C. Philo (eds) *Selling Places: The City as Cultural Capital, Past and Present*, Pergamon Press, Oxford, pp. 1–32.

Pigram, J.J. 1985, *Outdoor Recreation and Resource Management*, 2nd edn, Croom Helm, London.

Pigram, J.J. and Jenkins, J. 1999, *Outdoor Recreation Management*, Routledge, London.

Pilger, J. 1996, The land of fear, *The Sydney Morning Herald*, Spectrum, 1 June.

Pine, B.J. 1993, *Mass Customization: The New Frontier in Business Competition*, Harvard University Press, Cambridge, MA.

Pine, P.J. and Gilmore, J.H. 1999, *The Experience Economy: Work is Theatre and Every Business a Stage*, Harvard Business School Press, Boston, MA.

Piven, F.F. 1995, Is it global economics or neo-laissez-faire? *New Left Review* 213 (September/October), 107–14.

Pizam, A. 1999, A comprehensive approach to classifying acts of crime and violence at tourism destinations, *Journal of Travel Research* 38, 5–12.

Pizam, A. and Fleischer, A. 2002, Severity versus frequency of acts of terrorism: which has a larger impact on tourism demand? *Journal of Travel Research* 40, 337–9.

Pizam, A. and Mansfield, Y. (eds) 1996, *Tourism, Crime and International Security Issues*, John Wiley, Chichester.

Plan Canada (edition on planning capital cities) 2000, *Plan Canada* 40(3).

Pohl, N. 2001, *Mobility in Space and Time: Challenges to the Theory of International Economics*, Springer Verlag, Heidelberg.

Pol, M., Zoutendijk, D. and Blom, U. 1995, Influence of Dutch mobility policy on emancipation process for women and men, *Transportation Research Record* 1493, 136–42.

Polzin, S.E., Chu, X. and Rey, J.R. 2001, Mobility and mode choice of people of color for non-work travel, in *Personal Travel: The Long and Short of It, Conference Proceedings* June 28–July 1, 1999 Washington, DC, TRB Transportation Research Circular E–C026, Transportation Research Board, Washington, DC.

Poole, Jr., R.W. 2001, *A Better Approach to Airport Security*, The Heritage Foundation, 19 October, http://www.heritage.org/views/2001/ed101901 b.html (accessed 17 March 2002).

Pooler, E. 1994, An extended family of spatial interaction models, *Progress in Human Geography* 18, 17–39.

Pooler, J.A. 1995, The use of spatial separation in the measurement of transportation accessibility, *Transport Research A* 29A(6), 421–7.

Pooley, C. and Turnbull, J. 2000, Modal choice and modal change: the journey to work in Britain since 1890, *Journal of Transport Geography* 8, 11–24.

Poon, A. 1989, Competitive strategies for a 'new tourism', in C.P. Cooper (ed.), *Progress in Tourism, Recreation and Hospitality Management*, Belhaven Press, London, pp. 91–102.

Poon, A. 1990, Flexible specialization and small size: the case of Caribbean tourism, *World Development* 18, 109–23.

Porell, F. 1982, Interurban migration and quality of life, *Journal of Regional Science* 22, 137–58.

Porter, M. 1990, *The Competitive Advantage of Nations*, Macmillan, London.

Porter, M. 2000a, Locations, clusters and company strategy, in G. Clark, M. Feldman and M. Gertler (eds), *The Oxford Handbook of Economic Geography*, Oxford University Press, Oxford, pp. 253–75.

Porter, M. 2000b, Location, competition and economic development: local clusters in a global economy, *Economic Development Quarterly* 14(1), 15–34.

Poston, T. and Stewart, I. 1978, *Catastrophe Theory and Its Implications*, Pitman, London.

Pottinger, M. 2004, Why SARS didn't return, *The Far Eastern Economic Review*, 8 April, pp. 34–5.

Powell, W. 1990, Neither market nor hierarchy: network forms of organization, in B. Straw and L. Cummings (eds), *Research in Organizational Behaviour*, Vol. 12, JAI Press, Greenwich, CT, pp. 295–336.

Pred, A.R. 1977, The choreography of existence, *Economic Geography* 53, 207–31.

Pred, A.R. 1981a, Social reproduction and the time-geography of everyday life, *Geografiska Annaler* 63B, 5–22.

Pred, A.R. 1981b, Production, family, and free-time projects: a time-geographic perspective on the individual and societal change in 19th century US cities, *Journal of Historical Geography* 7, 3–6.

Pred, A.R. 1984, Places as a historically contingent process: structuration and the time geography of becoming places, *Annals of the Association of American Geographers* 74, 279–97.

Pred, A.R. 1990, *Lost Words and Lost Worlds: Modernity and the Language of Everyday Life in Late 19th Century Stockholm*, Cambridge University Press, Cambridge.

Presser, H.B. 1995, Job, family, and gender: determinants of nonstandard work schedules among employed Americans in 1991, *Demography* 32(4), 577–98.

Pries, L. 2001, *New Transnational Social Spaces: International Migration and Transnational Companies in the Early Twenty-first Century*, Routledge, London.

Purdy, D.A. and Richard, S.F. 1983, Sport and juvenile delinquency: an examination and assessment of four major themes, *Pacific Sociological Review* 14, 328–38.

Putnam, R.D. 1993, *Making Democracy Work: Civic Traditions in Modern Italy*, Princeton University Press, Princeton, NJ.

Putnam, R.D. 1995a, Bowling alone: America's declining social capital, *Journal of Democracy* 6(1), 65–78.

Putnam, R.D. 1995b, Tuning in, tuning out: the strange disappearance of social capital in America, *Political Science and Politics* 28(4), 664–83.

Putnam, R.D. 2000, *Bowling Alone: The Collapse and Revival of American Community*, Simon & Schuster, New York.

Putnam, R.D. (ed.) 2002, *Democracies in Flux: The Evolution of Social Capital in Contemporary Society*, Oxford University Press, New York.

Qu, H. and Zhang, H. 1997, The projected inbound market trends of 12 tourist destinations in S.E. Asia and the Pacific 1997–2001, *Journal of Vacation Marketing* 3(3), 247–63.

Ravenstein, E.G. 1885, The laws of migration, *Journal of the Royal Statistical Society* 48, 167–227.

Ravenstein, E.G. 1889, The laws of migration, *Journal of the Royal Statistical Society* 52, 214–301.

Rawn, C.D. 1990, From smokestacks to stadiums: affluent sports fans are a clean industry in Indianapolis, *American Demographics* (October), 49–50.

Redmond, C.R. 1988, The effects of working nontraditional hours on life satisfaction, *Mid-American Review of Sociology* 13(1), 21–40.

Reed, J. 2003a, Safe haven in an unsettled world, *FT Special Report: Investing in South Africa*, 6 October, pp. 1–2.

Reed, J. 2003b, Growth at centre of public policy debate, *FT Special Report: Investing in South Africa*, 6 October, p. 2.

Regan, P. 2003, Privacy and commercial use of personal data: policy developments in the United States, *Journal of Contingencies and Crisis Management* 11(1), 12–18.

Reid, D.G. 1989, Changing patterns of work and leisure and the health community, *Plan Canada* 29(4), 45–50.

Reilly, K.T. 1994, Annual hours and weeks in a life-cycle labor supply model: Canadian evidence on male behavior, *Journal of Labor Economics* 12(3), 460–77.

Relph, E. 1976, *Place and Placelessness*, Pion, London.

Resource Assessment Commission 1992a, *Coastal Zone Inquiry: Government Approaches to Coastal Zone Resource Management*, Information Paper No. 1, Resource Assessment Commission, Canberra.

Resource Assessment Commission 1992b, *Coastal Zone Inquiry*, Background Paper, Resource Assessment Commission, Canberra.

Resource Assessment Commission 1992c, *Coastal Zone Inquiry: Draft Report*, Resource Assessment Commission, Canberra.

Rethinking Tourism Project 1999. Tourism development runs amuck while indigenous peoples, NGOs press governments for consultation, participation, accountability and sustainability, *Electronic News* 12 August.

Rethinking Tourism Project 2000, EPA solicits public input on cruise ship discharges – *EPA Water News, Electronic Newsletter* 29 August, 2000.

Reuters 1993, Cairo bomb a mystery, *New Zealand Herald*, 1 March, p. 7.

Reuters 2004, A paperless future for Continental tickets, *International Herald Tribune*, 8 April, p. 20.

Rhodes, R. 1996, The new governance: governing without government, *Political Studies* 44, 652–67.

Rhodes, R.A.W. 1997a, From marketisation to diplomacy: it's the mix that matters, *Australian Journal of Public Administration* 56(2), 40–53.

Rhodes, R.A.W. 1997b, *Understanding Governance: Policy Networks, Governance, Reflexivity and Accountability*, Open University Press, Buckingham.

Richardson, B. and Richardson, R. 1989, *Business Planning: An Approach to Strategic Management*, Pitman, London.

Richter, L.K. 1980, The political uses of tourism: a Philippine case study, *Journal of Developing Areas*, 14, 237–57.

Richter, L.K. 1984, A search for missing answers to questions never asked: reply to Kosters, *Annals of Tourism Research* 11, 613–15.

Richter, L.K. 1989, *The Politics of Tourism in Asia*, University of Hawaii Press, Honolulu.

Richter, L.K. 1999, After political turmoil: the lessons of rebuilding tourism in three Asian countries, *Journal of Travel Research* 38(August), 41–5.

Richter, L.K., and Waugh, Jr., W.L. 1986, Terrorism and tourism as logical companions, *Tourism Management* (December), 230–8.

Ringer, G. (ed.) 1998, *Destinations: Cultural Landscapes of Tourism*, Routledge, New York.

Ritchie, B.W. and Adair, D. (eds) 2004, *Sport Tourism: Interrelationships, Impacts and Issues*, Channelview, Clevedon.

Ritchie, J.R.B. and Crouch, G.I. 2003, *The Competitive Destination: A Sustainable Tourism Perspective*, CABI, Wallingford.

Ritchie, J.R.B. and Smith, B.H. 1991, The impact of a mega-event on host region awareness: a longitudinal study, *Journal of Travel Research* 30(1), 3–10.

Ritchie, J.R.B. and Hu, Y. 1987, The role and impact of mega-events and attractions on national and regional tourism: a conceptual and methodological overview, paper presented at the 37th Annual Congress of the International Association of Scientific Experts in Tourism (AIEST), Calgary, Canada.

Ritter, W., and Schafer, C. 1998, Cruise-tourism: a chance of sustainability, *Tourism Recreation Research* 23, 65–71.

Ritzer, G. 1996, *The McDonaldization of Society: An Investigation into the Changing Character of Contemporary Social Life*, Pine Forge Press, Newbury Park, CA.

Roberts, L. and Hall, D. (eds) 2001, *Rural Tourism and Recreation: Principles to Practice*, CABI, Wallingford.

Robertson, R. 1992, *Globalization: Social Theory and Global Culture*, Sage, London.

Robins, K. 1991, Tradition and translation: national culture in its global context, in J. Corner and S. Harvey (eds), *Enterprise and Heritage: Crosscurrents of National Culture*, Routledge, London, pp. 21–44.

Robinson, G.M. 1998, *Methods and Techniques in Human Geography*, John Wiley, Chichester.

Robinson, O. and Wallace, J. 1984, Earnings in hotel and catering industry in Great Britain, *Service Industries Journal* 4, 143-60.

Roche, M. 1992, Mega-events and micro-modernization: on the sociology of the new urban tourism, *British Journal of Sociology* 43, 563–600.

Roche, M. 1994, Mega-events and urban policy, *Annals of Tourism Research* 21(1), 1–19.

Roche, M. 2000, *Mega-Events and Modernity: Olympics and Expos in the Growth of Global Culture*, Routledge, London.

Roche, M. and Annesley, C. 1998, *Comparative Social Inclusion Policy in Europe: Report 1: Contexts*, Sheffield University, Sheffield.

Roehl, W.S. 1990, Travel agent attitudes toward China after Tiananmen Square, *Journal of Travel Research* 29(2), 16–22.

Roehl, W.S. and Ditton, R.B. 1993, Impacts of the offshore marine industry on coastal tourism: the case of Padre Island National Seashore, *Coastal Management* 21, 75–89.

Rojek, C. and Urry, J. 1997, Transformations of travel and theory, in C. Rojek and J. Urry (eds), *Touring Cultures: Transformations of Travel and Theory*, Routledge, London, pp. 1–19.

Rollings, N.M. and Brunckhorst, D.J. 1999, Linking ecological and social functions of landscapes: II Scale and modelling of spatial influence, *Natural Areas Journal* 18, 65–72.

Romeril, M. 1988, Coastal tourism and the heritage coast programme in England and Wales, *Tourism Recreation Research* 13(2), 15–19.

Romm, J.J. 1993, *Defining National Security: The Nonmilitary Aspects*, Council on Foreign Relations Press, New York.

Root, T.L., Price, J.T., Hall, K.R., Schneider, S.H., Rosenzweig, C. and Pounds, J.A. 2003, Fingerprints of global warming on wild animals and plants, *Nature* 421(2 January), 57–60.

Rosa, B. 2001, Skiing's end? *Skiing Winter Adventure*, 53(6), 32.

Rose, G. 1997, Situating knowledges: positionality, reflexivities and other tactics, *Progress in Human Geography* 21, 305–20.

Rosenberg, S. 1992, More work for some, less work for others: working hours in the USA, *Futures* 16(3287), 551–60.

Rosenbloom, S. 1989, The travel patterns of elderly women alone: a research note, *Specialized Transportation Planning and Practice* 3(3), 295–310.

Rosenbloom, S. and Waldorf, B. 2001, Older travelers: does place or race make a difference?, in *Personal Travel: The Long and Short of It, Conference Proceedings June 28–July 1, 1999 Washington, DC*, TRB Transportation Research Circular E–C026, Transportation Research Board, Washington, DC.

Rosenfeld, S.A. 1997, Bringing business clusters into the mainstream of economic development, *European Planning Studies* 5(1), 3–23.

Rosenkopf, L. and Almeida, P. 2003, Overcoming local search through alliances and mobility, *Management Science* 49(6), 751–66.

Rosentraub, M.S. 1996, Does the emperor have new clothes? A reply to Robert A. Baade, *Journal of Urban Affairs* 18(1), 3–31.

Rosentraub, M.S., Swindell, D., Przybliski, M. and Mullins, D. 1994, Sport and downtown development strategy: if you build it, will jobs come? *Journal of Urban Affairs* 16(3), 221–39.

Ross, G. 1994, *The Psychology of Tourism*, Hospitality Press, Melbourne.

Rosser, J.B. and Rosser, M.V. 1994, Long wave chaos and system economic transformations, *World Futures* 39, 197–207.

Rouphael, A.B. and Inglis, G.J. 2002, Increased spatial and temporal variability in coral damage caused by recreational scuba diving, *Ecological Applications* 12, 427–40.

Rudkin, B. and Hall, C.M. 1996, Off the beaten track: the health implications of the development of special-interest tourism services in South-East Asia and the South Pacific, in S. Clift and S. Page (eds), *Health and the International Tourist*, Routledge, London, pp. 89–107.

Ruhanen, L. and Cooper, C. 2004, Applying a knowledge management framework to tourism research, *Tourism Recreation Research* 29(1), 83–8.

Rural Development Commission 1991a, *Tourism in the Countryside: A Strategy for Rural England*, Rural Development Commission, London.

Rural Development Commission 1991b, *Meeting the Challenge of Rural Adjustment: A New Rural Development Commission Initiative*, Rural Development Commission, London.

Russell, R. and Faulkner, B. 1998, Reliving the destination life cycle in Coolangatta, in E. Laws, B. Faulkner and G. Moscardo (eds), *Embracing and Managing Changes in Tourism: International Case Studies*, Routledge, London, pp. 95–115.

Russell, R.C. 1987, Survival of insects in the wheel bays of a Boeing 747B aircraft on flights between tropical and temperate airports, *Bulletin of the World Health Organization* 65, 659–62.

Ryan, C. 1991, *Recreational Tourism: A Social Science Perspective*, Routledge, London.

Ryan, C. 1997, Tourism – a mature subject discipline? *Pacific Tourism Review* 1, 3–5.

Ryan, C. 2003, *Recreational Tourism: Demand and Impacts*, Channelview, Clevedon.

Ryan, C. and Montgomery, D. 1994, The attitudes of Bakewell residents to tourism and issues in community responsive tourism, *Tourism Management* 15(5), 358–70.

Sadler, D. 1993, Place-marketing, competitive places and the construction of hegemony in Britain in the 1980s, in G. Kearns and C. Philo (eds), *Selling Places: The City as Cultural Capital, Past and Present*, Pergamon Press, Oxford, pp. 175–92.

Sadler, D. 1997, The role of supply chain management in the 'Europeanisation' of the automobile production system, in R. Lee and J. Wills (eds), *Geographies of Economies*, Arnold, London, pp. 311–20.

Sagoff, M. 1988, *The Economy of the Earth*, Cambridge University Press, Cambridge.

Salomon, I. 1983, Life styles – a broader perspective on travel behaviour, in S. Carpenter and P. Jones (eds), *Recent Advances in Travel Demand Analysis*, Gower, Aldershot, pp. 290–310.

Salter, M.B. 2004, Passports, mobility and security: how smart can the border be? *International Studies Perspectives* 5(1), 71–91.

Sassen, S. 1991, *The Global City*, Princeton University Press, Princeton, NJ.

Saul, J.R. 1995, *The Unconscious Civilization*, Anansi, Concord, MA.

Saxenian, A. 1994, *Regional Advantage: Culture and Competition in Silicon Valley and Route 128*, Harvard University Press, Cambridge, MA.

Schafer, A. 2000, Regularities in travel demand: an international perspective, *Journal of Transportation and Statistics* 3(3), 1–31.

Schafer, A. and Victor, D. 2000, The future mobility of the world population, *Transportation Research A* 34(3), 171–205.

Scholte, J.A. 2000, *Globalization: A Critical Introduction*, St Martin's Press, New York.

Schreiner, J. 2000, Snowmakers hold key to 'core' business, *National Post*, 4 December, C1, C7.

Schwartz, J. 2003, The little spacecraft that could? *International Herald Tribune*, 26 August, pp. 1, 8.

Scott, A.J. (ed.) 2001, *Global City-Regions: Trends, Theory, Policy*, Oxford University Press, Oxford.

Scott, J. 2000, Peripheries, artificial peripheries and centres, in F. Brown and F. Hall (eds), *Aspects of Tourism: Tourism in Peripheral Areas*, Channelview, Clevedon, pp. 58–72.

Seamon, D. 1979, *A Geography of the Lifeworld: Movement, Rest and Encounter*, Croom Helm, London.

Selby, M. 2004, *Understanding Urban Tourism: Image, Culture and Experience*, Palgrave Macmillan, London.

Selke, A.C. 1936, Geographic aspects of the German tourist trade, *Economic Geography* 12, 206–16.

Selwyn, T. 1996, *The Tourism Image: Myths and Myth Making in Tourism*, Wiley, Chichester.

Seys, S.A. and Bender, J.B. 2001, The changing epidemiology of malaria in Minnesota, *Journal of Emerging Infectious Diseases* 7(6), 993–5.

Shafer, E.L., Moeller, G.H. and Getty, R.E. 1974, *Future Leisure Environments*, Forest Research Paper NE-301, USDA Forest Experiment Station, Upper Darby, PA.

Sharpley, R. and Craven, B. 2001, The 2001 foot and mouth crisis – rural economy and tourism policy implications: a comment, *Current Issues in Tourism* 4(6), 527–37.

Sharpley, R. and Telfer, D.J. (eds) 2002, *Tourism and Development: Concepts and Issues*, Channelview, Clevedon.

Shaw, G. and Williams, A.M. 1994, *Critical Issues in Tourism: A Geographical Perspective*, Blackwell, Oxford.

Shaw, G. and Williams, A.M. (eds) 1997, *The Rise and Fall of British Coastal Resorts: Cultural and Economic Perspectives*, Mansell, London.

Shaw, G. and Williams, A.M. 2002, *Critical Issues in Tourism: A Geographical Perspective*, 2nd edn, Blackwell, Oxford.

Shaw, G. and Williams, A.M. 2004, *Tourism and Tourism Spaces*, Sage, Beverly Hills, CA.

Sheldon, P.J. 1997, *Tourism Information Technology*, CABI, Wallingford.

Sheller, M. and Urry, J. 2003, Mobile transformations of 'public' and 'private' life, *Theory, Culture and Society*, 20, 107–25.

Shenkar, O. 2004, One more time: international business in a global economy, *Journal of International Business Studies* 35(2), 161–71.

Sheppard, E.S. 1984, The distance-decay gravity model debate, in G. Gaile and C. Willmot (eds), *Spatial Statistics and Models*, D. Reidel, Dordrecht, pp. 367–88.

Sheppard, E.S. and Barnes, T. (eds) 2002, *A Companion to Economic Geography*, Blackwell, Oxford, pp. 149–68.

Sherden, W.A. 1998, *The Fortune Sellers: The Big Business of Buying and Selling Predictions*, Wiley, New York.

Shucksmith, D.M. 1983, Second homes, *Town Planning Review* 54, 174–93.

Shuval, J.T. 2000, Diaspora migration: definitional ambiguities and a theoretical paradigm, *International Migration* 38(5), 41–55.

Sickman, P. 1995, Sports pork, *The American Enterprise* 6(3), 80–2.

Simmons, D. 1994, Community participation in tourism planning, *Tourism Management* 15(2), 98–108.

Simpson, E. 1997, *Scotland's Past in Action: Going on Holiday*, National Museums of Scotland, Edinburgh.

Simpson, K. 2004, $7m push to sell culture to tourists, *The Age*, 18 April, p. 5.

Sinclair, J. 1987, *Images Incorporated: Advertising as Industry and Ideology*, Croom Helm, London.

Sinclair, K. 1994. Colombo's hotels are on the move, *Asian Hotelier* (July), 12–13.

Sinclair, M.T. and Stabler, M. 1997, *The Economics of Tourism*, Routledge, London.

Singh, S. 1999, On tourism in Goa – NGOs can make a difference, *Tourism Recreation Research* 24, 92–4.

Singh, S. Timothy, D. and Dowling, R. (eds) 2003, *Tourism in Destination Communities*, CABI, Wallingford.

Skelton, T. and Allen, T. (eds) 1999, *Culture and Global Change*, Routledge, London.

Smith, A. and Hall, C.M. 2001, A stakeholder generated SWOT analysis of the New Zealand food and wine tourism industry, paper presented at the New Zealand Wine and Food Tourism Conference, November, Hawkes Bay, New Zealand.

Smith, J.M. 2004, Unlawful relations and verbal inflation, *Annals of the Association of American Geographers* 94(2), 294–9.

Smith, K. 1990, Tourism and climate change, *Land Use Policy* (April), 176–80.

Smith, K. 1993, The influence of weather and climate on recreation and tourism, *Weather* 48, 398–404.

Smith, M. and Duffy, R. 2003, *The Ethics of Tourism Development*, Routledge, London.

Smith, N. 1988, The region is dead! Long live the region! *Political Geography Quarterly* 7(2), 150.

Smith, P. 1992, The making of a global city: fifty years of constituent diplomacy – the case of Vancouver, *Canadian Journal of Urban Research* 1(1), 90–112.

Smith, P. 1993, Policy phases, subnational foreign relations and constituent diplomacy in the US and Canada: city, provincial and state global activity in British Columbia and Washington, in B. Hocking (ed.), *Foreign Relations and Federal States*, University of Leicester Press, London.

Smith, R.A. 1994, Planning and management for coastal eco-tourism in Indonesia: a regional perspective, *Indonesian Quarterly* 22(2), 148–57.

Smith, S.L.J. 1985, US vacation travel patterns: correlates of distance decay and the willingness to travel, *Leisure Sciences* 7(2), 151–74.

Smith, S.L.J. 1988, Defining tourism: a supply–side view, *Annals of Tourism Research* 15, 179–90.

Smith, S.L.J. 1995, *Tourism Analysis: A Handbook*, 2nd edn, Longman, Harlow.

Smith, V. (ed.) 1989, *Hosts and Guests: The Anthropology of Tourism*, 2nd edn, University of Pennsylvania Press, Philadelphia, PA.

Smith, V. 2003, Space tourism, paper presented at the International Academy for the Study of Tourism Conference, July, Savonlinna, Finland.

Smith, V.L. and Eadington, W.R. (eds) 1992, *Tourism Alternatives: Potentials and Problems in the Development of Tourism*, 2nd edn, University of Pennsylvania Press, Philadelphia.

Smyth, H. 1994, *Marketing the City: The Role of Flagship Developments in Urban Regeneration*, E & FN Spon, London.

Smyth, R. 1986, Public policy for tourism in Northern Ireland, *Tourism Management* (June) 120–6.

Soane, J. 1993, *Fashionable Resort Regions: Their Evolution and Transformation, with Particular Reference to Bournemouth, Nice, Los Angeles and Wiesbaden*, CABI, Wallingford.

Sönmez, S. and Graefe, A. 1998, Influence of terrorism risk on foreign travel decisions, *Annals of Tourism Research* 25, 112–44.

Sönmez, S., Apostolopoulos, Y. and Tarlow, P. 1999, Tourism in crisis: managing the effects of terrorism, *Journal of Travel Research* 38(1), 13–18.

Sorkin, M. 1992, Introduction: variations on a theme park, in M. Sorkin (ed.), *Variations on a Theme Park: The New American City and the End of Public Space*, Hill and Wang, New York, pp. xi–xv.

Spoonley, P. 2000, *Reinventing Polynesia: The Cultural Politics of Transnational Communities*, working paper (WPTC–2K–14), Transnational Communities Research Programme, Institute of Social and Cultural Anthropology, Oxford University.

Squire, S.J. 1994, Accounting for cultural meanings: the interface between geography and tourism studies re-examined, *Progress in Human Geography* 18, 1–16.

Stamboulis, Y. and Skayannis, P. 2003, Innovation strategies and technology for experience-based tourism, *Tourism Management* 24, 35–43.

Stansfield, C.A. 1972, The development of modern seaside resorts, *Parks and Recreation* 5(10), 14–46.

Stansfield, C.A. 1978, Atlantic City and the resort cycle: background to the legalization of gambling, *Annals of Tourism Research* 5(2), 238–51.

Stear, L. 1981, Design of a curriculum for destination studies, *Annals of Tourism Research* 8(1), 85–95.

Stebbins, R.A. 1979, *Amateurs: On the Margin Between Work and Leisure*, Sage, Beverly Hills, CA.

Stebbins, R.A. 1982, Serious leisure: a conceptual statement, *Pacific Sociological Review* 25, 251–72.

Stephenson, M. 2002, Travelling to the ancestral homelands: the aspirations and experiences of a UK Caribbean community, *Current Issues in Tourism* 5, 378–425.

Stewart, J.Q. 1947, Empirical mathematical rules concerning the distribution and equilibrium of population, *Geographical Review* 37, 467–85.

Stewart, J.Q. and Warntz, W. 1958, Physics of population distribution, *Journal of Regional Science* 1, 99–123.

Stopher, P. 1992, Use of an activity-based diary to collect household travel data, *Transportation* 19, 177–96.

Storper, M. 1995, The resurgence of regional economies, ten years after: the region as a nexus of untraded dependencies, *European Urban and Regional Studies* 2(3), 191–223.

Storper, M. 2000, Globalization, localization and trade, in G. Clark, M. Feldman and M. Gertler (eds), *The Oxford Handbook of Economic Geography*, Oxford University Press, Oxford, pp. 146–68.

Stouffer, S. 1940, Intervening opportunities: a theory relating to mobility and distance, *American Sociological Review* 5, 845–67.

Strapp, J.D. 1988, The resort cycle and second homes, *Annals of Tourism Research* 15, 504–16.

Stutz, P. 1973, Distances and network effects on urban social travel fields, *Economic Geography* 49, 134–44.

Sugden, J. and Yiannakis, A. 1982, Sport and juvenile delinquency: a theoretical base, *Journal of Sport and Social Issues* 6(1), 22–30.

Sui, D.Z. 2004, Tobler's first law of Geography: a big idea for a small world? *Annals of the Association of American Geographers*, 94(2), 269–77.

Suvantola, J. 2002, *Tourists' Experience of Place*, Ashgate, Aldershot.

Swarbrooke, J. and Horner, S. 1999, *Consumer Behaviour in Tourism*, Butterworth-Heinemann, Oxford.

Swyngedouw, E. 1989, The heart of the place: the resurrection of locality in an age of hyperspace, *Geografiska Annaler* 71B, 31–42.

Tagliabue, J. 1998, Preserving a heritage via bed and barns – European govts subsidize agrotourism, *New York Times*, 13 August, Business Day Section, pp. 1, 4.

Tanner, J.C. 1979, Expenditure of time and money on travel, *Transport Research A* 15A, 25–38.

Taylor, F.F. 1993, *To Hell with Paradise*: *A History of the Jamaican Tourist Industry*, University of Pittsburgh Press, Pittsburgh, PA.

Taylor, P. 1991, The European Community and the state, *Review of International Studies* 17, 109–25.

Taylor, P.J. 1971, Distance transformations and distance decay functions, *Geographical Analysis* 3, 221–38.

Telfer, D.J. 2000, The Northeast Wine Route: wine tourism in Ontario, Canada and New York State, in C.M. Hall, E. Sharples, B. Cambourne and N. Macionis (eds), *Wine Tourism Around the World: Development, Management and Markets*, Butterworth-Heinemann, Oxford, pp. 251–71.

Teye, V.B. 1986, Liberation wars and tourism development in Africa: the case of Zambia, *Annals of Tourism Research* 13, 589–608.

The Age 2004, *The Age Goodweekend magazine*, 17 April.

The Australian 2003, News value, *The Australian*, Media section, 16–22 October, p. 12.

Théret, B. 1994, To have or to be: on the problem of the interaction between state and economy in its 'solidaristic' mode of regulation, *Economy and Society* 23, 1–46.

Thiessen, T. 2004, Marketers make way for new age phenomenon, *The Age*, 9–10 April, p. 6.

Thomas, A. 1984, The spirit of '76?: Calgary, site of the 1988 Winter Games, is showing symptoms of 'Montreal disease' – the scandal and debt that followed in the wake of the Montreal Olympics, *Saturday Night* 99(3), 67–8.

Thomas, R. 2000, Small firms in the tourism industry: some conceptual issues. *International Journal of Tourism Research* 2, 345–53.

Thomas, R. (ed.) 2004, *Small Firms in Tourism: International Perspectives*, Elsevier, Amsterdam.

Thomas, R.W. and Huggett, R.J. 1980, *Modelling in Geography: A Mathematical Approach*, Harper & Row, London.

Thompson, J.B. 1991, *Ideology and Modern Culture*, Polity Press, Cambridge.

Thrift, N.J. 1977a, An introduction to time-geography, *Concepts and Techniques in Modern Geography*, 13.

Thrift, N.J. 1977b, Time and theory in human geography, part 2, *Progress in Human Geography* 1, 23–57.

Thrift, N.J. and Glennie, P. 1993, Historical geographies of urban life and modern consumption, in G. Kearns and C. Philo (eds), *Selling Places: The City as Cultural Capital, Past and Present*, Pergamon Press, Oxford, pp. 33–48.

Timothy, D.J. 2001, *Tourism and Political Boundaries*, Routledge, London.

Timothy, D.J. 2005, *Shopping Tourism, Retailing and Leisure*, Channelview, Clevedon (in press).

Tisdell, C.A. 1995, Issues in biodiversity conservation including the role of local communities, *Environmental Conservation* 22, 216–28.

Tisdell, C. and Wen, J. 1991, Foreign tourism as an element in PR China's economic development strategy, *Tourism Management* (March), 55–68.

Tobler, W.R. 1970, A computer movie, *Economic Geography* 46, 234–40.

Tobler, W.R. 2004, On the first law of Geography: a reply, *Annals of the Association of American Geographers* 94(2), 304–10.

Toffler, A. (ed.) 1972, *The Futurists*, Random House, New York.

Toffler, A. 1981, *The Third Wave*, Pan Books, London.

Tomlinson, J. 1991, *Cultural Imperialism: A Critical Introduction*, Johns Hopkins University Press, Baltimore, MD.

Tomlinson, J. 1999a, Globalised culture: the triumph of the West?, in T. Skelton and T. Allen (eds), *Culture and Global Change*, Routledge, London, pp. 22–9.

Tomlinson, J. 1999b, *Globalization and Culture*, University of Chicago Press, Chicago, IL.

Tourism Malaysia 2003, *Meet & Experience Malaysia Truly Asia*, Tourism Malaysia, Kuala Lumpur.

Towner, J. 1996, *An Historical Geography of Recreation and Tourism in the Western World 1540–1940*, John Wiley, Chichester.

Townsend, M. and Harris P. 2004, Now the Pentagon tells Bush: climate change will destroy us, *The Observer*, 22 February.

Transportation Research Board 2001, *Personal Travel: The Long and Short of It, Conference Proceedings June 28–July 1, 1999 Washington, D.C.*, Transportation Research Circular E–C026, March 2001, Transportation Research Board, Washington, DC.

Tratalos, J.A. and Austin, T.J. 2001, Impacts of recreational SCUBA diving on coral communities of the Caribbean island of Grand Cayman, *Biological Conservation* 102, 67–75.

TravelAsia 1996, Our say: balancing politics and tourism, *TravelAsia*, 26 July.

Tribe, J. 1997, The indiscipline of tourism, *Annals of Tourism Research* 24, 638–57.

Troughton, M.J. 1997, Social change, discontinuity and polarization in Canadian farm-based rural systems, in B. Ilbery, Q. Chiotti and T. Rickard (eds), *Agricultural Restructuring and Sustainability*, CABI, Wallingford, pp. 279–91.

Truly, D. 2002, International retirement migration and tourism along the Lake Chapala Riviera: developing a matrix of retirement migration behaviour, *Tourism Geographies* 4(3), 261–81.

Tsuchiya, M. 1996, Recreation and leisure programmes for delinquents: the non-custodial option, in M.F. Collins (ed.), *Leisure in Industrial and Post-Industrial Societies*, Leisure Studies Association, Eastbourne, pp. 287–302.

Tuan, Y.-F. 1998, *Escapism*, Johns Hopkins Press, Baltimore, MD.

Tucker, H. 2003, *Living with Tourism: Negotiating Identities in a Turkish Village*, Routledge, London.

Tunbridge, J.E. and Ashworth, G.J. 1996, *Dissonant Heritage: The Management of the Past as a Resource in Conflict*, John Wiley & Sons, Chichester.

Turner, B.L., Clark, W.C., Kates, R.W., Richards, J.F., Mathews, J.Y. and Meyer, W.B. (eds) 1990, *The Earth as Transformed by Human Action*, Cambridge University Press, Cambridge.

Turner, G. 2004, Letters to the Editor: holiday homes and everyday reality, *The Times*, 30 March, p. 19.

Turner, L. and Ash, J. 1975, *The Golden Hordes: International Tourism and the Pleasure Periphery*, Constable, London.

Turner, T. and Niemeier, D. 1997, Travel to work and household responsibility: new evidence, *Transportation* 24(4), 397–419.

Ullman, R.H. 1983, Redefining security, *International Security* 8, 129–53.

United Nations 1994, *Recommendations on Tourism Statistics*, United Nations, New York.

United Nations 1999, The world at six billion, http://www.un.org/esa/population/publications/sixbillion/sixbilpart1.pdf (accessed on 1 November 2003).

United Nations, Division for Social Policy and Development 1998, *The Ageing of the World's Population*, United Nations, New York, http://www.un.org/esa/socdev/agewpop.htm.

United Nations Environment Programme, World Tourism Organisation, Foundation for Environmental Education in Europe 1996, *Awards for Improving the Coastal Environment: The Example of the Blue Flag*, United Nations Environment Programme, Paris; World Tourism Organisation, Madrid; and Foundation for Environmental Education in Europe, Kobenhaum, Denmark.

United Nations Population Division 1998, *World Population Projections to 2150*, United Nations, New York.

Unwin, T. 2000, A waste of space? Towards a critique of the social production of space, *Transactions, Institute of British Geographers* 25, 11–29.

Urry, J. 1987, Some social and spatial aspects of services, *Environment and Planning D: Society and Space* 5, 5–26.

Urry, J. 1990, *The Tourist Gaze: Leisure and Travel in Contemporary Societies*, Sage, London.

Urry, J. 1995, *Consuming Places*, Routledge, London.

Urry, J. 2000a, Mobile sociology, *Sociology* 51(1), 185–203.

Urry, J. 2000b, *Sociology Beyond Societies: Mobilities for the Twenty-First Century*, Routledge, London.

Urry, J. and Lash, S. 1987, *The End of Organised Capitalism*, Polity Press, Cambridge.

Valenzuela, M. 1988, Spain: the phenomenon of mass tourism, in A.M. Williams and G. Shaw (eds), *Tourism and Economic Development: Western European Experiences*, Belhaven Press, London, pp. 39–57.

Van Treeck, P. and Schumacher, H. 1998, Mass diving tourism – a new dimension calls for new management approaches, *Marine Pollution Bulletin* 37, 499–504.

Veblen, T. 1934, *The Theory of the Leisure Class*, Modern Library, New York.

Veijola, S. and Jokinnen, E. 1994, The body in tourist studies, *Theory, Culture and Society* 6, 125–51.

Verstraete, G. 2001, Technological frontiers and the politics of mobility in the European Union, *New Formations: A Journal of Culture/Theory/Politics* 43, 26–43.

Verstraete, G. and Cresswell, T. (eds) 2002, *Mobilizing Place, Placing Mobility: The Politics of Identity in a Globalising World*, Rodopi, Amsterdam.

Vidal, J. 2003, Every third person will be a slum dweller within 30 years, UN agency warns, *The Guardian*, 4 October, p. 13.

Vilhelmson, B. 1999, Daily mobility and the use time for different activities: the case of Sweden, *Geojournal* 48, 177–85.

Viner, D. and Agnew, M. 1999, *Climate Change and Its Impacts on Tourism*, report prepared for WWF-UK by the Climate Research Unit, University of East Anglia, Norwich.

Visser, N, and Njuguna, S. 1992, Environmental impacts of tourism on the Kenya coast, *Industry and Environment* 15(3/4), 42–52.

von Bertalanffy, I. 1950, An outline of general systems theory, *British Journal of the Philosophy of Science* 1, 134–65.

Vukonic, B. 1997, Selective tourism growth: targeted tourism destinations, in S. Wahab and J. Pigrim (eds), *Tourism, Development and Growth: The Challenge of Sustainability*, Routledge, London, pp .95–108.

Waits, M.J. 2000, The added value of the industry cluster approach to economic analysis, strategy development, and service delivery, *Economic Development Quarterly* 14, 35–50.

Walker, J.L. 1977, Setting the agenda in the US Senate, *British Journal of Political Science* 7, 423–45.

Wall, G. and Badke, C. 1994, Tourism and climate change: an international perspective, *Journal of Sustainable Tourism* 2(4), 193–203.

Walle, A.H. 1997, Hospitality/tourism education: generic vs. specialized perspectives, *Hospitality & Tourism Educator* 9(1), 73–6.

Walmesley, D.J. and Jenkins, J. 1992, Tourism cognitive mapping of unfamiliar environments, *Annals of Tourism Research* 19(3), 268–86.

Walmesley, D.J. and Lewis, G.J. 1993, People and Environment: *Behavioural Approaches in Human Geography*, 2nd edn, Longman, Harlow.

Walton, J.K. 1983, *The English Seaside Resort: A Social History 1750–1914*, Leicester University Press, Leicester.

Walton, J.K. 2002, British tourism between industrialization and globalization, in H. Bergoff, B. Korte, R. Schneider and C. Harvie (eds), *The Making of Modern Tourism: The Cultural History of the British Experience 1600–2000*, Palgrave, Basingstoke, pp. 109–31.

Wang, N. 2000, *Tourism and Modernity: A Sociological Analysis*, Elsevier Science, Oxford.

Ward, N, and Almå, R. 1997, Explaining change in the international agro-food system, *Review of International Political Economy* 4(4), 611–29.

Warner, J. 1999, North Cyprus: tourism and the challenge of non-recognition, *Journal of Sustainable Tourism* 7(2), 128–45.

Warnes, A. 1992, Migration and the life course, in A. Champion and A. Fielding (eds), *Migration Processes and Patterns*. Vol. 1: *Research Progress and Prospects*, Belhaven, London, pp. 175–87.

Warnken, J. and Buckley, R. 1998, Scientific quality of tourism environmental impact assessment, *Journal of Applied Ecology* 35, 1–8.

Warnken, J. and Buckley, R. 2000, Monitoring diffuse impacts: Australian tourism developments, *Environmental Management* 25, 453–61.

Watson, S. 1991, Gilding the smokestacks: the new symbolic representation of deindustrialised regions, *Environment and Planning D: Society and Space* 9, 59–70.

Watt, N. 2004, Tories to axe log cabin holidays, *The Guardian*, 29 July.

Watts, J. 2003, China sets sights on the moon, *The Guardian*, 6 October, p. 13.

Weaver, B.B. 1998, Peripheries of the periphery: tourism in Tobago and Barbuda, *Annals of Tourism Research* 25(2), 292–313.

Weaver, D.B. 2000, The exploratory war-distorted destination life cycle, *The International Journal of Tourism Research* 2, 151–61.

Weaver, D.B. (ed.) 2001, *The Encyclopedia of Ecotourism*, CABI, Wallingford.

Weiler, B. and Kalinowski, K.M. 1990, Participants of educational travel: a Canadian case study, *The Journal of Tourism Studies* 1(2), 43–50.

Weiler, B., Shaw, R. and Faulkner, W. 1991, Research in the tourism curriculum: extra or essential', in B. Ward, J. Wells and M. Kennedy (eds), *Tourism Education: National Conference*, Bureau of Tourism Research, Canberra, pp. 144–50.

Weiss, L. 1997, Globalization and the myth of the powerless state, *New Left Review* 225(September/October), 3–27.

Wells, J. 1996, The tourism curriculum in higher education in Australia, *Journal of Tourism Studies* 7(1), 20–30.

Western Australian Tourism Commission (WATC) 1997, *Tourism Research Brief on Daytripping*, WATC, Perth.

Whatmore, S. 1993, Sustainable rural geographies, *Progress in Human Geography* 17(4), 538–47.

Wheatcroft, S. 1998, The airline industry and tourism, in D. Ioannides and K. Debbage (eds), *The Economic Geography of the Tourist Industry: A Supply-side Analysis*, Routledge, London, pp. 159–79.

Wheeler, J.O. 1972, Trip purposes and urban activity linkages, *Annals of the Association of American Geographers* 62, 641–54.

Wheeler, J.O. and Stutz, P. 1971, Spatial dimensions of urban social travel, *Annals of the Association of American Geographers* 61, 371–86.

White, A.T., Barker, V. and Tantrigama, G. 1997, Using integrated coastal management and economics to conserve coastal tourism resources in Sri Lanka, *Ambio* 26(6), 335–44.

Whitford, D. 1993, *Playing Hardball: The High-Stakes Battle for Baseball's New Franchises*, Doubleday, New York.

Whitney, R.B. 1989, The ethical orientations of hotel managers and hospitality students: implications for industry, education and youthful careers, *Hospitality Education and Research Journal* 13(3), 187–92.

Whitson, D. and Macintosh, D. 1996, The global circus: international sport, tourism, and the marketing of cities, *Journal of Sport and Social Issues* 23, 278–95.

Wigan, M.R. and Morris, J.M. 1981, The transport implications of activity and time budget constraints, *Transportation Research Part A – General* 15(1), 63–86.

Wight, P.A. 1998, Tools for sustainability analysis in planning and managing tourism and recreation in the destination, in C.M. Hall and A. Lew (eds), *Sustainable Tourism Development: A Geographical Perspective*, Addison-Wesley Longman, London, pp. 75–91.

Wilkins, M. and Hall, C.M. 2001, An industry stakeholder SWOT analysis of wine tourism in the Okanagan Valley, British Columbia, *International Journal of Wine Marketing* 13(3), 77–81.

Wilkinson, P.F. 1997, *Tourism Policy and Planning: Case Studies from the Commonwealth Caribbean*, Cognizant, New York.

Wilks, J. and Atherton, T. 1994, Health and safety in Australian marine tourism: a social, medical and legal appraisal, *Journal of Tourism Studies* 5(2), 2–16.

Wilks, J. and Page, S. 2003, *Managing Tourist Health and Safety in the New Millennium*, Elsevier Science, Oxford.

Williams, A.M. and Hall, C.M. 2000, Tourism and migration: new relationships between production and consumption, *Tourism Geographies* 2(1), 5–27.

Williams, A.M. and Hall, C.M. 2002, Tourism, migration, circulation and mobility: the contingencies of time and place, in C.M. Hall and A.M. Williams (eds), *Tourism and Migration: New Relationships Between Consumption and Production*, Kluwer, Dordrecht, pp. 1–52.

Williams, A.M., King, R. and Warnes, A.M. 1997, A place in the sun: international retirement migration from northern to southern Europe, *European Urban and Regional Studies* 4(2), 115–34.

Williams, A.M., King, R., Warnes, A. and Patterson, G. 2000, Tourism and international retirement migration: new forms of an old relationship in southern Europe, *Tourism Geographies* 2, 28–49.

Williams, A.M. and Shaw, G. (eds) 1988, *Tourism and Economic Development: Western European Experiences*, Belhaven Press, London.

Williams, A.M. and Shaw, G. (eds) 1999, *Tourism and Economic Development: European Experiences*, 3rd edn, Wiley, Chichester.

Williams, D.R. and Kaltenborn, B.P. 1999, Leisure places and modernity: the use and meaning of recreational cottages in Norway and the USA, in D. Crouch (ed.), *Leisure/Tourism Geographies: Practices and Geographical Knowledge*, Routledge, London, pp. 214-30.

Williams, R. 1983, *Keywords*, Fontana, London.

Williams, S. 1998, *Tourism Geography*, Routledge, London.

Williamson, O. 1981, The modern corporation: origin, evolution attributes, *Journal of Economic Literature* 29, 1537–68.

Wilson, A.G. 1989, Classics, modelling and critical theory: human geography as structured pluralism, in W. Macmillan (ed.), *Remodelling Geography*, Basil Blackwell, Oxford, pp. 61–9.

Wilson, E.O. 1998, *Consilience: The Unity of Knowledge*, Little, Brown and Company, London.

Wilson, M.E. 1995, Travel and the emergence of infectious diseases, *Journal of Emerging Infectious Diseases* 1(2), 39–46.

Wilson, R.D. and Jolman, R.H. 1984, Time allocation dimensions of shopping behaviour, *Advances in Consumer Research* 11, 29–34.

Wine Institute of California 2002, *Pierce's Disease Update*, Wine Institute of California, San Francisco.

Wirral Partnership 2001, *Economic Regeneration Strategy 2001–2, Priority 4 Infrastructure and the Environment*, http://irdss.wirral.gov.uk/ecregen/prior4.asp (accessed 1 April 2002).

Wisch, R.J.A. 1991, The general education vs. careerism debate: developing a hospitality education perspective, *Hospitality & Tourism Educator* 4(1), 65–8.

Witt, P.A. and Crompton, J.L. (eds) 1996, *Recreation Programs that Work for At-Risk Youth*, Venture Publishing, Philadelphia, PA.

Witt, S.F. and Witt, C.A. 1992, *Modeling and Forecasting Demand in Tourism*, Academic Press, New York.

Wolfe, R. 1952, Wasaga Beach: the divorce from the geographic environment, *Canadian Geographer* 1(2), 57–65.

Wolfe, R. 1966, Recreational travel: the new migration, *Canadian Geographer* 10(1), 1–14.

Womack, J.P., Jones, D.T. and Roos, D. 1990, *The Machine that Changed the World*, Macmillan, New York.

Wong, P.P. 1986, Tourism development and resorts on the east coast of Peninsular Malaysia, *Singapore Journal of Tropical Geography* 7(2), 152–62.

Wong, P.P. 1990, Coastal resources management: tourism in Peninsular Malaysia, *ASEAN Economic Bulletin* 7(2), 213–21.

Wong, P.P. 1993, *Tourism vs Environment: The Case For Coastal Areas*, GeoJournal Library Vol. 26, Kluwer, Dordrecht.

Wong, P.P. 1998, Coastal tourism development in Southeast Asia: relevance and lessons for coastal zone management, *Ocean and Coastal Management* 38, 89–109.

Wood, B.D. and Peake, J.S. 1998, The dynamics of foreign policy agenda setting, *American Political Science Review*, 92, 173–84.

Wood, D.J. and Gray, B. 1991, Toward a comprehensive theory of collaboration. *Journal of Applied Behavioral Science* 27(2), 139–62.

Wood, R.E. 1993, Tourism, culture and the sociology of development, in M. Hitchcock, V.T. King and M.J.G. Parnwell (eds), *Tourism in South-East Asia*, Routledge, London, pp. 48–70.

Wood, R.E. 2000, Caribbean cruise tourism: globalization at sea, *Annals of Tourism Research* 27(2), 345–70.

World Commission on Environment and Development (the Brundtland Report) 1987, *Our Common Future*, Oxford University Press, London.

World Health Organisation (WHO) 2003, *International Travel and Health*, Information Resource Centre Communicable Diseases, WHO, Geneva.

World Population 2003, World Population, http://www.ibiblio.org/lunarbin/ worldpop (accessed on 1 November 2003).

World Tourism Organisation 1991, *Resolutions of International Conference on Travel and Tourism*, Ottawa, Canada, WTO, Madrid.

World Tourism Organisation 1995, *East Asia and the Pacific*, WTO, Madrid.

World Tourism Organisation (WTO) 1996a, Rural tourism to the rescue of Europe's countryside, *WTO News* 3 (August/September), 6–7.

World Tourism Organisation 1996b, *Tourist Safety and Security: Practical Measures for Destinations*, WTO, Madrid.

World Tourism Organisation 1997a, *Tourism 2020 Vision*, WTO, Madrid.

World Tourism Organisation 1997b, *Yearbook of Tourism Statistics*, Vol. 1, 49th edn, WTO, Madrid.

World Tourism Organisation 1998a, Asia warned about too much red tape, *WTO News* September/October.

World Tourism Organisation 1998b, Governments' role in tourism, *WTO News* September/October.

World Tourism Organisation 1998c, Public private partnerships, *WTO News* May/June.

World Tourism Organisation 1998d, Austria streamlines its national tourism organization, *WTO News* January/February.

World Tourism Organisation 1998e, Public-private strategy group formed, *WTO News* May/June.

World Tourism Organisation 1998f, Baltic Sea destinations poised for tourism growth, *WTO News*, September–November.

World Tourism Organisation 1999, *Changes in Leisure Time*, WTO, Madrid.

World Tourism Organisation 2002a, International tourist arrivals by sub (region), http://www.world-tourism.org/market_research/facts&figures/latest_data/tita01_07–02.pdf (accessed on 1 November 2003).

World Tourism Organisation 2002b, *WTO Tourism Recovery Committee*, WTO, Madrid, http://www.world-tourism.org/market_research/recovery/home (accessed 1 February 2002).

World Travel and Tourism Council (WTTC) 1998, APEC *Travel & Tourism Millennium Vision*, WTTC, London.

World Travel and Tourism Council 2003, *Blueprint for New Tourism*, WTTC, London.

Wrangham, R. 1999, Management or domination? Planning tourism in the Banda Islands, Eastern Indonesia, *International Journal of Contemporary Hospitality Management* 11(2/3), 111–15.

Wrigley, N. 1980, A second course in statistics, *Progress in Human Geography* 4, 133–8.

Wrigley, N. (ed.) 1988, *Store Choice, Store Location and Market Analysis*, Routledge, London.

Yates, C. 1998, Defining the fault lines: new divisions in the working class, *Capital and Class* 66, 119–47.

Yiftachel, O. 1989, Towards a new typology of urban planning theories, *Environment and Planning B: Planning and Design* 16, 23–39.

Young, C. 1977, *The Family Life Cycle*, ANU Press, Canberra.

Zakai, D. and Chadwick-Furman, N.E. 2002, Impacts of intensive recreational diving on reef corals at Eilat, northern Red Sea, *Biological Conservation* 105, 179–87.

Zarza, A.E. 1996, The LEADER programme in the La Rioja Mountains: an example of integral tourist development, in B. Bramwell, I. Henry, G. Jackson, A.G. Prat, G. Richards and J. van der Straaten (eds), *Sustainable Tourism Management: Principles and Practice*, Tilburg University Press, Tilburg, pp. 103–20.

Zhang, J. and Cameron, G.T. 2003, China's agenda building and image polishing in the US: assessing an international public relations campaign, *Public Relations Review* 29(1), 13–28.

Zipf, G.K. 1949, *Human Behaviour and the Principle of Least Effort*, Prentice-Hall, Reading, MA.

Zmud, J.P. and Arce, C.H. 2001, Influence of consumer culture and race on travel behavior, in *Personal Travel: The Long and Short of it, Conference Proceedings June 28–July 1, 1999 Washington, DC*, TRB Transportation Research Circular E–C026, Transportation Research Board, Washington, DC.

Zukin, S. 1991, *Landscapes of Power: From Detroit to Disney World*, University of California Press, Berkeley.

Index